HISTORIC U.S. COURT CASES
AN ENCYCLOPEDIA

SECOND EDITION

HISTORIC U.S. COURT CASES
AN ENCYCLOPEDIA

SECOND EDITION

John W. Johnson,

Editor

Volume II

Published in 2001 by
Routledge
Taylor & Francis Group
270 Madison Avenue
New York, NY 10016

Published in Great Britain by
Routledge
Taylor & Francis Group
2 Park Square
Milton Park, Abingdon
Oxon OX14 4RN

© 2001 by Taylor & Francis Group, LLC
Routledge is an imprint of Taylor & Francis Group

Printed in the United States of America on acid-free paper
10 9 8 7 6 5 4 3 2

International Standard Book Number 0-415-93019-7 (Set)
International Standard Book Number 0-415-93755-8 (Vol.1)
International Standard Book Number 0-415-93756-6 (Vol. 2)
Library of Congress Card Number 2001031651

Library of Congress Cataloging-in-Publication Data

Historic U.S. court cases : an encyclopedia / John W. Johnson, editor.—2nd ed.
     p. cm.
     Rev. ed. of: Historic U.S. court cases, 1690-1990. 1992.
     Includes bibliographical references and index.
     ISBN 0-415-93019-7 (set : alk. paper— ISBN 0-415-93755-8 (v. 1 : alk. paper—
     ISBN 0-415-93756-6 (v. 2 : alk. paper)
     1. Law—United States—History. 2. Law—United States—Cases. I. Title: Historic U.S.
court cases. II. Johnson, John W., 1946- III. Historic U.S. court cases, 1690-1990.
KF385.A4 J64   2001
349.73'0264—dc21

2001031651

Taylor & Francis Group is the Academic Division of T&F Informa plc.

Visit the Taylor & Francis Web site at
http://www.taylorandfrancis.com

and the Routledge Web site at
http://www.routledge-ny.com

Contents

———◄◦►———

x   Contents

xii   Contents

PART IV

RACE, GENDER, SEXUAL ORIENTATION, AND DISABILITY

- Slavery
- African Americans Since 1865
- Native Americans
- Other Racial Minorities
- Women
- Gays and Lesbians
- Americans with Disabilities

Despite the stirring affirmations of equality in the Declaration of Independence and the U.S. Constitution, thousands of legal disputes in the history of the American colonies and the United States have involved discrimination or perceived discrimination against racial minorities, women, homosexuals, and persons with disabilities. Since 1750, the general tendency has been for American courts to extend incrementally, albeit at a glacial pace, rights to racial minorities and women that most white men enjoyed from the beginning. Only within the last few years have gay men and women and persons with disabilities begun to receive any protection under the law.

Most experts would agree that the American courts have been more sympathetic to the rights of the "historically disadvantaged" than have this country's legislative or executive bodies. Courts, in other words, have been the focus and the forums for the most significant advances in the legal rights of the people whom the "founding fathers" (an appropriate term for fifty-five white males who attended the 1787 Constitutional Convention in Philadelphia) largely left out of the great democratic experiment. The forty-three selections in this portion of the *Encyclopedia* examine a sample of some of the most important U.S. cases involving discrimination and its remedies.

Slavery

By any quantitative or qualitative standard, the greatest injustice to a racial minority in American history was the chattel slavery of African Americans. It is important to emphasize that slavery was a legally protected institution from the earliest colonial times until well into the nineteenth century in virtually all jurisdictions of North America. "The End of Slavery in Massachusetts" presents a discussion of an early set of cases that helped extinguish slavery in New England.

The other five selections in this section deal with the vexing legal issues presented when slaves were taken out of the American South. "Emancipation of Slaves in Transit" describes a famous ruling in which a Massachusetts court held that any slave, except a fugitive, becomes free the moment he or she enters a free jurisdiction. The fugitive slave exception is covered in "Upholding the Fugitive Slave Law of 1793." The landmark case of *Dred Scott v. Sandford*, sometimes called the U.S. Supreme Court's "greatest self-inflicted wound," is examined in "They Have No Rights." Efforts by northern states to resist fugitive slave laws on the eve of the Civil War are discussed in "Slavery, Freedom, and Federal Judicial Power" and "Slaves-in-Transit and the Antebellum Crisis."

African Americans Since 1865

The advancement of African Americans from slavery to freedom has taken over a century. And the process is still not completed. The twelve selections in this section chart the ebb and flow of legal rights of black Americans. The retreat from black civil rights in the Reconstruction is discussed in "No 'Right' to Vote: The Reconstruction Election Cases" and "Civil Rights or Last Rites?" The selection "'Separate But Equal' Approved" presents a discussion of the case that provided the inglorious justification for the segregation of blacks from whites.

"Race, Law, and Gender in South Carolina" and "Justice Vindicated: The Case of William Harper" describe two little-known but revealing state cases involving black defendants in the years between World War I and World War II. Perhaps the most notorious example of racism in the southern courts of the Jim Crow years is discussed in "The Scottsboro Cases."

The appointment of Earl Warren as Chief Justice of the United States in 1953 proved to be one of the most important events in the modern American civil rights movement. Warren, as discussed in "Separate Education Is Not Equal Education," was able to convince all his judicial brethren to join in his 1954 opinion in *Brown v. Board of Education*, striking down school segregation. The initial resistance to the implementation of the *Brown* decision was massive, as noted in "The Little Rock Crisis: State Interposition Against the Supreme Court." Most southern states further limited the freedom of African Americans by prohibiting marriage between blacks and whites. As noted in "A Case of Black and White: Removing Restrictions Against Interracial Marriages," such "anti-miscegenation laws" were not voided by the U.S. Supreme Court until 1967.

In the late 1960s, as discussed in "The School Busing Case," courts began to approve complex busing plans to attempt to integrate the public schools. Since the 1970s, however, as examined in "Desegregation Heads North" and "Far Enough? The Rehnquist Court and Desegregation," courts have been increasingly hesitant to use legal compulsion to remedy patterns of school segregation.

Native Americans

Native Americans have been involved in several significant U.S. court cases since 1800. The first selection in this section, "The Cherokee Cases," deals with the attempt of one Indian tribal unit to have its status as a "nation" respected by American law. Although the Cherokees did technically win certain legal rights before the Supreme Court, the momentum of white migration and executive policy forced the Cherokees to suffer removal from their ancestral lands the and to relocate by traveling the brutal "Trail of Tears."

The next two selections in this section, "The 'Death Knell of the Nations'" and "Why Native Americans Can No Longer Count on Treaties with the U.S. Government," illustrate how the Supreme Court in the post-Civil War era allowed Congress to override stipulations in Indian treaties. However, a recent spate of Indian land claim litigation has reversed the pattern of legal defeat by Native Americans. One of the leading cases is profiled in "Native American Land Claims: The Indians Finally Win."

Other Racial Minorities

Although African Americans and Native Americans have been the parties to most of the important U.S. court cases involving racial discrimination, there are a number of historically significant cases growing out of disputes involving other racial minorities. In "Chinese Laundries and the Fourteenth Amendment," the late nineteenth-century U.S. Supreme Court uncharacteristically ruled in favor of a Chinese litigant. However, in "The Japanese Internment Cases," an essay focusing upon a set of cases which tested the legality of the imprisonment of over 100,000 Americans of Japanese background (most of whom were U.S. citizens) during World War II, the Court found against the Japanese American plaintiffs. "How Should We Pay for Our Schools?" discusses a 1973 case involving public school financing and the Fourteenth Amendment in which the plaintiff children were Mexican Americans.

The last two essays in this section, "Affirmative Action: Can a White, College-Educated Male Be a Victim of Discrimination?" and "Is Race Still a Compelling Factor?" examine the leading appellate cases on affirmative action, the most controversial dimension of civil rights public policy today.

Women

Although not a numerical minority, throughout most of the country's history American women have enjoyed fewer rights and privileges than their male counterparts. Many legal experts would argue that women have been forced to suffer a pattern of discrimination similar to that of racial minorities.

The nine selections in this section provide a glimpse of some of the leading cases on women's rights. "Should a Woman Be Admitted to the Bar?" discusses a nineteenth-century case in which the then typical practice of excluding women from the highest paying and highest status professions was upheld. In the early twentieth century, some state legislatures passed "protective" or "compensatory" legislation, allegedly for the benefit of women. "Aberration in the Movement Toward an Eight-Hour Day" discusses a state case in which a protective maximum hours law for women was struck down. But, in "The Law Recognizes 'Women Are Different,'" the U.S. Supreme Court, benefiting from the pioneering "Brandeis Brief," upheld the constitutionality of another state maximum hours law for women.

The next two essays—"A Supreme Court First: Equal Protection Applied to Women" and "Sex Discrimination: Reasonable or Suspect?"—provide illustrations of how the modern Supreme Court is attempting to struggle with state statutes that allegedly deny women equal protection of the laws under the Fourteenth Amendment. "Law Upheld Guaranteeing Right to Return to Work after Childbirth Leave of Absence," discusses a 1980s case in which a California pregnancy leave statute was upheld by the U.S. Supreme Court. A recent corporate attempt to "protect" women in their childbearing years from employment in a high-paying but hazardous industry, reminiscent of the compensatory practices of the early twentieth century, is discussed in "The Fetus and the Workplace." Another selection, "Do Women Belong in Military Academies?," examines the constitutionality of prohibiting women from attending state-supported military schools. The final selection in this section, "Protecting Students from Sexual Harassment," examines two U.S. Supreme Court decisions of the 1990s that interpreted a category of congressional legislation passed primarily for the benefit of females.

Gays and Lesbians

In this section are three selections—one from the 1970s, one from the 1980s, and one from the 1990s—examining cases involving the legal rights of homosexuals. In the first two—"When Consenting Adults Can't: Privacy, the Law, and Homosexual Conduct" and "Does the Right to Privacy End Where Sexual Preference Begins?"—the U.S. Supreme Court upheld state legislation challenged by homosexual plaintiffs. In the third, " 'Animus' or Moral Justification?: Anti-Gay Laws and Equal Protection," the Court struck down a controversial amendment to the Colorado state constitution that sought to remove protections recently extended to gays and lesbians.

Americans with Disabilities

The Americans with Disabilities Act (ADA), passed by Congress and signed by President George Bush in 1990, transformed the legal landscape for persons with physical or mental handicaps. The first essay in this section, "Three Generations of Imbeciles Are Enough," is illustrative of the glib prejudice against a person with a disability that existed prior to the passage of the ADA. The other three essays—"School Medical Services for Children with Disabilities," "Mitigating Measures and the Definition of Disability," and "Is Walking an Integral Part of the Game of Golf?"—present discussions of recent cases, only one of which found in favor of the disabled plaintiff.

Slavery

The End of Slavery in Massachusetts

<o>

David Thomas Konig

Department of History
Washington University in St. Louis

Walker v. Jennison (1781), *Jennison v. Caldwell* (1781), and *Commonwealth v. Jennison* (1783)
[Massachusetts state courts]

-o- THE CASE IN BRIEF -o-

Date
1781, 1783

Location
Massachusetts

Court
Massachusetts state courts

Principal Participants
Quock Walker
Nathaniel Jennison
Seth and John Caldwell
Levi Lincoln and other counsel
Chief Judge William Cushing

Significance of the Case
Although this series of cases did not, in fact, end slavery in Massachusetts, they revealed that it would have little legal protection in the state.

As the Revolutionary generation in Massachusetts looked back on its accomplishments, the abolition of slavery seemed to be one of its most tangible achievements. The federal census of 1790 listed no slaves in Massachusetts because, claimed opponents of slavery, the Declaration of Rights in the state constitution of 1780 stated that "all men are born free and equal." According to a belief widespread in Massachusetts at the turn of the nineteenth century, the state's highest court had cited that provision in declaring slavery unconstitutional in the 1780s when a black man, Quock Walker, successfully challenged his alleged owner's property rights in him. In truth, the Walker litigation (known collectively as the *Quock Walker Cases*) did not establish any constitutional principle and did not end slavery in Massachusetts. Nonetheless, the litigation did have a significant impact, and it stands as a landmark in the legal attack on slavery.

Quock Walker was nine months old in 1754, when he and his nineteen-year-old mother,

Dinah, were sold to James and Isabell Caldwell of Barre, Massachusetts. According to Quock, James Caldwell promised him his freedom at the age of twenty-four or twenty-five, whereas Mrs. Caldwell spoke of manumission at twenty-one. Unfortunately for Walker, James Caldwell died in 1770; three years later Isabell died, leaving Walker to her second husband, Nathaniel Jennison. Just before his twenty-first birthday, Walker learned that Jennison had no intention of honoring either of the Caldwells' promises.

Walker patiently worked for Jennison until 1781, when he finally abandoned any hope of manumission and fled to Seth and John Caldwell, younger brothers of his former owner. Presumably, they would corroborate James's promise and convince Jennison to manumit him. To Walker's disappointment, Jennison reacted angrily. Brushing aside the Caldwells' assertion that their brother had, indeed, promised Walker his freedom by 1778, Jennison confronted the alleged runaway working for the Caldwells. With the help of several of his servants, Jennison whipped Walker, returned him to the Jennison farm, and locked him in a barn for several hours. As soon as he could, Walker sought out a county justice of the peace and entered a trespass complaint against Jennison, seeking damages for injuries suffered in the whipping. Lacking jurisdiction, the local justice referred the complaint to the Worcester County Inferior Court of Common Pleas.

At the county court, Jennison entered his own complaint, suing the Caldwells in trespass upon the case for luring away his employee and depriving him of services. Jennison's action and Walker's were both heard at the June 1781 session of the court before a three-judge bench. Like most county judges, the three men were not trained lawyers but respected local leaders: the merchant Moses Gill, and farmers Joseph Dorr and Samuel Baker.

In the first action, *Walker v. Jennison*, the defendant produced a bill of sale to argue that Walker was his slave and that as owner he had the right to discipline a runaway. The jury thus had a straightforward and simply framed factual question: Was Walker Jennison's slave, or not? Its verdict was equally clear: it reported

that the plaintiff "was a Freeman, and not the proper Negro slave of the Defendant," and it awarded Walker £50 in damages. The sum was less than the £300 demanded but, more important, the jury had established Walker's freedom. Jennison, frustrated in his attempt to regain Walker as his slave, nevertheless gained a small measure of recompense in the other action, *Jennison v. Caldwell*, in which the jury, finding that Jennison had lost the services of an employee, awarded him the sum of £25.

A powerful array of legal talent had taken up Walker's and the Caldwells' causes. Jennison had capable counsel, too, in John Sprague and William Stearns, but they lacked the stature of those pleading for his opponents. Levi Lincoln, who argued Walker's case, was probably the most eminent attorney in the county and later served as U.S. Attorney General. For the second cause, Lincoln was joined by Caleb Strong, a member of the state convention that had drafted the constitution of 1780 with its Declaration of Rights; Strong later served as Governor of Massachusetts.

To gain Walker's freedom in *Walker v. Jennison*, Lincoln did not raise any constitutional issues. Rather, he chose an increasingly common antislavery device, the "freedom suit," which drew on the jury's power to interpret the law as it saw fit. In eighteenth-century Massachusetts, juries often acted, in effect, to settle legal issues by treating the question as a factual matter within their authority. During the Revolution, for example, accused violators of the hated Navigation Acts had charged customs officials with trespass for wrongful use of force in arresting them and seizing cargoes; juries hostile to Crown regulation would then return verdicts finding that the men making the seizures were not customs officials, and awarding damages to the complainants. From this tactic grew the antislavery freedom suit, which Walker, like many other slaves, was now using against his master. Walker sued Jennison in trespass for wrongful use of force—wrongful because Walker was not his slave. The freedom suit bypassed any larger question of whether or not slavery was legal; instead, it put to a jury a simple question: Was *their particular plaintiff* free, or not? Even in the case he had won at the county court, Jennison had established only that the Caldwells had deprived him of *service;* he could have recovered in any such action involving a freeman.

Although *Walker v. Jennison* decided only Walker's freedom and did not touch the status of other slaves in Massachusetts, it served an important larger purpose. Through this case and others like it, judges, lawyers, and jurors were stating unequivocally that they would not permit the machinery of the law to support a system of which they disapproved. For this reason, John Adams could recollect in 1795, "I never knew a Jury by a Verdict to determine a negro to be a slave—they always found them free." Walker's case, therefore, encouraged other such suits and reinforced the message that slave owners would have difficulty maintaining a distasteful system.

Appeals were necessary, however, for the verdict in *Jennison v. Caldwell* might appear to contradict that of *Walker v. Jennison,* and Jennison was a contentious individual unwilling to let the matter rest. Moreover, until reformed in 1859, the Massachusetts legal system allowed trial de novo (i.e., trying the matter anew) on appeal, thus making lower court decisions precarious and in many instances merely an elaborate form of pretrial discovery. The losing parties in the two cases therefore appealed to the Massachusetts Superior Court of Judicature, which heard the cases at its Worcester session in September 1781.

The trespass case, *Walker v. Jennison,* was on the docket first, but Jennison defaulted. Why he did so is unclear; perhaps he wished to have all the issues settled in one case, *Jennison v. Caldwell,* which he had won in the lower court. Whatever the reason, Levi Lincoln was well prepared for Jennison. Aware of the larger significance of freedom suits, and eager to strike a blow for more than just Walker's freedom, Lincoln embellished his argument. In addition to arguing that Walker was free by James Caldwell's promise of manumission, he brought in the question of whether slavery was legal under natural law and the law of God. "Is it not a law of nature that all men are equal and free?" he asked. "Is not the law of nature the law of God? Is not the law of God then against slavery?" Although he raised the constitutional question, too, only in passing did he argue that the Massachusetts Declaration of Rights had made slavery unconstitutional by declaring all men "free and equal."

The bench, with Judge Nathaniel Peaslee Sargent presiding, did not rule such arguments out of order. Although he and the other Superior Court judges hearing the case were, unlike their counterparts on the county bench, professional lawyers, they were receptive to the moral dimensions of the case. In any event, the jury was to decide, not they, and both sides addressed the broader question of slavery's legality. Sargent, an opponent of slavery, not only permitted Lincoln to plead natural, divine, and constitutional law, but he, too, raised the constitutional issue when he mentioned the "free and equal" clause of the state constitution in his jury instructions. The jury responded by reversing the lower court verdict: the Caldwells were not guilty of enticing Walker from Jennison and depriving him of services. Yet it is still unclear *why* they so decided. They may have responded to the natural law argument, or they may have believed, as other juries did, that slavery was morally repugnant. It is possible, too, that they may have merely regarded the matter as settled by appellant's default in *Walker v. Jennison;* with that judgment affirmed (namely, that Walker "was a Freeman"), the jury may have decided that Walker was neither the servant nor the slave of Jennison. Nothing exists in the record to indicate the grounds for their verdict, however.

Uncertain of the outcome of the Caldwells' appeal, however, and before it came to trial in the Superior Court, opponents of slavery obtained a criminal indictment of Jennison for beating Walker. When the appellate jury verdict in *Jennison v. Caldwell* seemed to assure Walker's freedom, *Commonwealth v. Jennison* did not go to trial. But when the litigious Jennison refused to accept defeat and in June 1782 petitioned the legislature to order the defaulted *Walker v. Jennison* reopened, abolitionists saw to it that *Commonwealth v. Jennison* would be tried. At the April 1783 term of the Supreme Judicial Court (successor to the Superior Court), both sides once again debated the legality of slavery—"as far as their fancy would lead them," recalled the court clerk when asked about the case in 1798, "although not directly on the point."

More directly to the constitutional question, however, and the reason that historians for so long mistakenly viewed this case as having abolished slavery in Massachusetts, was the charge to the jury prepared by Chief Judge William Cushing. In the final draft of his charge, Cushing wrote that the state constitution declared that *every subject is entitled to liberty.* He saw no need to construe the unconstitutionality of slavery, or to address the factual question of whether or not James or Isabell Caldwell had promised manumission. Rather, he wrote, "Slavery is in my judgment as effectively abolished as it can be by the granting of rights and privileges wholly incompatible and repugnant to its existence. The court are therefore fully of the opinion that perpetual servitude can no longer be tolerated in our government."

It is not clear that Cushing ever delivered this charge, nor is it apparent that the jury followed it if he did. For the record, they only "found the master guilty," recalled the clerk in 1798, and nothing of the charge or legal argument was committed to the record. Because the jury technically had decided only the facts at issue, the clerk explained, "nothing could be recorded to distinguish this case from any other common assault and battery."

Judge Cushing's charge nevertheless remains powerful evidence of the antislavery attitudes that prevailed among Massachusetts judges, lawyers, and jurors. Although Walker's cases produced no judicial decision that could operate as determinative constitutional law, they stood as three more highly visible demonstrations that slavery would have little legal protection in Massachusetts. Jennison, in fact, had to remove his slaves (one of whom was Quock's brother Prince) to Connecticut in order to sell them. Meanwhile, whites continued to hold slaves in Massachusetts after 1783, but Jennison's failures discouraged many other slave owners from contesting the legal efforts that slaves might exert to gain their freedom. In that limited but important regard, they signaled the death knell for slavery in Massachusetts.

Selected Bibliography

Cushing, John D. "The Cushing Court and the Abolition of Slavery in Massachusetts: More Notes on the 'Quock Walker Case.'" *American Journal of Legal History* 5 (April 1961): 118–144.

Davis, David Brion. *The Problem of Slavery in the Age of Revolution.* Ithaca, NY: Cornell University Press, 1975.

O'Brien, William. "Did the Jennison Case Outlaw Slavery in Massachusetts?" *William and Mary Quarterly* 17 (April 1960): 219–240.

Spector, Robert M. "The Quock Walker Cases (1781–1783)—Slavery, Its Abolition, and Negro Citizenship in Early Massachusetts." *Journal of Negro History* 53 (January 1968): 12–32.

Wiecek, William M. *The Sources of Antislavery Constitutionalism in America, 1760–1848.* Ithaca, NY: Cornell University Press, 1977.

Zilversmit, Arthur. "Quock Walker, Mumbet, and the Abolition of Slavery in Massachusetts." *William and Mary Quarterly* 25 (October 1968): 614–624.

Emancipation of Slaves in Transit

◄◦►

Paul Finkelman

College of Law
University of Tulsa

Commonwealth v. Thomas Aves, 18 Pick. 193 (1836)
[Supreme Judicial Court of Massachusetts]

◄◦► THE CASE IN BRIEF ◄◦►

Date
1836

Location
Massachusetts

Court
Supreme Judicial Court of Massachusetts

Principal Participants
Thomas and Med Aves
Chief Justice Lemuel Shaw
Commonwealth of Massachusetts

Significance of the Case
Chief Justice Lemuel Shaw ruled that
a slave became free upon entering
Massachusetts not because his or her
status changed but because the state
outlawed slavery. The case became a
precedent adopted by most northern
states.

*C*ommonwealth v. Aves was the first important northern state case to determine the
status, under common law, of a slave brought
into a free state. In *Aves* Chief Justice Lemuel
Shaw of the Massachusetts Supreme Judicial
Court ruled that any slave, except a fugitive,
became free the moment he or she entered a
free jurisdiction. By 1860 all but four northern
states had adopted the *Aves* precedent through
court decisions, statutes, or both. The legislatures in New Jersey, Indiana, and Illinois explicitly rejected the *Aves* precedent through
statutory law, and a California court adopted a
modified version of the *Aves* doctrine.

Chief Justice Shaw's holding in *Aves* can be
understood only in the context of three prior
developments in law and society: the 1772 English case of *Somerset v. Stewart*, the ending of
slavery in the North, and the growth of a revi-
talized northern antislavery movement after
1831.

James Somerset was the slave of Charles
Stewart, a British customs officer living in the
American colonies. In 1769 Stewart returned to

England and took Somerset with him. In 1771 Somerset escaped from Stewart, but was captured and consigned to a sea captain named Knowles, who was directed to transport the troublesome slave to Jamaica and sell him there. Somerset was confined to the hold of Knowles's ship, but before the ship sailed, the great English abolitionist Granville Sharp convinced Lord Chief Justice Mansfield of the Court of King's Bench to issue a writ of habeas corpus in order to test Somerset's status.

Mansfield initially suggested that Stewart manumit Somerset, in order to moot the case. Stewart stubbornly pursued the case, and after five hearings Mansfield ruled that whereas English courts would uphold contracts for slaves in the colonies, the actual practice of slavery was contrary to the common law of England. "The state of slavery is of such a nature," Mansfield wrote, "that it is incapable of being introduced on any reasons, moral or political; but only positive law [statutory law], which preserves its force long after the reasons, occasions, and times itself from whence it was created, is erased from memory; it's so odious, that nothing can be suffered to support it, but positive law."

The narrow holding of this case was that an alleged slave could not be forced out of England against his will. The decision meant that there was no law that would maintain slavery in England. Slaves could claim their freedom and no law could intervene. Although *Somerset* did not lead to an immediate end to slavery in England, most people in America thought it did.

For American purposes the *Somerset* precedent meant this: if a master brought his slave into a free jurisdiction, the slave could refuse to return to a slave jurisdiction, and no law could intervene to aid the master. On the contrary, the law would side with the slave.

Of course in 1772 there were no free jurisdictions in the American colonies: at the outbreak of the Revolution all of the thirteen colonies allowed slavery. This began to change during the struggle for independence.

Between 1780 and 1804 all the northern states took steps to end slavery within their respective jurisdictions. In 1780 Massachusetts adopted a constitution which declared that all people were "free and equal." Quickly this clause was interpreted to mean that no slavery could exist in the state. New Hampshire and Vermont (the fourteenth state) similarly abolished slavery in their constitutions. By 1800 no slaves were living in any of these places. In 1780 Pennsylvania adopted a gradual emancipation statute, under which the children of slaves would be born free. Connecticut (1784), Rhode Island (1784), New York (1799), and New Jersey (1804) followed Pennsylvania's lead. Although slaves could be found in some of these states well into the nineteenth century, by 1804 the "North" had defined itself as those states which either had ended slavery outright or had set it on a course of ultimate extinction.

The northern assault on slavery was led by a group of abolition societies which formed during and immediately after the Revolution. This first wave of abolition societies concentrated on four goals: the end of slavery in the North, the end of the African slave trade, the amelioration of conditions for free blacks in the North, and the protection of free blacks from kidnapping. By 1810 these societies had made a great deal of progress toward the first two goals and some progress toward the other two. However, by this time their leadership had died out and the societies began to lose their vigor. With the exception of various charitable projects—such as schools and orphanages for blacks—these societies ceased to have any impact on northern life.

In the early 1830s a new antislavery movement emerged around the leadership of William Lloyd Garrison in Boston, the brothers Arthur and Lewis Tappan in New York, and Theodore Dwight Weld and James G. Birney in Ohio. This movement called for the immediate end to slavery everywhere in the United States. Abolitionists in Massachusetts were particularly active in seeking ways to attack slavery. In 1836 such an opportunity arose.

In May 1836 Mary Aves Slater, the wife of a New Orleans slaveowner, returned to her native Boston to visit her father. She brought with her a six-year-old slave girl named Med. In July, Slater became ill and left Boston for a short time, leaving Med with her father, Thomas Aves.

At this point the Boston Female Anti-Slavery Society obtained a writ of habeas corpus for

Med. In August the case came before Chief Justice Shaw. Although he had been on the bench for only a few years, Shaw was already emerging as one of the most important state jurists in the nation. The case was argued by two distinguished lawyers. Benjamin R. Curtis, who would eventually serve on the United States Supreme Court, where he would write a vigorous antislavery dissent in *Dred Scott v. Sandford*, represented Aves. Ellis Gray Loring, who would devote much of his life to antislavery, as well as serving as a member of the Harvard Corporation, presented the case for Med's freedom on behalf of the Boston Female Anti-Slavery Society. After reading the arguments in the case, Justice Joseph Story commented to Loring: "I have rarely seen so thorough and exact arguments as those made by Mr. B. R. Curtis and yourself. They exhibit learning, research and ability of which any man may be proud."

Curtis argued that Massachusetts should grant comity (respect) to the law of Louisiana, under which Med was held as a slave. He argued that there was no reason not to give a "qualified effect" to Louisiana law. He argued that Aves could hold Med in his custody without bringing into Massachusetts all of the "consequences" of slavery. Curtis pointed out that under the fugitive slave clause of the U.S. Constitution, the judges of Massachusetts were bound to recognize the slave status of fugitives captured within the state. He argued that recognizing Med's status, for the purpose of preserving interstate harmony, would not overly burden Massachusetts.

Loring's main argument centered on the immorality of slavery. He argued that, for the people of Massachusetts, slavery "offends their morals," "contravenes their policy," and "offers a pernicious example." Equally important, he argued that any slavery in the state "violates a public law." Loring further argued that *Somerset* was part of the common law of Massachusetts, and under it Med had to be set free. He answered Curtis's arguments about the fugitive slave clause by asserting that the clause was "a barter of conscience, a violation of the express law of God" to which the North had unfortunately agreed, but that this compromise did not affect slave transit. Loring finished his

argument with a poetic and emotional plea: "Let not the accursed system thrive amongst us. If we are to be restrained from attacking the giant trunk—if we have even consented to let a single bough shoot over us, to taint our air—I trust by the blessing of Heaven we have yet strength and virtue enough to lop its luxuriance. God forbid that the deadly branches should bend over and strike root, to become in their turn, a parent stock, growing up on the soil of Massachusetts."

Chief Justice Shaw stated the legal issues concisely: "The Precise question presented . . . is, whether a citizen of any one of the United States, where negro slavery is established by law, coming into this State, for any temporary purpose of business or pleasure, staying some time, but not acquiring domicil here, who brings a slave with him as a personal attendant, may restrain such slave of his own liberty during his continuance here, and convey him out of this State on his return, against his consent."

Shaw expressed surprise that this was a novel issue. He thought it the common belief of all lawyers in the state that slaves became free when brought into Massachusetts. This was so "not so much because his coming within our territorial limits, breathing our air, or treading on our soil, works any alteration in his *status*, or condition, as settled by his domicil, as because by the operation of our laws, there is no authority on the part of the master, either to restrain the slave of his liberty, whilst here, or forcibly to take him into custody in order to effect his removal."

After reviewing English and American cases on this subject, including *Somerset*, Shaw concluded that this was in fact the law of his jurisdiction, even though no case on the subject had previously arisen. Shaw was also pleased to note that cases in Louisiana and Kentucky had also held that a slave gained freedom when brought to a free state.

Shaw carefully distinguished this case from one of a fugitive slave, pointing out that Massachusetts had an obligation to return runaways. The logic of this distinction was clear to Shaw. A master could choose to bring a slave into Massachusetts or not, but a master could not control a runaway slave. Thus, "It is only when they [slaves] escape, without the consent of their owners, into other States, that they [masters] require the aid of other States, to enable them to regain their dominion over the fugitives."

Although Shaw's opinion set a precedent followed by most other northern states, beginning in the 1830s some southern states would reject the concept that slaves gained their freedom by living in free states. However, not until the 1850s would this become a major political issue. In *Strader v. Graham* and *Dred Scott v. Sandford*, Chief Justice of the U.S. Supreme Court Roger Taney would rule that slaves brought to free jurisdictions did not necessarily become free. By 1860 most southern states would no longer recognize the *Somerset-Aves* principle that slavery was a status based on local law, and once the slave was taken from the locality, the status disappeared. However, the Supreme Court had not yet decided if the free states had the right to emancipate slaves brought into their jurisdiction. A case which might have raised this question, *Lemmon v. The People,* was making its way through the New York courts in the 1850s. However, the election of Abraham Lincoln as President and the outbreak of the Civil War prevented any final decision on the question of slave transit in the North.

Selected Bibliography

Finkelman, Paul. *An Imperfect Union: Slavery, Federalism, and Comity.* Chapel Hill: University of North Carolina Press, 1981.

Levy, Leonard. *The Law of the Commonwealth and Chief Justice Shaw.* Cambridge, MA: Harvard University Press, 1957.

Wiecek, William M. *The Sources of Antislavery Constitutionalism in America, 1760–1848.* Ithaca: Cornell University Press, 1977.

Zilversmit, Arthur. *The First Emancipation.* Chicago: University of Chicago Press, 1967.

Upholding the Fugitive Slave Law of 1793

—◄○►—

Paul Finkelman

College of Law
University of Tulsa

Edward Prigg v. The Commonwealth of Pennsylvania, 16 Peters 539 (1842) [U.S. Supreme Court]

◄○► THE CASE IN BRIEF ◄○►

Date
1842

Location
Pennsylvania

Court
U.S. Supreme Court

Principal Participants
Margaret Morgan
Edward Prigg
Commonwealth of Pennsylvania
Associate Justice Joseph Story

Significance of the Case
The ruling was the first case in which the U.S. Supreme Court upheld the validity of the 1793 Fugitive Slave Law.

Prigg v. Pennsylvania was the first decision by the U.S. Supreme Court interpreting the meaning of the fugitive slave clause of the U.S. Constitution (Art. IV, Sec. 2, Par. 3) and the validity of the federal Fugitive Slave Law of 1793. In a complicated decision with seven separate opinions, the Court upheld the validity of the 1793 law.

The case began with an alleged fugitive slave named Margaret Morgan. Margaret was in fact the daughter of two slaves who had once been owned by a Marylander named Ashmore. Ashmore had allowed these two slaves to live as if they were free, and he had never exerted any claim over Margaret, who lived her life as if she were free and eventually married a free black named Jerry Morgan. In 1832 the couple moved to Pennsylvania.

When Ashmore died, his estate went to his niece, a Miss Ashmore. In 1837 she hired Edward Prigg, a professional slave catcher, to seize Margaret and bring her back from Pennsylvania. Miss Ashmore claimed Margaret as a slave because Margaret's mother had been her uncle's slave, and because neither Margaret nor her mother was formally manumitted, Margaret had never been legally free. This was in fact a correct understanding of Maryland law.

Because Margaret had always lived as a free person, she made no attempts to hide her whereabouts. Prigg easily found her and seized her as a fugitive slave. At the time that Prigg acted, the seizure of a fugitive slave in Pennsylvania was regulated by both the federal law of 1793 and a state act of 1826. The state law was one of many "personal liberty laws" passed in the North throughout the antebellum period. This law, "An Act to Give Effect to the Provisions of the Constitution of the United States Relative to Fugitives from Labor, for the Protection of Free People of Color, and to Prevent Kidnapping," had been adopted to fulfill the state's obligation to aid in the rendition of fugitive slaves and also to protect the state's free black population from kidnapping. Complying with the law, Prigg applied to Justice of the Peace Thomas Henderson for an arrest warrant. Acting under this warrant, Prigg arrested Margaret and brought her back to Henderson to obtain a certificate of removal, which was required by both the 1826 law and the federal act of 1793.

At this point Henderson "refused to take further cognizance of the case." Why he did this is unknown, although any one or all of three explanations seem likely. He may have been offended by the notion that a woman who had lived her entire life as a free person could now be seized as a slave. He may also have objected to the seizure of Morgan's youngest child, who had been conceived and born in Pennsylvania and, thus, was a free person under Pennsylvania law. Finally, it is quite likely that Prigg was unable to produce the documentation necessary to prove Ashmore's title to Margaret. The evidentiary requirements under the Pennsylvania law were far more exacting than those of the federal law.

Prigg probably was not really interested in following all the procedures of the 1826 law because, among other provisions, the law required a formal trial of the status of an alleged

fugitive. Instead, Prigg simply forced Margaret back to Maryland. For this act a York County (Pennsylvania) court soon indicted Prigg for kidnapping. In 1839 Maryland extradited Prigg following an agreement that, if he was convicted, no sentence against Prigg would be enforced until after the case had been heard by the U.S. Supreme Court. The agreement further stipulated an expedited appeals process in Pennsylvania. This allowed for Prigg's trial and conviction, which the Pennsylvania Supreme Court upheld. The contrived nature of the Supreme Court case is illustrated by the fact that Prigg's counsel also represented the state of Maryland.

In reversing Prigg's conviction, Justice Joseph Story's "Opinion of the Court" made four major points. First, Story held that the federal law of 1793 was constitutional. This conclusion rebuffed those who argued that the text of Article IV of the Constitution clearly indicated that fugitive slave rendition was strictly a state issue and Congress was incompetent to act under the cause. Second, Story held that the power to regulate the rendition of fugitive slaves was exclusively within the prerogative of Congress. This meant that the Pennsylvania personal liberty law of 1826 (and similar statutes from other states) was unconstitutional because it interfered with the enforcement of the federal law by placing additional (and stricter) burdens on masters seeking fugitive slaves. Story's opinion, however, allowed the continued existence of state laws that did not add new steps or requirements to the rendition process. Third, Story asserted that state officials had a moral obligation to help enforce the Fugitive Slave Law of 1793, but Congress could not require any state official to act. This stemmed from the prevalent notions of Federalism that state officials might not interfere with federal law enforcement, but that the federal government could not force any state official to take a particular action. Finally, Story found that the fugitive slave clause of the Constitution guaranteed slave owners a common-law right of self-help in capturing their runaway slaves. This meant that under the Constitution "the owner of a slave is clothed with entire authority, in every state in the Union, to seize and recapture his slave." Because this right "may be properly said to execute itself," Story's opinion meant masters or kidnappers could remove fugitive slaves (or kidnapped free blacks) from a free state without any judicial supervision, as long as it could be accomplished "without any breach of the peace, or any illegal violence."

Story's opinion jeopardized the liberty of all blacks, both free and fugitive, in the North. Most personal liberty laws, which had been designed to protect free blacks, were now void. The North could still pass antikidnapping laws, but these laws could not be used to prevent the surrender of fugitive slaves. Thus, any free black who was seized would have to be able to prove his or her freedom quickly in order to get the state to interfere in a rendition. Without state supervision, any free black might be seized under the federal law and claimed as a fugitive slave. Even more dangerous to free blacks was Story's assertion that anyone who could seize a black without a "breach of the peace" could remove that person to the South and sell him or her as a slave. This was an open invitation to kidnapping, if it could be done secretly and quietly. Without any judicial superintendence no black could rest secure.

Though not a "holding" in the case, part of Story's rationale for his opinion was critical to the evolving antebellum crisis. His notion of a common-law right of recaption for slave owners implied that slavery was a national institution. Story stated this clearly, declaring that "the owner must, therefore, have the right to seize and repossess the slave, which the local laws of his own state confer upon him as property; and we all know that this right of seizure and recaption is universally acknowledged in all the slaveholding states." This, in effect, nationalized slavery. It applied the law of the slave states to the free states. *The Philanthropist,* an abolitionist paper, complained that this decision "establishes slavery as the law of the whole Union, on the ruins of state sovereignty, habeas corpus, and the jury trial." In the opinion Story argued "that it cannot be doubted that" the fugitive slave clause "constituted a fundamental article, without the adoption of which the Union could not have been formed." Story based this analysis on James Madison's *Notes of the Federal Convention,* even though those *Notes* show that, unlike all of the other slavery-related compromises at the Constitutional Convention, the fugitive slave clause was added near the end of the Convention without any debate or even a recorded vote. This assertion by Story, based on a faulty analysis of the Convention, gave slavery a protected status within the constitutional and political framework of antebellum America.

At the same time that Story's opinion undermined the liberty of free blacks, it may also have undermined the ability of owners to capture legitimate fugitive slaves. Although the Pennsylvania personal liberty law toughened the evidentiary standard necessary for the return of a fugitive slave, it also involved some state officials in the rendition process. Under Story's ruling, most of the existing personal liberty laws were unconstitutional, and thus most states no longer had valid legislation directing state officials to aid in the rendition process. States could, of course, pass such laws. Story urged them to do so. But Story's opinion noted that the states could not be required to do so.

Only Justice John McLean of Ohio dissented from this opinion. The rest of the Court agreed with the result of the opinion and most of its ramifications. However, Chief Justice Roger B. Taney wrote a long concurrence in which he clearly misrepresented and bitterly attacked Story's opinion.

Taney did not like that aspect of Story's opinion which held that Congress could not require state officials to enforce the federal law. Taney claimed that under this holding "all laws upon the subject [of fugitive slaves] passed by a State, since the adoption of the Constitution of the United States, are null and void, even although they were intended, in good faith, to protect the owner in the exercise of his property rights, and do not conflict in any degree with the act of Congress." He complained that under Story's ruling "no State, since the adoption of the Constitution can pass any law in relation" to the return of fugitive slaves.

Taney made this point and misstated Story's opinion for one apparent reason. He wanted to stress the importance of state cooperation in the return of fugitive slaves. He argued that under the "police powers" of a state, it was permissible for a state to order "the arrest and confinement of the fugitive in the public prison . . . until he could be delivered to his owner."

This portion of Taney's opinion totally misrepresented Story's opinion. Story held unconstitutional only state laws which conflicted with the act of Congress by adding further requirements to the rendition of fugitive slaves. In fact, Story explicitly asserted that "to guard, however, against any possible misconstruction of our views, it is proper to state that we are by no means to be understood in any manner whatsoever to doubt or to interfere with the police power belonging to the States by virtue of their general sovereignty. . . . We entertain no doubt whatsoever that the States, in virtue of their general police power, possess full jurisdiction to arrest and restrain runaway slaves, and remove them from their borders and otherwise to secure themselves against their depredations and evil example, as they certainly may do in cases of idlers, vagabonds, and paupers." Furthermore, he asserted that "the operations of this police power . . . may essentially promote and aid the interests of the owners."

Taney's real complaint was Story's assertion that state officials could not be required to enforce the 1793 law. The Chief Justice wrote that "if a State could not authorize its officers, upon the master's application, to come to his aid, the guaranty contained in the Constitution was of very little practical value." Taney decried the fact that under the "Opinion of the Court," the "State officials are absolved from all obligation to protect this right." This again misrepresented Story, who in fact urged states to help enforce the law.

Taney took this extreme position because he feared that under Story's opinion, states would decline to help in fugitive slave cases. With few federal judges and marshals in the nation, rendition might prove impossible.

Ironically, Taney's scathing concurrence provided ammunition for northerners who did not want to enforce the 1793 law. Some northern legislatures explicitly prohibited state officials

from aiding in the rendition process in any way. Some northern judges, who refused to hear fugitive slave cases, cited Taney's assertion that they lacked jurisdiction in such a case. It is quite possible that if Taney had not drawn attention to the ability of northerners to opt out of the enforcement process, fewer northerners would have done so. But Taney's opinion did draw attention to the antislavery possibilities of the case, and northerners acted on them. Taney, in fact, so misrepresented Story's opinion that he may have led some Northerners to believe that they were in fact not permitted to enforce the 1793 law. Northern noncooperation with fugitive slave rendition after *Prigg* led to intensified southern demands for a new and stronger fugitive slave law. This was achieved in 1850 with a law that created a system of federal enforcement through commissioners, U.S. marshals, and, if necessary, the army and navy.

Selected Bibliography

Cover, Robert M. *Justice Accused: Antislavery and the Judicial Process.* New Haven: Yale University Press, 1975.

Finkelman, Paul. "*Prigg v. Pennsylvania* and Northern State Courts: Antislavery Use of a Proslavery Decision." *Civil War History* 25 (March 1979): 5–35.

Finkelman, Paul. *Slavery in the Courtroom.* Washington, DC: U.S. Government Printing Office, 1985.

Leslie, William R. "The Pennsylvania Fugitive Slave Act of 1826." *Journal of Southern History* 18 (November 1952): 429–445.

Morris, Thomas D. *Free Men All: The Personal Liberty Laws of the North.* Baltimore: Johns Hopkins University Press, 1974.

Newmyer, R. Kent. *Supreme Court Justice Joseph Story: Statesman of the Old Republic.* Chapel Hill: University of North Carolina Press, 1985.

Nogee, Joseph. "The Prigg Case and Fugitive Slavery, 1842–1850." *Journal of Negro History* 39 (January 1954): 27–42.

Wiecek, William M. *The Sources of Antislavery Constitutionalism in America, 1760–1848.* Ithaca: Cornell University Press, 1977.

Wiecek, William M. "Slavery and Abolition Before the United States Supreme Court." *Journal of American History* 65 (June 1978): 34–59.

"They Have No Rights"

—◄◦►—

Kermit L. Hall

President and Professor of History
Utah State University

Dred Scott v. Sandford, 19 Howard 393 (1857) [U.S. Supreme Court]

◄◦► THE CASE IN BRIEF ◄◦►

Date
1857

Location
Missouri

Court
U.S. Supreme Court

Principal Participants
Dred Scott; Dr. John Emerson; Eliza Irene Emerson; John Sanford; State of Missouri; Chief Justice Roger B. Taney

Significance of the Case
In one of the most infamous cases in U.S. history, the Supreme Court for the second time declared a federal law unconstitutional, outlawing the Missouri Compromise of 1820, and declared that slaves had no rights under the Constitution.

Only a handful of U.S. Supreme Court cases can claim the status of true landmarks, points along the path of our history that genuinely separate one constitutional epoch from the next. Although scholars agree that *Dred Scott* fulfills this definition, they have differed about why. Until the 1960s, most of them tied the case to the coming of the Civil War, arguing that had it not been for the Court's decision, war might have been averted. Cast in this light, the Court seemingly suffered a self-inflicted wound that diminished its authority to shape the great constitutional controversies of the war and, later, of Reconstruction. Since the 1960s, however, a new generation of scholars, molded by events of the "Second Reconstruction" and the Supreme Court's constitutional revolution in civil rights, have adopted a different perspective on *Scott*. They have stressed that what the justices did in *Scott* not only was racist but also involved an unprecedented usurpation of power by the High Court. They have discounted the case's importance in bringing on the war, emphasizing that the judicial power remained intact throughout the war and Reconstruction. These scholars have insisted that *Dred Scott* was especially critical in establishing the authority of the justices to review acts of Congress on constitutional grounds. The case, they have cogently observed, was only the second instance before the Civil War—the first was *Marbury v. Madison* (1803)—in which the High Court struck down a federal law.

The litigants who began the case in the mid-1840s had little idea that their dispute would eventually assume such monumental proportions. Scott was a Missouri slave who, along with his family, accompanied his owner, Dr. John Emerson, an army officer, to his various duty posts. The most significant of these travels involved prolonged stays at military posts in Illinois and in federal territory at Fort Snelling, in what became present-day Minnesota. Both Illinois and Minnesota territory lay in free soil, the latter above the line 36°30', where the Missouri Compromise of 1820 had banned slavery in the Louisiana Purchase. There is no evidence that Scott ever demanded his freedom while residing in either place, and he and his wife, Harriet, returned with Emerson to Missouri.

After leaving the military in 1842, Dr. Emerson made fitful attempts to establish a private practice in St. Louis. In the spring of 1843 he moved to Davenport, Iowa Territory, where he died at year's end. The attending physician listed the cause as consumption, but Emerson most likely succumbed to the late stages of syphilis. Emerson's will bequeathed almost all of his estate, including Dred Scott and family, to his wife, whose maiden name had been Eliza Irene Sanford. Some historians have argued that Emerson actually left his estate to his daughter and designated his wife only a trustee with limited powers. The truth is that Mrs. Emerson enjoyed a life estate that included authority to diminish the principal of her inheritance and that gave her full control over Scott and his family.

Emerson also designated John F. A. Sanford, his brother-in-law, executor of the will. Sanford was a prominent St. Louis businessman connected by marriage to the upper levels of that city's social elite. Despite his designation as executor, Sanford played only a marginal role in the disposition of Dr. Emerson's estate, which

involved lands in Missouri and Iowa, and slaves (the Scotts) in Missouri. Rather, Mrs. Emerson assumed control over the property, including the slaves, with a minimum of legal fuss.

Three years after Dr. Emerson's death, Dred Scott and his wife filed separate suits for freedom in the state circuit court in St. Louis against Irene Emerson, not John Sanford. They did so only after Mrs. Emerson refused to allow them to purchase the family's freedom. Why she refused is unclear. By 1846 the Scotts were middle-aged slaves for whom Mrs. Emerson had little personal use. Perhaps she doubted her legal authority to grant the request; perhaps the terms offered by the Scotts (partial payment with security for the remainder) were unsatisfactory, especially because the value of slaves was rising. Perhaps she simply wanted to maintain the income they produced when hired out.

The Scotts' suits were typical of actions brought by slaves in Missouri. The laws of that state, as in most other southern states, had long embraced the rule that slaves who traveled into free territory and set up residences were emancipated. The circuit court judge quite predictably granted them leave to sue. The Scotts' declarations charged that Mrs. Emerson had "beat, bruised and ill-treated" them and had falsely imprisoned them. They sued not only for their freedom but also for damages of $10.

The trials dragged on for more than four years, during which time Mrs. Emerson continued to hire out the Scotts. After an abortive first trial, which the Scotts lost on a legal technicality, a second trial commenced in January 1850. Thanks to a highly favorable charge from the presiding judge, the jury found in favor of the Scotts. The counsel for Mrs. Emerson promptly appealed to the Missouri Supreme Court. Lawyers on both sides agreed that this and other appeals would be based on Dred's case alone, with the findings applying equally to Harriet. What had been two cases became one, and the Scotts, with a judgment in their favor, remained enslaved while they waited for a decision from the state's highest court.

Until 1850 the Scott case attracted little attention beyond the immediate circle of litigants. It had no political implications, and the legal precedents were clearly in Scott's favor. Against the unfolding sectional crisis of the 1850s, however, the case assumed increasingly momentous proportions. Events conspired to propel Scott's case into the national spotlight and to rob him and his wife of their earlier courtroom victory.

Until the 1830s American judges had fashioned a seemingly workable legal compromise over what to do with sojourning slaves, but it was a compromise that departed significantly from the nation's English common-law inheritance, which favored the slave. The celebrated 1772 British case of *Somerset v. Stewart*, for example, had held that slavery was a local institution and that a slave who came to free territory became free. Following independence, American judges refused to follow *Somerset* exactly. Masters were able to *sojourn* with their slaves into free territory and return with them to the slave states without interference by free-state authorities. Slave-state courts, at the same time, accepted the general principle that slaves *domiciled* in free states became forever free. This tacit arrangement began to collapse in the 1830s under the weight of growing antislavery agitation. Several northern states passed personal liberty laws that withdrew the long-standing privilege of masters to maintain their slaves while sojourning. The Supreme Judicial Court of Massachusetts in 1836 added insult to injury when, in *Commonwealth v. Aves*, it abandoned the domicile requirement altogether and held that a slave other than a fugitive from justice became free the moment he or she set foot on free soil.

The highest appellate court of Missouri was also in the process of hardening its position, although in a completely different direction from that of Massachusetts. The appeal taken by Emerson's counsel to the Missouri Supreme Court required two years to decide, just long enough for the political cast of Missouri politics to change dramatically in reaction to the growing controversy over the expansion of slavery into the western territories. Missouri was peculiarly exposed to the crosscurrents of sectional wrangling. Three free states bordered it, and Democrats who were moderates on the slavery expansion question, such as Senator Thomas Hart Benton, were constantly assailed by a small but articulate band of antislavery advocates. These antislavery pressures pushed moderates in the Democratic party increasingly into the slaveholders' camp, a development that was reflected in the composition of the popularly elected Missouri Supreme Court. In 1852, by a vote of 2–1, that Democrat-dominated body overturned the jury verdict in favor of Scott. The majority did so through a dramatic rejection of legal precedent, holding that the state could no longer enforce the antislavery laws of other jurisdictions against Missouri's citizens. In short, the fact that Scott had once been on free soil had no effect on his slave status in Missouri.

Normally, the next step should have been an appeal by Scott's counsel to the U.S. Supreme Court, but such a course of action was blocked by the justices' actions. By 1850 the climate of opinion, especially in the border states, had shifted against slaves bringing freedom suits, and the High Court's opinion in *Strader v. Graham* (1851) acknowledged as much. This Kentucky case involved slave musicians who were taken briefly into Ohio for performances, and later fled from Kentucky to Canada. Their owners sued several men who had allegedly aided the escape. Counsel for the defendants argued that the slaves had been freed as a result of their travel in free territory (and hence the defendants had committed no crime), but the Kentucky Court of Appeals rejected that argument. So, too, did the Supreme Court, with Chief Justice Roger B. Taney, a Democrat from Maryland, writing a unanimous opinion.

Taney concluded in *Strader* that the Court lacked jurisdiction to decide the case, and his opinion saved the justices from entering directly into the growing sectional dispute over slavery. On close examination, however, the decision was more than an exercise in judicial self-restraint, because its holding meant that each state supreme court alone could decide the question of whether a slave became free upon entering free territory. Amid growing sectional rancor over the "peculiar institution," a slave-state judge had no incentive to find that slaves from his state had become free as a result of sojourning on free soil. The High Court's holding in *Strader* meant that once a slave reentered a slave state from free territory, he or she reverted to slave status, and that the federal Supreme Court had no authority even to hear the case, let alone find for the slave.

The Court's *Strader* decision prompted Scott's lawyers to adopt a new strategy. A direct appeal from the Missouri Supreme Court to the justices in Washington would not bring relief. Instead, they initiated an entirely new lawsuit for freedom in the federal circuit court for Missouri against John F. A. Sanford, who had moved to New York. Because the case would begin in a federal rather than a state court, the *Strader* precedent would not apply.

Sanford's exact legal relationship to Scott is unclear. There is much evidence to indicate that Sanford handled some of his sister's business dealings and that he may have acted as her agent in the previous Scott litigation. There is even some additional evidence, although it is inconclusive, that by this time Sanford actually owned Scott. An earlier generation of scholars lavished great attention on the question of ownership because they believed that the suit against Sanford was part of some grand conspiracy, although they disagreed on the exact lineup of conspirators. Some insisted that abolitionists manufactured a counterfeit suit, especially because in 1850 Mrs. Emerson married Calvin Chaffee, a Massachusetts antislavery congressman. Chaffee, however, publicly and privately disavowed any knowledge of such a scheme. Others argued that the suit was part of a proslavery plot that succeeded. Because the historical evidence is shaky on several key points, we likely will never have a conclusive answer to the ownership question. It is largely irrelevant in any case. Whether Sanford owned Scott was immaterial to the slave's bringing suit in federal court. All that mattered was that Sanford had authority over Scott and that, in keeping with the requirement for diversity of citizenship, he resided in a state other than Missouri. So began the case of *Dred Scott v. Sandford* (with Sanford's name misspelled in the official record).

The federal suit for freedom was a customary form of an action of trespass. Scott's decla-

A front-page newspaper drawing of Dred Scott and his wife. The Supreme Court decision to deny Scott his freedom after he had moved to a nonslave state was a major factor in the onset of the American Civil War. *Hulton Getty Collection/Archive.*

ration asserted that he was a citizen of Missouri and complained that Sanford, a citizen of New York, had assaulted and wrongfully imprisoned him, his wife, and his children. The suit also sought damages of $9,000. The case was brought before Judge Robert W. Wells, a slaveholding ex-Virginian and former attorney general of Missouri, who did not suffer from the same sectional hubris that had infected the justices of the state supreme court.

Until the case reached Judge Wells's court, the principal issue had been how Scott's previous travel on free soil affected his status as a slave in Missouri. But the decision of Scott's counsel to proceed in federal court raised an entirely new and very explosive issue: Could a slave be a citizen? If Scott was not a citizen, then he would be barred, under the diversity of citizenship provision of the Constitution, from bringing suit. Sanford's counsel attacked Scott's claim of citizenship by filing a plea in abatement, a procedural device which contended that because Scott was not a citizen, the federal circuit court lacked jurisdiction to hear the case. Scott was incapable of suing, the plea asserted, because a Negro, descended from slaves of "pure African blood," could never be a citizen, either of Missouri or of the United States. The cost to Scott's counsel of proceeding in the federal court was that this strategy invited the slave regime to advance racist arguments to attack a seemingly technical jurisdictional question.

Judge Wells sustained Scott's demurrer to the plea and ruled that, for purposes of bringing a suit in federal court, citizenship implied only residence in a state and the legal capacity to own property. Wells's ruling was quite narrow. He did not, for example, sketch any comprehensive grounds upon which to rest Negro citizenship, such as the privilege and immunities clause of Article IV, Section 2, of the U.S. Constitution. A Negro was enough of a citizen to be covered by the diversity of citizenship clause, but it did not follow that he was a citizen in any broad, general sense. The rights of citizenship, in sum, were entirely contextual. On the merits of the case, however, Wells instructed the jury that established Missouri law should hold, and that once Scott had returned to that state, his fate depended entirely on its laws and not on any residence on free soil. The jury quickly returned a verdict in favor of Sanford.

Scott then appealed to the U.S. Supreme Court on the basis of a writ of error, charging that Judge Wells had improperly instructed the jury. The case was first argued in February 1856 before a Court composed on five southern Democrats, two northern Democrats, one northern Whig, and one Republican. This time it was Sanford's counsel who dramatically altered strategy by introducing the claim that Scott had not become free in federal territory because the law forbidding slavery there (the Missouri Compromise) was unconstitutional. Such an argument further

fueled the surging sectional conflict that had already inflamed national politics. The Kansas-Nebraska Act of 1854 and the ensuing struggle over "Bleeding Kansas" had already ignited a new round of constitutional debate about the authority of Congress over slavery in the territories and had given birth to the Republican party.

Many scholars have argued that the Kansas-Nebraska Act mooted the issue of the Missouri Compromise's constitutionality in *Dred Scott*. Such was not the case. The 1854 act repealed only part of the Missouri Compromise and applied only to Kansas and Nebraska. What Sanford's counsel wanted was to extend the principle of that legislation to all of the territories and, in so doing, to open vast new stretches of formerly free territory to slaveholders. The seemingly limited jurisdictional question actually offered, as the most recent scholarship has concluded, an opportunity for the slave power to plead an expansive view of masters' rights before the nation's highest court.

The justices disagreed sharply about how to dispose of the case after first hearing arguments in early 1856. With the sectional crisis at fever pitch and the presidential campaign under way, several of them sought shelter in the seemingly safe technical question of whether the Court could review a plea in abatement. They ultimately decided to buy time by directing counsel to reargue the case, and the new proceedings began on December 15, 1856, after James Buchanan had been elected president but before his inauguration.

The Court's call for reargument heightened political expectations, and the Washington press corps and members of Congress lavished great attention on it. The oral arguments consumed twelve hours spread over four days. Montgomery Blair and George T. Curtis, the brother of sitting Justice Benjamin R. Curtis, presented Scott's case; Henry S. Geyer and Reverdy Johnson furnished counsel for Sanford. The courtroom struggle, however, was almost entirely between Blair and Geyer. Blair argued that the *Strader* precedent did not apply in *Scott* because the case had begun as a matter of original jurisdiction in the federal courts and that Scott, though not a complete citizen, was, as Judge Wells had concluded, sufficiently endowed with citizenship to sue in a federal court. Geyer asserted that Congress had no authority to exclude slaveholders' property from the territories and that Scott, as a black who had never been naturalized, could not claim citizenship and therefore could not sue in a federal court.

A majority of the Court decided in the initial conference to skirt the larger issues and draw as heavily as possible on the *Strader* precedent. Justice Samuel Nelson, a New York Democrat, composed a brief draft of approximately five thousand words that kept Scott a slave and sidestepped the constitutionality of the Missouri Compromise. Nelson's draft, however, immediately encountered resistance, both from the Southern Democrats on the Court, notably Justice James Moore Wayne, and from the two Northern antislavery justices, Curtis, of Massachusetts, and John McLean, of Ohio. Not surprisingly, explanations of why the Court abruptly changed direction paralleled political sentiments. Wayne subsequently explained that public expectations were so high that the justices simply decided they could not leave the issue unresolved. But it was Wayne who made the vital motion to abandon Nelson's draft, to explore the issues fully, and to have Chief Justice Taney write the opinion. Justice John Catron offered another explanation of events. He charged, in a confidential communication to about-to-be inaugurated President Buchanan, that Curtis and McLean were prepared to issue dissents from Nelson's opinion that would discuss all of the issues raised in the case. The Southern Democratic wing, in this view, had no choice but to respond.

Whatever the reason for the reversal in the Court's behavior, President Buchanan was kept well informed. When he learned from Catron that the Court would decide the broad constitutional issue in a way favorable to the South, he included a sentence in his inaugural address that urged Americans to abide by the justices' ruling, without saying what it would be. The Court's opinion followed two days later, on March 6, 1857.

Although Taney spoke officially for the Court, every other justice wrote an opinion and only one, Wayne, concurred with the chief justice in every particular. Despite this jumble of opinions, one result was clear: Scott lost. Moreover, the welter of opinion writing could not obscure the fact that a majority of the Court fully agreed with Taney. On the critical issue of excluding Negroes from citizenship, a majority of the justices joined Taney, and seven of the justices (Curtis and McLean were the exceptions) concluded that as a matter of law, Scott was still a slave. Taney devoted more than 40 percent of his opinion to the question of citizenship. He ruled that slaves were not citizens, and neither were free blacks. All persons of African descent, he explained, were "regarded [by the founding fathers] as beings of an inferior order, and altogether unfit to associate with the white race." "[T]hey have no rights," the Chief Justice continued, "which the white man [is] bound to respect," and the framers of the Constitution had intended "that the negro might justly and lawfully be reduced to slavery for his benefit." Taney's excursion into history was clearly wrong. Free blacks had not, as a matter of law, been reduced to slavery; to the contrary, they had enjoyed a modest guarantee of rights in some states and, in any case, their ranks were regularly swollen by slaves who either purchased their freedom or were manumitted by their masters. But the correctness of Taney's argument was less important than its purpose, which was to place blacks—all blacks—in an inferior legal position.

Republicans at the time, and many historians subsequently, blasted Taney's discussion of the constitutionality of the Missouri Compromise as mere *obiter dictum*. That is, what he had to say did not hold as a matter of law. Having settled the citizenship question, the argument runs, Taney should have avoided any discussion of Congress's constitutional authority over the territories. His choice to discuss it, therefore, was not part of the Court's holding—it was just so much speculation by the Chief Justice. This argument had particular appeal to moderate Republicans because it permitted them to blast Taney's opinion and thereby sustain one of the main planks in their platform—that Congress could keep slavery out of the territories—without making a radical attack upon judicial authority. But, correctly understood, Taney's discussion of the Missouri Compromise was not obiter dictum. It was a central part of the Court's holding, a holding that the chief justice designed to be comprehensive and, therefore, definitive. Having concluded that Scott could not be a citizen because he was a Negro, the chief justice fortified that position by demonstrating to a majority of the Court's satisfaction that Congress could not interfere with the rights of slaveholding citizens in the territories. Some scholars have argued that Taney rested this portion of his decision on the due process clause of the fifth amendment, which required compensation for the taking of property (in this instance, the property of slaveholders). But the due process argument was weakly stated and buried in the middle of his opinion. In the end, Taney simply did not provide any coherent explanation for why the Missouri Compromise was invalid. Nonetheless, his ruling was authoritative and not mere *obiter dictum*.

The decision had powerful political implications. It meant that the Republican party, which strongly advocated congressional control over slavery in the territories, had been organized on an unconstitutional premise. It also struck a powerful blow against the northern wing of the Democratic party and Stephen A. Douglas, the apostle of popular sovereignty. Douglas and his followers had maintained that each territory should be allowed to decide whether it would accept slavery. Taney's opinion slammed the door shut on that option; according to Taney, Congress could not authorize a territorial legislature to prohibit slavery. But this portion of Taney's opinion was dictum. The chief justice was absolutely determined to cover all of the possible bases in providing judicial protection to slavery.

McLean and Curtis responded by insisting on the constitutionality of the Missouri Compromise and denouncing Taney's blanket rejection of Negro citizenship. Their dissenting opinions added grist to the Republican and antislavery propaganda mills, and an earlier generation of scholars gave great credence to this rhetoric by maintaining that the decision actually precipitated the Civil War. In the light of more recent historiography, however, this exercise in causation lacks merit. There is no doubt that the majority's decision further irritated rather than soothed already frayed sectional nerves. The decision also drove a wedge between the Douglas and Southern wings of the Democratic party, snapping the last threads of bisectional party cooperation. Radicals in the South assumed that the decision meant the federal government could pass a territorial slave code. Yet, given the strong Negrophobic cast of the Republican party, it seems doubtful that the decision either enhanced Republican recruiting or aided greatly in the election of Abraham Lincoln.

The constitutional effect of the decision was even more modest. As an unsuccessful candidate for the Senate in 1858 and as the successful presidential standard-bearer of the Republican party in 1860, Abraham Lincoln asserted that he was not bound by the *Scott* decision. The Court, he insisted, simply lacked authority to act unilaterally on a matter of such constitutional breadth. Lincoln's position was at least partly expedient; he did not suggest that the Court could not settle these matters, only that it had to wait for the proper time to do so. Lincoln knew that Republican justices were likely to reach positions different from those of Taney and his southern Democratic brethren. As president, Lincoln proceeded as if the decision had never been rendered. In 1862, Attorney General Edward Bates issued an official opinion holding that free men of color born in the United States were citizens of the United States. In the same year, Congress abolished slavery in all the federal territories. The Thirteenth Amendment (1865), which invalidated slavery, and the Fourteenth Amendment (1868), which, among other provisions, extended citizenship to newly freed slaves, completed the burial of Taney's handiwork.

Recent scholarship has argued persuasively that Taney's opinion is best understood as a powerful demonstration of judicial review and a model of sorts for the modern development of a policy-directed, end-oriented form of judicial authority. Taney went far beyond what John Marshall had done in 1803 in *Marbury v. Madison*, offering no explicit reason why the federal law at issue was unconstitutional. Yet we should not be too quick to cast Taney and his Court in entirely modern judicial garb. Taney clothed his political and racial proclivities in rhetoric which stressed the inherent limitations of judicial power as an appropriate means of adjusting the Constitution to a world that was quickly rejecting human slavery. Despite the fifty-five pages of text, Taney's message was simple: Dred Scott remained a slave because the framers had "constitutionalized" slavery and subsequent generations could do nothing through the judicial process to alter that fact.

Furthermore, Taney's opinion invoked the traditional departmental theory of constitutional adjudication. This theory, which had precedents in the debates of the founders and in early state judicial proceedings, held that each department—branch—of government could construe the Constitution where its powers were involved. Constitutional interpretation was a defensive and preserving practice in which the judiciary's authority to act was strictly limited. Courts and judges could not do anything that they wanted. "No one supposes," Taney wrote, "that any change in public opinion . . . should induce the court to give to the words of the constitution a more liberal construction . . . than they were intended to bear when the instrument was framed. . . . Any other rule of construction would abrogate the judicial character of this court, and make it the mere reflex of the popular opinion or passion of the day." The Constitution, in Taney's view, might change, but the justices could not change it; they could only interpret those values constitutionalized by the framers, one of which was slavery. "If any of its provisions are deemed unjust," Taney wrote, "there is a mode prescribed in the constitution itself by which it may be amended."

Some scholars have refused to accept Taney's assertions at face value, preferring to see in the opinion an example of the new, policy-making scheme of review that first appeared in the 1890s and has become a controversial feature of the present constitutional era. Taney, these scholars suggest, simply read his values into the Constitution. In one sense, this was true. Taney and his proslavery colleagues certainly understood that they were making social

choices, and their willingness to decide the case—quite apart from the opinion itself—indicated that the Court had moved toward embracing what has become the modern, liberal conception of judicial review.

Yet this argument explains too much. Taney's opinion, despite its innovation in legal doctrine, was an exercise in strict construction. In this context, the invocation of more power culminated in less authority for the Court. Taney was no modern-day jurist exalting his special knowledge over that of Congress. Taney could not, and did not, seek to legitimate his invalidation of the Missouri Compromise based on his own will. Rather, he is better understood as the agent of jurisprudential values that were themselves undergoing rapid change and of political forces that had thrust upon the Court the responsibility for deciding an issue that neither Congress nor the president wished to resolve. That the collapse of the departmental theory was under way seems certain; it seems equally plausible that Taney's Dred Scott opinion was rooted as much in a traditional as in a modern conception of the role of appellate judges.

Dred Scott was the first case in which the public had to consider the consequences of judicial review of a federal law. Marshall's Marbury opinion was self-liquidating and altogether defensive of the Court's authority. Marbury required no executive enforcement, and it placed no inhibition on Congress (and thus on the exercise of popular will). Dred Scott did both.

For the principals in the case, the verdict of the Court made little difference. John Sanford died in an insane asylum two moths after Taney read his opinion. Dred Scott was soon manumitted, but he lived only sixteen months as a free man before succumbing to tuberculosis.

Selected Bibliography

Ehrlich, Walter. *They Have No Rights: Dred Scott's Struggle for Freedom.* Westport, CT: Greenwood Press, 1979.

Fehrenbacher, Don E. *The Dred Scott Case: Its Significance in American Law and Politics.* New York: Oxford University Press, 1978.

Hall, Kermit L. *The Supreme Court and Judicial Review in American History*. Washington, DC: American Historical Association, 1985.

Morgan, Donald G. *Congress and the Constitution: A Study in Responsibility*. Cambridge, MA.: Harvard University Press, 1966.

Potter, David M. *The Impending Crisis, 1848–1861*. New York: Harper & Row, 1976.

Swisher, Carl B. *History of the Supreme Court of the United States: The Taney Period, 1836–1864*. New York: Macmillan, 1974.

Slavery, Freedom, and Federal Judicial Power

———◄o►———

Thomas D. Morris

Professor of History, Emeritus
Portland State University

Ableman v. Booth, 21 Howard 506 (1859) [U.S. Supreme Court]

◄o► THE CASE IN BRIEF ◄o►

Date
1859

Location
Wisconsin

Court
U.S. Supreme Court

Principal Participants
Sherman M. Booth
U.S. Marshal Stephan V. R. Ableman
Members of Wisconsin Supreme Court
Chief Justice Roger B. Taney

Significance of the Case
This case dealt with the relationship between federal and state judicial power and the issue of slavery versus freedom. As part of the ruling, the Court found the fugitive slave law of 1850 constitutional.

Neither Benammi S. Garland nor Joshua Glover could have known that when Glover fled Garland's farm outside of St. Louis in 1852, they would set in motion a series of events that led to one of the more important jurisdictional rulings by the Supreme Court in the nineteenth century. Sherman M. Booth, a hot-tempered abolitionist newspaper editor in Milwaukee, Wisconsin, could not have known it either. In March 1854 these three, along with others, had a violent meeting.

Glover, a runaway slave, was playing cards with two black friends in a cabin on the outskirts of Racine, Wisconsin, where he had fled earlier. On March 10, 1854, Garland, two U.S. deputy marshals, and four other men captured Glover. There was a struggle; Glover was badly hurt, manacled, and taken to a jail in Milwaukee. When Booth heard that the runaway was in jail "all bruised and bloody," he rode a horse through the city, stopping at each street corner and yelling, "To the rescue! Slave catchers are in our midst! Be at the courthouse at two o'clock!" That evening a mob gathered to listen to an impassioned speech by Booth, and then it demanded the release of Glover. When that was refused, the mob broke into the jail, took the battered slave out, and put him aboard a steamer bound for Canada. Joshua Glover was free at last, but for Booth the legal drama had just begun.

On March 15, 1854, Sherman M. Booth was arrested for aiding the escape of a fugitive in violation of the federal fugitive slave law. He was arrested by U.S. Marshal Stephan V. R. Ableman. Shortly thereafter, Booth's case became a cause célèbre among abolitionists, and a test of the constitutionality of the fugitive slave law of 1850. That statute had been a clear victory for the South. It provided for the appointment of fugitive slave commissioners by lower federal judicial officials. They would sit throughout the North, hearing claims by slave owners, and granting certificates authorizing the removal of the alleged runaways. These commissioners could also summon the aid of bystanders, a *posse comitatus*, to help in the recovery of fugitives. A commissioner would hear the proofs offered by the slave owner or his agent. The testimony of the alleged fugitive would not be admitted, and once a certificate of removal was granted, it was conclusive evidence of the right to remove the person and would "prevent all molestation . . . by any process issued by any court, judge, magistrate, or other person whomsoever." What this meant was that the basic presumption of freedom which underlay the law of the free states and the laws of those states designed to secure the personal liberty of freemen could not be used to defeat a claim that a person was a slave, whether it was true or false. And anyone who obstructed a claimant making a seizure "with or without" a legal process or who rescued a runaway would be guilty of a federal offense. Finally, antislavery people in Congress had tried, without success, to require that an alleged slave would be granted the right to a writ of habeas corpus and the right to a trial by jury.

Booth and the others had violated this law, but a question remained: Was the law itself constitutional? Ultimately, the question was Who shall decide? On May 27, 1854, by which time Joshua Glover was safely in Canada, Sher-

man M. Booth, who was still in jail, asked Associate Justice Abram D. Smith of the Wisconsin Supreme Court to issue a writ of habeas corpus and free him, on the ground that the fugitive slave law was unconstitutional. Byron Paine, Booth's counsel, delivered a searing indictment of that law and of the federal judicial power that had affirmed a duty and a power in the federal government to provide for the return of runaways.

Paine contended that the so-called fugitive slave clause of the U.S. Constitution (Article IV, Section 2, Paragraph 3) was addressed not to the federal government but to the states. "The trampling of the gathering hosts is already heard," Paine intoned, "the murmuring of the rising storm is wafted upon every gale. The North is snapping asunder the bands that have bound it in subjection to the slave power, as Sampson broke the withs of tow! The last link that binds it, is the judicial sanction that power has received! Let that be broken, and the people are free!" What Paine received in 1854 was a favorable state judicial decision. But it ultimately led to another judicial sanction of the slave power and of federal judicial power.

At the end of May, Associate Justice Smith freed Booth on the ground that the federal law was unconstitutional, in that it denied trial by jury to alleged fugitives, and it took their liberty without due process of law. Upon the request of the federal marshal, Smith's ruling was heard by the full Wisconsin Supreme Court, which upheld Smith's decision on July 19, 1854. The marshal, Ableman, appealed this decision to the U.S. Supreme Court. While this appeal was pending, Booth was rearrested for violating the federal fugitive slave act in January 1855. He was tried by a jury in a trial presided over by U.S. District Judge Andrew Miller. Miller was determined to uphold the federal law and its enforcement, lest there be a serious erosion of order and stability. Booth was found guilty and was sentenced to serve one month in jail and to pay a fine of $1000. Once again he appealed to the Wisconsin Supreme Court for release, on the ground that he was held under an unconstitutional federal statute.

On February 3, 1855, the Wisconsin Supreme Court again freed Booth. It ruled that he was illegally confined under an unconstitutional law and that a state was empowered to protect its citizens. Without this authority "the state would be stripped of one of the most essential attributes of sovereignty." This decision also was appealed to the U.S. Supreme Court.

Booth's original idea was to present a vigorous defense before the U.S. Supreme Court in an argument made "in behalf of liberty." Booth sought the help of Charles Sumner, the powerful U.S. Senator from Massachusetts, to argue the case on his behalf. Although he did not agree to serve as Booth's attorney, Sumner did write to Byron Paine that "it were well that the self-defensive power of the States should be recognized." The Wisconsin Supreme Court began to obstruct the process in May 1855. It ordered its clerk to make no return whatsoever to the writ of error issued by the U.S. Supreme Court. The clerk, however, had already handed over a certified copy of the record to the federal District Attorney. On March 6, 1857, the same day that it handed down one of the most significant decisions in its history, *Dred Scott v. Sandford*, the Court granted the motion of the U.S. Attorney General to file the copy of the record despite the order of the state court. The earlier appeal was consolidated, and the two cases were decided two years later, on March 7, 1859.

The only argument presented was that of Jeremiah S. Black of Pennsylvania, the Attorney General of the United States. No one appeared to present an argument "in behalf of liberty." Among the more critical points Black raised were that the fugitive slave law of 1850 was constitutional, that a judgment of a federal court was conclusive of all questions of constitutional law or statutory construction, and that no state court could free a man on a writ of habeas corpus when he was held by a federal court of exclusive jurisdiction.

The power of a state court under its habeas corpus jurisdiction was controversial at that time. A leading treatise on the writ, for instance, held that a state court could free a person who was illegally detained, even if that might involve "questions of the constitutionality of acts of Congress, or of the jurisdiction of a court of the United States."

In a very brief and unanimous opinion for the Court, Chief Justice Roger Taney flatly rejected this notion. It was an opinion of considerable importance in terms of federal judicial power that, in one sense, reads like a brief essay in arcane jurisdictional law. But it involved more than disembodied technicalities; it upheld national supremacy and fed the raging fires of controversy over slavery. One scholar called Taney's opinion in *Ableman v. Booth* "the most powerful of all his notable opinions." Another observed that it was "thoughtful, measured, and disciplined to the last degree." Whatever its ultimate significance, it should not be wholly abstracted from the context within which it was decided. It was the affirmation not so much of national supremacy in general as it was of federal *judicial* supremacy at a time when the federal judiciary was prepared to diminish federal legislative power in the interests of the institution of slavery, as in the *Dred Scott* case.

Taney began his opinion with the assertion that the Wisconsin Supreme Court had claimed far too much; it had claimed that the state courts were supreme over the courts of the nation. What it had actually claimed was that the state must possess the authority to protect its citizens on its own soil from being jailed under an unconstitutional law. Broadly stated, this harkened back to the position of Thomas Jefferson and James Madison in the Virginia and Kentucky Resolutions, adopted to undermine the enforcement of the Alien and Sedition Acts, which directly threatened civil liberty. The Wisconsin court claimed only that it had authority to protect personal liberty. It did not claim a general supervisory power over all federal legislation.

Still, the sweeping and controversial claim made by the Wisconsin Supreme Court, Taney reasoned, could lead to chaos. There would be conflicting decisions throughout the country, and decisions would be affected by "local influences." Under such a situation, federal supremacy could not be maintained peacefully unless there were a federal "judicial power equally paramount in authority to carry it into execution." Taney did admit that a state court could use its habeas corpus jurisdiction to inquire into any and all imprisonments. However, once it was informed that the person was held under federal authority, the case would end. Habeas corpus authority did "not pass over the line of division between the two sovereignties." This was the heart of the decision.

Although it was not necessary to the judgment in Ableman v. Booth, the Court, without full argument by counsel or discussion by the Court, announced that the Fugitive Slave Law of 1850 was "fully authorized by the Constitution of the United States." The Court's assertion about the Fugitive Slave Law seems to have escaped the notice of many scholars, but it did not escape that of some contemporaries. When Byron Paine, Booth's counsel, was elected to the Wisconsin Supreme Court, Charles Sumner wrote to him that "Trial by Jury, *habeas corpus,* and the other safeguards of the rights of all . . . will again become realities." The Wisconsin legislature, moreover, condemned *Ableman v. Booth* as an "arbitrary act of power" that abrogated the writ of habeas corpus, and left the liberties of the people defenseless beneath "unlimited power."

Federal officials in Wisconsin obviously confronted a rather delicate situation, and they moved with less than dispatch. In the spring of 1860 they finally acted. Booth was arrested yet again for violating the fugitive slave act. Sherman Booth had a little bit of John Brown in him. He considered himself a martyr and refused to pay the fine that had been levied against him. A little over a year after this arrest, after war had broken out, the Wisconsin Supreme Court, with a new set of jurists, ended the case of Sherman M. Booth when they upheld a judgment against his printing press to cover his fine.

Perhaps a more telling conclusion to the matter, however, came the following year. In a minority report of a special legislative committee of the Wisconsin legislature, the remarks of G. W. Hazelton made clear what was at stake in the jurisdictional battle that was *Ableman v. Booth.* Jurisdiction is power, the power to decide, but we should not forget that the substantive issues involved are also important. Hazelton did not forget. The federal government, in his view, had long been under the control of proslavery elements. But, with the secession

and the outbreak of war, it had "passed from the grasp of the slave power," and it would never be repossessed by that power. Because freedom and not slavery now controlled the institutions of the nation, the "true interests of freedom are to be developed in our nation, not . . . by States acting in their individual spheres . . . but by the whole body of the people operating through a national organization."

Buried deep within jurisdictional law are often issues of profound significance. In the case of *Ableman v. Booth* the issues were the relationship between federal and state judicial power and the issue of freedom or slavery. Caught in between were the free blacks whose liberty might be protected by the states or who might fall victim to a claim that the individual was a slave. Also intertwined, but not expressed in the opinion, were the divergent moral perceptions of the North and the South. The latter believed fervently that the ownership of human beings was proper and defensible, and the former, that it was not. There was no way that a judgment such as *Ableman v. Booth* could possibly resolve the division. As important as the case was for the affirmation of a nation, and of a federal judicial supremacy, the case was but one more element in the deterioration of the relationships between the sections. In the end it was not federal judicial supremacy that resolved that problem. Despite Chief Justice Taney's hope, the sectional divisions could not be resolved peacefully.

Selected Bibliography

Bestor, Arthur. "State Sovereignty and Slavery: A Reinterpretation of Proslavery Constitutional Doctrine, 1846–1860." *Journal of the Illinois State Historical Society* 54 (Summer 1961): 117–180.

Hagan, Horace H. "Ableman vs. Booth." *American Bar Association Journal* 17 (January 1931): 1–20.

Hyman, Harold M., and William M. Wiecek. *Equal Justice Under Law: Constitutional Development, 1835–1875.* New York: Harper & Row, 1982.

Schafer, Joseph. "Stormy Days in Court—The Booth Case." *Wisconsin Magazine of History* 20 (1936): 89–110.

Swisher, Carl B. *History of the Supreme Court of the United States: The Taney Period, 1836–1864.* New York: Macmillan, 1974.

Slaves-in-Transit and the Antebellum Crisis

—◄o►—

Paul Finkelman

College of Law
University of Tulsa

Lemmon v. The People, 20 N.Y. 562 (1860) [New York Court of Appeals]

◄o► THE CASE IN BRIEF ◄o►

Date
1852, 1860

Location
Virginia
New York

Court
New York Court of Appeals

Principal Participants
Jonathan and Juliet Lemmon
State of New York
Judge Hiram Denion

Significance of the Case
New York allowed slaves passing through the state to be freed. The outbreak of the Civil War in 1861 prevented the case from reaching the Supreme Court, where, Lincoln and Republicans feared, it would become "another Dred Scott," leading to the nationalization of slavery.

In 1852 Jonathan and Juliet Lemmon prepared to move from Virginia to Texas. At that time the easiest way to make such a move was to travel by steamboat to New York City and then board a steamboat going directly to New Orleans. On November 5, 1852, the Lemmons arrived in New York and rented a hotel room while awaiting passage for New Orleans. They expected to stay in New York for only a few days. Along with their baggage and other property, the Lemmons had eight slaves. They locked these slaves in their hotel room.

On November 6 a black man named Louis Napoleon secured a writ of habeas corpus on behalf of "eight colored persons lately taken from the steamer *City of Richmond.*" The Lemmons responded that the eight people were slaves owned by Juliet Lemmon and that she "never had any intention of bringing the said slaves or persons into the State of New York to remain therein, and that she did not bring them into said State in any manner nor for any purpose whatever, except *in transitu* or transit from the State of Virginia . . . through the port or harbor of New York." The Lemmons essentially argued that, as citizens of one state, they had a right of unmolested travel with their property through another state. This argument did not impress Judge Elijah Paine of the New York Superior Court. On November 13 Judge Paine discharged "the colored Virginians." While the Lemmons prepared their appeal to a higher court, the eight ex-slaves quickly disappeared.

The Lemmons felt that they had suffered a great injustice, and that the position of Judge Paine threatened the American Union. They had not wanted to establish slavery in New York. They had not even allowed their slaves to leave their hotel room. All they sought was to exercise their rights, under the U.S. Constitution, to travel from one state to another, through a third state.

Judge Paine acted under a New York law of 1841 which amended earlier statutes dealing with slavery. In 1810 New York adopted legislation allowing visitors and transients to bring slaves into the state for up to nine months. In 1841 the legislature repealed this nine-month exemption. The statutes of New York now read that any slave (except a fugitive) entering the state became instantly free. Judge Paine, the first New York jurist to construe this repeal, interpreted it literally, and freed the slaves.

The Lemmons were especially depressed by this result because their slaves constituted most of their property. The *New York Journal of Commerce* immediately established a fund to recompense the Lemmons, and in the process show Southerners that not all Northerners were abolitionists. The newspaper soon raised $5,000, far more than the five slave children, two women, and one adult man were worth. Before returning to Virginia with this large sum of money, the Lemmons formally manumitted their slaves, so that the outcome of any litigation would not turn on the actual fate of the eight "colored Virginians," who by this time had become "colored Canadians."

Although the Lemmons no longer had a personal stake in the case, the state of Virginia felt obliged to appeal Paine's decision, and employed a distinguished New York attorney and prominent Democrat, Charles O'Conor. Meanwhile the New York legislature appropriated special funds to William M. Evarts and Chester A. Arthur as special counsel. Governors of both states declared their determination to vindicate the rights of their respective states. This increasingly politicized background was exacerbated by the 1857 decision of the U.S. Supreme Court in *Dred Scott v. Sandford.* That same year the New York Supreme Court upheld Paine. Finally, in 1860, the state's highest court, the New York Court of Appeals, reached the same conclusion.

Speaking for the New York Court of Appeals, Judge Hiram Denion conceded that under the commerce clause, Congress might have the power to regulate the interstate movement of slaves. But until Congress passed such a law, he asserted, the state was free to act. Denion argued that New York was in full compliance with the privileges or immunities clause of the U.S. Constitution because Virginians could "hold property by the same titles by which every other citizen may hold it, and by no other." Denion argued that if the right of transit with slaves was constitutionally protected, "it would naturally be supposed that . . . [this right] would be adjusted in connection with the provision [in the Constitution] looking specially to that case instead of being left to be deduced by construction from clauses intended primarily for cases to which slavery had no necessary relation." Absent such a clause, no right existed.

In dissent, Judge Thomas Clerke asked, "Is it consistent with this purpose of perfect union, and perfect and unrestricted intercourse, that property which the citizen of one State brings into another State, for the purpose of passing through it to a State where he intends to take up his residence, shall be confiscated in the State through which he is passing, or shall be declared no property, and liberated from his control?" He pointed out that under international law, New York's action might lead to war. But "relations of the different States of this Union . . . are of a much closer and more positive nature . . . war between them is legally impossible." He condemned his judicial brethren for "forgetting . . . the compact, by which" the American states were governed, and thus undermining the Union.

Lemmon was the last important slavery-related case to be decided by a northern state supreme court. The election of Abraham Lincoln as President and the outbreak of the Civil War prevented the Supreme Court from hearing the case. Given its proslavery biases, it is quite likely that the Taney Court would have overturned the New York decision and ruled that all Americans had a constitutional right to travel with their property through other states. *Lemmon* was probably the "next Dred Scott" case that Abraham Lincoln predicted in his "House Divided" speech. In the late antebellum period Lincoln and other Republicans feared that *Lemmon* would lead to a nationalization of slavery. Lincoln's election and the outbreak of the Civil War made this speculation moot.

Selected Bibliography

Finkelman, Paul. *An Imperfect Union: Slavery, Federalism, and Comity.* Chapel Hill: University of North Carolina Press, 1981.

Finkelman, Paul. *Slavery in the Courtroom.* Washington, DC: U.S. Government Printing Office, 1985.

Foner, Eric. *Free Soil, Free Labor, Free Men.* New York: Oxford University Press, 1970.

Hyman, Harold M., and William M. Wiecek. *Equal Justice Under Law: Constitutional Development, 1835–1875.* New York: Harper & Row, 1982.

Wiecek, William M. *The Sources of Antislavery Constitutionalism in America, 1760–1848.* Ithaca: Cornell University Press, 1977.

Zilversmit, Arthur. *The First Emancipation.* Chicago: University of Chicago Press, 1967.

African Americans Since 1865

No "Right" to Vote:
The Reconstruction Election Cases

—◦—

Robert M. Goldman

Department of History-Political Science
Virginia Union University

United States v. Reese et al., 92 U.S. 214 (1876) and
United States v. Cruikshank et al., 92 U.S. 542 (1876)
[U.S. Supreme Court]

◦ THE CASE IN BRIEF ◦

Date
1876

Location
Louisiana
Kentucky

Court
U.S. Supreme Court

Principal Participants
Hiram Reese; William J. Cruikshank;
Reverdy Johnson and David Dudley Field;
Attorney General George H. Williams and
Solicitor General Samuel Field Phillips;
Chief Justice Morrison R. Waite

Significance of the Case
The rulings affirmed national authority, but
in limited terms and with deference to state
authority and political realities. Black voting
rights were set back for almost a century.

By some accounts the slaughter was reminiscent of the worst Civil War massacres. On April 13, 1873—Easter Sunday—at least 105 blacks and 3 whites were brutally murdered by a force of white Democrats in and around the Grant Parish courthouse in Colfax, Louisiana. Almost half of those killed had been shot after they surrendered, and some of the bodies were mutilated and looted.

The Grant Parish Massacre (or Colfax Riot) was one of the worst of many instances of violence and intimidation directed against the recently emancipated slaves in the South after the end of the Civil War. To protect the civil and political rights of the freedmen, Republicans in Congress had passed the Civil Rights Act of 1866 and added the Fourteenth Amendment to the Constitution in 1868. When those proved insufficient to guarantee that blacks in the South would be allowed to participate in the political process of Reconstruction, Republicans passed and ratified the Fifteenth Amendment in 1870.

Under the Fifteenth Amendment, "The right of citizens of the United States to vote shall not be denied or abridged by the United States or by any State on account of race, color, or previous condition of servitude." A second section gave Congress authority to enforce the provisions of the amendment "by appropriate legislation."

It quickly became evident that the amendment alone was not enough. Reports poured into Congress from throughout the South of continued terrorism directed against blacks attempting to vote or participate in political activities. Often the acts were committed by organized groups of southern white conservatives, most frequently the Ku Klux Klan. In response, Republicans in Congress passed a series of three acts in 1870–1871 known as the Enforcement Acts. These measures defined in great detail a wide variety of crimes directed against potential voters, and provided the machinery for the federal government and Justice Department officials to punish them.

Prosecutions were begun in the South under the Enforcement Acts, and during the first two years achieved some real success in protecting civil and voting rights. What was not yet clear was whether the U.S. Supreme Court would find these measures constitutional, and appeals were brought by defendants convicted under the acts in the federal courts. In one early lower court ruling, Circuit Court Judge William B. Woods of Alabama upheld a series of indictments brought under the acts. Judge Woods used the privileges or immunities clause of the Fourteenth Amendment to affirm the conviction of a group of white Alabamians accused of breaking up a political rally of blacks.

On the basis of extensive federal investigations, District Attorney James R. Beckwith of New Orleans used provisions of the May 1870 Enforcement Act to bring indictments against ninety-seven men who had participated in the Grant Parish massacre. Only nine of those indicted, however, were brought to trial. That trial lasted from February 23 to March 16, 1874, and resulted in the acquittal of one defendant and a mistrial for the eight others. In a second trial William J. Cruikshank and two others were found guilty of conspiracy. Following a division over the constitutional issues raised, the presiding judges on the circuit court, Supreme Court Justice Joseph Bradley and Judge Woods, certified the case for appeal to the U.S. Supreme Court.

An impressive array of legal counsel, including former Attorney General Reverdy Johnson and David Dudley Field, brother of Supreme Court Justice Stephen J. Field, argued the defendants' case before the Court in March and April 1874. Attorney General George H. Williams and Solicitor General Samuel Field Phillips represented the federal government.

In their briefs and oral arguments before the Supreme Court, the defendants' attorneys argued that the primary issue was whether Congress had the power to protect individual rights from infringement by private individuals. Using what one historian has called a "states' rights view of American federalism," defense counsel insisted that Congress had no such power, and that the Enforcement Acts were an unconstitutional infringement of state authority. Murdering a group of black men may have been a denial of their rights, but it was a denial that could be protected by only the states. The Attorney General and the Solicitor General confined their arguments to the narrowest possible grounds, arguing that the defendants were properly accused and convicted of a crime, that of conspiracy, cognizable under federal law.

While *Cruikshank* was making its way through the courts, federal officials brought another case involving prosecutions under the Enforcement Acts that dealt even more directly with the scope of the Fifteenth Amendment. The case began during the municipal elections in Lexington, Kentucky, in January 1873. A state law required voters to pay a $1.50 "capitation tax" and present a receipt for the same to election officials before being allowed to vote. Two Lexington officials, Mathew Foushee and Hiram Reese, were indicted by a federal grand jury for refusing to allow William Garner, a citizen "of African descent," to vote. They claimed he had failed to present the required receipt. Following a division of opinion among the circuit court judges reviewing the indictments in December 1873, the case was docketed for review by the Supreme Court shortly thereafter.

Reese was not argued before the Court until January 1875. Representing the defendants were two prominent Democratic attorneys, Henry Stanbery and B. F. Buckner of Kentucky. Attorney General Williams and Solicitor General Phillips again presented the government's case. Buckner and Stanbery contended that Sections 3 and 4 of the 1870 Enforcement Act were unconstitutional under the Fifteenth Amendment because there was no allusion in those sections to discrimination "on account of race." Foushee and Reese had prevented Garner from voting, but the indictment did not allege that the refusal had been because of his race. Williams and Phillips, on the other hand, argued that the act was constitutional inasmuch as the Fifteenth Amendment had given Congress broad affirmative powers to prevent any racially motivated interference with voting rights. The Enforcement Act made race an element of all its provisions, they insisted, and though the sections being reviewed "have a much wider application" than was necessary for the defendants in the case, they certainly covered the crimes that were committed.

At the time both cases were argued before the Supreme Court, the Chief Justice was Morrison R. Waite, an Ohio Republican appointed by President Ulysses Grant. Serving with Waite were Republican appointees Joseph Bradley, Samuel F. Miller, William Strong, Noah H. Swayne, Ward Hunt, and David Davis, along with Democrats Nathan Clifford and Stephen J. Field. The Supreme Court had already rendered one significant decision on the scope of the Reconstruction amendments in 1873, in the *Slaughterhouse Cases.* There, the Court had limited the meaning and scope of the privileges or immunities clause of the Fourteenth Amendment. But the *Slaughterhouse* decision involved a Louisiana butcher monopoly law: *Reese* and *Cruickshank* presented questions that dealt directly with the postwar amendments as they related to the protection of the rights of blacks in the South.

After initial hearings, the Court continued the cases for further argument in October 1875. A month later the Court agreed to affirm the lower court judgments in each case, thus overturning the convictions of both sets of defen-dants. The Court also agreed to keep the grounds of the decisions so narrow as "not [to] have any intimation in the opinion upon the constitutional questions" raised. The chief justice assigned Justice Clifford to write the opinion in the two cases on that basis. On November 20 the Court rejected Clifford's draft, and Waite assumed responsibility for preparing the final opinions. Three months later the Court approved Waite's version, and the decisions were announced together on March 27, 1876.

In *U.S. v. Reese* the Supreme Court declared Sections 3 and 4 of the May 1870 Enforcement Act unconstitutional. The key issue confronted by the Court's opinion was whether or not the two sections went beyond the "appropriate legislation" necessary to enforce the provisions of the Fifteenth Amendment. Waite did not deny Congress's power to provide for such legislation. On the contrary, he stated that "Rights and immunities created by or dependent upon the Constitution of the United States can be protected by Congress. The form and the manner of the protection may be such as Congress, in the legitimate exercise of its legislative discretion, shall provide."

The problem, according to Waite, was that the Fifteenth Amendment "does not confer the right of suffrage upon anyone." What it did do was prevent the states from discriminating or "giving preference" in the exercise of franchise rights on account of race or color. The statutes in question had gone beyond that protection and were so "general" in their import as to be beyond both the intention and the powers of Congress. They encroached upon the traditional right of states to determine voter qualifications for their own citizens. Given the generality of the statutes, it might have been possible for the Court itself to limit their meaning and scope by reading racial motivation into them, as the government attorneys had suggested. This Waite declined to do, because it would "substitute the judicial for the legislative department of government." Having decided that Congress had not as yet legislated against the crimes charged in the indictments (i.e., discrimination based on race), the lower court was correct in finding the indictments faulty and giving judgment for the defendants.

In a lone dissenting opinion, Justice Hunt pointed out that the majority had in fact ignored the constitutional issues at stake and based their opinion on a narrow and inaccurate reading of the statutes. The purpose of the Enforcement Act as a whole, insisted Hunt, was to protect blacks against violations of their right to vote. This purpose was clearly set forth in the first two sections of the act, which made explicit reference to race as the basis for the crimes specified. Though Sections 3 and 4 did not specifically mention race, the crimes listed concluded with the words "as aforesaid," referring back to the first two sections, in which race and the Fifteenth Amendment were mentioned. In other words, the majority had seen fit to throw out part of an act as a way of notifying Congress that "unless it crossed every 't' and dotted every 'i' the Court would not sustain its civil rights legislation."

Chief Justice Waite's opinion in *United States v. Cruikshank* reached an even more narrow conclusion than that in *Reese*. The Court reversed the convictions of the defendants without voiding the relevant sections of the Enforcement Act. Waite admitted that the right to assemble peacefully was an attribute of national citizenship which Congress, under the Fifteenth Amendment, was empowered to protect from infringement on account of race. Congress, in fact, had done this in Section 6 of the Enforcement Act under review.

The crucial issue was whether the indictments under which defendants had been prosecuted were sufficient in law to the extent that they set forth the same elements of the crimes committed as the crimes proscribed in Section 6 of the act. The Court ruled that they did not, because the indictments failed to allege that the murders in Grant Parish were committed because of the victims' race. "We may suspect that race was the cause of the hostility," Waite concluded, "but it is not so averred." For the Supreme Court this flaw was fatal to the indictments. Moreover, the omission was one of substance and not of form, making the indictments so "defective" as to be useless in supporting a conviction based on them.

Court fears of a negative public and congressional reaction to the decisions proved groundless. Northerners who had condemned the Grant Parish massacre made no outcry, and the Republican press actually approved of the way the Court reached its decision. Southerners and Democrats praised the decision and went so far as to compare the recently appointed Waite with the great chief justices of the past, such as John Marshall and Roger B. Taney.

Most twentieth-century constitutional scholars have concluded that the decisions left the federal laws "almost wholly ineffective to protect the Negro." The two cases were part of a series of Supreme Court rulings in the late nineteenth century that limited the effectiveness of the Fourteenth and Fifteenth Amendments in protecting the civil and political rights of southern blacks. Moreover, by placing strict limits on federal authority, the Court signaled southern states, by now back in the hands of the Democratic party, that they were essentially free to do what they would with their own citizens. For southern states this meant the establishment by law of "Jim Crow" segregation and the virtually complete disfranchisement of black voters.

A careful reading of the opinions and their immediate impact suggests an alternative view. In one case only two sections out of a comprehensive body of legislation were voided, and in the other case only the indictments were dismissed by the Court. This hardly constituted a total rejection of national authority. Furthermore, prior to the Court's announcement of the decisions, Congress incorporated both sections voided in *Reese*, along with the rest of the Enforcement Acts, as part of the new federal Revised Statutes. The new sections were more specific than the original ones, but were still based on the Fifteenth Amendment. In 1883 Virginia Circuit Court Judge Hugh Bond upheld a conviction based on these statutes. A year later, the Supreme Court upheld a series of convictions based on the same laws and, in the process, issued a strong affirmation of federal authority to protect voters in federal elections. Until most of the legislation was repealed by Congress in the 1890s, federal Justice Department officials continued to bring prosecutions in the South under these statutes.

The Supreme Court's decisions in *Reese* and *Cruikshank* represented an attempt to "preserve federalism" as it had come to be understood by the 1870s. This meant acceptance of a strong national authority, confirmed by the Civil War and Reconstruction, and at the same time it meant recognition of the limits of that power in deference to state authority and the political realities necessary for sectional reconciliation. The price was high, for it meant that those like the perpetrators of the Grant Parish murders and Hiram Reese went unpunished. The "heritage of sanctioned congressional power" to protect the voting rights of blacks in the South would remain dormant for another eighty to ninety years, to be revived with the struggles and achievements of the civil rights movement of the 1950s and 1960s. In that sense it is not surprising that the sections of the Enforcement Acts reviewed by the Supreme Court in 1867 could be found in almost identical wording and form in the opening sections of the Voting Rights Act of 1965.

Selected Bibliography

Benedict, Michael Les. "Preventing Federalism: Reconstruction and the Waite Court." *The Supreme Court Review* (1978): 39–79.

Cummings, Homer, and Carl McFarland. *Federal Justice: Chapters in the History of Justice and the Federal Executive.* New York: Macmillan, 1937.

Fairman, Charles. *Reconstruction and Reunion, 1864–88, Part Two.* New York: Macmillan, 1987.

Goldman, Robert M. *A "Free Ballot and a Fair Count": The Department of Justice and the Enforcement of Voting Rights in the South, 1877–1893.* New York: Garland, 1990.

Goldman, Robert M. *Reconstruction and Black Suffrage: Losing the Vote in Reese and Cruikshank.* Lawrence: University Press of Kansas, 2001.

Kaczorowski, Robert J. *The Politics of Judicial Interpretations: The Federal Courts, Department of Justice and Civil Rights, 1866–1876.* New York: Oceana Publications, 1985.

Magrath, C. Peter. *Morrison R. Waite: The Triumph of Character.* New York: Macmillan, 1963.

Wang, Xi. *The Trial of Democracy: Black Suffrage and Northern Republicans, 1860–1910.* Athens: University of Georgia Press, 1997.

Williams, Low. *The Great South Carolina Ku Klux Klan Trials, 1871–1872.* Athens: University of Georgia Press, 1996.

Civil Rights or Last Rites?

——◄o►——

Jonathan Lurie

Department of History
Rutgers University at Newark

Civil Rights Cases, 109 U.S. 3 (1883) [U.S. Supreme Court]

◄o► THE CASE IN BRIEF ◄o►

Date
  1883

Location
  Various states and the District of
  Columbia

Court
  U.S. Supreme Court

Principal Participants
  Litigants in five cases touching on the
    legality of the Civil Rights Act of 1875
  Associate Justice Joseph P. Bradley
  Associate Justice John Marshall Harlan

Significance of the Case
  The Court found the Civil Rights Act of
  1875 unconstitutional, ruling, among
  other things, that no congressional power
  existed to bar private discrimination.

The several cases decided together under the collective title *Civil Rights Cases* represent an epilogue to the Civil War era. The 1883 decision concerned the constitutionality of the Civil Rights Act of 1875, the last civil rights statute of Reconstruction. Understanding its significance requires some discussion of events between 1861 and 1883.

The Civil War began in 1861 as nothing more than an attempt to prevent an illegal act: secession by the southern states. By 1865, however, the conflict had become one for freedom for the slaves, as well as for restoration of the Union. Lincoln had not intended this result. "I claim," he wrote, "not to have controlled events, but confess plainly that events have controlled me." After four years of carnage, the intangible goal of a permanent Union merged with the very tangible aim of abolitionism.

The North strongly supported freedom for the slaves, as is shown in the Thirteenth Amendment. Yet the issue of exactly what this freedom actually involved, represented (and remains) a much more difficult challenge. For many northerners, racial antipathy toward African Americans seemed fully compatible with their strong pro-Union and antislavery sentiments. In no way did they envisage abolition as providing social equality within a newly integrated society. Nor did the great majority believe that the traditional operation of federalism, with the states assuming "local control of the character of daily experience," would change with a Union victory. This strong belief in traditional federalism, coupled with a very real and deep-seated streak of northern racism, represented a truly potent obstacle to new national efforts at racial integration. Given the rapidly shifting political currents after 1865, a variety of motives—reconciliation, revenge, restoration, reconstruction, racism, and republicanism—were in evidence.

We do not know how Lincoln would have handled the awesome challenge of integrating the former slaves into the American polity, although there is no doubt of his racial conservatism. We do know that his sudden death deprived the Union of consummate and tactful political leadership—skills notably absent in his successor, Andrew Johnson, a southern Unionist with a traditional racial bias. Others in the Republican party, especially Massachusetts Senator Charles Sumner, took a much more radical stand, calling for total racial equality in public facilities, including schools. To be sure, Sumner and his supporters were always in the minority. But he persisted, much to the discomfiture of the Republican party as a whole. From 1867 until his death seven years later, Sumner continually sought to have a civil rights act providing for such equality enacted into law. The fact that such a statute was not passed while he lived indicates the racial ambivalence of the Reconstruction era.

This ambivalence was also reflected in the Fourteenth Amendment, sent to the states by Congress for ratification in 1866. Although intended to provide some sort of federal protection for former slaves, the first section of the amendment (and the only section of major constitutional significance) made no mention either of equality or of any political and civil rights. It forbade the states to make any law

"which shall abridge the privileges or immunities of citizens of the United States," and it further held that no State could "deprive any person of life, liberty, or property, without due process of law; nor deny to any person within its jurisdiction the equal protection of the laws." Another section gave Congress power to enforce, "by appropriate legislation," the provisions of the new amendment.

The Supreme Court first interpreted this amendment in 1873 in the famous *Slaughterhouse Cases,* a dispute that appeared in no way to involve former slaves. For a bare majority of the Court, Justice Samuel F. Miller held that the amendment protected only federal privileges and immunities of U.S. citizens, and that these did not include what were usually referred to as "civil rights or liberties." For protection of *these* rights, one had to look to the states for relief, as had been primarily the case since adoption of the federal Constitution. In other words, the majority was unwilling to hold that American federalism had itself been fundamentally reconstructed during the Civil war era.

The decision gravely troubled politicians like Sumner, who had assumed that the new amendment provided protection to the former slaves from improper state, and possibly even private, action. One possible solution to the problems posed by the interpretation of the Constitution in the *Slaughterhouse Cases* would be a federal statute specifying the rights that states had to protect. Here, Sumner confronted the racial ambivalence of his party, many of whose members did not favor legislation that named specific rights, such as public school integration. But some members of Congress were equally unwilling (by voting against such a measure) to indicate support for segregation. The ideal solution, from their point of view, was to do nothing. Against such pragmatic prejudice, Sumner's eloquence was inspirational but ineffectual.

In 1872, Sumner argued that emphasis on separate facilities was in reality a fake substitute for equality, a "contrivance by which a transcendent right, involving a transcendent duty, is evaded." There can be, he insisted, "no substitute for equality; nothing but itself. Even if accommodations are the same, as notoriously they are not, there is no equality. In the process of substitution the vital elixir exhales and escapes. It is lost and cannot be recovered; for equality is found only in equality."

More than the racial ambiguity noted above explains Sumner's failure to gain this legislation he considered so vital. By 1872, the Republican party had split over the issue of a second term for President Ulysses S. Grant, under whose leadership the presidency had evolved, according to Henry Adams, to a level that "would have upset even Darwin!" Sumner and other "liberal Republicans" had supported a third-party candidate in 1872, when issues focused on budgets and corruption, not blacks and civil rights. Soundly trounced in the election, Sumner's wing had even less influence within the party after 1872 than the little it had enjoyed before. To make matters worse, the Democrats, who as a national party were even more opposed to racial progress than the Republicans, won enough congressional seats in the midterm elections of 1874 to control the House—something that had not happened since before the Civil War.

Given these facts, one might have expected that the lame duck session of Congress that convened in December 1874 would do nothing in the area of civil rights. In fact, their congressional defeat may have galvanized the Republicans into a belated if not final attempt to gather support on behalf of southern blacks. Moreover, Sumner's death in March 1874 could now justify as a memorial tribute the legislation to which he had devoted the last years of his political career. Finally, Republicans, though far less sympathetic to issues of integration than Sumner had been, had to admit that there *was* a need for some sort of federal statute. Benjamin Butler noted, for example, that the Supreme Court's decision in *Slaughterhouse* "allowed the nation to protect American citizens anywhere in the world except in the states." Thus, for a variety of reasons, the Republicans tried to enact a civil rights law.

The result, accomplished through traditional political methods of compromise, all-night sessions, and lengthy partisan wrangling, was far from what Sumner had sought. It held that "all persons are entitled to the full and equal enjoy-

ment of public accommodations in inns, transportation facilities, and places of public amusement." The statute made no mention of public schools, and thus in reality was more a mockery of than a memorial to Charles Sumner. Indeed, "the widely understood assumption that the measure would never operate effectively was the reason the bill had passed." The law, accepted by the Senate without change, was signed into law by President Grant on March 1, 1875, without comment.

Contemporary reaction to the new statute confirms that little positive value was to be expected from it. According to the *Baltimore Sun*, the law "represented buncombe, pure and simple." *Harper's Weekly* correctly observed that, shorn of application to public schools, the bill "indirectly sanctioned the very prejudice it was intended to combat." The *Southern Law Journal* commented "that such a law can be practically enforced . . . no intelligent person of either race or color believes." The *Mobile Register* called the statute "infamous, tyrannical, malicious, insolent," and added for good measure that it was unconstitutional.

Privately, Supreme Court Justice Joseph P. Bradley agreed. He drew a distinction between protecting one's privileges as a citizen, an appropriate area for federal intervention, and matters of social preference, an inappropriate area for federal legislation. In 1875–1876, Bradley recorded his thinking on the 1875 statute: "Surely Congress cannot guarantee to the colored people admission to every place of gathering and amusement. To deprive white people of the right of choosing their own company would be to introduce another kind of slavery. The civil rights bill [of 1866] had already guaranteed to the blacks the right of buying, selling and holding property, and of equal protection of the laws. Are not these the essentials of freedom?"

For Bradley, and probably the vast majority of white Americans, to ask such a question was to answer it. He further insisted that "[it] never can be endured that the white shall be compelled to lodge and eat and sit with the negro. The latter can have his freedom and all legal and essential privileges without that. The antipathy of race cannot be crushed and annihilated by legal enactment. The Constitutional amendments [referring here to the Thirteenth, Fourteenth, and Fifteenth] were never intended to aim at such an impossibility." Bradley concluded his statement by emphasizing that "surely it is no deprivation of civil rights to give each race the right to choose their own company." Thus Bradley had formulated his own distinct viewpoint about the inappropriateness, if not unconstitutionality, of the 1875 law soon after it was enacted. His views should be kept in mind, for what he wrote privately would later appear publicly as the opinion for the Court in the *Civil Rights Cases,* handed down in 1883.

It is not clear why the Supreme Court waited until 1883 to consider the Civil Rights Act of 1875. There is no doubt that the longer it waited, the more sentiment in favor of racial integration dissipated. A desire for national reconciliation and northerners' growing willingness to concede that southern attitudes toward blacks were not very different from their own seemed more important. Moreover, the famous "compromise of 1876" that ensured the election of Republican Rutherford Hayes in 1877, also ensured white control of the deep South and reinforced the view that the era of the federal government's active involvement in protecting the civil rights of black Americans had ended.

The *Civil Rights Cases* actually consisted of five separate suits. Four were the result of federal criminal indictments, and one was an action brought by a black plaintiff for damages against a southern railroad because she had been refused access to the "ladies" car. Perhaps reflecting an assumption that the Civil Rights Act was constitutionally insignificant, the defendants in the criminal cases did not even bother to file briefs before the Court. Such was not the case for the federal government, nor for the plaintiff against the Memphis and Charleston Railroad.

In separate briefs, both the U.S. government and the Solicitor General asserted the constitutionality of the Civil Rights Act of 1875. The "business to be carried on [in theaters and hotels] is quasi public in its nature, and for the general accommodation of the people." Because it was thus a public right, appropriate

federal legislation "may be raised to meet the necessities of the particular right to be protected." Freedom from racial discrimination by private owners serving the public had become a "right" of federal citizenship, and "what the United States has the right to give, it necessarily has the right and duty to preserve and protect."

The Solicitor General emphasized that the conduct of innkeepers and operators of passenger carriers was frequently "a mere reflection of the views of the community." Their action "testifies to and at the same time tends to enlarge, a particular current in *public opinion,* and this in its turn is fruitful of *public, i.e. State* institutions." A problem could arise if this opinion was contrary to the national will as reflected by Congress. "*Is it not a mere matter of legislative discretion to decide upon the stage of growth at which it will be best to suppress such vegetation?*" [Emphasis in original brief.]

The counsel for the black passenger noted that his case "involves the rights of a citizen of one State traveling [via public carrier] through another State, for the purpose of reaching a place in a third State." Existing constitutional authority, such as the interstate commerce clause, "leave[s] very little room for argument." In other words, this attorney did not feel it necessary to rely on the Fourteenth Amendment as the constitutional basis for the 1875 statute. Rather, he insisted that it could be justified by well established legal precedents. He added, however, that the civil rights law did give the right to "the full and equal enjoyment" of the *"very same"* accommodations enjoyed by other persons similarly circumstanced.

By a vote of 8-1, the Supreme Court, speaking through Justice Bradley, gutted the 1875 statute. Bradley based his opinion on a disarmingly simple proposition, one that Justice John Marshall Harlan in dissent described as "a subtle and ingenious verbal criticism." It was "state action of a particular character that is prohibited" by the Fourteenth Amendment. Congress could indeed adopt legislation to correct "the effects of such prohibited state laws and state Acts," but that was the full extent of congressional authority. "And so . . . until some state law has been passed or some state action through its officers and agents has been taken, adverse to the rights of citizens . . . no legislation of the United States under [the Fourteenth Amendment] . . . can be called into activity."

Bradley conceded that Congress did indeed possess the power to redress conditions of slavery or servitude, but he insisted that "the refusal to any persons of the accommodations of an inn or a public conveyance or a place of public amusement, by an individual and without any sanction or support from any state law or regulation" did not "inflict upon such persons any manner of servitude, or form of slavery, as those terms are understood in this country." Therefore, Congress had no authority on which to enact this statute. Well reflecting the racial realities of 1883, which he strongly supported, Justice Bradley claimed that "it would be running the slavery argument into the ground, to make it apply to every act of discrimination which a person may see fit to make as to the guests he will entertain, or as to the people he will take into his coach or cab or car, or admit to his concert or theatre, or deal with in other matters of intercourse or business."

Almost twenty years after the end of the Civil War, Bradley concluded that "there must be some stage in the process of the [former slave's] elevation when he takes the rank of a mere citizen, and ceases to be a special favorite of the laws." In truth, many free blacks "were not admitted to all the privileges enjoyed by white citizens," yet they possessed "all the essential rights of life, liberty and property." Because private discrimination was not barred by the Fourteenth Amendment, no congressional power had existed on which to construct the 1875 law. Hence, it was unconstitutional.

Justice Harlan, a former slave owner, found Bradley's conclusions unwarranted, unconvincing, unfortunate, and inaccurate. He emphasized that it was state approval, if not state action through issuance of a license, that enabled an innkeeper or theater proprietor or railroad operator to function in the first place. Such private property, when affected with a public interest, ceased to be purely private property. Here Harlan quoted Chief Justice Waite in the famous case *Munn v. Illinois*, decided in 1877. When one uses his property for a purpose in which the public has an interest, "he, in effect, grants to the public an interest in that use and must submit to be controlled by the public for the common good to the extent of the interest he has thus created." Bradley, it might be noted, strongly supported *Munn*, and indeed had aided Waite in formulating this argument.

Because there could be no doubt that such private enterprises as inns, theaters, and railroads were thus clothed with a public interest, they were legitimate subjects for state regulation. Furthermore, if Congress had the power to abolish slavery, why could it not also forbid private discrimination "based merely upon race or color" in public conveyances, inns, and places of public amusement? For Harlan, Bradley's insistence on state action as the required trigger for federal intervention was more than fulfilled by the obvious fact that proprietors of these types of businesses could not operate without state sanction, in the form of either a corporate charter (common to the railroads) or a state license (common to inns and places of public entertainment).

Harlan, no less a child of his era than Bradley, also conceded that government "has nothing to do with social, as distinguished from technically legal, rights of individuals. . . . Whether one person will permit or maintain social relations with another is a matter with which government has no concern." Indeed, "for even upon grounds of race, no legal right of a citizen is violated by the refusal of others to maintain merely social relations with him." But the actions involved in these cases were of individuals or corporations "wielding power under state authority for the public benefit or the public convenience." They were far from mere social relations.

Finally, Harlan emphasized a point made by federal attorneys in the briefs submitted to the Court. Under the Fourteenth Amendment, Congress had an affirmative power to intervene to "guard, secure and protect" a constitutionally protected right. Unlike Bradley, Harlan saw *both* affirmative and prohibitive provisions within its mandate. It was "a grave misconception to suppose" that the enforcement section "has reference exclusively to express prohibitions upon state laws or state action."

Harlan may have had the better argument, but Bradley had the votes. Harlan spoke alone, and for the most part contemporary reaction to the decision strongly supported Bradley's position. Perhaps this was because the 1875 statute had had virtually no effect on existing discrimination. The *Chicago Tribune* had called the measure harmless, but unnecessary; *The Nation* had described it as both "amusing" and an example of "tea-table nonsense." In 1883, *The Nation* observed that the "calm" with which the country accepted Bradley's conclusions revealed "how completely the extravagant expectations . . . of the war have died out." The great majority of those who voted for the law "knew very well," according to the writer, "that whenever it came before the Supreme Court it would be torn to pieces." Actually, it may be that the law was never effectively enforced at all, even between 1875 and 1883.

The *Civil Rights Cases* and the weakened statute that inspired them illustrate that law is frequently an accurate reflection of the society from which it comes. A logical corollary to Bradley's reasoning would be to permit a state requirement of separate but equal facilities while denying that such action violated the Fourteenth Amendment. The Court took this step in 1896 in *Plessy v. Ferguson*. Again, Justice Harlan dissented, and again he spoke alone. *Plessy*, however, was unanimously overruled in 1954. On the other hand, two problems raised in Bradley's 1883 decision continue to plague American public policy.

In terms of civil rights, American constitutional doctrine still confronts the twin challenges of affirmative action and state action. To what extent does the Constitution permit private discrimination based upon race? To what extent can the legal order use the force of law to affirmatively redress such discrimination? Indeed, does the public community have any obligation to pursue affirmative action as a matter of public policy? Or must it merely correct discrimination that has already occurred? Where does one draw the line between private discrimination and discrimination somehow sanctioned by state action? Much of our constitutional history since 1883 has focused on these questions. If one seeks the ways in which American society has answered them, one needs only to look around.

Selected Bibliography

Brown, Bertram Wyatt. "The Civil Rights Act of 1875." *Western Political Quarterly* 18 (1965): 763–775.

Donald, David H. *Charles Sumner and the Rights of Man.* New York: Knopf, 1970.

Fairman, Charles. *Reconstruction and Reunion, 1864–88, Part Two.* New York: Macmillan, 1963.

Gillette, William. *Retreat from Reconstruction.* Baton Rouge: Louisiana State University Press, 1979.

Hyman, Harold M., and William M. Wiecek. *Equal Justice Under Law: Constitutional Development, 1835–1875.* New York: Harper & Row, 1982.

Kelly, Alfred H. "The Congressional Controversy over School Segregation." *American Historical Review* 64 (1959): 537–563.

Lurie, Jonathan. *Law and the Nation, 1865–1912.* New York: Knopf, 1983.

Lurie, Jonathan. "Mr. Justice Bradley: A Reassessment." *Seton Hall Law Review* 16 (1986): 343–375.

McPherson, James M. "Abolitionists and the Civil Rights Act of 1875." *Journal of American History* 52 (1965): 493–510.

"Separate But Equal" Approved

—◦—

Robert P. Green Jr.

College of Health, Education and Human Development
Clemson University

Plessy v. Ferguson, 163 U.S. 537 (1896) [U.S. Supreme Court]

◦ THE CASE IN BRIEF ◦

Date
1896

Location
Louisiana

Court
U.S. Supreme Court

Principal Participants
Honor Adolph Plessy
Judge John H. Ferguson
Associate Justice Henry Billings Brown

Significance of the Case
The Court ruled that "separate but equal" accommodations for whites and blacks were constitutional, thus further chipping away at the protections guaranteed by the Fourteenth Amendment.

On June 7, 1892, Homer Adolph Plessy, a light-skinned African American man, boarded an East Louisiana Railway train and took a seat designated for whites. When asked by the conductor to move to the "colored" car, he refused and was immediately arrested. Tried before Judge John H. Ferguson of the Criminal District Court for the Parish of Orleans, Plessy was found guilty of violating an 1890 Louisiana statute titled "An Act to Promote the Comfort of Passengers." Plessy's subsequent appeal of Ferguson's decision ended up before the U.S. Supreme Court. The High Court's decision, delivered in 1896, profoundly influenced judicial application of the Fourteenth Amendment to the Constitution, permitting the practice of racial segregation in "separate but equal" facilities.

The Louisiana statute under which Plessy was tried stated that "all railway companies carrying passengers in their coaches in this State, shall provide equal but separate accommodations for the white, and colored, races, by providing two or more passenger coaches for each passenger train, or by dividing the passenger coaches by a partition so as to secure separate accommodations." Passengers who refused to cooperate with railroad officials charged with implementing the statute faced a possible $25 fine or a sentence of up to twenty days in jail. Before Judge Ferguson, Plessy argued that this law denied his privileges and immunities, and violated the equal protection clause of the Fourteenth Amendment. Judge Ferguson rejected this argument, as did, on appeal, the Louisiana Supreme Court. The Louisiana chief justice, however, granted Plessy's petition for a writ of error, thus allowing his case to be heard by the U.S. Supreme Court. The Court's opinion in *Plessy v. Ferguson* culminated a process that for over twenty years had chipped away at the original meaning of the Fourteenth Amendment.

Proposed in June 1866 and ratified in July 1868, the Fourteenth Amendment was an attempt to ensure the basic rights of U.S. citizenship for the newly freed slaves. Mainly designed as a response to the development of the infamous "Black Codes" in the South after the Civil War—state laws which returned freedmen to virtual slave status—the first section of the amendment declared: "All persons born or naturalized in the United States, and subject to the jurisdiction thereof, are citizens of the United States and of the State wherein they reside. No State shall make or enforce any law which shall abridge the privileges or immunities of citizens of the United States; nor shall any State deprive any person of life, liberty, or property, without due process of law; nor deny to any person within its jurisdiction the equal protection of the laws."

The historical record clearly shows that the Fourteenth Amendment was adopted to protect the civil rights of freedmen. Proposed during the height of tension between Congress and President Andrew Johnson over Reconstruction, the amendment was designed to remove questions of constitutionality raised by legislation like the Civil Rights Act of 1866. That act, passed over the president's veto, recognized the citizenship of persons born in the United States, guaranteed them certain rights and privileges, and provided penalties when any

person, because of color or race, was deprived of those protected rights. Many believed, as did President Johnson, that acts like the Civil Rights Act infringed upon state sovereignty and were unconstitutional. Johnson, for example, argued that such measures would lead to "an absorption and assumption of power by the general government which, if acquiesced in, must sap and destroy our federative system of limited powers and break down the barriers which preserve the rights of the states." Proponents of the Fourteenth Amendment and potential enabling legislation, such as John A. Bingham of Ohio, believed that the amendment's language would resolve any constitutional issue. Through it, they believed, the national government would become the protector of individual civil rights. That, however, would prove not to be the case.

Almost from the beginning, the Supreme Court's interpretation of the Fourteenth Amendment undermined its original intent. In the 1873 *Slaughterhouse Cases*, Justice Samuel F. Miller, writing for the Court, drew a distinction between national and state citizenship as treated in the amendment. The first sentence, he argued, clearly gave citizenship to the freedmen, but in the second sentence, "the distinction between citizenship of the United States and the citizenship of a State is clearly recognized and established. . . . It is quite clear, then, that there is a citizenship of the United States, and a citizenship of a State, which are distinct from each other." Despite the obvious history of the amendment, Miller argued that it was "not the purpose of the Fourteenth Amendment . . . to transfer the security and protection of . . . civil rights . . . from the states to the federal government." Rather, the intent had been to place national rights under the protection of the federal government, and "those fundamental civil rights for the security and establishment of which organized society is instituted" under the care of the state! What, then, *were* the rights the amendment was designed to protect? They were rights such as the right to vote in federal elections, the right to go to the seat of government and gain access to federal buildings, the right to petition the federal government for redress of grievances.

Even that paltry list of rights was soon undermined by the Supreme Court. For example, Chief Justice Waite argued for the Court in the 1876 case *United States v. Cruikshank* that "the right of suffrage is not a necessary attribute of national citizenship" and that the Fourteenth Amendment protected individual rights—life, liberty, privileges, immunities, due process of law, and equal protection of the laws—only when a *state* deprived citizens of those rights, not when citizens deprived other citizens of those rights. The fact that the state had failed to guarantee the rights of one group of its citizens against another remained an issue for the state. It was not a matter for the federal courts.

The reasoning in *Cruikshank* was reinforced a few years later in the 1883 *Civil Rights Cases*. In the face of a growing number of reported instances of discrimination against blacks, the Republican leadership pushed the Civil Rights Act of 1875 through Congress. Given the understanding that John Bingham and Charles Sumner (who had died in 1874) had of Section 5 of the Fourteenth Amendment, which states that "Congress shall have power to enforce, by appropriate legislation, the provisions of this article," the Civil Rights Act would seem to have been an appropriate action on the part of the national government. Section 1 of that act declared that "all persons within the jurisdiction of the United States shall be entitled to the full and equal enjoyment of the accommodations . . . of inns, public conveyances on land or water, theaters and other places of public amusement; subject only to the conditions and limitations established by law, and applicable alike to citizens of every race or color." In the *Civil Rights Cases*, the Court reviewed a number of discrimination cases originating in violations of this law. Writing for the Court, Justice Joseph P. Bradley argued that the Civil Rights Act exceeded the authority of Congress under the Fourteenth Amendment and was thus unconstitutional. The Fourteenth Amendment, he argued, was designed to address state deprivations of rights and was not meant to encompass individual acts of discrimination.

Why had the Court retreated from defense of the freedmen? Evidently the nation had tired of the turmoil surrounding the Civil War and Reconstruction. Its attention had shifted to other matters, and the Court reflected that trend. Many of the older "Radical Republicans" had passed from the political scene, and concern over issues such as economic growth and government reform captured the attention of those who remained. Popular pseudoscientific theories purporting to explain racial differences—to the discredit of anyone of non-Anglo-Saxon stock—tended to reinforce doubts concerning the assimilation of blacks into the broader society. Social theory, based upon these and other "scientific" ideas, suggested that government should avoid involvement in society and allow the "fittest" to succeed and survive. These changes were reflected in the Court's decision in the *Civil Rights Cases* when Justice Bradley argued that the time had come when the black American no longer needed to be "a special favorite of the law," and instead should take on the "rank of a mere citizen." Unfortunately, this decision came at the very time when southern politicians were beginning to rediscover and exploit racial fear and the call for white supremacy in shaping electoral majorities.

It was in this atmosphere that Louisiana passed the statute to provide for the "comfort of passengers" on railways within the state. In the early 1890s, however, blacks refused to be cowed by their losses, and the black community in New Orleans—composed of many men and women of culture and learning—decided to challenge the new state statute. Evidence suggests that the Plessy incident was planned in advance, with the cooperation of the East Louisiana Railway. In any event, the black community sought a test case over the issue, and *Plessy* provided just such a vehicle.

Plessy's case was argued before the Court by attorney Albion Tourgée, a well-known novelist who, as a carpetbagger, had been a leader of the North Carolina Radical Republicans during Reconstruction. Tourgée argued that the law in question was incompatible with the Fourteenth Amendment. Pointing out that it served only to perpetuate distinctions "coincident with the institution of slavery," he rejected the argument that the concept of "separate but equal" was, indeed, equal and impartial. Rather, he argued, "the object of such a law is simply to debase and distinguish against the inferior race. . . . Its object is to separate the Negroes from the whites in public conveyances for the gratification and recognition of the sentiment of white superiority and white supremacy of right and power." Decrying the obvious intent of the law, Tourgée declared in an oft-quoted passage, "Justice is pictured blind and her daughter, the Law, ought at least to be color blind."

The Court did not render its decision until 1896. In the interim, the pace of Jim Crow legislation quickened in the South as conservatives, frightened by Populist gains built in part upon black and poor-white political solidarity, frantically exploited racial fears. They were soon joined in the practice by their erstwhile white opponents. The segregation, disfranchisement, and lynching of blacks spread. The Supreme Court's decision in *Plessy* acquiesced in these developments.

On May 18, 1896, Justice Henry Billings Brown delivered the opinion of a near unanimous Court. Focusing on interpretation of the Fourteenth Amendment as central to the issue, Brown cited the distinction that the Court had earlier made in the *Slaughterhouse Cases* between "the rights and immunities of citizens of the United States, as distinguished from those of citizens of the States," and sought to clarify the kinds of rights protected from hostile state legislation. He concluded: "The object of the amendment was undoubtedly to enforce the absolute equality of the two races before the law, but in the nature of things it could not have been intended to abolish distinctions based upon color, or to enforce social, as distinguished from political equality, or a commingling of the two races upon terms unsatisfactory to either. Laws permitting, and even requiring, their separation in places where they are liable to be brought into contact do not necessarily imply the inferiority of either race to the other, and have been generally, if not universally, recognized as within the competency of the state legislatures in the exercise of their police power."

In support of this new distinction between political and social rights, Brown cited cases which protected the political rights of blacks—like the right to sit on juries—and those (both judicial and legislative) which ostensibly recognized or sustained segregation. The case, then, devolved to a question of the "reasonableness" of the Louisiana action. But, in determining the question of reasonableness, argued Brown, the legislature "is at liberty to act with reference to the established usages, customs and traditions of the people, and with a view to the promotion of their comfort, and the preservation of the public peace and good order." Gauged by that standard, Brown opined, "We cannot say that a law which authorizes or even requires the separation of the two races in public conveyances is unreasonable."

Adding insult to injury, Brown came to an incredible—and from today's perspective, disingenuous—conclusion: "We consider the underlying fallacy of the plaintiff's argument to consist in the assumption that the enforced separation of the two races stamps the colored race with a badge of inferiority. If this be so, it is not by reason of anything found in the fact, but solely because the colored race chooses to put that construction upon it."

Brown's opinion for the Court ignored the historical origin of the Civil War amendments and the political atmosphere in which segregation laws were passed. He cited cases as precedent which had only the most superficial relationship to the issue at hand. For example, in support of his point concerning the common nature of the state sanction of segregation, he cited the Massachusetts Supreme Judicial Court case of *Roberts v. City of Boston* (1849). That case arose when, in the late 1840s, the family of a black child, Sarah Roberts, argued that city maintenance of a separate school for blacks violated her rights under the state constitution. Attorney Charles Sumner argued for the plaintiffs not only that the school was inferior to those maintained for whites, but also that the segregation of black children "branded a whole race with the stigma of inferiority and degradation." Segregation based on some reasonable relationship to the educational endeavor—by age, by sex, by intellectual capacity—might be justifiable, but segregation by race was not. Such discrimination stigmatized the minority while it "hardened" the hearts of the white children. Despite Sumner's eloquence, Chief Justice Lemuel Shaw upheld the city's discriminatory policy. Though the case was cited as precedent in many later decisions, its relevance to *Plessy* was questionable at best because it was decided *before* the Fourteenth Amendment became part of the Constitution. Other "precedents" cited by Brown had little or nothing to do with the issue of equal protection under the Fourteenth Amendment.

The lone voice of dissent to the majority opinion in *Plessy* was that of John Marshall Harlan of Kentucky, the "Great Dissenter." Ironically, Harlan, who had once been a slave owner, argued that the Louisiana statute at issue was clearly a violation of the Civil War amendments. Accepting the reasoning of Tourgée and rejecting the idea that the law was not discriminatory because it applied equally to both races, he wrote, "Every one knows that the statute in question had its origin in the purpose . . . to exclude colored people from coaches occupied by or assigned to white persons. . . . The thing to accomplish was, under the guise of giving equal accommodation for whites and blacks, to compel the latter to keep to themselves while traveling in railroad passenger coaches. . . . The fundamental objection, therefore, to the statute is that it interferes with the personal freedom of citizens." He continued eloquently: "Our constitution is color-blind, and neither knows nor tolerates classes among citizens. In respect of civil rights, all citizens are equal before the law. The humblest is the peer of the most powerful. The law regards man as man, and takes no account of his surroundings, or of his color when his civil rights as guaranteed by the supreme law of the land are in-

volved. . . . We boast of the freedom enjoyed by our people above all other peoples. But it is difficult to reconcile that boast with a state of law which, practically, puts the brand of servitude and degradation upon a large class of our fellow citizens—our equals before the law. The thin disguise of 'equal' accommodations for passengers in railroad coaches will not mislead any one, nor atone for the wrong this day done."

With a great deal of prescience, Harlan predicted that "the judgment this day rendered will, in time, prove to be quite as pernicious as the decision made by this tribunal in the *Dred Scott* case. . . . The present decision, it may well be apprehended, will not only stimulate aggressions, but will encourage the belief that it is possible, by means of state enactments, to defeat the beneficent purposes which the people of the United States had in view when they adopted the recent amendments of the Constitution." As the sad history of race relations in the United States attests, it would be nearly sixty years before the Court would begin to undo the "pernicious" effects of its decision in *Plessy v. Ferguson*.

Selected Bibliography

Kluger, Richard. *Simple Justice: The History of Brown v. Board of Education and Black America's Struggle for Equality.* New York: Knopf, 1975.

Lurie, Jonathan. *Law and the Nation, 1865–1912.* New York: Knopf, 1983.

Woodward, C. Vann. *The Strange Career of Jim Crow.* 3rd ed. New York: Oxford University Press, 1974.

Race, Law, and Gender in South Carolina, 1925–1927

Henry Lewis Suggs
Department of History
Clemson University

South Carolina v. Demon Lowman, Bertha Lowman and Clarence Lowman, (1927)
[South Carolina state court]

◄◦► THE CASE IN BRIEF ◄◦►

Date
1927

Location
South Carolina

Court
South Carolina state court

Principal Participants
Demon, Bertha, and Clarence Lowman
N. J. Frederick

Significance of the Case
The lynching of members of the Lowman family, including a woman, shocked even the white establishment of South Carolina and revealed the gross racial justices in the judicial system in the South.

There is a fine distinction between murder and lynching. In order for an act of violence to qualify as a lynching, several factors must occur in concert. First, a group of three or more must have participated, and the group must have acted under the pretext of service to justice, race, or tradition. Moreover, the victim's body must have been found or other legal evidence must prove that the victim was killed.

If one accepts the above characteristics of a lynching, then what became known as the Lowman Case in South Carolina in the late 1920s is clearly a lynching. In the 1920s it was not unusual for a Southern mob to lynch a black male accused of a capital offense such as rape or murder. But the Lowman Case is different for two reasons.

First, a black woman was lynched. Therefore, remarked the black intellectual W.E.B. DuBois, "there can be no mention of the usual crime." He characterized the lynching as "a black stain upon the American South." And inasmuch as DuBois at the time was editor of *The Crisis*, official organ of the National Association for the Advancement of Colored People (NAACP), his opinion probably mirrored that of other black intellectuals.

Next, unlike other lynchings, the perpetrators of the violence did not go unnoticed. The Governor of South Carolina and other high officials not only condemned the lynching but also used their power to pursue a grand jury indictment.

The events leading to this uncharacteristic resolution commenced on April 25, 1925, when Aiken County Sheriff Henry Howard and deputies Nollie Robinson, A. D. Sheppard, and Robert McElheney visited the home of Sam Lowman, a black tenant farmer, to investigate charges of bootlegging. As they approached Sam Lowman's home on foot, they observed Lowman's wife, Annie, age fifty-five, and her daughter Bertha working in the backyard. Annie Lowman was making soap in an iron pot; her daughter was sweeping the yard with a brush broom.

When Bertha Lowman observed four white men in "civilian dress" approaching the house, she reflected upon an incident two weeks earlier in which her brother Demon was beaten severely by several robed and hooded Klansmen. She quietly alerted her mother to the presence of the armed and unfamiliar men in civilian dress. As Bertha and her mother attempted to retreat to their farmhouse, the men drew their weapons and ran toward the house. Sheriff Howard stopped Bertha Lowman within a few feet of the back door and began to pistol-whip her as he ordered her to "stand back." Meanwhile, Annie Lowman hit Sheriff Howard with an ax handle. In retaliation for the attack on Sheriff Howard, Deputy Sheriff Nollie Robinson "emptied his gun into Annie Lowman's body."

As Annie Lowman "crumpled" to the ground in what Walter White, the Executive Secretary of the NAACP, later termed "a lifeless heap," her son Demon and her nephew Clarence arrived on the scene. An exchange of gunfire occurred between the Lowmans and Sheriff Howard and his deputies. Within seconds, Annie Lowman and the sheriff lay dead.

Bertha Lowman was seriously wounded by shots in her breast and abdomen. Her brother Demon and her cousin Clarence lay gravely wounded as well.

Almost immediately Bertha, Demon, and Clarence Lowman were arrested and housed in the Aiken County jail. Sam Lowman, the father, who was at a local mill when the shooting occurred, returned home to find himself a widower, his two children and his nephew gravely wounded. Three days later, three-fourths of a quart of liquor was found buried in the yard of the Lowman home. Sam Lowman was arrested, tried, and sentenced to two years on the chain gang. Meanwhile, rumors persisted that the Ku Klux Klan was going to lynch the Lowman children. For their safety, Bertha and Demon Lowman, although seriously injured, were transferred to the state prison in Columbia, South Carolina.

Approximately two hundred Klansmen in full regalia attended Sheriff Howard's funeral. And when the Lowmans' trial began on May 12, 1925, an atmosphere of fear pervaded the courtroom and the Aiken community. And like the more famous Scottsboro cases of the following decade, an "ugly mood" permeated the daily crowd outside of the courtroom.

The outcome of the trial of Bertha, Clarence, and Demon Lowman was never in doubt. The defense attorneys asserted that they were "assigned" to defend the Lowmans, and Judge H. F. Rice apologized to the jury for the defense attorneys. "Don't hold it against them because they defended these Negroes," Judge Rice said. "They were ordered by the court to take the case; the ethics of their profession force them to defend a man when the courts assign them such a task," he continued. "None of them wanted to do it."

The jury found Demon and Clarence Lowman guilty of murder, and on June 12, 1925, Judge Rice sentenced them to die. Although Bertha Lowman was found guilty of murder, she was sentenced to life imprisonment because the jury recommended mercy.

Meanwhile, in Columbia, South Carolina, newspaper accounts of the trial angered black attorney N. J. Frederick. He became outraged after examining the court's procedure and decided to appeal the Lowmans' conviction to the South Carolina Supreme Court. Inasmuch as South Carolina did not have an NAACP chapter until the mid-1930s, it is safe to assume that he consulted on strategy with Walter White, Executive Secretary of the NAACP, and national NAACP officials in New York.

Frederick's objectives were threefold. First, he wanted to save the Lowmans from execution. Next, he wished to use this travesty of justice to highlight inequities in the South's judicial system and, at the same time, to encourage a more palatable social and political atmosphere for what black journalist P. B. Young called "the South's proscribed people." A final objective was to exploit the case in order to organize an NAACP chapter in Columbia, South Carolina. Even though the organization of an NAACP chapter seems inconsequential in the 1990s, in 1925 the NAACP was regarded as a subversive organization in communities throughout the South. NAACP chapters in Virginia, for example, were forced to use oral communication only to announce meetings. The NAACP met under the guise of the "Helping Hand Club" or some other fictitious or innocuous-sounding organization. The speaker was often a prominent minister from the North or an official of the NAACP.

Although a South Carolina black newspaper, *The Palmetto Leader,* dutifully reported on the Lowman Case, there was no attempt to organize a defense fund or to sponsor a mass meeting in support of the Lowmans. As the Lowmans' attorney for the appeal, Frederick shouldered most of the burden of the defense, both personally and financially.

As the South Carolina Supreme Court deliberated on Frederick's motion for a new trial, the Klan held "a great celebration" on April 25, 1926, the anniversary of the death of Sheriff Howard. The *State* newspaper reported that fifteen hundred people were in attendance. Eyewitnesses, however, estimated the crowd at four thousand to five thousand. Within days after the "great celebration," the South Carolina Supreme Court reversed the Lowmans' conviction and ordered a new trial on the grounds that the warrant was improperly drawn and executed. Also, the court rebuked Judge Rice

for his unethical conduct and hostility to the prisoners in the first trial.

On October 6, 1926, the *State* ran the headline: "New Trial Opens in Lowman Case." No excitement prevailed, the *State* recorded, as the black attorney Frederick and L. G. Southard, a white attorney whose grandfather had been a Confederate Army general, presented the Lowmans' defense. Interestingly, the defense did not petition the court for a change of venue. When the trial began, Frederick and Southard hammered away at the prosecution's attempt to introduce evidence that the Lowmans had conspired to murder Sheriff Howard. The defense also questioned the legality of the warrants and charged that Sheriff Howard had trespassed upon the property of a peaceable, law-abiding family. Besides, argued Frederick, "A man's home is his castle." The Lowmans, he continued, had every legal and human right to repel invaders of that home. Accordingly, one day after the trial began, the defense petitioned for a directed verdict of "not guilty" for the three defendants, on the ground that the state had failed to prove an act of conspiracy.

On October 7, 1926, the judge in the Lowman case directed a verdict of "not guilty" against Demon Lowman, the principal defendant, but denied the petitions of Bertha and Clarence Lowman. Demon Lowman was immediately rearrested on a charge of assault and battery, and was returned to the Aiken County jail along with Bertha and Clarence Lowman.

Although both court and law enforcement officials had assured South Carolina Governor Thomas McLeod, who called several times during the trial, that there was "no danger of any violence," they were wrong. On October 9, 1926, the *State* had the headline "Negro Prisoners Lynched at Aiken." Apparently, several Aiken County whites felt a need to avenge the death of Sheriff Howard. Also, Sheriff Howard's supporters were angered by the presence of black attorney Frederick and his cross-examination of witnesses. An embarrassed and angry Governor McLeod lamented, "I regret it exceedingly more than I can express." The prosecutor and the jury foreman demanded a thorough investigation.

In 1927, Governor-elect John G. Richards termed the Lowman lynching "a miscarriage of justice." He promised to stand for the "majesty of the law." And in his inaugural address, he promised the South Carolina electorate that "if it lies within my power, the Aiken lynchers shall be brought to justice." The governor's remarks were applauded by the Commission on Interracial Cooperation, a liberal southern organization, and by white editors in South Carolina who expressed anger over the Aiken lynching. In scathing editorials, white publishers demanded that the lynchers be tried and convicted for what the Columbia (South Carolina) *Record* called "one of the most bestial crimes that has ever happened in our state." The Spartanburg *Herald* called the lynching a "murderous defiance of the law by a few men," and the Charleston *News and Courier* urged Governor Richards "to defend the state's honor."

Vigilant NAACP publicity efforts kept the story of the Lowman lynching before the South Carolina public. In particular, black newspapers carried numerous stories about this "typical southern tragedy." Nevertheless, justice was not served. Although several lynchers were identified and ordered before an Aiken grand jury, no true bill of indictment was returned against any of them.

In March 1927, a man whom the Palmetto *Leader* characterized as "a man of sorrow," left for Philadelphia. Sam Lowman had served all but seventy-two days of his sentence on the charge of bootlegging. But his real crime was that he was the father of Demon and Bertha Lowman. When asked why he was leaving the South, Sam Lowman replied, "I can't live among these people."

Selected Bibliography

Brown, Richard Maxwell. *Strain of Violence.* New York: Oxford University Press, 1975.

Smith, Lillian. *Killers of the Dream.* New York: W. W. Norton, 1949.

Suggs, H. Lewis. *The Black Press in the South, 1865–1979.* Westport, CT: Greenwood Press, 1983.

Zangrado, Robert L. *The NAACP Crusade Against Lynching, 1909–1950.* Philadelphia: Temple University Press, 1980.

Justice Vindicated:
The Case of William Harper, 1931

◄○►

Henry Lewis Suggs
Department of History
Clemson University

The Commonwealth of Virginia v. William L. Harper, (1931) [Virginia state court]

◄○► THE CASE IN BRIEF ◄○►

Date
1931

Location
Virginia

Court
Virginia state court

Principal Participants
William L. Harper
William H. Starkey
Dorothy Skaggs

Significance of the Case
Harper, a black man, was acquitted by an all-white jury of raping Skaggs, a white woman. The outcome was almost unheard of in the South, where black men were executed for assaults—many of which did not occur—on white women.

One of the most unusual cases in southern legal history is that of William L. Harper. The Harper case, like the much more publicized cases of the same era—the Scottsboro Nine, Angelo Herndon, and Claude Neal—involved a black man or men accused of raping a white southern woman or women. All record the failure of the South's criminal justice system. Each provoked intense national indignation and became a rallying point for the struggle to push antilynching and civil rights legislation through Congress. What distinguishes the case of William Harper is that he was acquitted by a southern trial court.

The Harper case began on January 7, 1931, when Dorothy Skaggs, a young white resident of Portsmouth, Virginia, claimed that she was raped in Upton Lane in the city of Norfolk. The following day, William Harper, a black man arrested on an unrelated assault charge, confessed to the crime. In his original confession, Harper acknowledged that he waited for Skaggs in Upton Lane, "hit her in the stomach," and started "messing with her." He also admitted that he took one dollar and a half ($1.50) from Skaggs's pocketbook. At the time, the Norfolk police described Harper's crime to a reporter from the Norfolk *Virginian-Pilot* who was present during Harper's interrogation as one of "the most daring and brutal acts" in Norfolk's history. The Norfolk paper later reported that Dorothy Skaggs was "hysterical" and confined to bed with a badly bruised body.

Harper's family had retained W. H. Land, a black Norfolk attorney, to defend Harper on the assault charge. Land noted that Harper was "not of normal mentality," and asked the court for a "continuance" and for time to investigate. However, after Harper's confession and indictment for rape, Land withdrew from the case, and the court appointed a white attorney, William H. Starkey, to represent Harper. Starkey later emerged as one of Harper's strongest defenders; however, at the time he indicated that he was "not anxious" to defend a black man and that he would not oppose Harper's scheduled trial date of January 15.

Harper was declared sane by three court-appointed physicians on January 12. When his trial began on January 28, 1931, spectators were prohibited. The Norfolk *Journal and Guide,* a black weekly, was the black community's only source of information on the trial. The judge instructed the jurors to find Harper guilty if they determined that he possessed the capacity to distinguish right from wrong, and understood the nature, character, and consequences of his act. Apparently the jury was convinced of Harper's guilt, for they found him guilty on January 29, and fixed his punishment as death. The case might have slipped into obscurity had it not been for the efforts undertaken on Harper's behalf by Starkey and by P. B. Young, publisher of the *Journal and Guide.* Because of their interest, the Harper-Skaggs controversy became one of the most historic and celebrated cases in the city of Norfolk and tidewater Virginia.

Shortly after Harper's trial, attorney Starkey introduced a motion for a new trial on the basis of "after discovered evidence." Starkey presented to the Norfolk court affidavits from Skagg's landlords, Rex and Virginia Rogers, who maintained that they were knowledgeable of Skaggs's "habits and customs," and that it was impossible for Dorothy Skaggs to have been in Norfolk between 6:30 and 6:45 P.M. on the night of January 6. Their affidavits called Skaggs's testimony "false, perjured, without foundation, and wholly and completely designed to injure Harper." On the strength of the affidavits, Judge Allan R. Hanckel set aside Harper's conviction and ordered a new trial.

During the interim period, the Norfolk Branch of the National Association for the Advancement of Colored People (NAACP) and the *Journal and Guide* were busy organizing a defense fund for Harper. The national NAACP saw the Harper case as an excellent opportunity to resurrect its dormant Norfolk chapter, to increase black Virginians' lackadaisical support of the NAACP, and to enhance the struggle for blacks to serve on juries in Virginia.

P. B. Young had organized the Norfolk chapter of the NAACP in 1917, but by 1925 it was inactive due to internal bickering and a lack of confidence in Young's leadership. Young and his friends saw the Harper case was a unique opportunity to unite a divided black community, to reestablish Young's reputation as an "able and safe" black leader, and to enlarge the circulation of the *Journal and Guide.*

Although it was not unusual for a southern black man "without friends or funds" to receive a death sentence for sexual assault upon a white female, many whites were skeptical of the charge. And after Harper was found guilty by an all-white jury, the white citizens of Norfolk and Portsmouth, in the words of P. B. Young, "revolted at the prospect of a legal lynching." They were concerned because an innocent man was being sent to the electric chair. John Jordan, a Portsmouth native and former editor in chief of the *Journal and Guide,* recalled that in an unusual display of interracial cooperation, both whites and blacks labeled Harper's case "a frame-up" and supported the *Journal and Guide*'s call for "a careful inquiry" and a new trial.

In a virtually unprecedented action in the South between the World Wars, the Virginia legal system acceded to pressure brought by those outraged at the conviction of a black man on the charge of raping a white woman. A new trial was ordered, and it began on March 5. At this trial, white citizens in the vicinity of Upton Lane testified that they neither saw an attack nor heard cries for help during the time of the alleged assault. A strong point for the defense was the testimony by the police, which noted that on the night in question, Upton Lane was patrolled three times between 6:30 P.M. and 11:00 P.M., and "no victim was laying there." It was demonstrated that Dorothy Skaggs was a woman of questionable character. Several whites testified that at the time of the alleged attack, Skaggs was with her lover at the Caroon Dance Hall in Elizabeth City, North Carolina. Her lover, W. P. Kidd, testified that he accompanied her to North Carolina on the night of January 6, and they returned at 6:00 A.M. the following day. Dorothy Skaggs's landlords testified that Skaggs "suffered from delusions," drank heavily, and once claimed that she had been kidnapped. Dr. D. K. Howard, a prominent white physician, testified that he found no bruises or other evidence that Mrs. Skaggs had been "attacked or roughly handled." In fact, more than a hundred defense witnesses eventually came forward to testify on Harper's behalf.

Meanwhile, Skaggs sat beside her sailor husband and frequently dabbed tears from her eyes with a handkerchief. The prosecution characterized her as "an example of a fine Southern woman" who was "wantonly attacked by an imbecilic black brute." And when Skaggs took the stand to describe how Harper, who was only five feet, six inches tall, had assaulted her, spectators were barred from the courtroom.

Later, the trial judge reminded the jury that they were not bound to consider the evidence as "equally balanced." Moreover, he noted, establishing the credibility of a witness was exclusively the duty of a jury, and that a jury had the right to determine from the appearance of witnesses "their candor and fairness." More important, the judge explained that Harper was presumed to be innocent, and the burden of proof was upon the state. Also, he continued, if reasonable doubt existed, then Harper must be acquitted. The judge asked the jury to take into account Harper's mental capacity, the embarrassment occasioned by his arrest and

confinement, and the prospect of execution or a long term of imprisonment.

After thirty-five minutes of deliberations on March 5, an all-white male jury found Harper not guilty. The *Journal and Guide*, which maintained reporters inside the courtroom throughout both trials, called the judge "absolutely fair," and Harper's acquittal, an act of "Justice Vindicated." Harper was released from police custody, and his attorney, William Starkey, was later paid $25 from Norfolk's treasury.

Had the Harper case ended at this point, it would have been only an anomaly in southern justice. However, it did not, and within a few weeks would evolve into one of the most complicated cases in Virginia's judicial history.

Shortly after Harper's acquittal, Dorothy Skaggs was indicted by an all-white male grand jury for perjury. At the same time, William Harper was indicted for robbing Skaggs of the $1.50 in her pocketbook. In June 1931, Dorothy Skaggs was tried in Norfolk's Corporation Court No. 1. During the trial, Catherine Ketchum, a white Portsmouth resident, testified that Skaggs arrived at her home on January 6 at 11:00 P.M. and remained until the next day. Ketchum's testimony was rebutted by numerous white witnesses who observed that Skaggs had arrived the following morning, about 7:00 A.M. Skaggs was found guilty and sentenced to five years in prison. Within weeks of Skaggs's conviction, Catherine Ketchum was indicted for perjury. After a week of testimony, the Ketchum case went to the jury. But the jury could not agree on a verdict and a mistrial was declared. On the second day of the Ketchum trial, William Starkey, who had defended Harper in his first trial, announced his candidacy for the South Carolina Senate at the suggestion of "a number of personal friends."

The second trial of Dorothy Skaggs for perjury began on September 15, in Norfolk. Unlike the first perjury trial, the jury was impaneled from Norfolk instead of Newport News. Verbal clashes and intense heat marked this second trial. Men were forced to keep on their coats "to preserve dignity in the temple of justice." Spectators listened intently to testimony that many had heard three times before. Harper's confession was deemed "irrelevant." Interestingly, the defense did not call Skaggs to testify. After one full week of testimony, Dorothy Skaggs was acquitted of perjury. Shortly thereafter the state prosecutor dropped the robbery charges against Harper, and indicated that he would not prosecute Ketchum again.

Thus, one of the most curious legal battles in southern history came to a close. The Harper-Skaggs legal controversy opened a new chapter in the administration of southern justice by alerting whites to the dubious nature of what the *Journal and Guide* called "Negro-Did-It" crimes.

Selected Bibliography

Bardolph, Richard. *The Civil Rights Record: Black Americans and the Law, 1849–1970.* New York: Thomas Y. Crowell, 1970.

Buni, Andrew. *Robert L. Vann of the Pittsburgh Courier: Politics and Black Journalism.* Pittsburgh: University of Pittsburgh Press, 1974.

Carter, Dan T. *Scottsboro: A Tragedy of the American South.* New York: Oxford University Press, 1969.

Martin, Charles H. *The Angelo Herndon Case and Southern Justice.* Baton Rouge: Louisiana State University Press, 1976.

McGovern, James R. *Anatomy of a Lynching: The Killing of Claude Neal.* Baton Rouge: Louisiana State University Press, 1976.

Suggs, Henry Lewis. *The Black Press in the South, 1865–1979.* Westport, CT: Greenwood Press, 1983.

Suggs, Henry Lewis. *P. B. Young, Newspaperman: Race, Politics, and Journalism in the New South, 1910–1962.* Charlottesville: University of Virginia Press, 1988.

The Scottsboro Cases

—◄○►—

Robert F. Martin

Department of History
University of Northern Iowa

Powell v. Alabama, 287 U.S. 45 (1932) and *Norris v. Alabama,* 294 U.S. 587 (1935)
[U.S. Supreme Court]

◄○► THE CASE IN BRIEF ◄○►

Date
1932, 1935

Location
Alabama

Court
U.S. Supreme Court

Principal Participants
"Scottsboro Nine"; International Labor Deference (ILD); Scottsboro Defense Committee; Associate Justice George Sutherland; Chief Justice Charles Evans Hughes

Significance of the Case
In a turgid case stretching from 1931 until 1950, the High Court substantially expanded the scope of the due process clause of the Fourteenth Amendment and challenged the de facto exclusion of blacks from juries in the South.

Early on the morning of March 25, 1931, a freight train pulled out of the railroad yards of Chattanooga, Tennessee, and wound its way westward toward Memphis. Like many other freights of the Depression era, it carried not only the usual load of raw materials and manufactured goods but also an illicit cargo of unemployed men and women in search of opportunity and adventure. As the train moved through the hills of northern Alabama, a fight broke out among some of the black and white youths on board. During the struggle, the black combatants forced most of the whites to leap from the gondola car in which they had sought shelter from the wind.

By the time the train pulled into the station at Paint Rock, Alabama, news of the fight had reached the authorities there, and they immediately began searching the cars for unauthorized persons. The police rounded up a dozen people, nine of whom were black youths ranging from twelve to twenty years of age. Two of the three whites discovered on the train were young women from Huntsville who had reportedly been seeking work in the textile mills of Chattanooga and were now returning home. Victoria Price and Ruby Bates related a story that transformed a relatively inconsequential brawl among hoboes into a culturally and constitutionally significant incident.

Price and Bates charged that, after having driven all but one of the white males from the gondola, the blacks had raped them. On the basis of this testimony, the authorities jailed the nine accused rapists—Haywood Patterson, Olen Montgomery, Clarence Norris, Willie Roberson, Andrew Wright, Ozie Powell, Eugene Williams, Charley Weems, and Leroy Wright—in Scottsboro, county seat of Jackson County.

As news of the alleged rape spread throughout the county, a lynch mob bent on punishing those who had violated the virtue of the white women of the South gathered outside the jail. The courageous and determined efforts of the local sheriff, assisted after a few hours by a small contingent of Alabama National Guardsmen, prevented the mob from seizing the prisoners. On March 31, less than a week after the arrests, a special session of the Jackson County grand jury indicted the nine black youths. Judge Alfred E. Hawkins appointed all seven members of the Scottsboro bar as counsel for the defense. Within a few days, however, all but one had excused themselves from service. Meanwhile, Dr. P. A. Stephens, a black physician of Chattanooga, read with concern newspaper accounts of developments in Scottsboro. Because four of the Alabama defendants were from Chattanooga, Stephens had little difficulty persuading the city's black ministerial alliance to assist in obtaining counsel for "the Scottsboro boys," as they were called by both their supporters and their critics. The alliance secured the services of Stephen R. Roddy, a local attorney of modest ability who had represented members of the city's black community on several occasions.

Roddy appeared in Scottsboro on the morning of April 6, shortly before the trial began. Although he had been in town a few days earlier for the grand jury hearing, he had not previously met with his clients and was unfamiliar with both the details of the case and Alabama law. He was reluctant to assume responsibility for the defense of the nine youths until a sixty-nine-year-old Scottsboro attorney, Milo Moody, agreed to assist him.

The state chose to try Clarence Norris and Charley Weems first. In a tension-filled courthouse protected by Alabama National Guardsmen, Roddy and Moody attempted to defend their clients by questioning the character and undermining the credibility of Price and Bates. Their tentative efforts were complicated by the dramatic testimony of Victoria Price and by the fact that Clarence Norris testified that he had not been involved, but he had seen the other eight defendants attack the two white women. The jury deliberated scarcely an hour before returning a verdict of guilty with the recommendation that the defendants be sentenced to death.

The trial of Haywood Patterson was already under way when the jury reached its decision in the Weems-Norris case. The judge excused the Patterson jury from the courtroom while the verdict in the initial trial was rendered. However, the reaction of the spectators in the courtroom and that of the crowd waiting outside was so loud and enthusiastic that the jury in the Patterson case could not escape hearing the reaction. Roddy hoped to turn the unruly behavior of the spectators to the advantage of his client. Charging that the atmosphere surrounding the proceedings was so hostile and intimidating that Patterson could not receive a fair trial, he asked that the judge declare a mistrial. Judge Hawkins rejected the attorney's request and the trial proceeded, going to the jury at eleven o'clock the next morning. Within a quarter-hour thereafter, the trial of Ozie Powell, Willie Roberson, Andy Wright, Eugene Williams, and Olen Montgomery began. Less than twenty-five minutes later the Patterson jury concluded its deliberations, and the proceedings were halted long enough for the court to hear the verdict of guilty with the recommendation of the death penalty.

The third trial resumed after lunch and went to the jury at 4:20 P.M. The remaining Scottsboro defendant, Leroy Wright, was only thirteen years of age. Under Alabama law he could be tried only in a juvenile court unless the state brought waiver proceedings. Solicitor H. G. Bailey offered Roddy a deal. In exchange for a guilty plea, he would ask only for life imprisonment rather than the death penalty. Roddy refused, knowing that a guilty plea would mean forfeiture of the right of appeal. He did, however, agree to make his defense brief. Within an hour this case, too, went to the jury. In his summation, Bailey asked for life imprisonment in view of the defendant's youth. The juries were unable to reach a decision until the next day. On Thursday morning, Powell, Roberson, Andy Wright, Williams, and Montgomery were all found guilty with the recommendation that they be sentenced to death. The jury was unable to reach a verdict regarding Leroy Wright because seven of the twelve members wanted the death penalty in spite of the state's request for life imprisonment. Therefore, Judge Hawkins declared a mistrial in the Leroy Wright case. Then, only four days after the trials had begun, he sentenced the remaining eight defendants to death.

The events that transpired in the Scottsboro, Alabama, courthouse in the spring of 1931 were merely the first scene of an ideological, cultural, and legal drama that unfolded before the nation throughout most of the remainder of the decade. During the late 1920s the Communist Party had begun laying plans to woo the black masses of the South. The leaders of the International Labor Defense (ILD), the legal arm of the party, recognized the potential value of the Scottsboro cases. The ILD temporarily won the backing of the black ministers of Chattanooga and secured the services of George W. Chamlee, an able Tennessee lawyer, to represent the Scottsboro defendants.

The National Association for the Advancement of Colored People (NAACP), which might have been expected to take up the boys' cause, moved rather slowly. It lacked reliable information about developments in Jackson County and was reluctant to risk its reputation by becoming involved in a sordid rape case. However, when NAACP Executive Secretary Walter White learned of the ILD's involvement in the cases, he moved swiftly to thwart what he believed were Communist efforts to capitalize on the situation. The battle for control of the Scottsboro defense which followed was heated, bitter, and public. The NAACP charged that the ILD was merely using the Scottsboro boys as pawns in an ideological struggle for the hearts and minds of the South's black population. The ILD countered with the accusation that the NAACP was a reactionary tool of the white capitalist class and out of touch with the black masses.

The inexperienced, poorly educated defendants were confused and uncertain about who should represent them in the appellate process. During the summer and fall of 1931 they vacillated between the ILD and the NAACP. Although Walter White engaged such able attorneys as Clarence Darrow and Arthur Garfield Hays to help in the presentation of the case before the Alabama Supreme Court, by late 1931 the ILD had won the confidence of the defendants and their families, and had gained control of the defense. The Alabama Supreme Court heard the Scottsboro appeals in early 1932. ILD attorney Joseph Brodsky, with the assistance of George Chamlee, presented the defense's case before the court. The two lawyers contended that the mob atmosphere surrounding the trials, the exclusion of blacks from the jury, the speed with which the verdicts were reached, and the lack of adequate counsel combined to deny the defendants a fair trial.

Attorney General Thomas G. Knight, son of one of the Alabama Supreme Court justices, responded to the defense case. He paid little attention to allegations of inadequate counsel or systematic exclusion of blacks from jury service. Rather, he concentrated on the charge that the atmosphere surrounding the trial had been detrimental to the defendants. Brodsky had cited Oliver Wendell Holmes's dissent in the Leo Frank case, in which he had declared that a trial conducted in the midst of mob pressure was invalid. In responding to this reference to the eminent jurist, Knight declared, "I have the deepest reverence for Justice Holmes, but I wonder if he had lived a little closer to the South whether he would have written these decisions, had he known how jealously we have striven to uphold our rights and protect our womanhood."

The court's ruling on March 24, 1932, surprised no one. The majority of the judges upheld the sentences of seven of the eight defendants. They granted Eugene Williams a new trial on the grounds that he had been a minor at the time of his conviction. The justices commended the speed with which the Scottsboro court had proceeded. They argued that the presence of Alabama National Guardsmen had guaranteed the defendants a fair trial. Contending that, within limits, the state of Alabama had the right to fix qualifications for jury service, the justices rejected the charge that the exclusion of blacks from Jackson County juries had violated the Fourteenth Amendment or had in any way been detrimental to the defendants. Only Chief Justice Anderson dissented. He could find no single legal basis on which to ground a reversal, but concluded that the weight of the collective evidence suggested that the ends of justice had not been served. After the ruling of the Alabama Supreme Court, the International Labor Defense retained Walter Pollak, a nationally known constitutional lawyer, and prepared to take the case of the Scottsboro defendants to the U.S. Supreme Court. Following a preliminary hearing on May 27, 1932, the High Court agreed to hear the appeal. The arguments presented five months later were much like those made before the Alabama Supreme Court, but with one notable difference. Pollak stressed the exclusion of blacks from Alabama juries since the days of Reconstruction.

On November 7, 1932, the U.S. Supreme Court handed down its ruling in the case known as *Powell v. Alabama.* Justice George Sutherland, one of the most conservative of the judges, read the majority opinion. The Court did not address the socially volatile matter of the exclusion of blacks from Alabama juries. It concentrated instead on the issue of whether or not the defendants had been denied the right of counsel and, if so, whether this denial constituted a violation of the due process clause of the Fourteenth Amendment. Most of the justices considered the way in which counsel had been provided for the defendants to be unacceptable. It quickly became clear as Sutherland read the majority opinion that the Court was going to reverse the convictions on the grounds of inadequate counsel, but the constitutional basis for the ruling was not immediately apparent.

The Sixth Amendment guaranteed the right to counsel, but the Supreme Court, in the 1884 case of *Hurtado v. California* (1884), had held that the defendant's right to due process in a state court did not include the first eight amendments to the Constitution. In the *Hurtado* decision the Court described due process in vague terms and suggested that the people could establish new procedures as long as these were in "furtherance of the general public good." The Supreme Court was, of course, the ultimate judge of what constituted "furtherance of the general public good," and in 1925, in *Gitlow v. New York,* it had already begun to undermine the *Hurtado* ruling by extending the application of the First Amendment to the states. In *Powell v. Alabama* it went a step farther. After an extensive review of precedents, Sutherland asserted that the right to counsel had been so accepted by the states that it was now an integral part of due process. He maintained that the "right to have counsel appointed when necessary is a logical corollary from the constitutional right to be heard by counsel." Therefore, on the grounds that the Scottsboro defendants' guarantee of due process had been violated, their convictions were reversed and their cases remanded to the lower courts. For almost half a century the Court had used the due process clause of the Fourteenth Amendment to protect property rights and to obstruct state and federal economic regulatory efforts. Now, however, the justices were interpreting the Fourteenth Amendment in a way consistent with its original intent, that of protecting the civil rights of black Americans.

Justices Pierce Butler and James C. McReynolds dissented, arguing that the defendants had received a fair trial. Butler, who wrote the minority opinion, declared that even had there been a miscarriage of justice, the Court's ruling marked "an extension of Federal authority into a field hitherto occupied exclusively by the several states." Legal authorities later maintained that *Powell v. Alabama* was indeed the first time that the U.S. Supreme Court had set aside a state criminal conviction on any grounds.

Though many moderates hailed the Court's decision, radicals condemned it. The Communists charged that the Court had provided Alabama authorities with the means to engage in legal lynching. Some Socialists complained that the Court had avoided the socially significant issues raised by the case and had based its opinion on narrow legal grounds. Most white Southerners regarded the ruling as an unwarranted intrusion into their region's race relations.

As preparation for the new trial began, the International Labor Defense hired Samuel S. Leibowitz, an eminent criminal lawyer, to handle the Scottsboro defense. Leibowitz had little interest in the ideology of the ILD and tried to distance himself from the Communists, but he believed that the civil rights of the Scottsboro boys must be protected. ILD attorneys obtained a change of venue and the new trials were held in Decatur, Alabama, about fifty miles west of Scottsboro. The atmosphere there was not markedly different from that in Scottsboro. Nevertheless, the defense, although somewhat disappointed, hoped that the relocation of the proceedings would be beneficial to their clients.

When the first of the new trials, that of Haywood Patterson, began, Leibowitz tried to discredit the testimony of Victoria Price by questioning her character and revealing inconsistencies in her story. Leibowitz's treatment of Price as little more than a common prostitute was probably a mistake because he failed to recognize the degree to which she had become a symbol of white southern womanhood. In spite of the contradictions in Price's testimony and the doubt which Leibowitz cast on her character, the jury and spectators remained convinced of the defendants' guilt. Patterson was convicted with a recommendation of the death sentence. However, the presiding judge, James Edwin Horton, had serious misgivings about the verdict. Discrepancies in Price's testimony, questions about the accuracy of the statements of some of the witnesses, and the fact that one of the doctors who had examined the two women told the judge privately that he doubted their story so troubled Horton that on June 22, 1933, he set aside the verdict and granted a new trial.

Attorney General Knight immediately announced that the state would retry Patterson as soon as possible. A new trial began in November 1933. Judge Horton had been removed from the case and replaced by Judge William Washington Callahan. From the outset Callahan appeared prejudiced against Patterson and the other defendants. He made it difficult for Leibowitz to challenge either the credibility or the character of Price and Bates. The judge's bias was evident in his instructions to the jury. He initially failed to include the form for an acquittal. The judge's oversight was inconsequential because the jury required little time before reaching a verdict of guilty with a recommendation of the death penalty. The trial of Clarence Norris was equally swift, and his fate was the same as that of Patterson. Leibowitz asked for a postponement of the remaining trials, and a weary Judge Callahan granted the request. The ILD appealed the Patterson and Norris convictions, but in June 1934, the Alabama Supreme Court refused to set aside the lower court's decisions.

During the summer of 1934 the International Labor Defense was caught in an attempt to bribe Victoria Price to change her testimony. When Leibowitz, who had been unaware of the effort, learned of it, he was furious and accused the organization of having "assassinated" the Scottsboro boys. Leibowitz's public criticism of the ILD caused it to drop him from the defense, on the grounds that he was inexperienced in constitutional appeals. Leibowitz then attempted to seize the case from the International Labor Defense. There followed another complicated tug of war over the Scottsboro boys. During October and November 1934, the frightened and confused young men changed their minds about whom they wished to represent them no less than five times. In October a group consisting primarily of New York supporters of Leibowitz established the American Scottsboro Committee to champion the cause of the nine youths.

In early 1935 the U.S. Supreme Court agreed to hear appeals in the Patterson and Norris cases. In order to avoid undermining the defense, Leibowitz and the ILD worked out a compromise. Leibowitz and George Chamlee, who had now broken with the ILD, would represent Norris, and ILD attorneys Osmond

Fraenkel and Walter Pollak would represent Patterson.

On February 15, 1935, Leibowitz appeared before the Supreme Court to begin presenting his case. He contended that his client had been denied a fair trial because, although Alabama law did not actually exclude blacks from jury duty, they were in fact denied the right to serve. He charged that the roll books had been fraudulently altered to make it appear that blacks were indeed eligible for jury service. Attorney General Knight argued that the small number of blacks serving on Alabama juries was not the result of discrimination but the consequence of a careful selection process.

In 1880 the Supreme Court had ruled, in *Strauder v. West Virginia*, that any systematic exclusion of blacks from jury service constituted a violation of the equal protection clause and due process clause of the Fourteenth Amendment. Over the years, however, in several decisions the Court had emasculated this guarantee. On April 1, 1935, in *Norris v. Alabama* the Court issued a dramatic reversal of the stance which had evolved over the previous half-century. Chief Justice Charles Evans Hughes delivered the majority opinion. The justices ruled that the exclusion of blacks from jury service deprived a black person of equal protection of the law guaranteed by the Fourteenth Amendment. The Court contended that Alabama was guilty of systematic exclusion of black people from jury service and that local officials had attempted to conceal this fact by fraudulently tampering with the jury rolls. They rejected the contention of Alabama officials that there were no qualified black jurors in Morgan County. Therefore, Norris's rights under the equal protection clause and due process clause of the Fourteenth Amendment had been violated, and they overturned his conviction.

Haywood Patterson's case presented the Court with a problem. Although the point was debatable, the Alabama Supreme Court had ruled that the defense's bill of exceptions in the Patterson case had not been filed within the ninety days required by state law. The Supreme Court rarely overturned lower court decisions which were technically correct, but in this instance it was possible that, because of a technicality, one person might go free, and another might be executed, on the same evidence. Without actually overturning the decision, the Court strongly suggested that the Alabama Supreme Court review its judgment in the Patterson case. Following the U.S. Supreme Court's ruling, yet another struggle for control of the Scottsboro defense developed between the International Labor Defense and the American Scottsboro Committee. Out of this contest there eventually emerged a new, somewhat more stable and effective organization. On December 19, 1935, representatives of the NAACP, ILD, League for Industrial Democracy, American Civil Liberties Union, and Methodist Federation for Social Service established the Scottsboro Defense Committee, representing a broadly based coalition of individuals and groups interested in the fate of the nine black prisoners. Leibowitz, whose intemperate remarks about Alabama's system of justice had alienated many of the state's residents, continued to act as chief counsel but agreed to remain in the background while a prominent southern attorney played the primary role in the courtroom.

On November 13, 1935, a Jackson County grand jury, consisting of thirteen whites and one black, returned another indictment against the nine defendants. Judge Callahan announced that a new trial would begin on January 20, 1936. Haywood Patterson was tried first. As expected, the jury found Patterson guilty but, to the surprise of everyone including the prosecution, recommended seventy-five years in prison. Although the defense was disappointed, the verdict represented something of a victory because it was rare, if not unprecedented, for a black man in the South to be convicted of the rape of a white woman and to escape the death penalty. The trial of the other eight defendants was postponed due to the illness of one of the state's witnesses.

During 1936, Alabama showed signs of a willingness to compromise on the Scottsboro cases. In October, Governor David Bibb Graves suggested that the youths plead guilty to the less serious charge of miscegenation. Though the defense rejected this proposal, the attorneys were heartened that the state appeared willing to ask for less than the death penalty. On October 13, 1936, Clarence Watts, the Southern lawyer retained by the Scottsboro Defense Committee to assist Leibowitz, met with Attorney General Carmichael and attempted to have all charges against Olen Montgomery, Willie Roberson, Eugene Williams, and Leroy Wright dropped. Watts indicated that if the state agreed to this proposal, the committee would be willing to have the remaining five defendants plead guilty to a lesser charge, with the understanding that they would serve relatively short sentences. Carmichael told Watts that he would accept nothing less than a sentence of twenty years on a charge of rape for each of the youths.

Over the Christmas holidays of 1936, Knight and Carmichael visited Leibowitz in New York. They proposed to release some of the defendants if Norris, Patterson, and several others would plead guilty to rape. Leibowitz declined the offer, declaring that the defendants had told him on a number of occasions that they would rather die in the electric chair than confess to a crime they had not committed. Leibowitz offered to have the boys plead guilty to vagrancy or to the fight on the train. This compromise would enable the state to have a conviction while resulting in a minimal penalty for the boys.

At a later meeting in Washington, Leibowitz and Carmichael reached an agreement. Haywood Patterson's appeal was to be withdrawn. Ozie Powell would be tried only for assault on a deputy sheriff whom he had attacked. Charley Weems, Andy Wright, and Clarence Norris were to plead guilty to some form of assault. They would then receive sentences of less than five years. Eventually Haywood Patterson would be released so that his term in prison would be no longer than those of Weems, Wright, and Norris.

The Scottsboro Defense Committee was not happy with the compromise, and threatened to reject it. Leibowitz himself did not like the arrangement, but warned the committee that the alternative might be death or life imprisonment because the defendants' grounds for appeal were running out. The committee therefore agreed that it would neither endorse nor oppose the compromise.

However, for reasons that are not entirely clear, Alabama authorities seem to have had a change of heart. Judge Callahan announced that he intended to proceed with the trial of the remaining defendants, and in the summer of 1937 they found themselves in court again. In mid-July Clarence Norris was tried for a third time. After only two and a half hours of deliberation, the jury found him guilty and recommended the death penalty. When the trial of Andy Wright began, there were hints that a compromise might still be in the offing. The prosecution announced that the state would not seek the death penalty. The proceedings were brief, and the jury found Wright guilty and recommended ninety-nine years in prison. In the subsequent trial of Charley Weems, the state again failed to ask for the death penalty. Once again the jury convicted the defendant and sentenced him to a lengthy prison term. Ozie Powell was to be tried next, but the state announced that it was charging him not with rape but only with assault on a deputy sheriff, the penalty for which was twenty years. Powell pleaded guilty and received the maximum sentence.

Then, to the surprise of many observers, charges against Olen Montgomery, Leroy Wright, Willie Roberson, and Eugene Williams were dropped. The state contended that the fact that Willie Roberson had a severe case of venereal disease and that Olen Montgomery was nearly blind cast serious doubt upon their guilt. Victoria Price's identification of them was apparently a matter of mistaken identity. In the case of Eugene Williams and Leroy Wright, one of whom was twelve and the other thirteen at the time of the alleged crime, the state argued that the six and a half years they had served in jail was sufficient punishment, and agreed to release them on the condition that they would leave Alabama and never return.

On October 26, 1937, the U.S. Supreme Court refused to review the conviction of Haywood Patterson. Defense attorneys knew that they had no better grounds on which to appeal the verdicts in the Norris, Weems, and Wright cases, and decided not to do so.

The Scottsboro Defense Committee hoped to persuade Governor Graves to pardon the remaining prisoners. Graves appeared sympathetic to the idea, but indicated that he wished to allow the appeals process to run its course before taking any action. In mid-June 1938, the Alabama Supreme Court upheld the death sentence of Norris and the prison terms of Weems and Wright. Graves then commuted Norris's sentence to life imprisonment but made no move to free any of the Scottsboro boys. In August the Alabama Parole Board met and refused to grant paroles to any of the prisoners. There was now considerable support in the Alabama press for clemency, and Governor Graves appeared ready to grant pardons in the fall. However, after a meeting with the Scottsboro boys during which they were quarrelsome and one was found to be carrying a homemade knife, the governor refused to pardon them. He reportedly concluded that the character and level of intelligence of the prisoners were such that they would be an embarrassment to all those who had come to their defense. This unfavorable impression may well have determined Graves's final decision, but some members of the Scottsboro Defense Committee also felt that he had begun to worry about the unfavorable political ramifications of a pardon for the controversial prisoners.

Over the next few years, negotiations continued between Alabama officials and those working on behalf of the Scottsboro boys. On several occasions apparent compromises failed to materialize. Finally, on November 7, 1943, the Alabama Board of Pardons and Paroles released Charley Weems, and in January freed Clarence Norris and Andrew Wright, on the condition that they would not leave the state. After working for some time for an Alabama lumber company for $13 a week, Norris and Wright fled the state, violating their parole. Allan Knight Chalmers, chairman of the Scottsboro Defense Committee, persuaded them to return to Alabama, believing that the state would give them another chance. However, the two young men were returned to prison. In late 1946 Ozie Powell was released, and Clarence Norris was granted a second pardon. The Parole Board judged Haywood Patterson to be incorrigible and refused to parole him. In the summer of 1948, Patterson slipped away from a work gang and made his way north. After remaining in hiding for two years, he was finally arrested in Detroit. Michigan Governor G. Mennen Williams refused to extradite Patterson, and Alabama dropped extradition proceedings. In May 1950 the Parole Board unanimously agreed to grant Andrew Wright another pardon.

With Wright's release on June 9, 1950, a saga of injustice that had begun almost two decades earlier came to a rather anticlimactic end. The decision of nine young black Southerners to catch a westbound freight train on a cool spring morning in 1931 had a devastating impact upon their lives but a salutary effect upon the constitutional law of the United States. The experiences of the Scottsboro boys led the Supreme Court to substantially expand the scope of the due process clause of the Fourteenth Amendment and to challenge the de facto exclusion of blacks from the juries of the South.

Selected Bibliography

Carter, Dan T. *Scottsboro: A Tragedy of the American South.* Rev. ed. Baton Rouge: Louisiana State University Press, 1979.

Klehr, Harvey. *The Heyday of American Communism.* New York: Basic Books, 1984.

Norris, Clarence, and Sybil D. Washington. *The Last of the Scottsboro Boys.* New York: G. P. Putnam's Sons, 1979.

Record, Wilson. *Race and Radicalism: The NAACP and the Communist Party in Conflict.* Ithaca, NY: Cornell University Press, 1964.

Zangrando, Robert L. *The NAACP Crusade Against Lynching, 1909–1950.* Philadelphia: Temple University Press, 1980.

Separate Education
Is Not Equal Education

—◄◦►—

Robert P. Green Jr.

College of Health, Education, and Human Development
Clemson University

Brown v. Board of Education of the City of Topeka, 347 U.S. 483 (1954)
[U.S. Supreme Court]

◄◦► THE CASE IN BRIEF ◄◦►

Date
1954

Location
Kansas

Court
U.S. Supreme Court

Principal Participants
Oliver Brown and other plaintiffs
Topeka Board of Education
Thurgood Marshall
NAACP
Chief Justice Earl Warren

Significance of the Case
The *Brown* decision, one of the most
momentous cases in American history,
ended legal segregation in public schools.

On May 17, 1954, the Supreme Court of the United States issued a decision that many have described as its most dramatic and far-reaching of the twentieth century. In a unanimous opinion, the Court held that separate educational facilities were inherently unequal, that "in the field of public education the doctrine of 'separate but equal' has no place." With that ruling, the Court overturned its 1896 decision in *Plessy v. Ferguson* and set the stage for further dramatic developments in the field of civil rights. The decision in *Brown v. Board of Education* was a moral victory in the realm of American ideals; it was a victory for African Americans in their attempt to promote racial justice; but more particularly, it was a legal victory for a bright and persevering group of black lawyers who convinced the Court to do that which it is most hesitant to do, overturn longstanding precedent. The road to that victory, however, was both long and tortuous.

In *Plessy v. Ferguson*, the U.S. Supreme Court had reviewed a Louisiana statute requiring "separate but equal" accommodations in railway cars. Dismissing the argument that such legislation violated the equal protection clause of the Fourteenth Amendment, Justice Henry Billings Brown, writing for the Court, drew a distinction between "laws interfering with the political equality of the negro and those requiring the separation of the two races in schools, theatres and railway carriages." Whereas the former clearly violated Fourteenth Amendment rights, the latter did not. Legislatures, he argued, are at "liberty to act with reference to the established usages, customs and traditions of the people, and with a view to the promotion of their comfort, and the preservation of the public peace and good order." In that context, the Louisiana law was not unreasonable and did not violate the rights of the minority. Reflecting the racial attitudes of his day, Justice Brown went on to argue that "legislation is powerless to eradicate racial instincts or to abolish distinctions based upon physical differences. . . . If the civil and political rights of both races be equal one cannot be inferior to the other civilly or politically. If one race be inferior to the other socially, the Constitution of the United States cannot put them upon the same plane." In a lone voice of dissent, Justice John Marshall Harlan decried the "pernicious" nature of the majority decision and predicted that it would "stimulate aggressions, more or less brutal and irritating, upon the admitted rights of colored citizens, [and] encourage the belief that it is possible, by means of state enactments, to defeat the beneficent purposes which the people of the United States had in view when they adopted the [Civil War] amendments of the Constitution."

Justice Harlan could not have been more prescient, for the next three decades saw a litany of abuses—ranging indeed from the "irritating" to the "brutal"—against the rights of black Americans. This was a period when racism ran rampant, fueled by pseudoscientific theories concerning racial differences. From popular cultural expressions such as Thomas Dixon's *The Clansman* (the basis for the 1915 movie *The Birth of a Nation*) to academic tracts such as those from the pens of historian Ulrich Bonnell Phillips (*American Negro Slavery*) and political

scientist William Graham Sumner (*Folkways*), racial stereotypes were supported, and blacks and their roles in and contributions to American society were disparaged. Jim Crow legislation flourished: separate railway cars were followed by separate streetcars, restaurants, boardinghouses, public washrooms and water fountains, separate neighborhoods, and even separate ballparks. Discrimination spread to the workplace as blacks were kept in the most menial positions, in part because of their poor education (separate but equal was anything but equal) and in part because even the union movement discriminated against them. But the darkest aspect of the story of the first quarter of the twentieth century was the sheer brutality that blacks frequently faced. Race riots (whites rioting against blacks) and lynchings claimed the lives of many innocent victims. The true flavor of the times can be captured only with a realization of the barbarisms to which blacks were periodically subjected. Richard Kluger recounted one such incident: "[T]he South's ongoing disfigurement of the Negro as a human being reached the zenith of heartlessness during the summer of 1911 when one of the more barbaric lynchings of the era was literally staged in Livermore, Kentucky. A Negro charged with murdering a white man was seized and hauled to the local theater, where an audience was invited to witness his hanging. Receipts were to go to the murdered white man's family. To add interest to the benefit performance, seatholders in the orchestra were invited to empty their revolvers into the swaying black body while those in the gallery were restricted to a single shot. And so it happened."

Black educational opportunity was a particular victim of segregation and discrimination, a development that seemed to be fostered by Supreme Court decisions in the decades after *Plessy*. A series of decisions during the period entrenched "separate but equal" in a way that was both unequal and particularly discriminatory. In the late 1890s, Richmond County, Georgia, maintained three high schools: one for white boys, one for white girls, and one for blacks. When the student population at the black elementary school outgrew the accommodations there, the school board converted the black high school into another elementary institution, leaving black high school students without a school. Advised by the school board that they should send their children to church-sponsored schools, the protesting parents of the black high school students instead took their case to court, arguing that the white high school should be closed down as long as there was no black high school available. Though the case appeared to be a clear violation of the *Plessy* "separate but equal" doctrine, the courts treated only the demand of the plaintiffs that the white high school be closed. Thus, in *Cumming v. Richmond County Board of Education* (1899), the U.S. Supreme Court upheld the school board: "While all admit that the benefits and burdens of public taxation must be shared by citizens without discrimination against any class on account of their race, the education of people in schools maintained by state taxation is a matter belonging to the respective states, and any interference on the part of Federal authority with the management of such schools cannot be justified except in the case of a clear and unmistakable disregard of rights secured by the supreme law of the land. We have here no such case to be determined." Not only was segregation recognized in the *Cumming* decision, but unequal facilities (in fact, the absence of facilities) clearly were condoned.

Even more disturbing was the Court's decision in *Berea College v. Kentucky* (1908). Berea College, a private institution, had held racially mixed classes since its incorporation in 1859. During the height of racist mania, however, the state of Kentucky passed a law stating that an institution could teach members of both races at the same time only if classes were held separately, at least twenty-five miles apart. Berea College sued, but the Court upheld the state, thus establishing a further precedent: not only did the states have the right to establish separate educational facilities, they also had the right to prohibit mixed facilities in institutions they had chartered—even when those institutions were private.

Finally, in *Gong Lum v. Rice* (1927), any question of a state's right to segregate "colored" children in its schools seemed ultimately put to rest. When Gong Lum, an American of Chinese

descent living in Bolivar County, Mississippi, challenged the white superintendent's placement of his daughter in the county's obviously inferior black school, the courts again upheld the school system. Gong Lum had challenged his daughter's classification as "colored," but Chief Justice William Howard Taft, citing *Plessy* and *Cumming* (among other cases) as precedent, wrote for the Supreme Court: "The right and power of the state to regulate the method of providing for the education of its youth at public expense is clear." Again, the federal courts would not intervene.

Of course, inequities in educational policy simply mirrored inequities in other aspects of life. Just as blacks were segregated socially even before the *Plessy* decision, so, at least in the South, they were disfranchised politically. As the basic civil rights of blacks—tenuous at any time—eroded further, it was no wonder that resentment in the black community grew. Ray Stannard Baker captured some of that sentiment when he interviewed blacks for his *Following the Color Line* (1908): "How would you feel, if with our history, there came a time when, after speeches and papers and teachings, you acquired property and were educated, and were a fairly good man, it were impossible for you to walk the street (for whose maintenance you were taxed) with your sister without being in mortal fear of death if you resented any insult offered to her? How would you feel if you saw a governor, a mayor, a sheriff, whom you could not oppose at the polls, encourage by deed or word or both, a mob of "best" and worst citizens to slaughter your people in the streets and in their own homes and in their places of business? Do you think that you could resist the same wrath that caused God to slay the Philistines and the Russians to throw bombs? I can resist it, but with each new outrage I am less able to resist it."

Yet even as resentment grew, blacks were beginning to address these ills. At the same time that oppression was greatest, changes were taking place in the black community. Traditionally a rural phenomenon, black communities were growing in urban areas of the South and the North. Like so many others seeking a better life, blacks were driven from the land by hardship and drawn to the cities by perceptions of economic opportunity. In these urban black communities, a new middle and professional class appeared, educated and ready to do battle against an unjust system. Here was the "Talented Tenth" for which W.E.B. DuBois had called.

From the black middle class, the backbone of the National Association for the Advancement of Colored People (NAACP) would be drawn. Formed in 1909–1910 by both white sympathizers and black leaders like DuBois, the NAACP would play a leading role in the civil rights struggle ahead. Recognizing the need to support blacks in legal proceedings, the NAACP early began to take part in court cases involving Fourteenth and Fifteenth Amendment issues. During the 1920s, the NAACP's efforts met with mixed success, but more important, during the period, bright young black lawyers became more and more involved in its work. Principal among these was Charles Hamilton Houston, a graduate of Amherst Phi Beta Kappa, and of Harvard Law School, who was Dean of the Howard Law School. In the mid-1930s, Houston was appointed chief legal counsel in the NAACP's desegregation efforts. In that position, he attracted a number of sharp minds to the NAACP's cause: William Hastie, later to become the nation's first black federal judge; James Nabrit, successor to Houston as Dean of the Howard Law School, and then President of Howard University; Ralph Bunche, later U.S. delegate to the United Nations; Spotswood Robinson III, later a federal judge; and, most significant of all, Thurgood Marshall, later the first black justice of the U.S. Supreme Court.

Although throughout its early life the NAACP had, in essence, been fighting a holding action, a singular development in the 1920s provided it with funds to go on the offensive. In 1922, Charles Garland, son of a Boston millionaire, had devoted a substantial share of his inheritance to a fund for liberal causes. In 1929, the directors of that fund provided a grant of $100,000 to the NAACP to initiate a campaign "to give the southern Negro his constitutional rights." Educational equality—obviously lacking in the most segregated states, where fund-

ing for black schools ranged from one half to one tenth that of white schools—was to have been a particular emphasis of the effort. In 1931, attorney Nathan Margold created a plan that would form the basis for the NAACP's effort over the next two decades. In essence, the Margold Plan called for a series of suits that would focus on the inequalities of facilities in segregated schools in the South, especially where they were habitually so, and would emphasize, in particular, the absence of statutory requirements in the several states that such schools be equal. The Court, reasoned Margold, operating under the doctrine of separate but *equal*, would certainly force states to equalize funding for black schools.

The Margold Plan, though conservative in nature—it attempted only to enforce the principle of *Plessy*, not challenge separation—still had drawbacks. In order to address some of these shortcomings, Houston modified the plan to focus at first on graduate and professional schools. At that level, evidence of inequality was obvious. State-supported black graduate and professional schools were nonexistent in the segregated states. Because the students involved were adults, white sensibilities would be least offended by black legal victories. Finally, Houston hoped that each victory would build upon the previous one, establishing a series of precedents upon which broader action might be pursued. During the next fifteen years, the NAACP pursued the Margold Plan as modified by Houston, first under the direction of Houston himself and then, increasingly, through the efforts of Thurgood Marshall.

In February 1935, Donald Murray, a fully qualified black, was refused admission to the University of Maryland Law School because of his race. Maryland had a segregated system of higher education, but it had no law school for blacks. Rather, it had established partial scholarships for black students who wanted to pursue programs not offered by Maryland's black schools. In *Murray v. Maryland* (1936), Houston demonstrated that the partial scholarships were inadequate and that they would fail to provide an education comparable to that provided at the University of Maryland. The Maryland Court of Appeals upheld a lower

"All the News That's Fit to Print"

The New York Times.

LATE CITY EDITION
Fair and cool today. Mostly sunny, continued cool tomorrow.

Copyright, 1954, by The New York Times Company.

VOL. CIII...No. 35,178.   NEW YORK, TUESDAY, MAY 18, 1954.   FIVE CENTS

HIGH COURT BANS SCHOOL SEGREGATION; 9-TO-0 DECISION GRANTS TIME TO COMPLY

McCarthy Hearing Off a Week as Eisenhower Bars Report

SENATOR IS IRATE

President Orders Aides Not to Disclose Details of Top-Level Meeting

President's letter and excerpts from transcript, Pages 24, 25, 26.

By W. H. LAWRENCE

WASHINGTON, May 17—A secrecy directive by President Eisenhower resulted today in an abrupt recess for at least a week of the Senate's Army-McCarthy hearings.

Democratic and Republican Senators, some publicly and some privately, predicted that the investigation might never resume in earnest. However, there were other Senators who insisted that the investigation would go on to completion.

The recess was voted after Herbert Brownell Jr., the Attorney General, disclosed formally he had instituted prosecutions that might be involved in the "preparation and dissemination" of an altered, condensed but still confidential Federal Bureau of Investigation report. This was offered in evidence last week by Senator Joseph R. McCarthy, Republican of Wisconsin.

Communist Arms Unloaded in Guatemala By Vessel From Polish Port, U. S. Learns

State Department Views News Gravely Because of Red Infiltration

WASHINGTON, May 17—The State Department said today that it had reliable information that "an important shipment of arms" had been sent from Communist-controlled territory to Guatemala.

It said the arms, whose origin it would not disclose, had been unloaded at Puerto Barrios, Guatemala, had been shipped from Stettin, a former German Baltic seaport, which has been occupied by Communist Poland since World War II.

REACTION OF SOUTH

'Breathing Spell' for Adjustment Tempers Region's Feelings

By JOHN N. POPHAM

CHATTANOOGA, Tenn., May 17—The South's reaction to the Supreme Court's decision outlawing racial segregation in public schools appeared to be tempered considerably today.

1896 RULING UPSET

'Separate but Equal' Doctrine Held Out of Place in Education

Text of Supreme Court decision is printed on Page 15.

By LUTHER A. HUSTON

WASHINGTON, May 17—The Supreme Court unanimously outlawed today racial segregation in public schools.

Chief Justice Earl Warren read two opinions that put the stamp of unconstitutionality on school systems in twenty-one states and the District of Columbia where segregation is permissive or mandatory.

The court, taking cognizance of the problems involved in the integration of the school systems concerned, put over until the next term, beginning in October, the formulation of decrees to effectuate its 9-to-0 decision.

LEADERS IN SEGREGATION FIGHT: Lawyers who led battle before U. S. Supreme Court for abolition of segregation in public schools congratulate one another as they leave court after announcement of decision. Left to right: George E. C. Hayes, Thurgood Marshall and James M. Nabrit.

SOVIET BIDS VIENNA CEASE 'INTRIGUES'

Envoy Warns Austrian Chief on Inciting East Zone—Raab Denies Charges

By JOHN MacCORMAC

VIENNA, May 17—The Soviet Union warned Austria today to put an end to "hostile and subversive intrigues" against the Soviet occupation forces.

City Colleges' Board Can't Pick Chairman

The Board of Higher Education was unable to elect a chairman at its annual meeting last night at Hunter College.

2 TAX PROJECTS DIE IN ESTIMATE BOARD

Beer Levy and More Parking Collections Killed—Payroll Impost Still Weighed

By CHARLES G. BENNETT

INDO-CHINA PARLEY WEIGHS TWO PLANS

French and Rebel Peace Bids Will Be Studied Jointly as a Basis for Settlement

By THOMAS J. HAMILTON

GENEVA, May 17—The Far East conference decided today to take up French and Vietminh proposals jointly as a basis for settlement.

MORETTIS' LAWYER MUST BARE TALKS

Jersey Court Orders Counsel to Racketeers in Bergen to Divulge Data to Grand Jury

By GEORGE CABLE WRIGHT

TRENTON, May 17—The New Jersey Supreme Court today ordered a lawyer who once had represented two Morettis to divulge to a Bergen County grand jury the substance of confidential talks with those clients.

RULING TO FIGURE IN '54 CAMPAIGN

Decision Tied to Eisenhower —Russell Leads Southerners in Criticism of Court

By WILLIAM S. WHITE

WASHINGTON, May 17—Congress as a whole grappled gingerly today with the profound political implications of the Supreme Court's anti-segregation decision.

It became clear at once—and by both parties was accepted in silence—that the court's action would figure importantly in the coming Congressional election campaigns.

New York Times front-page headline shows unanimous victory for anti-segregation in *Brown v. Board of Education.*

court ruling that Murray be admitted to the university's law school.

In a similar case in Missouri, Lloyd Lionel Gaines was rejected by the University of Missouri Law School. Missouri officials argued that he should apply to the state's institution of higher education for blacks, Lincoln University, where a black law school would, given his application, in time be established. Furthermore, a legal education equivalent to that offered at the university could be pursued by black students through an out-of-state tuition supplement. On appeal in *Missouri ex rel Gaines v. Canada* (1938), the U.S. Supreme Court rejected the state's argument and ruled that Gaines be admitted to the university: "The basic consideration is not as to what sort of opportunities other states provide, or whether they are as good as those in Missouri, but as to what opportunities Missouri itself furnishes to white students and denies to Negroes solely upon the ground of color. The admissibility of laws separating the races in the enjoyment of privileges afforded by the State rests wholly upon the equality of the privileges which the laws give to the separated groups within the State. . . . By the operation of the laws of Missouri a privilege has been created for white law students which is denied to Negroes by reason of their race."

Early success in forcing equality within separate facilities laid the foundation for a broader argument against segregation, but roadblocks remained. In *Sipuel v. Oklahoma State Board of Regents* (1948), Thurgood Marshall began to attack segregation itself: "Segregation in public education helps to preserve a caste system which is based upon race and color. It is designed and intended to perpetuate the slave tradition. . . . The terms 'separate' and 'equal' cannot be used conjunctively in a situation of this kind; there can be no separate equality." Nevertheless, the Court approved a jerry-built "law school" for the plaintiff.

Thus stimulated to further effort, Marshall consolidated earlier gains in *Sweatt v. Painter* and *McLaurin v. Oklahoma State Board of Regents*, both decided by the U.S. Supreme Court in 1950. In each case, the Court reviewed makeshift accommodations for the professional and graduate education of blacks. In *Sweatt*, the University of Texas Law School had denied admission to Herman Sweatt on the basis of race, but, to provide "equal" facilities, the state had created a "law school" in the basement of a downtown Austin office building. In *McLaurin*, George W. McLaurin was admitted to the University of Oklahoma to work on a doctorate in education, but he was segregated from the rest of the students: he was required to sit outside the regular classrooms, assigned a segregated desk in the library, and even required to sit at a separate table and dine at a different time in the university cafeteria!

Again, Marshall used the cases in an attempt to broaden the attack on segregation. In *Sweatt*, Marshall called upon Professor Robert Redfield, a distinguished University of Chicago anthropologist, to testify that modern anthropology had discarded the old arguments concerning racial differences, and that where they did exist, they might readily be attributed to such factors as segregation itself. When the relevance of this line of testimony was challenged by the state's attorney, Marshall's thinking became apparent: "[W]e have a right to put in evidence to show that segregation statutes in the state of Texas and in any other state, actually when examined—and they have never been examined in any lawsuit that I know of yet—have no line of reasonableness. There is no understandable factual basis for classification by race, and under a long line of decisions by the Supreme Court, not on the question of negroes, but on the Fourteenth Amendment, all courts agree that if there is no rational basis for the classification, it is flat in the teeth of the Fourteenth Amendment." Later, when *Sweatt* was appealed to the Supreme Court, Marshall arranged for an amicus curiae brief for the plaintiff by a coalition of law professors. That brief directly attacked the principle of "separate but equal": "Laws which give equal protection are those which make no discrimination because of race in a sense that they make no distinction because of race." In *McLaurin*, Marshall's challenge to segregation was implicit in the case itself: McLaurin had been admitted to the white school, so on the face of it, the facilities were equal. What remained was the question of his segregation within the school.

Yet a unanimous Court took a narrow stand on both cases. Chief Justice Fred M. Vinson wrote, "Broader issues have been urged for our consideration, but we adhere to the principle of deciding constitutional questions only in the context of the particular case before the Court." Given the efforts of Texas to provide separate but "equal" facilities for Sweatt, Vinson wrote, "we cannot find substantial equality in the educational opportunities offered white and negro law students by the state." He continued: "What is more important, the University of Texas Law School possesses to a far greater degree those qualities which are incapable of objective measurement but which make for greatness in a law school . . . reputation of the faculty, experience of the administration, position and influence of the alumni, standing in the community, traditions and prestige. It is difficult to believe that one who had a free choice between these law schools would consider the question close." Sweatt was ordered admitted to the University of Texas Law School. Given the restrictions place upon McLaurin, restrictions which clearly impaired "his ability to study, to engage in discussions and exchange views with other students, and, in general, to learn his profession," Vinson wrote: "State imposed restrictions which produce such inequalities cannot be sustained." Oklahoma had to remove such restrictions. The Court, however, refused to step beyond the confines of *Plessy.* Marshall and his colleagues had gone as far as they could with Houston's modification of the Margold Plan—separate facilities had to be clearly equal—but bolder legal action would be needed to attack segregation itself.

The time was ripe for bolder action. Despite continued outrages against the rights of blacks in many parts of the country, the nation was slowly moving away from old prejudices. In part, this movement was due to a newfound political power among black Americans. Black urban communities had begun to wield some political power—albeit of a local nature—in the late 1920s, and during the 1930s black Americans became an important part of Franklin D. Roosevelt's New Deal coalition. In later decades it was due in part to two Chief Executives, Roosevelt and Harry Truman, who sympa-

thized with black efforts for racial justice and, through actions and appointments, began to move the vast federal machinery in their support. In part it was due to World War II. Black soldiers and sailors contributed to the military effort. Black industrial workers played an important role on the home front, increasing their economic and political power. But more important, the war was fought for democracy, against German totalitarianism and racism. The all-too-obvious contrast between America's ideology and her treatment of black citizens spurred reform. And, finally, this movement was reinforced by developments in the social sciences showing that intelligence and educational performance were related much more closely to environmental factors than they were to race. Scientific research was undermining old racial stereotypes.

These changes were accompanied by a broad range of NAACP successes in the courts and dramatic moves by the White House. In *Mitchell v. United States* (1941), the Supreme Court applied the principle achieved in *Gaines* to the railroads, requiring equality of facilities; in *Smith v. Allwright* (1944), the Court threw out the all-white election primary; in *Morgan v. Virginia* (1945), the Court struck down segregation on buses operating across state lines; and in *Shelley v. Kraemer* (1948), the Court held that although racially restrictive housing covenants were in themselves not illegal, such covenants could not be enforced by the state. At the same time, President Harry Truman aggressively pushed civil rights, asking Congress for action on a broad range of issues: antilynching laws, poll taxes, segregation in interstate transportation, discriminatory hiring practices, and, on the positive side, creation of a permanent civil rights commission. Requests for legislation were followed by executive orders ending racial discrimination in federal employment and in the armed forces. The time was indeed ripe for a bolder move against segregation in schooling, and in 1950, Thurgood Marshall announced that NAACP legal efforts would reflect just such a redirection in emphasis.

The shift away from equalization within *Plessy* to an attack upon the fundamental principle of *Plessy* was not without risk. Important precedents had been achieved with *Sweatt* and *McLaurin*, and clearly the Court would have to extend those principles to elementary and secondary education. Furthermore, the Court had repeatedly reconfirmed *Plessy* and had approved a state's "right" to classify students by race. The Supreme Court was exceedingly averse to overturning clear precedent, and if it chose not to overturn *Plessy*, black America's struggle for equality might be set back for years. Marshall was quite aware of the risks he was taking and at times had second thoughts, but by late 1950 the die was cast. In a series of cases, the NAACP would challenge *Plessy*.

Four cases pursued by the NAACP would ultimately be decided by the Supreme Court in the decision known to history as *Brown v. Board of Education of Topeka* (a fifth would be included in the decision, but it was not an NAACP case). In each case, Marshall's strategy was twofold. First, the NAACP would attempt to show that segregated schools clearly were, and historically had been, unequal. Second, and more important, the NAACP would argue that race was not a reasonable basis for the classification of students, that racial separation caused severe psychological damage and antisocial tendencies, and that segregation was, in fact, discriminatory and therefore in violation of the Fourteenth Amendment. The first element of the strategy was conservative, relying on *Sweatt* and *McLaurin*; the second challenged *Plessy* directly. In a controversial but very significant attempt to buttress that second element of the strategy, the NAACP in each case introduced the testimony of social scientists concerning the adverse effects of segregation. With little hope for success at the state or district court level, the strategy was designed to build cases for appeal to the U.S. Supreme Court.

There was no clearer example of inequality in educational opportunities than that in Clarendon County, South Carolina. During the 1949–1950 school term, the average expenditure for white students was $179 and that for blacks was $43. The valuation of sixty-one black schools (often no more than wooden shacks) housing 6,531 students was $194,575; that of twelve white schools (brick and stucco) housing 2,375 students was $673,850. The county provided no transportation for the black students, whereas busing was provided for whites. The average salary for white teachers was two thirds more than that for black teachers. There was also no clearer example of the racial prejudice that lay behind such inequality: the black minister/teacher who, in the late 1940s, had begun the effort for equal treatment that would ultimately end before the Supreme Court was fired from his job (his wife, two of his sisters, and a niece also lost their jobs), physically threatened, and sued and convicted on trumped-up charges; saw his house burned down and his church stoned; and finally was chased out of the county. Other blacks involved in the case received similar treatment. Undaunted, black plaintiffs, backed by the NAACP, sought an injunction abolishing segregation.

Briggs v. Elliott, the South Carolina case, was the first in which Marshall pursued his new strategy. The evidence of inequality was overwhelming, but the heart of the black case was the attack on *Plessy*. In support of that effort, Marshall introduced the testimony of witnesses such as social psychologist Kenneth Clark. Clark's groundbreaking research with "projection tests" using pictures of dolls suggested a detrimental effect of school segregation on personality development, the essence of which, according to Clark, was "a confusion in the child's concept of his own self-esteem—basic feelings of inferiority, conflict, confusion in his self-image, resentment, hostility towards himself, hostility towards whites." Nevertheless, the Court of Appeals denied the plaintiff's plea for an injunction. Judge John J. Parker wrote for the court: "[W]hen seventeen states and the Congress of the United States have for more than three quarters of a century required segregation of the races in the public schools, and when this has received the approval of the leading appellate courts of the country including the unanimous approval of the Supreme Court of the United States . . . it is late in the day to say that such segregation is violative of fundamental constitutional rights." However, the decision did require the school district to "promptly" provide equal educational facilities for the black students. It was an empty victory, and Marshall appealed.

Meanwhile, in Topeka, Kansas, black citizens sued to have their children enrolled in white grammar schools. The first name on the list of plaintiffs was that of Oliver Brown, so the case was entitled *Brown v. Board of Education of Topeka*. Again, the NAACP attorneys pursued Marshall's strategy. Again, data suggesting inequality were presented (although to a much lesser degree than in the South Carolina case), and expert witnesses testified that "separate but equal" was a contradiction in terms. Again, the district court deferred to *Plessy*. This time, however, because the physical facilities of the white and black schools were deemed comparable, no relief was given the plaintiffs. Despite the loss, an important step was taken in the attempt to build a case for the Supreme Court. One of the "Findings of Fact" attached to the district court's opinion was the following: "Segregation of white and colored children in public schools has a detrimental effect upon the colored children. The impact is greater when it has the sanction of law; for the policy of separating the races is usually interpreted as denoting the inferiority of the Negro group. A sense of inferiority affects the motivation of a child to learn. Segregation with the sanction of law, therefore, has a tendency to retard the educational and mental development of Negro children and to deprive them of some of the benefits they would receive in a racially integrated school system." For the first time, a court had questioned Justice Henry Billings Brown's incredibly callous statement in *Plessy*: "We consider the underlying fallacy of the plaintiff's argument to consist in the assumption that the enforced separation of the two races stamps the colored race with a badge of inferiority. If this be so, it is not by reason of anything found in the act, but solely because the colored race chooses to put that construction upon it."

The third case which would finally appear before the Supreme Court began as two cases, *Belton v. Gebhart* and *Bulah v. Gebhart,* in Wilmington, Delaware. The first case concerned inferior facilities for blacks, and the second, the absence of transportation. As in the earlier cases, expert witnesses testified regarding the impact of segregation. Psychiatrist Frederick Wertheim,

for example, reported on Delaware children he had studied: "Most of the children we have examined interpret segregation in one way and only one way—and that is they interpret it as punishment." Unlike the two earlier cases, however, the Court of Chancery of Delaware, Chancellor Collins Seitz presiding, found in favor of the plaintiffs and ordered the immediate admission of their children to the previously all-white schools. Yet Chancellor Seitz avoided *Plessy*: "I do not believe a lower court can reject a principle of United States Constitutional law which has been adopted by fair implication by the highest court of the land. I believe the 'separate but equal' doctrine in education should be rejected, but I also believe its rejection must come from that Court." The defendants appealed to the Supreme Court.

The fourth case, *Davis v. County School Board*, came from Prince Edward County, Virginia. There, conditions comparable to those of Clarendon County, South Carolina, prevailed. A series of events which included a student boycott of classes at an inferior black high school led to a suit requesting that the Virginia law requiring segregated schools be struck down. By this time, the other cases had been tried, and the Virginia legal establishment was familiar with the NAACP's approach. For the first time, expert witnesses were challenged—albeit weakly— by experts testifying for the defense, and the state argued that attempts to provide equal facilities were moving forward. In words that seem incredible to modern eyes, the state even claimed that its segregation policy had benefited Virginia blacks. Defense counsel Justin Moore argued that "in these eighty years . . . there has been an outstanding piece of work done in building up the Negro in every way—socially, politically and economically—where today he occupies a position of importance in economics and politics, in many ways, all due to the opportunities that have been given to him in this land in which we live and love." The district court panel, composed of three Virginians, found that segregation was neither prejudiced nor capricious, and rejected the plea of the plaintiffs. The court required merely that district and state plans for equalization of facilities continue. The NAACP appealed.

The final case considered under *Brown* came from the District of Columbia. There, in *Bolling v. Sharpe*, black parents represented by James Nabrit sued District of Columbia school officials. The plaintiffs argued that their Fifth Amendment rights were violated by the practice of segregation in the nation's capital, and that the burden was upon school officials to prove any reasonable basis for segregated schools. The district court threw out the suit, arguing that the constitutionality of segregation itself was at issue, and on that issue the precedents were clear. The plaintiffs appealed.

The Supreme Court scheduled the oral argument in the five cases dealing with segregation for December 1952. In the interim, South Carolina attempted to strengthen its position before the Court. Governor James F. Byrnes had pushed through a bond issue which, the state argued, would go a long way toward equalizing black facilities (the district court had approved these efforts), and the state had retained the services of John W. Davis, former presidential candidate and perhaps the most distinguished constitutional lawyer in the country. Davis was confident of victory. The lines were clearly drawn: given the equalization efforts of the segregationist states, the legal issue devolved to the reasonableness of segregation. The legal precedent, thought Davis, was clearly on the side of segregationists. Furthermore, the current Court was not distinguished by civil libertarian decisions.

By the same token, the NAACP legal staff was concerned. Criticism from the black press reminded them of their precarious position should the Court decide that *Plessy* must stand. In the light of that possibility, the NAACP's brief tried to make a case for deciding the segregation issue outside *Plessy*. *Plessy* itself had dealt with transportation, not education, and many of the precedents—including *Gong Lum*—did not deal directly with the question of the reasonableness of segregation in education. On the other hand, the Court had clearly denied race as a basis for classification in other circumstances. In *Nixon v. Herndon* (1927), for example, Justice Oliver Wendell Holmes, Jr., had argued that color could not be "made the basis for a statutory classification" with regard to qualifications for participation in primary elections. Marshall and his team hoped that with this line of reasoning, they might give the Court a way to decide in the plaintiff's favor without dealing directly with *Plessy*.

In the event, however, it was clear that the Court recognized what was at stake. Probing questions by Justice Felix Frankfurter, for example, revealed that the justices were troubled. Overturning precedent was a weighty matter. Other issues were also significant: Given the clear resistance among southern whites to desegregation, what might be the impact of a desegregation decision—especially if the Court, as it seemed to be—was badly divided on the issue? Were the efforts to equalize facilities promoted by southern leaders like James Byrnes legitimate? What was the position of the incoming Republican presidential administration of Dwight D. Eisenhower? In fact, the issue was so troublesome that the Court decided to postpone a decision until several issues were pursued in greater depth. In June 1953, the five segregation cases were restored to the Court's docket for reargument in October. At that time, the parties to the litigation were invited to discuss a series of questions ranging from the original intent of the authors of the Fourteenth Amendment to the extent of judicial power to abolish segregation in schools and, given that abolition, the best means to achieve it. Also, the Eisenhower administration was invited to file a brief in the cases.

The summer's delay was significant. Marshall organized an intensive research effort by historians and social scientists to solidify the NAACP's interpretation of the original intent of the Fourteenth Amendment's authors. The evidence was cloudy, but a strong case was made for a broad, egalitarian purpose. In the fall, the Eisenhower administration's brief was filed, calling for desegregation but requesting a transitional period. Finally, and most significantly, in September, Chief Justice Fred Vinson—perhaps the staunchest proponent of *Plessy*—died. In his place, President Eisenhower appointed Earl Warren of California.

Chief Justice Warren, was a shrewd politician whose personality and tact soothed a fractious Court, felt that segregation was wrong. Reargument in early December (after yet another postponement) convinced the chief justice and a number of other justices that the issue of public school segregation could be avoided no longer. Consequently, Warren argued in conference, "I don't see how, in this day and age, we can set any group apart from the rest and say that they are not entitled to exactly the same treatment as all others. To do so would be contrary to the Thirteenth, Fourteenth, and Fifteenth Amendments. They were intended to make the slaves equal with all others. Personally, I can't see how today we can justify segregation based solely on race." By taking the high moral ground, Warren, for all practical purposes, shifted the justices' debate from *what* to do to *how* to do it. As Justice Robert Jackson argued, "Our problem is to make a judicial decision . . . [and find] a judicial basis for a congenial political conclusion."

Thus the problem remained: How could the Court, in the face of precedent, reverse itself? The Court's greatest advocate of judicial restraint, Felix Frankfurter, had earlier grappled with the question and seemed to have resolved it in his own mind. In notes to himself before the 1952 conference, he wrote that respect for earlier decisions did not mean that the reasoning and principles upon which they were based could not be reexamined: "The equality of laws enshrined in the Constitution is not a fixed formula defined with finality at a particular time. It does not reflect as a congealed formulation the social arrangement and beliefs of a particular epoch. . . . It is addressed to the changes wrought by time and . . . must respond to transformation of views as well as to that of outward circumstances. The effect of the change in men's feelings of what is right and just is equally relevant in determining whether discrimination denies the equal protection of the laws." Justice Frankfurter's thoughts portended the direction the Court would take.

On May 17, 1954, Chief Justice Earl Warren read his opinion for a unanimous Court, an opinion described by historian Alfred H. Kelly as "remarkable both for its simplicity and for the extraordinary fashion in which it avoided all legal and historical complexities." Warren recognized that there was "little in the history of the Fourteenth Amendment relating to its intended effect on public education" and dismissed as inconclusive the arguments dealing with the intent of its authors. Rather, in order to consider the "effect of segregation itself on public education," Warren argued that the Court could not "turn the clock back to 1868 when the Amendment was adopted, or even to 1896 when *Plessy v. Ferguson* was written. We must consider public education in the light of its full development and its present place in American life throughout the Nation." That place was central, and where educational opportunity was provided by the state, it was "a right which must be made available to all on equal terms." Did segregation based on race deprive minority children of equal educational opportunities? Yes, argued Warren. Alluding to the social science evidence suggesting the detrimental impact of segregation on children, Warren argued for the Court: "We conclude that in the field of public education the doctrine of 'separate but equal' has no place. Separate educational facilities are inherently unequal."

Marshall and his associates had won their biggest case. The constitutional foundation for segregation in education had been destroyed. Yet the Court did not order immediate desegregation. Rather, recognizing the complexities inherent in desegregation under a "great variety of local conditions," the Court postponed implementation until it could hear recommendations from the parties involved. A year later, in a supplementary decision, generally known as *Brown II,* the Court ordered desegregation carried out under local federal court direction "with all deliberate speed."

Although it would be years before meaningful desegregation would come to many schools in the country, the decision in *Brown* set the stage for important developments in black America's struggle for civil rights and, ultimately, the rights of other groups suffering from unreasonable classification. Under Warren, the Court became a major player in those developments as it continued to strike down racial segregation in its variety of forms: on public beaches, in municipal parks, public buildings, housing, transportation, and eating facilities. By 1963, the Court would declare: "It is no longer open to question that a State may not constitutionally require segregation of public facilities." The nation was beginning to redress the "brutal and irritating aggressions" so accurately predicted by John Marshall Harlan.

Selected Bibliography

Graglia, Lino A. *Disaster by Degree: The Supreme Court Decisions on Race and the Schools.* Ithaca, New York: Cornell University Press, 1976.

Kluger, Richard. *Simple Justice: The History of Brown v. Board of Education and Black America's Struggle for Equality.* New York: Knopf, 1975.

LaMorte, Michael W. *School Law: Cases and Concepts.* Englewood Cliffs, NJ: Prentice-Hall, 1982.

Schwartz, Bernard, with Stephen Lesher. *Inside the Warren Court.* New York: Doubleday, 1983.

Wilkinson, J. Harvie III. *From Brown to Bakke: The Supreme Court and School Integration, 1954–1978.* New York: Oxford University Press, 1979.

The Little Rock Crisis: State Interposition Against the Supreme Court

—◦—

F. Thornton Miller

Department of History
Southwest Missouri State University

Cooper v. Aaron, 358 U.S. 1 (1958) [U.S. Supreme Court]

—◦— THE CASE IN BRIEF —◦—

Date
1958

Location
Arkansas

Court
U.S. Supreme Court

Principal Participants
John Aaron and 32 other plaintiffs;
William G. Cooper; NAACP;
Governor Orville Faubus;
Associate Justice William J. Brennan

Significance of the Case
The Supreme Court struck down the attempt by the state of Arkansas to prevent the implementation of the *Brown* decision through the doctrine of "interposition," or a state preventing a federal law from being enforced.

The *Cooper v. Aaron* litigation was, in general, typical of the slow, gradual, and, for the most part, orderly process of the racial desegregation of the public schools of the South in compliance with *Brown v. Board of Education of Topeka*. However, the significance of the *Cooper* case lies elsewhere. Beyond the schools and school boards, extreme segregationists and politicians, such as Orval E. Faubus, Arkansas's incumbent governor running for reelection, wished—or felt it was necessary for their political survival—to tap the potential popularity of a strong segregationist stand. The attempt by the Arkansas state government to prevent desegregation caused a constitutional crisis.

The burdensome task of implementing the *Brown* decision fell upon the federal district judges. It had been the practice for presidents to defer to a state's U.S. Senators for appointments of district judges in that state. The appointees were generally from the area and shared the community's ideas and values. Most white southerners and southern federal district judges had doubts about the propriety of the *Brown* decision. But the judges and many mod-

Nine black students being escorted into Central High School by National Guard troops in Little Rock, Arkansas, September 1957. *AP Photo.*

erates believed that, regardless, the decision was the law of the land, as determined by the highest court, and would have to be carried out. They hoped that it could be done gradually and with the least public disturbance. They knew that extreme segregationists would attempt to create problems at every step of the way. The judges were caught between their duty to carry out a law of desegregation and their place in a society where segregation was fully entrenched.

In the late 1950s and early 1960s, a pattern emerged in the implementation of *Brown*. The NAACP would organize attempts by black parents to register their children in racially segregated public schools, the students would be turned away, and then, on their behalf, the NAACP would bring a suit against the school district in federal district court. The federal judge would follow a course of studied vacillation, delay, and compromise, giving the school districts time to draft plans to gradually desegregate their schools. The school boards were relieved to have court-ordered plans to follow, because they could tell extreme segregationists that they were only complying with the law. Long after the original *Brown* case, through years of tokenism and phases from elementary to high school (or vice versa), racial segregation in the public schools of the South was slowly being dismantled.

In its early stages, *Aaron v. Cooper* seemed to fit this pattern. The Little Rock school board in the mid-1950s was dominated by moderates who did not like, but were willing to carry out, the *Brown* decision. Indeed, they voluntarily agreed to a plan—called the "Blossom Plan," prepared by Virgil Blossom, the district superintendent—for the gradual desegregation of Little Rock's public schools, beginning with Central High School. The local NAACP chapter believed the plan was inadequate, because desegregation would begin in only one school, and much of the timing of the phases was left indefinite. After black parents tried to enroll their children in another public high school and were turned away, a suit was filed by the NAACP in the U.S. District Court for the Eastern District of Arkansas on behalf of John Aaron and thirty-two other students against William G. Cooper, president of the school board, and other officers of the board and the school district. The case went before Judge John E. Miller, a native of Arkansas. He thought the *Brown* opinion was wrong and sympathized with local dislike for it, but he believed he was duty bound to carry it out as the law of the land.

The attorneys for the Little Rock school board argued that the only issue was whether the board had, in good faith, devised a reasonable plan to carry out the *Brown* decision. The counsel for the NAACP argued that the actions of the board had merely complied with an Arkansas law that was segregationist and unconstitutional. Judge Miller, ruling in favor of the board, decided that the "Blossom Plan" was not based on state segregation laws and was a reasonable attempt to comply with federal law. He maintained jurisdiction in the matter, however, to assure that the board continued to implement its plan in good faith, and that the schedule in the plan was made definite. After an NAACP appeal, the U.S. Court of Appeals for the Eighth Circuit upheld Miller's decision. At this point, the *Cooper* litigation was similar to many suits that were part of the slow process of desegregation in the schools. It became different and highly significant when the Supreme Court had to deal with forces beyond the control of a school board that, in effect, created a situation in which no plan of desegregation could, in good faith, be carried out.

Southern moderates and extremists disagreed over whether they should comply with the Supreme Court's *Brown* decision. They agreed, however, in raising serious objections to the decision. The separate-but-equal doctrine had been accepted as constitutional by the Supreme Court, Congress, and the states for decades. If the doctrine had not been in line with the original intention of the framers of the Fourteenth Amendment, it had since become an accepted part of constitutional law. Southerners thought the Supreme Court would need ample grounds to alter it. The Court's agreement with sociological arguments in the *Brown* decision was disturbing, because the whole question along those lines was debatable. Segregation had been ingrained in southern society and law since the late nineteenth century. Social upheaval in reaction to the implementation of the *Brown* decision was to be expected. The chance that desegregation could weaken more than strengthen the public school system in the South had to be taken into account. Moreover, by what authority could the Court act in an area that most white southerners in the 1950s believed was outside the proper sphere of the federal government? Public education was the domain of the states. Southerners seriously questioned the Supreme Court's constitutional authority to make the *Brown* decision.

The moderates believed the decision was unwise but hoped that Congress or the Court would later correct the mistake and prayed, in the meantime, that change would be gradual and peaceful. But the extremists wished to take their stand against what they saw as a misguided attempt by the federal government to intervene in their internal affairs. To fight this threat to their racially segregated society by a "foreign" court, they brushed off and invoked the old states' rights doctrine of interposition.

Interposition went back to Thomas Jefferson's and James Madison's resolutions of 1798–1799 when the Kentucky and Virginia legislatures voiced their opinion that the Alien and Sedition Acts were unconstitutional. The question was raised, at the time, of whether the states could constitutionally challenge federal law. Later, in the Nullification Crisis of 1832, John C. Calhoun and South Carolina proposed that a state could challenge and, indeed, nullify federal law within its jurisdiction. Secession carried this line of reasoning to its logical conclusion, and the Civil War determined that a state could not defy federal law. But could a state government, drawing on the original and milder Madison/Jefferson model, declare its opinion on the constitutionality of a Supreme Court decision? For a while, Arkansas officials merely voiced their disagreement with the *Brown* decision. They appeared ready to carry it out. Yet when Governor Faubus and the majority of the Arkansas legislature tried to thwart the action of the lower federal courts, then the further ramifications of interposition became clear: Arkansas crossed the line from the Madison/Jefferson model of the doctrine, as a statement of constitutional opinion, to the Calhoun/nullification model, as an act of direct opposition by a state to the enforcement of federal law within its jurisdiction. This state challenge would have to be met by the U.S. Supreme Court.

After desegregation was set to begin in the Little Rock school district in the fall of 1957, Governor Faubus placed the Arkansas National Guard at Central High School, he claimed, to keep order. Afraid that the troops would be used, instead, to prevent the black children from entering the school, the federal district court ordered them removed. Faubus did so, and after desegregation began, disturbances forced the Little Rock mayor to call on President Dwight Eisenhower for federal assistance. Eisenhower, instead of relying on federalized National Guard and U.S. marshals, sent in the 101st Airborne paratroopers. This heavy-handed federal action allowed nine black students to attend Central High School, but it made Faubus even more popular. Ironically, it proved he had been right in claiming that the federal courts' actions were leading to social unrest and that the National Guard troops had been necessary to keep order. The Governor's "secret orders," however, and his subsequent public actions brought about a constitutional crisis.

An FBI report, made available to the federal district court, charged that Faubus had ordered the National Guard not to allow black students to enter Central High School. This maneuver, if in fact it occurred, was a clear violation of a federal court order. With federal troops in Little Rock outraging extreme states' righters and segregationists and demoralizing the moderates, the legislature passed, and Faubus signed into law, a bill authorizing the governor to close all public schools that had come under federal court order to desegregate. This state law stipulated that the schools must remain closed until the voters could decide whether or not to reopen them. The state had now crossed that line between making public its constitutional disagreement with the federal government and placing its own state law counter to federal law. Arkansas was directly challenging the uniformity and enforcement of American constitutional law. Chief Justice Earl Warren called the Supreme Court into a special session.

The appeal of *Cooper v. Aaron,* from the U.S. Court of Appeals for the Eighth Circuit, had been on the docket, but there was no urgency in deciding the case until Faubus and the Arkansas legislature acted to prevent desegregation. The school board's plan was not the issue. No school board could possibly continue a plan of desegregation, given the actions of the state government. The onus rested on Faubus and the legislature. The main issue was interposition. Could a state government interpose itself between its citizens and the national government in order to prevent the implementation of a decision of the Supreme Court?

Cooper answered this question, clearly and resoundingly, in the negative. The Warren court was unanimous in its decision. Justice William J. Brennan wrote the majority opinion. Justice Felix Frankfurter wrote a concurring opinion. As stated by the Court, the major question at issue was of the "highest importance to the maintenance of our federal system of government. It squarely presents a claim by the Governor and Legislature of a State that there is no duty on state officials to obey federal court orders resting on this Court's deliberate and considered interpretation of the United States Constitution." The Court would not allow any southern state to directly prevent the implementation of Brown. De jure (legal) segregation of the public schools had to end.

Cooper was but one case in the desegregation story of southern public schools. Desegregation was brought about through a combination of forces, with hesitancy, vacillation, and postponement occurring at every level and in every branch of government. In the courts, there were continuous motions made, hearings, and appeals. After the *Cooper* case was finally decided by the Supreme Court, the Little Rock NAACP chapter was still at work in the federal district court, trying to get a desegregation plan implemented. The process continued, and some success could be claimed. But there was a concurrent development of private schools for whites. Through either public neighborhood or suburban school systems or private schools, the premise of *Brown*—that separate was inherently unequal—would still be thwarted. Also, the accomplishment of the law in bringing about desegregation was mixed. Going through a gradual, legal process had the advantage of making desegregation possible with minimum public disturbances, though it also allowed de facto (actual) discrimination and inequality to continue. But the significance of *Cooper* is in the prevention of de jure segregation in the public schools by a state's resort to the old constitutional doctrine of interposition.

Selected Bibliography

Freyer, Tony. *The Little Rock Crisis: A Constitutional Interpretation.* Westport, CT: Greenwood Press, 1984.

Huckaby, Elizabeth. *Crisis at Central High: Little Rock, 1957–58.* Baton Rouge: Louisiana State University Press, 1980.

Jacoway, E., and C. F. Williams, eds. *Understanding the Little Rock Crisis: An Exercise in Remembrance and Reconciliation.* Fayetteville: University of Arkansas Press, 1999.

Peltason, J. W. *Fifty-eight Lonely Men: Southern Federal Judges and School Desegregation.* New York: Harcourt, Brace & World, 1961.

A Case of Black and White: Removing Restrictions Against Interracial Marriages

Roger D. Hardaway
Department of History
Northwestern Oklahoma State University

Loving v. Commonwealth of Virginia, 388 U.S. 1 (1967) [U.S. Supreme Court]

⊸ THE CASE IN BRIEF ⊸

Date
 1967

Location
 Virginia
 District of Columbia

Court
 U.S. Supreme Court

Principal Participants
 Richard Loving
 Mildred Jeter
 State of Virginia
 Chief Justice Earl Warren

Significance of the Case
 In striking down a Virginia state law banning interracial marriages, the Supreme Court extended the protection of the equal protection and due process clauses of the Fourteenth Amendment to the U.S. Constitution.

Richard Loving and Mildred Jeter committed a felony when they got married. The state of Virginia considered the marriage illegal, but the District of Columbia recognized it as valid. The question of whether these two people who loved each other could legally stay married and live wherever they chose had to be decided by the U.S. Supreme Court.

The "problem" with the Loving-Jeter marriage was that Loving was white and Jeter was black. In 1958, when they decided to wed, such interracial marriages were legal in only about half of the states in the country. The couple lived in Virginia, one of those jurisdictions with a restriction against interracial relationships. On June 2, 1958, Loving and Jeter went to Washington, D.C., where such marriages were sanctioned, and exchanged vows. They then returned to Virginia to live.

A general rule of law holds that a marriage which is legal where it is contracted is legal everywhere. In Virginia, however, a law was in effect creating an exception to that rule in the case of biracial marriages. If two people who lived in Virginia left the state with the intent of circumventing the ban on interracial marriage and returned to the state as a "married" couple, their marriage was illegal and they were as guilty of felonious behavior as though they had participated in a marriage ceremony in the state. This was, of course, the exact conduct in which Loving and Jeter had engaged.

The Lovings were arrested and appeared in the Circuit Court of Caroline County on January 6, 1959. Both entered pleas of guilty to the state's charges and were duly convicted. The court could have confined them for five years each in the state penitentiary. However, the judge sentenced each of them to only one year in jail, such sentences to be suspended for a twenty-five-year period provided they left the state and did not return together or separately at the same time during those twenty-five years.

Although another Virginia statute made the Lovings' marriage "absolutely void without any decree of divorce or other legal process," the circuit court did not mention this law in its decision. Apparently, the state was content to allow the couple's marriage to continue so long as they moved out of Virginia. Not surprisingly, the Lovings decided to relocate. They moved to the District of Columbia to continue their life together.

In 1963 the Lovings filed a motion with the sentencing court, asking that the judgments against them be vacated and their sentences be set aside. Their theory was that the Virginia miscegenation laws under which they had been convicted violated the due process and equal protection clauses of the Fourteenth Amendment of the U.S. Constitution. Judge Leon M. Bazile of the Caroline County Circuit Court denied the motion, whereupon the Lovings appealed to the state's highest court, the Supreme Court of Appeals.

The Virginia high court had upheld the validity of the state's ban on interracial marriages several times before. Thus, the attorneys for the Lovings had to construct a novel attack upon the miscegenation statutes to present to the court.

That argument began with the allegation that miscegenation laws were unconstitutional because of the U.S. Supreme Court's holding in its landmark 1954 decision of *Brown v. Board of Education*. The Lovings argued that the *Brown*

case, in effect, struck down all statutes which were based upon the "separate but equal" reasoning of segregation, including the ultimate statute—that prohibiting the sexual integration of the races. Consequently, the Lovings submitted, the Virginia Supreme Court should reverse its prior decisions on the issue and invalidate the law which the Lovings had violated.

The Virginia court shrugged off such reasoning in a 7-0 decision handed down on March 7, 1966. Associate Justice Harry L. Carrico, writing for the unanimous court, noted that six months after the *Brown* decision, the U.S. Supreme Court had refused to consider an appeal filed by an Alabama woman who had been convicted of violating that state's miscegenation ban. Consequently, Justice Carrico wrote, the Court obviously had not meant for the *Brown* decision to "have the effect upon miscegenation statutes which the defendants claim for it."

Undaunted, the Lovings petitioned the U.S. Supreme Court, which agreed to hear their case and decide the constitutionality of the Virginia statutes. The Japanese American Citizens League was allowed to file an amicus curiae brief in support of the Lovings, an indication of the fact that miscegenation laws in some states prohibited interracial sex and marriages between individuals of many different races, not just between blacks and whites.

The arguments presented to the U.S. Supreme Court by the Lovings' attorneys differed somewhat from the position they had taken before the Virginia court. The basis of that argument, of course, remained the same—that the laws denied due process and equal protection to those who were not allowed to marry because they were of different races. But, instead of trying to show that the *Brown* case had already outlawed all segregation laws, the Lovings simply asked the Court to state emphatically that miscegenation laws violated the Fourteenth Amendment and to outlaw those statutes with its decision. On June 12, 1967, the Court, in a unanimous opinion written by Chief Justice Earl Warren, did just that. In doing so, the Court overturned one of its prior cases and relied to some degree upon another.

The rejected case was *Pace v. State of Alabama*, a decision issued in 1883. *Pace* had upheld an

Married couple Mr. and Mrs. Richard Perry Loving went to court to fight a Virginia law against interracial marriages. *Bettmann/CORBIS.*

Alabama miscegenation law because the penalty provided for the offending black person was the same as for the white sexual partner. Thus, because the two violators were treated equally, the Court had said the law did not contravene the Fourteenth Amendment.

The decision the justices followed was the 1964 case of *McLaughlin v. State of Florida,* in which the Supreme Court had overturned a miscegenation law dealing with cohabitation outside of marriage even though both offending parties were punished equally under the statute. Because the people involved in that case were not married, the Court had sidestepped the question of the constitutionality of statutes that prohibited interracial marriages. The decision in *Loving* thus extended the Court's distaste for antimiscegenation statutes. Now such statutes, whether they proscribed interracial cohabitation in *or* outside of marriage, were held to be unconstitutional.

The *McLaughlin* court also enunciated a new test for the validity of statutes based upon racial distinctions. Racial statutes would no longer be automatically constitutional just because the parties were punished equally. Rather, a state must show "some overriding statutory purpose" in prohibiting interracial conduct that would be legal if the parties were of the same race. Florida had no statute prohibiting two whites or two blacks of different sexes from habitually living in and occupying

the same room at night. Thus, black-white couples in Florida were being singled out for special punishment to which other couples were not subjected. When Florida chose to punish one group of people (black-white couples) for conduct permitted to other groups (black-black and white-white couples), it was engaging in discrimination based solely on race, the Court said. The statute therefore "must be viewed in light of the historical fact that the central purpose of the Fourteenth Amendment was to eliminate racial discrimination emanating from official sources in the States." The Court could find no "overriding" purpose for the law and found that it was unconstitutional; McLaughlin's conviction was overturned.

In *Loving v. Virginia,* Chief Justice Warren maintained that states were free to regulate marriage without federal interference, but that such regulation could not violate the Fourteenth Amendment. The fact that the Virginia laws punished both parties in an interracial marriage equally was a hollow argument, considering the Court's decision in *McLaughlin v. State of Florida.* The laws in question, Chief Justice Warren said, were designed merely to perpetuate white supremacy in Virginia, and there was no other purpose in their enactment. Such legislative intent could not be justified under the equal protection clause of the Fourteenth Amendment.

In straightforward and forceful language, the chief justice methodically attacked the Virginia statutes and interpreted the Constitution to outlaw rather than sanction racial discrimination in the marital relationship: "The Equal Protection Clause requires the consideration of whether the [racial] classifications drawn by any statute constitute an arbitrary and invidious discrimination. The clear and central purpose of the Fourteenth Amendment was to eliminate all official state sources of invidious racial discrimination in the States. . . . There can be no question but that Virginia's miscegenation statutes rest solely upon distinctions drawn according to race. The statutes proscribe generally accepted conduct if engaged in by members of different races. . . . If [laws drawing racial distinctions] are ever to be upheld, they must be shown to be necessary to the accomplishment of some permissible state objective. . . . There is patently no legitimate overriding purpose independent of invidious racial discrimination which justifies this classification."

Further, Warren held that the Virginia miscegenation laws violated the due process clause of the Fourteenth Amendment by depriving interracial couples of a "fundamental" liberty interest—"the freedom of choice to marry" whomever they wished. Such a decision, the chief justice concluded, "resides with the individual and cannot be infringed by the State." Thus, the convictions of the Lovings were overturned, and racial distinctions in laws governing the institution of marriage were removed from the statute books of the United States.

Loving v. Virginia struck a blow for individual freedom by limiting the authority of state governments to prohibit certain people from engaging in acts which are legal for most of the population. Its immediate impact was to outlaw miscegenation laws not only in Virginia but also in fifteen other (mostly southern) states.

By extending the coverage of the due process and equal protection clauses to additional persons targeted by criminal laws because of their race, *Loving v. Virginia* was a logical and appropriate step in the civil rights movement of the 1950s and 1960s.

Selected Bibliography

Drinan, Robert F. "The *Loving* Decision and the Freedom to Marry." *Ohio State Law Journal* 29 (1968): 358–398.

Greenberg, Jack. *Race Relations and American Law.* New York: Columbia University Press, 1959.

Reuter, Edward B. *Race Mixture: Studies in Intermarriage and Miscegenation.* New York: McGraw-Hill, 1931.

Wadlington, Walter. "The *Loving* Case: Virginia's Anti-Miscegenation Statute in Historical Perspective." *Virginia Law Review* 52 (October 1966): 1189–1223.

The School Busing Case

——◄◦►——

Robert P. Green Jr.

College of Health, Education, and Human Development
Clemson University

Swann v. Charlotte-Mecklenburg Board of Education, 402 U.S. 1 (1971) [U.S. Supreme Court]

◄◦► THE CASE IN BRIEF ◄◦►

Date
 1971

Location
 North Carolina

Court
 U.S. Supreme Court

Principal Participants
 Darius and Vera Swann
 Charlotte-Mecklenburg school system
 Judge James B. McMillan
 Chief Justice Warren E. Burger

Significance of the Case
 For the first time, the Supreme Court endorsed specific proposals, including court-ordered busing, to desegregate a school system that had previously been segregated.

Though *Brown v. Board of Education of Topeka* (1954) was a significant victory in the battle for African Americans' civil rights, it was not a complete victory. Declaring "that in the field of public education the doctrine of 'separate but equal' has no place," the Court in *Brown* struck down legally segregated school systems. At the same time, however, the Court postponed implementation of its decision. In fact, full implementation of the *Brown* decision in the South would require nearly twenty more years of legal struggle. The Court's decision in *Swann v. Charlotte-Mecklenburg Board of Education* (1971), endorsing busing as a tool for desegregation, played a major role in that struggle.

During the course of the Supreme Court's deliberations in *Brown*, two issues of particular concern arose. First, the justices were aware of the potentially explosive impact of an antisegregation decision on an unwilling white South. "It will take all the wisdom of this Court to dispose of the matter with a minimum of emotion and strife," argued Chief Justice Earl Warren. The Court recognized that whereas border states

666

might desegregate relatively quickly and without friction, white resistance in the deep South might be violent. A good deal of sentiment appeared to exist among the justices for a decree flexible enough to allow different handling of the decision in different places. A second issue, closely related to the first, was the question of the degree to which the Supreme Court should involve itself in shaping the details of plaintiff's relief. Several of the justices wanted to avoid Supreme Court entanglement in enforcement, yet some guidelines for lower courts were obviously necessary. Given the divisiveness of these two issues, and in order to achieve a unanimous opinion on the overriding issue of segregation, Chief Justice Warren agreed to postpone a decision on implementing the Court's ruling in *Brown*. Thus in 1955, over a year after the first decision of *Brown v. Board of Education,* and after hearing further arguments from interested parties, the Supreme Court issued its relief decree in a second decision titled *Brown v. Board of Education* (generally known as *Brown II*).

Brown II reflected a compromise designed to impose the constitutional principles enunciated in *Brown* in a way that would give school districts and states time to adjust. The Court recognized that "full implementation of these constitutional principles" might require varied solutions, so local school districts were given the primary responsibility for "elucidating, assessing, and solving" particular problems that might arise as they desegregated. District courts were given the task of considering "whether the action of school authorities constitutes good faith implementation" of the constitutional principles. The district courts were directed to "require that the defendants make a prompt and reasonable start toward full compliance"; however, once such a "good faith" start had been made, "the courts may find that additional time is necessary to carry out the ruling in an effective manner." Such extensions of time might be based upon a variety of problems, ranging from those related to administration and transportation to the need for "revision of local laws and regulations." Thus, the Supreme Court remanded the original *Brown* cases to the district courts to ensure that black students were admitted to public schools on a

"racially nondiscriminatory basis . . . with all deliberate speed."

Taken together, *Brown I* and *Brown II* held that certain constitutional rights were being violated, but that these violations need not be fully and immediately redressed. Although such conceptual ambiguity might have been good politics, it was not good law. Furthermore, leaving the burden of review to district judges—judges closest to, sometimes products of, and certainly more subject to sanctions from, the white communities that so disliked the High Court's decision—invited problems. The intent of the Supreme Court in *Brown* had been to end dual school systems, but the lower courts often interpreted the decision in a way that fell far short of that goal. The influential Circuit Court Judge John J. Parker, for example, interpreted *Brown* narrowly: "What [*Brown*] has decided, and all that it has decided, is that a state may not deny to any person on account of race the right to attend any school that it maintains. . . . The Constitution, in other words, does not require integration. It merely forbids discrimination." Supreme Court ambiguity and the consequent lack of aggressiveness on the part of lower court judges combined to form an open invitation to southern delay. In fact, the history of litigation from *Brown* to *Swann* became a history of ever more specific guidelines from the Supreme Court, guidelines designed to combat southern intransigence.

That intransigence took a number of forms. In some areas, schools were closed or blacks attempting to enroll in previously all-white schools were intimidated. More typically, southern states adopted complicated pupil placement laws which provided for assignment of students to schools according to nonracial factors ranging from the capacities of the various schools to the level of a pupil's academic preparation or characteristics of a pupil's home environment. A student dissatisfied with a particular assignment had to pursue a detailed administrative procedure in order to request a change. The net effect of all of this was, of course, to inhibit large-scale desegregation.

At first, as black plaintiffs challenged the pupil placement laws, the courts upheld such statutes. In a 1956 case, Circuit Court Judge

Parker declared North Carolina's pupil placement statute constitutional "upon its face." That is, pupils were enrolled in schools on the basis of factors other than race. In *Shuttlesworth v. Birmingham Board of Education* (1958), the U.S. Supreme Court upheld a lower court ruling on the Alabama pupil placement law: "The School Placement Law furnishes the legal machinery for an orderly administration of the public schools in a constitutional manner by the admission of qualified pupils upon a basis of individual merit without regard to their race or color. We must presume that it will be so administered."

The presumption that these laws would be administered without racial bias was, however, obviously inaccurate. Under the North Carolina law approved by Judge Parker, there were only three blacks in Charlotte "white" schools in 1957, four in 1958, and one in 1959. Records indicate that, during the period under the Alabama statute considered in *Shuttlesworth*, only one black was assigned to a "white" Alabama school, and that student transferred under pressure after only a few weeks. By the early 1960s, it was clear that if the Supreme Court were to foster enforcement of the principles in *Brown I*, more active judicial measures were necessary. Over the next decade a series of rulings demonstrated that the Court was tired of delay, and that more precise direction would be given the lower courts in desegregation cases.

In June 1963, the Court decided two desegregation cases that signaled the changes to come. In *McNeese v. Board of Education*, it ruled that plaintiffs challenging failure to desegregate need not exhaust unpromising state administrative remedies before bringing suit in federal court. The same day, in *Goss v. Board of Education*, the Court ruled against a provision of the Knoxville, Tennessee, desegregation plan allowing students to transfer from a school that had previously served the other race, or where the student's race was in a minority. The decision clearly noted that, nine years after *Brown I* and eight after *Brown II*, the Court's patience with Southern delaying tactics was running out.

The message from the Court became clearer over the next few years. One of the original de-

fendants in the Brown case, Prince Edward County, Virginia, had closed its public schools rather than desegregate under a circuit court order, and provided tuition grants to white families who sent their children to private schools. In *Griffin v. County School Board* (1964), the Court declared that such a device deprived the black students of equal protection of the laws. More important, the Court argued, "There has been entirely too much deliberation and not enough speed in enforcing the constitutional rights which we held [had been denied] in *Brown v. Board of Education*." Furthermore, for the first time, the Supreme Court gave lower courts more specific administrative guidelines. Not only was the district court called upon to enjoin the county from giving tuition grants and tax credits to families sending their children to private schools; it was also to "require the Supervisors to exercise the power that is theirs to levy taxes to raise funds adequate to reopen, operate, and maintain without racial discrimination a public school system in Prince Edward County." The *Griffin* decision was followed a year later by *Bradley v. Richmond School Board* (1965). In *Bradley*, the Court prohibited further delay in desegregating faculties. Reflecting the language in *Griffin*, the Court argued, "More than a decade has passed since we directed desegregation of public school facilities 'with all deliberate speed.' . . . Delays in desegregating school systems are no longer tolerable."

As it became apparent that the pupil placement laws of southern states would no longer meet the Supreme Court's criteria for desegregation, many southern systems adopted "freedom of choice" plans. On their face, these plans allowed students to choose freely the schools they wished to attend. In practice, very little desegregation took place. For example, New Kent County, Virginia, maintained two schools: one traditionally white and one traditionally black. In theory, under a freedom of choice plan instituted in 1965, students could choose to attend either school. However, students remained in the school in which they were currently enrolled. As a result of this policy, all of the white students in the county attended the traditionally white school, and 85 percent of the black students attended the traditionally black school. Only token desegregation took place.

In *Green v. New Kent County School Board* (1968), such tokenism was challenged and found inadequate. Writing for the Court, Justice William Brennan declared, "A plan that at this late date fails to provide meaningful assurance of prompt and effective disestablishment of a dual system is . . . intolerable. . . . The burden on a school board today is to come forward with a plan that promises realistically to work, and promises realistically to work *now.*" In order to foster real desegregation, district courts were directed to evaluate desegregation plans "in practice" and "retain jurisdiction until it is clear that state-imposed segregation has been completely removed." Finally, Brennan suggested positive steps, such as pairing or geographic zoning, that the school board might pursue to aid desegregation.

Green was a turning point in the history of school desegregation in the South. It marked the Supreme Court's transition from the passivism of *Brown II* to an activism characterized by specific guidelines and positive suggestions. This new activism was extended in *United States v. Montgomery County Board of Education* (1969), in which the Court endorsed the use of numerical goals in faculty desegregation, and *Alexander v. Holmes County Board of Education* (1969), in which the Court reversed a Fifth Circuit Court delay of implementation of a desegregation plan and reasserted its position that desegregation must take place immediately. It was in this atmosphere of activism that the Court considered *Swann v. Charlotte-Mecklenburg Board of Education.*

Swann began as a result of black dissatisfaction with a desegregation plan proposed for the Charlotte-Mecklenburg school system, a unified system composed of largely black, inner-city schools in Charlotte and predominantly white schools in what formerly had been the Mecklenburg County system. The plan entailed the closing of a number of traditionally black schools, the creation of geographic attendance zones (which would leave a great majority of blacks in separate schools), and a watered-down freedom of choice provi-

sion. Arguing that the plan placed the burden of desegregation on black students and thus perpetuated a dual system, black plaintiffs brought suit in January 1965. When a federal district court approved the plan and, a year later, that decision was affirmed in circuit court, the plaintiffs decided to appeal no further. The 1968 *Green* decision, however, suggested that the Supreme Court might not accept Charlotte-Mecklenburg's plan. In September 1968, the *Swann* plaintiffs reopened the case.

The reopened case was tried before District Judge James B. McMillan. He found that a large majority of the school system's black students attended schools in which the enrollments were either totally or more than 99 percent black. Influenced by the *Green* decision, he ordered the school board to devise a new plan. The board delayed, but finally came up with a weak plan in July. Judge McMillan approved that plan on an interim basis, but ordered the board to file another plan that would desegregate the schools "to the maximum extent possible" for the 1970–1971 school year. In November, the school board filed for an extension of time, but McMillan, influenced by *Alexander,* denied the request. The board then presented another unsatisfactory plan. In December, recognizing that he was getting nowhere with the board, Judge McMillan appointed an educational consultant to develop a satisfactory desegregation plan. In February 1970, Judge McMillan adopted the consultant's plan.

The consultant's plan desegregated all of Charlotte-Mecklenburg's schools by pairing and clustering groups of white and black schools so that enrollment in each school would roughly reflect the white-black ratio in the system at large. Attendance zones were shaped like wedges of a pie, extending from the black, urban center out into the suburban and rural areas of the county. Through the use of busing, black, inner-city students would be transported to predominantly white suburban schools, and white students from the suburbs would be transported to the inner city. Roughly a quarter of the busing in Charlotte-Mecklenburg would be solely for the purpose of desegregation.

The school board appealed Judge McMillan's order, and the Fourth Circuit Court of Appeals, in a mixed vote, affirmed those portions of the plan dealing with secondary education but overturned those portions affecting elementary students. The black plaintiffs appealed the circuit court's decision to the U.S. Supreme Court.

The Supreme Court that heard *Swann* was no longer "the Warren court." Upon the retirement of Earl Warren in 1969, President Richard Nixon had appointed Warren Burger as Chief Justice. Court watchers expected the Burger appointment, in keeping with the President's conservative political philosophy—which promoted the idea of neighborhood schools and rejected busing to achieve racial balance—to move the Court to the right. Indeed, Burger's position in the *Swann* conference was that Judge McMillan's remedies were too sweeping. Despite indications that his view was in the minority, Chief Justice Burger ignored Court precedent and assigned himself the responsibility for writing a draft opinion. However, Court supporters of Judge McMillan's order, led by Justices Brennan and John Marshall Harlan II, were able to influence a final, unanimous opinion affirming the district judge.

The key elements of the opinion centered on the specific remedies prescribed by Judge McMillan: the use of ratios as beginning guidelines for desegregation; the remedial altering of attendance zones through gerrymandering, clustering, or grouping schools in noncontiguous areas; and the use of bus transportation. Though rejecting the idea of mathematical ratios as an inflexible requirement, the Court ruled that "awareness of the racial composition of the whole school system is likely to be a useful starting point in shaping a remedy to correct past constitutional violations." With regard to the manipulation of attendance zones, the Court pointed out that, in the absence of a con-stitutional violation, "there would be no basis for judicially ordering assignment of students on a racial basis." However, in the presence of a history of segregation, and when "school authorities present a district court with a 'loaded game board,' a remedial altering of attendance zones is proper to achieve truly nondiscriminatory assignments." Finally, though recognizing that objections to busing might be valid when "the time or distance of travel is so great as to either risk the health of the children or significantly impinge on the educational process," such was not the case here, and "the remedial techniques used in the District Court's order were within that court's power to provide equitable relief."

Thus, nearly seventeen years after *Brown*, the Supreme Court outlined specific measures that might be required in order to desegregate school systems that had, by law, previously been segregated. Those measures included the use of ratios as beginning guidelines for desegregation, the remedial altering of attendance zones, and busing.

Selected Bibliography

Douglas, Davison M. *Reading, Writing, & Race: The Desegregation of the Charlotte Schools.* Chapel Hill: University of North Carolina Press, 1995.

Graglia, Lino A. *Disaster by Decree: The Supreme Court Decisions on Race and the Schools.* Ithaca, NY: Cornell University Press, 1976.

LaMorte, Michael W. *School Law: Cases and Concepts.* Englewood Cliffs, NJ: Prentice-Hall, 1982.

Schwartz, Bernard. *Swann's Way: The School Busing Case and the Supreme Court.* New York: Oxford University Press, 1986.

Wilkinson, J. Harvie III. *From Brown to Bakke: The Supreme Court and School Integration, 1954–1978.* New York: Oxford University Press, 1979.

Desegregation Heads North

———◄○►———

Sonia Ingles
Issaquah, Washington

Keyes v. School District No. 1, 413 U.S. 189 (1973) and *Milliken v. Bradley*, 418 U.S. 717 (1974)
[U.S. Supreme Court]

◄○► THE CASE IN BRIEF ◄○►

Date
1973, 1974

Location
Colorado
Michigan

Court
U.S. Supreme Court

Principal Participants
Keyes; Milliken; Bradley; Chief Justice
Warren E. Burger

Significance of the Case
Keyes made it easier for African
Americans to get court-ordered busing
for desegregation, but *Milliken*
represented a loss of momentum for
court-ordered desegregation—an end of
a kind of judicial activism in civil rights.

In 1968 desegregation was barely fifteen years old, but it was taking the South by storm. In *Green v. New Kent County School Board* (1968), the U.S. Supreme Court assigned to school officials "the *affirmative* duty to take whatever steps might be necessary to convert to a unitary system." *Green* and several subsequent cases brought desegregation to the South swiftly and meaningfully. By 1971, according to government statistics, the South was significantly more integrated than the North and the West. At that time the Court began to explore issues which were not uniquely Southern. Its decision in *Swann v. Charlotte-Mecklenburg Board of Education* (1971) recognized the effect of residential segregation upon *urban* schools, a recognition which had profound implications for the North and West.

On the other hand, *Swann* left some significant loopholes. It allowed a distinction between de facto (incidental) segregation, commonly seen in the North, and the de jure (state-sanctioned) segregation of the South. Schools were to be held responsible only for rectifying the latter. Furthermore, the conduct of *school* officials was the only relevant state action the courts were willing to review. As a result, the crucial issues of housing and residential discrimination were avoided. This judicial double standard was not lost on the South.

Finally, in 1973, a city outside the South—Denver, Colorado—was legally compelled to account for the segregated condition of its schools. Denver had been a relatively progressive community in terms of race relations until its initially small black population expanded into a previously white section of town. As that area became less white, moderate steps were taken to integrate the local schools. When blacks began to advocate more radical steps toward school integration, including busing to achieve racial balance, the white community balked and black families were forced to seek redress in the courts.

In *Keyes v. School District No. 1* (1973) the Supreme Court confirmed that Denver authorities had used numerous subtle tactics to restrict integration. Denver claimed that only one of its neighborhoods was substantially segregated, but the Court held that when intentional segregation is found in a significant part of a district, nothing less than a districtwide remedy will do. The Court now recognized that, at the very least, racially motivated actions in one part of a district have a ripple effect that could ultimately be cited to illustrate a school board's intentions throughout the school system. The case was remanded to the district court, where a comprehensive busing plan was eventually ordered.

The *Keyes* case made it easier for blacks to win busing orders from the courts because they were no longer required to prove that discrimination was present in every school in a district. Still, plaintiffs in northern districts bore a heavier burden of proof than those in the South. Over the years, segregation in southern schools had been simple to spot because it was written into law. But northern plaintiffs could point to no such smoking guns. They were forced to sift through mountains of school records in an attempt to identify patterns of segregation. The tedium and expense were quite discouraging for blacks contemplating court action. Nevertheless, go to court they did. Ultimately, many

of the African American plaintiffs were successful in convincing federal courts to compel desegregation, as in the Denver case, through busing.

Although Denver experienced a relatively untroubled transition period, other northern and western communities suffered considerable unrest over busing. Complicating the issue in the North and West was the reality of carefully drawn school district lines. Large cities did not always have unitary school systems, and the suburbs almost always possessed school systems separate from those of the core cities. If residential segregation had produced racially identifiable districts, as was almost always the case within a larger community, could integration take place across district lines? Detroit, Michigan, provided the first opportunity for an answer to this question in a northern metropolitan area.

Detroit's African American population had grown as a result of black migration from the South after both world wars. Over the decades, the expanding black population was channeled, via residential segregation, into the core of the city, and whites moved to the outer portions of town and into the suburbs. By 1970 the Detroit School District (the boundaries of which are coterminous with the city limits) was two-thirds black, and most of its students were attending racially identifiable schools. Suburban districts, largely as a result of "white flight," were virtually all white.

Despite the dwindling white population, the Detroit School Board decided to proceed with a small-scale, Detroit-only integration plan known as the April 7, 1970, Plan. For the first time in Detroit's history, white students were to be bused to historically black schools. Predictably, white families balked, and pressured the state legislature to scuttle the plan. The Michigan legislature responded by passing Public Act 48, which nullified the April 7 Plan and imposed a different pattern of pupil assignment in Detroit.

The local chapter of the NAACP challenged the constitutionality of Act 48 and charged that the Detroit public school system was racially segregated. During the district court trial, the plaintiffs' lawyers effectively exposed the existence of substantial residential segregation through the manner in which school boundaries conveniently coincided with single-race neighborhoods. The NAACP presentation was so effective that it convinced conservative District Court Judge Stephen Roth and Alex Ritchie, counsel for a white Detroit homeowners group, of the merits of cross-district busing.

Judge Roth eventually ruled that both government and private institutions had acted (or failed to act) so as to create and maintain residential segregation in the Detroit area. This, combined with significant discriminatory conduct by state and local school officials, he found, had resulted in a thoroughly segregated school system. Upon evaluating several Detroit-only desegregation plans, the district court determined that even the most promising would likely worsen the situation by sparking more white flight. Given the state's complicity and its power over individual districts, a metropolitan solution was not only justifiable, it was also the only solution which would yield reasonable results and stabilize white enrollment. A metropolitan panel was appointed, and directed to design a plan that would achieve maximum integration by pairing portions of the city with districts in the suburbs.

Predictably, the defendants appealed to the Sixth Circuit Court of Appeals, another court known for its conservative predisposition. Nevertheless, both a three-judge panel and an en banc (full-court) review panel affirmed Judge Roth's rulings. In 1973, certiorari was granted by a Supreme Court which had recently become less sympathetic to desegregation because of the addition of four conservative justices appointed by Republican President Richard Nixon between 1969 and 1972. Oral argument in the Detroit case took place early in 1974, in a packed Supreme Court chamber simmering with the political tension.

Five months later, the Court handed down a 5-4 defeat for desegregation. The new conservative block—Chief Justice Warren Burger and Associate Justices Harry Blackmun, Lewis Powell, and William Rehnquist—had been joined by "swing" Justice Potter Stewart in voting to reverse the lower courts on the issue of multidistrict desegregation. Justice Stewart offered a concurring opinion which was only marginally gentler than Burger's in its rejection of metropolitan remedies. Justices Thurgood Marshall, Byron White, and William Douglas all penned blistering dissents.

The justices in the majority did not attempt to contest the findings of segregation in Detroit, but they shrank from accepting a remedy which was, in their view, disproportionate to the violation found. The majority submitted that an "educational conglomerate," such as established by the cross-district plan, would jeopardize local control, cause an unwelcome expansion of judicial power, lead to financial and administrative hardship, and violate the due-process rights of innocent districts against which no evidence of racial discrimination had been found. The Court accepted Michigan's characterization of its own actions as "isolated" and "incidental." Further, the majority discerned nothing in the way of interdistrict segregative effects resulting from the actions of either state or suburban officials. The Court did not offer any analysis of the reciprocal effects of Detroit's segregatory practices. Rather, the Court determined that the demographics of the Detroit area were beyond the state's control.

Justice Marshall insisted that the state's actions must be evaluated in the contextual reality of the situation. Certain local districts, he argued, had carried out the bulk of segregatory policy, allowing the state to stand aloof and claim no responsibility. When a district "strayed," as Detroit did by attempting the limited April 7, 1970, desegregation plan, the state moved swiftly through its Act 48 to restore the status quo. Moreover, the "confinement" of blacks to Detroit, for which the state was derivatively responsible, had preserved the suburbs as a haven for retreating whites. Clearly, suburban school officials had not participated in this process—they had no need to. As long as residential segregation was a valid excuse for school segregation, Marshall maintained, suburban officials could simply incorporate the reciprocal effects of black containment into neighborhood schools. The resulting one-race schools *throughout* the metropolitan area further exacerbated residential segregation by affecting housing choices made by both blacks and whites, producing an endless spiral of apartheid. Marshall blamed the state of Michigan, in part, for the fact that effective desegregation could no longer be achieved within Detroit. The state's largest city had fostered an environment in which the races were not accustomed to living and learning together. Hence, the white flight made Detroit-only integration an exercise in futility.

As for the logistics of the proposed remedy, Marshall and the other dissenters pointed to frequent use throughout the twentieth century of metropolitan area solutions to solve metropolitan area problems, both educational and noneducational. The involvement of the suburbs in a final remedy, regardless of their complicity, was no more unreasonable than the involvement of certain electoral districts in the reapportionment of other over- and underrepresented districts. The district court had gone out of its way, after all, to leave the actual planning to the parties involved. Indeed, Justice White found great irony in the fact that "the least local court in the land" was professing to know better about the feasibility of interdistrict relief than the local courts, which were "on the scene and familiar with local conditions."

Marshall's dissent underscored the pointlessness of taking the Detroit situation, applying a remedy which would essentially do nothing to change it, and then deeming it constitutional. The arbitrary nature of the *Milliken* ruling is also evident in the way that desegregation played out in different cities: the Charlotte metropolitan area happened to encompass one school district, whereas Richmond's suburbs were districts unto themselves. Thus students in Richmond could not be integrated, even though a busing plan for them would be no more complex or costly than the one in effect for Charlotte. Further comparison of these two cities also validates fears concerning white flight: whereas the white student population stabilized after metropolitan desegregation in Charlotte, in Richmond it continued to dwindle after desegregation of the inner city.

Justice Douglas brought the entire issue full circle by pointing out that because blacks were likely to be poorer, and because *San Antonio Independent School District v. Rodriguez* (1973) regrettably had permitted the continuance of financial disparities between school districts, the Detroit schools, as a result of the *Milliken* decision, would be not only separate but also, almost certainly, inferior. Douglas's observation has been borne out in urban America as a whole: cities, with their poor and minority populations, have in fact been left to bear the brunt of reform while affluent suburbs remain aloof and impregnable. Thanks to conservative policies limiting government pursuit of desegregation, further progress has been dependent largely on private organizations with limited resources. Meanwhile, the desegregation plans that have survived litigation have increasingly been formulated to minimize white hostility in the interest of achieving *some* successful integration.

Racial discrimination has proven intractable, in large part, because the means to perpetuate it are so mutable. In the 1960s and early 1970s, it seemed that the federal courts were finally making inroads against long-standing patterns of segregation. But in 1974, in *Milliken v. Bradley,* the momentum in favor of court-ordered desegregation came to a halt. The political heat was too intense, even for the heavily insulated Supreme Court. The Court could not risk losing its authority and prestige among the politically powerful suburban middle class. Instead, it gambled that black achievement and white tolerance had developed enough that judicial activism was no longer necessary to break down segregated schools in the North and West.

Selected Bibliography

Dimond, Paul R. *Beyond Busing: Inside the Challenge to Urban Segregation.* Ann Arbor: University of Michigan Press, 1985.

Graglia, Lino A. *Disaster by Decree: The Supreme Court Decisions on Race and the Schools.* Ithaca, NY: Cornell University Press, 1976.

Kalodner, Howard I., and James J. Fishman, eds. *Limits of Justice: The Courts' Role in School Desegregation.* Cambridge, MA: Ballinger, 1978.

Metcalf, George R. *From Little Rock to Boston: The History of School Desegregation.* Westport, CT: Greenwood Press, 1983.

Orfield, Gary. *Must We Bus? Segregated Schools and National Policy.* Washington, D.C.: Brookings Institution Press, 1978.

Wilkinson, J. Harvie III. *From Brown to Bakke: The Supreme Court and School Integration, 1954–1978.* New York: Oxford University Press, 1979.

Far Enough? The Rehnquist Court and Desegregation

Robert P. Green Jr.

College of Health, Education, and Human Development
Clemson University

Freeman v. Pitts, 503 U.S. 467 (1992) and *Missouri v. Jenkins,* 515 U.S. 70 (1995)
[U.S. Supreme Court]

◄o► THE CASE IN BRIEF ◄o►

Date
  1992, 1995

Location
  Georgia
  Missouri

Court
  U.S. Supreme Court

Principal Participants
  Freeman; Pitts; Jenkins; State of Missouri;
  Chief Justice William Rehnquist

Significance of the Case
  These cases involving school
  desegregation led to rulings that sharply
  blunted court-sanctioned remedies to
  integrate and revealed that a conservative
  Supreme Court had, in effect, limited the
  judicial arena as a place for correcting the
  problems of inner-city schools.

In his dissent from the majority opinion in *Milliken v. Bradley* (1974), Justice Thurgood Marshall wrote, "Today's holding, I fear, is more a reflection of a perceived public mood that we have gone far enough in enforcing the Constitution's guarantee of equal justice than it is the product of neutral principles of law." In *Milliken,* the Burger court, restricting federal district courts' remedial discretion, provided a bellwether for the more conservative Rehnquist Court in the 1990s. As a result of the Rehnquist court's decisions in *Freeman v. Pitts* (1992) and *Missouri v. Jenkins* (1995), many legal scholars, as well as civil rights advocates, felt the Supreme Court had indicated, with regard to court-ordered desegregation, that indeed "we have gone far enough."

The history of school desegregation from the Supreme Court's remedial decree in *Brown v. Board of Education* (*Brown II,* 1955) to the Court's decision in *Swann v. Charlotte-Mecklenburg Board of Education* (1971) was characterized by intransigence in the South and more specific directives from the Supreme Court to district courts concerning their remedial powers. In *Green v.*

New Kent County School Board (1968), the Supreme Court finally drew the line on stalling in the South. Justice William Brennan, writing for the Court, argued that school boards had to take affirmative steps to eliminate the effects of prior discrimination and that schools had an affirmative duty to desegregate. Though Brennan stated that schools should "take whatever steps might be necessary to convert to a unitary system in which racial discrimination would be eliminated root and branch," such as pairing or geographic zoning, more dramatic remedies were not approved until *Swann*.

In the late 1960s, the Charlotte-Mecklenburg school system exhibited characteristics found in many metropolitan areas in the South. The school system encompassed the whole county, and residential patterns based on race were obvious. Black schools and neighborhoods were found in certain parts of the county; white, in others. Responding to a suit by black parents to desegregate the Charlotte-Mecklenburg schools, District Court Judge James McMillan required the school board to adopt a plan that included busing, remedial altering of attendance zones, and the use of racial ratios. In *Swann*, the Supreme Court endorsed McMillan's order. With this decision, the Supreme Court had identified dramatic measures that might be required of school boards with a history of de jure (statutory) segregation.

By the time *Swann* was decided, however, conservative politicians outside the South had begun to question some aspects of school desegregation. President Richard Nixon, for example, presented himself as an advocate of neighborhood schools and an opponent of busing. Conservative legal scholars had begun to criticize the "judicial activism" of the Warren court, calling for judicial restraint. Nixon's appointment of Warren E. Burger as Chief Justice just prior to the Court's deliberations in *Swann* had led many to believe the Court would begin to take a more conservative turn. In fact, with the exception of the Carter administration, during which no Supreme Court vacancies occurred, conservative Republicans dominated the White House until the election of Bill Clinton in 1992. That domination provided opportunities for the appointment of conservative justices. Al-though Burger surprised many by writing the majority opinion in *Swann*, the influence of more conservative justices came to be felt in Supreme Court decisions as desegregation suits began to be served against northern school systems.

Some of the most segregated school systems in the country were found in urban areas in the North and West, where there had been no history of de jure segregation. On its face, such segregation derived from individuals making decisions about where they would work and live, not upon the state's imposition of a dual system. Could the measures endorsed in *Swann* be required in cases of de facto segregation? In *Keyes v. School District No. 1* (1973), the Supreme Court answered in the affirmative. Fact-finding by the district court had revealed that the school board, through its building plans and the gerrymandering of attendance zones, had engaged in deliberate racial segregation within the school district. "Where plaintiffs prove that the school authorities have carried out a systematic program of segregation affecting a substantial portion of the students . . . ," wrote Justice Brennan for the Court, "it is only common sense to conclude that there exists a predicate for a finding of the existence of a dual school system." *Keyes* opened the door to desegregation suits throughout the North and West.

In *Keyes*, however, unlike previous major desegregation cases, the Court was divided. Nixon appointees Lewis Powell (in partial dissent) and William Rehnquist (in dissent) began to make an argument for the more careful tailoring of judicial remedies in cases of segregation. Powell, for example, pointed out the legitimacy of neighborhood schools, argued that predominantly white or predominantly black schools did not necessarily reflect segregative intent (rather, de facto housing patterns), and that widespread busing could be an inappropriate constitutional remedy. Where widespread busing was ordered, argued Powell, the burden of redressing the constitutional violation was borne not by the violating agency but by children and parents who did not participate in any constitutional violation.

The more careful tailoring suggested by Powell and Rehnquist in *Keyes* was adopted by the majority in *Milliken v. Bradley* (1974). In *Milliken*, plaintiffs were able to demonstrate that the city of Detroit, Michigan, had maintained a de jure segregated school system. However, the proportion of minority students in Detroit (64%) precluded any meaningful desegregation within that district. All Detroit schools were predominantly minority. In order to desegregate these schools, the district court designed a remedy requiring busing between Detroit and suburban (majority white) school districts. The circuit court concurred, despite the fact that there was no evidence of the suburban districts' complicity in segregative acts, pointing out that the plan provided the only meaningful way to desegregate the Detroit schools.

Four Nixon appointees—Burger, Powell, Rehnquist, and Harry Blackmun—were joined by Potter Stewart in a majority opinion overturning the lower courts' rulings. In the absence of evidence of de jure segregative actions on the part of the outlying suburbs, argued the majority, the remedy was inappropriate: "To approve the remedy ordered by the court would impose on the outlying districts, not shown to have committed any constitutional violation, a wholly impermissible remedy based on a standard not hinted at in *Brown I* and *II* or any holding of this Court."

Central to the majority's reasoning was the idea that local school districts were autonomous units. The majority rejected the lower courts' rationale that, in fact, all districts were instrumentalities of the state. In a spirited dissent, Justice Marshall, joined by Justices William Douglas, Brennan, and Byron White, agreed with the lower courts' reasoning. "In sum," wrote Marshall, "several factors in this case coalesce to support the District Court's ruling that it was the State of Michigan itself, not simply the Detroit Board of Education, which bore the obligation of curing the condition of segregation within the Detroit city schools." Given such reasoning, a multidistrict remedy made sense. The conservative majority, however, thought otherwise. For the first time since *Green*, the Supreme Court had restricted rather than expanded district courts' remedial powers.

Later, in approving a revised Detroit desegregation plan in *Milliken II* (1977) that included

compensatory education programs, the Court outlined a three-part test to guide district courts in their application of remedies. Chief Justice Burger, writing for the Court, declared: "In the first place, like other equitable remedies, the nature of the desegregation remedy is to be determined by the nature and scope of the constitutional violation. . . . Second, the decree must indeed be remedial in nature, that is, it must be designed as nearly as possible 'to restore the victims of discriminatory conduct to the position they would have occupied in the absence of such conduct.' Third, the federal courts in devising a remedy must take into account the interests of state and local authorities in managing their own affairs, consistent with the Constitution."

As the 1970s and 1980s progressed, turnover in justices provided an even more solidly conservative majority to deal with desegregation issues. Two of those issues, resegregation in Southern school systems and desegregation efforts in the North, given the restrictions in *Milliken*, were addressed in *Freeman v. Pitts* (1992) and *Missouri v. Jenkins* (1995).

In 1969, the DeKalb County, Georgia, school system fell under court order to desegregate. For many years, desegregation strategies were pursued by the school district, following guidelines established in *Green*. In 1986, the school district filed a motion in district court for unitary status and the repeal of court supervision. By the time of this motion, however, the county had undergone significant demographic changes. A massive influx of black residents to the southern part of the county, and the migration of many white families to the northern part, left a number of predominantly black and predominantly white schools. Despite this fact, the district court granted the school district's motion, although it also found that in principal and faculty assignment, further desegregation work remained. On appeal by black plaintiffs, the circuit court overturned the district court's decision, requiring that unitary status depend on desegregation of all elements of the school system and that affirmative steps be taken to desegregate the predominantly black and white schools that remained.

Thus, when *Freeman* reached the Supreme Court, the Court faced two issues: Could a school system be released from a court order in a piecemeal fashion? Was a system responsible for resegregation that occurred as a result of demographic patterns? The Supreme Court answered yes to the first and no to the second.

In a previous case, *Oklahoma City v. Dowell* (1991), the Supreme Court had outlined the conditions under which a district court might withdraw its supervision of a court-ordered desegregation plan or grant unitary status to a previously dual system. Those conditions included good-faith compliance with the desegregation decree from its onset and elimination of the vestiges of past discrimination to the extent practicable. In making its determination, the district court had to consider six factors outlined in *Green*: pupil assignment, faculty assignment, administration, transportation, facilities, and extracurricular activities. Significantly, once a school district was declared unitary, it was under no obligation to maintain busing and racial balancing indefinitely, despite the reemergence of racially identifiable schools.

In *Freeman*, the Supreme Court clarified its position in *Dowell*. The Court argued that district courts could indeed release school systems from desegregation decrees incrementally, as had been the case with the DeKalb County schools. Furthermore, wrote Justice Anthony Kennedy for the Court, "once the racial imbalance due to the de jure violation has been remedied, the school district is under no duty to remedy imbalance that is caused by demographic factors. . . . Where resegregation is a product not of state action but of private choices, it does not have constitutional implications. It is beyond the authority and beyond the practical ability of the federal courts to try to counteract these kinds of continuous and massive demographic shifts."

Unlike *Dowell*, a 5–3 decision of the Court, *Freeman* was a unanimous decision. Thurgood Marshall, perhaps the Court's strongest advocate of integration and a dissenter in *Dowell*, had retired. The kind of argument that Marshall had made in that dissent—that the Court "equivocated" when claiming that residential patterns were the result of individual choice and not vestiges of prior segregation to which the school system itself had contributed—was gone. The Rehnquist Court of the early 1990s (Rehnquist having been promoted to Chief Justice in 1986 by President Ronald Reagan) was composed almost entirely of appointees of Republican presidents. Reagan appointees Sandra Day O'Connor, Antonin Scalia, and Anthony Kennedy, along with Bush appointee Clarence Thomas (who did not participate in *Freeman*), joined the chief justice in an ideologically conservative core that helped shape Court decisions in the direction of judicial restraint. That was clearly the case in *Missouri v. Jenkins*.

In a 1977 suit, both the local school district and the state of Missouri were found complicit in operating a segregated school system in Kansas City. Beginning in 1985, the district court issued a series of remedial orders intending the "elimination of all vestiges of state imposed segregation," including reduced student achievement. To that end, the district court ordered the most comprehensive set of remedial measures in the history of school desegregation, including compensatory educational programs such as full-day kindergarten, expanded summer school, before- and after-school tutoring, an early childhood development program, a massive capital improvement program, and increased salaries for school personnel. The total cost of these measures, borne by the school district and, principally, the state, was over a billion dollars.

Under the principle established in *Milliken I*, the district court found that the constitutional violation in Kansas City was an intradistrict violation; thus no interdistrict movement of students could be forced. In an attempt to integrate schools in a system in which 68.3% of the students were minority, a magnet school program was devised. The district court reasoned that such a plan would attract private school students and white suburban students to the school district.

By 1989, the school district and state had implemented all the programs prescribed by the district court. At that point, the state of Missouri challenged the district court's orders to fund salary increases and to continue to fund remedial programs that addressed low student achievement. Both the district court and, on review, the circuit court rejected Missouri's claims. Missouri appealed to the U.S. Supreme Court.

The Supreme Court overturned both lower courts. Writing for the majority, Chief Justice Rehnquist endorsed Missouri's claim that the scope of the remedy went beyond the violation. "Instead of seeking to remove the racial identity of the various schools within the KCMSD [Kansas City, Missouri, School District], the District Court has set out on a program to create a school district that was equal to or superior to the surrounding SSD's [suburban school districts]." To do this, the district court had focused on the principles of "desegregative attractiveness" and "suburban comparability." Applying principles derived from *Milliken I* and *II*, Rehnquist argued that using magnet schools to attract students from outlying districts (desegregative attractiveness) was "beyond the scope of the intradistrict violation identified by the District Court." The district court's contention that "white flight" was a vestige of segregation, and thus permitted the interdistrict remedy, was rejected. "[T]he District Court's order of salary increases, which was 'grounded in remedying the vestiges of segregation by improving the desegregative attractiveness of the KCMSD,' is simply too far removed from an acceptable implementation of a permissible means to remedy previous legally mandated segregation," Rehnquist wrote.

A similar line of reasoning led the Court to conclude that continued funding of remedial programs also was inappropriate. "Just as demographic changes independent of de jure segregation will affect the racial composition of student assignments, so too will numerous external factors beyond the control of the KCMSD and the State affect minority student achievement," wrote Rehnquist. "So long as these external factors are not the result of segregation, they do not figure in the remedial calculus. Insistence upon academic goals unrelated to the effects of legal segregation unwarrantably postpones the day when the KCMSD will be able to operate on its own."

Rehnquist reminded the district court that its objective was not only to remedy the constitutional violation "to the extent practicable," but also "to restore state and local authorities to the control of a school system that is operating in compliance with the Constitution." This reminder of the importance of local control reflected the conservative direction the Court had taken. In fact, separate concurring opinions by Justices Thomas and O'Connor reiterated conservative themes.

The two concurring opinions pointedly suggested that the courts had gone too far. Thomas, declaring amazement "that the courts are so willing to assume that anything that is predominantly black must be inferior" (and thus a violation of equal protection), found fault with that assumption as well as with the federal courts' exercise of "virtually unlimited equitable powers to remedy this alleged constitutional violation." Reminding the district court of the distinction between de jure violations and private decision making, Thomas declared: "Even if segregation were present, we must remember that a deserving end does not justify all possible means. The desire to reform a school district, or any other institution, cannot so captivate the Judiciary that it forgets its constitutionally mandated role. Usurpation of the traditionally local control over education not only takes the judiciary beyond its proper sphere, it also deprives the States and their elected officials of their constitutional powers. At some point, we must recognize that the judiciary is not omniscient, and that all problems do not require a remedy of constitutional proportions." In similar terms, O'Connor wrote: "The necessary restrictions on our jurisdiction and authority contained in Article III of the Constitution limit the judiciary's institutional capacity to prescribe palliatives for societal ills. The unfortunate fact of racial imbalance and bias in our society, however pervasive or invidious, does not admit of judicial intervention absent a constitutional violation."

The clear message of the conservative majority was that if the country wants to address the problems of minority-dominated, inner-city schools, from this time forward it will have to do so outside the judicial arena. The courts had gone far enough.

Selected Bibliography

Armor, D. J. *Forced Justice: School Desegregation and the Law.* New York: Oxford University Press, 1995.

Brubaker, R. "*Missouri v. Jenkins*: Widening the Mistakes of *Milliken v. Bradley*." *Case Western Reserve Law Review* 46 (1996): 579–601.

Lundin, J. "The Call for Color-Blind Law." *Columbia Journal of Law and Social Problems* 30 (1997): 407–457.

Parkman, C. "*Missouri v. Jenkins*: The Beginning of the End for Desegregation." *Loyola University Chicago Law Journal* 27 (1996): 715–764.

Native Americans

The Cherokee Cases

—◄◦►—

John R. Wunder

Department of History
University of Nebraska-Lincoln

Cherokee Nation v. State of Georgia, 5 Peters 1 (1831) and
Samuel A. Worcester v. State of Georgia, 6 Peters 515 (1832)
[U.S. Supreme Court]

—◦— THE CASE IN BRIEF —◦—

Date
1831, 1832

Location
Appalachian areas of the East coast
Oklahoma

Court
U.S. Supreme Court

Principal Participants
Cherokee Nation
Government of the United States
William Wirt
Chief Justice John Marshall

Significance of the Case
The Court's opinion in the 1831 case, although repudiated a year later, became the basis for which Native Americans were regarded in American law, namely, as domestic, dependent nations.

A-ni-tsa-la-gi' (the Cherokee people); *Ge-wa-ne:-ga* (They are near the horizon, walking away). Such were the circumstances after the fateful decisions of the U.S. Supreme Court in 1831 and 1832 and the subsequent refusal of Andrew Jackson's administration to prevent the ultimate outcome of these cases, the "Trail of Tears." Perhaps at no other time in American history has the failure of law been so evident. Here a people, *A-ni-tsa-la-gi'*, were forced to walk from their homelands in the Appalachian foothills of North Carolina, South Carolina, Georgia, and Tennessee to new lands in Indian Territory, now Oklahoma. It was a forced migration fraught with great hardships, including the lack of food and clothing, and brutal winter travel. Some estimates suggest as many as ten thousand Cherokees perished. What were the legal circumstances that led up to this tragedy?

The Cherokee nation is one of the largest Native American nations in North America. By the time of their first contact with British traders in the seventeenth century, they probably numbered at least twenty thousand. The Cherokees lived as hunters and farmers in five regions along the eastern edge of the Appalachian Mountains. These five regions contained at least sixty independent towns. The regions extended from the northernmost point on the upper Little Tennessee River, where the Overhill towns were located, to the southernmost point on the Keowee River in southwestern South Carolina.

By 1700 the Cherokees had begun to spread their influence beyond their traditional Appalachian homelands. They had moved as far north as Kentucky and Virginia, and as far south as Georgia and Alabama. They controlled over seventy million acres of rich lands. It is not specifically known how the Cherokees came to the point of being a significant nation of North America. In the Cherokee oral tradition, they are said to be the People of the Fire. It is conceivable that their migration may have occurred in concert with volcanic eruptions of an earlier period.

Cherokee history prior to the constitutional crisis of the Jacksonian era had three stages. The initial stage was "frontier contact" (1540–1785). During this time, the Cherokees first encountered Europeans, the introduction being to Hernando de Soto's expedition. This period also witnessed the encroachment on Cherokee lands by British, French, and Spanish colonials; the introduction of more sophisticated weaponry and horses; and the destructive forces of a fur trade economy. The challenge for the Cherokees was to develop a national consensus to combat the serious pressures they were experiencing. Moving from independent city-states to a nation state was an extremely difficult and delicate process. This era closed with the first treaty, the Treaty of Hopewell, signed with the new United States. The agreement guaranteed Cherokee hegemony over Cherokee homelands.

The second stage was the rise of white ascendancy (1786–1828). White ascendancy took various forms. It included attempts by Caucasians to take Cherokee lands, to end Cherokee cultural practices, and to destroy Cherokee legal institutions; the increase of the power of mixed bloods in the Cherokee political system; the creation of the Cherokee Republic; and the attempts of many Cherokees to adapt Cherokee traditions to European institutional forms. For

example, the Cherokees developed their own syllabary, they published their own newspapers, they set up a constitutional convention which adopted a republican form of government, and they selected a national capital site at New Echota, near present-day Calhoun, Georgia.

The Cherokee cases occurred during the third stage, tribal dislocation (1829–1846). During this stage, all Cherokee attempts to adapt to U.S. political and legal institutions were attacked. The administration of Andrew Jackson encouraged this hostility with the passage of Indian removal acts and the sanctioning of the state of Georgia's extension of Georgia law over the Cherokee nation. The Cherokees were not the only Indian nation under these pressures, but they were the only Indian nation to fight for cultural survival and retention of their homelands through the American court system. This resulted in two landmark decisions, both written by Chief Justice John Marshall: *Cherokee Nation v. State of Georgia* (1831) and *Samuel A. Worcester v. State of Georgia* (1832).

The immediate evolution of the *Cherokee Nation* case began with the U.S. efforts to come to grips with the theory and reality of Native American sovereignty. From its beginning, the United States had negotiated treaties with Indians that treated each tribe as an independent nation. Land titles, boundaries, and legal rights punctuated these treaties. Nevertheless, actual practice provided for the abrogation of these treaties when lands were sold and Indians were forced to move away from their homelands.

The U.S. Supreme Court first began to consider this conflict in *Fletcher v. Peck*, decided in 1810. In this case, Chief Justice John Marshall decided an issue which attracted little attention compared to other aspects of the dispute. Georgia, according to Marshall, held a fee simple interest (absolute title) in lands occupied by Indian nations. This interest emerged as a complete right once lands were obtained by the United States from Native Americans. Thus, states had specific realty interests which could not be extinguished.

In 1823 the Marshall Court once again looked into an Indian sovereignty matter. In *Johnson and Graham's Lessee v. McIntosh*, Marshall decided that Indians held a peculiar place within the U.S. legal system. Indians possessed rights of occupancy and concurrent rights of dependency. The United States had the ultimate right to the soil, but Native Americans could occupy the soil and sell it—only to the United States. Where the states fit into this equation was not explicitly noted.

The basic inconsistency of the theory and practice of United States-Native American relationships came under the glare of national consciousness in the 1820s, when Southern tribes refused to sign any more treaties which required them to cede land. In addition, the Cherokees took the United States as a model and created their own democratic institutions. This process allowed them to claim absolute sovereignty within their homelands. The state of Georgia chose to react.

To meet this diplomatic and domestic dilemma, Georgia adopted laws which placed Cherokee lands within organized Georgia counties. Georgia law was to be enforced in these counties, and Cherokee law was to be rendered void. Other legal restrictions on Indian rights also were passed. The laws were not enforced at first, while Georgians waited to see how the new administration in Washington would react. They were not disappointed. Andrew Jackson made it clear that Cherokees and other Indian nations had only two choices: move to Western lands set aside for them or live under state law.

The Cherokees did not plan to let this matter rest. They petitioned Congress to protect their rights. They traveled throughout the Northeast, encouraging memorials on their behalf. And they hired a respected Washington, D.C., attorney, William Wirt, to begin planning for a Supreme Court challenge. In spite of this lobbying effort, a removal law was passed in 1830. This law went farther than previous removal laws because it lessened the requirement of Native American permission before removals could be ordered.

Once the removal law was passed, it became imperative that Wirt challenge Georgia's aggressive anti-Cherokee behavior in court. Wirt first publicly offered the Governor of Georgia, George Gilmer, a joint opportunity to appear before the Supreme Court to settle any differences. Gilmer refused. Wirt then composed an extensive legal brief arguing that the Cherokees were a foreign nation. He attempted to prove that they were sovereign against the world, except that they could not sell their lands to any other nation but the United States, and they could not have diplomatic relations with any nation other than the United States. He reasoned that the Georgia laws were unconstitutional because they impaired the obligation of contracts, violated existing treaties, and constituted a violation of a legislative sphere reserved exclusively for the federal government. This argument was published in newspapers John Marshall and Andrew Jackson no doubt read.

Even so, William Wirt was cautious. Though he remained confident about the constitutional arguments on behalf of the Cherokees, he was worried about finding a way to achieve standing before the Supreme Court. He thought he had only two possible avenues to the Court: either through a suit to be instituted by Chief John Ross against a Georgia officeholder in a lower federal court, or by means of a direct appeal by the Cherokees to the Supreme Court based upon original jurisdiction. He was less confident about the latter, but it was this road he chose to take.

In many ways the Cherokees had no choice. While they were considering their possible legal options, the state of Georgia took direct action. A Georgia court convicted a Cherokee, George Tassel, of murder in Cherokee country. Even though this conviction was appealed to the U.S. Supreme Court, Georgia went ahead and executed Tassel in January 1831, before the Court could act. Such belligerent action necessitated an immediate response.

By January 1, 1831, the Cherokee nation served notice on the officials of the state of Georgia, asking them to appear before the U.S. Supreme Court. A hearing was to be held to determine if Georgia should be prevented from any further attempts at enforcement of state law in Cherokee country. When, on March 5, 1831, William Wirt appeared before the Supreme Court justices to present the Cherokee nation's case, the state of Georgia refused to answer the motion or to participate in the argument.

The Supreme Court was composed of seven justices in 1831. Chief Justice John Marshall presided. Also sitting were Federalist Joseph Story, Jeffersonian partisan William Johnson, and the relatively new justices Smith Thompson, Henry Baldwin, and John McLean. Gabriel Duval could not attend.

Wirt asked for an injunction to prevent further actions by the state of Georgia. He predicated this request upon the basis that the Cherokees were a sovereign nation and, as such, were entitled to the original jurisdiction of the Supreme Court, the exclusive right to their territory, and the exclusive right of self-government within their territory. To hold otherwise would be to violate the treaties made between the Cherokee nation and the United States. In addition, Wirt argued, if the Court did not prevent Georgia from further outrages, the Cherokees would be forced either to move to western lands, where their "progress" toward Christianity and "civilization" might be lost, or "to arm themselves in defence [sic] of these sacred rights, and fall sword in hand, on the graves of their fathers."

The Supreme Court did not rule in favor of the Cherokees even though it clearly expressed a sympathy for their position. In *Cherokee Nation v. State of Georgia*, the majority opinion was, not surprisingly, penned by John Marshall (the great chief justice wrote over half of all the Court opinions during his long tenure). However, there were three other opinions submitted, including a dissent. This was a most remarkable situation, because Marshall did not tolerate a great deal of diversity of opinion on his court. Rare were the occasions on the Marshall court when four separate opinions were officially published.

On March 19, 1831, Marshall began reading his opinion by letting his audience know his agony. "If courts were permitted to indulge their sympathies," Marshall wrote, "a case better calculated to excite them can scarcely be imagined." But Marshall would never reach the merits of the case. Instead, he chose to discuss whether the Supreme Court had jurisdiction.

In order for the Supreme Court even to consider this matter, the Cherokees had to be officially considered a "foreign state." Marshall then embarked upon a historical survey of the relationship of the Cherokees to the United States. He found that the Cherokees and all other Indians had a unique relationship with the United States. Their treaties put them under federal protection. They allowed the United States to have the right to regulate their trade agreements, and they could send a deputy to the Congress to observe, but not to vote. On the other hand, Indians, according to Marshall, had the unquestioned right to the lands unless they voluntarily agreed that the United States could extinguish that right. Only the United States could negotiate with Native Americans over this matter.

Marshall then set in stone three words that have come to characterize the relationship of the United States to Native American peoples. He decided that Native Americans should be considered under American law to be "domestic, dependent, nations." This was a typical Marshallian move. He combined the meaning of three contradictory words to denote a new legal concept. "Domestic" signified internal, "dependent" suggested subordinate, and yet "nation" implied sovereign independence.

He then went on to clarify his meaning. "They [referring to the Cherokees and all other Indians] are in a state of pupilage." To Marshall, Native Americans were the wards of their guardian, the United States. Marshall had accepted the myth of the Indian as child that was shared by many educated Americans during the nineteenth century.

Thus, an Indian tribe could not be a foreign nation, because it was both not foreign to the United States and, like a child, it lacked complete sovereignty. Even the Constitution, according to Marshall, did not use words to imply that Native Americans were members of foreign nations. The commerce clause stated that Congress could "regulate commerce with foreign nations, and among the several states, and with the Indian tribes." Marshall suggested that had the framers thought of Indians as foreign nations, they would not have added them to the clause.

Marshall, therefore, had disposed of the case before he could reach the merits. Because the Cherokees were a domestic, dependent nation, they could not sue for an injunction under the original jurisdiction of the Supreme Court. Any rights to be asserted by the Cherokees would have to be brought into another court first. Still, Marshall had carved out a third, new position for the Cherokees. They were not at the total mercy of the state of Georgia, nor were they released from federal control. This third dimension remained to be devised.

After Marshall announced his opinion, Justices Johnson and Baldwin read theirs. Marshall's six pages paled when compared to Johnson's twelve and Baldwin's twenty. William Johnson was well known as a dissenter. Johnson, after all, had been Thomas Jefferson's man on the Court. In his concurring opinion, Johnson stressed a much stronger view toward the Cherokees. He set up the same questions as Marshall, but he answered them with a decidedly anti-Cherokee stance.

As to whether the Cherokees were a state, Johnson intoned that "to a people so low in the grade of organized society as our Indian tribes most generally are," no statehood could be imagined. Johnson did grant that the Cherokees had "improved," but he found that this new development had not been in place long enough to know whether it was simply a fleeting moment. Johnson also disputed Marshall's notion of occupancy. He wrote that Indians had never been recognized as holding any form of sovereignty over their occupied territory. They had never been known to any other nations except the United States, and in any agreements they made with the United States, they gave up every attribute of sovereignty they might once have had.

Having disposed of the foreign nation argument, Johnson turned to the practical implications of any other decision. He worried that if Indians were ever recognized as foreign nations, or even as domestic, dependent nations, this would overburden the family of nations. It would constitute a folly of a few people holding on to a few acres that would disrupt and make needlessly complex all foreign relations of the United States. Johnson then noted that the U.S. Constitution specifically referred to Indians not as nations but as tribes. Thus, he concluded that the law of nations would interpret this declaration as seeing Native Americans as

what Johnson thought they truly were: "wandering hordes, held together only by ties of blood and habit, and having neither laws or government, beyond what is required in a savage state." Johnson's hostility was clear to all. He agreed with Marshall only in the chief justice's results. To Johnson, the Cherokees were under the jurisdiction of the state of Georgia, and should the merits be reached under a future case, that is how he would hold.

Henry Baldwin took an even stranger tack. He agreed with Marshall's result, but he found that there was no plaintiff in the suit. To Baldwin, Indians could never sue in federal court as Indians. They could come to court only as Americans or as citizens of a particular state, such as Georgia. Even so, Baldwin felt compelled to address the same issue Marshall and Johnson confronted. Baldwin went on for many pages, trying to decide if, as a matter of debate, Indians were independent nations or "tribes of savages." The history of the Iroquois Confederation, the Catawbas of South Carolina, and other Native Americans was interpreted by Baldwin to prove any lack of sovereignty.

Perhaps Baldwin's most novel point was that because the treaties signed with the Cherokees by the United States did not use the word "nation," the Cherokees were not in fact a nation. This led Baldwin to discuss whether the treaties signed were really treaties. He decided that even though the word "treaty" was mentioned in these agreements, they were not treaties because Indians were not nations. Thus, a treaty was not a treaty even if it called itself a treaty, and Indians were not nations because the treaties did not specifically delineate them as nations. Baldwin declared that these "treaties" should instead be termed "indentures of servitude."

Baldwin next belittled William Johnson. Baldwin thought it useless to consult legal theorists or *The Federalist*. This kind of exercise was pointless to him and, of course, was very important to Johnson. Plain reasoning was all that Baldwin needed, and he found it in previous Supreme Court cases, such as *Sturges v. Crowninshield* and *Cohens v. Virginia*.

Baldwin concluded as if he anticipated some action by Marshall. He could see no means of denying the sovereignty of Georgia over the Cherokees, and he could not contemplate any action by the Supreme Court that might change matters. "Foreign states," warned Baldwin, "cannot be created by judicial construction; Indian sovereignty cannot be roused from its long slumber, and awakened to action by our fiat."

No further opinions were announced that day. One has the sense that John Marshall probably was not happy with the outcome. He no doubt found much to dislike in the concurring opinions. This can be discerned from the fact that Marshall set about encouraging Justices Thompson and Story to write down their objections. They did so, and they were later printed with the other three opinions.

As author of the dissent, Thompson strongly rejected the reasoning of all three opinions, especially Baldwin's and Johnson's. He stated at the beginning of his dissent that the Supreme Court had jurisdiction, and that he was going to address the merits of the Cherokee claim. In so doing, he considered the issue all of the previous opinions had, that is, whether the Cherokees were a competent party before the Court. Once he handled this matter, he went on to determine whether a sufficient case had been made to warrant court action and whether an injunction was the appropriate form.

Of course, it was the first issue that mattered. Thompson set up several criteria for the determination of what constituted a foreign nation, relying heavily upon Emerich de Vattel, a noted international law theorist. To Thompson, a group of people constituted a nation if (1) they governed themselves, under any possible form, and (2) if they were without any significant dependence upon a foreign power. Under this second requirement, the key interpretation hinged on a stronger state. Thompson explained this matter by citing a maxim: no weak state that for its safety places itself under the protection of a strong state can lose its right to self-government or sovereignty.

Thompson, once he had set up a model for the determination of a foreign nation, sought to apply the Cherokees to the model. Not surprisingly, he concluded that the Cherokees were a foreign nation. They had a form of governance that provided them with a basic political entity,

and they were powerful enough to exercise control over a significant area of land. Moreover, once they became weakened, they signed treaties protecting themselves from a stronger nation, the United States, but this did not lessen their sovereignty.

In recent times, Thompson noted, that Cherokee government had changed in form. It now more closely resembled that of the United States. Thompson reasoned that for him, at least, progress made in national governance by the Cherokees should not be allowed to destroy their national character. Indeed, he seemed to tie this recent development to the treaty guarantees of which the United States was a party. To attack Cherokee sovereignty was to attack Cherokee progress, and this in turn was attacking the very fundamentals of the American constitutional experience.

This brought Thompson to confront the nature of treaties, something Baldwin had dwelt upon earlier. Thompson found treaties to be contracts between sovereign nations. The subjects of treaties included war, prisoners, territorial cessions, and peace. The United States, according to Thompson, entered into treaties with Native Americans, and these agreements contained all of the normal components found in treaties. Thus, the Cherokee agreements had to be honored if the United States was to be a member of the family of nations. In particular, Thompson cited the twelfth article of the Treaty of Hopewell between the United States and the Cherokees. This contained language which recognized the sovereign and independent character of the Cherokee nation, and it allowed the Cherokees to send a representative to the Congress to make known their positions. Thompson, perhaps stretching his argument, said it made no difference whether such a representative was called a minister, such as an ambassador, or a deputy, such as a territorial delegate.

Thompson's last important point in his thirty-page dissent pertained to citizenship. The Cherokees could not be sovereign if they were citizens of the state of Georgia. If they were not sovereign, then they could not be a foreign nation and appear before the Supreme Court. If the state of Georgia was to claim jurisdiction over Cherokee lands, as both Johnson and Baldwin had agreed to (although Baldwin also suggested a slavery-type analogy), then those persons within that jurisdiction would be citizens. But Georgia did not wish that to be the case, nor did the concurring opinions. Consequently, Thompson concluded that Cherokees were not citizens of Georgia, and that was because Georgia could not exercise jurisdiction over the Cherokees. It was circular reasoning of a spectacular nature.

Once Thompson had found the Cherokees to be a foreign nation, it was a simple matter to dispose of whether an injunction could be issued. Thompson, and his fellow dissenter, Story, agreed that an injunction should be brought against the state of Georgia prohibiting it from any further attempts to erode the sovereignty of the Cherokees. Domestic, dependent nationhood did not concern Thompson, nor did wards and guardianships. These concepts were Marshall's alone.

Given Marshall's own discomfort and the strength of the Thompson-Story dissent, the majority decision in *Cherokee Nation* was tenuous at best. It had been a marriage of strange bedfellows, and Marshall wanted out. One year later the opportunity presented itself. Thompson's dissent and Marshall's dicta encouraged William Wirt and the Cherokees to find another case to attempt to resolve the constitutional status of Native Americans.

In March 1831, Samuel A. Worcester and several other whites were arrested by the Georgia militia after church services in Cherokee country. Worcester was a white Congregational missionary who was backed by the American Board of Commissioners for the Foreign Missions, one of the most powerful mission organizations in the United States. Moreover, Worcester was the postmaster for New Echota, capital of the Cherokee nation.

Worcester had deliberately violated Section 7 of a Georgia statute that prohibited "all white persons [from] residing within the limits of the Cherokee nation . . . without a license or permit from his excellency the [Georgia] governor." Violation of this section constituted the commission of a high misdemeanor with a punishment of not less than four years at hard labor in the penitentiary.

To prevent Worcester from claiming he was a federal employee, the Georgia governor had President Andrew Jackson fire Worcester as postmaster of New Echota. Worcester and his friends were then rearrested, recharged, and tried before a Georgia state court in September. Worcester and the others were found guilty and sentenced to four years in the penitentiary. Worcester appealed, and the Supreme Court accepted the case.

Politics was even more interwoven into the Georgia-Cherokee confrontation this time than in the case decided the previous year. The Cherokees' attorneys were especially active in anti-Jackson groups. One was running for vice president in the election of 1832 on the Whig Party ticket. William Wirt was the presidential candidate of the Anti-Masonic Party. President Jackson was also the subject of many rumors, the most antagonistic being that he would never allow Worcester to leave prison without serving out his term. Cherokee leaders toured throughout the country, seeking support for their cause. They even met with Justice Joseph Story, who later mentioned that he was most impressed with their understanding of the legal issues.

On February 20, 1832, the U.S. Supreme Court heard arguments in the case of *Worcester v. State of Georgia*. William Wirt and his cocounsel once again argued for the Cherokee nation, and the state of Georgia once again stayed away. The composition of the Court had not changed since the *Cherokee Nation* decision, but this time Gabriel Duval was present and William Johnson was ill. The delicate balance of the court on this issue could easily be altered, and it was.

Worcester's attorneys argued that the Georgia act asserting jurisdiction over Cherokee country was void. It was void because it was repugnant to various United States-Cherokee treaties, the contract and commerce clauses of the U.S. Constitution, and the sovereign national authority of the Cherokees. The strategy was to suggest indirectly to the justices that the Cherokees were a foreign nation, but that the protection of their sovereignty necessitated the declaration of Georgia's laws unconstitutional.

In *Worcester v. State of Georgia,* John Marshall, joined by Story, Duval, and Thompson, wrote the majority opinion. Justice McLean added a concurring opinion. Baldwin dissented, and he wrote down his views, but they were not included in the official printed reports. It was assumed that Justice Johnson agreed at least in part with Justice Baldwin. The court had moved from a split decision denying the Cherokees access to the Supreme Court in *Cherokee Nation* in 1831 to a clear 5-1 decision in favor of Worcester and the Cherokees in 1832.

Because it was Marshall who had changed his mind and now gathered a clear majority, it fell to him to attempt to write a majority opinion that dealt with the *Cherokee Nation* precedent. Just as Justice Robert Jackson did with *West Virginia State Board of Education v. Barnette* in 1943, when the Supreme Court found it wanted to reverse the recent precedent of the *Minersville School District v. Gobitis* (1940), so Marshall more than rose to the occasion. In his opinion, he simply refused to acknowledge or even mention *Cherokee Nation v. State of Georgia.*

Marshall began his decision by looking at the Court's jurisdiction. "It behooves this court," he wrote, "in every case, more especially this, to examine into its jurisdiction with scrutinizing eyes." Citing *Martin v. Hunter's Lessee* and *McCulloch v. Maryland,* Marshall appeared to poke gently at the previous concurrence of Justice Baldwin in the *Cherokee Nation* case. Because Worcester was a citizen of Vermont and because he was appealing the action of another state, Georgia, he easily came within the ambit of the Supreme Court's diversity jurisdiction.

Marshall then turned to the merits of Worcester's position, which required examining the constitutionality of the Georgia statute. To determine constitutionality, Marshall chose to look at the effect of the statute. In doing so, he brought up the nature of the Cherokees as a nation through a discussion of the history of the Indian-British and Indian-United States relations. Many treaties were surveyed. Throughout, Marshall emphasized what he called "the language of equality." Indians, to Marshall, were viewed in the treaty process and within the treaties themselves as if they were similar to European nations.

Marshall borrowed heavily from Thompson's dissent in the *Cherokee Nation* case. For Marshall, as it had for Thompson, one nation asking for the protection of another power in a treaty did not imply the destruction of sovereignty. It was simply a basic part of the nature of nations. Some were stronger than others. Furthermore, to agree upon safety did not mean that self-government was necessarily surrendered. That, Marshall noted, would be "a perversion of . . . necessary meaning," and, by looking at the effect of such an interpretation, it would convert a peace treaty into "an act annihilating the political existence of one of the parties." This was neither intended nor desired.

At this point Marshall essentially divorced himself from his own opinion in the *Cherokee Nation* case. He concluded that the Cherokees were a nation, a nation able to negotiate basic national issues such as maintaining peace or war and setting boundaries. This was recognized in the Treaty of Hopewell. Additional pledges of support from the United States came in the Trade and Intercourse Act of 1802 and subsequent laws. Moreover, the Constitution itself recognized Indians as special foreign nations. The Georgia act clearly was unconstitutional.

Thus, from treaties, U.S. statutes, and the Constitution, Marshall derived a conclusion he had specifically rejected in the *Cherokee Nation* decision. Indian nations, according to Marshall, were always "distinct, independent political communities, retaining their original natural rights." An Indian nation was "a people distinct from others." It should be viewed like "other nations of the earth." This was a significant distance from Marshall's "domestic, dependent nation" language just one year previously. In essence, Marshall constructively reversed *Cherokee Nation*'s majority opinion. Worcester, decided the majority, should be released, and the Georgia lower court decision was reversed.

John McLean, who had agreed with Marshall in *Cherokee Nation,* felt compelled to concur and to set his views apart from those of the "new" Marshall. McLean spent a significant part of his concurring opinion on procedural matters, but then he turned to a discussion of the nature of the Cherokee nation. McLean did not dissociate himself from his *Cherokee Nation* views. He wrote that the Georgia statute under consideration was unconstitutional because it violated treaties and federal powers, but Indians were not like other nations of the world. "[I]t is equally clear," determined McLean, "that the range of nations or tribes, who exist in the hunter state, may be restricted within reasonable limits." Such restrictions included amounts of land they could claim, areas over which Native Americans could travel, and hunting and fishing rights.

McLean concluded by noting that Indians never held full sovereign power over their lands and that they did not constitute a foreign state. He continued to believe that under American law Indians should be treated as domestic, dependent nations. Moreover, they were also wards of the guardian United States. "The humane policy of the [federal] government towards these children of the wilderness," observed McLean, "must afford pleasure to every benevolent feeling." This was a subtle hint to Marshall. He could still derive his moral sympathies from McLean's views without creating international legal confusion by declaring Native Americans to be foreign nations.

McLean also worried about the implications of the *Worcester* case. What if President Jackson refused to back the Supreme Court's pronouncement? In strong language, McLean warned the President, "It is in vain, and worse than in vain, that the national legislature enact laws, if those laws are to remain upon the statute book as monuments of the imbecility of the national power." If the executive refused to enforce a declaration by the Supreme Court of unconstitutionality, "the existence of the federal government is at an end."

Because of the crucial element of the timing, the need for specific papers, and the lack of cooperation from the state of Georgia, the Supreme Court was not in a position to obtain Worcester's release. William Wirt realized this, and he attempted to have new laws drafted so that the problems presented by this specific case could be resolved. Such laws would make it difficult for a state to resist a federal court's

mandate. Of course, the United States was not yet ready for this major constitutional change, and President Jackson was not about to use force to make Georgia comply (although later he would need to do so in South Carolina because of the nullification controversy). Worcester eventually served out his sentence, and the Cherokees were forced to move to Oklahoma.

The importance of these two cases to Indian law cannot be overstated. Marshall's opinion in *Cherokee Nation* came to represent the fundamental basis on which Native Americans were to be regarded in American law. This is somewhat ironic, in that this opinion was never shared by more than two out of seven justices at any one time, and the author himself repudiated it one year later. Nevertheless, the legal concept of an American Indian domestic, dependent nation has endured.

After *Cherokee Nation* and *Worcester*, Indian law went through a series of evolutionary attempts to interpret the meaning of "domestic." Post-World War II revivals of civil rights, plus the creation and implementation of the Indian Claims Commission, led to notions of Indian home rule and a greater focus on the word "nation" in U.S. governmental relations with Native Americans.

These recent developments in federal Indian law no doubt would have been positively received by Chief John Ross and the Cherokees. It might have made their attempts to preserve their homelands and nationhood in the early nineteenth century more meaningful to them. Nothing, of course, can blur the memories of the Trail of Tears and the inability of America's greatest legalist, John Marshall, to will a resolution to the legal place of Native Americans within the geopolitical confines of the Untied States. Nor should it.

Selected Bibliography

Burke, Joseph C. "The Cherokee Cases: A Study in Law, Politics, and Morality." *Stanford Law Review* 21 (February 1969): 500–531.

McLoughlin, William G. *Cherokee Renascence in the New Republic*. Princeton, NJ: Princeton University Press, 1986.

Reid, John Phillip. *A Better Kind of Hatchet: Law, Trade, and Diplomacy in the Cherokee Nation During the Early Years of European Contact.* University Park: Pennsylvania State University Press, 1976.

Strickland, Rennard. *Fire and the Spirits: Cherokee Law from Clan to Court.* Norman: University of Oklahoma Press, 1974.

Wunder, John R. *"Retained by the People": A History of American Indians and the Bill of Rights.* New York: Oxford University Press, 1994.

The "Death Knell of the Nations"

———◄○►———

Thomas Burnell Colbert
Department of History
Marshalltown Community College

Elias C. Boudinot, et al. v. United States, 11 Wallace 616 (1871) [U.S. Supreme Court]

◄○► THE CASE IN BRIEF ◄○►

Date
1871

Location
Cherokee Nation (Arkansas)

Court
U.S. Supreme Court

Principal Participants
Elias C. Boudinot
Government of the United States
Associate Justice Noah Swayne

Significance of the Case
The ruling gave Congress the power to override provisions in existing Indian treaties through legislation, and it led to the reversal of the long-time policy of making treaties with Indian tribes.

Mixed-blood Cherokee Elias Cornelius Boudinot was often embroiled in controversy. Indeed, he made many enemies among his Native American brethren with his "progressive" views and actions. Ironically, though, it was his conflict with the federal government over taxing tobacco manufactured in the Cherokee Nation that not only moved him to advocate legal absorption of Indians into white society but also, and more important, led to a change in federal policy toward Indian treaties.

The seed of the legal imbroglio was sown in 1867 when Boudinot and his uncle Stand Watie established a tobacco factory in the Cherokee Nation. They made a deal with the owners of a factory in Missouri to move the operation into the Cherokee Nation, near Maysville, Arkansas. The Missourians would receive $5,000 for their machinery and expenses. However, Boudinot lacked cash, so he offered them two-thirds of the profits.

The site of the factory, only 100 yards from the Arkansas state line, received the name

Boudyville. Tobacco would be purchased in Missouri, and Cherokee farmers in Arkansas would be encouraged to grow the plant. Furthermore, Boudinot could undersell white competitors because of the Cherokee Treaty of 1866. Article 10 of the treaty stated that a citizen of the Cherokee Nation "shall have the right to sell any products of his farm . . . or any manufactured products, and to ship and drive the same to market without restraint, paying tax thereon, which is now or may be levied by the United States on the quantity sold outside of the Indian Territory."

The business was so successful that Boudinot expanded his operations in 1868. By then he had erected two two-story frame buildings and several one-story log-and-frame houses. He also owned state-of-the-art hydraulic equipment and employed several workers.

However, Boudinot feared that tobacco manufacturers in St. Louis might use their political influence to hinder his endeavors. Therefore, on May 8, 1868, he asked John R. Risley, Deputy Commissioner of Internal Revenue, for an opinion on the legality of selling his tobacco outside of Indian Territory. Risley answered that "under *existing* laws, no tax can be legally assessed and collected upon tobacco manufactured at such a factory, whether it be sold in the Cherokee country or elsewhere in any of the United States." But he cautioned that he did not feel able to remark upon how a revenue bill under congressional consideration would affect the situation.

On July 20, 1868, the new law was enacted, and Section 107 of the legislation provided for collecting taxes on liquor and tobacco produced within the "exterior boundaries of the United States." Boudinot concluded, though, that the Cherokee Treaty of 1866 exempted his goods from coming under this statute. But, apprehensive nonetheless, in November he informed James Marr, Supervisor of Internal Revenue for the region, that he was a Cherokee by birth and the owner of a tobacco factory in the Cherokee Nation, and that tobacco sold in the Cherokee Nation was exempt from taxation if produced there. He further stated that he did sell some tobacco outside of Indian Territory and did pay taxes on it when the tobacco was sold. He asked to be allowed to continue this practice.

Marr referred Boudinot's request to the Office of Internal Revenue, recommending that officials "be instructed to assess and collect this tax upon requiring Major Boudinot to report all tobacco to them that he intends offering for sale in this state [Missouri]." Thomas Harland, the acting Commissioner of Internal Revenue, replied that although Boudinot did not have to pay tax on tobacco sold in the Cherokee Nation, he had to affix revenue stamps before selling it in the states. He could do so, however, by purchasing stamps at the nearest collection point before selling his product. Consequently, on January 4, 1869, Marr informed E. A. Rollins, the new Commissioner of Internal Revenue, that under instructions from Harland, Boudinot could "go on with his business without molestation."

In February 1869, Boudinot communicated with Rollins. After reminding him of Article 10 of the Cherokee Treaty of 1866 and noting that there was not much of a market for tobacco in the Cherokee Nation, he stated his desire to sell outside of the Cherokee Nation. "No one manufacturing tobacco in the nation," he wrote, "can pay taxes on the same until he gets into a market where he can anticipate the proceeds on the sale of the same." In fact, he contended, to pay such taxes while his tobacco was still at the factory, as the law stipulated, would violate the treaty. Therefore, he asked to be allowed to put the tobacco he intended to sell outside of Indian Territory in the custody of revenue collectors until he had a buyer. Then he would pay the tax. Rollins, who agreed that the treaty held precedence over statutory law, gave Boudinot permission to ship his tobacco to specified towns, "provided that the packages indicate . . . the place of manufacture, the name of the manufacturer, and [are] shipped to the care of the collector of the district." Boudinot would have to inform the collector of where and when the tobacco would be sold, and to pay the tax before removing it.

Less than a month later, Columbus Delano replaced Rollins, and under Delano's leadership, Internal Revenue Service (IRS) authorities decided to take action against those who sold unstamped tobacco. Boudinot engaged his old friends Albert Pike and Robert W. Johnson as his attorneys. They contacted Delano, who stated that the government did not intend to tax goods made and sold in the Cherokee Nation, only products shipped into the United States from there.

Regardless of Delano's remarks, on December 20, 1869, IRS officials John McDonald and John A. Royce arrested Boudinot and seized his factory. On January 1, 1870, Boudinot, in a signed statement, confirmed that he had purchased thousands of pounds of leaf tobacco in Missouri and Arkansas and that he had sold thousands of pounds of processed tobacco in Indian Territory, paying taxes only to the Cherokee Nation. He also declared that he had affixed stamps only to two hundred pounds, which he had sent to James E. Trott in Fayetteville, Arkansas. That was all he had sold outside of Indian Territory. Nonetheless, he did admit that he had not complied with the Revenue Act of 1868.

Pike and Johnson demanded that Delano return Boudinot's property. When he refused, they argued that arresting Boudinot was an illegal act because it violated Article 10 of the Cherokee Treaty of 1866. Boudinot was released but refused to post bond, declaring that his arrest had been accomplished illegally. He publicly contended that McDonald refused to acknowledge the Cherokee Nation as a legal entity and that he served the interests of Missouri tobacco manufacturers.

Many years later, McDonald asserted that he had received instructions "to investigate gigantic frauds which it was reported were being perpetrated by tobacco manufacturers in the Indian Territory." He claimed that President Ulysses Grant told him to proceed "without fear." Eventually, McDonald confiscated four factories. And, although Delano ordered him several times to release the property, he refused, believing that he had good cases against the offenders. As for agent Royce, he remembered officials concluding that "the Indians were simple figure-heads for the brains and capital of cunning white men."

Whatever prompted the actions of McDonald and Royce, Boudinot did not waste time speculating about their motives. He needed to save his property. First, he tried without success to draw the Attorney General into the conflict. Boudinot then announced in Washington that he was an escaped prisoner from Arkansas, for he had not given bail. He wanted to be arrested in that city so he might test the case under habeas corpus law. The Treasury Department, however, refused to call for his arrest. Next, he offered to compromise with Delano, saying that he would "conform strictly hereafter . . . with all regulations respecting collection of tax on tobacco in the United States," and also would "pay the . . . tax on all tobacco . . . hitherto sold unstamped whenever the courts shall determine that such tax is due."

The Treasury Department, however, was already taking stronger steps to enforce tax collection in Indian Territory. In fact, the day before Boudinot made his plea to Delano, a tax assessor and a collector had been appointed for Indian Territory. A few days later, Treasury Secretary George Boutwell informed Boudinot that "the action taken by Mr. Delano in the matter [confiscating the tobacco factory] was after consultation with me." In desperation, through Senator Alexander McDonald of Arkansas, Boudinot begged Delano to allow him to continue doing business. Delano rejected his request in mid-February 1870.

In May, Boudinot's case was tried in the U.S. District Court for the Western District of Arkansas. Judge Henry C. Caldwell decided against Boudinot. Although Caldwell believed that Boudinot had acted in good faith, he concluded that the Internal Revenue Act of 1868 abrogated Article 10 of the Cherokee Treaty. Boudinot's factory and tobacco were declared forfeited, and his only recourse lay in appealing to the U.S. Supreme Court.

By now, Boudinot lacked money to pursue the case, but fortunately the Cherokee National Council authorized the hiring of lawyers to represent him. Not only was Boudinot a Cherokee citizen but, more important, the case involved "great principles of international law and rights of foreign nationality vital to the interests and security of the Cherokee Nation and people."

In April 1871, the Supreme Court heard the case. The lawyers for Boudinot included himself, Augustus H. Garland, Albert Pike, Robert Johnson, and Benjamin F. Butler. Boudinot sued the government on writ of error, offering several points in his argument. It was pointed out that as a Cherokee, he was not a citizen of the United States and not represented in Congress. Therefore Congress had no right to tax him. In addition, Delano officially extended IRS authority in Indian Territory after the arrest of Boudinot. Furthermore, not only did Article 10 of the Cherokee Treaty of 1866 have precedence over an act of Congress, but also the Court had earlier opined that "all provisions of laws and treaties in regard to the Indians shall be construed most favorably to that people." The attorneys argued that Boudinot was on "impregnable ground" under the rule of construction. That is, there was no indication that Congress intended the Internal Revenue Act to cover Indian Territory, nor had the Cherokees ever agreed to give the U.S. government the right to tax Indian property.

Attorney General Amos Akerman presented the government's side. He argued that the United States and the Cherokee Nation were not equals, and that the federal government had the power to levy and collect taxes in Indian Territory under proper legislation, such as the Internal Revenue Act of 1868.

The six sitting justices voted 4-2 against Boudinot. Justice Noah Swayne, delivering the majority decision, said that the language in the law was quite clear, and he advanced the argument that Indians were implicitly under the authority of congressional power unless statutes expressly excluded them. Swayne further submitted that if the disputed revenue law caused an injustice, it was a political matter. Congress, not the Court, would have to resolve that conflict. Justice Joseph P. Bradley, in dissent, maintained that it was clear Congress had not intended the law to affect Indian Territory, and that the case reflected on the honor of the federal government to uphold the integrity of Indian treaties.

In effect, the Supreme Court destroyed the supposed binding power of a treaty. The ruling, Boudinot informed Stand Watie, "is the Death Knell of the Nations." In fact, though, partly due to the effect of Boudinot's case, in

March 1871 Congress had attached a rider to the Indian Appropriations Act, declaring that no new treaties would be made with Indian tribes, and tribal concerns would be controlled by the federal government. Indian tribes would no longer be considered independent powers. Although existing treaties were to be honored, the decision on the tobacco case brought new fears. The Grand Council of Indian Territory declared that Indian treaties "are now dependent wholly upon the forbearance of the government for we are powerless to enforce their fulfillment." The federal government could, if it desired, abrogate a treaty, and then the tribe would be at the mercy of government policy without the safeguard of another treaty.

As for Boudinot, he now became a strong proponent of territorial government for Indian Territory. He concluded that the Indian, especially an enterprising one such as himself, needed legal protection—citizenship—and personal ownership of his real property, not merely use of land held in common by the tribe. Had he been protected by the Constitution in an official territory of the United States, Boudinot reasoned, he would not have lost his property. He spent much of the next twenty years lobbying Congress and making speeches across the nation promoting his views—much to the chagrin of most Cherokees and other Indians.

With regard to his tobacco factory and his losses, Boudinot memorialized Congress for compensation. Eventually, Congress voted to dismiss civil proceedings against him, and, upon the request of the House Judiciary Committee, the Attorney General withdrew the criminal counts. Finally, in 1880 Congress allowed Boudinot to sue United States for damages in the Court of Claims.

The Court of Claims acted on Boudinot's petition in 1883. Boudinot asked for $175,000. The court awarded him only $3,272.25. This amount covered the tobacco lost, damage to his property, and his legal expenses, because the buildings and machinery had been returned to Boudinot. In rendering this decision, the court offered the following commentary: "In no instance, probably, in the history of this court has a special act authorizing a party to sue the United States here, been couched in terms so liberal to the claimant. . . . It removes any ground for questioning the right of an Indian to sue in this court, and gives jurisdiction to this tribunal, which it would not otherwise have, of a claim against the Government based on an alleged tort committed by its officers. . . . and declares an act done by the internal revenue officers . . . which had been sustained by a verdict of a jury and . . . affirmed by a solemn judgment of the Supreme Court . . . on a grave constitutional question, to have been 'a *wrong done*' to the claimant." Certainly, Congress's allowing Boudinot to receive damages was testimony to his influence in Washington. Thus, after fourteen years of controversy, the Court of Claims finally ended Boudinot's case.

Boudinot's financial claim, however, was ultimately of secondary importance. The specific issue in *Boudinot* was whether Boudinot had violated the Internal Revenue Act of 1868, but the ramification of the Supreme Court's verdict was far-reaching. The case did deal with a "grave constitutional question," and the Court's

ruling gave Congress the power to override stipulations in existing Indian treaties through legislation. At the same time, the concerns raised by the case, even before the Supreme Court heard it, helped prompt Congress to reverse its longtime policy of making treaties with Indian tribes. Congressional Indian policy would hereafter be more authoritarian, and it could be so with the concurrence of the Supreme Court.

Selected Bibliography

Colbert, Thomas Burnell. "Prophet of Progress: The Life and Times of Elias Cornelius Boudinot." Ph.D. dissertation, Oklahoma State University, 1982.

Heimann, Robert K. "The Cherokee Tobacco Case." *Chronicles of Oklahoma* 41 (Autumn 1963): 299–322.

Wilkins, David E. *American Indian Sovereignty and the U.S. Supreme Court: The Masking of Justice.* Austin: University of Texas Press, 1997.

Why Native Americans Can No Longer Count on Treaties with the U.S. Government

—‹o›—

John R. Wunder

Department of History
University of Nebraska-Lincoln

Lone Wolf v. Hitchcock, 187 U.S. 535 (1903) [U.S. Supreme Court]

‹o› THE CASE IN BRIEF ‹o›

Date
  1903

Location
  Oklahoma
  Kiowa-Comanche Reservation

Court
  U.S. Supreme Court

Principal Participants
  Lone Wolf; Hampton L. Carson; Secretary of the Interior Ethan A. Hitchcock; Justice Edward D. White

Significance of the Case
  The Court ruled that an act of Congress could abrogate an earlier treaty between the U.S. government and Indians, thus leaving Native Americans as wards of the government with no right to function outside that relationship.

Lone Wolf v. Hitchcock is to the Kiowa people and Native Americans as *Plessy v. Ferguson* (1896) is to African Americans and *United States v. Ju Toy* (1902) is to Chinese Americans. It represented a direct legal attack upon the fundamental basis governing U.S.-Indian relationships—the treaty. After *Lone Wolf,* treaties of the past were not perceived within the American legal system as inviolable instruments of law until the decisions of the Indian Claims Commission during the 1950s and 1960s tentatively began the long legal road back.

Approximately twelve thousand years ago, the first ancestors of the Kiowa people migrated from Asia to North America. These ancestors were hunters who eventually resided in the forests of what is today Canada. Approximately nine thousand years ago, the forests that predominated in much of North America began to die out due to a change in climate. The Great Plains region became an area characterized by lush grasslands, and Native Americans began to move there. Here the Kiowas settled.

Although anthropological explanations of Kiowa migration are for the most part theoretical, most Kiowas believe that their nation began on the northern Great Plains in western Montana. Their neighbors were Flatheads, Crows, and Sarcis. The Sarcis, an Apachean people, and the Kiowas lived and traveled together. During the seventeenth century, Kiowas moved to the Black Hills, where they obtained the horse, a significant cultural, technological, and military breakthrough.

By the beginning of the eighteenth century, the Kiowa controlled much of the area around the Black Hills. However, this hegemony was not to last. A new nation entered what the Kiowas considered to be their homelands. This nation, the Comanches, launched a series of wars against the Kiowas from the south. At the same time, the Shoshones attacked the Kiowas from the west, the Cheyennes and their Arapaho allies put pressure on the Kiowas from the north, and the Sioux, the Kiowas' greatest threat, menaced them from the east. These pressures, plus a smallpox epidemic in 1781, weakened the Kiowas and forced them to evacuate the Black Hills. They moved south, encountering French traders, Spanish settlers, and the Comanche.

The Kiowas were known to other Plains Indians as the diplomats of the Great Plains. A relatively small nation, the Kiowas relied upon diplomatic skills in order to survive in a volatile region. The move onto the southern Great Plains necessitated making agreements with the Comanches, which the Kiowas successfully pursued. This alliance, made around 1790, continues today. It also was through a diplomatic approach that the Kiowas met the new nineteenth-century invaders of the Great Plains, the United States.

Kiowa foreign policy relationships with the United States officially began in 1835. The Kiowas and other Plains Indians listened to a proposed treaty of peace and friendship with the United States. Some tribes agreed to share a common hunting territory and to allow U.S. citizens safe passage through the southern Great Plains. They also promised to pursue peaceful relations with Mexico. Although the Kiowas were interested, they chose not to sign such an agreement. This did not deter the United States. Two years later, the United

States and the Kiowas formally entered into a similar agreement. Each nation claimed that its people had been attacked and injured by people of the other, and these past disputes were forgiven. A treaty proclaiming peace and friendship was signed.

For the next thirty years, the southern Great Plains proved to be a very unstable area. Numerous wars were waged by Mexico, an independent Texas, the United States, and the Comanches, Utes, and Kiowas. Attempts were made by all parties to bring stability to the region, but were unsuccessful. The Civil War brought a respite for the Kiowas, but after the war the United States turned its attention to the full military capitulation of all Indian nations on the Great Plains.

In the fall of 1867, the United States again tried to make an agreement with the Kiowas and other southern Great Plains tribes. The Treaty of Medicine Lodge Creek was the result. Ten Kiowa chiefs signed the document, which created a reservation between the Canadian and Red rivers in southwestern Oklahoma. Two provisions of this treaty would prove important in the future. The first allowed heads of Indian families to select up to 320 acres of reservation land to own, if they so desired. The second provision of significance was Article 12, which stated, "No treaty for the cession of any portion or part of the reservation herein described [the Kiowa-Comanche Reservation], which may be held in common, shall be of any validity or force as against the said Indians, unless executed and signed by at least three fourths of all the adult Indian males occupying the same." Because he did not trust the United States to keep its word, young chief Lone Wolf did not sign.

Many Kiowas continued to range beyond the reservation lands because of the scarcity of buffalo. This did not sit well with U.S. settlers or military leaders. Before long, war broke out once again on the southern Great Plains, with both sides violating the terms of the Medicine Lodge Creek Treaty. The U.S. Army was particularly effective. Winter campaigns were very destructive; the message to the Indians was that unless they ceased fighting and remained on the reservation, they would face annihilation. Shortly after the Battle of the Washita (1868), Lone Wolf and another chief delivered a message from the Indian agent assigned to the Kiowas to General George Armstrong Custer. The message stated that the Kiowas had not taken part in the battle. The two chiefs, who were carrying a white flag of truce, were immediately seized, and the rest of the Kiowas fled. After the army threatened to hang Lone Wolf and others in custody, the Kiowas returned to the reservation.

Life on the reservation was not easy. The land in southwestern Oklahoma was not particularly conducive to economic activities within the range of Kiowa experiences. Government officials sought to alter Kiowa cultural values in particularly punitive ways rather than to place a positive emphasis on training in farming and ranching. White settlers tried to invade the reservation to occupy lands, and they sought long-term leases for the valuable grasslands on the reservation. Lone Wolf and other Kiowas tried to resist these attacks.

Perhaps the greatest force to threaten Kiowa culture came from the General Allotment Act (Dawes Severalty Act) of 1887. This law allowed reservation lands to be divided into separate units that were distributed or allotted to individual Indians, who were to farm or live on their allotments. After each person from a tribe received a plot, the remaining lands were sold. The money from the sale of this land was to be held in trust for the particular Indian tribe.

From the beginning, the Kiowas, like many other reservation Indians throughout the country, strongly opposed allotment. The tribe's chief, Lone Wolf, notified Washington that his people would go to war if allotment were forced on them. Nevertheless, non-Indians wanted the reservation lands, and in 1889 Congress set up a three-member committee to negotiate allotment with all twenty Indian reservations in Oklahoma. The delegation, known as the Jerome Commission (after its chairman, David Jerome), arrived at Fort Sill in September 1892.

At the Fort Sill hearings, many Kiowas expressed their opposition. They did not want allotment. They cited the Medicine Lodge Creek Treaty as binding. Jerome persisted, offering each member of the three tribes (the Kiowas,

Comanches, and Apaches) on the Kiowa-Comanche Reservation 160 acres each plus a total payment of $2 million for the surplus lands. Lone Wolf and others were opposed. Lone Wolf said, "Look on Quanna's [Quanah Parker was the primary negotiator for the Comanche] people, they are Indians; look on Lone Wolf's people and Whiteman's [leader of the Apache] people, they are Indians; they are not educated, they do not know how to till the ground. They do not know how to work. Should they be forced to take allotments it means sudden downfall for the three tribes." Even though most Kiowas had objections and Lone Wolf feared that the worst danger was losing tribal lands, Quanah Parker succeeded in persuading Lone Wolf and others to sign the document. They realized that no one could return to the way things were, and that they had to accept change. Lone Wolf himself favored building schools and houses.

Lone Wolf and others thought that Quanah Parker's proposals were a part of the original agreement. These included payment for two sections in every township that were set aside for education, 320-acre allotments, payment of up to $2.50 per acre for leftover lands, and retention of mineral rights to the reservation lands. Soon after the Fort Sill meeting, however, it became clear that Jerome did not believe the agreement included these provisions. Opposition developed, and Lone Wolf now opposed the agreement, which he considered to be based upon fraud. In order for Congress to begin the assignment of Kiowa-Comanche Reservation lands, three-fourths of all tribal members had to sign the agreement. This was based upon the provision in the Medicine Lodge Creek Treaty. With the collusion of the Indian agent, whites were added to tribal rolls and Indians were deleted. The commission certified that there were 562 eligible signers, but in reality that figure was closer to 725. It claimed to have 456 signatures, but many of the 456 who had originaly signed, did so under false pretenses and now wished to have their names removed from the document. Nevertheless, the commission presented the document to Congress.

After seven years, the agreement was accepted by Congress on June 6, 1900. Lone Wolf and other Indians had spent a great deal of time lobbying against ratification, but their efforts were to no avail. Secretary of the Interior Ethan A. Hitchcock was charged with implementing the allotments. Shortly after the bill had been passed by Congress, representatives of three tribes met with President William McKinley. He refused to modify the bill. This split the tribes, some of whom refused to acknowledge defeat. Lone Wolf was among those who vowed to fight on in the courts.

In June 1901, Lone Wolf went to Washington, D.C., and retained former Congressman and federal judge William Springer as the tribe's attorney. Springer encouraged the Indian Rights Association, a private, humanitarian, reform group organized in the late nineteenth century, to help with the case, and they did. Unfortunately, Springer was not a very good attorney, was short of funds, and was looking for an easy case. He demanded funding from the Department of the Interior, and he was refused. The Indian Rights Association was alerted to what were perceived to be Springer's shortcomings.

Springer, however, pushed ahead, filing a complaint for Lone Wolf in the federal district court in the District of Columbia. Secretary Hitchcock was named as the defendant. Lone Wolf's suit sought an injunction to prevent the Secretary of Interior from allotting the Kiowa-Comanche Reservation. The brief argued that the Jerome Commission report ratified by Congress was unconstitutional because it was contrary to the provisions of the Treaty of Medicine Lodge Creek and, if the allotment was allowed, it constituted a taking of property without due process. Two weeks later, Springer added seven more plaintiffs who had been named representatives of the three tribes by a general council held on the reservation.

The district court ruled against Lone Wolf. It denied the injunction and the assertion that property would be taken without due process of law. The judge, A. C. Bradley, ruled that the allotment procedures were "the usual process," and he held that it did not make any difference if misunderstandings or deception was involved. He did not see irregularities as relevant, because Congress had spoken. Springer appealed the decision to the Court of Appeals,

but by the time the court met in August 1901, the Kiowa-Comanche Reservation had been divided and opened for settlement.

On December 4, 1901, the Court of Appeals for the District of Columbia rejected Lone Wolf's appeal. The appellate judges held that U.S. treaties with Indians were not a proper judicial subject for scrutiny. Instead, this was a policy matter which was the sole function of Congress. Moreover, they found that "lands and reservations are held by the Indians subject to the control and dominion of the United States." Indians, according to the appellate court, had no title in reservation lands. They were simply occupants, subject to the will and whim of the federal government.

The appellate opinion caused great consternation among groups favoring Indian rights, as well as among the Indians themselves. The Indian Rights Association (IRA) concluded that an appeal had to be made in order to overturn the extremely damaging appellate opinion. The IRA hired Hampton L. Carson, professor of law at the University of Pennsylvania, to argue the case. The competence of Springer was subject to question, and now that the case had gone this far with an unmitigated disaster near at hand, more experienced and stronger counsel was needed. Meanwhile, Lone Wolf and two hundred others refused to accept the first land payment.

Lone Wolf's attorneys had a challenging argument to make. Recent U.S. Supreme Court decisions had moved steadily toward rendering U.S. treaty agreements with Indians unenforceable. Under American law, Indians were being reclassified from members of sovereign nations to dependent wards of the federal government. For example, in *United States v. Kagama* (1886) the Supreme Court ruled that crimes committed by Indians on reservation land were subject to federal criminal jurisdiction because Indians were now wards of the federal government. *Kagama* was interpreted by lower courts to mean that Congress had total authority to do as it wished, even if it disregarded specific provisions of Indian treaties.

Oral arguments before the U.S. Supreme Court began on October 23, 1902. Carson presented the bulk of Lone Wolf's case. Those present at the hearing remarked that his presentation was outstanding. Representing the Department of Interior was Assistant Attorney General Willis Van Devanter, a lawyer from Wyoming and a future Supreme Court justice. Lone Wolf supporters reported that Van Devanter's argument was dull and unexciting, and that the justices did not pay much attention to it.

Lone Wolf argued that the allotment act dividing the Kiowa-Comanche Reservation was unconstitutional for three reasons. First, the agreement violated the Medicine Lodge Creek Treaty because fewer than three-fourths of the adult Indian males on the reservation signed it. Second, those who did sign were fraudulently misled by the Jerome Commission. And third, the agreement allowed only $1 per acre for surplus lands reimbursement, which was significantly below the value of the real estate and also abrogated the $2.50 per acre promise. Thus, the attorneys concluded that the allotment act violated Kiowa and Comanche property rights and deprived them of due process of law.

Van Devanter, for Secretary of the Interior Hitchcock, relied upon recent cases to conclude that Indians were wards of the U.S. government and, as such, were totally dependent upon Congress. Thus, when Congress acted, treaty obligations might be revised or voided. Indian legislation was essentially a political matter, not a judicial issue.

Justice Edward D. White wrote a nearly unanimous opinion for the Court. His holding agreed with the appellate court and Van Devanter, but he went even farther. White decreed that Congress was to have unlimited power over Indian property, regardless of treaty guarantees. He reached the conclusion that Indian treaties were not valid legal instruments if they conflicted with congressional action. Indians were dependent upon the federal government, White maintained, and therefore they had neither power nor ability to function outside a guardianship relationship. Congress also might need to dispose of Indian land in an emergency, so it could not afford to be inhibited by Indian consent. White quoted an 1877 case involving a claim of reservation status on disputed lands,

in which the Court ruled, "It is to be presumed that in this matter the United States would be governed by such considerations of justice as would control a Christian people in their treatment of an ignorant and dependent race." Finally, White reasoned that the Resolution of 1871, a law whereby the United States was prevented from making any future treaties with Native American nations, should be interpreted as meaning that past treaties were revokable by Congress at any time and for any reason.

Thus, the Court found that Congress had total control over Lone Wolf and the Kiowas because Indians were a dependent, racially inferior group capable of challenging congressional power. Such a challenge might be rendered in a treaty, and therefore treaties as legal contracts were no longer enforceable if voided by Congress. With this holding, it made no difference whether fraud or deceit was used by the Jerome Commission. In essence, the allotment act nullified the Treaty of Medicine Lodge Creek. All the judicial branch could do was presume that Congress would act in good faith. Any remedy the Kiowas might seek would have to occur within the legislative branch, not with the judiciary.

Lone Wolf v. Hitchcock was a devastating opinion for Native Americans. The only protection Indians had traditionally had for individual and tribal rights was through their treaty agreements, and now treaties were no longer given credence. With one stroke of the pen, a new doctrine was articulated, authorizing the unilateral termination of treaties. It would be over half a century before this new doctrine began to fade, although it has never been overruled.

In the interim, the Kiowa-Comanche Reservation was divided and abolished. The Kiowas concentrated in seven communities in Caddo and Kiowa counties of southwestern Oklahoma. The descendants of Lone Wolf settled in the most isolated and westward of the communities and named the settlement after him. Awarded $2 million by the Indian Claims Commission in 1960 for past treaty abrogations, the Kiowa Nation today strives to overcome the legacy of rural poverty and the destruction of their land base that was their heritage from *Lone Wolf v. Hitchcock.*

Selected Bibliography

Barsh, Russel L., and James Y. Henderson. *The Road: Indian Tribes and Political Liberty.* Berkeley: University of California Press, 1980.

Clark, Blue. *Lone Wolf v Hitchcock: Treaty Rights and Indian Law at the End of the Nineteenth Century.* Lincoln: University of Nebraska Press, 1994.

Estin, Ann Laquer. "*Lone Wolf v Hitchcock*: The Long Shadow." In *The Aggressions of Civilization: Federal Indian Policy Since the 1880s,* ed. Sandra L. Cadwalader and Vine Deloran, Jr., 215–245. Philadelphia: Temple University Press, 1984.

Wilkinson, Charles F. *American Indians, Time, and the Law: Native Societies in a Modern Constitutional Democracy.* New Haven, CT: Yale University Press, 1987.

Wunder, John R. *The Kiowa.* New York: Chelsea House Press, 1989.

Native American Land Claims:
The Indians Finally Win

John R. Wunder
Department of History
University of Nebraska-Lincoln

Joint Tribal Council of the Passamaquoddy Tribe et al. v. Rogers C. B. Morton,
528 F. 2d 370 (1975) [U.S. Circuit Court of Appeals]

◄◦► THE CASE IN BRIEF ◄◦►

Date
1975

Location
Maine
Passamaquoddy reservations

Court
U.S. Circuit Court of Appeals

Principal Participants
Joint Tribal Council of Passamaquoddy tribe; Secretary of the Interior Rogers C. B. Morton; State of Maine; Circuit Court Judge Levin H. Campbell

Significance of the Case
The courts served as a catalyst to an agreement between the Passamaquoddy tribe, the federal government, and the state of Maine that remedied decades of injustice and served as a model for Native American-government relations.

An old Passamaquoddy tale concerns the scarcity of tobacco. A young Passamaquoddy sees his grandmother smoking, and he wants to smoke with her. She says that she will share the tobacco, but she worries that it is very rare. He says he will get some tobacco, and she tells him he must go to an island. The young man journeys to the island, where he confronts a woman who tries to prevent him from obtaining any tobacco. A struggle ensues between the boy and the woman, and the woman changes into a crow. The boy becomes a large bird, and the two fight in the air. Eventually the crow/ woman drops the tobacco she has in her claws. The bird/boy swoops down and seizes it. Then he brings it to his grandmother and says, "Ho'k'mi yut, t'ma'wei kwuskwe'sul [My grandmother, here is the tobacco]." His grandmother wisely replies, "Ndege'k'ma'jehan; k'dunlogo'kw [You'd better go your way; she will be after you]."

This story certainly applies to the relationships of the Passamaquoddy with other nations over time, and with the state of Maine and the United States in particular. These relationships have taken a variety of twists, the most recent resulting in a pathbreaking federal court decision, *Joint Tribal Council of the Passamaquoddy Tribe et al. v. Rogers C. B. Morton,* which forced an unusual federal-state legislative package, the Maine Indian Claims Settlement Act and the Maine Implementing Act.

The Passamaquoddy are an eastern woodlands people who have lived in Maine for at least three thousand years. The earliest evidence of their occupation is found around Passamaquoddy Bay on what is today the U.S.-Canadian border. There is evidence of agricultural cultivation. The Passamaquoddy lived a seminomadic life of hunting and fishing, migrating up and down the St. Croix River basin. In the summer they raised corn, beans, and tobacco. Linguistically, the Passamaquoddy spoke the Algonquian language. They shared a dialect with their neighbors, the Maliseet, and they were related linguistically and culturally to other neighbors, the Micmac and the Penobscot.

The first major European contact with the Passamaquoddy occurred in the early seventeenth century. The French established missions in Passamaquoddy country, and they involved the Indians in the fur trade. Unfortunately for the Passamaquoddy, many pressures built up by the mid-seventeenth century. Disease took its toll; British and French rivalries required northern New England tribes to choose sides; and to the west the Iroquois Confederacy became a power that threatened the existence of eastern tribes. A combination of British atrocities and French diplomacy led to the Passamaquoddy becoming French allies. Moreover, a confederation of Algonquian-speakers termed the Wabanaki (People of the Dawnland) was formed among the Micmac, Maliseet, Penobscot, and Passamaquoddy. The Wabanaki Confederacy remained at war with the British from the end of King Philip's War in 1676 to the end of the American Revolution in 1781. In 1700 it made peace with the Iroquois Confederacy. Even though the Iroquoian-speakers remained staunch allies of the English, this did not cause a breach in the peace. In 1749 the Great Council Fire began between the two confederacies. Such diplomacy established the basis for Indian-European relations on the eastern American continent for two centuries.

The victory of the British over the French at Quebec in 1759 caused a strain in the Wabanaki Confederacy. The Passamaquoddy and others concluded that they had to make peace with the British. They did so in 1760, but they did not give up their autonomy or swear loyalty. At first British officials tried to protect Passamaquoddy lands. But the Proclamation of 1763 and other promises could not hold off white settlement. By 1764 the Passamaquoddy were complaining to the governor of Massachusetts that whites were illegally taking land on islands in Passamaquoddy Bay, selling alcohol, and committing trading frauds. The British ignored them.

Thus, it was an easy choice for the Passamaquoddy and the Wabanaki Confederacy when war broke out between the patriots and loyalists in 1776. The Passamaquoddy and Maliseet signed a treaty of alliance with the patriots in 1777 at Aukpaque. The patriots promised the Indians trade, supplies, a priest, payment for military service, and a beaver monopoly. The alliance was further secured when the French joined the patriot cause in 1778. During the war, the Passamaquoddy helped repulse a British naval attack at Machias, but when the negotiations were begun and concluded with the Treaty of Paris in 1783, Passamaquoddy interests were neither represented nor protected. This oversight occurred even though John Allan, George Washington's agent on the eastern frontier, reported to the Continental Congress in the spring of 1783 that the Wabanaki Confederacy had been crucial to the holding of Maine for the patriots: "These Indians, particularly St. John's [Maliseet] and Passamaquoddy are very tenacious of their liberties; delegacious and subtle people and may be very dangerous if not attended to; their zeal in the cause and their virtue in persevering through many difficulties throughout the war with the attachments and affections the subscriber has experienced himself commands attention."

The boundary agreed to by the British and Americans was the St. Croix River, but they did not agree as to where that river was. The

British, before the treaty was formally signed, confiscated the Passamaquoddy summer camps, and the Americans allowed this. The final determination of the Maine boundary did not occur until the Webster-Ashburton Treaty of 1842. Still, the choice the St. Croix River divided the Wabanaki Confederacy, with the Passamaquoddy and Penobscot plus one band of Maliseet living in Maine, and the rest of the Maliseet and the Micmac residing in Canada.

In 1790 the United States enacted the first Indian Trade and Intercourse Act (many courts and historians have incorrectly labeled this the Nonintercourse Act). This law was designed to prevent confusion over Indian land cessions and to establish federal control over Indians within the United States. Section 4 of the Act provided: "That no sale of lands made by any Indians, or any nation or tribe of Indians within the United States, shall be valid to any person or persons, or to any state, whether having the right of pre-emption to such lands or not, unless the same shall be made and duly executed at some public treaty, held under the authority of the United States." The act was further strengthened in 1793, when it was amended to provide that no representatives of state governments could negotiate for Indian land cessions. The burden was placed on a state to stay out of these negotiations. Nevertheless, states ignored the Indian Trade and Intercourse Act. They made tribes subject to state law. In 1794 Massachusetts concluded a treaty with the Passamaquoddy whereby the latter ceded all of their lands except twenty-seven thousand acres, located at two reservations on the Canadian border. When Maine became a state in 1820, Massachusetts gave Maine $30,000 to use as a trust fund for taking on the responsibilities of providing for Indians in the new state.

From 1820 to 1964, the Passamaquoddy land base was nibbled away, and the conditions of the people deteriorated significantly. Maine assumed complete power over the Passamaquoddy without federal interference. The Maine legislature gave out 999-year leases to whites on Passamaquoddy reservation lands, sold timber rights, and granted railroad, highway, and utility rights-of-way over Passamaquoddy lands without consultation or compensation. A portion of the Passamaquoddy lands was used for German internment during World War II. After the war the federal government returned control of the reservation land to the state, and Maine sold the land to whites.

Maine hoped that the Passamaquoddy would simply go away. At first the state dealt directly with the Passamaquoddy Council and the two reservation chiefs or governors. But in 1927 Maine stopped dealing directly with the Passamaquoddy and placed all state activity with them in the Forestry Department. This lasted until 1933, when Passamaquoddy affairs were shifted to the Health and Welfare Department. Then, in 1965, Maine created the Department of Indian Affairs. The money in the state trust fund was not used for Maine Indians. Maine decided who could be a Passamaquoddy, and it restricted hunting, fishing, and trapping rights. The state went so far as to declare the Passamaquoddy no longer an Indian tribe. Beginning in 1823, the Passamaquoddy had chosen a nonvoting representative to the Maine legislature. The state abolished the position in 1941. In 1953 Maine became the last state to allow Indians the right to vote, and the Passamaquoddy finally achieved the franchise for state legislature elections in 1967. The Passamaquoddy had to pay all state taxes but the property tax, and they paid federal income taxes. They could be drafted, but they could not receive veterans' benefits.

By 1964 the Passamaquoddy had two reservations, which had come to provide them with a strong sense of community and continuity. One was at Pleasant Point or Sebayick, a one hundred-acre tract between Eastport and Perry on Passamaquoddy Bay. This second most easterly point of the United States is treeless and barren. In 1964 nearly four hundred Passamaquoddy resided at Pleasant Point. The other reservation was located at Indian Township or Medakinegook, a seventeen thousand-acre, heavily wooded, undeveloped tract near Princeton. Freshwater streams and lakes dot Indian Township, which extends to the shore of the St. Croix River. Two Indian towns, Peter Dana Point and Indian Strip, contained most of the three hundred Passamaquoddy living in Indian Township. The rest of the Passamaquoddy, some five hundred, lived off the reservations. Both reservations border Canada, and both are in Washington County, the poorest county in all of the New England states. The average annual income for the Passamaquoddy in the 1960s was approximately $430. Part-time work existed in logging operations and sardine factories, and the Passamaquoddy had seasonal opportunities in potato picking and blueberry raking. Nearly one-third of all Passamaquoddy were unemployed, and they had a 99.5% high school dropout rate. Some scattered welfare programs reached the reservations, and the state of Maine spent some funds on food and health programs for the Passamaquoddy. Still, the reservation settlements had no running water, electricity, or sewage disposal. Only two pay phones were on each reservation; there were no private phones.

Given these very difficult conditions, the Passamaquoddy still had not been disruptive to Maine authorities prior to 1964. In part, this was because of a cultural taboo on criticism. Most Passamaquoddy accepted authority without question unless a group consensus reflected a need for change. There was a strong sense of loss—the loss of land, of self-sufficiency, and of aspects of culture. This loss, combined with the physical conditions of Passamaquoddy life and the cultural tradition of consensus, brought widespread depression.

Change was set in place for the Passamaquoddy at a poker game in February 1964. William Plaisted, a white man, held a 999-year lease on property in Indian Township between Lewey's Lake and U.S. Route 1. On this property he had built some tourist cabins. In the poker game, Plaisted won the rights to a 999-year lease held by a neighbor. The next morning Plaisted set out stakes around the adjoining land to mark the course of a new road, and he hired some Passamaquoddy to cut down trees. This property was inhabited by a Passamaquoddy named George Stevens, and he did not like what was happening. He contacted his brother, John Stevens, who worked at the Georgia-Pacific Corporation paper mill. John Stevens was the Passamaquoddy tribal governor for the Indian Township Reservation. He had served in Korea and had spent some time

off the reservations, and he had been encouraging his people to stand up to white confiscation of Passamaquoddy lands. Moreover, John Stevens's wife's great-aunt, Louise Sockabesin, had shown John several documents she had been keeping in a shoebox. Among the documents were letters from George Washington to the Passamaquoddy written during the American Revolution, and the original copy of the 1794 Passamaquoddy-Commonwealth of Massachusetts treaty. Stevens discovered a disparity of six thousand acres and several islands between the lands guaranteed by the treaty and the lands actually held by the Passamaquoddy. He had tried to find a Maine lawyer to look into this matter, but he had been unsuccessful.

The next evening John Stevens called a meeting of the Indian Township tribal council at Peter Dana Point. Everyone already knew about Plaisted's plans. The hall was packed with angry Passamaquoddy who recalled many other instances of white takings of Passamaquoddy property. The council decided to go see Maine Governor John Reed and ask for his help. Governor Reed did not take the Passamaquoddy seriously. The council returned and called another meeting. Now the Passamaquoddy identified the state of Maine as the primary problem, and they decided to block construction of Plaisted's planned road. Seventy-five Passamaquoddy took up positions the next morning. After a standoff for several hours, five men, including George Stevens, and five women remained. The men were arrested by a Princeton policeman, who took them to Woodland and released them. The five women were arrested by state troopers and taken to Calais, where they were booked, charged with trespass, and put in the city jail. That afternoon John Stevens bailed the women out. He then sought legal counsel.

The charge against the women was eventually dismissed, but in the process the attorney and Passamaquoddy leaders decided to look into the loss of Passamaquoddy land. Initially the strategy was to attempt to find a means to obtain the missing six thousand acres by upholding the 1794 treaty with Massachusetts. The Passamaquoddy now turned to a young attorney, Thomas Tureen, who had only recently graduated from law school and was working with the Indian Legal Services Unit of Pine Tree Legal Assistance, a program funded by the federal Office of Economic Opportunity. First, Tureen helped the tribe set up corporations so it could receive grants from federal agencies. In the process he discovered that the Passamaquoddy had never been recognized by the federal government. This led him to see that the federal government had attempted to protect the Passamaquoddy and other tribes with the 1790 Indian Trade and Intercourse Act. The act prohibited the private sale of Indian lands, and if it was still in force, it superseded the Massachusetts treaty. Thus, the Passamaquoddy might well be entitled to *several million acres*, because their title to land in Maine had never been extinguished. In 1970 Tureen began to plan a suit to recover these lands for the Passamaquoddy. Other eastern tribes watched the litigation closely, because they believed they could recover land by making the same arguments regarding their own claims.

Because the Passamaquoddy could not sue the state of Maine, they needed the assistance of the Department of the Interior. This would be a problem because they were not a federally recognized tribe and, after contact with several Washington officials, it became obvious that the Department of the Interior was not very interested. Its delays took on even greater significance when Tureen and the Passamaquoddy discovered that on July 18, 1966, Congress had passed a statute of limitations on damages for which Indians might sue, which meant that any suit the Passamaquoddy wished to initiate had to be filed by July 18, 1972. They were eight months from the expiration of their claim, and the Department of the Interior appeared to be deliberately stalling.

After a great deal of frantic research, on June 2, 1972, Tureen filed a suit for the Passamaquoddy against Secretary of the Interior Rogers C. B. Morton in federal district court at Portland, Maine. The Passamaquoddy sought a declaratory judgment that they were protected by the Indian Trade and Intercourse Act of 1790. They also wanted an injunction ordering the Department of the Interior to file a court action for monetary damages and return of acreage against the state of Maine. The district court judge, Edward T. Gignoux, held two hearings. After the first hearing, he ordered the Department of the Interior to decide within a week whether it would voluntarily file suit or not. The Department of Interior appeared one week later and said it would not file voluntarily, and Judge Gignoux ordered it to do so. In late June, the Department of Justice presented Judge Gignoux with a $150 million damage suit against the State of Maine on behalf of the Passamaquoddy. Two weeks later the Penobscot and the Houlton Band of Maliseet also joined the suit. All of Maine's Indians were now represented, and they had beat the deadline by one day. Ironically, Congress then extended the deadline for Indian lawsuits.

In the winter of 1973, Judge Gignoux heard arguments on the substantive issues raised by the Passamaquoddy suit. The plaintiffs argued that the Indian Trade and Intercourse Act of 1790 must be applied to the Passamaquoddy, and that it created a trust relationship for all Indians with the new nation, the United States. The defendants, which now included the state of Maine, urged the judge to hold that no trust relationship existed because the Passamaquoddy had never been officially recognized. On January 20, 1975, Judge Gignoux issued his opinion, which found that the Indian Trade and Intercourse Act was applicable to the Passamaquoddy even though there had never been federal recognition of the tribe; that a trust relationship had been created by the act, and that a right existed on the part of the Passamaquoddy to use the courts to attain land and damages based upon the holding. The defendants appealed.

The three-judge panel of the U.S. Court of Appeals for the First Circuit heard arguments from all parties beginning in September 1975. The Passamaquoddy reiterated their district court position, and Maine offered several refinements of its basic arguments. Each side agreed that there were three issues: (1) whether the Indian Trade and Intercourse Act of 1790 applied to the Passamaquoddy; (2) whether the Indian Trade and Intercourse Act of 1790 created a trust relationship between the United States and the Passamaquoddy; and (3) what remedies, if the first two issues were decided in the affirmative, were afforded the Passamaquoddy. Circuit Court Judge Levin H. Campbell wrote a unanimous opinion for the panel in favor of the Passamaquoddy.

The opinion began with a history of the Passamaquoddy relationship to the United States and the state of Maine. The court seemed particularly impressed with the supportive role the Passamaquoddy played in the American Revolution and the legal relationship the tribe had with Maine and the United States. Maine, since its statehood, had passed nearly 350 laws relating to the Passamaquoddy, whereas the United States dealt with the Passamaquoddy only briefly during the 1820s, when it supported the bringing of education to the Passamaquoddy reservations.

The circuit court then identified what it considered the basic issue of the case: whether the United States had a trust relationship with the Passamaquoddy. To determine this, the court asked three questions. First, given the Indian Trade and Intercourse Act of 1790, were the Passamaquoddy to be considered a tribe within the meaning of the act? The act referred to "any tribe of Indians." Maine argued that a tribe included only those officially recognized by the federal government. Even if the Passamaquoddy were a tribe in the sense of a racially and culturally separate entity, Maine argued that when it became a state, the United States, through ignoring the terms by which Maine took over the administration of the Indians within its borders, tacitly agreed not to recognize Passamaquoddy tribal status. The court rejected this contention, finding that the word "tribe" was to be broadly defined in the act, and that it applied to all groups of Indians, regardless of whether they were recognized by the federal government. Eventually the U.S. Department of the Interior would issue guidelines for the determination of tribal status. In addition, the court ruled that the act was designed so that the federal government protected the right of Indians to occupy lands that they claimed or were agreed upon by United States-Native American treaties. No Maine-Massachusetts agreement could extinguish the federal responsibilities under the act.

The second question probed whether the United States had a specific trust relationship with the Passamaquoddy. Because the court had held that the Indian Trade and Intercourse Act of 1790 did apply to the Passamaquoddy, it was relatively simple to reason that a federal duty existed to investigate and protect Passamaquoddy interests, regardless of whether Congress recognized the Passamaquoddy as a tribe in the future. The third question then asked whether time or Passamaquoddy-Maine relationships precluded any trust relationship. The court reasoned that no action on the part of Maine or neglect on the part of Congress could mitigate or deny federal responsibility. Even Maine's argument that an old judicial ruling that the Passamaquoddy were not an Indian tribe was dismissed by the court. The federal government, stated Judge Campbell, was under no obligation to react to a state court's opinion.

Thus, the Passamaquoddy had won an important decision. Even though the First Circuit Court refused to discuss how the Passamaquoddy might go about seeking a remedy, an important precedent had been established. Moreover, neither side sought to appeal, and the decision stood as law. By this point there was much political fallout in Maine and in Washington, D.C. What would the Passamaquoddy want? Would they desire lands already occupied? What would other eastern tribes affected by the 1790 act do? It was a time of great political passion and negotiation.

The governor of Maine, James Longley, and his political rival, Attorney General Joseph Brennan, sought to score political points at the expense of the Passamaquoddy. Maine's Washington delegation was also caught up in the hysteria, particularly after Ropes & Gray, a Boston law firm and legal adviser to New England municipal bond companies, refused to give unqualified approval to municipal bonds to be issued in Maine's disputed area. Only Senator William Hathaway tried to assist the Passamaquoddy in receiving a fair settlement, but he lost his bid for reelection to the Senate to Congressman William Cohen.

After much maneuvering, Maine passed legislation approved by the Passamaquoddy. The

Indians agreed that serious crimes committed by Indians on reservations would be tried in state courts, that Indians who lived on reservations and made their living on reservations would pay state income taxes, and that Maine's environmental laws would apply to the reservations. Maine agreed not to regulate tribal membership; that all reservations now fell under the Indian Trade and Intercourse Act, thereby preventing any land losses without congressional action; and Indians could regulate fishing, hunting, and trapping on reservation lands without state interference.

Senators George Mitchell and Cohen then introduced the Maine Indian Claims Settlement Act in the Senate. The Passamaquoddy agreed not to press claims for occupied lands. Instead, timberlands would be obtained from lumber companies, and they agreed to set aside a maximum of two hundred thousand acres for sale. After several hearings, the bill was approved and sent to the House, which also approved it. President Jimmy Carter signed the Settlement Act on October 10, 1980, and an appropriations bill on December 12, 1980 (after his defeat by Ronald Reagan). This act established the Maine Indian Claims Settlement Trust Fund of $27 million, to be administered by the Department of the Interior. The Maine Indian Claims Land Acquisition Fund was also created ($26.8 million each for the Penobscot and the Passamaquoddy plus $900,000 for the Houlton Band of Maliseet). This fund could be used to purchase up to three hundred thousand acres. The tribes were officially recognized by the federal government and, as such, could receive the benefits afforded other recognized tribes. Since then the Penobscots have purchased 150,000 acres in five large tracts. The Passamaquoddy have been more deliberative. They acquired a five thousand-acre blueberry farm and four thousand acres previously taken away in Indian Township.

Joint Tribal Council of the Passamaquoddy Tribe et al. v. Morton and the accompanying legislation proved to be a very important step in the evolution of Native American law. It demonstrated the significance of negotiations combined with court action. No settlement would have been possible without federal participa-tion. In a sense, the courts acted as a catalyst. The federal courts ruled that the Indian Trade and Intercourse Act applied to all Indian tribes. This case led to other cases, and to determinations concerning tribal status. In a 1978 case, a jury decided the Mashpee were not a tribe; this was upheld later with specific applications of tribal qualifications. The Mashpee setback did not deter the Narragansett from gaining federal recognition and $3.5 million to purchase nine hundred acres through the Rhode Island Claims Settlement Act of 1978. A 1981 case led to the Mashantucket Pequot Indian Claims Settlement Act of 1982 in Connecticut. The Gay Head Wampanoag of Massachusetts, the Schaghticoke and Mohegan of Connecticut, and the Catawba of South Carolina have also pressed claims.

In the aftermath of the Maine litigation and the settlement acts, it is important to recognize that land is viewed by the Passamaquoddy as a means of self-identity. It was not necessarily seen as an economic entity. There is a Passamaquoddy trade song that explains the court case and legislation. A Passamaquoddy goes to the wigwam of another person. Near the entrance he sings a song. He then enters, continuing to sing the song, and begins to dance. At the end of the song he points to an object in the room that he wants to buy, and offers a price. The owner is then obliged to sell the object selected or to barter something of equal value. For thousands of years the Passamaquoddy have lived on the northern coast of Maine. Although they had lost most of their homelands, they were patient but firm. When the opportunity was presented, when the courts allowed them to sing and dance in Augusta, Maine, and Washington, D.C., they were reasonable people. The Maine Indian Claims Settlement Act became the result and a reality, and it enhanced the life of the Passamaquoddy and many other Native Americans.

Selected Bibliography

Brodeur, Paul. "Annals of Law: Restitution." *The New Yorker,* October 11, 1982, 76–155.

Brodeur, Paul. *Restitution: The Land Claims of the Mashpee, Passamaquoddy, and Penobscot Indians of*

New England. Boston: Northeastern University Press, 1985.

Calloway, Colin G. *The American Revolution in Indian Country: Crisis and Diversity in Native American Communities*. New York: Cambridge University Press, 1995.

Paterson, John M. R., and David Roseman. "A Reexamination of *Passamaquoddy v. Morton*." *Maine Law Review* 31 (1979): 115–151.

Tureen, Thomas N., and Francis J. O'Toole. "State Power and the Passamaquoddy Tribe: 'A Gross National Hypocrisy'?" *Maine Law Review* 23 (1971): 1–39.

Vollmann, Tim. "A Survey of Eastern Indian Land Claims: 1970–1979." *Maine Law Review* 31 (1979): 5–16.

Wallace, Harry B. "Indian Sovereignty and Eastern Indian Land Claims." *New York Law School Law Review* 27 (1982): 921–950.

Other Racial Minorities

Chinese Laundries
and
the Fourteenth Amendment

---⊸o⊶---

John R. Wunder
Department of History
University of Nebraska-Lincoln

Yick Wo v. Hopkins, 118 U.S. 356 (1885) [U.S. Supreme Court]

⊸o⊶ **THE CASE IN BRIEF** ⊸o⊶

Date
1885

Location
California

Court
U.S. Supreme Court

Principal Participants
Yick Wo
Hall McAllister
Sheriff Hopkins
Justice Stanley Matthews

Significance of the Case
In striking down a city law that discriminated against Chinese people, the Court expanded the meaning of the Fourteenth Amendment and restricted local police powers.

In the summer of 1885, Yick Wo and over 150 other Chinese residents of San Francisco deliberately violated two ordinances in order to challenge an infringement upon what they considered to be a basic right: the right to engage in economic activity. The San Francisco county and city ordinances, passed in May and July 1880, placed restrictions upon laundry operators that were designed to prevent Chinese laundries from functioning. This challenge eventually was resolved by the U.S. Supreme Court in the unanimously decided *Yick Wo v. Hopkins.*

Yick Wo had come from China in 1861 and settled in San Francisco, as did many other Chinese. The period from 1820 to 1882 was a time of free Chinese immigration. By 1870 over forty-nine thousand Chinese lived in California, and that number increased to over seventy-five thousand by 1880. This amounted to nearly 10 percent of California's population. Approximately 40 percent of all Chinese in California lived in the six counties of the San Francisco Bay area.

Many Caucasian and Hispanic Californians did not like this influx of Chinese. As a result, laws were passed that discriminated against the Chinese. The first California anti-Chinese law levied the foreign miner's license tax (1853), a head tax of $4 per month to mine. A foreign fishing license tax of $4 per month was passed in 1860, and two years later the Chinese police tax charged Chinese not engaged in mining a monthly $2.50 fee.

The legal assault on Chinese living in San Francisco became especially acute in the 1870s. The city and county passed ordinances that specified the minimum amount of living space in an apartment building ("Cubic Air" Ordinance of 1870), called for cutting off the hair of Chinese prisoners ("Queue Ordinance" of 1876), and denied the Chinese police protection for their homes and businesses ("No Special Police for Chinese Quarter Ordinance" of 1878). An 1876 ordinance required all hand laundries with horse-drawn delivery vehicles to pay a license fee of $2.25 per month.

Outright banning of the Chinese from certain economic activities also started in the 1870s. In 1879 Chinese were prohibited from working for state, county, or city governments, and this provision was placed in the new California Constitution. The next year the California legislature made it a misdemeanor for any corporation chartered in California to employ Chinese workers. Thus, these state laws and local ordinances made life extremely difficult for the Chinese in California. One historian concluded, "So severe and strident were the local laws that sought to banish the Chinese people from American life that in some ways they equaled the slave ordinances of the South."

Anti-Chinese feeling manifested itself nationally in 1876 when a committee of California legislators memorialized Congress to restrict Chinese immigration. Six years later, Congress passed the first of several Exclusion Acts aimed at stopping Chinese from coming to the United States. These laws were enforced, and Chinese immigration was significantly curtailed.

Simultaneously, political agitation and violence struck California. In 1877 Denis Kearney led the Workingmen's party in protests against the Chinese in San Francisco. This group eventually took over the California Democratic party, which embraced anti-Chinese rhetoric and action. The Workingmen's party played an important role at the California Constitutional Convention by obtaining insertion of anti-Chinese sections into the new constitution. It also took over San Francisco government with the election of Isaac Kalloch as mayor in 1879. Political agitation eventually led to the expulsion of the Chinese from Eureka and Truckee, and to the first organized massacre of Chinese, at Rock Springs, Wyoming, in 1885.

Federal and local laws and anti-Chinese violence caused many Chinese to abandon rural areas and congregate in urban Chinatowns. The Chinese were also forced to leave farming, mining, manufacturing, railroading, and the professions for self-employment in marginal and noncompetitive occupations. In 1881–1882, a Trades' Assembly labor census was taken in San Francisco. Chinese labor was concentrated in four areas: cigarmaking (8,500 Chinese, 97 percent of all persons in this occupation), boot-and shoemaking (5,700 Chinese, 84 percent), garment making (7,510 Chinese, 88 percent), and laundry operation (5,107 Chinese, 89 percent).

The Chinese did not go into laundry work by choice. It was a difficult job which caused social isolation from the Chinese community, because the laundry owner had to do business primarily with non-Chinese customers. In addition, Chinese laundries were not liked by many whites. Missionaries believed laundries to be centers of moral perversion. Visions of white females captured by Chinese and forced into prostitution operations headquartered at Chinese laundries were readily propagated. Such was the fear and loathing that California mobs began attacking isolated Chinese laundries in the 1870s. Even so, the laundry business attracted many Chinese. It afforded a modest and steady income. Few skills, little capital, and minimal English were needed. To some degree, their dealing with selected portions of the white community cushioned the violence of the anti-Chinese era.

Most laundries were family operations. Three kinds of laundries evolved. The hand laundry with one or two persons was most common. The other two types required specialization and a greater investment: shirt-processing firms specialized in ironing only, and wet-washing firms only washed clothes. All of these laundries required backbreaking labor, and they operated day and night.

Yick Wo knew this life. He had been in the laundry business for twenty-two years prior to his arrest. He had been in California for twenty-four years but had never became an American citizen, a process which in the 1860s and 1870s would have been very difficult for him. As the owner of a laundry, Yick Wo was quite familiar with the ordinances governing laundry operations in San Francisco. He had a license dated March 3, 1884, from the Board of Fire Wardens certifying that his stoves, irons, and washing machines were safe. He also had a certificate from the health officer that his laundry was sanitary and that it drained properly. His city license to operate a laundry was dated to expire on October 1, 1885.

In order to comply with local law, on June 1, 1885, Yick Wo applied to the Board of Supervisors for renewal of his general license to operate his laundry. His request was rejected on July 1. The ordinance (No. 1569) which allowed the Supervisors to grant laundry licenses was passed in 1880. This local law provided that all persons who established a laundry within the city limits of San Francisco had to obtain the consent of the Board of Supervisors. Violation of this ordinance was a misdemeanor punishable by a fine of up to $1,000 or a county jail sentence of not more than six months or both. The ordinance also prohibited certain scaffoldings. Laundries in brick buildings did not need the license, whereas laundries in wooden buildings did. This allowed the Board of Supervisors to claim that the ordinance was necessary as a fire protection measure.

Yick Wo was not the only Chinese laundry owner who was denied a license. Two hundred Chinese owners who also had petitioned the Board of Supervisors had not been granted a license. Eighty laundry licenses had been granted, all but one to non-Chinese owners. The only exception was a permit given to one Mary Meagles, and no doubt this exception had merely slipped past the Supervisors. The lack of permits issued to Chinese laundry owners did not seem to be related to the structure of the buildings. Of the 320 laundries listed in San Francisco in 1880, the year the ordinance was passed, 310 were housed in wooden buildings. Approximately 240 laundries were Chinese-owned. By 1885, 200 of the 240 Chinese-owned laundries had been denied licenses to operate.

Shortly after his license request was denied, Yick Wo was arrested for operating a laundry without a license. He was taken to Police Court No. 2 in San Francisco, was found guilty, and was fined $10. Yick Wo refused to pay the fine, and he was jailed for ten days. He then petitioned the Supreme Court of California for a writ of habeas corpus. This was denied by California's highest court, and he appealed to the U.S. Supreme Court, naming Sheriff Hopkins in his suit.

Yick Wo had a difficult case. He knew that San Francisco would argue the ordinances in question were designed to protect the health and safety of its residents. Yet clearly the result of enforcing this law was discriminatory. Thus, he had to address this twofold problem in his argument.

In a masterful presentation, Yick Wo's attorneys, led by a prominent San Francisco Republican, Hall McAllister, conceded that the state and city had the right to regulate certain businesses that posed potential health and safety problems. Laundries came under this category. However, laundries were not dangerous or unhealthy per se, and therefore they could not be prohibited. They argued that the best evidence of this conclusion was the existence of the ordinances themselves, which regulated rather than banned laundry operations. The purpose of the statutes was to ensure the health and safety of San Francisco's residents *and* the continued operation of laundries.

The plaintiff next cited the results of the enforcement of the ordinances. What had in effect happened was the curtailment of the laundry business through a blatantly discriminatory practice of not granting licenses to Chinese laundry owners. Statistics presented showed that of the 280 license petitions received by the Board of Supervisors, eighty were granted. Only 25 percent of the laundries in San Francisco could operate, and only one of the 201 Chinese applicants was granted a license. Thus, in a bold move, pre-Brandeis brief and pre-*Brown v. Board of Education* (1954) statistical evidence was presented before the Court.

Having proven the discriminatory result of the administration of these ordinances, Yick Wo then claimed that this state action violated an 1880 treaty between China and the United States and the Fourteenth Amendment. More specifically, he argued that the due process clause of the Fourteenth Amendment had been abrogated by the ordinances and their enforcement.

San Francisco claimed it was only exercising a traditional right of every governing body—the duty to protect the health and safety of its citizens. This police power, it was argued, was "indestructible and inalienable," and it had been granted at the beginnings of American governance. Thus, to the defendant, it was too late to question the existence of the police power, even with the Fourteenth Amendment. The police power was sufficiently strong to allow discriminatory interpretations.

It was a haughty argument. San Francisco virtually dared the Supreme Court of the United States to limit the police powers of state and local government. It tried to force the Court to choose between abolishing police power and ratifying any police power. If the Court could find a middle ground, it would have to adopt a position never before taken—extending the Fourteenth Amendment to prevent discriminatory municipal actions, and this is precisely what it did.

On May 10, 1886, Justice Stanley Matthews read the unanimous opinion of the U.S. Supreme Court in the case of *Yick Wo v. Hopkins*. He began by dismissing the issue of the plaintiff's imprisonment, his jail term having expired. The Court might have stopped here, but Matthews asserted that the "meaning of the ordinances" of San Francisco had attracted the Court's concern.

The Court found that the ordinances were so vague as to vest a power broader than police power in the Board of Supervisors. This power constituted "a naked and arbitrary power to give or withhold consent, not only as to places, but as to persons." Thus, the Court saw this power as discriminatory, a form of class legislation prohibited by the Fourteenth Amendment.

To reach this conclusion, the Court specifically noted that the Fourteenth Amendment applied to all persons, citizens and aliens alike. Moreover, Justice Matthews developed a test for legislation to see whether it was prohibited by the Fourteenth Amendment. Legislation must specifically regulate an economic activity in terms of safety and health practices, and such laws must be applied fairly. For Yick Wo, the San Francisco ordinances failed both tests, but the Court was most offended by the discriminatory application by the Board of Supervisors. Wrote Matthews, "The very idea that one man may be compelled to hold his life, or the means of living, or any material right essential to the enjoyment of life, at the mere will of another, seems to be intolerable in any country where freedom prevails, as being the essence of slavery itself." Thus, the Court ruled the ordinances unconstitutional. The actions of the Board of Supervisors were discriminatory and violated the due process clause of the Fourteenth Amendment.

The significance of this case was especially important to the evolution of constitutional law and to the Chinese. In its opinion the Court expanded the Fourteenth Amendment. With one stroke of the pen, Justice Matthews limited state police powers, activated the due process clause to prohibit discriminatory action, broadly construed the coverage of the Fourteenth Amendment to include aliens, and placed state and local governments on notice that the Fourteenth Amendment would be applied to actions heretofore not associated with slavery and the Civil War.

The effect of this case upon the anti-Chinese movement in California and throughout the West was profound. The Supreme Court answered the question posed by Yick Wo's attorneys: "That it [the enforcement of the ordinances] does mean prohibition, as to the Chinese, it seems to us must be apparent to every citizen of San Francisco who has been here long enough to be familiar with the cause of an active and aggressive branch of public opinion and of public notorious events. Can a court be blind to what must be necessarily known to every intelligent person in the State?" The U.S. Supreme Court was not blind, and by condemning the official actions of the city and county of San Francisco, it placed public officials on notice that the anti-Chinese agitations of Californians and other Westerners would no longer be tolerated. The anti-Chinese movements lessened in the next decade partly because of the stand taken by the Court in the *Yick Wo* decision.

Yick Wo v. Hopkins did not, however, bring an immediate end to discrimination, nor did it activate the Fourteenth Amendment. Shortly after 1886 the Supreme Court composition changed, and the new Court saw the Fourteenth Amendment more as a vehicle to prevent broad social change. It extolled property rights, and attempts by states and localities to use regulatory powers to restrict property rights and economic activities were thwarted. The Fourteenth Amendment became a haven for substantive economic theory protected by the due process clause. The *Yick Wo* case would reassert itself in the twentieth century when the Fourteenth Amendment was reactivated to destroy the Jim Crow system of discrimination against blacks which had been erected in the border states and the South after the Civil War.

Selected Bibliography

Barth, Gunther. *Bitter Strength: A History of the Chinese in the United States, 1850–1870.* Cambridge, MA: Harvard University Press, 1964.

Chan, Sucheng, ed. *Entry Denied: Exclusion and the Chinese Community in America, 1882–1943.* Philadelphia: Temple University Press, 1991.

Chan, Sucheng, and Kevin Scott Wong, eds. *Claiming America: Constructing Chinese American Identities During the Exclusion Era.* Philadelphia: Temple University Press, 1998.

Fritz, Christian G. *Federal Justice in California: The Court of Ogden Hoffman, 1851–1891.* Lincoln: University of Nebraska Press, 1991.

Konvitz, Milton R. *The Alien and the Asiatic in American Law.* Ithaca, NY: Cornell University Press, 1946.

McClain, Charles J. *In Search of Equality: The Chinese Struggle Against Discrimination in Nineteenth-Century America.* Berkeley: University of California Press, 1994.

Salyer, Lucy E. *Laws Harsh as Tigers: Chinese Immigrants and the Shaping of Modern Immigration Law.* Chapel Hill: University of North Carolina Press, 1995.

Saxton, Alexander. *The Indispensable Enemy: Labor and the Anti-Chinese Movement in California.* Berkeley: University of California Press, 1971.

Shih-shan, Henry Tsai. *The Chinese Experience in America.* Bloomington: Indiana University Press, 1986.

The Japanese Internment Cases

Paul Finkelman
College of Law
University of Tulsa

Hirabayashi v. United States, 320 U.S. 81 (1943), *Yasui v. United States*, 320 U.S. 115 (1943), *Korematsu v. United States*, 323 U.S. 214 (1944), and *Ex parte Endo*, 323 U.S. 283 (1944)
[U.S. Supreme Court]

⊸ THE CASE IN BRIEF ⊸

Date
1943, 1944

Location
California

Court
U.S. Supreme Court

Principal Participants
Gordon Hirabayashi; Minoru Yasui; Fred Korematsu; Mitsuye Endo; Government of the United States

Significance of the Case
In four cases before the Court in 1943 and 1944, the internment of Japanese Americans during World War II was basically upheld, although forty years later this action came to be seen as blatant racism and a violation of the Constitution.

In 1941 approximately 112,000 Japanese-Americans, about three-quarters of whom were citizens, lived on the West Coast of the United States. At the beginning of World War II, civilian and military officials expressed concern about the presence of these Japanese-Americans. General John L. DeWitt, head of the Western Defense Command, very quickly began to argue for military control of aliens and citizens of Japanese ancestry. He added to a growing hysteria by constantly—and always erroneously—reporting acts of Japanese-instigated sabotage and military actions off the coast of California by the Japanese Navy.

In late 1941 and early 1942, newspaper columnist Walter Lippman urged a relocation of all Japanese Americans in California. Another columnist, Westbrook Pegler, declared "To hell with habeas corpus" in arguing for "concentration camps" for Japanese Americans. Politicians, including California Attorney General Earl Warren, demanded federal action against the Japanese Americans. In January 1942, for example, Congressman Leland Ford, a

California Republican, wrote to Secretary of War Henry L. Stimson, urging that "all Japanese, whether citizens or not, be placed in inland concentration camps." Congressman Ford argued that an American citizen of Japanese ancestry would prove he is "patriotic" and "make his contribution to the safety and welfare of this country . . . by permitting himself to be placed in a concentration camp." Noting that such an enterprise "presents a very real problem," Stimson suggested that Congressman Ford make his views known to the Attorney General.

Attorney General Francis Biddle resisted any mass evacuation of American citizens on the grounds that such a procedure would violate their constitutional rights. However, in cabinet-level discussions, Biddle was outmaneuvered by Assistant Attorney General Tom C. Clark, who favored internment, and by a former corporate lawyer, Assistant Secretary of War John J. McCloy. According to Major General Allen W. Gullion, the Provost Marshal General of the Army, when Biddle made it clear that the Justice Department would not support military evacuation of civilians who were not charged with any crimes, Assistant Secretary of War McCloy told the attorney general, "You are putting a Wall Street lawyer in a helluva box, but if it is a question of the safety of the country [and] the constitution . . . why the constitution is just a scrap of paper to me."

Despite Attorney General Biddle's protests, on February 19, 1942, President Franklin D. Roosevelt signed Executive Order no. 9066, which empowered the Secretary of War and various military commanders to create "military areas" from which civilians might be excluded. President Roosevelt issued the order under authority granted to him by the Espionage Act of 1917 and various acts passed in 1940 and 1941. Acting in his capacity as commander in chief, Roosevelt declared "that the successful prosecution of the war requires every possible protection against espionage and against sabotage to national defense material." Thus, the President authorized "the Secretary of War and the Military Commanders who he may from time to time designate . . . to prescribe military areas in such places and of such extent as [they] . . . may determine, from

which any or all persons may be excluded and with respect to which, the right of any person to enter, remain in, or leave shall be subject to whatever restrictions the Secretary of War or the appropriate Military Commander may impose in his discretion." Roosevelt ordered the Secretary of War "to provide for residents of any such area who are excluded therefrom, such transportation, food, shelter, and other accommodations as may be necessary." The President further authorized the Secretary of War to take "such other steps" as he might deem "advisable" to enforce this order in designated military areas, "including the use of Federal troops and other Federal Agencies, with authority to accept assistance of state and local agencies." All other executive departments and federal agencies were also ordered "to assist the Secretary of War or the said Military Commanders in carrying out this Executive Order, including the furnishing of medical aid, hospitalization, food, clothing, transportation, use of land, shelter, and other supplies, equipment, utilities, facilities, and services." Finally, Roosevelt declared that this order superseded any authority of the Attorney General or any other agency of the government over civilians in areas designated "military" under the order, with the exception that the F.B.I. was still empowered to investigate "alleged acts of sabotage." And the Attorney General was still authorized to regulate "the conduct and control of alien enemies" in nonmilitary areas.

On March 18 the President issued Executive Order no. 9102, establishing the War Relocation Authority for the purpose of relocating persons named in Order 9066. On March 21, President Roosevelt signed a law which Congress had unanimously passed to implement these orders. The Japanese internment quickly followed.

There were five stages to the internment process. First, a curfew was imposed on all persons of Japanese ancestry living in particular areas of the West Coast. Second, Japanese Americans living in those areas were forbidden to leave the areas in which they lived. The third order prohibited Japanese Americans from remaining in designated areas. Thus, they could neither leave their homes nor stay in their homes. Instead, they had to comply with the

Japanese American citizens in Manzanar, California, after being forced from their homes in Los Angeles by the U.S. Army during World War II. *AP Photo.*

fourth stage of the process, to report to an assembly center, or civilian control center (the official name). The assembly center was the starting point of the fifth stage—the evacuation of the Japanese Americans to "relocation centers" or "relocation camps."

On March 24, General DeWitt imposed an 8 P.M. to 6 A.M. curfew on all enemy aliens and persons of Japanese ancestry on the West Coast. Gordon Hirabayashi refused to obey this curfew, and his conviction for this unlawful act was upheld by a unanimous Supreme Court. DeWitt's proclamation of March 24 also declared that at all other times these persons were not permitted to be more than five miles from their homes. On March 27, DeWitt issued a new proclamation prohibiting Japanese Americans

from moving away from where they lived. Starting on March 24, and continuing through May, General DeWitt issued a series of "civilian exclusion orders" for various parts of the West Coast. Under these orders Japanese Americans were required to report to civilian control centers, from which they were, virtually without exception, removed to relocation camps. Fred Korematsu was convicted of failing to report to such a center.

The internment camps were surrounded by barbed wire, guarded by armed soldiers, and located in isolated parts of the country. Except for those men who were drafted, virtually all the Japanese Americans sent to these camps were forced to remain in them until 1945. Those people sent to the camps were forced to abandon most of their possessions, except for a few personal items and some clothing they were allowed to take with them. Many sold their homes, farms, and businesses for a fraction of their real value. Many of those who boarded up their property or left it in the hands of neighbors lost their possessions to thieves and vandals.

Four major internment cases reached the U.S. Supreme Court: *Hirabayashi v. United States* (1943), *Yasui v. United States* (1943), *Korematsu v. United States* (1944), and *Ex parte Endo* (1944). In the first three the Supreme Court upheld convictions for violating the internment laws. In the last case the Court ordered the release of the plaintiff and set the stage for dismantling of the internment camps.

In the spring of 1942 both Gordon Hirabayashi and Minoru Yasui refused to obey the curfew orders issued by General DeWitt. Hirabayashi, an American-born citizen of Japanese ancestry, was a senior at the University of Washington. He violated the 8 P.M. to 6 A.M. curfew imposed on Japanese Americans and also failed to report to a civilian control center, where his presence was "required" as "a preliminary step to the exclusion from that area of persons of Japanese ancestry." Hirabayashi intentionally disobeyed the curfew and exclusion orders because he believed that if he obeyed them, "he would be waiving his rights as an American citizen." A jury found him guilty on both counts, and the court sentenced him to two concurrent terms of three months.

Yasui was also an American-born child of Japanese immigrants. In 1941 Yasui was a member of the Oregon bar and a second lieutenant in the U.S. Army Infantry Reserve. When the war broke out, he was an employee of the Japanese consulate in Chicago. He immediately left that job, and in mid-January reported for active duty at Camp Vancouver, in Washington state. However, when he arrived there, he was told to go home and await further orders. These orders never came. Yasui returned to Oregon. When the first curfews were put in place, Yasui informed the F.B.I. that he would violate the curfew in order to test its constitutionality. At 11 P.M. he went for a walk, in violation of the curfew. A policeman confronted, but refused to arrest, him. Yasui later said, "I had to go on down to the Second Avenue police station and argue myself into jail." The district court in Oregon ruled that the Act of March 21, implementing Roosevelt's two executive orders, could not be constitutionally applied to American citizens. However, the Court also ruled that through his actions in disobeying the law, Yasui "must be deemed to have renounced his American citizenship." The court then imposed the maximum sentence of one year in prison and a $5,000 fine.

Hirabayashi and Yasui appealed their convictions. The cases were argued on May 10 and 11, 1943, and both were decided on June 21, 1943.

The Court dealt with Hirabayashi first. He had appealed both his conviction for curfew violation and his conviction for failure to report to a civilian control (assembly) center. However, because of the concurrent sentences, the justices ruled that if they upheld one conviction—the curfew violation—they would not have to consider the constitutionality of the order to go to the assembly center.

Speaking for the Court, Chief Justice Harlan F. Stone gave a detailed legislative history of the curfew and the military situation in 1942 in order to justify the constitutionality of the curfew. Stone argued that, under the "power to wage war successfully," Congress and the president had the right to delegate authority to military commanders. Furthermore, it was clear that a curfew was a reasonable and constitutional act under that authority. The big question, however, was whether a single group of people—the Japanese Americans—could be singled out for the curfew.

Stone noted that Japanese aliens were ineligible for U.S. citizenship; that American-born citizens of Japanese parents were considered, under Japanese law, also to be citizens of Japan; and that "social, economic and political conditions" in the nation had, over the years, "intensified their solidarity and have in large measure prevented their assimilation as an integral part of the white population." He pointed out that large numbers of Japanese American children had been "sent to Japanese language schools outside the regular hours of public schools," and that some of these schools were "generally believed to be sources of Japanese nationalistic propaganda." There had, the Chief Justice observed, "been relatively little social intercourse between them and the white population."

Stone found that "Congress and the Executive could reasonably have concluded that these conditions have encouraged the continued attachment of members of this group to Japan and Japanese institutions," and that it was reasonable for "those charged with . . . the national defense" to "take into account" these factors in "determining the nature and extent of the danger of espionage and sabotage, in the event of an invasion or air raid attack." Stone declared that the Court "cannot reject as unfounded the judgment of the military authorities and of Congress that there were disloyal members of that population, whose number and strength could not be precisely and quickly ascertained."

Stone acknowledged that "racial discriminations are in most circumstances irrelevant" but argued that "in dealing with the perils of war, Congress and the Executive" were not "precluded from taking into account those facts which are relevant to measures for our national defense . . . which may in fact place citizens of one ancestry in a different category from others."

Stone declared, "We cannot close our eyes to the fact . . . that in time of war residents having ethnic affiliations with an invading enemy may be a greater source of danger than those of a different ancestry." In essence, Stone and the Court refused to question the authority of the military. In reaching this decision, on the narrow question of the curfew, Stone specifically declared that the Court was not considering whether more drastic measures "differing from the curfew order" would be permissible.

Although the decision was unanimous, not all the judges agreed to share in Stone's opinion. Justices William O. Douglas, Wiley Rutledge, and Frank Murphy qualified their support and sought to narrow the scope of the opinion. Murphy's concurrence in fact reads more like a dissent. He noted that this "is the first time . . . that we have sustained a substantial restriction of the personal liberty of citizens of the United States based on the accident of race or ancestry. Under the curfew order here challenged no less than 70,000 American citizens have been placed under a special ban and deprived of their liberty because of their particular racial inheritance. In this sense it bears a melancholy resemblance to the treatment accorded to members of the Jewish race in Germany and in other parts of Europe. . . . In my opinion this goes to the very brink of constitutional power."

Having decided the constitutionality of the curfew in *Hirabayashi*, the Court had little problem disposing of *Yasui v. United States*. The Court reversed the ruling of the district court that the curfew was unconstitutional when applied to citizens, and also reversed the ruling that Yasui had effectively renounced his citizenship. His conviction stood, and the case was remanded for resentencing. On remand, U.S. District Judge James A. Fee reduced the one-year sentence he had previously imposed to time served and removed the $5,000 fine. After about eight months in jail, Yasui was removed to a relocation camp.

The shaky unanimity of *Hirabayashi* disappeared in *Korematsu*. Like Hirabayashi and Yasui, Fred Korematsu was an American-born citizen of Japanese ancestry. However, Korematsu did not resist the relocation out of constitutional conviction. Korematsu had lived all his life in Alemeda County, in northern California. When the war began, he volunteered for military service, but he was rejected for health reasons. He then obtained a job in a defense industry, after using his own funds to learn to become a welder. On May 3, 1942, the day Japanese Americans in Alemeda County were required to report to an assembly center, Korematsu had a good job and a non-Japanese girlfriend unaffected by the relocation orders. He had no reason to want to leave his home, no reason to think he was a threat to the nation, and many good reasons for staying.

Rather than report to an assembly center, Korematsu moved, changed his name, and attempted to avoid arrest by claiming to be of Mexican ancestry. He was now in violation of a new order, for after May 9 it was no longer legal for Japanese Americans to remain in the area where Korematsu lived. On the other hand, it was also illegal for him to leave the area where he lived. As Justice Robert Jackson noted in his dissent, "Korematsu . . . has been convicted of an act not commonly a crime. It consists merely of being present in the state whereof he is a citizen, near the place where he was born, and where all his life he has lived." How did he get into this situation? Because, as Jackson wrote: an "unusual . . . series of military orders . . . forbid" Korematsu "to remain, and they also forbid him to leave." In his dissent Justice Owen Roberts explained the problem in greater detail: "The predicament in which the petitioner thus found himself was this: He was forbidden, by Military Order, to leave the zone in which he lived; he was forbidden, by Military Order, after a date fixed, to be found within that zone unless he were in an Assembly Center located in that zone. General DeWitt's report to the Secretary of War . . . makes it entirely clear . . . that an Assembly Center was a euphemism for prison. No person within such a center was permitted to leave except by Military Order."

Faced with this dilemma, "that he dare not remain in his home, or voluntarily leave the area, without incurring criminal penalties, and that the only way he could avoid punishment was to go to an Assembly Center and submit himself to military imprisonment, the petitioner did nothing." On June 12 he was arrested and charged with violating the orders excluding all Japanese Americans from the area. Following his conviction, the trial court sentenced Korematsu to five years in prison, then immediately paroled him. He was taken to an assembly center, and from there to the internment camp at Topaz, Utah.

As a major case in constitutional law, *Korematsu* is remembered for the assertion in Justice Black's majority opinion that "all legal restrictions which curtail the civil rights of a single racial group are immediately suspect" and should be given "the most rigid scrutiny." Significantly, this case is only one in which the Supreme Court has applied the "rigid scrutiny" test to a racial restriction *and still upheld* the restrictive law.

As in *Hirabayashi,* the Court in *Korematsu* never questioned the assertion of the military

that the Japanese on the West Coast posed a special problem for the nation. Black wrote: "Like the curfew, exclusion of those of Japanese origin was deemed necessary because of the presence of an unascertained number of disloyal members of the group, most of whom we have no doubt were loyal to this country. It was because we could not reject the finding of the military authorities that it was impossible to bring about an immediate segregation of the disloyal form the loyal that we sustained the validity of the curfew order as applying to the whole group. In the instant case, temporary exclusion of the entire group was rested by the military on the same ground. The judgment that exclusion of the whole group was for the same reason a military imperative answers the contention that the exclusion was in the nature of group punishment based on antagonism to those of Japanese ancestry." Thus, Black upheld the exclusion order "as of the time it was made and the petitioner violated it."

In reaching this conclusion, the Court turned a blind eye to what was really happening. Korematsu argued that if he had gone to an assembly center, as ordered, he would have been immediately shipped to a relocation camp. These arguments did not impress Justice Black, who asserted: "Had the petitioner here left the prohibited area and gone to an assembly center we cannot say either as a matter of fact or law that his presence in that center would have resulted in his detention in a relocation center." In fact, this is what happened to virtually every Japanese American who went to such a center.

Black blithely asserted that reporting to an assembly center could be separated from being forced to go to a relocation camp. Since Korematsu was charged only with failing to report to the assembly center, Black and the majority of the Court would not examine the constitutionality of the military forcing people into relocation camps. Black asserted, "It will be time enough to decide the serious constitutional issues which the petitioner seeks to raise when an assembly or relocation order is applied or is certain to be applied to him, and we have its terms before us." In other words, Korematsu could litigate the constitutionality of the internment only after he had been incarcerated in a camp.

Finally, Black bristled with indignation at the assertion by counsel for Korematsu and the dissenting judges that this decision was based on racism and that the "relocation centers" were concentration camps. In his concluding paragraph Black declared: "It is said that we are dealing here with the case of imprisonment of a citizen in a concentration camp solely because of his ancestry, without evidence or inquiry concerning his loyalty and good disposition toward the United States. Our task would be simple, our duty clear, were this a case involving the imprisonment of a loyal citizen in a concentration camp because of racial prejudice. Regardless of the true nature of the assembly and relocation centers—and we deem it unjustifiable to call them concentration camps with all the ugly connotations that term implies—we are dealing specifically with nothing but an exclusion order. To cast this case into outlines of racial prejudice, without reference to the real military dangers which were presented, merely confuses the issue. Korematsu was not excluded from the Military Area because of hostility to him or his race. He *was* excluded because we are at war with the Japanese Empire, because the properly constituted military authorities feared an invasion of our West Coast and . . . decided that the military urgency . . . demanded that all citizens of Japanese ancestry be segregated from the West Coast temporarily."

Justices Owen Roberts, Frank Murphy, and Robert Jackson found Black's reasoning and analysis unacceptable. In dissent, they argued that the requirement of reporting to a relocation center differed substantially from the constitutionally permissible curfew approved in *Hirabayashi*. Furthermore, they had little patience with Black's fine distinction between the exclusion order and the internment. Justice Roberts remarked: "The Government has argued this case as if the only order outstanding at the time the petitioner was arrested and informed against was Exclusion Order 34 ordering him to leave the area in which he resided." But, the justice noted, "We cannot shut our eyes to the fact that had the petitioner attempted to . . . leave the military area in which he lived he would have been arrested and tried and

convicted under Proclamation No. 4. The two conflicting orders, one which commanded him to stay and the other which commanded him to go, were nothing but a cleverly devised trap to accomplish the real purpose of the military authority, which was to lock him up in a concentration camp. . . . We know that is the fact. Why should we set up a figmentary and artificial situation instead of addressing ourselves to the actualities of the case?"

Justice Murphy, meanwhile, challenged Black's blind support for military expertise and his denial of racism. Murphy pointed out that the internment was not based on any military analysis; rather, "justification for the exclusion" was based "mainly upon questionable racial and sociological grounds not ordinarily within the realm of expert military judgment." Murphy found no compelling evidence that tied the Japanese American community to sabotage or espionage. He charged: "The main reasons relied upon by those responsible for the forced evacuation . . . appear . . . to be largely an accumulation of much of the misinformation, half-truths and insinuations that for years have been directed against Japanese Americans by people with racial and economic prejudices—the same people who have been among the foremost advocates of the evacuation. A military judgment based upon such racial and sociological considerations is not entitled to the great weight ordinarily given the judgments based upon strictly military considerations."

Murphy argued that the Japanese Americans should have been treated "on an individual basis" through "investigations and hearings to separate the loyal from the disloyal, as was done in the case of persons of German and Italian ancestry." He noted that the first exclusion order was not issued until "nearly four months elapsed after Pearl Harbor," and that "nearly eight months went by until the last order was issued; and the last of these 'subversive' persons was not actually removed until almost eleven months had elapsed." Concluding that "Leisure and deliberation seem to have been more of the essence than speed," Murphy undermined the claim of military necessity. Thus, Murphy dissented "from this legalization of racism."

The Court's majority in favor of the government disappeared in *Endo*. On the same day it upheld Korematsu's conviction, the Court ordered the release of Mitsuye Endo, who at the time was held in the relocation center at Topaz, Utah. Endo, an American citizen of Japanese ancestry, had complied with all of the relocation orders. In July 1942, shortly after she was removed to the Tule Lake relocation center, Endo petitioned for a writ of habeas corpus. When a U.S. district court rejected her petition, the relocation authorities moved her to Topaz, Utah. This transfer was designed to frustrate her legal efforts and to punish her for attempting to gain freedom. From Topaz she appealed to the Circuit Court of Appeals and then to the U.S. Supreme Court.

Endo asserted that she was a "loyal and law-abiding citizen of the United States, that no charge has been made against her, and that she is being unlawfully detained, and that she is confined to the Relocation Center under armed guard and held there against her will." The United States did not deny her loyalty, nor did the government claim a right "to detain citizens against whom no charges of disloyalty or subversiveness have been made for a period longer than that necessary to separate the loyal from the disloyal and to provide the necessary guidance for relocation." Rather, the government argued that the whole purpose of the program was to determine which Japanese Americans were loyal, and to relocate them beyond military areas. The government argued it needed more time because "a planned and orderly relocation was essential to the success of the evacuation program," and an immediate release of Endo and others in the camps would lead to "a dangerously disorderly migration of unwanted people to unprepared communities" which would result in "hardship and disorder." The program's success "was thought to require the knowledge that the federal government was maintaining control over the evacuated population except as the release of individuals could be effected consistently with their own peace and well-being and that of the nation."

Speaking for a unanimous Court, Justice William O. Douglas rejected these arguments, asserting that the exclusion orders were for the "single aim" of "protection of the war effort against espionage and sabotage." Douglas found that Executive Orders 9066 and 9102 and the legislation supporting them only authorized the military "to formulate and effectuate a program for the removal" of the Japanese Americans. Douglas would not say that detention was unconstitutional per se, but only that it was unauthorized by statute. Thus, because no one doubted Endo's loyalty, there was no reason or statutory authority to incarcerate her. The Court ordered her released.

Within a month after the *Endo* decision, the military cleared about fifty thousand internees, who were allowed to return to their homes. Some twenty thousand remained interned, mostly at Tule Lake, the camp designated for troublemakers and those suspected of disloyalty. Some remained scattered in other camps until after the war ended.

In 1948 Congress passed the Japanese American Evacuation Claims Act, which authorized compensation to internees who could prove property losses by means of records. Claims under this law totaled $148 million, but because of the strict proof requirements, the treasury paid out only $37 million. One scholar noted: "The Federal Reserve Bank had estimated the Japanese Americans lost $400 million in property. Losses of earnings and profits from businesses and farms sold in 1942 under distress conditions, and compensations for deprivations of constitutional rights, were not covered by the 1948 law."

In 1980 Congress established the Commission on Wartime Relocation and Internment of Civilians to make recommendations on restitution for the victims of the internment and their heirs. During the commission hearings, John J. McCloy, the Wall Street lawyer who had been the most forceful high-level government advocate of the plan, admitted that the internment had been "retribution for the attack that was made on Pearl Harbor." Thus, almost forty years after the internment began, the man who helped bring it about admitted what lawyers for Hirabayashi, Yasui, Korematsu, and Endo had argued all along: that it was not "stern military necessity" that forced the internment, as the army and government had argued before the Supreme Court. Rather, it was racism which allowed the white majority to punish American-born citizens for the actions of people of the same ethnic background, from another country. These hearings revealed that the F.B.I. and the Office of Naval Intelligence consistently opposed the internment because both intelligence organizations believed the Japanese Americans were fundamentally loyal and, as a group, posed no threat to the nation's security. And, while the internment was being planned and carried out, lawyers in the Justice Department had branded as "lies" the assertions of the War Department that the Japanese posed a threat to the nation. The hearings revealed that the alleged incidents of sabotage and espionage by Japanese Americans were fabrications or fantasies of General DeWitt and his staff. In 1983 the commission concluded that the internment was a "grave injustice."

The manipulation of facts by government lawyers in the internment cases, revealed by the commission hearings and private investigations by lawyers and scholars, made it clear that these cases were wrongly decided. In the first three cases the Court had deferred to military judgments, but those judgments were based on lies and incomplete information. For example, there had been a power outage in Oregon at the beginning of the war that was blamed on Japanese sabotage. But, in fact, the government knew it was actually caused by cattle scratching their backs on electrified fences. Similarly, the military asserted that Japanese farmers were using flashlights to guide enemy planes at night, although the F.B.I. had established that in the areas in question, flashlights were used by people going to their outhouses. Information like this was suppressed during the internment cases.

In January 1983, Hirabayashi, Korematsu, and Yasui reopened their cases in Federal District Court in San Francisco. In November, Korematsu's conviction was overturned. In February 1986, a federal court reversed Hirabayashi's conviction. Meanwhile, numerous Japanese Americans began receiving checks for back pay for federal, state, and local government jobs they held at the time the internment began, on the grounds that they were illegally fired. How-

ever, a reparations suit for $24 billion failed, because the courts ruled that a six-year statute of limitations had expired. The plaintiffs argued that because the government concealed vital evidence in the internment cases, the statute of limitations should not have begun to run until after the plaintiffs discovered the illegal activity of the government. In August 1988, Congress passed a law, which the president signed, establishing a $1.25 billion trust fund to pay $20,000 in reparations to each survivor of the internment or his/her survivors.

In 1945, Professor Eugene D. Rostow published an article in the *Yale Law Journal* titled "The Japanese American Cases—A Disaster." Also in that year an article by Nanette Dembitz, titled "Racial Discrimination and Military Judgment: The Supreme Court's *Korematsu* and *Endo* Decisions," appeared in *Columbia Law Review*. The titles of these two articles aptly characterize the High Court's response to these cases.

By the time the Court heard these cases, it was clear that there had been no espionage or sabotage by the Japanese Americans on the West Coast. In the Hawaiian Islands, which were thousands of miles closer to the Pacific war and where Japanese Americans made up a much greater percentage of the population, there were no mass arrests, evacuations, or internments. There was also no sabotage or espionage perpetrated by members of the Japanese American community. In Europe, the "Nisei Brigade," made up entirely of Japanese Americans, was on its way to becoming the most decorated military unit in American history. The Court took no notice of these facts. Nor did the Court even question the "facts" of sabotage presented by the government. Instead, the Court accepted, without hesitation, the assertions of military necessity.

During the congressional hearings in 1983, John J. McCloy defended the internment, in part, because the Supreme Court had upheld it. In fact, of course, in *Endo* the Court did not uphold interning people. The Court did, however, uphold the curfew, the evacuation, and the right of the government to force citizens to leave their homes solely on the basis of their race and ethnicity. The 1943–1944 Supreme

Court, in essence, agreed with McCloy that, at least for nonwhites during World War II, the Constitution was "just a scrap of paper."

Selected Bibliography

Daniels, Roger. *Concentration Camps USA.* New York: Holt, Rinehart and Winston, 1971.

Dembitz, Nanette. "Racial Discrimination and the Military Judgment: The Supreme Court's *Korematsu* and *Endo* Decisions." *Columbia Law Review* 45 (March 1945): 175–239.

Irons, Peter. *Justice at War: The Story of the Japanese Internment Cases.* New York: Oxford University Press, 1983.

Rostow, Eugene V. "The Japanese American Cases— A Disaster." *Yale Law Journal* 54 (June 1945): 489– 533.

Tateishi, John. *And Justice for All: An Oral History of the Japanese American Detention Camps.* New York: Random House, 1984.

How Should We Pay for Our Schools?

—◦—

John R. Wunder

Department of History
University of Nebraska-Lincoln

San Antonio Independent School District et al. v. Demetrio P. Rodriguez et al., 411 U.S. 1 (1973)
[U.S. Supreme Court]

—◦— THE CASE IN BRIEF —◦—

Date
1973

Location
Texas

Court
U.S. Supreme Court

Principal Participants
Demetrio P. Rodriguez and co-plaintiffs;
Mexican American Legal Defense and
Education Fund; San Antonio Independent
School District and co-defendants;
Associate Justice Lewis Powell

Significance of the Case
By refusing to overturn Texas's method of
financing public education, the Court
limited the reach of the *Brown* decision of
1954 and preserved inequities in the state
financing of public education.

On March 21, 1973, five members of the U.S. Supreme Court issued a directive in the case of *San Antonio Independent School District et al. v. Demetrio P. Rodriguez et al.* Their opinions placed a clamp over the hemorrhage of school litigation released after *Brown v. Board of Education*, decided nearly two decades earlier. But in *Rodriguez*, the children were Mexican Americans, not African Americans; the primary issue was whether education was a fundamental right under the U.S. Constitution, not whether separate but equal facilities were inherently unequal; and the legal threat was to school finance systems nationwide, rather than to segregated Southern school districts. Clearly the stakes were high, and the Court, led by Chief Justice Warren Burger, had an agenda it was ready to act upon.

Demetrio Rodriguez was one of several Mexican American parents who sent their children to Edgewood Independent Schools, an urban district in San Antonio, Texas. Their families had been in Texas since the late seventeenth century, and in 1718 they had founded San Antonio de Bexar, a mission outpost to East Texas.

732

By 1820, 2,500 Texas Mexicans, or Tejanos, lived in three settlements, one of them San Antonio. The next year Texas officially became a part of the Mexican nation.

Significant Anglo migration occurred to Texas during the next fifteen years, to the point that, by the time of the Texas Revolution in 1835, Anglos outnumbered Tejanos. At this time Anglos began to assert political control over county and local governments except in San Antonio, which developed a tradition of Tejano political activity.

The Mexican-American War (1846–1848) increased local racial tensions in Texas. During the 1850s, Anglo lynchings of San Antonio Tejanos occurred. After the war, hostility also took the form of legal discrimination, especially against the use of Spanish. Laws could not be officially printed in Spanish, Spanish could not be used in Texas courts, and in 1870 Spanish was officially banned in the schools.

By 1900, large numbers of Tejanos began to desire education. At first they had gravitated to Catholic parochial schools, but they were expensive and Catholic officials refused to integrate. That left the public schools, which also were segregated but much cheaper. San Antonio's first public school was opened in 1875, and it included several Tejano children from wealthy families. After the push for education, two schools of limited quality were established in the barrio for Mexican Americans only, but this would not prove sufficient.

The twentieth century brought a huge migration of Mexicans to their lost province. These new immigrants had greater burdens than their Tejano relatives. They almost always could not speak English, they were extremely poor, they had few skills, and they came in large, refugee-like numbers. The number of Mexican school districts so designated in Texas doubled from twenty in 1920 to forty by 1930. Mexican American children represented 13 percent of the Texas school population. Only 40 percent of the Texas school districts maintained separate "Mexican schools." In San Antonio, at least eleven thousand Mexican American pupils were attending elementary schools.

The 1940s witnessed World War II, with strong Mexican American participation in the war effort, and the beginnings of a significant Latino organized attack on "separate but equal" education. As early as 1929, with the founding of the League of United Latin American Citizens (LULAC), Mexican Americans had challenged segregation. LULAC, centered in San Antonio, was joined in 1948 by the G. I. Forum, organized by Mexican-American veterans in Corpus Christi, Texas. The Forum investigated education in Texas, and concluded, "We, as Veterans, did not fight a system like the Nazi Socialist system in order to come back to our own state and live and tolerate such humiliation and suffering of our own children and the children of those soldiers who died fighting for the rights and privileges of our great Democracy." Until *Brown v. Board of Education,* Hispanic organizations kept up pressure to eliminate discrimination.

Although education in Texas was supposed to be integrated for Mexican Americans by 1948, a Texas court struck down a Mexican American desegregation plan. The following year, Texas Attorney General Price Daniel issued an opinion forbidding the segregation of Mexican American children in public schools by race, but language discrimination was still acceptable. Thus, no changes were made. Culture became the discrimination tool of Texas school districts.

Nevertheless, most Texas districts ignored these legal pronouncements until after the *Brown* decision. By the early 1960s integration was piecemeal, and Mexican Americans had moved from wanting an integrated education to expecting good quality public education. High quality education, however, would be an elusive target. The *Brown* decision may have helped put an end to segregated schools, but it did not solve the educational economic disparity that had grown over the years of segregation.

By 1960, San Antonio was the second largest U.S. city in terms of Hispanic population. Within ten years its Hispanic population had increased to over 40 percent of the total city population of nearly 250,000. Most Chicanos were very poor and uneducated. Annual income averages for Mexican Americans in San Antonio was $968; for Anglos, $2,047; for other nonwhites, $1,044. Thirty percent of Mexican Americans lived in deteriorated housing. San Antonio had the highest rate of tuberculosis of any U.S. city. Fewer than 10 percent of Mexican Americans finished high school, and half of all Chicanos in San Antonio did not have more than a fifth grade education.

These conditions and the restlessness they generated led to the organization of a more activist group, the Political Association of Spanish-Speaking Organizations (PASSO). At first PASSO achieved rapid success, its most highly visible achievement being the political takeover of Crystal City, Texas, in 1963. One of the first controversies in Crystal City came with the firing of teachers who had exhibited overt racist behavior. Factions in PASSO evolved, disagreeing over moderate versus militant approaches to social change. Those desiring more immediate change channeled their activity into the Mexican American Legal Defense and Education Fund (MALDEF). MALDEF, much like the legal arm of the NAACP, began to file civil rights lawsuits. Its primary goal was to eliminate discrimination in public education in Texas and to stop the assimilationist thrust of the public schools. Thus, MALDEF sought to reinforce Mexican culture through traditional American philosophical and political forms.

Brown v. Board of Education, the 1961 election of San Antonian Henry Gonzalez to Congress, the civil rights legislation of the 1960s, and the 1968 Bilingual Education Act all encouraged Mexican Americans to seek remedies for their basic problems. MALDEF decided to challenge the Texas system for financing public education. As one political figure observed, Texas was notorious "for providing the least amount of public education for Mexican Americans while fiercely defending its record of inferior and separate schooling." On behalf of Demetrio Rodriguez, several San Antonio parents and other minority or poor families in Texas, MALDEF sued the state of Texas.

The original lawsuit, filed in the summer of 1968 by MALDEF, charged that the Texas system of financing schools was unconstitutional under the equal protection clause of the Fourteenth Amendment. The system was complex. It provided for a redistribution of funds and a collection of taxes based both upon ability to pay and enrollment. The Minimum Foundation Program required every school district to pay a set amount, based upon ability to pay, into a common state fund. This money was then redistributed to school districts, and it constituted up to 80 percent of a school district's operationing budget. Each district was expected to pay the remaining amount of the budget. If it could levy additional taxation, an even greater amount could be devoted to local education.

At the time of the lawsuit, Demetrio Rodriguez lived in the Edgewood School District. Located in the core of San Antonio, Edgewood was a poor district without a large property tax base. No factories or significant stores were located in the district. Ninety percent of Edgewood's students were Mexican American, and 6 percent were black. In 1968 the school district contributed $26 per pupil, the Texas Minimum Foundation Program gave $222 per pupil, and federal funds contributed $108 per pupil, for a total of $356 per pupil.

Across the city was the Alamo Heights School District. It was the richest district in San Antonio, with a more than 80 percent Anglo, 18 percent Mexican American, and 1 percent African American pupil population. In 1968, Alamo Heights raised $333 per pupil locally. It received $225 per pupil from the Texas Minimum Foundation Program and $36 per pupil from federal funds. Thus, Alamo Heights had $594 per pupil to spend, compared to Edgewood's $356 per pupil—a significant disparity.

At the time of this case, litigation attacking state public school financing was occurring throughout the country. The argument accepted by those who wished to equalize educational funding centered on the principle of fiscal neutrality. That is, the quality of public education must be a function of the wealth of an entire state rather than that of a single community. Thus, a state had an obligation not to discriminate against poor school districts.

Tying this principle to the Constitution was another matter. Those who wanted state intervention to rectify educational disparities argued that state educational laws fell under a "strict scrutiny" test. If a state policy created a class of people or if it restricted a fundamental right, then the state had to show its policy was necessary for a compelling purpose. The onus was on the state to defend its education laws. If it could not, then the equal protection clause of the U.S. Constitution was abrogated, and the state policy was unconstitutional. Three phrases were important to this test: class of people, a fundamental right, and compelling purpose. *Brown* established race as one category of class. Certainly in *Rodriguez* race was evident, but the class went beyond one race to encompass wealth. *Brown* found that integrated education was a fundamental right guaranteed in the Constitution, but *Rodriguez* plaintiffs went farther. They argued that quality education was a fundamental constitutional right. In *Brown*, the Supreme Court found that separation of the races was not a legitimate compelling interest to justify the basic violations of the Fourteenth and Fifth Amendments. MALDEF fought for a determination that state aid to education, because of an expanded class and a fundamental right to quality education, had to be fiscally neutral.

Between the time the *Rodriguez* suit was filed in 1968 and the time a three-judge panel convened by the federal district court rendered its opinion, two cases challenging other state education finance systems had been decided. Both would affect the ultimate outcome of *Rodriguez*.

In Illinois, the federal courts held that the state's school finance system did not violate the Fourteenth Amendment. A district court in that state ruled that the proper constitutional test to use in this kind of case was the "rational basis" test. Here, in the absence of special circumstances, such as blatant racial discrimination, the burden was on a plaintiff to prove that state policy caused an unequal treatment not rationally related to a legitimate purpose. Differences in school district funding allocations were constitutional if the overall goal was legitimate. In reaching the conclusion that Illinois had acted responsibly, the court decided that the Fourteenth Amendment did not require a state to base expenditures solely on need, that funding levels were not the sole measure of a student's opportunities in public education, and that no standards could be applied that might be manageable on a national scale. Thus, there was no constitutional mandate for change, and even if

there was, no constitutional remedy existed to implement change.

A 1971 California decision stood in contrast. Here the state relied almost exclusively on local property taxes to fund public education. In the California case, a federal district court ruled that this system was not fiscally neutral; that education was a right guaranteed by the U.S. Constitution; and that California's method unfairly discriminated against poorer school districts. Thus, the district courts were divided. The Illinois system, which channeled most funds through the state, was found constitutionally compatible when subjected to the "rational basis" test, whereas the California system, which left school districts to fund local education mostly from local sources, was constitutionally deficient when put to the "strict scrutiny" test. The Texas system was somewhere in the middle.

Shortly after these cases were decided, a West Texas judicial panel ruled in favor of Demetrio P. Rodriguez, other parents, and MALDEF. It accepted the California district court's rationale and, holding the Texas school finance system to the "strict scrutiny" test, found the Texas system to be unconstitutional. The state of Texas appealed.

Was the Texas system of public school finance unconstitutional? How should one measure the constitutionality of state public school finance systems? What tests and remedies should be applied? These issues were paramount when the U.S. Supreme Court agreed to hear arguments in *San Antonio Independent School District et al. v. Rodriguez et al.* in October 1972. At stake was the fundamental basis for financing most primary and secondary education in the entire nation.

At oral argument, Charles Alan Wright, a noted Texas conservative constitutionalist, articulated the positions of the state of Texas. He argued that the Texas school finance system could not pass the "strict scrutiny" test, and that test should not be applied. Nowhere, posited Wright, did Texas arbitrarily single out a class of people for discrimination (a "suspect class") or suppress a fundamental right. Given acceptance of this twofold argument, the only test to be applied was the "rational basis" test, which the Texas educational finance system met. The issue was not quality education, but basic education. Moreover, if the Court found differently, Wright noted, the effect would be to throw the nation's schools into disarray.

MALDEF countered these arguments by relying upon the findings in the California case and by showing the financial disparities within the Texas school system. The class of the poor was deemed a suspect class, and education was termed a fundamental right under the Constitution as it related to the rights of free speech and voting. Unfortunately for San Antonio's Mexican American community, the U.S. Supreme Court did not agree with MALDEF's position.

In a split opinion, the Court held for Texas, reversing the lower court. Justice Lewis Powell wrote the majority opinion and was joined by Justices Warren Burger, Harry Blackmun, and William Rehnquist. Justice Potter Stewart concurred, helping to put together the slim five-person majority. Justices William Brennan, Byron White, and Thurgood Marshall wrote dissenting opinions which were joined by Justice William Douglas.

Justice Powell accepted the arguments of Charles Alan Wright. He found that the "strict scrutiny" test could not be applied because no class was being implicitly discriminated against; that wealth or lack thereof did not constitute a suspect class in noncriminal cases; and that education, as important as it is, was not a fundamental right protected in the Constitution. Moreover, Powell stressed that basic, not quality, education was the requirement. He also worried about limits. If education were elevated as a fundamental right, then what else might the Court find to set aside? And if the Texas system were struck down, where would the funding come from for all of the school districts? How could the Court supervise the local chaos that Powell saw as inevitable? Powell then had to deal with the California district court ruling. He noted that the Supreme Court had not yet reviewed that case, but that quite possibly the lower court holding would not stand up. Nevertheless, he seemed to suggest that California needed to take a long look at its school financing system, and it needed to do so with an eye to the new *Rodriguez* precedent.

Justice Marshall's thirty-seven-page dissent castigated the Powell majority opinion. Marshall accused the majority of adopting a "rigidified approach to equal protection analysis" and of arguing with "labored efforts." He pointed to numerous elevations of fundamental rights requiring the "strict scrutiny" test, and he noted the dangerous precedent that appeared to be law—that education as a right was not constitutionally guaranteed. Marshall sarcastically concluded, "The Court seeks solace for its actions today in the possibility of legislative reform. The Court's suggestions of legislative redress and experimentation will doubtless be of great comfort to the schoolchildren of Texas's disadvantaged districts, but considering the vested interests of wealthy school districts in the preservation of the status quo, they are worth little more."

What Marshall recognized was the end of an era. Had this case been heard in 1968, the justices of the majority opinion would have been practicing rather than interpreting law. In that short time Earl Warren, Abe Fortas, Hugo Black, and John Marshall Harlan were replaced by the signers of the *Rodriguez* majority opinion, Powell, Burger, Blackmun, and Rehnquist.

Perhaps this case, more than any other, symbolized the emergence of the Burger court and the end of the Warren court. The breadth of *Brown v. Board of Education* was now limited. Only basic education would be monitored by the Supreme Court. In addition, matters regarding the financing of education and other school issues became the focus of state courts, not federal courts. Some state courts ruled that their education financing systems violated their constitutions (Wyoming, New Jersey, Connecticut, West Virginia), but others upheld their systems (Oregon, Ohio). A crazy quilt matching the variety of traditions of the states emerged with no sense of a national educational system.

In Texas, the education finance system continued unchanged. During the post-*Rodriguez* years of the 1970s and 1980s, predominantly Mexican American schools received three-fifths of the appropriations given to predominantly Anglo schools. In San Antonio, Chicano districts received less state funding than did the Anglo districts. The landmark *Rodriguez* decisions clearly placed limits upon any attempts to alter fundamental aspects of American education.

Selected Bibliography

Acuna, Rodolfo. *Occupied America: A History of Chicanos.* 3rd ed. New York: Harper & Row, 1988.

Cortes, Carlos E., ed. *Education and the Mexican American.* New York: Arno Press, 1974.

DeLeon, Arnoldo. *They Called Them Greasers: Anglo Attitudes Toward Mexicans in Texas, 1821–1900.* Austin: University of Texas Press, 1983.

Madsen, William. *The Mexican-Americans of South Texas.* New York: Holt, Rinehart and Winston, 1964.

San Miguel, Guadalupe, Jr. *"Let All of Them Take Heed": Mexican Americans and the Campaign for Educational Equality in Texas, 1910–1981.* Austin: University of Texas Press, 1987.

Shockley, John Staples. *Chicano Revolt in a Texas Town.* Notre Dame, IN: University of Notre Dame Press, 1974.

Affirmative Action:
Can a White, College-Educated Male
Be a Victim of Discrimination?

—◁◦▷—

Mike Healy
Monona, Iowa

Regents of the University of California v. Bakke, 438 U.S. 265 (1978)
[U.S. Supreme Court]

◁◦▷ THE CASE IN BRIEF ◁◦▷

Date
1978

Location
California

Court
U.S. Supreme Court

Principal Participants
Allan Bakke
University of California
Justices of the U.S. Supreme Court in six
separate opinions

Significance of the Case
The most prominent "reverse discrimination" case led to a mixed decision on how race should be considered in academic admissions but provided little constitutional clarification on affirmative action.

Allan Bakke was raised in Minnesota; his father was a postal employee and his mother was a teacher. He graduated with honors from the University of Minnesota in 1962 with a B.S. in mechanical engineering. He then entered the Marine Corps to fulfill his ROTC commitment and eventually served a tour of duty in Vietnam. In 1967, he was hired by the National Aeronautics and Space Administration (NASA) as a research engineer. He continued graduate work at Stanford University, earning an M.S. degree in mechanical engineering in 1970.

Despite Bakke's apparent success as an engineer, he had a further goal. He wanted to become a physician. To this end, he attended night school to complete needed undergraduate science courses and performed volunteer work in a hospital emergency room. In 1973 Bakke applied for admission to the University of California–Davis Medical School (UCDMS). He was turned down.

In 1973, UCDMS had 2,464 applicants for 100 vacancies. The regular admissions formula took into account Medical College Admissions

Test scores, transcripts, grade point averages, applicant-supplied descriptions of activities and work, and letters of recommendation. The admissions committee was required to sift through these credentials and extend personal interviews to selected candidates (38 percent of the applicants in 1973 were interviewed). On the basis of the credentials and the interview, candidates were given "benchmark scores." Because the practice was for candidates to apply to a number of schools, a list of alternates was compiled of those not admitted but standing high in the process. Regular admissions filled eighty-four of the one hundred vacancies.

A special admissions program, begun in 1972, was designed "to increase opportunities in medical education for disadvantaged citizens." Sixteen vacancies were filled from a list of minority applicants. The process was the same as with regular admissions, but grade point average was not considered. From this separate list sixteen vacancies were filled.

In 1973 Allan Bakke was interviewed by Dr. West of UCDMS. Dr. West found Bakke a very desirable candidate and recommended him for admission. In the rating process, Bakke scored 468 on a 500 scale. Earlier in the year UCDMS had accepted some applicants with lower scores. But Bakke's application came late in the year, and a score of 470 was then being required for acceptance. In early May 1973, Bakke received the UCDMS rejection.

Allan Bakke wrote to Dr. Lowrey, the UCDMS Admissions Committee chairman. In that letter he asked to be placed on a waiting list or to be allowed to audit classes until a vacancy might occur. Dr. Lowrey did not reply. Bakke wrote again in July 1973, questioning Dr. Lowrey on the justice of racial quotas in admissions. Bakke indicated that he would consider legal action.

Dr. Lowrey directed his assistant, Peter Storandt, to reply to Bakke's letters. Storandt already had expressed personal doubts about whether the UCDMS special admissions program was hurting qualified nonminority candidates. In his letter to Bakke, Storandt urged him to apply early for the 1974 admissions process. He also encouraged Bakke to continue researching legal actions, noting that a discrimi-

nation case, *DeFunis v. Odegaard,* was then before the U.S. Supreme Court. In a series of letters, Bakke and Storandt discussed possible legal action, and Storandt offered advice on the best course to follow.

Allan Bakke reapplied for admission to UCDMS in 1974. His preliminary scores were comparable to those of his 1973 application. In 1974 there were 3,737 applicants for 100 vacancies at UCDMS. A student member of the Admissions Committee interviewed Allan Bakke. The interviewer gave Bakke a strong recommendation. Bakke was also interviewed by Dr. Lowrey, the admissions chairman and a strong supporter of special admissions. Dr. Lowrey's evaluation was that Bakke was self-centered and showed difficulty reaching independent conclusions. He devoted the majority of his written analysis to Bakke's views on special admissions. Dr. Lowrey concluded that Bakke was an acceptable candidate but not an outstanding one. Bakke's overall benchmark score in 1974 was 549 on a 600 scale. His application was again rejected.

In April 1974, Allan Bakke sued in California state court, seeking admission to UCDMS. He contended the school's affirmative action program had unconstitutionally reduced the number of vacancies for which he was allowed to compete. If all one hundred vacancies had been open to him, would Allan Bakke have been admitted? Bakke said yes; the university said no.

The UCDMS affirmative action program of 1974 was similar to programs at many colleges and universities. Its purpose was to compensate for past or present discrimination by giving special consideration to certain classes of individual applicants. Based upon the alleged cultural bias of standardized tests, special standards for minority students were then being applied in most professional school admissions. Thus, minority inclusion occasionally meant majority exclusion. Some individuals, like Allan Bakke, questioned whether affirmative action was going too far, becoming "reverse discrimination."

Shortly before the *Bakke* case went to trial, the U.S. Supreme Court heard an appeal from Marco DeFunis, a student at the University of Washington Law School. DeFunis claimed to be a victim of reverse discrimination. The Supreme Court considered the case but did not rule on the merits of the affirmative action issue. The Court declared that because DeFunis was already attending the University of Washington Law School under a lower court order, and law school officials testified that he would complete his legal degree soon, he had "nothing to lose." Thus, there was no live case or controversy.

Bakke had repeatedly maintained that he was not an anti-affirmative action crusader; that he just wanted to attend medical school. Regardless of his motives, Bakke's challenge to the UCDMS admissions policies presented a challenge to the constitutionality of affirmative action that could not be avoided as easily as it had been in the *DeFunis* case.

The *Bakke* case was heard in rural Yolo County, California, before Judge F. Leslie Manker. The University of California was worried that the case would be settled without a definitive ruling on affirmative action. The university therefore filed a cross complaint requesting that the court declare the UCDMS special admissions program legal. Judge Manker agreed with Bakke's attorney that UCDMS had a racial quota. He ruled that Bakke's rights under the equal protection clause of the Fourteenth Amendment were violated. Judge Manker also felt that Title VI of the Civil Rights Act of 1964 applied. It reads: "No person in the United States shall, on the ground of race, color, or national origin, be excluded from participation in, be denied the benefits of, or be subjected to discrimination under any program or activity receiving Federal financial assistance."

The UCDMS continued to maintain that Bakke would not have been accepted into the Davis Medical School even with all one hundred vacancies available. Judge Manker agreed, ruling that UCDMS could not be compelled to admit Bakke to its student body. In 1973, he noted, Bakke had applied to, and had been rejected by, two medical schools. In 1974 he had applied to, and had been rejected by, eleven schools. The burden of proof, Judge Manker concluded, rested on Bakke to prove he would have been accepted by UCDMS if he had been eligible to compete for all one hundred vacan-

cies. Because Bakke had not fully documented that issue in his case, Judge Manker would not command Bakke's admission.

A direct appeal was made to the California Supreme Court. In hearing the case, that court had to select a standard of judicial review to weigh the merits of the issue. If a "rational basis test" was selected, state action was permissible if a reasonable public policy purpose was served. A "balancing test" had been proposed in a 1976 discrimination case in the New York courts. The balancing test required (a) that a "substantial state interest" be present and (b) that no nonracial classification could serve the same purpose. The California Supreme Court rejected both tests. The Court relied on a form of judicial review called "strict scrutiny," which required (a) that a "compelling state interest" be served and (b) that "no less onerous means" was available to fulfill the state's interest. The California State Supreme Court found the UCDMS policy wanting on the basis of this test. Therefore, it declared the Davis special admissions program unconstitutional under the equal protection clause of the Fourteenth Amendment. The Court's decision, rendered in September 1976, was by a 6-1 vote. In its opinion, the California Supreme Court ruled that UCDMS had not offered sufficient proof that Bakke should be denied a vacancy. It therefore ordered that Allan Bakke be admitted. Finally, the court eliminated the consideration of race as a criterion for admissions. The court directed UCDMS to discontinue its present special admissions process.

The University of California appealed to the U.S. Supreme Court, and Allan Bakke was not admitted to medical school immediately. The university feared a repeat of the *DeFunis* case. If Bakke was admitted to UCDMS, could the Supreme Court rule the case moot?

Several organizations, representing the rights of women and racial minorities, tried to stop the University of California from appealing. These organizations distrusted the sincerity of UCDMS and its affirmative action policy. They believed that the *Bakke* case was a "poor vehicle" to test affirmative action. The UCDMS special admissions was different from other affirmative action programs in that it used "dis-

Allan Bakke, whose landmark U.S. Supreme Court decision struck down minority admissions quotas, receives his degree in medicine at the University of California in Davis. *AP/Wide World Photo.*

advantaged citizens" in defining groups targeted for special consideration. If a minority student was not sufficiently "disadvantaged," he/she was not considered for special admissions. However, only nonwhite students were admitted as "disadvantaged." Finally, experts questioned the use of test scores to give an accurate benchmark score. The standardized tests were designed with a statistical error margin that UCDMS did not consider in evaluating candidates.

The Supreme Court received fifty-seven amicus curiae briefs in the *Bakke* case. Constitutional experts cannot recall another Supreme Court case generating so many separate briefs. Some briefs came from friends of *Bakke*, but most were foes. Some organizational constituencies were divided. For example, the National Education Association's brief was against Bakke, but the American Federation of Teachers' brief was for Bakke. The Justice Depart-

ment's brief was the product of intense politics. It condemned racial quotas but strongly supported affirmative action. Minority organizations, legal groups, labor unions, government agencies, professional groups—all were "friends of the court." On appeal, the University of California retained Archibald Cox, a former Solicitor General of the United States and a victim of President Richard Nixon's "Saturday night massacre," to head its legal team.

The Supreme Court heard oral arguments on October 12, 1977. A steady stream of newspaper, magazine, radio, and television attention was directed at the *Bakke* case. When the Supreme Court ruled, confusion reigned. Six justices delivered opinions. The June 28, 1978, *New York Times* headline read "NO ONE LOST."

The Supreme court ruled that Allan Bakke should be admitted to UCDMS. Chief Justice Warren Burger, and Associate Justices John Paul Stevens, Potter Stewart, William Rehnquist, and Lewis Powell voted to agree with the California Supreme Court. The Court also held that the university had the right to take race into account when setting admissions criteria. Associate Justices William Brennan, Byron White, Thurgood Marshall, Harry Blackmun, and Lewis Powell voted to overturn the California Supreme Court ruling on admissions criteria. Thus, the Court held that Allan Bakke's rights were violated by the consideration of race, but the university could continue to use race as an admissions criterion. This seeming contradiction came because of the mediating vote of Justice Powell. Powell voted with the Stevens group on the Bakke admission-to-school question, but he voted with the Brennan group on the admissions-criteria question.

The Stevens opinion (Burger, Stewart, and Rehnquist concurring) did not address the question of constitutionality. The Stevens group took a narrow view of the case. Stevens felt that Title VI of the Civil Rights Act had been violated. He ruled that Allan Bakke must be admitted to UCDMS.

The Brennan opinion (White, Marshall, and Blackmun concurring) considered both Title VI of the Civil Rights Act and the equal protection clause of the Fourteenth Amendment. Justice Brennan felt that broad remedial measures were possible: "We cannot let color-blindness become myopia which masks the reality that many 'created equal' have been treated within our lifetimes as inferior both by the law and by their fellow citizens."

The Brennan group rejected a "strict scrutiny" judicial review standard. The Brennan opinion proposed use of a standard review taken from sex discrimination cases: "[The classification] must serve important governmental objectives and must be substantially related to the achievement of those objectives." Justice Brennan wrote that correcting past societal discrimination was a valuable objective, but no group or individual could be stigmatized as inferior by this process. In the *Bakke* case, no one claimed that whites were inferior. Since all the minority students admitted to UCDMS were qualified candidates, no stigma was being attached. Brennan viewed affirmative action as the only way to reduce underrepresentation of racial minorities in medical schools.

The Brennan group felt that displaced whites, such as Allan Bakke, were not really "innocent victims" of racial preferences in admissions. Rather, these whites would not have won out in competition had the minorities not been handicapped by previous discrimination. The Brennan group seemed to view the equal protection clause of the Fourteenth Amendment as the protector of group rights.

Justices White, Marshall, and Blackmun all wrote additional opinions. Justice White added that the enforcement of Title VI was the responsibility of the government. Justice Marshall, in a strongly worded opinion, held that past discrimination required affirmative action. Justice Blackmun emphasized that educators were those best qualified to determine admissions.

The opinion most analyzed was written by Justice Lewis Powell, the swing justice. It is ironic that the opinion most consulted was Powell's, because his view was not completely shared by any of the other justices. Powell agreed with the Brennan group that race was a permissible criterion in admissions, but he agreed with the Stevens group on admitting Bakke to UCDMS, basing his judgment on the equal protection clause of the Fourteenth Amendment (the Stevens group relied on Title

VI). Thus, Powell created the majority, but he disagreed in some form with both factions.

Justice Powell rejected goals and quotas. He felt that both resulted in racial classifications based on race and ethnic group. He viewed the equal protection clause as the guarantor of individual rights. Powell felt that the *Bakke* case required a "strict judicial scrutiny." The UCDMS special admissions program supposedly was enacted to (1) reduce the deficit of minority students in medical schools, (2) increase the number of physicians in minority communities by training minority doctors, (3) remediate past societal discriminations, and (4) obtain the educational benefits of a diverse student body. Justice Powell rejected the first three as not substantial enough to merit a separate classification system. The Brennan group had based its judgment on the remediation of past societal discriminations, but Powell rejected that argument.

In Powell's mind, Allan Bakke should not pay for society's past discriminations. Powell did offer an exception. If a specific institution was guilty of past discriminations, that institution could try to correct its own past shortcomings. Justice Powell accepted the fourth goal, the attainment of a diverse student body, as being sufficiently important so as not to fall prey to the "strict scrutiny" requirements. He felt that the First Amendment has a special concern with academic freedom. Such academic freedom necessitated a diverse student body. However, in Powell's view, racial quotas were a constitutionally impermissible means of obtaining that diverse student body. Powell did hold that race could be used on an individual basis as one of the criteria for admissions. He cited the Harvard College admissions process as an example of such a program. Harvard desired a diverse student body and viewed each applicant on an individual basis. Harvard used a variety of criteria in its review, including race. Thus, Powell voted with the Brennan group to allow *consideration* of race in college admissions. He did so, however, for a different reason and to a lesser extent.

Powell continued his strict scrutiny review of the UCDMS admissions policy. Because Allan Bakke could compete for only eighty-four vacancies, and minority students could compete for all one hundred vacancies, Powell found that Bakke's rights had been violated. Thus, Powell voted with the Stevens group to admit Bakke to UCDMS, and he did so on equal protection grounds.

What was the end result of *The Regents of the University of California v. Bakke*? Allan Bakke was admitted to UCDMS. The UCDMS special admissions policy was declared unconstitutional. The California Supreme Court's race-neutral admissions standard was overturned. Who was victorious?

Attorney General Griffin Bell called the decision "a great victory for affirmative action." The Reverend Jesse Jackson called it "a devastating blow to our civil-rights struggle." A. E. Howard of the University of the Virginia School of Law viewed the *Bakke* decision as a "Solomonic compromise." Lawrence Tribe of Harvard Law School called it an "act of statecraft." Eleanor Holmes Norton of the Equal Employment Opportunity Commission felt "that we are not compelled to do anything differently from the way we've done things in the past."

Good, bad, neutral—the *Bakke* case was a mixed decision. Some expert commentators saw the Court decision as reflecting larger society's split on how to resolve historic racial injustice with today's desire for equal opportunity. As society was split, so was the Supreme Court. Did *Bakke* have an impact? For Allan Bakke, most assuredly! He entered UCDMS amid protests, and graduated in 1982. He interned at the Mayo Clinic in Rochester, Minnesota, and later served as an anesthesiology resident there. Bakke is now a practicing physician. He refuses to discuss the case.

Bakke appears to have had minimal impact on college admissions. A survey of college admissions programs in 1982 found that 83% had made no forced change in their programs as a result of the Supreme Court's *Bakke* decision. Many experts saw a wide range of discretion possible for admissions officials. In reality *Bakke* has not prohibited race-conscious admissions; rather, it has licensed such programs.

Later court cases did little to provide constitutional clarification for affirmative action. In *Kaiser Aluminum and Chemical Corporation v.* *Brian F. Weber et al.,* a 1979 labor case involving minority quotas for entrance into a special training program, the Supreme Court held 5-2 that the use of quotas was permissible under the Civil Rights Act of 1964. In overruling the Circuit Court of Appeals, the majority opinion of Justice Brennan saw the equal protection clause of the Fourteenth Amendment as applying only to actions by states, not private individuals or companies. However, when consenting parties to a labor agreement decide on private action to ameliorate past discrimination, those affirmative action measures are permissible.

The Regents of the University of California v. Bakke thus provided a complex compromise to a vexing public policy concern. Subsequent court decisions on affirmative action in higher education, especially the Fifth Circuit Court of Appeals' decision of *Hopwood v. Texas* (1996), have undercut much of the precedential value of *Regents v. Bakke*. As Allan Bakke's medical career progresses, the courts continue to struggle with the issues he raised.

Selected Bibliography

Ball, Howard. *The Bakke Case: Race, Education and Affirmative Action.* Lawrence: University Press of Kansas, 2000.

Dreyfus, Joel, and Charles Lawrence III. *The Bakke Case: The Politics of Inequality.* New York: Harcourt Brace Jovanovich, 1979.

Eastland, Terry, and William J. Bennett. *Counting by Race: Equality from the Founding Fathers to Bakke and Weber.* New York: Basic Books, 1979.

Schwartz, Bernard. *Behind Bakke: Affirmative Action and the Supreme Court.* New York: New York University Press, 1988.

Simmons, Ron. *Affirmative Action: Conflict and Change in Higher Education after Bakke.* Cambridge, MA: Schenkman, 1982.

Sindler, Allan P. *Bakke, DeFunis, and Minority Admissions: The Quest for Equal Opportunity.* New York: Longman, 1978.

Tribe, L. H. "Perspectives on Bakke: Equal Protection, Procedural Fairness, or Structural Justice?" *Harvard Law Review* 92 (February 1979): 864–877.

Wilkenson, J. Harvie. *From Brown to Bakke: The Supreme Court and School Integration, 1954–1978.* New York: Oxford University Press, 1979.

Is Race Still a Compelling Factor?

———◁○▷———

Melvin I. Urofsky

Center for Public Policy
Virginia Commonwealth University

Hopwood v. Texas, 78 F.3d 932 (1996) [U.S. Circuit Court of Appeals]

◁○▷ **THE CASE IN BRIEF** ◁○▷

Date
  1996

Location
  Texas

Court
  U.S. Circuit Court of Appeals

Principal Participants
  Cheryl Hopwood and co-plaintiffs
  Center for Individual Rights (CIR)
  University of Texas Law School
  Judge Jerry E. Smith

Significance of the Case
  A circuit court judge circumvented the
  framework of the Bakke Supreme Court
  ruling and eliminated an affirmative
  action program.

Following the *Bakke* decision of 1978, in which a divided Supreme Court condemned the use of racial quotas but permitted race-conscious evaluations, many schools adopted entrance policies that favored minority applicants. For universities that had practiced overt discrimination against African Americans, Hispanics, or women, affirmative action provided a means to redress past sins. For schools that lacked such a record, affirmative action represented a balm to the social conscience, as well as a chance to construct student bodies reflective of the general population.

Throughout the 1980s and early 1990s, affirmative action became standard practice at a majority of the nation's colleges and universities, even as the Reagan and Bush administrations railed against race, ethnic, and gender preferences. But Presidents Reagan and Bush were to have the last word because, for the most part, the appointments they made to the federal bench, shared their antipathy to affirmative action. The U.S. Supreme Court, although it has not reversed *Bakke,* did strike down minority business set-aside programs and so-called minority-majority districting, a form of electoral affirmative action. The stage was set for a challenge to university affirmative action programs. That challenge came in Texas in 1994.

The University of Texas Law School is the most prestigious in the state, and one of the top law schools in the country. Each year it typically received four thousand applications, of which about nine hundred were offered acceptance, yielding a first-year class of about five hundred. Because of the large applicant pool, numbers mattered. The school used the "Texas Index," comprised of grade point average (GPA) plus score on the standardized Law School Admissions Test (LSAT). The university aimed for a class with 10% Mexican Americans and 5% African Americans. To achieve this, it took all applications from these two groups and put them into a separate pool. According to figures introduced at the trial, an in-state white applicant would need a minimum GPA of 3.53 and an LSAT score of 164 to get into the law school. A Mexican American would need scores of 3.27 and 158, and a black would need 3.25 and 157. Apparently some five hundred to six hundred white applicants were passed over for admission in preference for minority applicants with lower scores.

Cheryl Hopwood and three other disappointed applicants to the University of Texas Law School—Douglas Carvell, Kenneth Elliott, and David Rogers—asked the Center for Individual Rights (CIR), a formidable nonprofit law firm adamantly opposed to affirmative action, to represent them. The CIR sued on their behalf in federal district court, arguing that the school's use of a separate admissions subcommittee to evaluate minority applicants too closely resembled the quota system that the High Court had condemned in *Bakke.* This, the CIR argued, violated the Fourteenth Amendment's equal protection clause as well as several federal civil rights statutes.

The district court agreed that the admissions system violated the *Bakke* guidelines and ordered that Ms. Hopwood and the others be

given nominal damages of $1 apiece and be allowed to reapply to the law school without fee. By this point, however, the law school had already changed its admissions policies to fit the *Bakke* criteria more closely. However, in its opinion the district court noted the that the entire Texas public school system, from primary grades through the university system, bore the continuing imprint of prior de jure discrimination, thus making race-conscious remediation allowable. In addition, as late as 1994—the year Cheryl Hopwood went to court—the Office of Civil Rights within the U.S. Department of Education had notified the state that it was "continuing to oversee Texas's effort to eliminate all vestiges of *de jure* segregation." With its admissions policy now comporting with the *Bakke* standards, as well as a district court and federal government imprimatur on its efforts to compensate for past prejudice, all seemed well in Austin.

But Ms. Hopwood appealed. She, and especially the CIR, wanted to get rid of affirmative action at the university completely. They found a sympathetic five-judge panel in the Fifth Circuit that was willing to grant their wish. In his opinion for the panel, Judge Jerry E. Smith noted that the U.S. Supreme Court had recently declared that all governmental race classifications, including affirmative action programs, had to meet strict scrutiny standards. He then posed two questions: (1) Did the racial classification employed by the law school meet some compelling governmental interest? (2) If so, was it narrowly tailored to achieve that goal?

The district court had found a compelling interest—obtaining "a racially and ethnically diverse student body"—which comported with Justice Lewis Powell's opinion in *Bakke.* The circuit panel was unwilling to accept that rationale, but in doing so it had to find a way to ignore *Bakke,* which the Supreme Court has never overruled. It did so by noting that, in *Bakke,* Justice Powell wrote only for himself. Four justices joined Powell in rejecting the quota system at the University of California Davis Medical School, and the other four members of the *Bakke* Court joined Powell in allowing race as a "plus" factor that could be taken into account in decisions. The unusual voting arrangement, according to Judge Smith, meant that Powell's *Bakke* opinion should not be considered a true majority opinion or a binding precedent. Instead, he claimed, the Supreme Court had gradually come to the conclusion that only the *remedial* use of race (i.e., to compensate for past discrimination) is compelling. The use of race to achieve a diverse student body, on the other hand, "cannot be a state interest compelling enough to meet the steep standard of strict scrutiny."

Did the Texas admissions policy serve a remedial function, and thus a compelling governmental interest? The court said that it did not, because the university had failed to show any present effects of past discrimination. Judge Smith brushed away as uncompelling the district court's finding that there were indeed present effects resulting from past discrimination (e.g., the law school's poor reputation with minority students, minorities' perception of the law school as a hostile environment, and the underrepresentation of minorities in the student body). Racial tension, he stated, had more to do with general societal problems than with particular past policies, and the record did not support the claim that minority underrepresentation had been caused by past discrimination.

Interestingly, the panel did not issue an injunction forbidding the school to use race in future admissions decisions. It assumed that school administrators would comply, and suggested that punitive damages might be awarded if they did not. The Fifth Circuit denied a rehearing en banc, and the U.S. Supreme Court denied certiorari, with Justices Ruth Bader Ginsburg and David Souter noting that certiorari had been denied not on the merits of the case, but because the admissions program that had been challenged was no longer "genuinely in controversy."

The decision in *Hopwood* sent shock waves through the civil rights community and the chambers of state legislatures. The Supreme Court had given indications that it found affirmative action more and more problematical, but in none of its decisions had the justices implied that they had abandoned *Bakke*. Although state and lower federal courts will sometimes try to distinguish between a case before them and a Supreme Court precedent, they will rarely challenge the precedent head-on. In effect, Judge Smith overruled *Bakke* in the Fifth Circuit. In 1994, in *Podberesky v. Kirwan,* the Fourth Circuit had struck down a racially exclusive scholarship program administered by the University of Maryland at College Park. However, in the First Circuit in 1998, a judicial panel in *Wessman v. Gittens* found that achieving diversity to remedy minority underrepresentation was legitimate.

It is one thing when national candidates and representatives of upper- middle-class districts condemn affirmative action; it is another when one's constituents start to complain that their children are now effectively precluded from admission to the state's flagship university. Once again, the numbers could not be ignored. In 1996, in the last first-year class admitted to the University of Texas at Austin under affirmative action, there were 266 blacks and 932 Hispanics out of a total of 6,430 admittees. The following year, these numbers dropped to 154 and 781, and minority faces practically disappeared from the law school.

One widely respected black state senator raised the question of whether the legislature ought to continue its generous support of the university if it became an elite, all-white institution: "That won't reflect the face of Texas, and we ought to send the money where the people are." But very few people in Texas wanted the university to become all-white; they wanted the school to "look like the people," and the legislature came up with a plan that may prove effective in securing minority representation.

In March 1997, the Texas legislature enacted the "10% plan." It entitles the top 10% of the graduating class of each accredited high school in Texas to attend the University of Texas at Austin or any other UT or Texas A&M campus. Because the plan is color-blind, it will likely pass constitutional challenge. But the fact of the matter is that it favors minorities far more than did the set-aside program that was at the heart of the original suit. Graduates from some of the substandard schools in poorer urban and rural neighborhoods may well rank in the top 10% of their classes, but, in terms of standardized test scores, they may well fall below those in the top 10% in the richer schools.

Texas, according to most observers, is a highly segregated state, both regionally and neighborhood by neighborhood. The majority of its schools are almost entirely white or brown or black. The law, according to a scholar conversant with this situation, "uses our bitter history of segregation to promote diversity." At the same time, it attempts to addresses the broader inequities which have kept UT-Austin from enrolling few of the brightest kids of any color from the state's poorer counties.

The 10% plan seems to be working unevenly so far, at least in terms of the number of black and Hispanic students attending the university. Some numbers are up, at least in relation to the post-*Hopwood* drop, and most observers believe it is too early to tell whether the plan will get minorities into school and keep them there.

One of the ironies of the *Hopwood* decision is that, at least in Texas, it will likely make it harder for individuals like Cheryl Hopwood to be admitted to the school of their choice.

Selected Bibliography

Holley, Danielle, and Delia Spencer. "The Texas Ten Percent Plan." *Harvard Civil Rights-Civil Liberties Law Review* 34 (1999): 245–278.

Pratt, Carla D. "In the Wake of *Hopwood*: An Update on Affirmative Action in the Education Arena." *Howard Law Journal* 42 (1999): 451–467.

Urofsky, Melvin I. *Affirmative Action on Trial: Sex Discrimination in Johnson v. Santa Clara.* Lawrence: University Press of Kansas, 1997.

"Whose Mosaic Now? Political Devolution and the Future of Affirmative Action." *Stanford Law & Policy Review* 10 (Spring 1999): 129–214.

Women

Should a Woman Be Admitted to the Bar?

—◄◦►—

Fara Y. Driver
Clemson, South Carolina

Bradwell v. Illinois, 18 U.S. 130 (1873) [U.S. Supreme Court]

◦► THE CASE IN BRIEF ◄◦

Date
1873

Location
Illinois

Court
U.S. Supreme Court

Principal Participants
Myra Colby Bradwell
Matthew H. Carpenter
State of Illinois
Associate Justice Samuel L. Miller

Significance of the Case
The Supreme Court refused a woman's effort to overcome an Illinois ban on admitting women to the bar, thus establishing a precedent for regulation of females in occupations.

Since 1850 American women have taken significant steps toward legal recognition and legal independence: they have received the right to vote, the right to own and control property, the right to make contracts, the right to control their own income, and the right to practice a self-chosen profession. This latter right was hard-won, and nowhere was it more resisted than within the legal profession.

In the 1860s, Myra Colby Bradwell, the wife of practicing lawyer James Bradwell, was the chief editor and president of the *Chicago Legal News*, a weekly newspaper that soon became, according to one authority "the most important legal publication west of the Alleghenies." Mrs. Bradwell had been studying law under her husband. Through her work with the *News*, charitable organizations, and the women's suffrage movement, she was aware of the legal restrictions placed upon women by society. Her husband had already secured a special charter for her to be president of the law publication because Illinois law placed restrictions on the ability of a married woman to make

Myra Bradwell, whose efforts to be admitted to the bar went before the Supreme Court in 1873. *Archive Photos.*

contracts. Mrs. Bradwell herself was responsible for drafting legislation in Illinois to allow married women to control their own earnings.

In 1869, the same year that Arabella Mansfield was admitted to the bar in Iowa, Bradwell applied to practice law in Illinois. She passed the required examination but was denied the right to practice, on the ground that she was a married woman. This meant that she could not enter into the necessary contracts between attorney and client. When she appealed the lower court decision to the Supreme Court of Illinois, that court decided that the mere fact that she was a woman could prevent her from the practice of law. With this decision, Bradwell petitioned to have her case heard by the Supreme Court of the United States.

The Supreme Court did not make a decision in her case until 1873. Coincidentally, the case was decided the same day as the more famous *Slaughterhouse Cases.* Both the butchers in the *Slaughterhouse Cases* and Myra Bradwell were represented by Matthew H. Carpenter, and these two cases were the first Fourteenth Amendment cases heard by the Supreme Court. Carpenter attacked the Illinois law as an infringement on the privileges and immunities clause of the Fourteenth Amendment, section 1: "No State shall make or enforce any law which shall abridge the privileges or immunities of citizens of the United States." In contrast to his strategy in the *Slaughterhouse Cases,* Carpenter argued for a broad interpretation of this passage in *Bradwell,* stating in his brief that the Fourteenth Amendment "executes itself in every State of the Union." He carefully stayed away from the suffrage issue, going so far as to say that "the right to vote is not one of those privileges" protected by the amendment.

In presenting his case, Carpenter laid great stress upon a statement of Justice Stephen J. Field in *Cummings v. Missouri* (1867): "[I]n the pursuit of happiness all avocations, all honors, all positions, are alike open to everyone, and that in the protection of these rights all are equal before the law." Anticipating the Court's use of the Fourteenth Amendment for the protection of African-Americans, Carpenter used the following argument: "The legislature may say at what age candidates shall be admitted, may elevate or depress the standard of learning required. But a qualification, to which a whole class of citizens never can attain, is not a regulation of admission to the bar, but is, as to such citizens, a prohibition.... If the legislature may, under the pretence of fixing qualifications, declare that no female citizen shall be permitted to practice law, it may as well declare that no colored citizen shall practice law; for the only provision in the Constitution of the United States which secured to colored male citizens the privilege of admission to the bar ... is the provision that 'no State shall make or enforce any law which shall abridge the privileges or immunities of a citizen.' And if this provision does protect the colored citizen, then it protects every citizen, black or white, male or female."

Associate Justice Samuel F. Miller, wrote the opinion of the Court in *Bradwell*. He ruled: "There are privileges and immunities belonging to citizens of the United States . . . and that it is these and these alone which a State is forbidden to abridge. But the right to admission to practice in the courts of a State is not one of them." Whereas Justice Miller avoided discussion of the specifics of gender and the practice of law, the subject was covered in great detail in Justice Joseph Bradley's concurring opinion: "Man is, or should be, woman's protector and defender. The natural and proper timidity and delicacy which belongs to the female sex evidently unfits it for many of the occupations of civil life. The constitution of the family organization, which is founded in the divine ordinance, as well as in the nature of things, indicates the domestic sphere as that which properly belongs to the domain and functions of womanhood. The harmony, not to say identity, of interests and views which belong, or should belong, to the family institution is repugnant to the idea of a woman adopting a distinct and independent career from that of her husband. . . . The paramount destiny and mission of woman are to fulfill the noble and benign offices of wife and mother."

The Court's decision in *Bradwell v. Illinois* is significant in that it established a precedent for state regulation of women in occupations. Later decisions, especially the 1875 case of *Minor v. Happersett*, denying women the right to vote, reinforced the attitude of the American majority in the late 1800s toward women and the role they should play in society.

As a final note, in 1872, one year before the Court's decision in *Bradwell*, the Illinois legislature passed a bill that made it illegal to prevent the entrance of anyone into any profession or employment (except the military) on the grounds of sex. Although Myra Bradwell did not reapply for admission to the Illinois bar, she was finally admitted in 1890, by a motion of the Supreme Court of Illinois.

Selected Bibliography

Bredstein, Burton J. *The Culture of Professionalism: The Middle Class and the Development of Higher Education in America.* New York: W. W. Norton, 1976.

Harris, Robert J. *The Quest for Equality.* Westport, CT: Greenwood Press, 1960.

Riley, Glenda. *Inventing the American Woman: A Perspective on Women's History, 1865 to the Present.* Arlington Heights, IL: Harlan Davidson, 1986.

Stevens, Robert. *Legal Education in America from the 1850's to the 1980's.* Chapel Hill: University of North Carolina Press, 1983.

Aberration in the Movement Toward an Eight-Hour Day

Robert A. Waller

Professor of History, Emeritus
Clemson University

Ritchie v. People, 155 Ill. 98 (1895) [Illinois Supreme Court]

⟡ THE CASE IN BRIEF ⟡

Date
1895

Location
Illinois

Court
Illinois Supreme Court

Principal Participants
Illinois Manufacturers' Association
(IMA)
State of Illinois

Significance of the Case
The supreme court of a major state struck down a law mandating an 8-hour workday for women, but the setback for reform was an aberration that was reversed a decade later.

Among the most celebrated state court cases impeding the movement toward an eight-hour day is *Ritchie v. People,* in which reformers in Illinois sought to improve working conditions by using the state's police power to restrict property rights. The supporters of laissez-faire resisted such constraints by arguing for "freedom of contract" between employer and employee.

In 1893, the General Assembly of Illinois passed a law limiting women's hours in factories or workshops to no more than eight hours in any single day and forty-eight hours in a week. This Factory Act established a system of inspectors charged with the responsibility of enforcing the eight-hour clause for female workers. Among the inspectors was the noted social reformer Florence Kelley. She and her colleagues successfully prosecuted several violators. In response, a number of factory owners formed the Illinois Manufacturers' Association (IMA) in order to resist the eight-hour provision. By January 1894, the IMA and the inspectors agreed to a test case in the state courts.

IMA counsel Levy Mayer argued that the clause was unconstitutional on two grounds. First, he argued that the law was discriminatory in applying only to factories and workshops. Second, Levy employed the conventional wisdom that the clause denied freedom of contract to both employer and employee. The attorney for the state, Alexander Bruce, responded that the eight-hour clause was a legitimate exercise of the state's police power for the protection of health and morals of women as childbearers and mothers. An estimated thirty thousand women were affected.

On May 4, 1894, the Illinois Supreme Court heard the arguments of the attorneys. However, the court took almost a year to consider the case before rendering an opinion. In that interval, employers violated the law with impunity. Finally, on March 15, 1895 (almost one year after the famous Pullman strike), the Illinois Supreme Court declared the clause unconstitutional because it impaired a woman's right to contract for her labor without due process of law. While conceding that the police power of the state is extensive, the court declared that it must be directly related to the comfort, welfare, or safety of the society. In the opinion of the court, the law under consideration did not meet this test. "It is not the nature of the things done," the opinion reads, "but the sex of the persons doing them, which is made the basis of the claim that the act is a measure for the promotion of the public health." *Ritchie v. People* became the model of how courts opposed to protective legislation would react.

The decision became one of the most celebrated of the late nineteenth century. Opponents of reform like the *Chicago Tribune* announced that the decision meant "an end to the vexatious suits, begun by overzealous Inspectors to enforce a provision they must have known would be held illegal." The opposition newspaper, the *Chicago Times-Herald*, countered that the decision was "nothing but a setting back [of] the hands of progress on the dial of time." In writing her third annual report, Kelley observed that the court had become "an in-

superable obstacle to the protection of women and children." She hoped that this case would "be added to the reversed decisions in which the Supreme Court of Illinois is so rich." Ultimately, her wish was granted.

The ramifications spread beyond the confines of the Prairie State. Supporters of laissez-faire found confirmation that a principal canon had been supported by the highest court of a major industrial state. Proponents of freedom of contract hailed the decision as anchoring the cornerstone of the free enterprise system. Agents of reform believed that this opinion against protective legislation concerning hours of work had a stultifying effect upon child labor legislation, another progressive measure. The reformist press pilloried the decision as an obstacle to achieving an eight-hour day.

The conventional interpretation has held that *Ritchie v. People* was representative of the judicial opinion in the nation. Recent research, however, indicates that this much praised and much maligned case rarely served as a precedent for other decisions. Most state courts tended to reflect "the mildly reformist views of the country at large." The Progressives of the early twentieth century, in spite of the loud complaints of their opponents, were making significant gains. The *Ritchie* case was an aberration. In *Muller v. Oregon* (1908) the U.S. Supreme Court affirmed the principle of women's hours legislation by upholding an Oregon law.

The Illinois Supreme Court had the opportunity to reconsider its position. In 1910, a second Ritchie case was considered, *Ritchie and Company v. Wayman*, in which the validity of the ten-hour law for women was revisited. The court reversed itself; Kelley was vindicated. The judges held that a limit of ten hours per day was more reasonable than the proviso for eight. Conservatives now accepted the principle that inequalities existed between employers and employees, and that the state had a role to play in placing limitations upon the contractual powers of private parties. Two years later, the same bench upheld another Illinois statute which expanded the ten-hour day to women employed in hotels. The times, indeed, had changed. *Ritchie v. People* had been an exception rather than the rule.

Selected Bibliography

Baer, Judith A. *The Chains of Protection: The Judicial Response to Women's Labor Legislation.* Westport, CT: Greenwood Press, 1978.

Goldmark, Josephine. *Impatient Crusader: Florence Kelley's Life Story.* Urbana: University of Illinois Press, 1953.

Harmon, Sandra D. "Florence Kelley in Illinois." *Journal of the Illinois State Historical Society* 74 (Autumn 1981): 162–178.

Urofsky, Melvin I. "State Courts and Protective Legislation During the Progressive Era: A Reevaluation." *Journal of American History* 72 (June 1985): 63–91.

The Law Recognizes "Women Are Different"

—◄◦►—

Melvin I. Urofsky
Center for Public Policy
Virginia Commonwealth University

Muller v. Oregon, 208 U.S. 412 (1908) [U.S. Supreme Court]

◄◦► THE CASE IN BRIEF ◄◦►

Date
1908

Location
Oregon

Court
U.S. Supreme Court

Principal Participants
Louis D. Brandeis; National Consumer's League; State of Oregon; Associate Justice David J. Brewer

Significance of the Case
The Court upheld a state law regulating working hours for women, but for the first time a substantial brief was submitted (by Louis Brandeis) with nonlegal supporting documentation; the outcome further legitimized economic regulation of the labor market.

Joseph H. Choate, a pillar of the New York bar, listened patiently and courteously as the two women explained their request. Florence Kelley, the Chief Factory Inspector of Illinois, and Josephine Goldmark of the National Consumers' League, wanted the eminent New York attorney to defend, before the U.S. Supreme Court, an Oregon law restricting the working hours of women to ten a day. "I can see no reason," he told them, "why a big husky Irishwoman should not work more than ten hours day in a laundry if she and her employer so desired."

The Oregon ten-hour law was part of that great spurt of reform activity which dominated American political life for the two decades prior to World War I, and which has often been described as a "response to industrialism." Whether this characterization is true in all areas of Progressive reform, there is no doubt that it marked the various statutes known as protective legislation, which established maximum hours and minimum wages, restricted child labor, and created workmen's compensation plans. In the eyes of reformers, protective legislation would redress, in large measure, the perceived imbalance between the lords of big business and their ill-used workers.

These campaigns had begun in the latter part of the nineteenth century, as state after state passed some or all of the reformers' proposals. But in just about every state, conservatives challenged these measures as violating one or both of the great constitutional shibboleths, substantive due process and freedom of contract. The former rested on the due process clause of the Fourteenth Amendment, and had been interpreted by state and federal courts to mean that certain property interests could not be diminished through regulation by the state acting under its police power. What these interests were and how great their protection was, depended on the particular court, but the common thread of interpretation held that property interests were the backbone of society and progress, to be defended against wild-eyed reformers at all cost.

Freedom of contract derived from the pre-Civil War doctrine of free labor, originally designed to distinguish northern industrial workers from southern slaves. Free workers could choose the terms of their employment, whereas slaves could not; free workers could bargain with their employers, but slaves could not. Free workers could leave if they found employment more to their liking or advantage; slaves could not. After the war, the free labor idea was converted into freedom of contract, in which nothing could be allowed to interfere with the voluntary bargaining between employer and employee. The fact that conditions had changed—that no actual bargaining took place between the owners of big factories and the thousands of men they employed—did not penetrate the judicial consciousness; judges continued to decide cases as if each worker in a steel mill or coal mine had individually bargained out his employment contract with the owner.

As courts first began to hear constitutional challenges to protective legislation, conservative attorneys appealed to the doctrines of substantive due process and freedom of contract. Laws regulating factories, they claimed, interfered with the owners' free use of property, depriving them of that property without due process of law. Statutes controlling working conditions, on the other hand, deprived workers of their right to make any arrangement they wanted with their employers. Jurists unsympathetic to the goals of protective legislation could rely upon either or both of these arguments to find the statutes unconstitutional.

One should not assume that all judges and all lawyers opposed protective legislation; they did not. But courts are by nature conservative, and even if late nineteenth-century judges had been prescient about the direction of a rapidly changing society, it is unlikely they would have rushed to approve a wide spectrum of innovative laws, many of which ran counter to established common-law principles. The courts did eventually accept the need for protective legislation, and they did so under the rationale of the states' police powers.

As part of its sovereign powers, a state could employ its police power to override both property and individual rights in order to protect public order and maintain minimum standards of health, safety, and welfare for its citizens. Even property-conscious jurists such as Stephen J. Field recognized the great range of the state's powers "to prescribe the regulations to promote the health, peace, morals, education and good order of the people, and to legislate so as to increase the industries of the state, develop its resources and add to the wealth and prosperity." In the famous 1877 Granger case of *Munn v. Illinois,* one of the first cases involving the police power to reach the Supreme Court, the majority made it clear that under proper circumstances, even the sanctity of contract and property rights, might be restricted for the public good, an idea that sent paroxysms of terror through conservative ranks.

The range of police powers, as well as the extent of property rights and freedom to contract, formed a central debate in American jurisprudence from the 1880s to the 1930s. Reformers applauded the statement by Justice Oliver Wendell Holmes Jr., in 1911 that the police power "may be put forth in aid of what is sanctioned by usage, or held by the prevailing morality, or strong and preponderant opinion to be greatly and immediately necessary to the public welfare." By that reading, the police power could reach almost anything the legislature wished to regulate.

Conservatives, on the other hand, while conceding the existence of the police power, argued that it had only limited range, and the state could interfere only minimally with property and individual rights. Thomas M. Cooley, the leading law writer of the late nineteenth century, admitted the need for police regulations in any well-ordered society, but these rules "must have reference to the comfort, safety, or welfare of society . . . and they must not, under pretense of regulation, take from the corporation any of the essential rights and privileges which the charter confers." Rather than deny the existence of the police power and the state's authority to pass protective legislation, opponents argued that the power had been misused, that it had been extended in an illegitimate manner to matters beyond its reach. The states, on the other hand, often prefaced their statutes with a claim that the legislation met a legitimate state interest. The preamble to an Oregon minimum wage law, for example, declared: "The welfare of the State of Oregon requires that women and minors should be protected from conditions of labor which have a pernicious effect on their health and morals, and inadequate wages . . . have such a pernicious effect."

The general perception of courts as a bastion of antireform sentiment is somewhat at variance with the facts. Although in some well-known state cases, such as *In re Jacobs* (New York, 1885) and *Ritchie v. People* (Illinois, 1895), state courts went out of their way to deny the applicability of the police power, the fact is that by the early years of the twentieth century, nearly all state courts approved protective legislation. Moreover, in the Supreme Court a similar pattern emerged; with few exceptions, the Court rebuffed challenges to the states' police powers. One of the most famous—or infamous—of those exceptions was the 1905 case of *Lochner v. New York*.

In that case Justice Rufus Peckham, perhaps the most conservative member of the Court, spoke for a 5-4 majority in striking down a New York statute prescribing maximum hours

for bakery workers. "Is this a fair, reasonable and appropriate exercise of the police power of the State," Peckham asked, "or is it an unreasonable, unnecessary and arbitrary interference with the rights of the individual?" Peckham's phrasing of the question left no doubt as to his answer, and he went on to denounce the law, whose real object, he claimed, was "to regulate the hours of labor between the master and his employees . . . in a private business, not dangerous in any degree to morals or in any real and substantive degree, to the health of the employees."

The *Lochner* decision cheered conservatives, and it quickly became a classic statement of the defense of property and contract rights against the allegedly overweening power of the state. There is probably little doubt that the *Lochner* ruling led Curt Muller to appeal his conviction under the Oregon ten-hour law.

In 1903 Oregon had established a maximum of ten hours' work a day for women employed in manufacturing, mechanical establishments, and laundries. On September 4, 1905, Joe Haselbock, the manager of Curt Muller's Grand Laundry in Portland, required Mrs. Elmer Gotcher to work more than ten hours. She complained to the authorities, and two weeks later Muller was charged with violating the law, found guilty of a misdemeanor, and fined $10. He appealed to the Oregon Supreme Court, and when that body upheld the statute as a legitimate exercise of the state's police power, Muller appealed to the U.S. Supreme Court. Reformers around the country noted the appeal with alarm, for if the Court struck down the Oregon statute, it might well mean the end of hours legislation. That is when Florence Kelley and Josephine Goldmark began seeking an eminent attorney to defend the statute; the day after Joseph Choate rebuffed them, the two women traveled to Boston to meet with Louis D. Brandeis.

By late 1907 Brandeis had already earned the title "People's Attorney." After establishing a successful Boston practice, he had become interested in reform. He began, as did so many of the Progressives, on the local scene, fighting corrupt traction companies and opposing the giveaway of important municipal franchises.

Brandeis then moved to the state level. In Massachusetts he considered his most important reform contribution to be the establishment of savings bank life insurance. Following the great insurance scandals of 1905, Brandeis had condemned the insurance companies for their scandalous treatment of poor workers, who paid exorbitant premiums for so-called industrial life policies which provided very limited protection. As an alternative, Brandeis proposed, and then secured approval of, a plan under which low cost life insurance would be sold through the state's savings banks.

The campaign for savings bank insurance illustrated a pattern Brandeis would employ not only in his career as a reformer and lawyer, but also later, as a member of the Supreme Court. First, identify the problem; second, gather all the facts available on that problem; and third, from those facts deduce an appropriate remedy. One of his favorite maxims was *ex facto jus oritur*, "out of facts springs the law," and this would be the strategy he employed in *Muller*.

Brandeis had, in fact, been the first choice of both Mrs. Kelley and Ms. Goldmark; both knew him through a network of reformers, and beyond that, he was married to Ms. Goldmark's sister. But an aide in the Consumers' League office had made the appointment with Choate while Mrs. Kelley was out of town, so the two women felt bound at least to ask Choate to take on the case. When he refused, they gladly turned to Brandeis.

After listening to the two women, Brandeis agreed to take on the case, provided certain conditions could be met. First of all, Oregon would have to designate him as its official counsel; second, the Consumers' League would have to research certain areas for him very quickly, and provide extensive documentation; third, he would accept no fee. Although the conditions struck the two women as somewhat unusual, they agreed, without any idea of how Brandeis would proceed.

Actually, the three conditions were not so unusual. Brandeis already had in mind a rather unorthodox strategy, and in order for it to be successful, he had to be in control of the litigation. The official counsel plans the brief and determines what form the main arguments, both

written and oral, will take. Had he been just an amicus curiae, a friend of the court, he would have been allowed to submit a brief, but it would have been ancillary to the main arguments. He doubted that Oregon's Attorney General would be comfortable with the innovative strategy he had in mind, or that he would be willing to let Brandeis control the case. Oregon, as it turned out, was more than delighted not only to be spared the cost of the appeal, but also to let Brandeis and the Consumers' League act on its behalf.

Brandeis's refusal to take a fee was perhaps the most unusual of the demands. Early in his career as a reformer, Brandeis had accepted fees for his work, and then had turned them over to charity. But so long as he accepted payment for his work, he was an employee of a client, and thus his primary responsibility was to that client. He came to realize that in many cases, a difference existed between the specific interests of the client, even that of a reform group, and the larger interests of the public. By not accepting a fee, Brandeis could work for solutions that he believed were in the public interest, without being held accountable to a particular client.

The request for data derived from Brandeis's belief that he had to know all the facts surrounding an issue before he could frame a workable solution. But in this particular case, the strategy, though certainly innovative, had in fact been suggested by Justice Peckham in his *Lochner* decision. The New York law, he claimed, exceeded the state's police power because it had no relation to health or safety; the state's saying it had a relation did not constitute proof. By implication, if a law could be shown to have a direct relation to health, safety, or public welfare, then the courts would recognize it as a legitimate exercise of state power.

Brandeis told Ms. Goldmark that he wanted "*facts,* published by anyone with expert knowledge of industry in its relation to women's hours of labor, such as factory inspectors, physicians, trade unions, economists [and] social workers." Aided by ten readers, she began to scour the holdings of the New York Public Library, Columbia University, and the Library of Congress. She enlisted a young medical stu-

dent to research material on the hygiene of occupations. They had about two weeks to gather
the material; Brandeis had agreed to take the
case in mid-November 1907, and it would have
to be argued before the Court in January 1908.
After they presented the mass of data to him,
he had to assimilate it, arrange it in an orderly
and persuasive manner, and have the brief
printed by the Court's deadline.

Brandeis recognized, as many people at the
time did not, that *Lochner* represented a departure from the Supreme Court's earlier decisions
on the police power. In *Holden v. Hardy* (1898),
the Court had upheld a Utah law establishing
an eight-hour day for miners; a few years later,
in *Atkin v. Kansas* (1903), the Court confirmed a
state law mandating an eight-hour day on all
public projects and for all private employers
contracting to do state business. In response to
the argument that the state had exceeded its
authority, Justice John Marshall Harlan declared that "regulations on this subject suggest
only considerations of public policy. And with
such considerations the courts have no concern." Only a few months after its *Lochner* decision, the Court reaffirmed its *Holden* ruling
with a per curiam decision upholding a similar
Missouri statute and then, in 1907, extended
Atkin by validating a federal eight-hour law for
government laborers.

Brandeis had to get the majority of the Court
to return to this earlier line of decisions without asking them to overrule *Lochner*. He recognized, as a matter of strategy, that the Court
would be unwilling to reverse itself so quickly
(even though *Lochner* had been a 5-4 decision),
and that even those justices who had voted to
sustain earlier protective legislation still believed in freedom of contract and protection of
property. So instead of rebutting *Lochner*, he
quoted selectively from it in the two pages he
devoted to legal argument. Rather than deny
the idea of freedom of contract, he acknowledged it, but then cited *Lochner* to claim that
freedom of contract could be abridged in order
to protect health, safety, and the public welfare.

In his *Lochner* opinion Justice Peckham had
tried to show that the conservative majority
was not placing its own social and economic
views above the legislative judgment, and so

he had declared that "when the validity of a
statute is questioned, the burden of proof"
would be on the challenger rather than the
state. The Court itself, according to Peckham,
would not strike down a statute unless it found
no "fair ground, reasonable in and of itself, to
say that there is material danger to the public
health [or safety], or to the health [or safety] of
the employees [or to the general welfare]." In
Lochner, Peckham had claimed that the Court
had been unable to find the connection between the statute and the public health and
safety. The "Brandeis brief" set out to show that
connection.

After the two pages of legal citations, Brandeis set out to show the reasonableness of and
the factual basis for the Oregon law. He devoted fifteen pages to showing that Oregon
was not alone in believing that long hours of
labor adversely affected women's health, and
cited the laws of other states as well as foreign
countries to show that responsible people believed limiting hours was a reasonable exercise
of the state's power.

Then came a ninety-five-page section titled
"The World's Experience upon Which the Legislation Limiting the Hours of Labor for Women
Is Based," with sections titled "The Dangers of
Long Hours" and "Laundries." Here Brandeis
marshaled the facts which he had asked Ms.
Goldmark and her researchers to find, and he
utilized sources which, until then, had rarely
been cited in legal briefs or judicial opinions—
the British *Reports of Medical Commissioners on
the Health of Factory Operatives* (1833), reports of
the Massachusetts Bureau of Labor Statistics
and the Commissioners on the Hours of Labor,
the *Journal of the Royal Sanitary Institute*, an 1892
treatise titled *The Hygiene, Diseases, and Mortality of Occupations*, and many others. In fact,
nearly all of this section consisted of lengthy
quotations organized to prove the basic contention that contemporary knowledge justified
restricting the hours that women worked in
order to preserve their health.

The Court heard oral argument in *Muller v.
Oregon* on January 15, 1908. William D. Fenton,
counsel for the laundry owner, took the traditional view that freedom of contract should not
be abridged, and that a law which restricted

hours only for women was unconstitutionally discriminatory. "Women equally with men," he declared, "are endowed with the fundamental and inalienable rights of liberty and property, and these rights cannot be impaired or destroyed by legislative action under the pretense of exercising the police power of the state. Difference in sex alone does not justify the destruction or impairment of these rights."

The gist of Brandeis's argument, however, and the whole point of nearly one hundred pages of economic, medical, and sociological data, had been to show that people outside the courts recognized that women in fact *were* different from men. By now Brandeis had completely mastered the voluminous data he had requested, and, according to Ms. Goldmark's recollection, "slowly, deliberately, without seeming to refer to a note, he built up his case from the particular to the general, describing conditions authoritatively reported, turning the pages of history, country by country, state by state, weaving with artistic skill the human facts—all to prove the evil of long hours and the benefit that accrued when these were abolished by law." In his oral presentation, as in the brief, he let the facts speak for themselves, and he invited the justices to take judicial notice of them, so they might understand the reasonableness of the state's action in passing the law.

The justices listened carefully, and recognized that Brandeis had given them an opportunity to sidestep the *Lochner* decision (which had been overwhelmingly criticized by all but the most hidebound conservatives) without actually overruling it. Brandeis had proposed no radical jurisprudential doctrine, nor even an erosion of accepted principles. He merely asked the justices to recognize in law what everyone knew: the "common knowledge" that women differed from men.

Brandeis's innovative strategy worked. Justice David J. Brewer wrote the brief opinion for the Court upholding the Oregon ten-hour law, and in an unusual comment referred to counsel by name. "It may not be amiss, in the present case," he declared, "before examining the constitutional question, to notice the course of legislation as well as expressions of opinion from other than judicial sources. In the brief filed by

Mr. Louis D. Brandeis . . . is a very copious collection of all these matters, an epitome of which is found in the margin." In a footnote Brewer listed the state and foreign laws, and the fact that over ninety separate reports had been cited to justify this legislation. Though constitutional issues could not be decided by "a consensus of present public opinion," the Court did "take judicial cognizance of all matters of general knowledge." The particular aspect of "general knowledge" referred to by Brewer was that "women's physical structure and the performance of maternal functions place her at a disadvantage in the struggle for existence."

The *Muller* decision, and especially Brandeis's strategy, received widespread praise in the press. *The Outlook* of March 7, 1908, called the decision "unquestionably one of the [most] momentous decision[s] of the Supreme Court . . . immeasurable in its consequences, laden with vast potential benefit to the entire country for generations to come." Similar puffery from reformers such as Josephine Goldmark and Felix Frankfurter have obscured the fact that in its holding, the Court did not hand down a revolutionary decision at all. If one looks at the long list of protective legislation cases which came before the high bench between 1897 and 1917, one finds that it is *Lochner*, not *Muller*, which is the exception.

Lochner, with its extreme assertions of property rights, soon became the epitome of judicial activism, condemned by reformers for the next thirty years. But in terms of holding, the Court approved nearly all the hours laws which it heard; *Muller* fits into the pattern, and is noteworthy primarily for the Court's backtracking from *Lochner*. Many scholars, in fact, thought that the Court would just bury *Lochner*, but in 1923 the reactionary bloc resurrected the case in *Adkins v. Children's Hospital*.

The "Brandeis brief," as it would henceforth be known, remains the most important legacy of the case. So long as courts insisted on reviewing the reasonableness of state police regulations, lawyers would be able to utilize nonlegal materials to secure judicial cognizance of the facts of real life. Before his own appointment to the Supreme Court in 1916, Brandeis, working with the National Consumers' League and Ms. Goldmark, defended a number of protective statutes before both state courts and the Supreme Court. In cases where Brandeis could not direct the litigation personally, the League gave local attorneys the factual data and suggestions on how to prepare a "Brandeis brief."

In the long run, the introduction of factual material became commonplace, and today many law schools offer courses on law and social sciences with the aim of utilizing these disciplines in legal proceedings. After *Muller,* the most noteworthy case to employ the Brandeis brief was the great school desegregation decision of 1954, *Brown v. Board of Education.* In that case, the NAACP amassed as much factual data as it could find to support its contention that discrimination inflicted psychological damage on black children.

The "Brandeis brief" also epitomized what Roscoe Pound, Oliver Wendell Holmes, Ernst Freund, and others had been advocating for nearly a generation: that the law could not be divorced from facts. In his Lowell Institute lectures on the common law in 1881, Holmes had argued that "the life of the law has not been logic but experience." This assertion greatly impressed Brandeis, who was in the audience. In his own practice, Brandeis had made it a rule to know, as he put it, all the facts which surround a case. In his regular work as well as in the cases he argued for reform groups, he had always brought facts to bear in his arguments; the *Muller* brief may have been revolutionary to many attorneys, but it represented a logical culmination of Brandeis's own work.

In *Muller,* Brandeis opened the door wide for the entry of facts of all kinds into the courtroom. His strategy also affected how legislation would henceforth be written. Now, instead of merely declaring that a certain statute affected health or safety, the assembly could create a "legislative history" which litigants and judges could rely upon for determining the reasons and the reasonableness of the laws. For better or for worse, the "felt necessities of the time," expressed in judicially cognizable facts, would henceforth be an essential component of American law.

Since the rise of the new feminist movement in the 1960s, *Muller's* reputation has fallen.

Some critics charged that the decision embedded the notion of female difference in constitutional law, and thereby legitimized treating women differently than men. The principle of sex as a legitimate basis for differentiation provided a rationale for gender discrimination in other areas as well, such as family law. For some feminist critics, *Muller* was not a high point of progressive reform and sociological jurisprudence, but an enormous error that in the long run harmed women far more than it did them any good, and retarded the arrival of a true equality of the sexes in American law.

One cannot deny that both the arguments put forward by Brandeis and Goldmark, and the Court's opinion, viewed women as different from men, and in some respects inferior to them. But discrimination based on gender had been firmly grounded in Anglo-American law long before 1908. Women had been forbidden to own or convey property, to testify in court, to sit on juries, and to vote long before *Muller.* Liberty of contract, that core ingredient of classical legal thought, belonged solely to adult males. The idea that women, especially married women, needed special protection had long been a staple of common law. As for viewing women as inferior, the law had frequently classified women, along with children and mental incompetents, as "persons under a disability" and unable to care for themselves legally.

That the *Muller* decision reaffirmed existing gender biases in the law may be true; that it placed them there is not; and that it raised them to a new high is questionable. The true significance of the case may be less what it said about women than its legitimization of economic regulation of the labor market by the government.

Selected Bibliography

Brandeis, Louis D., assisted by Josephine Goldmark. *Women in Industry.* New York: National Consumers' League, 1908.

Cahill, Marion C. *Shorter Hours: A Study of the Movement Since the Civil War.* New York: Columbia University Press, 1932.

Goldmark, Josephine C. *Impatient Crusader: Florence Kelley's Life Story.* Urbana: University of Illinois Press, 1953.

Johnson, John W. *American Legal Culture, 1908–1940.* Westport, CT: Greenwood Press, 1981.

Semonche, John E. *Charting the Future: The Supreme Court Responds to a Changing Society, 1890–1920.* Westport, CT: Greenwood Press, 1978.

Strum, Philippa. *Louis D. Brandeis: Justice for the People.* Cambridge: Harvard University Press, 1984.

Urofsky, Melvin I. "Myth and Reality: The Supreme Court and Protective Legislation in the Progressive Era." *Yearbook of the Supreme Court Historical Society* (1983): 53–72.

Woloch, Nancy. *Muller v. Oregon: A Brief History with Documents.* Boston: Bedford Books, 1996.

A Supreme Court First:
Equal Protection Applied to Women

—◦—

Nancy S. Erickson
Brooklyn, New York

Reed v. Reed, 404 U.S. 71 (1971) [U.S. Supreme Court]

—◦— THE CASE IN BRIEF —◦—

Date
1971

Location
Idaho

Court
U.S. Supreme Court

Principal Participants
Sally and Cecil Reed
American Civil Liberties Union (ACLU)
State of Idaho
Associate Justice Ruth Bader Ginsberg

Significance of the Case
Reed signaled a judicial tendency, still not fully realized, to require formal legal equality between men and women.

Most cases are brought to the Supreme Court because a litigant believes that he or she has not received a correct decision from a lower court and wants the Supreme Court to rectify that error. However, there is another category of cases—sometimes called test cases—that are handpicked and specially groomed by organizations litigating for broad changes in the law and its application to society. The famous school desegregation case, *Brown v. Board of Education*, was one of these cases. It was the culmination of a two decade-long litigation strategy by the NAACP Legal Defense Fund, which carefully chose each case it took to the Court, and the order in which it took them, to achieve its goals. *Reed v. Reed* was the result of a more modest effort.

In 1970, the American Civil Liberties Union set up a Women's Rights Project, headed by Ruth Bader Ginsburg, a professor at Rutgers Law School (and now a justice on the U.S. Supreme Court), to devise and implement a litigation strategy to pursue equality for women under the equal protection clause of the Fourteenth Amendment. In 1970, that clause had never been used by the U.S. Supreme Court to overturn a law that discriminated on the basis of sex, although state courts and lower federal courts had begun to use it in that way. In fact, existing Supreme Court precedent had consistently upheld sex-based laws on the ground that such laws were valid unless the challenger could show they were not rationally related to valid governmental objectives (the "rational basis" test). Heretofore, the Court had never viewed a sex-based law as irrational.

The "rational basis" test was applied by the Court in almost all equal protection cases. One of the few exceptions to this general rule involved cases in which race-based statutes were challenged as violative of the equal protection clause. To such cases, because race was considered a "suspect classification," the Court applied a more rigorous standard—"strict scrutiny." Strict scrutiny meant that the burden was on the government to demonstrate that the race-based law was necessary (not just rationally related) to the achievement of a compelling (not just valid, but extremely important) governmental purpose. Desegregation laws and virtually all other race-based laws had failed to pass this test.

The ACLU Women's Rights Project (WRP) set out to convince the Court that sex discrimination, like race discrimination, should be judged by the strict scrutiny test. This appeared to be the only way for women to achieve equality under the Constitution, because in the past the outcome of a particular case had always depended on the test applied: if the rational basis test was used, the law would be upheld; if the strict scrutiny test was applied, the law would be invalidated.

The WRP also knew, however, that to convince the Court that race discrimination and sex discrimination are analogous would not be an easy task. After the civil rights movement, courts were prepared to see race discrimination for the evil that it was, but the women's movement had not progressed to the point where society and the courts saw sex discrimination in the same light. Treating women differently

from men was viewed as "natural" or "normal," not as harmful or evil to women (or to men). Women's biological differences from men were seen as valid reasons for the attribution of different sex-based roles to men and women, and these stereotyped roles were the underpinnings of sex-based laws.

For these reasons, the WRP knew that it would have to choose very carefully the cases it would bring to the Court, starting with the most simple, blatant examples of sex discrimination in the law. *Reed* fit that bill perfectly. The case arose after the death in 1967 of Richard Reed, who was survived only by his estranged parents. He left no will and less than $1,000 in property. His mother, Sally Reed, petitioned an Idaho court for appointment as administrator of her son's estate; Richard's father, Cecil, filed a similar petition. The court ordered that Cecil be appointed. The court's order was based not on a finding that Cecil was better qualified than Sally, but rather on a section of the Idaho Code which provided that, of persons related in the same manner to the deceased, "males must be preferred to females." Sally appealed, and the appellate court held that section of the Idaho Code to be in violation of the Equal Protection Clause. But Cecil appealed to the Idaho Supreme Court, which reinstated the original order. Sally then petitioned for a hearing by the U.S. Supreme Court.

It was the perfect case for the WRP to use to initiate its litigation campaign because there appeared to be no reasonable explanation for the statutory distinction between males and females. During the litigation, only two rationales for the law had been identified, and neither could withstand any scrutiny. First, an Idaho court had indicated that the preference for males served the purpose of efficiency, because if two persons of the opposite sex related in the same degree to the deceased both applied to be administrator of the estate, the court could avoid the time and trouble of a hearing to determine which was better qualified by simply preferring the male over the female. This rationale clearly made no sense, because the court could just as easily use any other arbitrary measure, such as preferring the older one or the taller one. The second rationale was enunciated by Cecil Reed in his briefs to the Idaho courts. He argued that giving preference to males was reasonable because "men [are] as a rule more conversant with business affairs than . . . women," and "it is a matter of common knowledge, that women still are not engaged in politics, the professions, business or industry to the extent that men are." This rationale was based on cultural notions of male and female sex roles and did not allow any individual woman to demonstrate that she did not fit the pattern.

The brief presented to the Supreme Court by the WRP was almost seventy pages long, plus a twenty-page appendix of laws similar to the Idaho law. Out of the seventy pages, fewer than ten were devoted to the argument that the Idaho law could not pass the "rational basis" test. The greatest part of the brief developed the argument that sex, like race, should be a "suspect classification" under the law. It supported this argument by offering historical, sociological, and economic data which documented both the traditionally inferior legal status of women in the United States *and* the modern legal trend away from that position. The brief quoted at length from a recent decision of the California Supreme Court, which had explicitly designated sex as a suspect classification and, on that basis, had held a sex-based California statute unconstitutional. The California Supreme Court clearly and eloquently explained its decision to hold sex a suspect classification: "Sex, like race and lineage, is an immutable trait, a status into which the class members are locked by the accident of birth. What differentiates sex from non-suspect statuses, such as intelligence or physical disability, and aligns it with the recognized suspect classifications is that the characteristic frequently bears no relation to ability to perform or contribute to society. . . . The result is that the whole class is relegated to an inferior legal status without regard to the capabilities or characteristics of its individual members. . . .

"Another characteristic which underlies all suspect classifications is the stigma of inferiority and second class citizenship associated with them. . . . Women, like Negroes, aliens, and the poor have historically labored under severe legal and social disabilities. Like black citizens, they were, for many years, denied the right to vote and, until recently, the right to serve on juries in many states. They are excluded from or discriminated against in employment and educational opportunities."

In contrast to the voluminous brief submitted by the WRP, the Court's unanimous opinion is surprisingly short. And its failure to mention the "suspect classification" argument is striking. The Court declined to hold that sex is a suspect classification entitled to strict scrutiny, but it nonetheless held the statute violative of the equal protection clause under the "rational basis" standard. Ignoring Cecil Reed's argument that men are generally better versed in business affairs, the Court addressed only the "efficiency" argument. While conceding that it was a valid legislative purpose, the Court held that the method of achieving that purpose did not pass muster. "To give a mandatory preference to members of either sex . . . merely to accomplish the elimination of hearings on the merits, is to make the very kind of arbitrary legislative choice forbidden by the equal protection clause of the Fourteenth Amendment."

The Court's conclusion—that the statute did not survive the "rational basis" test—was unexpected. Although not an ideal outcome, it was viewed by the WRP as a step in the right direction. In fact, some commentators believed that in *Reed* the Court had formulated a new test, one more rigorous than the old "rational basis" test but less strict than the "strict scrutiny" test. The WRP hoped that the next time the Court was presented with a sex discrimination case, it would take one step farther and declare sex a suspect classification.

Two years later, a plurality of the Court did precisely that in *Frontiero v. Richardson,* but a majority of the Court has never done so. In fact, the Court seems to have settled on a middle level of scrutiny for sex-based classifications since its 1976 decision in *Craig v. Boren.* It appears that the dream of the WRP—that sex would be declared a suspect classification like race—may not be achieved. Nonetheless, the Court's decisions from *Reed* to the present have laid down a general rule requiring formal legal equality between women and men. The exceptions to that general rule are problematic, but the establishment of the general rule is an enormous achievement for American women and men.

Selected Bibliography

Cowan, Ruth. "Women's Rights Through Litigation: An Examination of the American Civil Liberties Union Women's Rights Project, 1971–1976." *Columbia Human Rights Law Review* 8 (1976): 373–412.

Gunther, Gerald. "The Supreme Court 1971 Term, Foreword. In Search of Evolving Doctrine on a Changing Court: A Model for a Newer Equal Protection." *Harvard Law Review* 86 (1972): 1–48.

Sex Discrimination:
Reasonable or Suspect?

—◦—

Elizabeth E. Traxler

Department of Social Sciences
Greenville Technical College

Frontiero v. Richardson, 411 U.S. 677 (1973) [U.S. Supreme Court]

-◦- THE CASE IN BRIEF -◦-

Date
1973

Location
District of Columbia

Court
U.S. Supreme Court

Principal Participants
Sharon Frontiero
Department of Defense
Associate Justice William J. Brennan

Significance of the Case
A gender-discrimination case, the ruling in *Frontiero* did not fully define gender as a "suspect classification" but furthered the movement toward the elimination of sex discrimination in government.

As a resurgent women's movement arose in the 1960s and 1970s, it was inevitable that challenges to the government's treatment of women would arise in the courts as well as in the executive and legislative branches. One of the more significant court challenges to discrimination based on gender was initiated by Sharron Frontiero, a lieutenant in the U.S. Army.

Consider the temerity displayed by a mere lieutenant, breaking ranks to take the Secretary of Defense to court! At issue was a federal statute providing for additional quarters allowance and medical and dental care for dependents of members of the armed forces. The lieutenant's claim of her husband as a dependent for medical and dental benefits had been denied. Though the law allowed all service*men* to claim their wives as dependents without offering any evidence, service*women* were required to prove that their spouses were, in fact, dependent on them for over half of their income. Because Joseph Frontiero, a full-time college student, received $205 a month in veteran's benefits to put toward his $354 expenses, he did not meet the test. Lt. Frontiero sued in federal district court, arguing discrimination on the basis of sex.

Previous legal challenges to gender-specific state laws were generally based on the Fourteenth Amendment's prohibition of a state's denying equal protection of the laws to its residents. Because the statute in question in the *Frontiero* case was federal, this avenue was not open. Instead, the lieutenant's attorneys based their challenge on the due process clause of the Fifth Amendment. Though there is no explicit guarantee of equal protection under the laws in this amendment, previous Court opinions had interpreted due process to include equal protection. Both concepts are tied to the notion of fairness in the government's treatment of individuals. This interpretation was so widely accepted that the Court felt no need to rule on its applicability. Instead, the dispute arose over which test should be used to evaluate the constitutionality of legislation providing for classification based on sex.

This was only the second case claiming gender discrimination to be decided by the U.S. Supreme Court, but there existed a substantial body of opinions relating to other types of discrimination—race being the best known. As the courts had been confronted with a variety of claims of discrimination, they had developed two tests for evaluation purposes. The "rational basis" test found the legislation constitutional as long as the differing treatment served a reasonable purpose. The burden of proof here was on the plaintiff to demonstrate that no such purpose existed. This burden shifted to the government when the "strict scrutiny" or "compelling interest" test was imposed. In this case, the government had to demonstrate that the distinction made on the basis of sex was necessary to fulfill a compelling interest of government.

As the Supreme Court's rulings in other equal protection cases had demonstrated, the choice of test almost invariably determined the outcome of the constitutional challenge. If the Court chose the "rational basis" test, the

statute in question would be upheld. Some reason could almost always be found for the different treatment. On the other hand, a statute subjected to strict scrutiny almost never survived. Therefore, the focus of argument in discrimination cases centered on the test to be employed. The Court, over time, had identified two categories for which the more demanding test would be used. Classifications based on an immutable characteristic bearing little or no relationship to an individual's abilities were labeled "suspect" and subjected to strict scrutiny. At the time of *Frontiero*, the U.S. Supreme Court had identified several such classifications, including race, alien status, and national origin, but not sex. The other use of this test arose when "fundamental rights" were in question. Because economic rights were not so designated, Sharron Frontiero's challenge did not raise this issue, but it asked that sex be labeled a "suspect" classification. If it was successful in this, the odds were high that the law would be held unconstitutional. Even more significant, a whole host of other laws which distinguished between the sexes would fall prey to similar equal protection lawsuits.

The district court, however, in ruling against the Frontieros, argued that the issue was not one which turned on classification by sex. The district court judge noted that other sections of the statute ascribed dependency without relation to gender (minor children, for example) and that, therefore, the treatment varied with relationship to the serviceperson, not in regard to the dependent's sex. Despite this holding, the judge added the opinion that, were sex the determining factor, the differing requirements had a rational basis in providing for administrative efficiency and saving money, and thus would still be constitutional. His choice of a test was clearly the less demanding "rational basis" one.

On appeal to the U.S. Supreme Court, Sharron Frontiero was more successful. In an 8–1 opinion, the Court ruled in favor of the Frontieros. On the paramount question of whether sex would be included as a suspect classification, the Court was less forthcoming. Justice William Brennan, joined by Justices William Douglas, Byron White, and Thurgood Marshall, held sex to be "suspect" and found no compelling interest served by the different treatments mandated in this statute. The other four justices in the majority stopped short of this position and suggested that the issue was before the states with the pending ratification of the Equal Rights Amendment. Legal commentators in the case's aftermath found evidence of a third test evolving for use in sex discrimination cases—one which would demand more than the assumption of a rational basis, but less than a compelling interest. This intermediate standard would require the government to show that the distinction made between the sexes was, in fact, closely related to achieving the underlying goals of the statute. Lieutenant Frontiero's willingness to confront her superiors and the system initiated a period of successful court challenges to many classifications based on gender, albeit fewer than would have been the case if the "strict scrutiny" standard had been applied.

Selected Bibliography

Cole, David. "Strategies of Difference: Litigating for Women's Rights in a Man's World." *Law and Inequality: A Journal of Theory and Practice* 2 (February 1984): 33–96.

Dixon, Joyce. "Case Notes. Constitutional Law—Due Process—United States Supreme Court in Plurality Opinion Names Sex a Suspect Classification Requiring Compelling Interest Test." *Creighton Law Review* 7 (Fall 1973): 69–91.

Matthews, Donna Meredith. "Avoiding Gender Equality." *Women's Rights Law Reporter* 19 (Winter 1998): 127–154.

Walters, Susan Vitullo. "Constitutional Law—*Frontiero v. Richardson.*" *Loyola University Law Journal* 5 (Winter 1974): 295–313.

Wiesenberger, Leslie Dolin. "Recent Case. Constitutional Law—Equal Protection—Discrimination Based on Sex in the Provision of Armed Service Dependents' Benefits." *Case Western Reserve Law Review* 24 (Summer 1973): 824–845.

Law Upheld Guaranteeing Right to Return to Work after Childbirth Leave of Absence

Nancy S. Erickson

Brooklyn, New York

California Federal Savings and Loan Association v. Guerra, 479 U.S. 272 (1987)
[U.S. Supreme Court]

◂◦▸ THE CASE IN BRIEF ◂◦▸

Date
 1987

Location
 California

Court
 U.S. Supreme Court

Principal Participants
 Lillian Garland
 California Federal Savings and Loan
  Association
 State of California
 Associate Justice Thurgood Marshall

Significance of the Case
 The ruling gave women in California
 some limited protection against job loss
 on account of pregnancy.

Sex discrimination is still a major problem in the United States, and one type of sex discrimination—pregnancy discrimination—has proved to be especially difficult to eradicate. The *California Federal* case illustrates some of the complexities of the legal issues involved in pregnancy discrimination cases.

Lillian Garland, a receptionist at California Federal Savings and Loan (Cal-Fed) in Los Angeles, took a leave of absence in January 1982 to have a baby. The child was delivered by cesarean section. When her doctor certified that she was able to return to work in April, she requested reinstatement to her old job, but Cal-Fed informed her that her job had been filled and that there were no positions available for her.

A black single mother, Garland was unable to pay her rent without an income, so she was evicted from her apartment. Then, with no home or resources to care for her child, she lost custody to the child's father. To further complicate matters, her subsequent job-hunting attempts were unsuccessful.

Finally she contacted the California Department of Fair Employment and Housing. She was informed that part of the California Fair Employment and Housing Act required an employer to reinstate an employee returning from pregnancy leave of four months or less to the job she previously held, unless the job was no longer available, in which case the employer was obligated to make a good faith effort to place the employee in a substantially similar job. The California reinstatement provision had been enacted in 1978 as part of a larger statutory scheme designed to remedy pregnancy discrimination in employment, which was not, at that time, prohibited by Title VII of the Civil Rights Act of 1964. Title VII prohibited sex discrimination in employment, but in 1976 the U.S. Supreme Court had ruled that an employer's disability insurance plan's failure to cover pregnancy-related disabilities did not violate Title VII. The Court relied upon a 1975 case which upheld a similar plan against a Fourteenth Amendment attack. In the 1975 case the Court had reasoned that discrimination against pregnant people is not sex discrimination. Not wanting to leave the women in its workforce unprotected against pregnancy discrimination, the California legislature enacted a pregnancy discrimination law which included the reinstatement law. Later in 1978, Congress passed an amendment to Title VII, the Pregnancy Discrimination Act (PDA), thereby superseding much of the California statute, but the reinstatement provision remained.

Because Cal-Fed had failed to comply with the reinstatement law, the state of California brought an action against Cal-Fed on Ms. Garland's behalf. Cal-Fed decided to turn its defensive posture into an offensive one by going into federal court (along with another large employer and the California Chamber of Commerce) to challenge the California law. Cal-Fed claimed that the California reinstatement statute conflicted with the PDA because the federal act required employers to treat men and women the same—not to give women preferential treatment. Cal-Fed argued that if two employees took leaves of absence—one, a man to recover from a heart attack, and the other a woman, to recover from childbirth—the employer would be required to reinstate the woman but not the man. This would be discrimination against men and would violate Title VII's prohibition on sex discrimination. Thus, the California law must be held preempted by Title VII.

The federal district court agreed with Cal-Fed. However, in 1985 the Court of Appeals overturned that decision, reasoning that the PDA does not "demand that state law be blind to pregnancy's existence." The Court of Appeals held that in enacting the PDA, Congress intended "to construct a floor beneath which pregnancy disability benefits may not drop—not a ceiling above which they may not rise."

Cal-Fed appealed the case to the U.S. Supreme Court, which was presented with an unusual array of arguments. Cal-Fed argued, of course, that the California law was preempted by the federal law, and that the state law should therefore by nullified. The American Civil Liberties Union and some feminist lawyers and groups—including the National Organization for Women, the National Women's Law Center, and the Women's Legal Defense Fund—agreed with Cal-Fed that the state law was invalid as written because Title VII prohibits preferential treatment based on sex or pregnancy and supersedes any inconsistent or conflicting state legislation. They based their arguments on what has become known as the "equal treatment" approach, that is, that the most effective way to prevent unfair treatment of pregnant workers is to treat them like others subject to temporary incapacities, not to segregate them for special treatment. Even well-intentioned legislation, they reasoned, pointing to nineteenth- and early twentieth-century "protective" labor legislation, has not served women's interests in equality. However, unlike Cal-Fed, these "friends of the court" argued that the Court should extend the state law to all disabled employees rather than take away the benefits from pregnant employees.

Other feminist groups—such as "9 to 5" (the national association of working women)—and several trade unions supported the California law, even though it applied only to women. Their "special treatment" or "treatment as equals" approach was that although both women and men suffer from most medical conditions, pregnancy and childbirth are medical conditions suffered only by women, and thus harm women's job opportunities while they do not harm men's. Special laws protecting job opportunities for pregnant women are therefore as justifiable as, for example, laws requiring ramps for use by individuals who need wheelchairs. As Marian Johnston, deputy attorney general of California, stated to the Court during oral argument in the *Cal-Fed* case, "It's really irrelevant to male employees whether the employer provides pregnancy benefits. The male employee is going to keep his job when he has children."

Six members of the Supreme Court, in an opinion written by Justice Thurgood Marshall, held that the California reinstatement law was not preempted by federal law because it does not require or permit employers to violate Title VII, as amended by the PDA, and is not inconsistent with the purposes of the federal statute. The PDA, they reasoned, was intended to "provide relief for working women and to end discrimination against pregnant workers. In contrast to the thorough account of discrimination against pregnant workers, the legislative history is devoid of any discussion of preferential treatment of pregnancy, beyond acknowledgments of the existence of state statutes providing for such preferential treatment." Thus, the Supreme Court agreed with the Court of Appeals that Congress intended the PDA to be "a floor . . . not a ceiling," and that the state law was not preempted by the PDA.

As a result of the *Cal-Fed* case, women in California and the two other states with similar laws, Connecticut and Montana, gained some limited protection against job loss on account of pregnancy. However, such "special" laws for women have the potential of leading to backlash that could harm women workers. For example, male employees may become resentful of the benefits that pregnant women receive, and employers may be disinclined to hire women if they know they must provide pregnant women with reinstatement benefits.

The Family and Medical Leave Act, passed by Congress in 1993, avoids these problems. Modeled on an "equal treatment" approach, it supplements the PDA by giving limited reinstatement rights to employees who take a disability leave of absence (up to twenty-six weeks), including women disabled by pregnancy and childbirth. The act goes beyond traditional disability leaves in that it grants a qualified right to an employee to be reinstated after a leave of absence (up to eighteen weeks) for the purpose of caring for a newborn, adopted, or sick child or a seriously ill parent. The act does not require that the leave of absence be paid. Although women still suffer economic losses to bear children, this law helps to decrease those losses.

As an epilogue to the *California-Federal* case, Lillian Garland was hired back by Cal-Fed, but only after she had been unemployed for seven months. "I don't want this to happen to another woman," she said. "What are we supposed to do, have babies, stay home, and go on welfare? That's not me."

Selected Bibliography

Krieger, Linda, and Patricia Cooney. "The Miller-Wohl Controversy: Equal Treatment, Positive Action and the Meaning of Women's Equality." *Golden Gate Law Review* 13 (1983): 513–572.

Rust, Mark. "Maternity Leave Caught in the Crossfire." *American Bar Association Journal* 72 (August 1986): 52–55.

Williams, Wendy. "Equality's Riddle: Pregnancy and the Equal Treatment/Special Treatment Debate." *New York University Review of Law and Social Change* 13 (1984–1985): 325–380.

The Fetus and the Workplace

—<o>—

Philippa Strum
Department of Political Science
Brooklyn College-City University of New York

International Union, United Automobile, Aerospace and
Agricultural Implement Workers of America v. Johnson Controls, 499 U.S. 187 (1991)
[U.S. Supreme Court]

-o- THE CASE IN BRIEF -o-

Date
1991

Location
Vermont

Court
U.S. Supreme Court

Principal Participants
Employees of Johnson Controls
Johnson Controls
Various labor unions
Associate Justice Harry Blackmun

Significance of the Case
The Court banned an employer's sex-specific fetal protection program; the decision also affirmed the right of women to make decisions themselves about the well-being of future children.

The piece of paper Ginny Green received at her job in the Johnson Controls plant in Brattleboro, Vermont, wasn't quite as bad as a pink slip. She wasn't fired, but she had been demoted. She would no longer work on the battery assembly line, as she had been doing for the last eleven years. Now her job title would be "respirator sanitizer"—a position she saw as no better than that of a glorified laundress. Although her basic wage would remain the same, her new job did not permit extra hours. Hence, she would not have the opportunity to receive the time and a half she had been earning for overtime. That extra money was crucial for Ms. Green, then fifty years old, divorced, and supporting a nine-year-old daughter.

Battery assembly line workers were exposed to high levels of lead, and Johnson Controls knew that direct exposure had been found to stunt children's physical and mental development. Very little was known about the ways lead might be transmitted from a pregnant mother to her fetus or, in fact, whether lead in a mother's blood actually endangered a fetus.

The company, nonetheless, had a policy that workers of both sexes had to be informed about the possibility of harm. The policy included this language: "Protection of the health of the unborn child is the immediate and direct responsibility of the prospective parents. While . . . the company can support them in the exercise of this responsibility, it cannot assume it for them without simultaneously infringing their rights as persons."

The company changed its mind about parental responsibility in 1982, the year Ginny Green and other women at Johnson Controls were removed from the assembly line. A new policy now excluded from the line itself, and from any job that might lead to promotion to work on the line, all women "capable of bearing children" except for "those whose inability to bear children is medically documented." The words "capable of bearing children" were defined to apply to all women between seventeen and seventy, which meant women were effectively denied 95% of the company's jobs. Employee Mary Craig, frightened at the economic consequences of having to leave the line, had herself sterilized so she could stay. She eventually would sue Johnson Controls.

The company said that the new policy reflected increased knowledge about the risks associated with lead exposure, the "failure" of voluntary measures, and the lack of less restrictive alternatives that would adequately protect unborn children. Eight Johnson Controls workers with blood levels above those deemed safe by the Occupational Safety and Health Administration (OSHA) had become pregnant. This made the company conclude that its policy of letting women decide for themselves whether they ought to work on the line was not functioning as it had hoped. The company said that it feared suits by employees or by their children who had been exposed to lead as fetuses. Although OSHA had warned that lead at high levels is potentially dangerous to the newborn, whether carried by the mother *or* the father, Johnson Controls' doctors dismissed the evidence about risks of male-to-fetus transmission as too speculative. They chose to be less skeptical about the effects on women, ignoring the experience of one Johnson Controls medical consultant who had treated an estimated fifty thousand workers and their families. He testified that he had encountered only one child with abnormal symptoms whose mother worked on the battery assembly line, and he was not certain that the harm had been caused while the mother was pregnant.

Though "protective" of women, Johnson Controls seemed hostile to male workers concerned about possible effects of exposure to lead. Donald Penney, a mechanic at the company's Wilmington, Delaware, plant, frequently worked in the high-lead areas. When he and his wife decided to start a family, Penney asked for three months' unpaid leave under the company's parental leave policy, so as to be sure their child would not be contaminated. The company turned him down, its personnel director berating him for making the request and telling him to quit. Penney, too, would sue Johnson Controls.

Also signing on as plaintiffs in the suit against Johnson Controls were Mary Craig, Elsie Nason (a woman who had been compelled to leave the battery assembly line), and the employees' union, the United Automobile, Aerospace and Agricultural Implement Workers of America (UAW). The claim was that the company's policy discriminated on the basis of sex in violation of Title VII of the Civil Rights Act of 1964 and the Pregnancy Discrimination Act (PDA).

Women had been entering the work force in large numbers and had been demanding access to all jobs, including those requiring manual labor, since the 1970s. Their decision to do so, frequently a result of economic necessity, ran up against societal stereotypes that saw women as defined by their childbearing capacity and men as defined by their ability to earn money. Ignoring the fact that poorer women had worked in factories for decades, voices now proclaimed that the biological future of the race would be imperiled by the massive entry of women into the workplace and that women, as a result of nature or nurture or some combination of the two, could not be trusted with decisions about the best interests of themselves and their progeny. In addition, information about environmental dangers, coupled with the litigious nature of American society, led to corporate fears of lawsuits by employees claiming that they were harmed in the workplace.

One reaction was the adoption of fetal protection policies by many major American corporations. In 1980, employment experts estimated that one hundred thousand jobs were already closed to women on that basis, and they suggested that something like twenty million positions eventually might be at stake if potential fetal damage became a criterion for exclusion of women. The question of whether sex-specific fetal protection policies were legal was therefore of major concern both to women and to employers.

Though Congress did not have fetal protection in mind when it passed the Civil Rights Act of 1964, it knew that race and sex had operated for years to exclude many Americans both from better-paying jobs and from the workplace in general. Title VII of the act, therefore, prohibited racial, religious, ethnic, and gender discrimination in employment. A narrow exception, however, permitted discriminatory policies "in those certain instances where religion, sex, or national origin is a bona fide occupational qualification [BFOQ] reasonably necessary to the normal operation of that particular business or enterprise." Interpreting that clause, the Supreme Court held in *Griggs v. Duke Power* (1971) that a neutral policy which results in a disparate impact on members of a racial, religious, ethnic, or gender group can be permissible if the employer demonstrates that there is a "manifest relationship" between the policy and the employment in question. In other words, both Congress and the Court had said that legitimate business necessity is a defense against an employment discrimination claim.

In 1976, in *General Electric v. Gilbert,* the Supreme Court declared that an employer's disability benefits plan that compensated employees for temporary disabilities, including elective surgery, but excluded pregnancy-related disabilities, did not violate Title VII. An outraged Congress responded by enacting the Pregnancy Disability Act of 1978 (PDA), which brought policies that deprive women of employment opportunities and benefits on the basis of pregnancy or related medical conditions under the prohibitions of Title VII.

Before the Johnson Controls case reached the Supreme Court, the justices had made it fairly easy for employers to claim a BFOQ. An employment practice did not have to be "indispensable" to the particular occupation to qualify as a business necessity, the Court said in *Wards Cove Packing Co. v. Atonio* (1989), as long as the practice served the legitimate employment goals of the employer in a "significant" way. Johnson Controls would argue that industrial safety was part of the essence of its business, and that its fetal protection policy was reasonably necessary to further that concern.

The federal district court which heard the Johnson Controls case found in favor of the company. It relied on rulings by various circuit courts of appeals which held that policies excluding women from certain jobs were legal, provided employers could show that the jobs in question entailed a significant risk of harm to fetuses, that the hazards were transmitted only through women, and that there were no alternative, less restrictive policies that would minimize the risk to fetal health. The Seventh Circuit Court of Appeals agreed, holding that the policy was a BFOQ. The Supreme Court, however, thought otherwise.

"The bias in Johnson Controls' policy is obvious," Justice Harry Blackmun wrote in 1991 for the unanimous Court: "Fertile men, but not fertile women, are given a choice as to whether they wish to risk their reproductive health for a particular job," in spite of the evidence that potential fathers might be equally affected by exposure to lead. He considered the policy analogous to the one struck down by the Supreme Court in *Phillips v. Martin Marietta* (1971), in which a company excluded mothers, but not fathers, of preschool children from its workforce. Whether or not Johnson Controls acted from benign motives, Blackmun said, the policy discriminated on the basis of sex.

Title VII's BFOQ exception was insufficient to save the policy. The exception applied only to "bona fide occupational qualifications," which Blackmun read as meaning that "permissible distinctions based on sex must relate to ability to perform the duties of the job." Fertile or pregnant women, however, were as capable of performing battery assembly line jobs as were men or infertile women. The Court had held in *Dothard v. Rawlinson* (1977) that, under Title VII, potential danger to a woman herself rather than to others did not justify an employer's decision that she was not qualified for a job. The only acceptable reason for exclusion had to do with the company's ability to conduct business. Blackmun rejected Johnson Controls' contention that protecting fetuses was part of the "essence" of its business.

The PDA required pregnant employees to be "treated the same" as other employees, unless pregnancy interfered with their ability to work. "With the PDA," Blackmun declared, "Congress made clear that the decision to become pregnant or to work while being either pregnant or capable of becoming pregnant was reserved for each individual woman to make for herself." The Court thereby squarely rejected long-standing "protective legislation," laws that kept women out of various jobs, predicated on their supposed inability to make rational decisions for themselves about potentially harmful employment. Such laws had existed in the United States since the late nineteenth century. Obviously troubled by the continuing paternalism and assumption of female irrationality implicit in the Johnson Controls' policy, Blackmun added: "Decisions about the welfare of future children must be left to the parents who conceive, bear, support, and raise them rather than to the employers who hire those parents. . . . Title VII and the PDA simply do not allow a woman's dismissal because of her failure to submit to sterilization." Emphasizing that employers would not be liable for damages if they fully informed their employees about health risks and did not act negligently, Blackmun concluded by announcing a new rule: sex-specific fetal protection policies were illegal under Title VII and the PDA.

Justice Byron White wrote a concurrence for himself, Chief Justice Warren Burger, and Justice Anthony Kennedy which agreed that the company's policy was illegal, but argued that a sex-specific fetal protection policy might qualify for the BFOQ exception if excluding women from a job was necessary to avoid liability for damages. Justice Antonin Scalia, endorsing this concern, added that a company facing substantial expense as a result of hiring pregnant women would have a BFOQ.

Judge Frank Easterbrook had dissented from the Seventh Circuit Court's decision, calling the case "the most important sex-discrimination case in any court" since passage of the Civil Rights Act. The Supreme Court, in banning only sex-specific fetal protection policies, left employers free to adopt sex-neutral safety measures ranging from protective clothing to using less harmful chemicals. At the same time, the Court firmly established the equal right of women to make decisions for themselves about the well-being of any future children while, at the same time, receiving equal treatment in the workplace. That, as Judge Easterbrook recognized, constituted a landmark in the law.

Selected Bibliography

Becker, Mary E. "From *Muller v. Oregon* to Fetal Vulnerability Policies." *University of Chicago Law Review* 53 (1986): 1219–1273.

Helper, Allison L. *Women in Labor: Mothers, Medicine, and Occupational Health in the United States, 1890–1980.* Columbus: Ohio State University Press, 2000.

Kirp, David L. "Fetal Hazards, Gender Justice, and the Justices: The Limits of Equality." *William and Mary Law Review* 34 (1992): 101–138.

Miller, Sheryl Rosensky. "From the Inception to the Aftermath of *International Union, UAW v. Johnson Controls, Inc.*: Achieving Its Potential to Advance Women's Employment Rights." *Catholic University Law Review* 43 (1993): 227–277.

Riffaud, Marcelo L. "Fetal Protection and *UAW v. Johnson Controls, Inc.*: Job Openings for Barren Women Only." *Fordham Law Review* 58 (1990): 843–863.

Williams, Wendy W. "Firing the Woman to Protect the Fetus: The Reconciliation of Fetal Protection with Employment Opportunity Goals Under Title VII." *Georgetown Law Journal* 69 (1981).

Do Women Belong in Military Academies?

———◄◦►———

Philippa Strum
Department of Political Science
Brooklyn College-City University of New York

United States v. Virginia, 518 U.S. 515 (1996) [U.S. Supreme Court]

◄◦► THE CASE IN BRIEF ◄◦►

Date
1996

Location
Virginia
District of Columbia

Court
U.S. Supreme Court

Principal Participants
Government of the United States
State of Virginia
Associate Justice Ruth Bader Ginsburg

Significance of the Case
The ruling admitted women to a formerly all-male military academy.

On November 11, 1839, a teenager named John Logan became the first student to sign the matriculation book at the fledgling Virginia Military Institute (VMI). A century and a half later, in 1989, a female high school senior from northern Virginia asked for an application. VMI declined to send her one, citing the policy that had been in place since 1839: only men need apply.

The men who had applied successfully to VMI included illustrious figures in American history. George Marshall, the five-star general who was at various times Army Chief of Staff, Secretary of State, Secretary of Defense, and the only American military figure to win the Nobel Peace Prize, began his career at VMI. Among other distinguished VMI graduates were Rear Admiral Richard E. Byrd, Jr.; Brigadier General Frank McCarthy, who produced the movie *Patton*; General George Patton himself; and Marine

Corps Commandant General Lemuel C. Shepherd, Jr. There were important civilian alumni as well: Supreme Court Justice Tom Clark, Virginia Governor Harry F. Byrd, Sr., nine Rhodes scholars, and thirty-nine college and university presidents. VMI had graduated so many CEOs and other corporate executives that the *New York Times* described it as "heavily linked to future business success" in Virginia and the nation.

VMI was also tied to the history of the Confederate South. It still celebrated the courage of the young students who fought and died in the Civil War battle at New Market. General Stonewall Jackson taught at VMI until he left to fight in the war; one of Robert E. Lee's sons was a professor there after the war (Lee himself became president of what is now Washington & Lee University, just down the street). Statues of Jackson and Lee have long graced VMI's main quadrangle. The ethos of VMI was that of the Old South: white women required male protection, all women were unsuited to life in the public sphere, and orders from Washington designed to change the way life was conducted in the South were misguided.

VMI's official mission since 1839 had been to produce "citizen-soldiers": individuals who functioned primarily in civilian life but who could be called upon to serve in the nation's armed forces during emergencies. That, in 1839, excluded women. By 1989, however, more than twenty-five years into the women's liberation movement and all the legal changes that it had wrought, some found it outmoded to claim that women could not serve their country as well as men.

Among the people to whom the assertion rang false were attorneys in the Justice Department's Civil Rights Division, who received a letter of complaint from the young woman who had been denied an application to VMI. Women wanted to attend VMI for the same reasons as men: military discipline, leadership training, and access to a powerful alumni network. VMI was a publicly funded institution, and the Civil Rights Act of 1964 prohibited such institutions from discriminating on the basis of sex. The equal protection clause of the Constitution's Fourteenth Amendment ("No state shall . . . deny to any person within its ju-

risdiction the equal protection of the laws") had been held to mean that a state could not offer benefits to only one race or gender without substantial justification. Citing these legal bases, the Justice Department sided with the disappointed female applicant and took VMI to court.

VMI thought the case was by no means clearcut. For one thing, an amendment to the Civil Rights Act permitted colleges that had always been single-sex to remain that way. For another, VMI's proudest tradition was its "adversative method." The method, designed to break entering students down psychologically and rebuild them in the VMI image, included physical rigor, mental stress, absolute equality of treatment, minute regulation of behavior, and such lack of privacy that there were no stalls in bathrooms. The crucial egalitarianism and lack of privacy would be destroyed if women were admitted, VMI claimed. Moreover, it was alleged that women could not manage the adversative system's physically overwhelming demands.

One of VMI's defenses was innovative: it drew on feminist social science, emphasizing the work of Harvard University psychologist Carol Gilligan. Gilligan's 1982 book, *In a Different Voice,* maintained that men and women tend to develop ethical systems in different ways. VMI interpreted her work as evidence that women required a much more supportive educational system than the one it offered. To subject teenage women to the adversative system, VMI said, would be to ignore their real needs and to minimize their learning potential. The Supreme Court had held in *Mississippi v. Hogan* (1986) that single-sex educational institutions could be maintained under the equal protection clause only if there was an "exceedingly persuasive justification" for doing so. The differing educational requirements of men and women, VMI argued, constituted such a justification and made sense out of Virginia's decision to offer men a single-sex college. Virginia did not explain, however, why it had no publicly supported single-sex college for women.

Early litigation in the case resulted in a court decision that the equal protection clause required the state of Virginia to provide women with the same kind of education available to

Virginia Military Institute admitted the first female cadets in the academy's history in 1997 after the exclusion of women had been found unconstitutional by the U.S. Supreme Court. *AP Photos/Steve Helber.*

men at VMI. The state quickly put together a program at a nearby private women's institution, Mary Baldwin College (MBC). Although the program at MBC was designed to produce citizen-soldiers, it eschewed the adversative method and the military lifestyle and discipline that were at the core of the VMI program, substituting what it called "a cooperative method which reinforces self-esteem." VMI was renowned for its engineering programs, but MBC had none; nor did MBC possess faculty, library resources, or physical training facilities comparable to those at VMI.

Both the district trial court and the Fourth Circuit Court of Appeals nonetheless upheld the program as satisfying the demands of the equal protection clause, saying it offered "substantive comparability" to the VMI regimen. The Justice Department promptly appealed to the Supreme Court, contending that the MBC program did not offer a comparable military-style education and was based on "impermissible generalizations and stereotypes" about

women. In petitioning the High Court to overturn the lower courts' rulings, it was joined by groups at the forefront of women's struggle for equality, including the American Civil Liberties Union's Women's Rights Project, the National Organization for Women, the National Women's Law Center, and the Women's Legal Defense Fund. Carol Gilligan expressed outrage at what she labeled the misinterpretation and misapplication of her findings. VMI called the case a Washington power play; feminists saw it as an attempt to undo blatant gender discrimination.

The case arrived at a Supreme Court that had been gender-integrated only since 1981. The two women on the Court at the time of the appeal in *United States v. Virginia* were Justice Sandra Day O'Connor, the author of the Court's opinion in *Mississippi v. Hogan,* and Justice Ruth Bader Ginsburg, a distinguished appellate attorney.

In *Reed v. Reed* (1971) the Supreme Court had held that laws differentiating between men and women had to be based upon a compelling purpose, rather than merely upon traditional assumptions about gender-based abilities. Throughout the 1970s—in such decisions as *Frontiero v. Richardson* (1973), *Weinberger v. Wiesenfeld* (1975), and *Califano v. Goldfarb* (1977)—the Court had interpreted the Constitution as precluding government policies giving different levels of benefits to men and women in the military. And in *Edwards v. Healy* (1975) and *Taylor v. Louisiana* (1975), the Court had ruled unconstitutional laws that established male preference in jury service.

Most of these cases had been argued and won by Ruth Bader Ginsburg prior to her appointment to the Court. Ginsburg, more than any other attorney or author, had persuaded appellate courts that the kinds of "outmoded stereotypes" the Justice Department cited in the VMI case were insufficient justification for unequal legal treatment of women. Ginsburg was appointed to the Supreme Court in 1993. Fittingly, it was Justice Ginsburg who wrote the majority opinion in *United States v. Virginia*.

Ginsburg's goal as an attorney had been to convince the High Court that gender should be treated in a fashion similar to race in American constitutional law. That is, she wanted the courts to declare that any laws based on gender, like laws based on racial categories, were presumptively unconstitutional. The courts had declined to do so. This meant that contested gender-specific state actions were more easily defended than were race-specific laws. One of the questions, as the VMI case reached the Supreme Court, was whether that doctrine should now be changed. Another was whether the kind of difference between the sexes alleged by VMI was a legitimate defense when the differential treatment was supposedly in the best interests of women.

Ginsburg, speaking for herself and six other justices, voted to admit women to VMI. The Court retained *Hogan's* "exceedingly persuasive justification" standard, but did not declare gender, like race, to be a constitutionally "suspect category." Presumably, Ginsburg could not convince a majority to agree to the more expansive standard. But the Court, through Ginsburg, ruled that VMI had failed to meet even the *Hogan* standard in withholding its "extraordinary opportunities for military training and civilian leadership development" from women. The parties agreed that *some* women, like *some* men, might want, and be able to profit from, the adversative method of education. The Court concluded that if the state offered this method of instruction to one gender, it had to offer it to both. Public institutions that had always been single-sex could not remain that way if no truly equal educational opportunity was offered to members of the other sex.

The assumption that women would benefit from being excluded from VMI because they learned differently could not be maintained, Ginsburg continued. She compared VMI's assertion of "gender-based developmental differences" with the way medical "authorities" in the past had justified excluding women from all higher education on the basis of its supposed detrimental effect on their ability to reproduce. "Generalizations about 'the way women are,'" she wrote, "estimates of what is appropriate for most women, no longer justify denying opportunity to women whose talent and capacity place them outside the average description."

That sentence encompasses the notion at the heart of the opinion and the innovation it made in equal protection jurisprudence: the equal protection clause not only prohibits treating *groups* of people unequally but also forbids treating *individuals* unequally on the basis of characteristics of groups. " 'Inherent differences' between men and women," Ginsburg admonished, did not constitute adequate justification "for artificial constraints on an individual's opportunity." Taking note of the great differences between VMI and the MBC program in academic offerings, methods of education, and financial resources, the Court ordered VMI to admit women.

Chief Justice William Rehnquist wrote a concurrence expressing his discomfort with the "exceedingly persuasive justification" standard and arguing for retention of the traditional standard of a program's fulfilling an "important governmental objective." Even under the latter measure, however, he found Virginia's failure to provide equal educational opportunities unconstitutional.

In a stinging dissent, Justice Antonin Scalia chastised the majority for altering "our established standards for reviewing sex-based classifications" and placing no legal importance on "the long tradition, enduring down to the present, of men's military colleges" in the United States. Scalia found nothing in the language of the Fourteenth Amendment specifically forbidding public support for single-sex colleges. He viewed the case as one about the future of governmentally supported single-sex education, as did VMI, rather than about the perpetuation of stereotypes and the provision of equal educational opportunity, as did the Justice Department and the Court's majority. Justice Clarence Thomas recused himself from the case because his son was then a VMI student.

On August 19, 1997, almost 158 years after John Logan entered VMI, Beth Ann Hogan and thirty other women inscribed their names in VMI's matriculation book. A year earlier, after equally contentious litigation, The Citadel in South Carolina had admitted women. The history of single-sex military colleges in the United States, with their assumption that women had no place in the active defense of their country, had ended.

Selected Bibliography

Avery, Dianne. "Institutional Myths, Historical Narratives and Social Science Evidence: Reading the 'Record' in the Virginia Military Institute Case." *Southern California Review of Law & Women's Studies* 5 (1996).

Gilligan, Carol, and Joan E. Bertin. "Opposing All-Male Admission Policy at Virginia Military Institute: Amicus Curiae Brief of Professor Carol Gilligan and the Program on Gender, Science, and Law." *Women's Rights Law Reporter* 16 (1994).

Ginsburg, Ruth Bader. "The Burger Court's Grapplings with Sex Discrimination." In Vincent Blasi, ed., *The Burger Court*. New Haven: Yale University Press, 1983.

Ginsburg, Ruth Bader. "Interpretations of the Equal Protection Clause." *Harvard Journal of Law & Public Policy* 9 (1986).

Kerber, Linda K. *No Constitutional Right to Be Ladies: Women and the Obligations of Citizenship.* New York: Hill and Wang, 1998.

Pressman, Carol, "The House That Ruth Built: Justice Ruth Bader Ginsburg, Gender and Justice." *New York Law School Journal of Human Rights* 14 (1997): 311–337.

Smiler, Scott M. "Justice Ruth Bader Ginsburg and the Virginia Military Institute: A Culmination of Strategic Success." *Cardozo Women's Law Journal* 4 (1998): 541–584.

Protecting Students
from Sexual Harassment

Stephen Lowe
Greenville, South Carolina

Franklin v. Gwinnett County Public Schools, 503 U.S. 60 (1992);
Davis v. Monroe County Board of Education, 526 U.S. 629 (1999)
[U.S. Supreme Court]

◄◦► THE CASE IN BRIEF ◄◦►

Date
1992, 1999

Location
Georgia

Court
U.S. Supreme Court

Principal Participants
Christine Franklin; Gwinnett County
Public Schools; LaShonda Davis;
Monroe County Board of Education

Significance of the Case
Franklin determined that a plaintiff could
recover monetary damages in a sex
discrimination case. *Davis* held that
schools were responsible for sexual
harassment of students by other students
and represented an extension of sexual
harassment law beyond the workplace.

Over the past two decades sexual harassment has been an issue of vital importance in the American workplace. The body of law on sexual harassment has grown considerably, and harassment doctrine has now been extended beyond the workplace. For example, in the 1990s the legal principles of sexual harassment moved into American colleges and into elementary and secondary education.

Under Title IX of the Education Amendments of 1972, sexual discrimination in educational programs and activities is forbidden. Although this legislation was used almost from the beginning as a wedge to improve access for females to school programs, it was not until the 1990s that it began to serve as a means of identifying and punishing the harassment of students. The questions brought forth by the two cases under discussion here allowed the U.S. Supreme Court to interpret and extend Title IX to cover sexual harassment in the public schools.

In 1992, *Franklin v. Gwinnett County* determined that Title IX should permit the recovery of monetary damages in a sex discrimination action. The justices were unanimous, though the reasoning of the majority was not shared by the entire Court. In 1999, *Davis v. Monroe County* held that school boards were responsible for sexual harassment of students by students. This time, however, the decision was a narrow 5-4. Joining a dissent by Justice Anthony Kennedy were Chief Justice William Rehnquist and Associate Justices Antonin Scalia and Clarence Thomas.

Between 1985 and 1989, Christine Franklin attended high school in Gwinnett County, Georgia. In December 1989, she filed a complaint with the U.S. District Court against the school district, alleging that school administrators failed to deal effectively with the ongoing sexual harassment of her by a teacher, Andrew Hill. Among other allegations, Franklin said that Hill had once "forcibly" kissed her and, worst of all, had coerced her to have sexual relations with him in a private office at the school. Although Hill resigned after the school board began an investigation, Franklin alleged that the same school board had tried to discourage her from making the accusations and pressing charges.

The Office of Civil Rights (OCR) of the Department of Education was first to investigate the situation. The OCR determined that Franklin's rights under Title IX had indeed been violated but that subsequent actions by the school district, combined with the resignations of Hill and William Prescott (the other named defendant), brought the school into compliance. For Franklin, the district's belated establishment of a grievance procedure was not enough, and she filed her suit a few months after the OCR made its determination.

The district court dismissed the complaint, and that decision was upheld by the court of appeals. The decisions of the lower courts were based on precedents that did not mandate monetary damages under either Title IX or Title VI of the 1964 Civil Rights Act. The court of appeals, in fact, noted that it would await action by either Congress or the Supreme Court before awarding monetary damages under a Title IX claim. However, a decision from the Third Circuit Court of Appeals conflicted with the Eleventh Circuit opinion, so the time was ripe for a final determination by the U.S. Supreme Court.

Justice Byron White, writing for Justices Harry Blackmun, John Paul Stevens, Sandra Day O'Connor, Anthony Kennedy, and David Souter, held that the "availability of all appropriate remedies" was presumptive unless Congress "expressly" legislated otherwise. In short, if a cause of action existed, it was within the jurisdiction of the federal courts to provide relief. Citing *Marbury v. Madison* (1803) as well as William Blackstone's *Commentaries on the Laws of England,* White noted that the right to a remedy had existed as long as the republic. Attorneys for the Gwinnett County School District, joined by attorneys of the Justice Department, argued that the right had in fact faded away over the years, but White dismissed those arguments quickly.

The respondents argued for affirming the lower courts' decisions because Title IX had been enacted under the spending clause of Article I of the U.S. Constitution. The case of *Pennhurst State School and Hospital v. Halderman* (1981) held that, under the power granted to Congress by the spending clause, unintentional violations should result in limited remedies. The respondents argued that intentional violations should be held to the same standard. White countered that, since "Congress surely did not intend for federal moneys to be expended to support the intentional actions it sought by statute to proscribe," the very idea that intentional discrimination should not be subject to monetary remedy was unfounded.

Justice Antonin Scalia wrote a concurring opinion in which he was joined by Justice Thomas and Chief Justice Rehnquist. Scalia reluctantly concurred with the Court's opinion. Subsequent legislation amending Title IX, he believed, validated the Court's opinion, rather than the notion that a right of action necessarily led to the full judicial remedy.

Seven years following the disposition of the constitutional issue in *Franklin,* the issue of sexual harassment in public schools again came before the Court. This time the situation was more complex, partly because the individuals involved in the accusations of harassment were in the fifth grade. LaShonda Davis, starting in December 1992, was subjected to months of rude and harassing behavior by one of her classmates. The behavior continued through April 1993 and into May, when the boy was charged with sexual battery, a charge to which he pleaded guilty.

Despite informing her teacher, who allegedly informed the school's principal, Bill Querry, no action was ever taken against the alleged harasser, known only as G.F. In fact, G.F. had engaged in his behavior with several girls, and on one occasion a number of them, including LaShonda Davis, tried to see Principal Querry. They were told that "if [Querry] wants you, he'll call you." In fact, G.F. never was disciplined by the school, and it took three months of harassment before LaShonda was even allowed to have her classroom seat moved away from G.F.

Despite the evidence of harassment and the inaction of the school district, the district court dismissed the action because Title IX gave no basis for a private cause of action. In short, because the harassment was "student-on-student," or peer harassment, the court ruled that there was no remedy under Title IX. After a three-judge panel of the Eleventh Circuit Court of Appeals reversed the district court, the entire circuit judiciary, sitting en banc, reinstated the district court ruling.

The Eleventh Circuit's affirmation of the district court's original decision was based on the opinion that legislation passed under the spending clause of Article I must give recipients of federal money "unambiguous notice of the conditions they are assuming when they accept it." Title IX effectively did this with regard to employee-student harassment, but not in regard to student vis-à-vis student harassment. Not all circuits agreed on this issue, however, so as in *Franklin*, the U.S. Supreme Court accepted certiorari to resolve the differences.

The Supreme Court, in a decision written by Justice Sandra Day O'Connor and joined by Justices Stevens, David Souter, Ruth Bader Ginsburg, and Stephen Breyer, decided that the district court had been wrong all along. The Court's decision was qualified, however: only when a recipient of federal funds knows about the harassment and behaves indifferently toward it, and only when the harassment is "so severe, pervasive, and objectively offensive that

it effectively bars the victim's access to an educational opportunity or benefit," could the courts award damages under Title IX.

O'Connor admitted that the only condition for a cause of action against a recipient of federal funds was misconduct by the organization that received the funds. The recipient must discriminate in order to be held liable under Title IX. However, O'Connor agreed with Verna Williams, the attorney for Davis, and noted that the school board was not being held liable for the actions of G.F., but for its own actions in effectively ignoring the boy's long-term harassment of LaShonda Davis. When a funding recipient intentionally ignores its responsibilities under a statute, it can be held responsible. In fact, the Court's earlier decisions, such as *Franklin*, *Gebser v. Lago Vista Independent School District* (1998), and *Pennhurst*, had demanded a high standard of proof for a finding of sexual harassment against a school district. Negligence in itself would not be enough to warrant a holding for damages against a school district if it did not know of the harassment. Only deliberate indifference would cause the courts to take cognizance of the cause of action. The only difference between the Court's earlier decisions and *Davis* was that the harasser was a fellow student, not a school employee. The Court could theoretically have held that the *Gebser* standard would control the current case, but Justice O'Connor was not willing to go quite that far, choosing instead to place conditions on student-student harassment. For instance, Title IX requires that the funding recipient have some authority to remedy the situation. Absent that, they could not be held liable. In addition, Title IX makes it clear that only when the indifference of the recipient creates a situation where discrimination or harassment takes place can the recipient be held liable. Since most of G.F.'s harassing behavior took place in school classrooms, it could hardly be argued that the school did not have control over the situation.

O'Connor took great pains to explain that the majority opinion did not mean that schools would have to expel every accused student immediately to protect themselves against suits for sexual harassment. Nor would ordinary childishness be subsumed under the new standard. The standard, O'Connor repeated, was behavior that was "severe, pervasive, and objectively offensive." "Insults, banter, teasing, shoving, pushing, and gender-specific conduct" would not result in liability for the school: "Damages are not available for simple acts of teasing and name-calling among school children . . . even where these comments target differences in gender." Clearly, G.F.'s harassment of LaShonda Davis went well beyond the typical misbehavior common in school-age children everywhere. His harassment met the standards of severity, pervasiveness, and offensiveness. Furthermore, the evident indifference of the school district to behavior that ultimately led to charges of sexual misconduct against G.F. was enough to hold the district liable.

For Justice Anthony Kennedy, however, the majority opinion was a bitter pill. For Kennedy, the holding in the *Davis* decision presented a serious violation of federalism since it abrogated the rights of federal funding recipients to a clear knowledge of the conditions imposed upon them. What the Court did in its decision amounted to imposing a new condition for receiving federal funds, a condition that was neither explicit nor implied in the original mandate. "The remedial scheme the majority creates today," Justice Kennedy wrote, "is neither sensible nor faithful to Spending Clause principles. . . . The fence the Court has built [to qualify actions under the opinion] is made of little sticks, and it cannot contain the avalache of liability now set in motion."

Discrimination in schools, argued Kennedy, should violate Title IX only if it takes place under the auspices of the federal grant recipient. Mere indifference is not enough to justify a cause of action. Whereas O'Connor had argued that Title IX discrimination could take place "in a context subject to the school district's control," Kennedy countered that "the discrimination must actually be controlled by" the school. While sexual harassment by a teacher at a school would be considered "under" the school's control, harassment by a fellow student would not.

Kennedy also asserted that the majority's attempt to qualify student-on-student harassment as falling under Title IX amounted to "arbitrary line-drawing." To say that sexual harassment liability exists where the school has a "degree of control" over the situation violates not only constitutional principles but the Department of Education's own guidelines as well—at least those the department maintained until 1997. In those guidelines, liability extended only to cover people over whom the school delegated some authority.

Further, the prospective remedy of removing the harasser from the class would lead to unintended problems. Schools would have to hire tutors for individualized instruction or face the possibility of allegations of unfair treatment. Students with behavioral disorders might also come under the Individuals with Disabilities Education Act, which limits the ability of schools to discipline children even if their disorder was not previously diagnosed. Other problems proposed by Justice Kennedy included First Amendment difficulties: sexual harassment in the form of speech could very well be protected.

The most significant aspect of the decision in *Davis,* however, is the continued extension of sexual harassment law beyond the workplace. Although the school district's counsel—and Justice Kennedy—regarded this as a dangerous precedent, G.F.'s actions and the weak or nonexistent efforts of the school district to deal with the harassment indicates that a strong response was necessary in LaShonda Davis's case. Finally, the Supreme Court has enunciated a workable standard to deal with sexually harassing behavior in the nation's schools.

Selected Bibliography

Stein, Nan. *Classrooms and Courtrooms: Facing Sexual Harassment in K-12 Schools.* New York: Teachers College Press, 1999.

Gays and Lesbians

When Consenting Adults Can't:
Privacy, the Law, and Homosexual Conduct

—◄◦►—

Roger D. Hardaway
Department of History
Northwestern Oklahoma State University

Doe v. Commonwealth's Attorney for the City of Richmond, 425 U.S. 901 (1975)
[U.S. Supreme Court]

◄◦► THE CASE IN BRIEF ◄◦►

Date
1976

Location
Virginia

Court
U.S. Supreme Court

Principal Participants
Plaintiff "Doe"
City of Richmond, Virginia

Significance of the Case
The Supreme Court affirmed a lower court decision that refused to extend the right of privacy to persons engaged in homosexual conduct.

Since 1965, the U.S. Supreme Court has issued several landmark decisions in which it has enunciated that a constitutional right of privacy exists in matters of sex and intimacy. Together, these cases stand for the proposition that sexual activity is protected from governmental intrusion and regulation when the participants are consenting adults. The Court, however, has refused to extend that right of privacy to persons engaging in homosexual conduct. States are thus free to enact laws prohibiting homosexual behavior.

In 1975 Virginia had a statute which proscribed anal and oral sex, making the participants in such activity liable to conviction of a felony and subject to imprisonment of one to three years. Two male homosexuals filed suit against local and state authorities, asking for an injunction to prohibit the enforcement of the law and for a judgment that the statute was unconstitutional. The plaintiffs relied primarily upon the U.S. Supreme Court case of *Griswold v. Connecticut*, which had first articulated the right of privacy in 1965. That case had struck down a state statute forbidding the use of contraceptives by married couples. Subsequent Supreme Court opinions on privacy had, among other things, voided laws aimed at punishing the viewing of pornographic materials at home in *Stanley v. Georgia* (1969), the sale of contraceptives to minors in *Eisenstadt v. Baird* (1972), and the performing of most abortions in *Roe v. Wade* (1973).

Many observers believed that the Supreme Court would also rule against laws prohibiting homosexual activity. But, when given the opportunity to do so in 1976, the Court declined, opting to allow a decision of a three-judge federal panel in Virginia to stand as the Supreme Court's position on the matter.

Doe v. Commonwealth's Attorney for the City of Richmond was a 1975 decision of the U.S. District Court for the Eastern District of Virginia. Its 2-1 decision was written by Senior Circuit Judge Albert V. Bryan of the Fourth Circuit, U.S. Court of Appeals. He could find nothing in the statute, he said, which offended the U.S. Constitution.

The *Griswold* decision was not applicable, Judge Bryan asserted, because that case dealt with privacy in a marital situation, and homosexuality "is obviously no portion of marriage, home or family life. . . . If a State determines that punishment [for homosexual activity], even when committed in the home, is appropriate in the promotion of morality and decency, it is not for the courts to say that the State is not free to do so." The Virginia statute in question was justified by the state's police power to pass laws to protect the health, safety, and welfare of its citizens because homosexual "conduct is likely to end in a contribution to moral delinquency."

In a well-reasoned dissent, District Judge Robert R. Merhige, Jr., traced the steps the Supreme Court had taken in outlining the privacy doctrine. "I view those [Supreme Court] cases," he declared, "as standing for the principle that every individual has a right to be free from unwarranted governmental intrusion into one's decisions on private matters of intimate concern. . . . Private consensual sex acts between adults are matters, absent evidence that they are harmful, in which the state has no legitimate interest. To say, as the majority does, that the right of privacy, which every citizen has, is limited to matters of marital, home or family life is unwarranted under the law."

Judge Merhige would have held that homosexual conduct was protected under the Fourteenth Amendment's guarantee that the government cannot deny citizens liberty without due process of law. The majority's opinion, he concluded, had "misinterpreted the issue—the issue centers not around morality or decency, but the constitutional right of privacy."

On appeal, the U.S. Supreme Court affirmed the lower court's decision without comment. Only justices William Brennan, Thurgood Marshall, and John Paul Stevens wanted the Supreme Court to address the issue with its own opinion. Thus, in effect, the Supreme Court upheld the constitutionality of the Virginia statute by a 6-3 vote.

In 1986 the U.S. Supreme Court had the opportunity to overturn *Doe v. Commonwealth's Attorney*. However, it declined to do so, by a 5-4 vote, in the case of *Bowers v. Hardwick*. Once again, the Supreme Court refused to grant constitutional protection to homosexual conduct. As Chief Justice Warren Burger stated succinctly in his concurring opinion: "In constitutional terms there is no such thing as a fundamental right to commit homosexual sodomy."

Justice Harry Blackmun, joined by Justices Brennan, Marshall, and Stevens (the three dissenters in the *Doe* case), objected to the majority's interpretation of the issue. "The Court claims," he wrote, "that its decision today merely refuses to recognize a fundamental right to engage in homosexual sodomy; what the Court really has refused to recognize is the fundamental interest all individuals have in controlling the nature of their intimate associations with others'. . . . Indeed, the right of an individual to conduct intimate relationships in the intimacy of his or her own home seems to me to be the heart of the Constitution's protection of privacy."

Most commentators agree that sex between gays will not be curtailed by laws proscribing such conduct. Nevertheless, even at the beginning of the twenty-first century, states remain free to pass statutes which criminalize homosexual behavior.

Selected Bibliography

O'Neill, Tim. "*Doe v. Commonwealth's Attorney*: A Setback for the Right of Privacy." *Kentucky Law Journal* 65 (1976–1977): 748–763.

Richards, David A. J. "Homosexuality and the Constitutional Right to Privacy." *New York University Review of Law and Social Change* 8 (1978–1979): 311–316.

Sullens, Julia K. "Thus Far and No Further: The Supreme Court Draws the Outer Boundary of the Right to Privacy." *Tulane Law Review* 61 (March 1987): 907–929.

Does the Right to Privacy End Where Sexual Preference Begins?

Stephen Lowe

Greenville, South Carolina

Bowers v. Hardwick, 478 U.S. 186 (1986) [U.S. Supreme Court]

◄◦► THE CASE IN BRIEF ◄◦►

Date
  1986

Location
  Georgia

Court
  U.S. Supreme Court

Principal Participants
  Michael Hardwick
  Michael J. Bowers
  American Civil Liberties Union (ACLU)
  Associate Justice Byron White

Significance of the Case
  In another setback for gay rights, the Court ruled that a Georgia law banning sodomy did not violate the right of privacy.

In 1968, the state of Georgia enacted a criminal sodomy statute that translated the language of the previous statute of 1861 into modern parlance. Instead of "unnatural copulation," sodomy was now "any sexual act involving the sex organs of one person and the mouth or anus of another." The act was passed a mere three years after the Supreme Court's decision in *Griswold v. Connecticut*, which guaranteed the privacy of the marital bed. Although Georgia never claimed that the purpose of its 1968 statute was to single out homosexual activity, the fact that the Court had ruled on marital privacy seemed to indicate that gay sex was what Georgia officials had in mind to proscribe. As of the early 1980s, there had been no prosecution for sodomy in the Peach State since the 1930s or 1940s.

In early August 1982, an Atlanta police officer, attempting to serve a warrant on Michael Hardwick in his apartment, observed Hardwick and a male companion engaging in oral sex. The officer arrested Hardwick and his companion and took them to police headquarters.

Although worried about violent reprisals, Hardwick agreed to an offer of the American Civil Liberties Union (ACLU) to represent him in an action to test the legality of the Georgia sodomy law. Hardwick did not face prosecution for his alleged crime because the district attorney had not submitted the case to the grand jury and had no intention of doing so. However, Hardwick was willing to risk public scrutiny and physical jeopardy by initiating the challenge to the Georgia law himself. With the help of the ACLU, he sued the Atlanta police commissioner, the prosecutor who had refused to prosecute, and the state Attorney General, Michael J. Bowers.

At the trial, presiding Federal District Judge Robert Hall relied on the 1975 case of *Doe v. Commonwealth's Attorney* to grant the motion of the defendants to dismiss the case. In *Doe*, a three-judge panel had held that a sodomy statute in Virginia was constitutional. Hardwick appealed Judge Hall's ruling, and the U.S. Supreme Court agreed to hear the case. Unfortunately for Michael Hardwick and the ACLU, the result in *Bowers v. Hardwick* would mirror the earlier Virginia case.

Oral arguments in the case took place in March 1986, three and a half years after Hardwick's arrest in Georgia. Attorney General Michael Hobbs opened his argument for the state of Georgia by asserting that there could be no right of homosexuals to engage in sexual relations. The Court's previous decisions in the realm of privacy law had always dealt with marriage and procreation. An expansion of those rights to include homosexual sodomy, Hobbs maintained, would be anathema to legal precedent.

Further, Hobbs contended that opening the door for homosexual sodomy would call into question statutes dealing with "polygamy; homosexual, same-sex marriage; consensual incest; prostitution; fornication; adultery; and possibly even personal possession in private of illegal drugs." Recognizing the right of gay men to be sexually intimate, he argued, could destroy the right of Georgia "to maintain a decent society."

Laurence Tribe, a professor of law at Harvard, argued the appeal on behalf of Michael Hardwick. Presenting a case for liberty over morality, Tribe asserted that if government could outlaw certain types of homosexual intimacy because those involved were unmarried, it could go even further and outlaw caressing or kissing between unmarried people. Tribe also appealed to the notion of limited government: "If liberty means anything it means that the power of government is limited in a way that requires an articulated rationale by government for an intrusion on freedom as personal as this." If government is going to tell individuals how to behave and what they can and cannot do in their own homes, it must have a reason other than the morality of a political majority for it.

By the narrowest of constitutional margins, the Supreme Court ruled 5-4 that Georgia's sodomy law did not violate rights of privacy that the Court had been struggling to elaborate over the past twenty years. Justice Byron White, writing for a majority consisting of Associate Justices Lewis Powell, William Rehnquist and Sandra Day O'Connor, and Chief Justice Warren Burger, narrowly construed the question before the Court. The Supreme Court was not being asked to rule on the issue of privacy, but on the issue of homosexual conduct. "The issue . . . is whether the Federal Constitution confers a fundamental right upon homosexuals to engage in sodomy."

Sodomy, White argued, did not meet the standard for greater protection. Citing *Palko v. Connecticut* (1937) and *Moore v. East Cleveland* (1977), he concluded that sodomy was not a "fundamental liberty . . . implicit in the concept of ordered liberty," nor was the practice "deeply rooted in this Nation's history and tradition." White feared that the Court would be engaging in "judge-made constitutional law having little or no cognizable roots in the language or design of the Constitution" if the justices found in favor of Hardwick and overturned Georgia's sodomy law. Finally, White concluded his brief opinion with an appeal to morality. Tribe had argued on Hardwick's behalf that even if the Court could not find that a fundamental right existed, the Georgia law failed to meet a "rational basis" standard. The justification for such a law, Tribe asserted, could not depend solely on the moral stance of a majority of the population. White countered: "Law . . . is constantly based on notions of morality."

Two dissents were filed. Justice John Paul Stevens, joined by Justices William Brennan and Thurgood Marshall, published a brief dissent in which he addressed and rejected the "selective application" that the Georgia law seemed to require. Since the state could not totally forbid the kind of behavior in question, only a neutral interest in prohibiting sodomy could justify the continued existence of the law. Indeed, because the Georgia legislature did not single out homosexuals in the first place, neither could the Court.

A much longer dissent, written by Justice Harry Blackmun and joined by the other three dissenters, expanded on the basic theme of the case as laid out by Justice White. The case was not simply about the right of gay men to engage in sexual activity that the state defined as sodomy. Quoting with favor Louis Brandeis's dissent in *Olmstead v. United States* (1928), Blackmun argued that *Bowers* was about "the most comprehensive of rights and the right most valued by civilized men . . . the right to be let alone."

Blackmun's dissent chided the Court majority for its "obsessive focus on homosexual activity." Contrary to Blackmun's view, the statute in fact did not single out homosexual activity, but included all persons who might engage in such acts. Sexual orientation should not enter into the case: either the statute was constitutional, or it was not. Blackmun argued that it was not, because it interfered with the right to privacy. Privacy law had developed along two different lines: personal decisions and personal space. *Bowers*, in Blackmun's opinion, was problematic because it impeded the right to privacy in both spheres.

Privacy inheres in the individual, not in the family. If the rights of married couples are to be protected, as they were in *Griswold v. Connecticut*, it was not, according to Blackmun, because of a "social project," but because of the importance of the individuals in the marriage. If families were to be protected, it was not because of a "preference for stereotypical households,"

but because family life is essential to individual well-being. Thus, when sexuality enters the picture, it is not as something foreign to the happiness of the individual, but as something essential to being an individual. In refusing to overturn the Georgia sodomy law, Blackmun charged, the majority abrogated the right of all individuals to exercise control over "the nature of their intimate associations."

The right of individuals to be secure in their homes was also a key element of the Blackmun dissent. The right to privacy that the Court had developed since *Griswold* depended on the sanctity of the home. Whereas Justice White had argued that Hardwick was pressing for a right with no "support in the text of the Constitution," Blackmun believed that "the right of an individual to conduct intimate relationships in the privacy of his or her own home [was] the heart of the Constitution's protection of privacy."

Blackmun had already mounted a tough challenge to the majority opinion, but he went on to address the moral issues raised in White's opinion. The state, Blackmun said, must have some justification for law other than religion. The idea that "traditional Judeo-Christian values" alone could justify Georgia's sodomy law was akin to giving the state power to punish conduct because of race. Georgia's law, and the Court's affirmation of that law, threatened the nation's values to a "far greater" degree "than tolerance of nonconformity could ever do."

Despite the two stinging dissents, a slim majority was still a majority. *Bowers* established the principle that a state could criminalize intimate behavior if a political majority of the people believed that behavior was immoral. Standards designed to subject laws tending to abrogate the rights of certain classes of citizens to strict scrutiny could not apply to laws against gays. The *Bowers* decision was a stunning setback for gay rights when it was issued. Despite such later qualified victories as *Romer v. Evans* (1996), the rights of gays and lesbians are still unrecognized by many states and the federal government. The U.S. military's "don't ask, don't tell" policy, ostensibly a protection for gay and lesbian soldiers, merely perpetuates discrimination. Continued violence against gay men and lesbians makes it clear that a great deal more progress has to be made in this area of constitutional rights.

Interestingly, Justice Powell added a concurring opinion to the majority decision by Justice White. In it, he intimated that Hardwick and others facing prosecution for sodomy could invoke their Eighth Amendment protections against cruel and unusual punishment. The maximum twenty-year prison term for this particular crime specified by the statute seemed to him to be excessive. However, because Hardwick had not been tried, that issue was not before the Court. In 1990, three years after his retirement from the bench, Powell stated that he had initially sided with the minority in *Bowers*, but that he had changed his mind before the decision. He admitted then that he had "probably made a mistake."

In November 1998, the Georgia Supreme Court did what the U.S. Supreme Court had not done twelve years earlier. In a 6-1 decision, it struck down the 1968 sodomy law because it violated the right to privacy guaranteed under the state constitution. Overturning a decision the Georgia Supreme Court had made only two years earlier, the justices found that moral disapproval was not enough to legitimate the state law. The case had begun as one of heterosexual sodomy, but it was applied to everyone who might be subject to the law. Only one month earlier, a Maryland circuit court overturned that state's sodomy law on the grounds that the law violated the equal protection clause of the Fourteenth Amendment to the U.S. Constitution. Most recently, an Arkansas circuit court ruled that a case challenging that state's sodomy law could go forward. Arkansas is one of few states whose criminal sodomy statute targets only same-sex couples. Challenges to criminal sodomy statutes in Texas and Puerto Rico also are pending.

Some have argued that the 1996 case of *Romer v. Evans* effectively overruled *Bowers*. However, it seems likely that the U.S. Supreme Court will once again have to assume its role as final arbiter before the rights of gays and lesbians to intimate associations can be clarified.

Selected Bibliography

Cain, Patricia A. "Litigating for Lesbian and Gay Rights: A Legal History." *Virginia Law Review* 79 (October 1993): 1551–1641.

Gerstmann, Evan. *The Constitutional Underclass: Gays, Lesbians, and the Failure of Class-Based Equal Protection*. Chicago: University of Chicago Press, 1999.

Goldstein, Anne B. "History, Homosexuality, and Political Values: Searching for the Hidden Determinants of *Bowers v. Hardwick*." *Yale Law Journal* 97 (1988): 1073–1103.

Hayes, John Charles. "The Tradition of Prejudice Versus the Principle of Equality: Homosexuals and Heightened Equal Protection Scrutiny After *Bowers v. Hardwick*." *Boston College Law Review* 31 (March 1990): 375–475.

"Animus" or Moral Justification?:
Anti-Gay Laws and Equal Protection

—◄◦►—

Stephen Lowe

Greenville, South Carolina

Romer v. Evans, 517 U.S. 620 (1996) [U.S. Supreme Court]

◄◦► THE CASE IN BRIEF ◄◦►

Date
1996

Location
Colorado

Court
U.S. Supreme Court

Principal Participants
Roy Romer, Governor of Colorado
Richard Evans and co-defendants
Associate Justice Anthony Kennedy

Significance of the Case
The Court overturned an amendment to the Colorado constitution that prohibited the passage of laws granting special consideration to homosexuals, ruling that it denied equal protection to gays.

In 1977, Aspen, Colorado, passed an ordinance that protected the city's gay citizens, an important interest group, from discrimination in a number of areas of social and political interest. Ten years later, Boulder, the home of the University of Colorado, passed a similar ordinance, and in 1991 Denver, the state's capital and largest city, followed suit. The several city ordinances banned discrimination against gay men and women in housing, employment, education, and public accommodations.

Soon after the passage of the Denver ordinance, and in response to a proposed similar enactment in Colorado Springs—probably the most conservative city in the state—a group calling itself Colorado for Family Values pushed for a countervailing ballot initiative. Arguing that they stood for the idea that gays and lesbians should not receive special rights, the members of this Colorado Springs–based group championed an initiative that came to be known as "Amendment Two." The amendment, if passed and put into effect, would have invalidated all the protective ordinances already enacted and would have prevented any political entity in the state of Colorado from passing any new laws that would allow gays, lesbians, or bisexuals to claim discrimination. The amendment passed in the fall 1992 general election.

In anticipation of the passage of Amendment Two, a group of civil rights activists calling itself CLIP (Colorado Legal Initiatives Project) had been plotting a responsive strategy. Nine days following the passage of Amendment Two, CLIP filed a complaint in a state court in Denver. The state judge granted an injunction preventing Amendment Two from taking effect until the state supreme court could review the law. Shortly thereafter, the same judge ruled the amendment unconstitutional. The state appealed to the Colorado Supreme Court. After Colorado's highest court ruled against the state, the case was appealed to the U.S. Supreme Court.

Five justices joined Justice Anthony Kennedy in the majority opinion in *Romer v. Evans*. Justice Antonin Scalia filed a scathingly sarcastic dissent in which he was joined by Chief Justice William Rehnquist and Justice Clarence Thomas. Kennedy's majority opinion found that Amendment Two was indeed unconstitutional. However, whereas the state supreme court ruled that the amendment constituted a denial of access to the political process, Justice Kennedy for the Supreme Court majority found that Amendment Two had attempted to impose a denial of equal protection on a much broader scale. Amendment Two, he concluded, violated the rights of gays and lesbians to a protection against arbitrary discrimination in both the public and the private arenas. Without judicial intervention, the only recourse that gays and lesbians would have had in the face of Amendment Two would have been to amend the state constitution.

Kennedy found that Amendment Two did not meet constitutional requirements of reasonableness: "It is at once too narrow and too broad. It identifies persons by a single trait and then denies them protection across the board." Such a legal enactment, Kennedy stated, was "unprecedented" in the history of the Supreme

Court. Equally important to Kennedy's argument was the sad reality that the amendment was motivated by "animosity toward the class of persons affected." The only conclusion left for the Court to make was that Amendment Two's purpose was not to "further a proper legislative end but to make [gays and lesbians] unequal to everyone else. This Colorado cannot do."

Justice Antonin Scalia, the most conservative member of the Court, did not agree. He believed that Colorado had every right to pass Amendment Two, and he shared his opinion in a biting dissent. "The Court has mistaken a *Kulturkampf* for a fit of spite," he began, and went on to contend that Amendment Two represented an effort by "tolerant Coloradans to preserve traditional sexual mores." He asserted that the "prestige" of the Court was at stake: the majority had insinuated that prejudice on the basis of sexual preference was as bad as racism or religious animosity. With that he could not agree. Scalia adopted the argument of the Family Values group that the intent of the Amendment was merely to prevent special treatment for homosexuals.

Scalia went further, however, and next met the "rational basis" question head-on. Because *Bowers v. Hardwick* had not been overturned in the majority opinion, Scalia was left with a paradox: If a state can criminalize homosexual conduct, as the High Court ruled it could do in *Bowers*, why could a state *not* enact laws that did not go nearly as far as criminalizing that same conduct? Scalia thought the argument that supported such a paradoxical conclusion was weak at best. If the Court thought it rational to criminalize a certain conduct, Scalia maintained, it should have no difficulty with a measure that denied "special favors" to those with a "tendency or desire" to engage in such conduct. Scalia's argument, however, depended on his interpretation of the local ordinances. He, along with Colorado for Family Values, accepted the idea that by preventing discrimination based on sexual orientation, the local laws granted special favor to gays and lesbians just because of their sexuality.

After attacking the "rational basis" argument, Scalia turned to what he characterized as the "eminently reasonable" nature of Amendment Two. Comparing homosexuality to the constitutionally banned practice of polygamy, Scalia argued that there was nothing essentially un-American in anti-gay animus. "Hate," he said, was not part of "our moral heritage," but to consider some conduct "reprehensible" and thus subject to legal sanction—and here he mentioned murder, polygamy, and cruelty to animals—was certainly part of American tradition. The Court's decision, Scalia concluded, was ultimately "an act, not of judicial judgment, but of political will."

In the final analysis, the Supreme Court did not go so far as to guarantee gays and lesbians equal protection. The Court implied that anti-homosexual legislation was not, on its face, suspect. Contrary to legislation that discriminated against racial, ethnic, or religious minorities, legislation discriminating against gays and lesbians could be found constitutional if a legitimate, rational basis for such enactments could be found. On the other hand, the Court went much farther than many on the political right would have wished them to go. As a result of the majority opinion in *Romer v. Evans*, gays and lesbians can now utilize the political process to pass laws that protect their rights without fear of political reprisal through initiatives like Amendment Two.

Selected Bibliography

Eskridge, William N., Jr. "Democracy, Kulturkampf, and the Apartheid of the Closet." *Vanderbilt University Law Review* 50 (March 1997): 419–443.

Gerstmann, Evan. *The Constitutional Underclass: Gays, Lesbians, and the Failure of Class-Based Equal Protection.* Chicago: University of Chicago Press, 1999.

Hamill, Katherine. "*Romer v. Evans*: Dulling the Equal Protection Gloss on *Bowers v. Hardwick.*" *Boston University Law Review* 77 (June 1997): 655–685.

Keen, Lisa, and Suzanne Goldberg. *Strangers to the Law: Gay People on Trial.* Ann Arbor: University of Michigan Press, 1998.

Witt, Stephanie L., and Suzanne McCorkle, eds. *Anti-Gay Rights: Assessing Voter Initiatives.* Westport, CT: Praeger Publishers, 1997.

Americans with Disabilities

"Three Generations of Imbeciles Are Enough"

—◄o►—

William Lasser
Department of Political Science
Clemson University

Buck v. Bell, 274 U.S. 200 (1927) [U.S. Supreme Court]

◄o► THE CASE IN BRIEF ◄o►

Date
1927

Location
Virginia

Court
U.S. Supreme Court

Principal Participants
Carrie E. Buck
Mr. Bell, Superintendent of the State Colony for Epileptics and the Feeble-Minded
Associate Justice Oliver Wendell Holmes Jr.

Significance of the Case
The Supreme Court upheld the legality of a state law that allowed the mentally retarded to be sexually sterilized without their approval.

There are few more pathetic figures in the history of American law than Carrie E. Buck. After classifying her as "feeble-minded" in the mid-1920s, the state of Virginia committed her to a state hospital and then ordered that she be sexually sterilized—ostensibly for her own good and for the good of society. In 1927, this sterilization order was upheld by the U.S. Supreme Court: "Three generations of imbeciles," concluded Justice Oliver Wendell Holmes, "are enough."

Carrie Buck endured a miserable childhood. Her father, Frank Buck, left (or perhaps died) when she was an infant. Her mother, Emma Buck, led a dismal life of poverty and prostitution. When Carrie was three, she was taken in as a ward of J. T. and Alice Dobbs. Though Mr. and Mrs. Dobbs regarded their "adoption" of Carrie as an act of kindness, they treated the young girl poorly and never accepted her as a member of the family. After the sixth grade, they removed Carrie from school "to help with the chores at home."

Carrie's lot in life went from bad to worse when, at the age of seventeen, she became pregnant (according to her account, she had been raped by one of the Dobbses' nephews). When the Dobbses discovered the pregnancy, they turned Carrie out of the house and asked a local court to declare her "feeble-minded within the meaning of the law." The court agreed, and resolved to commit Carrie to the state Colony for Epileptics and Feeble-minded in Lynchburg, Virginia, where Carrie's mother was also an inmate. Carrie entered the facility shortly after the birth of her child; ironically, the Dobbs family took Carrie's baby into their home.

The doctors at Lynchburg had no doubts about Carrie's medical and mental condition: "[S]he is feeble-minded of the lowest grade Moron class," concluded Dr. Albert Priddy, the facility's superintendent. "Her mental age is nine years, or of the average child of nine years." Priddy believed that Carrie was "capable of earning her own living," but because she was "morally delinquent" and because "the baneful effects of heredity will be shown in descendants of all future generations," he recommended that she be sexually sterilized.

Virginia law set out clear procedures to be followed before inmates of state institutions could be involuntarily sterilized. The law required that the operation be approved by the hospital's board of directors, and gave the inmate (or her guardian) the right to appeal both to the state circuit court and to the Virginia Supreme Court. Still, there were questions about the constitutionality of the procedure, and Carrie Buck was chosen as the test case.

Neither the hospital board nor the two state courts had any difficulty concluding that Carrie Buck should be sterilized. Nor, ultimately, did the U.S. Supreme Court. In a four-page opinion by Justice Holmes, the Court concluded that the state's actions violated neither the due process clause nor the equal protection clause of the Fourteenth Amendment. The procedures required under the Virginia statute were more than adequate to protect the inmate's due process rights, and the equal protection clause claim—which was based on the different treatment accorded to inmates in state institutions and those living on the outside—were baseless: "The law does all that is needed when it does all that it can," Holmes wrote.

However misguided *Buck v. Bell* might seem in light of modern understandings of disability, Holmes's majority opinion in the case was consistent with his overall interpretation of the Constitution. The "Yankee from Olympus" favored giving the states wide discretion to adopt policies designed to meet social ills. A year later, Holmes's colleague Louis D. Brandeis cited *Buck v. Bell* as standing for the principle that the government is not prohibited "from meeting modern conditions by regulations which, 'a century ago, or even half a century ago, probably would have been rejected as arbitrary and oppressive.'"

There is no doubt, however, that the case was made easier for the justices because they agreed wholeheartedly with the science (or pseudoscience) on which it was based. As Holmes put it, "It is better for all the world if, instead of waiting to execute degenerate offspring for crime or to let them starve for their imbecility, society can prevent those who are manifestly unfit from continuing their kind." Unfortunately, by legitimating these views, the Court's opinion helped solidify support for both the theory and the practice of eugenics, in this country and abroad—most tragically, of course, in Nazi Germany.

Fifteen years after *Buck v. Bell*, however, in *Skinner v. Oklahoma*, the Court invalidated the Oklahoma Habitual Criminal Sterilization Act on equal protection grounds. Although *Skinner* did not explicitly overrule *Buck*, Justice William O. Douglas's majority opinion made it clear that the tide was turning. In language that would form the basis of the Court's later decisions on contraception and abortion, Douglas wrote: "We are dealing here with legislation which involves one of the basic civil rights of man. Marriage and procreation are fundamental to the very existence and survival of the race."

Although *Buck v. Bell* is still technically the law of the land, the constitutional status of laws permitting the sterilization of the mentally retarded is unclear. The Supreme Court held in 1985 that the mentally retarded are not a "suspect" or "quasi-suspect" class for equal protection purposes, but nonetheless indicated that states would have to justify carefully any laws aimed at such individuals. In the same year, the state of Virginia provided a modest settlement to some 8,300 men and women who had been sterilized under the law used in the case of Carrie Buck. But a 1976 case revealed that involuntary sterilization laws are not dead: "In rare and unusual cases," a federal court in North Carolina concluded, "it can be medically determined that involuntary sterilization is in the best interests of either the mentally retarded person or the State or both." The specter of poor Carrie Buck still haunts American constitutional law.

Selected Bibliography

Krais, William A. "Note and Comment. The Incompetent Developmentally Disabled Person's Right of Self-Determination: Right-to-Die, Sterilization and Institutionalization." *American Journal of Law and Medicine* 15 (1989): 333–361.

Smith, J. David, and K. Ray Nelson. *The Sterilization of Carrie Buck: Was She Feebleminded or Society's Pawn?* Far Hills, NJ: Far Horizons Press, 1989.

School Medical Services for Children with Disabilities

—◄◦►—

Larry D. Bartlett

College of Education
University of Iowa

Irving Independent School District v. Tatro, 468 U.S. 883 (1984);
Cedar Rapids Community School District v. Garret F., 526 U.S. 66 (1999)
[U.S. Supreme Court]

◄◦► THE CASE IN BRIEF ◄◦►

Date
1984, 1999

Location
Texas
Iowa

Court
U.S. Supreme Court

Principal Participants
Amber Tatro, a minor child; Irving Independent School District; Garret F., a minor child; Cedar Rapids Community School District; Members of the Supreme Court

Significance of the Case
In separate rulings fifteen years apart, the Supreme Court held that school districts were required to provide certain services that would allow physically handicapped children to attend school.

Two court decisions, rendered fifteen years apart, represent the U.S. Supreme Court's principal efforts to interpret a single statutory phrase. The first ruling was not well accepted by public schools, and, partly in consequence, the lower courts differed substantially on what the Supreme Court had meant. In the late 1990s, the issue came before the Court a second time for clarification.

In 1975, Congress enacted the Education for All Handicapped Children Act. Fifteen years later the name of the legislation was changed to the Individuals with Disabilities Education Act (IDEA). Under its terms, children with disabilities who needed assistance in obtaining an education were to be provided with a "free appropriate public education" (FAPE). A FAPE consisted of both special education and "related services" as determined by a team consisting of educators and the child's parents. The term "related services" was defined to include any supportive service required to help the child with a disability to benefit from his or her special education programming. Examples of required related services were physical and occupational therapy, rehabilitation counseling, and transportation. The most controversial among the services required have been those of a medical nature. The statutes and their supporting regulations required the provision of "school health services . . . by a qualified school nurse, or other qualified person," and the services of a licensed physician for the sole purpose of diagnosing and evaluating a child's medical disability.

Shortly after the initial implementation of the statute and its subsumed regulations, a number of legal disputes arose around the country which focused on the extent of school health services required by law for students with disabilities who were in an educational program. Many public schools resisted the concept that they would have to provide some students with medical services.

The first Supreme Court review of the medical services issue occurred in *Irving Independent School District v. Tatro* (1984). That case involved an eight-year-old girl born with spina bifida who had a number of impairments, including a neurogenic bladder, which prevented her from emptying her bladder voluntarily. Consequently, she needed a procedure known as a clean intermittent catheterization (CIC) every three to four hours, including the time she was in school. The CIC procedure involves the insertion of a catheter into the urethra to drain the bladder, and can be performed by a lay person with minimal training. The girl's school developed a FAPE which provided her with an education program and services, but did not include CIC for the girl. The girl's parents unsuccessfully sought to persuade the school to provide CIC during school hours. Failing this, they tried to obtain a court order requiring the school to provide that service.

A series of lower federal court rulings determined that CIC was a "related service" under the IDEA. Upon appeal, the U.S. Supreme Court concluded that the provision of CIC enabling the girl to attend school was a supportive service that must be provided by the school in order for her to benefit from special education. Second, the Supreme Court concluded that CIC was a school health service required under the IDEA to be provided to the girl while she was at school. Because CIC was a school health service similar to other services which may be prescribed by a physician and carried out by a school nurse—such as the administration of medications and injections—the Court was in unanimous agreement that CIC was required as a related service under the IDEA. The Court determined that medical services requiring a licensed physician, except for diagnosis and evaluation, were not services that schools should be required to provide for students with disabilities.

The Court attempted to soften its ruling by identifying several limitations to the requirement of school-provided health services for children with disabilities. First, it stated that entitlement must be based on a child's disability which requires special education; second, it determined that only those services necessary to allow a child to benefit from special education are required to be provided; and third, it submitted that services of a medical nature must be furnished only if they can be provided by a nurse or other qualified person, and not if they must be performed by a physician.

Unfortunately, in attempting to explain the legal distinction between the services of a school nurse and those of a physician, the Court used language which later became the basis of confusion among lower courts. The Court explained that, in enacting the related services requirement, Congress and the executive branch of the government acted reasonably in distinguishing between physician-provided medical services, other than diagnosis and evaluation, and medical and health services provided by nurses. The Court speculated that differences in costs and complexities of services "could" have been the reason for excluding the treatment services of a physician as a "related service" under the IDEA. The Court did not expressly say that cost and complexity were the reasons for the legislative distinction.

A number of subsequent lower court decisions took this Supreme Court digression from the facts in *Tatro* as a springboard to allow schools to use considerations of expensive and complicated medical services as a limitation on a school's obligation to provide related services under the IDEA. For example, in *Detsel v. Board of Education* (1989), the Second Circuit Court of Appeals upheld a district court ruling that a seven-year-old child with severe disabilities that presented potential life-threatening respiratory distress was not entitled to school medical services as a related service, even though the services of a physician were not required. The district court decision relied upon the Supreme Court's reference to costly and complex medical procedures as a justification for excluding extensive medical services from the definition of related services. Several subsequent court decisions expressly followed the *Detsel* ruling and concluded that in *Tatro* the Supreme Court had approved considerations of cost and complexity in the determination of whether a school medical service must be provided as a related service under the IDEA.

A shorter line of decisions remained faithful to the Supreme Court precedent in *Tatro* and based its determination of whether school-provided medical services were required solely on the question of whether or not a physician's services were necessary. In *Macomb County Intermediate School District v. Joshua S.* (1989), this distinction was referred to by a federal district court in Michigan as the "bright line" test, meaning that public schools were not responsible under the IDEA for medical services performed by a physician, except for diagnosis and evaluation, but were responsible for medical services performed by other health professionals.

The second case in the chain of court rulings following the "bright line" approach arose in Cedar Rapids, Iowa. Garret F., a twelve-year-old boy who was injured at age four while riding with his father on a motorcycle, was paralyzed from the neck down and had mobility only through the use of a motorized wheelchair controlled by a puff-and-suck straw. His primary medical needs in school included CIC once a day, hourly repositioning, and the assistance of a ventilator. Being ventilator-dependent meant that Garret could breathe only with the assistance of an electric ventilator or someone manually pumping an air bag attached to his tracheotomy tube. Garret was a friendly, verbal, well-liked, and creative person who performed at an above-average level in academic

subjects. When family and insurance resources were nearly exhausted in 1993, Garret's mother requested that the school assume responsibility for providing Garret's at-school nursing services.

Subsequent to the school's refusal of her request, Garret's mother filed a request for a due process hearing under the IDEA. The state administrative law judge ruled that the Supreme Court in *Tatro* had established a "bright line" test of need for services by a physician as the determining factor in a school's duty to provide medical services as a related service under the IDEA. Because the hearing record established that Garret's needed services did not require a physician, the nursing services required at school were a "related service" that the school was required to provide. The estimated cost of the services was between $20,000 and $30,000 per year. A school district administrator testified that if funding sources other than the school could not be identified to meet Garret's in-school medical needs, his likely placement for an educational program would be "homebound." The school appealed to the federal district court, and the ruling was upheld on the basis of the "bright line" physician service test. That decision was affirmed by the Eighth Circuit, which expressly adopted the "bright line" physician test. The school district then appealed to the Supreme Court in an effort to replace the "bright line" test with a multifactor test which would take into account medical service's cost, complexity, and other matters.

The Supreme Court heard the case and, by a majority of 7-2, upheld its previous ruling in *Tatro*. It held that only the treatment services of a physician were excluded from the IDEA's medical services requirement, and that a multifactor test was not required by the statute or related regulations. In response to the school district's concerns about the cost of medical services as a required "related service," the majority was mindful that a basic purpose of the IDEA was to provide the meaningful access for students with disabilities to public school programs and services. Because it was not disputed that Garret must have the services of a nurse, or other responsible adult, to supervise his ventilator in order to remain in school, the school district was required to fund the services in order to assure that students like Garret were integrated into school programs. Although the majority recognized the legitimacy of the school district's financial concerns in providing related services of a medical nature, it noted that the Court's role was to interpret existing statutes and not to create new law. It hinted strongly that the issue of excessive cost of related services should be taken up with Congress. The dissenting opinion did little to clarify the issue, basically calling for a reversal of the *Tatro* ruling. The majority brushed aside the dissent's approach as being unreasonable and a violation of the concept of stare decisis.

In a final settlement agreement between the parents of Garret and the Cedar Rapids School District, the parents received $174,237 to reimburse them for the six years of nursing services they had paid while Garret was in school and $129,296 for their attorney fees. The school district's legal fees and the cost of its own staff time were not, of course, covered by the settlement. The final word on the actual cost to school districts of the Supreme Court's interpretation of "related services" has not been written and, barring congressional action, will likely remain in dispute for some time. At best, schools and parents will no longer need to continue to do legal battle over the issue. These two rulings by the Supreme Court should, at least, assure that much.

Selected Bibliography

Osborne, A. G., Jr. "Supreme Court Rules That Schools Must Provide Full-Time Nursing Services for Medically Fragile Students." *Education Law Reporter* 136 (1999): 1–14.

Rebore, D., and Zirkel, P. A. "The Supreme Court's Latest Special Education Ruling: A Costly Decision?" *Education Law Reporter* 136 (1999): 331–341.

Mitigating Measures and the Definition of Disability

—◄◦►—

Robert F. Martin

Department of History
University of Northern Iowa

Sutton v. United Air Lines, Inc., 527 U.S. 471 (1999);
Murphy v. United Parcel Service, Inc., 527 U.S. 516 (1999);
Albertsons, Inc. v. Kirkingburg, 527 U.S. 555 (1999) [U.S. Supreme Court]

◄◦► THE CASE IN BRIEF ◄◦►

Date
1999

Location
District of Columbia

Court
U.S. Supreme Court

Principal Participants
Karen Sutton and Kimberly Sutton Hinton; United Airlines; Vaughn Murphy; United Parcel Service; Hallie Kirkingburg; Albertsons

Significance of the Case
In grappling with a legal definition of disability and its relationship to employment, the Court considered each of these cases on its own merits, thus refusing to create a general legal category of the disabled.

In 1990, the Americans with Disabilities Act (ADA) passed both houses of Congress by wide margins. President George Bush, as he signed the bill into law, described the new statute as "an historic opportunity" representing "the full flowering of our democratic principles." At the time of its passage, the legislation was relatively uncontroversial because a broad spectrum of Americans regarded it as a logical extension of civil rights guarantees begun with the passage of the Civil Rights Act of 1964. Millions of disabled citizens hailed the law as the dawn of a new era of expanded rights and opportunities in the tradition of those already protected minorities, women, and older Americans. Soon, however, a pall of controversy and disillusionment began to descend over the increasingly litigious landscape of disability law.

Nowhere has the confusion been greater than with regard to issues of employment. Any plaintiff in work-related cases under the ADA must prove that he/she is a "qualified individual," that is, one "who, with or without reasonable accommodation, can perform the essential functions of the employment position" in question. A plaintiff must also demonstrate that he or she has a disability, "a physical or mental impairment that substantially limits one or more of the major life activities," "a record of such impairment," or a record of "being regarded as having such an impairment." Unfortunately, several crucial terms—including "major life activity," "impairment," and "substantially limits"—are not defined by the ADA. Furthermore, the legislation does not address the issue of whether corrective or mitigating measures should be considered when determining whether an individual is disabled. Congress delegated to the Equal Employment Opportunity Commission (EEOC) the task of implementing Title I, the employment provision of the statute, thereby clarifying many of its ambiguities. Myriad problems have arisen, however, out of the sometimes imprecise and incomplete language of the ADA itself, the broad and at times inconsistent construction of the statute by the EEOC, and a complex and contradictory series of judicial decisions rendered by the federal courts.

For much of its history, neither employees nor employers have had a clear grasp of what constitutes compliance with the law. What was intended as a simple extension of justice to people who long had been consigned to the ranks of the underemployed or unemployed has developed into a legal maze from which few seem capable of escaping. So frustrating has the situation become that a federal judge in the Western District of Arkansas declared: "The court doubts that the ultimate result of this law will be to provide substantial assistance to persons for whom it was obviously intended, and that one of the primary beneficiaries of it will be trial lawyers who will ingeniously manipulate such ambiguities to consistently broaden its coverage so that federal courts may become mired in employment injury cases, becoming little more than glorified worker's compensation referees."

In three decisions handed down on June 22, 1999—*Sutton v. United Air Lines, Inc., Murphy v. United Parcel Service, Inc.,* and *Albertsons, Inc. v. Kirkingburg,* the U.S. Supreme Court took a significant although controversial step toward clarifying the issue of precisely who could claim occupational protection under the Americans with Disabilities Act.

In *Sutton v. United Air Lines,* the Court considered the case of extremely myopic twin sisters—Karen Sutton and Kimberly Sutton Hinton. In 1992 the Suttons sought employment as global pilots with United Air Lines. Without corrective measures the siblings had a visual acuity of 20/200 or worse and were unable to engage in a number of routine life functions, such as driving, watching television, or shopping. With contact lenses, however, their vision was correctable to 20/20 or better. Because United required that its global pilots have uncorrected vision of at least 20/100, the airline refused to hire the sisters for the positions they sought. In 1996 the Suttons sued United in federal court, claiming discrimination under the Americans with Disabilities Act. They alleged that the airline discriminated against them on the basis of their disability or because of what it regarded as a disability. When both the district court and the Tenth Circuit Court of Appeal decided against them, the plaintiffs took their case to the U.S. Supreme Court. In a 7-2 decision with important implications for disability law, the High Court also ruled against the sisters. A majority of the justices held that if a condition such as myopia is fully correctable, it does not significantly limit any major life activity and does not constitute a disability under the terms of the ADA. The Suttons were not, therefore, disabled and were not protected by the legislation.

The decision was contrary to the position of the EEOC, which had previously held that corrective measures should not be considered when determining whether a person was disabled. The Court concluded that the EEOC had construed the law more broadly than legislators had intended. In the view of a majority of the justices, if corrective or mitigating circumstances were not taken into account, the ADA would apply to four times as many Americans as the approximately forty-three million designated by Congress when it passed the measure. The Court also ruled that United's 20/100 standard of visual acuity for international pilots, which the plaintiffs claimed unfairly excluded them from the job, was not discriminatory but was merely an exercise of the company's legitimate right to impose physical conditions for employment. In its view, an employer violated the ADA only "when it makes an employment decision based on a physical or mental impairment, real or imagined, that is regarded as substantially limiting" to "a major life activity." The Court conceded that work is a major life activity, but determined that the Suttons were not significantly limited with regard to work because there were many jobs at United, including some as pilots, for which they were qualified.

In *Murphy v. United Parcel Service, Inc.* the Court followed the logic established in the *Sutton* case. Vaughn Murphy, a mechanic for United Parcel Service (UPS), had suffered from severe hypertension since childhood. His job with UPS required that he do some driving. He therefore was expected to meet U.S. Department of Transportation (DOT) health and safety standards for truck drivers. When UPS hired Murphy, it erroneously believed that his blood pressure was within DOT guidelines. When it discovered that, even with medication, this was not the case, the company fired the mechanic. Murphy then sued his former employer, alleging discrimination under the Americans with Disabilities Act. Lower courts ruled against Murphy, finding that, with medication, his hypertension was not sufficiently severe to substantially limit him in any major life activity; therefore his condition did not conform to the statutory definition of a disability. The Supreme Court noted and accepted the lower courts' position on this issue, but the primary question before it was Murphy's allegation that even though his hypertension was not a disability, UPS regarded it as such. In a 7-2 decision the Court ruled that the dismissal of Murphy was not based on the perception that he was disabled but merely on the grounds that he did not meet DOT health and safety standards. According to the justices, Murphy was eligible for other positions as a mechanic. Thus, he was not substantially limited in the major life activity of work, nor was he protected under the "regarded as" provision of the ADA.

In *Albertsons, Inc. v. Kirkingburg,* the Court took yet another step toward determining who

is and who is not protected under the ADA. Hallie Kirkingburg was a truck driver with a record of safe driving extending back over more than a decade. Kirkingburg, however, suffered from amblyopia which left him with a visual acuity of 20/200 in his left eye and what was, in effect, monocular vision. The Department of Transportation, since 1971, has required a distance visual acuity of at least 20/40 in each eye and comparable binocular distance vision. When Kirkingburg applied for a job with Albertsons, a doctor erroneously certified that he met the DOT's requirement and the grocery chain hired him. During a physical examination following a protracted leave due to injury, the examining physician discovered that the truck driver did not meet DOT vision standards. The doctor informed Kirkingburg that he could apply for a DOT waiver, but Albertsons fired him on the grounds that he failed to meet the DOT's minimum standards. Even after Kirkingburg received the DOT waiver in 1993, the grocery store chain refused to reinstate him. Kirkingburg then sued, claiming discrimination under the Americans with Disabilities Act.

A federal district court decided in favor of Albertsons on the grounds that Kirkingburg admittedly did not meet DOT requirements. The Ninth Circuit Court reversed the lower court. The appellate court judges reasoned that Kirkingburg had demonstrated that his vision was essentially monocular, and that monocularity constituted not only a different way of seeing but also a disability as defined by the ADA. The court acknowledged that Albertsons had a right to establish a vision standard for its drivers and that the use of DOT regulations to establish that standard was legitimate, but that the company had not justified its failure to take DOT's waiver program into account in its decision to dismiss Kirkingburg.

The U.S. Supreme Court overturned the appellate court ruling on several grounds. The justices concluded that physical differences do not necessarily constitute a disability. The appeals court, it determined, was in error when it held that Kirkingburg's essentially monocular vision was a different way of seeing and therefore constituted a disability. The High Court determined that the appellate judges had erroneously equated a difference with a disability, contrary to the intent of the ADA.

Furthermore, the High Court argued that monocularity, per se, did not constitute a disability. Kirkingburg's body had learned to compensate for his loss of vision, just as if he had taken some conscious corrective action. The Court contended that the ADA required monocular individuals, like others claiming the its protection, to prove a disability by offering evidence that the extent of the limitation in terms of their own experience, as in loss of depth perception and visual field, is substantial. Albertsons, the Court concluded, was within its rights to define certain physical standards for employment, and Kirkingburg had no legitimate claim because his impaired vision did not constitute a significant limitation on a major life activity.

The *Sutton, Murphy,* and *Kirkingburg* decisions are significant for several reasons. They establish the principle that medical or prosthetic measures—or even, as in the case of *Kirkingburg,* subconscious physiological adaptations that correct or compensate for a disabling condition—must be taken into account when determining whether an individual is eligible for protection under the Americans with Disabilities Act. Furthermore, they affirm, within broad limits, the right of employers to establish reasonable and relevant physical standards for employment. They also make the definition of disability a functional rather than a categorical one by requiring that each case must be decided on the basis of whether or not a condition substantially limits a major life function, rather than on the grounds that an individual suffers from a condition that may hypothetically do so.

The Supreme Court's opinions in these three cases have, not surprisingly, elicited varied reactions. Some disabled Americans and their advocates have expressed the concern that the justices, by permitting the consideration of mitigating measures in determining whether a person is or is not legally disabled, have denied millions of people the protection to which they are entitled. Others, however, believe that the Court, by not categorizing broad classes of people as disabled, has acted in a manner consistent with the spirit of the Americans with Dis-

abilities Act and that it has redirected the focus of disability law toward the interests of those more severely disabled Americans for whom its protections were originally intended. It is safe to say that the nation's employers desperately hope that the *Sutton, Murphy,* and *Kirkingburg* decisions mark the beginning of the unraveling of the legal complexities in which employer and employee alike have found themselves entangled since the early 1990s.

The Supreme Court, in a February 2001 decision that failed to cite any of the three 1999 disability cases discussed in this essay, nevertheless complicated disabilities law and further restricted the application of the Americans with Disabilities Act. In *University of Alabama v. Garrett* (2001), the Court, by a close 5-4 ruling, held that the ADA did not permit suits by disabled state employees against agencies of a state's government. The reasoning of Chief Justice William Rehnquist's majority opinion was that the legislative history of the ADA did not present evidence that state agencies had engaged in sufficiently demonstrable patterns of discrimination against persons with disabilities to overcome the state immunity from suits by citizens normally protected by the Eleventh Amendment. The Court made clear that its opinion in *Garrett* did not affect the protection that the ADA extends to disabled employees in the face of employment discrimination by private companies or even by local governmental agencies. It also indicated that state employees with disabilities could continue to seek legal remedies under state disability legislation. Limited as the holding of *Garrett* may be, it has served to heighten the suspicion, raised initially among the disabled and their advocates by the rulings in *Sutton, Murphy* and *Kirkingburg,* that a majority of the current High Court is unwilling to grant a broad sweep to the Americans with Disabilities Act.

Selected Bibliography

Barhorst, Stacie E. "What Does Disability Mean: The Americans with Disabilities Act of 1990 in the Aftermath of *Sutton, Murphy,* and *Albertsons." Drake Law Review* 48 (1999): 137–171.

Befort, Stephen F., and Holly Lindquist Thomas. "The ADA in Turmoil: Judicial Dissonance, the Supreme Court's Response, and the Future of Disability Discrimination Law." *Oregon Law Review* 78 (Spring 1999): 27–104.

Bland, Timothy, and Thomas J. Walsh, Jr. "U.S. Supreme Court Resolves Mitigating Measures Issue Under the ADA." *University of Memphis Law Review* 30 (Fall 1999): 1–27.

Is Walking an Integral Part of the Game of Golf?

Richard R. Broadie

Department of History
University of Northern Iowa

PGA Tour v. Martin, 532 U.S. ___ (2001);
Ford Olinger v. United States Golf Association, 205 F. 3d 1001 (1999)
[U.S. Supreme Court]
[U.S. Court of Appeals]

◄◦► THE CASE IN BRIEF ◄◦►

Date
1999, 2000, 2001

Location
District of Columbia

Court
U.S. Supreme Court

Principal Participants
Casey Martin
Professional Golf Association Tour
Associate Justice John Paul Stevens
Associate Justice Antonin Scalia

Significance of the Case
The Court ruled that the PGA tour must permit a disabled golfer the right to ride in a golf cart in its competitions; the majority opinion stated that a cart does not bestow an unfair advantage on a golfer.

When the Americans with Disabilities Act (ADA) was passed by Congress and signed by President George Bush in 1990, critics warned that its ambiguity would invite lawsuits testing what is meant by "disability" and the extent to which the law can be applied to groups, organizations, and entities outside the norm. To date, two court cases have tested the issue of whether golf associations are "private clubs" or organizations exempt from the provisions of the ADA.

Casey Martin is a disabled golfer. He suffers from a rare condition called Klippel-Trenaunay-Weber syndrome, an abnormal vascular condition, in his lower right leg. In simplest terms, Martin's right leg is much smaller and more brittle than his left. His condition is very painful even while he is at rest. While walking, he is at risk of fracturing his tibia, hemorrhaging, and developing blood clots. Martin's condition is worsening as he ages, and his orthopedist, Dr. Don Jones, has testified that he is "looking at the possibility of amputation eventually." It appears likely that Martin will—at best—have a short career as a touring professional.

As an amateur, Martin was able to compete by walking in some tournaments and riding in a golf cart in others. After a successful college career at Stanford University, in which he competed alongside Tiger Woods, Martin sought to play on the PGA tour while using a cart. This placed him directly in conflict with the tour policy of prohibiting competitors from riding in tournament competition. Could he have walked and competed on tour? Martin, in one interview, said, "If you put a gun to my head, I could walk. But it certainly takes a toll on me." For this reason and the likely possibility of serious injury, Martin decided to challenge the PGA tour's no-cart policy in court by using the Americans with Disabilities Act. In 1997, he won a temporary court order allowing him to play in a few Nike (minor league) tour events. He promptly won his first tournament. On February 19, 1998, Martin was granted the right to ride a cart on a permanent basis by federal Judge Thomas Coffin.

The official position of the PGA tour was endorsed by most of its competitors. Golfing legend Arnold Palmer, who, at seventy years of age still walks the course, testified that using a cart could provide a competitive advantage. Even Tiger Woods, Martin's college teammate, seemed to back tour officials: "As a friend, I'd love to see him have a cart. But from a playing standpoint, is it an advantage? It could be."

Golf commentator and former U.S. Open champion Curtis Strange made the case against Martin in detail in a 1998 article in *Golf Magazine*: "Despite what most people outside the game think . . . fitness and stamina are as much a part of championship golf as shot making ability." Because fitness is required to perform at a high level in all types of conditions, "an exception to the tour's walking-only rule would change the nature of the game and . . . give Martin an unfair advantage over the rest of the field." It might also open a can of worms by setting a precedent where competitors with "bad backs, bad hips and bad knees" would challenge the rule and be allowed to compete.

On the nature of Martin's condition, the plaintiff and the defendant were in agreement. Both accepted that Martin's condition is a disability under any reasonable definition of the

term, and that "as he has gotten older [Martin was twenty-five at the time of the ruling], his leg has steadily worsened because of his disability." The judge noted that the tour did not extensively review Martin's condition prior to trial because it believed that his "individual circumstances are irrelevant to the inquiry." Where the two sides did disagree was over the issue of whether the ADA applied to professional golf tournaments and if, as the PGA asserted, "the requirement of walking is a substantive rule of its competition and that a waiver of the rule would, accordingly, result in a fundamental alteration of its competitions which the ADA does not require."

On the first issue, Judge Coffin ruled that the PGA tour was not exempt from ADA coverage and that its tournaments were conducted at places—golf courses—that were clearly included within the definition of "public accommodations" subject to the statute. He noted that the "ADA does not distinguish between sports organizations and other entities when it comes to applying the ADA to a specific situation." Indeed, given that the disabled have as much right to be free of discrimination in athletics as they do in other aspects of everyday life, he seemed to suggest that the tour's position would be in conflict with the spirit of the law as well. Casey Martin's lawyers argued that the specific accommodation requested by Martin, a golf cart, was reasonable in light of the cases cited as precedents.

Judge Coffin also disagreed with the PGA position that a modification of the walking requirement would fundamentally alter the nature of the game being played on tour. In part, he noted professional golf's inconsistency in applying its own rule. Club professionals are allowed to ride in most of their tournaments, as are aspiring tour professionals in their qualifying schools. Senior golfers are also allowed to ride in most of their events, although many choose not to, and some, including soon-to-be senior Curtis Strange, have suggested that it no longer be permitted. Finally, Coffin challenged the tour's contention that "the purpose of the walking rule is to inject the element of fatigue into the skill of shot-making." Relying on the testimony of a professor of physiology from the

Golfer Casey Martin at the Greater Austin Open, March 5, 1998, after winning a lawsuit against the PGA Tour that allowed him to use a golf cart during competition. Martin has a circulatory disorder in his right leg that prevents him from walking long distances. *Archive Photos.*

University of Oregon, the plaintiff asserted that walking a golf course expends a relatively small amount of energy (fewer calories than in a Big Mac), and fatigue is often more related to dehydration, heat exhaustion, and even psychological factors than to walking. Judge Coffin, who has not walked a golf course under adverse conditions or in competition, may not have considered that walking might accelerate or exacerbate the effects of heat, loss of fluids, and competitive pressure.

On balance, Judge Coffin's ruling, though allowing Casey Martin the chance to compete, was somewhat limited. The judge found a clear distinction between temporary disabilities, or "non-chronic impairments," and Martin's condition. The PGA erred, in the judge's view, by

not considering the specifics of Martin's disability. Given his physical handicap, Martin would not possess a competitive advantage if his request to ride in a cart in competition was granted. The judge concluded that future cases should be decided on their own merits, thereby minimizing the risk of the "slippery slope" scenario feared by the tour.

The PGA tour appealed Judge Coffin's decision to the U.S. Court of Appeals for the Ninth Circuit. The case was argued on May 4, 1999, and a unanimous ruling of the three-judge appellate panel was handed down on March 6, 2000, shortly after Casey Martin had joined the PGA tour. The Circuit Court, in a forceful opinion written by Judge William Canby, upheld the lower court decision and essentially adopted its reasoning. In particular, Judge Canby accepted the notion that it is necessary to evaluate each case on its own merits. He concluded that "Nothing in the record establishes that an individual determination would impose an intolerable burden on the PGA [and] that providing Martin with a golf cart would not give him an unfair advantage over his competitors." Although both lower courts made it clear that some claims for accommodations in golf competition under the ADA could be rejected, given different sets of facts, neither court chose to craft guidelines for such determinations.

This was far from the final word on the Martin case. In May 1999 a U.S. federal district judge in Indiana ruled, in *Olinger v. United States Golf Association*, that the nation's major golf association did not have to permit Ford Olinger, a professional golfer with a degenerative condition called bilateral avascular necrosis, the use of an electric golf cart in a qualifying round for the U.S. Open, a tournament sponsored by the United States Golf Association (USGA). The *Martin* appeals court was aware of the *Olinger* case, but said in its opinion that it "respectfully" disagreed with the Indiana judge. To further muddy the legal waters, on the day after the Ninth Circuit Court of Appeals ruled in Casey Martin's favor, the Seventh Circuit Court of Appeals upheld the Indiana federal district court's denial of Olinger's appeal.

Thus, as of early 2001, there existed a classic "split in the circuits" on the issue of whether a golfer has the right to ride a cart in a sanctioned golf competition. To attempt to settle the matter, the PGA tour appealed to the U.S. Supreme Court. In mid-January 2001, teams of lawyers for the tour and Casey Martin teed it up at oral argument before the nation's highest court. Many legal observers at oral argument felt that the justices' questions indicated skepticism that Martin could be reasonably accommodated under the ADA without "fundamentally altering" the nature of competitive golf. In addition, the Court's February 2001 decision in *University of Alabama v. Garrett*, which denied coverage by the ADA to state employees suing for accommodations from agencies of state government, further hinted that the Court was not disposed toward a broad reading of the ADA. Thus, the May 29, 2001, decision in *PGA Tour v. Casey Martin* came as somewhat of a surprise.

By a vote of 7-2, the Court majority, in an opinion written by Justice John Paul Stevens, found in favor of Casey Martin. Stevens determined that the PGA tour's tournaments fit within the understanding of a "public accommodation" under Title III of the ADA and that Martin, as a "client or customer" of the tour, was legally entitled to a reasonable adjustment for his disability. Stevens emphasized that striking the golf ball is what is integral to the game of golf, not the walking between shots. He and his brethren in the majority discounted the testimony of several PGA stars that walking subjected one to a "fatigue factor" and, thus, was a necessary component of competitive golf. Pointing out that many U.S. golf competitions, including tournaments on the Senior PGA Tour, permit players to ride in carts, Stevens maintained that Martin's use of a cart would not "fundamentally alter the competition" to which he aspired. If there is fatigue in competitive golf, Stevens submitted, it is more psychological than physical.

In a strongly worded dissent, Justice Antonin Scalia spoke for himself and Justice Clarence Thomas. The majority decision, in Scalia's words, "exercises a benevolent compassion that the law does not place it within our power to impose. The judgment distorts . . . the structure of the ADA . . . and common sense."

Reaction to the decision in *PGA Tour v. Martin* was swift. PGA Tour Commissioner Tim Finchem asserted that the Stevens opinion should be read narrowly, simply permitting one accommodation for one golfer. By contrast, U.S. Senator Tom Harkin (Democrat, Iowa), one of the Senate sponsors of the ADA saw the ruling in broader terms: "We passed the ADA to give people with disabilities an equal opportunity to fully participate in American life. That includes the right to compete."

During the week following the ruling in the *Martin* case, the Supreme Court vacated the Seventh Circuit Court of Appeals judgment in *Olinger v. United States Golf Association*, remanding that case to the appeals court for disposition consistent with the holding in *PGA Tour v. Martin*.

Whether other disabled athletes will be able, even with reasonable accommodations, to compete at the highest levels of their sports remains to be seen. Casey Martin, himself, has struggled of late to find his game, perhaps distracted by the publicity of his lawsuit. In addition, given the current Supreme Court's conflicting opinions in recent disability litigation, future construction of the ADA is shrouded in a mist as thick as often faces a golfer with an early tee time.

Selected Bibliography

Koepke, Byron L. "The Americans with Disabilities Act and Professional Golf—Breaking Par for the Sake of Equality." *Washburn Law Journal* 38 (Spring 1999): 699–725.

Sharpe, Tanya R. "Casey's Case: Taking a Slice out of the PGA's No-Cart Policy." *Florida State University Law Review* 26 (Spring 1999): 783–808.

Strange, Curtis. "Protecting the Game." *Golf Magazine*, March 1998: 32–33.

PART V

CIVIL LIBERTIES

- Freedom of Speech
- Freedom of the Press
- Freedom of Religion
- Obscenity and Pornography
- Other Civil Liberties Issues
- Privacy

One of the distinctive features of the American legal system is the protection of freedoms of individuals against encroachment by government. Individual freedoms—generally termed "civil liberties"—can of course be protected by government. After all, the very purpose of criminal law is to safeguard the person and property of law-abiding people. But it is often the government—in its zeal for the enforcement of criminal laws and/or social policy—that may violate the freedoms of individuals. To guard against governmental infringement of individual liberty, such notable late-eighteenth-century Americans as Thomas Jefferson, James Madison and George Mason insisted on the passage of the Bill of Rights as a *quid pro quo* for the ratification of the U.S. Constitution.

For many years the Bill of Rights—the first ten amendments to the Constitution—lay dormant, seldom serving as the basis for challenges to governmental practices. That would change with World War I which sparked a series of legal questions that brought the Bill of Rights out of forgotten appendices to textbooks and into the fabric of American life. The forty-seven selections in Part V offer analyses of some of the most important federal and state civil-liberties decisions.

Freedom of Speech

The first selection in this section, "State Wrongs and the Bill of Rights," addresses the question of whether the Bill of Rights protects individuals against threats to civil liberties mounted by state governments as well as by the national government. In *Barron v. Mayor of Baltimore,* the 1833 case examined, the U.S. Supreme Court held that the Bill of Rights did not apply to the states. For almost one hundred years, this interpretation stood. It would be freedom-of-speech cases in the 1920s that would cause the Supreme Court to reconsider this nineteenth-century decision.

The first significant spate of freedom of expression cases reached the Supreme Court in the final stages of World War I. As discussed in "Defining Free-Speech Protection in the World War I Era," the initial efforts to challenge state and federal legislation restricting freedom of expression were upheld by the Supreme Court. Justice Oliver Wendell Holmes enunciated his famous clear-and-present-danger test for determining the constitutionality of controversial speech in these cases. This standard would be employed, revised, and twisted in many directions over the remainder of the twentieth century. The selection "Agrarian Reform and the Politics of Loyalty" provides an example of the Supreme Court siding with the government and not the individual in an early freedom-of-speech case.

With a case from New York discussed in "Expanding Free Speech to the States," the High Court noted that there exist "fundamental personal rights protected by the due process clause of the Fourteenth Amendment from impairment by the states." The rights the Court chose to identify were freedom of speech and of the press. Although the Supreme Court found in favor of the government in the case profiled, this was the beginning of what experts have called the selective "incorporation" of the Bill of Rights guarantees over and against state infringements.

Thus, the 1833 opinion discussed in *Barron v. Mayor of Baltimore* was finally undercut.

Throughout the 1920s and 1930s, the Court generally found ways to uphold legislation restricting the speech of those on the left of the political spectrum. However, as discussed in "Silencing Critics: Guilt by Association in the 1920s" and "The California Red Flag Law and Freedom of Speech," strong dissenting voices from Justices Louis Brandeis, Oliver Wendell Holmes, and Harlan Fiske Stone began to be raised in support of civil liberties.

Perhaps the case most clearly isolating polar positions on freedom of expression was *Dennis v. United States* (1951). In *Dennis*, the Supreme Court majority upheld the conviction of leading members of the American Communist Party for advocating the doctrine of violent revolution, but stinging dissents were filed to the *Dennis* majority by two of the Court's liberals, Hugo Black and William O. Douglas. The landmark *Dennis* ruling is examined in "Cold War, Communism, and Free Speech." A later selection in this section, "The Smith Act Narrowed," treats an important modification of the *Dennis* holding as enunciated by the Supreme Court in a 1957 decision.

This section also includes several selections on the fate of notable state and federal laws restricting different types of expression. The constitutionality of a "group libel" statute is discussed in " 'Breach of Peace' and Group Libel." Cases that tested the constitutionality of state statutes restricting advertizing are discussed in "Commercial Speech and the First Amendment" and "Free Speech and Legal Ethics: The Issue of Lawyer Advertizing." The controversy over the constitutionality of legislation prohibiting the burning of the American flag is discussed in "Flag Burning and the Constitution," and the debate over attempts to legislate against "hate speech" is addressed in "Reigniting the 'Fighting Words'/ 'Symbolic Speech' Debate: Cross Burning and the Constitution." Finally, a selection on symbolic speech, "The Constitution Finds Its Way Inside the Schoolhouse Gate," is included in this section because it raises important free speech issues stemming from student protests against the Vietnam War in the 1960s.

Freedom of the Press

The first selection in this section, "Myth and Reality: The Case of John Peter Zenger," deals with the well-known but often misunderstood libel trial of a colonial printer. The next selection, "The Sedition Act and the Price of a Free Press," examines a freedom-of-the-press case from the early national period involving a scurrilous journalist who blackened the reputation of a number of famous Americans. In the landmark case of *Near v. Minnesota* (1931), the Supreme Court held that freedom of the press was one of the "fundamental freedoms" that needed protection against state as well as national infringement; it is discussed in the essay "The Limits of Prior Restraint."

Five of the selections in this section probe Supreme Court decisions rendered since the mid-1960s involving public figures: "Public Officials, Libel, and a Free Press" deals with the suit of a Southern police officer who believed that his rights were violated by a civil-rights news story; "Public Personalities and the Right to Privacy" and "Public Disclosure of Private Facts" concern stories that exacerbated the trauma of "unwilling" public figures; and "Did CBS Libel General Westmoreland?" and "The 'Preacher' and the 'Smut Merchant' " discuss cases involving, respectively, a famous general and a controversial evangelist.

Perhaps the most important freedom of press case in the last third of the twentieth century involved the federal government's 1971 attempt to stop the publication by leading American newspapers of a series of confidential government reports on the origins of the Vietnam War. This case is analyzed in "The Pentagon Papers."

Freedom of Religion

Besides protecting speech and the press, the First Amendment to the Constitution also stipulates that "Congress shall make no law respecting an establishment of religion, or prohibiting the free exercise thereof." The establishment and free exercise clauses figure in some of the most interesting and controversial court decisions in American history.

The first selection in this section, "Religion, Cultural Pluralism, and the Constitution: Mormonism and Polygamy," notes how in the late nineteenth century the Supreme Court did not allow the religion clauses of the First Amendment to sanction a religious practice that offended secular public policy. "The Scopes Trial: A Collision of Cultures," delves into the famous 1925 evolution trial in Dayton, Tennessee. "The Flag Salute Cases" considers the question of whether the law can compel children to salute the flag even if such behavior violates personal religious beliefs; the Supreme Court struggled with this question during World War II and ended up reversing itself.

In "Religion in the Public School Day: The Released Time Cases," the issue of whether students can be released from public-school classes to participate in religious instruction is examined. In "To Pray or Not To Pray: The Supreme Court Says No to Prayer in the Public Schools," the Supreme Court's still controversial decision to ban organized prayer in public schools is discussed. In a decision handed down early in the Vietnam War, examined in "Conscientious Objection: A Right or a Privilege?," the Supreme Court considered whether a young man could avoid military service if his objections to such duty were primarily ethical rather than a product of conventional religious beliefs.

A test used by the late-twentieth-century Supreme Court to determine whether a state policy violates the principle of separation of church and state is examined in "Lemon Test, Not So Pretty." Whether a state's compulsory school-attendance law violates the right of free exercise of religion for the Amish is considered in "Expanded Exercise: The Amish, Compulsory Education, and Religious Freedom." The question of whether a state-mandated "moment of silence" during the school day is an establishment of religion is discussed in "The Pieties of Silence." Finally, whether the smoking of an hallucinogenic drug as part of a religious ritual can disqualify someone for state employment is probed in "Religious Practices and the First Amendment: The Peyote Case."

Obscenity and Pornography

Another First Amendment issue addressed in Part V is expression that may violate standards of good taste. American jurists have generally agreed that "obscene" or "pornographic" expression is not deserving of First Amendment protection. But how should these concepts be defined? Courts have been groping, with little success, for such definitions for over a century. Justice Potter Stewart may have put it best in a mid-1960s decision when he lamented that he could not define obscenity, but "I know it when I see it." The selection "Obscenity: 'I Know It When I See It!' " treats the Supreme Court's first modern attempt to set a standard for obscenity in *Roth v. United States* (1957). "A Book Named *Fanny Hill*" examines an extension of the *Roth* standard in a mid-1960s case. And "The Triumph of 'Community Standards' " delves into some of the major modifications in standards for determining obscenity propounded by the Supreme Court under the leadership of Chief Justice Warren Burger in a set of 1973 cases.

Another selection in this section, "Pornography, Feminism, and Free Speech," examines the fate of feminist-inspired attempts in the 1980s to ban expression deemed pornographic as well as offensive to women. And the final selection, "Cyberporn and the Constitution," discusses the challenges to the First Amendment and American standards of decency by the federal government's attempt to regulate the ubiquitous internet.

Other Civil Liberties Issues

The Fifth Amendment to the Constitution contains many critical phrases. Among them is the injunction that a person "shall [not] be compelled in any criminal case to be a witness against himself. . . ." Whether this protection extends to individuals called to testify before legislative committees is addressed in "The Court and the Committee" and "The Court and the Committee: Part Two." The Fifth Amendment's due process clause (similar to the Fourteenth Amendment's due process clause) has been found by the U.S. Supreme Court to protect a number of unspecified individual rights. The essay, "The Right to Travel," examines one such right. The privileges and immunities clause of the Fourteenth Amendment has also been identified by the Supreme Court as the seat of a right to travel, as discussed in "Family Welfare Rights and the Right to Travel."

Privacy

Neither the Constitution nor its amendments contain the term "privacy." Yet most Americans believe quite strongly that there exists a private realm into which the government should not enter. As early as 1890, Louis Brandeis and a collaborator wrote a famous essay defending the existence of a legal right to privacy. Constitutionally, the right to privacy was born in a 1965 decision, *Griswold v. Connecticut*, discussed in "Meaningful Shadows? The Right of Privacy Achieves Constitutional Status." Privacy dimensions of the so-called "right to die" are considered in two selections: "The Right of Guardians to Terminate

Life-Extending Medical Treatment" and "Physician-Assisted Suicide: Death with Dignity?"

The leading right to privacy decision and, perhaps, the most controversial Supreme Court decision of the last thirty years is *Roe v. Wade* (1973). *Roe* upheld, subject to certain state restrictions, a woman's legal right to abortion; the decision is examined in "Abortion: Who Shall Decide?" The constitutionality of recent state attempts to regulate abortion is discussed in "Preserving the 'Essence' of *Roe*: The Rehnquist Court and Abortion."

Freedom of Speech

State Wrongs and the Bill of Rights

—◄◦►—

Maxwell Bloomfield
Columbus School of Law
Catholic University of America

Barron v. Mayor of Baltimore, 7 Peters 243 (1833) [U.S. Supreme Court]

◄◦► THE CASE IN BRIEF ◄◦►

Date
1833

Location
Maryland

Court
U.S. Supreme Court

Principal Participants
John Barron; City of Baltimore;
Chief Justice John Marshall

Significance of the Case
The Supreme Court, citing the Constitution's Article I, refused to hear a case involving a property owner and the state of Maryland. Chief Justice Marshall concluded that the Bill of Rights could not be applied to protect the freedom of individuals faced with hostile actions by state governments.

Baltimore, Maryland, was a rapidly growing city in the early nineteenth century, with a severe shortage of municipal and public health services. To help meet these pressing needs, the city government launched an impressive public works program aimed in part at eliminating the health hazards associated with the old section of the harbor known as the Basin. As one contemporary reported, the slips between the docks in that area "often filled with stagnated water and every species of filth, which have not only been destructive to health but highly inconvenient in that part of the town to free mercantile intercourse." From 1815 to 1821, the city council passed a series of ordinances directing the extensive regrading and paving of streets near the Basin. In the process, embankments were built, and neighboring streams were diverted toward the harbor, causing soil and other debris to accumulate around the docks.

John Barron and John Craig owned one of the largest and most profitable wharves in the Basin. As the street construction progressed, they found that the surrounding water grew steadily shallower until no vessel of any size could use their facility. In 1822, Barron sued the city for compensatory damages, thereby profoundly influencing the future course of American civil rights and civil liberties.

Barron's lawyers argued that the city's acts had violated his property rights under state law. Alternatively, they contended that Barron, as a citizen of the United States, could claim protection under the Fifth Amendment to the Constitution, which prohibited the taking of private property for public use "without just compensation."

The attorneys for the city of Baltimore denied all liability. Maryland law, they asserted, did not require payment to property owners who suffered incidental damage as a result of needed public improvements; and the federal Bill of Rights did not apply to the states.

Barron won his case in the Baltimore County Court, which awarded him $4,500 in damages. On appeal, however, the Maryland Court of Appeals ruled against him on all points; and from this decision of the highest state tribunal, Barron's lawyers carried the case to the Supreme Court on a writ of error.

For reasons that are not disclosed in the record, the Marshall court did not hear the case until 1833, more than a decade after it began its progress through the state courts. By that time, federal-state relations had reached a point of crisis. During the previous year, a defiant South Carolina had purported to "nullify" a congressional tariff law, while the state of Georgia in *Worcester v. Georgia* had refused to enforce a Court decision affecting Indian rights. Although both controversies appeared to be heading toward a peaceful resolution, the justices could not have been unmindful of their potential consequences as they considered Barron's claims.

For a unanimous Court, Chief Justice John Marshall dismissed the *Barron* case for want of jurisdiction. The compensation clause of the Fifth Amendment did not apply to the states, he ruled, and the case thus presented no federal question that the Court was empowered to decide.

In reaching this conclusion, Marshall relied in part on constitutional construction. He pointed particularly to the contrasting language used in Article I, Sections 9 and 10. Section 9, whose restrictions clearly apply only to the federal government, makes extensive use of general provisions, of the sort found in many of the later amendments. Section 10, which limits state power, contains no such general terminology. Instead, each paragraph begins with a specific reference to state action ("No State shall . . ."). The argument from analogy, while reasonable, was scarcely conclusive, because Marshall presented no evidence that those who framed the amendments intended to emulate the style of the main text.

More compelling was his appeal to history. The opponents of the Constitution had pressed for amendments at the state ratifying conventions, he noted, out of fear of federal power: "These amendments demanded security against the apprehended encroachments of the general government—not against those of the local governments." Congress and the states later responded to these same pressures by adopting the first ten amendments. "These amendments contain no expression indicating an intention to apply them to the state governments," Marshall concluded. "This court cannot so apply them."

Barron was Marshall's last constitutional opinion, written when he was in failing health and despondent over the future of the Union. But it did not signal the Court's capitulation to the states' rights extremism of the time. Marshall's history, unfortunately, was quite accurate. The records of the ratifying conventions support his position, as do prior state-court decisions. Later courts extended the *Barron* holding by inevitable analogy to the rest of the Bill of Rights, and thus continued to prevent the federal government from interfering with state violations of civil rights.

Since the 1920s, however, successive Supreme Courts have found an indirect way to expand federal power in this area by resorting to the due process clause of the Fourteenth Amendment ("nor shall any State deprive any person of life, liberty, or property, without due process of law"). By defining specific guarantees of the Bill of Rights as fundamental rights implicit in the concept of due process, judges have gradually brought almost all of these guarantees under federal control. But the process of "selective incorporation" has been slow, erratic, controversial, and confusing. Had the *Barron* case been decided differently, these cumbersome maneuvers would not have been necessary.

In the 1990s, the Supreme Court showed renewed interest in protecting the property rights of individuals against a threatened "taking" by government agencies. In *Dolan v. City of Tigard* (1994), the Court, by a narrow 5-4 majority, ruled that the environmental safeguards imposed on a land developer by a municipal government amounted to a taking of his property without just compensation. The decision, like other evidence of a resurgent conservative constitutionalism since the "Reagan revolution" of the 1980s, may signal a more vigorous enforce-ment of the property clauses of the Constitution in the future.

Selected Bibliography

Currie, David P. *The Constitution in the Supreme Court: The First Hundred Years, 1789–1888.* Chicago, IL: University of Chicago Press, 1985.

Ely, James W., Jr. *The Guardian of Every Other Right: A Constitutional History of Property Rights,* 2d ed. New York: Oxford University Press, 1998.

Johnson, Herbert A. *The Chief Justiceship of John Marshall, 1801–1835.* Columbia: University of South Carolina Press, 1997.

White, G. Edward. *History of the Supreme Court of the United States, Vols. III–IV: The Marshall Court and Cultural Change, 1815–35.* New York, NY: Macmillan, 1988.

Defining Free-Speech Protection in the World War I Era

Carol E. Jenson

Minneapolis, Minnesota

Schenck v. United States, 249 U.S. 47 (1919) and *Abrams v. United States*, 250 U.S. 616 (1919) [U.S. Supreme Court]

◄◦► THE CASE IN BRIEF ◄◦►

Date
1919

Location
Pennsylvania
New York

Court
U.S. Supreme Court

Principal Participants
Charles Schenck
Jacob Abrams
Justice Oliver Wendell Holmes Jr.

Significance of the Case
In response to two Socialist Party leaflets distributed during World War I, the Court introduced a clear-and-present-danger doctrine as a test to evaluate challenges to the First Amendment protection of freedom of speech.

For over one hundred and twenty-five years, following the adoption of the Bill of Rights in 1791, the U.S. Supreme Court considered no First Amendment free-speech cases based on federal law. Then, the advent of U.S. involvement in World War I and the passage of the 1917 Espionage Act and its 1918 Sedition Act supplement led to High Court interpretation of the extent to which political speech might be protected in times of war. In initiating development of that interpretation, Justice Oliver Wendell Holmes Jr. introduced his clear-and-present-danger doctrine in March 1919 in the unanimous opinion in *Schenck v. United States*. He clarified it further in November of the same year when Justice Louis D. Brandeis joined him in the dissent in *Abrams v. United States*.

In June 1917, two months after the United States entered the war against Germany, Congress passed the Espionage Act. The act established three basic wartime offenses: conveying false information intending to interfere with U.S. military operations, causing insubordination in the military, and obstructing recruiting.

The statute also made it a criminal offense to use the U.S. mail for any of these purposes.

The Espionage Act did not satisfy a number of advocates of increased wartime zeal, who concluded that the statute did little to restrict what they saw as disloyal speech and activity. Accordingly, the Senate Judiciary Committee responded to Attorney General Thomas Gregory's modest request for amending the wording of the 1917 act by including sweeping statements adding nine additional offenses to the original list of three.

After Congress passed the Sedition Act in May 1918, no one was to say or write anything that might in any way bring contempt or disrepute upon the U.S. government, flag, uniform, or Constitution or intend to promote resistance to U.S. policies. These two pieces of legislation, the second an amendment and supplement to the first, were the statutes involved in the two most prominent free-speech cases of the World War I period: *Schenck* and *Abrams*.

On August 13, 1917, two months after the passage of the Espionage Act, Charles Schenck and other members of the Executive Committee of the Socialist Party, meeting in Philadelphia, voted to print fifteen thousand leaflets to be mailed to men who had passed the first phase of the conscription program. Within a few days, Schenck directed the printing of the pamphlets and purchased stamped envelopes for the mailing.

The pamphlet challenged the draft on grounds that it violated the Constitution's supremacy clause as well as the rights protected under the First and Ninth Amendments. The Socialists reasoned that officials who administered conscription contradicted the concept of the Constitution as the supreme law of the land as well as the philosophy of individual rights because "they refuse to recognize your right to assert your opposition to the draft." The leaflet also argued that the draft interfered with freedom of religion, as it forced individuals to disregard the Old Testament commandment, "Thou shalt not kill." The law exempted only clergy and Quakers on religious grounds; others were subject to the conscription law and therefore suffered discrimination.

Socialists argued that it was the citizens' duty to assert individual rights and to seek the election of officials opposed to the draft policy. The pamphlet used the classic anticonscription argument made by a number of politicians during debate over passage of the 1917 draft law. The leaflet pointed out that many immigrants settled in the United States because of opposition to European militarism and that President Woodrow Wilson had won reelection in 1916 by promising to keep the United States out of the European conflict.

The leaflet advocated resistance to the "moloch of militarism," which, according to Socialist contentions, was leading U.S. policy to undermine the Constitution and was presenting "jingoism masquerading under the guise of patriotism." The Socialist argument maintained that democracy could not be the result of war but only of education, thereby challenging President Wilson's idea of a "War to Make the World Safe for Democracy." Furthermore, the Socialists challenged the draft as a violation of the Thirteenth Amendment's ban on involuntary servitude.

The pamphlet denounced what it termed the tactics of governmental intimidation and appealed for an adherence to constitutional principles of free speech, assembly, and petition rather than a submission to the intimidating tactics of war zealots. Nowhere did the pamphlet mention anything about overthrow of the government. Rather, it supported the Constitution and advocated a more intensive forum for discussion of issues, using First Amendment rights of free speech and peaceful assembly, and urged people to come into the headquarters to sign an anticonscription petition to be sent to Congress. The words of the circular pleaded: "Help us re-establish democracy in America. Remember, eternal vigilance is the price of liberty." These Socialists saw the Constitution as the principal protector of the rights they were attempting to exercise.

Several persons who received the leaflets in the mail complained to Philadelphia postal inspectors, who then approached the U.S. Attorney's Office. The investigation led to a search of the Socialist Party headquarters on August 28. Agents seized as evidence a file of newspaper clippings with lists of names of draft inductees, a pile of circulars, and the minute book of the party's executive committee. The federal authorities questioned a number of young men and arrested Charles Schenck, the party's general secretary and the person in charge of the office. Later, police arrested four other members of the executive committee for violating the 1917 Espionage Act.

After a September arraignment at which Schenck pleaded "not guilty," the trial began on December 17, 1917, before Judge J. Whitaker Thompson in the U.S. District Court for the Eastern District of Pennsylvania. The United States contended that Schenck and others had used the post to send materials considered nonmailable under the Espionage Act. The prosecution presented testimony from postal inspectors and a number of young men who had received copies of the circular. In cross-examination by defense attorney Henry John Nelson, several of these young men testified that the pamphlet had not made them feel insubordinate to the United States. Several of them had not even read it. Others indicated they had not received letters addressed to them; this raised the possibility of post office intervention.

Attorney Nelson also raised objections, which led to repeated discussion regarding the introduction of the minute book as evidence. He contended that presentation of this material violated the constitutional protection of his clients' rights against self-incrimination. After some deliberation, Judge Thompson overruled the objection. Later, the court held that the prosecution could not introduce the minute book because it constituted hearsay evidence, inadmissible in federal criminal conspiracy trials.

When Judge Thompson made his charge to the jury, he asked for a directed verdict of not guilty for three defendants, but he pursued the charges against Charles Schenck and Elizabeth Baer for conspiracy and willful use of the mail to commit an offense against the United States. The jury was not to determine the constitutionality of the law but to decide if the leaflets "advocate forcible resistance," which would make them nonmailable. The judge pointed out that committing a conspiracy required an agreement to do something, but conspiracy was not determined by whether the objective was achieved. The jury agreed that advocacy had occurred and convicted Schenck and Baer on December 20.

The court sentenced Schenck to six months and Elizabeth Baer to ninety days.

After the court denied a motion for a new trial in March 1918, attorneys for Schenck and Baer requested an assignment of errors to the U.S. Supreme Court. The subsequent brief, filed in December 1918 (just after the armistice), questioned the constitutionality of the Espionage Act in relation to First Amendment protection of freedom of speech and petition. Attorneys Nelson and Henry Gibbons saw the act as an infringement upon necessary political discourse. "How can the citizens find out whether a war is just or unjust unless there is free and full discussion?" According to their analysis, the most critical statement in the Socialist circular contended that a "conscript is little more than a convict," a statement attributed to Missouri congressman Champ Clark in a speech on the floor of the House of Representatives. Such a statement hardly advocated interference with war aims.

Referring to the twelve hundred cases that had arisen under the Espionage Act, Schenck's attorneys contended that the law was out of step with English and American legal developments. In this tradition, a distinction had been drawn between (1) speech that involved sincere and honest communication of opinion and (2) speech that involved incitement of a "forbidden action." In their view, the Espionage Act destroyed this distinction and made honest discussion an indictable offense. Therefore, the statute violated the First Amendment.

Gibbons and Nelson challenged the trial procedures, questioning the conspiracy evidence and the seizure of the papers from the Socialist headquarters. They argued that the acts had been committed before the Supreme Court held the draft law to be constitutional and that the evidence introduced was insufficient to support conviction. Furthermore, they said the government presented no evidence that Schenck and Baer had mailed the leaflets, that the granting of the search warrant had not been based upon probable cause, and that the seizure of private papers violated Fifth Amendment protection against self-incrimination because private written words were introduced as evidence. They concluded that the case involved a political issue in which the law attempted to restrict a small group of citizens "steadfastly standing for what they honestly, conscientiously believe."

John Lord O'Brian, special assistant to the attorney general for war work, and Alfred Bettman, special assistant to the attorney general, prepared the government response. In their earlier careers, both men had subscribed to the concept of freedom of discussion, and they were knowledgeable about the content of left-wing literature. However, under the pressure of wartime circumstances, they came to view the Espionage and Sedition Acts as a way of calming the wartime hysteria, which advocated far more drastic action against those with dissenting views. O'Brian and Bettman feared mob action and believed these laws would calm the public.

In their brief, O'Brian and Bettman argued that the case did not involve the First Amendment; therefore, claims involving free-speech violations were frivolous. Consequently, the Supreme Court should refuse to hear the case because the issue had been settled in previous cases—particularly in the *Selective Draft Law Cases* in 1918. Apparently, O'Brian and Bettman saw no legal distinction between the refusal to comply with a draft summons and the discussion of the law as a matter of public policy and individual rights.

In the unanimous ruling of March 3, 1919, the Supreme Court presented Justice Holmes's clear-and-present-danger test, a doctrine much discussed and evaluated in subsequent years. Holmes's analysis tied the act of political speech to the "circumstances in which it is done." He argued that the persons who sent the document intended it to have the effect of obstructing persons from complying with the draft.

"The question in every case," Holmes wrote, "is whether the words used are used in such circumstances and are of such a nature as to create a clear and present danger that they will bring about the substantive evils that Congress has a right to prevent." According to Holmes, those arrested had been attempting to interfere with congressional conduct of war policy and therefore had committed "substantial evils." He went on to distinguish wartime circumstances from more peaceful contexts and argued that, since the statute punished conspiracies as well as ob-

struction, it was not necessary for the action to be successful in order to violate the law.

Shortly after his introduction of the clear-and-present-danger doctrine in *Schenck*, Holmes wrote two more unanimous opinions in Espionage Act cases. These discussions reveal a restricted view of the First Amendment and provide little clarification of the clear-and-present-danger test. In *Frohwerk v. United States* (1919), the Court upheld the conviction of Jacob Frohwerk, who had published a number of articles critical of the draft in a Missouri German-language newspaper. The justices determined that Frohwerk's words might "be enough to kindle a flame of resistance." This opinion presented a definite "bad tendency" application, which meant that one could be found guilty of violating a statute if what a person said produced a tendency to bring about an evil effect. Such a tendency did not rely on any causal relationship.

In *Debs v. U.S.* (1919), the Court upheld the conviction of the prominent Socialist Eugene Debs for delivering a speech in Canton, Ohio, in which he attacked capitalist wars. Also, Debs had informed the trial jury that he abhorred war, and his 1917 Socialist Party platform had advocated war opposition. On this basis, the Court held that Debs's speech intended to obstruct recruiting. However, Holmes did not apply any clear-and-present-danger analysis, but relied entirely upon the tendency of Debs's words.

In the years since 1919, much of the discussion generated by Holmes's famous doctrine has centered on just where he meant to draw the line between protected and unprotected speech. A forceful scholarly argument has concluded that, in subsequent months, Holmes honed his *Schenck* reasoning and developed the apparently more libertarian application written eight months later in his *Abrams* dissent in a case involving another group who challenged wartime restrictions on political expression.

Jacob Abrams, along with Socialist Samuel Lipman and fellow anarchists Hyman Lachowsky, Jacob Schwartz, and Mollie Steimer, were all Russian-born Jews struggling to make a new life in the traditional New York immigrant trades. The difficult working conditions and the resistance of employers to making any improvements brought Abrams and the others to consider anarchism and socialism as avenues in which to seek redress. The five became involved in a group that published a Yiddish-language anarchist paper, *Der Shturm* (The Storm), which had a limited circulation in the Jewish neighborhoods of East Harlem. Members of Abrams's group sometimes attended meetings of a No-Conscription League organized by better-known anarchists Emma Goldman and Alexander Berkman, who were supporters of the 1917 Russian Revolution.

During August 1918, the group reacted passionately when the United States decided to join the British and French Allies in intervening on behalf of Czechoslovakian troops trapped in the Ukraine when the Bolsheviks exited the war in the Treaty of Brest-Litovsk. In attempting to flee via Vladivostok, the Czechs had become involved in confrontations with the Red Army. President Wilson responded to pressure from those who blamed German influence for the Russian withdrawal from the war. On a pretext of self-defense, Wilson dispatched seven thousand troops to aid the Czechs in Siberia.

The Abrams group viewed Wilson's action as a violation of the concept of the 1917 revolution. They reacted by purchasing their own printing press and preparing two protest statements—one in English and one in Yiddish—critical of U.S. intervention. On August 22 and 23, fellow anarchist sympathizers distributed the leaflets by scattering them from rooftops at several Manhattan locations. The English version was entitled "The Hypocrisy of the United States and Her Allies" and included fewer than four hundred words. Author Samuel Lipman cautiously accused Wilson of deceiving the American people concerning the intervention. Lipman pointed to allied capitalism, combined with German militarism, as the enemy of the world and called upon workers to "Awake!" He closed by denouncing German militarism and disavowing any alleged pro-German connections on the part of his group. Nowhere did the leaflet advocate any specific action.

Jacob Schwartz wrote the more militant Yiddish flyer, entitled "Workers Wake Up!!" which

was not translated into English until after the indictment. He accused the United States of hypocrisy in misleading people into support of the war and of using Russian immigrants to produce munitions to shoot Russian revolutionaries as well as Germans. He perceived the "barbaric intervention" as a betrayal of workers and an attempt to destroy the Bolshevik revolution, and he called for a general strike, although he provided no organizational details. Subsequent translations of the leaflet have raised questions about the degree of militancy expressed in the version used at the trial. Some interpretations view the words as less harsh than the prosecution's version.

On August 23, New York police officers quickly traced the leaflets to Hyman Rosansky, one of the distributors and a fringe anarchist sympathizer. He confessed readily and agreed to serve as a police decoy when the members of the Abrams group made contact with him. By the end of the evening, police had arrested the five major participants as well as Rosansky and Gabriel Prober for violation of the 1918 Sedition Act.

Officers interrogated the group with assistance from the Military Intelligence Division (MID) of the U.S. Army, which had been integrated into the New York Police Department for the surveillance of radicals. Police successfully worked to obtain a confession from each person arrested. Procedures included beatings and other forms of mistreatment later implicated in the jailhouse death of Jacob Schwartz.

On September 12, a federal grand jury handed down a four-count indictment charging those arrested with conspiring to publish the leaflets, using "language intended to bring the government of the United States into contempt" and inciting resistance to the United States in the war. The fourth count charged that defendants attempted "to oppose the cause of the United States in said war." Francis Caffey, the U.S. attorney for the Southern District of New York and one who advocated "extermination" of war critics, revised the final count so that it included conspiracy "to urge . . . curtailment of things and products . . . necessary and essential to the prosecution of the war . . . with intent . . . to cripple and hinder the United States." According to Caffey's reasoning, opposition to intervention equaled a pro-Bolshevik position, which in turn was equivalent to a pro-German stand. He firmly believed all pro-Germans, and therefore all Bolsheviks, should be in prison. Caffey often relied upon rumors, particularly those connecting the Abrams group with well-known anarchist Emma Goldman. Caffey also was in the habit of submitting the names of potential jurors in espionage and sedition cases to the Justice Department's newly created Bureau of Investigation. Consequently, he could rely on these background checks as a basis for peremptory challenges during jury selection.

The Abrams trial began on September 30, 1918, in the midst of an influenza epidemic that many New Yorkers blamed on German agents. Harry Weinberger, associated with earlier anarchist clients, defended Abrams and his colleagues before Judge Harry DeLamar Clayton, a patriarchal Alabamian temporarily assigned to relieve a heavy New York court docket. A former congressman and the author of the antitrust law that bears his name, Clayton harbored an intense hatred of Germany, which intensified when his younger brother was killed in the Great War. He saw the activities of radicals as a threat to a system of paternalism and "one hundred percent Americanism."

During the proceedings, prosecution attorneys John M. Ryan and Sanford Miller focused only on attempting to show that the defendants wrote, printed, and distributed the leaflets involved. For four days, they called a parade of government witnesses that included a number of police officers as well as the man who had sold Abrams the printing press and the woman who had rented him the apartment where the meetings and printing activity took place. Police testified they found partially burned copies of the leaflets there as well. The prosecution used this information, as well as testimony that established Abrams's use of an alias at various times, to support the government's claim that the group acted surreptitiously.

Prosecutors also used witnesses' testimony to place into the record Mollie Steimer's earlier answer to a question indicating that she knew the leaflets were unlawful when she distributed them. With these trial tactics, prosecutors

attempted to demonstrate that the defendants conspired with criminal intent. However, Ryan and Miller did not attempt to show that the leaflets specifically intended to interfere with the American intervention or that they had any effect on U.S. policy. Essentially, the prosecution concentrated on depicting the Abrams group as dangerous, conniving radicals.

In conducting the defense, Weinberger cross-examined the government witnesses, but for the most part did not challenge their testimony. However, he contended, very strongly at times, that the acts were not criminal in nature. Furthermore, he claimed that the five principals were victims of police brutality, and he attempted to demonstrate this charge in his cross-examination of the officers. This tactic proved unsuccessful when Judge Clayton sustained several prosecution objections and later reprimanded Weinberger for overstepping his role as attorney. Several of the officers denied any improper behavior, and the judge accepted their denials at face value. Further demonstration of Judge Clayton's disposition in the trial occurred when he ordered Weinberger to take his seat as the defense attorney attempted to question an undercover MID agent who had been attending various radical meetings. Clayton then made an ethnic comment: "I have tried to out-talk an Irishman, and I never can do it, and the Lord knows I can not out-talk a Jew."

Weinberger also attempted to respond to prosecution assumptions that pro-Bolsheviks equaled pro-Germans. He called to the witness stand social reformer Raymond Robins and journalist and Congregational minister Albert Rhys Williams, two vigorous opponents of the Wilson intervention policy. Both men had observed the 1917 revolution firsthand, and they maintained that the Bolsheviks, prior to their withdrawal from the war, had sought military and economic cooperation with the United States. A counterview, based on information found in questionable documents released through the wartime Committee on Public Information, maintained that the Germans dictated the 1917 revolution as well as subsequent Bolshevik policies. Weinberger's goal was to discredit the German-Bolshevik link. Although Judge Clayton allowed Weinberger to question

Robins and Williams, he forbade the witnesses to answer the questions.

During the proceedings, Judge Clayton questioned witnesses, a rather common practice in federal trials in 1918. He interrogated the defendants in a hostile manner and inquired why they had not returned to Russia since they were so critical of the United States. He preached the virtues of an agrarian life to these New York workers and concluded verbally from the bench that they were not producers because they had never grown anything, not even a potato. While instructing the jury, Judge Clayton delivered a long lecture on intent, emphasizing what he saw as the attempted secrecy of the defendants' actions. He rejected a number of the points Weinberger had requested to be included in the charge, including a statement to the effect that the government had presented no evidence that the defendants had attempted to aid Germany. Instead, their objective had been to protest intervention in Russia. After a deliberation of only a little more than an hour, the jury convicted all of the defendants. On October 25, after delivering a two-hour tirade on the evils of German and Bolshevik agents, Judge Clayton sentenced Abrams, Lachowsky, and Lipman to twenty years and Mollie Steimer to fifteen years.

While awaiting a direct appeal to the U.S. Supreme Court, Weinberger managed to arrange bail, financed by friends of the defendants who ironically provided Liberty bonds as the principal security. The defendants were under continued surveillance as the post–World War I Red Scare went into full swing. The Federal Bureau of Investigation's J. Edgar Hoover proceeded with the early stages of establishing his master file of suspicious persons; and the government sought evidence of anarchist activity to serve as a basis for deportation—for the Abrams group as well as others.

In this atmosphere, the Supreme Court heard oral arguments in the Abrams case on October 21, 1919. Weinberger's brief argued that the evidence presented did not support a guilty verdict. His clients had been engaged in mere criticism involved with public discussion of a public policy, and according to his argument, such discussion enjoyed First Amendment immunity from government restriction. Because the United States was not at war with the Soviet Union, this discussion could not be interpreted as interference with the war effort in any way. Weinberger contended further that the Espionage Act of 1917 and its 1918 Sedition Act amendment were both unconstitutional, because they violated the natural right of liberty of discussion.

Originally, the argument for the defense of the Sedition Act had been assigned to O'Brian and Bettman of the Justice Department's Emergency War Division. However, with the war's end, O'Brian and Bettman had resigned their jobs in May 1919, after having urged pardons for all those convicted under the Espionage and Sedition Acts—including the Abrams group. The task of presenting the government's case then fell to Assistant Attorney General Robert T. Stewart. He and his assistant, W. C. Herron, put together arguments never used at the trial. They contended that the group had attempted to interfere with munitions production and had intended to overthrow the government by force. They argued a static constitutional view that subscribed to the doctrine of seditious libel and claimed that the First Amendment had been created merely to protect the press from prior restraint. Such a position reflected a narrow, eighteenth-century, English common-law view that provided no protection for public discussion and criticism of public policy.

On November 10, 1919, the Court in a 7-2 decision upheld the conviction of Abrams and his colleagues. Justice John Clarke's opinion rested on narrow, procedural grounds, which found the evidence sufficient to convict. He quoted the leaflets selectively and out of context to demonstrate the defendants' anarchist views, and he commented on their failure to apply for U.S. citizenship. Even though the trial prosecutors had not dealt with the issue of intent, Clark concluded that "men must be held to have intended, and to be accountable for effects which their acts were likely to produce."

In applying this "bad tendency" test, Clarke reasoned that the Abrams group's plan for aiding the Soviet cause involved support for defeat of the U.S. war effort because their leaflet advocated the tactic of a general strike. Bad-tendency reasoning would argue that, if such a strike had taken place, it could have interfered with munitions production and thus affected the war effort. According to Clark, the leaflets attempted to embarrass the U.S. government, to defeat U.S. war plans, and "to provoke and encourage resistance to the United States in the war." Such activity, regardless of outcome, violated the 1918 Sedition Act.

Justices Holmes and Louis Brandeis dissented. Holmes centered his argument on the government's failure to demonstrate intent in the case. In his words, "a deed is not done with intent to produce a consequence unless that consequence is the aim of the deed." Holmes did not recant the line of reasoning he applied earlier in the year in the *Schenck*, *Frohwerk*, and *Debs* opinions because he continued to acknowledge that dangers to the government were greater during wartime. However, he insisted in his dissent that a present danger must relate to an immediate evil, which in this case the defendants' words had not created because they had demonstrated no specific intent to damage the war effort. Their intention had been to aid Bolsheviks, not Germans. The key to creating a clear and present danger was a relationship between specific intent and a specifically evil effect. According to Holmes, "the defendants had as much right to publish [the leaflets] as the Government has to publish the Constitution of the United States."

Holmes went on in the final paragraph of the dissent to elaborate and clarify his ideas on freedom of speech, which he had wrestled with and developed in the months since his *Schenck* opinion. He granted that if a person were certain of his position, it was "logical" to try to "sweep away all opposition," because allowing discussion seemed to imply that the position is weak and fallible. But when men have realized that time has "upset many fighting faiths they may come to believe . . . that the ultimate good desired is better reached by free trade in ideas—that the best test of truth is the power of the thought to get itself accepted in the competition of the market and that truth is the only ground upon which their wishes safely can be carried out. That at any rate is the theory of our Constitution."

These now famous words became the cornerstone of much subsequent clear-and-present-danger doctrine application. In order for speech to be restricted, dangers must present an immediate evil and connect to a specific action. Unless those conditions exist, speech should be allowed to make its case against competing ideas.

Upon close examination, the reasoning in Holmes's *Abrams* dissent does not appear to follow from his *Schenck* opinion written eight months previously, especially concerning the crucial relationship between intent and result. In *Schenck*, he had written that "it was not necessary for the action to be successful in order to violate the law." This consideration of intent is not consistent with his insistence in *Abrams* on the necessity to establish a connection between specific words and specific and immediate evil results. During the eight months between the two opinions, Holmes devoted considerable time to clarifying his First Amendment views for himself and his Court colleagues. After all, neither Holmes nor any other jurist had focused significant attention on this issue since free-speech interpretation was not yet a main body of constitutional interpretation.

During the summer of 1919, Holmes discussed the *Schenck* reasoning with other legal thinkers, including Judge Learned Hand and Harvard Law School professor Zechariah Chafee Jr., both of whom shared libertarian views on the value of political discussion. Holmes also met with English socialist Harold Laski, often a visiting professor at Harvard. These discussions, together with Holmes's own thoughtful consideration focusing on questions of intent and effect, help to explain the difference between Holmes's *Schenck* and *Abrams* views, a fine-tuning in legal reasoning that makes the difference between restricting speech or allowing it to seek acceptance "in the competition of the market."

In his *Abrams* dissent, Holmes acknowledged one of the basic concepts in his legal philosophy, that the law as well as life is an experiment. Citizens should be "eternally vigilant" against silencing unpopular opinions unless the threat is so great and so imminent that "an immediate check is required to save the country." Holmes concluded that this emergency did not exist in the *Abrams* case and that the government had deprived the defendants of their First Amendment rights. As far as Holmes was concerned, the law of seditious libel reflected in the 1918 Sedition Act did not apply. Two years later, in 1921, Congress repealed the Sedition Act; the Espionage Act remained on the books to apply again in times of declared war.

The Holmes dissent caused a stir among legal scholars who, for the first time since the adoption of the Bill of Rights, began to analyze the First Amendment seriously in terms of the value of political discussion within a democratic society. In this sense, the World War I espionage and sedition cases helped to define a new area of constitutional development and discussion. It would lead eventually to a stronger position for First Amendment freedoms, as the clear-and-present-danger approach developed in the *Abrams* dissent became the position of the Court majority in the 1930s.

Of course, Holmes's eloquent dissent could not save the Abrams defendants who endured prison sentences and then deportation to the Soviet Union in 1921. Eventually, their home-land also rejected each of them, and they were forced to go elsewhere to seek acceptance of their political views.

Selected Bibliography

Chafee, Zechariah, Jr. "A Contemporary State Trial: The United States versus Jacob Abrams et al." *Harvard Law Review.* 33 (April 1920): 747–774.

———. *Free Speech in the United States.* Cambridge, MA: Harvard University Press, 1941.

Murphy, Paul L. *World War I and the Origin of Civil Liberties in the United States.* New York: Norton, 1979.

Polenberg, Richard. *Fighting Faiths: The Abrams Case, the Supreme Court, and Free Speech.* New York: Viking, 1987.

Ragan, Fred. "Justice Oliver Wendell Holmes, Jr., Zechariah Chafee, Jr., and the Clear and Present Danger Test for Free Speech: The First Year, 1919." *Journal of American History* 58 (June 1971): 24–45.

White, G. E. *Justice Oliver Wendell Holmes: Law and the Inner Life.* New York: Oxford University Press, 1993.

Agrarian Reform and the Politics of Loyalty

—◦—

Carol E. Jenson
Minneapolis, Minnesota

Gilbert v. Minnesota, 254 U.S. 325 (1920) [U.S. Supreme Court]

◦ THE CASE IN BRIEF ◦

Date
1920

Location
Minnesota
District of Columbia

Court
U.S. Supreme Court

Principal Participants
Joseph Gilbert; State of Minnesota;
Justice Louis Brandeis

Significance of the Case
The Supreme Court majority voted to uphold the Minnesota sedition statute that denied a citizen his freedom of speech during World War I. In his dissent, Justice Louis Brandeis linked the Fourteenth Amendment to the Bill of Rights—a position the Court would accept five years later.

When the Nonpartisan League (NPL) farmers' reform organization moved its campaign from North Dakota to Minnesota in 1917, the group encountered fierce opposition from incumbent politicians bent on using wartime loyalty issues to discredit any attempt to promote political change. The confrontation led to the arrest of Joseph Gilbert and others, as the state's insistence on prevention of conflict clashed with the constitutional protection of the rights of free speech and assembly. The Gilbert case represented a series of Minnesota arrests of NPL leaders who fought early civil-liberties battles at the state level, while the more publicized confrontations involved the federal Espionage and Sedition Acts.

Organized in North Dakota in 1915 by ex-farmer A. C. Townley, the Nonpartisan League won control of the state government in the 1916 election. The chief goal of the farmers' organization was to increase farm income through improved marketing facilities, stricter regulation of elevators, lower interest rates, and state-owned facilities for the processing of agricultural products.

By the time the league attempted to extend its political successes to neighboring Minnesota, the United States had entered World War I, and Minnesota had preceded Congress in passing a sedition statue, which vaguely outlawed any advocacy discouraging the war effort. The legislature also created a Commission of Public Safety (CPS) empowered to coordinate wartime programs down to the township level and designed to ensure statewide loyalty by stopping disloyalty before it appeared.

According to the CPS, much of the potential disloyalty existed within the ranks of the Nonpartisan League, which sponsored a Producers and Consumers Conference in St. Paul in September 1917. The meeting attracted considerable attention when one featured speaker, war-entry opponent Senator Robert La Follette of Wisconsin, was misquoted by the Associated Press as stating that the United States had no grievances against Germany. Only verbatim transcripts produced by the U.S. Attorney's Office in Minnesota forced the AP to change its story months later. The La Follette furor obscured the fact that the league had reaffirmed its support of both the war effort and Wilson administration policies, and had criticized "those who are making extortionate profits out of the necessities of the people in time of war."

The September incident made the league the principal target of CPS suspicions, and Commission Vice-Chair Charles W. Ames wrote that "any movement which seeks to crystallize discontent" could not be dealt with tolerantly. As a result, the commission proceeded to process 682 "sedition" cases during the war months and further exercised its broad arbitrary powers by sending field agents to check on league meetings. The spies reported back to a disappointed CPS that disloyal speeches had not occurred and that league organizers and members had endorsed the Wilson administration's war efforts and the sale of Liberty bonds. After November 1, the commission dispensed with the agents and thereafter relied on rumor and statements from frightened local officials as the main sources of information. As anti-league rumors spread, communities in twenty-one of Minnesota's eighty-seven counties eventually denied the league access to speaking facilities and forbade league meetings.

In early 1918, the league intensified its political campaign, focusing on precinct caucuses and the June primary. The state nominating convention selected former congressman Charles A. Lindbergh Sr. as the NPL gubernatorial candidate in the Republican primary, pitting him against incumbent J. A. A. Burnquist, a firm supporter of the CPS and an advocate of vigorous enforcement of the state sedition act.

Throughout the campaign, Lindbergh had to battle charges of disloyalty. He had served in Congress for ten years, and prior to April 1917, he had opposed U.S. entry into the war, although his decision not to seek reelection in 1916 prevented him from casting his vote against intervention. However, once the United States entered the conflict, Lindbergh, like many other anti-interventionists, supported the war effort. His 1918 campaign speeches revealed his firm support of Wilson administration policies, including the Liberty bond and Red Cross campaigns.

Violence as well as denunciation plagued Lindbergh as he sought the gubernatorial nomination. Spies followed him, and more than once mobs pulled him from the speaker's platform. He was banned from Duluth and hanged in effigy in the southeastern Minnesota community of Red Wing. On one occasion, he emerged from a meeting to find a mob beating his driver. After considerable negotiation, Lindbergh persuaded the crowd to allow him to leave, only to be escorted by a shower of bullets. At this point, Lindbergh reportedly said to his driver, "We must not drive so fast. They will think we are afraid of them if we do."

At the height of the league primary campaign, a Goodhue County grand jury, in Red Wing, indicted league organization manager Joseph Gilbert for violation of the state sedition act. Gilbert was charged for remarks made in a speech on August 18, 1917, in the village of Kenyon, where he allegedly advocated "that men should not enlist" and that people should not support the war effort.

Gilbert's May trial, held one month before the primary, reflected the anti-league political atmosphere of much of the state. Defense witness George Breidel, threatened and forcibly dragged from the St. James Hotel in Red Wing, was later dumped and shot at in a rural area of the county. Local authorities made no attempt to apprehend or arrest the kidnappers. The jury convicted Gilbert after six prosecution witnesses repeated verbatim ten sentences that appeared in the indictment, a feature one of Gilbert's attorneys called "the only parrot chorus in the history of jurisprudence." The trial judge relied on a broad "bad tendency" application of the statute and instructed the jury that it wasn't necessary to show that Gilbert had advocated directly that men should not enlist or aid the war effort. Gilbert could be convicted "if the natural and reasonable effect of the words spoken" would lead to such advocacy.

The jury convicted Gilbert on May 10, and his attorneys appealed to the Minnesota Supreme Court, contending that Gilbert had not intended to interfere with the war effort. The appeal also cited the unusual testimony of the state's witnesses, reiterating in word-for-word fashion remarks Gilbert denied making. On December 20, 1918, the Minnesota Supreme Court upheld the sedition statute, finding that the state has the power to protect the people's welfare and concluding that the "statute would be violated if the natural and reasonable effect of the words spoken is to teach or advocate that citizens should not aid or assist the United States," regardless of what Gilbert intended.

In late January 1919, Gilbert's lawyers approached the U.S. Supreme Court on a writ of error. They argued that the trial court, in convicting Gilbert, had not considered intent an element necessary under the Minnesota sedition law. The brief questioned the courtroom procedures involving the "parrot chorus," as well as the constitutionality of a state venturing into legislation involving wartime activities—normally an area reserved to the national government. Gilbert's lawyers emphasized the basic and natural rights involved in freedom of speech and argued that the state legislature had no power to curtail them.

Attorneys for Minnesota argued that the Supreme Court was without jurisdiction in the case because of a lack of a federal question. They defended the statute as a police regulation that applied regardless of Gilbert's intent, and they maintained that the Constitution did not protect seditious speech of the type attributed to Gilbert.

When the High Court ruled in the Gilbert case in December 1920, it was the first time since the 1868 ratification of the Fourteenth Amendment that the justices had considered the issue of state sedition legislation. Seven members of the Court voted to uphold the Minnesota statute as part of a cooperative venture within the federal system, a "simple exertion of the police power to preserve the peace of the State."

In the opinion of the Court, Gilbert's words had created disorder, and the state was justified in arresting him. Justice Joseph McKenna's majority opinion declared further that the World War I cases prosecuted under the federal Espionage and Sedition Acts had established that free speech was not an absolute, but was subject to "restriction and limitation," especially during wartime. The opinion made no attempt to establish a relationship between Gilbert's words and their effect. In his brief dissent, Chief Justice Edward White accepted the contention of Gilbert's attorneys that the subject matter was "within the exclusive legislative power of Congress."

In contrast, Justice Louis Brandeis's dissent raised important new questions, which would become part of a compelling body of constitutional development for the remainder of the twentieth century. In Brandeis's view, the Minnesota statute was unconstitutional because it provided no test to determine a relationship between ideas and action. More importantly, Brandeis also raised the issue of the application of the Fourteenth Amendment to circumstances involving possible state infringement of basic liberties. He saw the Minnesota sedition act as an attempt to "prevent not acts but beliefs," and in his analysis this restriction interfered with the privileges and immunities of an American citizen. In his dissent, Brandeis supported vigorously the federal protection of freedom of speech and other Bill of Rights guarantees from state encroachment, a position the Court majority would accept in theory five years later in the better-known case of *Gitlow v. New York*. The concept of a nationalization of the Bill of Rights, which has evolved since 1925, developed from Brandeis's *Gilbert* dissent when he linked the Fourteenth Amendment to the Bill of Rights: "I cannot believe that the liberty guaranteed by the Fourteenth Amendment includes only liberty to acquire and to enjoy property."

The Nonpartisan League lost out in the 1918 Republican primaries in Minnesota. It attempted to regroup for the fall elections by forming a third party, but this campaign also was unsuccessful. The political disaster of several of these contests damaged the NPL in Minnesota; however, the reform ideas lived on in the Farmer-Labor Party, which replaced the league in the agrarian protest tradition and eventually merged with Minnesota's Democratic Party in the 1940s. Arthur LeSueur, one of Gilbert's attorneys, and A. B. Gilbert, editor of the *Nonpartisan Leader*, became active in the American Civil Liberties Union in the 1920s, contributing an often overlooked midwestern and agrarian element to that movement.

Selected Bibliography

Chrislock, C. *Watchdog of Loyalty: The Minnesota Commission of Public Safety during World War I*. St. Paul, MN: Minnesota Historical Society Press, 1991.

Jenson, Carol E. *Agrarian Pioneer in Civil Liberties*. New York: Garland, 1986.

———. "Loyalty as a Political Weapon: The 1918 Campaign in Minnesota." *Minnesota History* 43 (Summer 1972): 42–57.

Morlan, Robert. *Political Prairie Fire*. Minneapolis: University of Minnesota Press, 1955.

Expanding Free Speech to the States

—◦—

Harold Josephson
Deceased Professor of History
University of North Carolina at Charlotte

Gitlow v. New York, 268 U.S. 652 (1925) [U.S. Supreme Court]

—◦— THE CASE IN BRIEF —◦—

Date
1925

Location
New York
District of Columbia

Court
U.S. Supreme Court

Principal Participants
Benjamin Gitlow
Clarence Darrow
State of New York

Significance of the Case
A communist manifesto case challenged states' rights and civil liberties, leading the Court to hold for the first time that state laws restricting speech were to be judged by a selective application of the language of the Bill of Rights.

Prior to World War I, the Supreme Court treated the freedom-of-speech provision of the Constitution with benign neglect, saying nothing about when state legislatures could or could not limit expression. For the most part, the American people embraced freedom of speech as a theoretical principle and took it for granted. Unfortunately, neither Congress nor the Supreme Court transformed this First Amendment concept into a legal doctrine that would guarantee expression to all citizens.

Because almost no litigation relative to freedom of speech reached the Supreme Court, the limits of constitutional expression lacked definition. To make matters worse, the Court held in *Barron v. Baltimore* (1833) that the federal restrictions and liberties guaranteed by the Bill of Rights did not apply to the states, thereby allowing them to abridge speech, as well as other liberties, at their discretion.

Restrictions on civil liberties increased at the turn of the century, as state governments and local communities sought to curtail the activities of the growing radical movement in the

845

United States. Socialists, anarchists, and other radical critics of American society found little sympathy within the general community and faced sharp limitations during the Progressive Era. World War I carried repression even further. Federal laws, such as the Espionage Act of 1917 and the Sedition Act of 1918, put pacifists, conscientious objectors, radicals, and aliens on the defensive.

The end of the war brought no decline in political repression. Instead, it led to increased anxiety in the face of political upheavals in Europe, unprovoked bombings, inflation, unemployment, and the outbreak of strikes throughout the country. Led by Attorney General A. Mitchell Palmer, federal, state, and local officials in the winter of 1919–1920 rounded up and arrested labor radicals, Socialists, and Communists in a series of spectacular raids.

Because the Espionage and Sedition Acts had lost the force of law when the war ended, states replaced the federal government as the primary agency for prosecuting radicals. By 1920, some thirty-five states had passed repressive measures. In New York, one of the first Communists arrested was Benjamin Gitlow, a former Socialist assemblyman and founder of the Communist Labor Party, one of two Communist parties organized in 1919. Instead of passing a new antiradical statute after the war, New York chose to resurrect a 1902 Criminal Anarchy Act, enacted shortly after the assassination of President William McKinley. Rarely used before 1919, the law defined *criminal anarchy* as the doctrine that organized government should be overthrown by force or violence, by the assassination of executive officials, or by any other unlawful means. The specific charge against Gitlow and several other leading Communists was that they had violated the Criminal Anarchy Act by their association with the radical publications *Revolutionary Age* and the "Left Wing Manifesto." The manifesto, according to the indictment, was not only a broad critique of capitalism and a general defense of revolutionary socialism, but it was also an inflammatory call for immediate revolution.

Of the many Communists arrested in New York, Gitlow stood trial first. Assistant District Attorney Alexander Rorke reasoned that Git-

low's position as business manager of the *Revolutionary Age* made him more vulnerable than the others to the charge of publishing the paper. At the trial, Rorke argued that the "Left Wing Manifesto" clearly called for the violent, unlawful overthrow of the government and thereby came under the provisions of the Criminal Anarchy Act. According to Rorke, Gitlow's central objective in publishing the manifesto was "the destruction, the conquest and the annihilation of the government of the United States."

The defense team, led by the renowned Clarence Darrow, admitted that Gitlow was a Communist, that he was the business manager of the paper, and that he had responsibility for its publication and circulation. Darrow denied, however, that the manifesto was a call for violent revolution or that it came within the prohibitions of the Criminal Anarchy Act. He also challenged the statute's constitutionality, declaring that it violated not only New York's guarantee of freedom of speech and press, but that it also violated the Fourteenth Amendment to the Constitution, which prohibited states from depriving persons of life, liberty, or property without due process of law.

This final argument, that the due process clause of the Fourteenth Amendment held state governments to the same standards of free speech as the First Amendment held Congress, was originally promulgated at Gitlow's preliminary hearing by Walter Nelles of the National Civil Liberties Bureau (the precursor of the American Civil Liberties Union). Both Nelles and Darrow hoped to use the Gitlow case to convince the Court that the Fourteenth Amendment reversed the legal doctrine, promulgated in *Barron v. Baltimore*, that the Bill of Rights did not apply to the states. They also wished to move Gitlow's defense from a narrow discussion of the contents of the manifesto to the broader issue of free speech and the repressive nature of laws like New York's Criminal Anarchy Act. Both attorneys emphasized that, because the law prohibited both actions and the promulgation of radical ideas, it threatened the constitutional guarantee of freedom of speech. In his trial summation, Darrow drove this point home. Communists, he declared, might be wrong, but they had to be given a chance to preach and to try to make the world a better place. The real danger to the nation was not in their ideas or publications, but in the government's attempt to curtail free expression. To send Gitlow to jail merely for holding unpopular views, he told the jurors, would be "to strike one blow which means the death of freedom in the United States."

Darrow's attempt to focus on the broader constitutional issues in the case was undermined by the presiding judge, Bartow S. Weeks. In his charge to the jury, Weeks declared that the New York Criminal Anarchy Act did not negate the right of free speech and that the constitutionality of the statute was not in question. The jury took only three hours to convict Gitlow, and on February 11, 1920, six days after the trial ended, Weeks sentenced him to five to ten years in prison, the maximum penalty allowed by law.

During the next several months, other Communists faced Justice Weeks, and they too were found guilty of violating the New York statute and joined Gitlow in prison. New York officials had found an effective method for removing antiestablishment leaders from public activity. All of those who followed Gitlow to jail, however, gained their freedom by 1923, either by having their convictions overturned on technicalities by the New York Court of Appeals or by being pardoned by Governor Alfred E. Smith. Smith postponed issuing a pardon for Gitlow, however, so that he and the American Civil Liberties Union could appeal his case to the Supreme Court and thus test the constitutionality of the state's criminal anarchy statute.

Both the Appellate Division and the New York Court of Appeals upheld Gitlow's conviction. Moreover, both rejected his contention that the New York statute violated the First Amendment and the due process clause of the Fourteenth Amendment. Gitlow did find some support on the court of appeals, where two of the justices, Benjamin Cardozo and Cuthbert W. Pound, dissented. Pound, who wrote the dissent, defined the term *anarchy* very narrowly and argued that, although the "Left Wing Manifesto" advocated the use of force and violence in overthrowing the government, it did not fall within the prohibitions of the New York statute. Gitlow had not sought to "establish" the Communist program, but rather to "teach" revolutionary doctrines and to "advocate" a fundamental change in the government. Strongly critical of Gitlow's aims, he pointed out that "although the defendant may be the worst of men; although left Wing socialism is a menace to organized government; the rights of the best of men are secure only as the rights of the vilest and most abhorrent are protected."

Both the ACLU and many radical organizations believed that a Supreme Court review of the case was important, for it would further clarify the rights of free speech and decide the extent to which Congress and state legislatures could suppress radical political dissent. Although the Supreme Court had offered little guidance as to the constitutional dimensions of the free-speech guarantee of the First Amendment prior to World War I, after the war it heard several cases that led to the establishment of new standards by which to judge the constitutionality of free-speech restrictions. In the first of these cases, *Schenck v. United States* (1919), Justice Oliver Wendell Holmes, writing a unanimous opinion, declared: "The question in every case is whether the words used are used in such circumstances and are of such a nature as to create a clear and present danger that they will bring about the substantive evils that Congress has a right to prevent."

Liberals and progressives cheered the clear-and-present-danger test, for it seemed to limit the curtailment of speech only to those instances where a direct and immediate relationship between expressed ideas and alleged acts could be proven. Unfortunately, while all of the justices agreed on the principle, they applied it very restrictively. Schenck, a prominent Socialist indicted for writing and circulating pamphlets counseling draft resistance in violation of the Espionage Act of 1917, found no relief, as the Court upheld his conviction. One week later, the Court again unanimously upheld lower-court convictions of violations of the Espionage Act in the cases of *Frohwerk v. United States* and *Debs v. United States*. Although the Court paid lip service to the clear-and-present-danger test, in each specific case it embraced the idea that legitimate abridgements of freedom of expression could be based upon the "bad tendency" of the words used, rather than upon their direct relation to illegal actions.

After considering the liberalizing potential of the clear-and-present-danger test, however, Justices Oliver Wendell Holmes and Louis D. Brandeis began to challenge the majority position. Eight months after the *Frohwerk* and *Debs* decisions, Brandeis and Holmes dissented in the case of *Abrams v. United States* (1919), the first of several famous dissents rejecting the doctrine of bad tendency and advocating a broader interpretation of the clear-and-present-danger test.

Although Gitlow's attorneys might have found some hope in the dissents of Holmes and Brandeis, they could find little encouragement in the Court decisions regarding challenges to state restrictions on individual rights. In 1920, in *Gilbert v. Minnesota*, the Court ruled that it had no authority to challenge a state's use of its police powers carried out in the public interest. Two years later, the Court formally rejected the concept that the Fourteenth Amendment prohibited states from abridging individual liberties.

Despite these rulings, the ACLU hoped to use the *Gitlow* case to move the Court majority toward the Holmes-Brandeis view of the First Amendment's guarantee of freedom of expression and toward an interpretation of the Fourteenth Amendment that would provide for federal protection against state abridgement of civil liberties. Unfortunately, on June 8, 1925, Justice E. Terry Sanford, writing for the Court's majority, found New York's Criminal Anarchy Act constitutional and upheld Gitlow's conviction. Sanford maintained that state legislatures, and not the courts, had responsibility for determining what kinds of utterances endangered society. They could not be required "to measure the danger from every such utterance in the nice balance of a jeweler's scale." States had a right and a duty to protect society from utterances that *might* lead to substantial danger, for "a single revolutionary spark may kindle a fire that, smoldering for a time, may burst into a sweeping and destructive conflagration." A state did not have to wait until that spark burst into a blaze before it could act.

On one issue and one issue only, the Court supported the ACLU arguments on behalf of

Gitlow. Without explanation or support, it held for the first time that state laws restricting speech were to be judged by the standards of the First Amendment. "For present purposes," wrote Sanford, "we may and do assume that freedom of speech and of the press—which are protected by the First Amendment from abridgment by Congress—are among the fundamental personal rights and 'liberties' protected by the due process clause of the Fourteenth Amendment from impairment by the states." Despite this important new principle, Sanford and the Court majority did not think that New York's Criminal Anarchy Act crossed the line of unconstitutionality, nor that Gitlow's conviction should be overturned.

In dissent, Holmes and Brandeis further clarified their argument, begun in *Abrams*, that unless speech posed a clear and present danger to society, there was more to be lost by its suppression than by its expression. Agreeing that the First Amendment should apply to the states, they stressed that no real threat was created by the distribution of the "Left Wing Manifesto." Holmes, writing the dissent, belittled the argument that the manifesto constituted an incitement. "Every idea," he argued, "is an incitement. It offers itself for belief, and, if believed, it is acted on unless some other belief outweighs it, or some failure of energy stifles the movement at its birth." Because the Court received no evidence that the manifesto would likely start an immediate conflagration, those responsible for its publication could not be prosecuted constitutionally. The dangers of suppression of speech far outweighed the state's desire to restrict expression that only remotely posed a threat to society. As in the *Abrams* case, however, Holmes and Brandeis could not move the Court majority to their position.

Reactions to the opinion were divided. Conservative newspapers and law journals found the majority opinion sound and appropriate. Radical and liberal commentators lamented the substitution of "bad tendency" for "clear and present danger" as the test for the constitutionality of legislative attempts to limit free speech. What few commentators perceived at the time, however, was how far the Court's new interpretation of the First and Fourteenth

Amendments would move it in the area of civil liberties. By the late 1960s, the Court, using the concept of "selective incorporation," had expanded the meaning of the due process clause of the Fourteenth Amendment so that states had to provide most of the guarantees and abide by most of the restrictions imposed upon the federal government in the Bill of Rights.

The Supreme Court's position on the proper limits of free speech also changed over time. As late as 1951, in the case of *Dennis v. United States*, the majority held that when the gravity of the evil was great enough, expression that threatened eventual violent revolution may be punished by the government without violating the Constitution. But first in *Yates v. United States* (1957) and then in *Brandenburg v. Ohio* (1969), the Court rejected the concept that the dangerous tendency of expression was sufficient to permit its suppression. In *Brandenburg*, the Court unanimously reaffirmed the distinction between advocacy of ideas and advocacy of illegal action. For speech to be constitutionally restricted, it had to pose an imminent danger that was real and not imaginary. The Court made clear that even threatening speech was protected unless it could be proved that the "advocacy is directed to inciting or producing imminent lawless action and is likely to incite or produce such action."

In 1925, when the Court issued the *Gitlow* decision, only Brandeis and Holmes called for a stronger defense of free speech, but not even they went so far as to advocate an incitement test for political expression. The Court majority, reflecting widespread popular opinion, believed that Communists and radicals should not be permitted to advocate ideas and policies that might eventually undermine public safety or the existing order of things. Gitlow returned to jail for a time, but was soon pardoned by

Governor Al Smith, after which he resumed active participation in the Communist Party.

It would take many years for the Holmes-Brandeis dissent in the *Gitlow* decision to become the majority opinion or for selective incorporation to apply key portions of the Bill of Rights to the states. Until that time, the Court, while embracing the principle that speech should be protected unless it posed a clear and present danger to society, nevertheless applied that principle in a limited fashion. This gap between legal doctrine and its application enabled conservative politicians to severely restrict the influence of radical organizations like the Communist Party by eliminating, through harassment and imprisonment, those who challenged American capitalism and the existing social structure. The *Gitlow* decision provided an opportunity for the future expansion of freedom, but in the context of the 1920s, it represented another triumph for unwarranted repression.

Selected Bibliography

Chafee, Zechariah, Jr. "Thirty-five Years with Freedom of Speech." *Kansas Law Review* 1 (November 1952): 1–36.

Curtis, M. K. *No State Shall Abridge: The Fourteenth Amendment and the Bill of Rights.* Durham, NC: Duke University Press, 1986.

Josephson, Harold. "Political Justice during the Red Scare: The Trial of Benjamin Gitlow." In *American Political Trials*, ed. Michal R. Belknap, 153–175. Westport, CT: Greenwood, 1981.

Kalven, Harry, Jr. *A Worthy Tradition: Freedom of Speech in America.* New York: Harper and Row, 1988.

Murphy, Paul L. *The Meaning of Freedom of Speech: First Amendment Freedoms from Wilson to FDR.* Westport, CT: Greenwood, 1979.

Warren, Charles. "The New 'Liberty' Under the Fourteenth Amendment." *Harvard Law Review* 39 (February 1926): 431–465.

Silencing Critics:
Guilt by Association in the 1920s

—◁◦▷—

Carol E. Jenson
Minneapolis, Minnesota

Whitney v. California, 274 U.S. 357 (1927) [U.S. Supreme Court]

◦► **THE CASE IN BRIEF** ◦►

Date
 1927

Location
 California

Court
 U.S. Supreme Court

Principal Participants
 Charlotte Anita Whitney
 State of California

Significance of the Case
 A civil rights activist challenged the California Criminal Syndication Act, an act that sought to silence advocates of violent political upheaval. The Supreme Court ruled that the law did not violate the Fourteenth Amendment's due process and equal protection clauses.

Charlotte Anita Whitney's concern for the poor and downtrodden led her to leave the security of her wealthy and influential family to pursue an activist career in social work and left-wing politics. Her involvement in socialist activities made her the focus of the first significant—and the most publicized—prosecution conducted under the April 20, 1919, California Criminal Syndicalism Act, an act that was designed to silence members of the Industrial Workers of the World (IWW), long active in California's agricultural fields and lumber camps.

The California statute, like a number of others passed by states in the early decades of the twentieth century, defined criminal syndicalism as "advocating, teaching or aiding . . . sabotage . . . or unlawful acts of force and violence . . . as a means of accomplishing a change in industrial ownership or control, or effecting any political change." From 1919 to 1924, California used the statute to arrest 504 people and to try 264, including Charlotte Whitney.

For a number of years, Whitney had been active in the Socialist Party in the United States and had participated in its Oakland, California, branch. At a convention in Chicago during the summer of 1919, she joined with other Oakland delegates to split from the main organization and form the Communist Labor Party (CLP). This group resolved to adhere to the principles of the Third International's manifesto to organize workers as a class movement. On November 9, Whitney and others held an Oakland convention to organize a California branch of the CLP. Whitney was active in convention proceedings, including the resolutions committee, which endorsed her views supporting traditional election procedures. This position clashed strongly with the views of the convention majority, who voted in favor of seizure of power through industrial unions and strikes.

On November 28, at the Oakland Center of the Civic League, Whitney delivered an address on the problems of American blacks. As she was leaving the meeting, authorities arrested her on a warrant that cited her attendance at the November 9 CLP convention. Later, the five counts brought against her for violation of the Criminal Syndicalism Act would charge her with illegal activities on or about November 28, the day of the Civic League speech, an event that had no connection to her CLP membership. This discrepancy was one of many confusing and contradictory aspects of the case.

Because none of the five charges brought against Whitney under the Criminal Syndicalism Act referred to any specific words or actions on her part, her attorney, J. E. Pemberton, filed a request for more precise and particular information. He contended that the charges were invalid because nothing Whitney had done constituted an offense under the act. The Alameda County Superior Court denied the motion as well as another defense request asking the judge to instruct the jury to acquit Whitney on grounds that the charges brought by the grand jury referred to the wrong date.

In the state's opening statement at the trial, which began in late January 1920, Deputy Alameda County District Attorney Myron Harris explained that it was his objective to make public the ideological positions of the CLP, even though it was Whitney who was on trial—not the party. The guilt by association procedures had begun.

Defense counsel Thomas M. O'Connor, a well-known San Francisco labor attorney, conducted the courtroom questioning in the early days of the trial, before his death from influenza on February 6. He objected repeatedly, and usually unsuccessfully, to a number of prosecution questions bearing no connection to Whitney and referring only to the CLP or the IWW. After O'Connor's death, Nathan Coghlan took over the courtroom defense of Whitney. He unsuccessfully protested the introduction of a long parade of IWW literature, including renditions of Joe Hill songs and organization history that predated the 1919 law. The court admitted these materials because the state presented evidence that demonstrated that at one point the CLP briefly and generally had endorsed IWW objectives.

Whitney served as the only defense witness, attempting to discount her influence in the CLP by explaining that the convention majority had voted down her position on political action. She did not deny her membership in the CLP, and that association led to her February 20 conviction on the first count, which referred to organizing and membership. The jury could not agree on the other four counts, and the state eventually dismissed them. Judge James Quinn sentenced Whitney to fourteen years in San Quentin for doing nothing more than attending the organizational meeting of the CLP, which in its founding Chicago convention had referred in passing to the debt that it felt workers owed to the IWW. The prosecution had convinced the jury of Whitney's guilt by association.

In her appeals to higher California courts, Whitney argued that her actions were insufficient to constitute a public offense and that there was insufficient evidence to demonstrate that the activities of the CLP were covered by the Criminal Syndicalism Law. In April 1922, the California Court of Appeals affirmed the trial court ruling, and in June 1923, the California Supreme Court denied Whitney a hearing. This provided her the opportunity to appeal to the U.S. Supreme Court.

When Whitney first brought her case to the High Court, the justices denied jurisdiction for lack of a federal question. Later, after attorneys successfully raised constitutional questions in the California Court of Appeals regarding the possible conflict of the California law with the Fourteenth Amendment's due process and equal protection clauses, the U.S. Supreme Court accepted the case on a writ of error.

Whitney's attorneys, which by this time included civil liberties advocates Walter Nelles and Walter Pollak, contended that California courts had denied Whitney equal protection of the law and numerous points of procedural due process because her accusation was not particularized and because of "subsequent acts of other persons—not her own acts." In the brief, they argued further that (1) presumption of intent to conspiracy based on mere presence was also a denial of due process, and (2) without a definite test of criminality, the California statute required "prophetic qualities" in order to determine what a group and its members might do in the future. Attorneys also contended that the law violated First Amendment freedom-of-assembly and freedom-of-speech protections because it imposed "penal consequences for joining and participating in an organization still in its formative stage." In other words, this application of the law assumed guilt by association.

In defending the California law, the state attorney general's office argued that the law was comparable with other state statutes on the subject and, therefore, could not be criticized for being indefinite. The state also relied on World War I case precedents involving the federal Espionage and Sedition Acts and accused the plaintiff of submitting a brief "devoted to political rather than legal argumentation."

On the contention involving the Fourteenth Amendment, California maintained that the case did not really raise constitutional issues because the state's power to provide for the public safety outweighed any protection of individual rights. Attorneys argued that, under the law, membership alone was sufficient to convict those involved with the IWW. They claimed the state had demonstrated that the CLP recognized the "immense effect" of the IWW upon the American labor movement generally and on the CLP in particular. Ac-

cording to this analysis, Whitney's continued membership in the CLP, even after her position was outvoted, constituted a violation of the law, even though there was no evidence that she either advocated or committed violent action. This was clearly guilt by association. California's attorneys cited the Supreme Court's upholding of the conviction of CLP associate Benjamin Gitlow in 1925 as further argument against Whitney's position.

On May 16, 1927, the Supreme Court ruled. Technically, the decision was unanimous in upholding the California law. However, Justice Louis D. Brandeis, joined by Justice Oliver Wendell Holmes Jr., wrote a concurring opinion, which raised crucial points of difference with the views of the majority. Justice Edward Sanford concluded for the Court that the California Criminal Syndicalism Law did not violate the Fourteenth Amendment due process clause on vagueness grounds; he cited numerous precedents, none of which involved civil liberties issues. He concluded that the California law did not violate equal protection guarantees because states had the power to classify their police laws. Finally, according to the majority, the state did not violate Fourteenth Amendment due process protection of free speech because this right was not absolute.

In his oft-quoted concurring opinion, Brandeis contended that the First Amendment, linked with the Fourteenth Amendment, limited the state legislature's authority to restrict free speech and assembly. In his analysis, he extended Fourteenth Amendment protection beyond the Court interpretation, which previously had involved only property rights. Brandeis advised that Whitney's attorneys should have argued for a clear-and-present-danger test to distinguish between ideas and dangerous action. "There must be reasonable ground to believe that the danger apprehended is imminent. There must be reasonable ground to believe that the evil to be prevented is a serious one." Whitney had maintained that the California law violated the U.S. Constitution, "but she did not claim that it was void because there was no clear and present danger of serious evil." Had it not been for this technical point, viewed as a mistake made by Whitney's lawyers, Brandeis and Holmes very likely would have dissented.

Brandeis went on to explain the value of allowing political discussion with opportunity for various views to be expressed and challenged. He saw such debate as the essence of the American political system. He stated, "Those who won our independence by revolution were not cowards. They did not fear political change." If a group presented a challenge to the governmental system, then it was important to discuss the differences of opinion; "the remedy to be applied is more speech, not forced silence." He concluded, "Only an emergency can justify repression." In Brandeis's view, freedom of assembly in a political party was protected from state regulation by the due process clause of the Fourteenth Amendment.

A few months after the Supreme Court decision, California governor C. C. Young pardoned Charlotte Whitney on grounds similar to those explained in Brandeis's reasoning. Young's action ended nearly eight years of a legal endurance contest that occurred because one prominent woman insisted on maintaining her political rights of speech and assembly de-

spite a state's interference. From 1924 to 1930, California prosecuted no one under its Criminal Syndicalism Law. Nevertheless, the publicity of the Whitney case caused left-wing political activity to decline to a very low ebb. In 1969, the Supreme Court overturned the *Whitney* precedent in a unanimous per curiam decision, which declared a similar Ohio criminal syndicalism law unconstitutional. However, a modified California law still remains in force, presenting the risk of possible use of guilt-by-association tactics at some future time.

Selected Bibliography

Chafee, Zechariah, Jr. *Free Speech in the United States.* Cambridge, Massachusetts: Harvard University Press, 1967.

Dowell, Eldridge. *A History of Criminal Syndicalism Legislation in the United States.* New York: Da Capo, 1969.

Jenson, C. *The Network of Control.* Westport, CT: Greenwood, 1982.

Whitten, Woodrow. "Trial of Charlotte Anita Whitney." *Pacific Historical Review.* 15 (September 1946): 284–294.

The California Red Flag Law and Freedom of Speech

Carol E. Jenson
Minneapolis, Minnesota

Stromberg v. California, 283 U.S. 359 (1931) [U.S. Supreme Court]

<table>
<tr><td>

◄◦► THE CASE IN BRIEF ◄◦►

Date
1931

Location
California

Court
U.S. Supreme Court

Principal Participants
Yetta Stromberg
John Beardsley
The state of California
Chief Justice Charles Hughes

Significance of the Case
The Supreme Court struck down a woman's sedition conviction, employing the language of the Fourteenth Amendment to protect speech against infringement by a state government.

</td></tr>
</table>

Events surrounding Yetta Stromberg's challenge to the California Red Flag Law reveal the conformist mentality of the decade of the 1920s and demonstrate the extent to which California state and local officials went in their attempts to impose political homogeneity upon the community.

During the summer of 1929, Stromberg, a nineteen-year-old former political science student at the University of California, Los Angeles, and the American-born daughter of Russian immigrant parents, became involved in the Pioneer Summer Camp Conference. A number of independent organizations, some Communist in ideology, others not, made up the group, which worked to make it possible for children of working-class parents to attend summer camp.

The selected campsite was part of a sixty-acre farm, leased from the owner, near Yucaipa, California, in San Bernardino County. It was located in a secluded area, one mile from a main highway and a distance from any town. The camp was accessible only by a private road, which passed through two gates. Seven young women and one elderly male custodian maintained the camp facilities. Stromberg, who was a member of the Young Communist League, led the campers in a daily study of history and economics, presented from a communist perspective. She also conducted a 6:30 A.M. flag-salute ceremony in the camp dormitory. Sleepy children emerged from their cots, observed the raising of a red flag with a hammer-and-sickle emblem, and recited a pledge acknowledging the red flag as a symbol of the freedom of the working class. During the remainder of the camp day, the children played baseball, hiked in the hills, and engaged in other typical summer activities.

Local organizations reacted negatively to the camp's presence, isolated as it was. The Better American Federation, a group determined to eliminate "dangerous" dissent from southern California, teamed up with the American Legion and succeeded in convincing the county authorities to raid the camp. On August 3, the San Bernardino County Sheriff's Department conducted a surprise search of the premises, confiscated camp materials including a small red flag, and jailed Stromberg and the other members of the staff. County officials then had to determine what charges to bring against the group. After considering and later rejecting a criminal syndicalism charge, the authorities discovered the previously unenforced California Red Flag Law passed in 1919.

Under this statute, created to supplement the California Criminal Syndicalism Act adopted at the same time, using or displaying a red flag in a public place was considered a felony. The California legislature perceived the red fabric as a sign and emblem of opposition to organized government and an invitation to anarchy and sedition.

In addition to finding the flag at the camp, authorities also discovered communist-oriented books and other reading materials in the camp library, which was under the supervision of Stromberg. As a result, on August 26, Stromberg and the other members of the staff were charged not only with violating the Red Flag Law but also with conspiracy to display a red flag.

When the trial began on September 30, Judge Charles Allison instructed the jury that "it is only necessary for the prosecution to prove to

you, beyond a reasonable doubt, that said flag was displayed for any one of the three purposes mentioned" in the charges. Those objectives included opposition to organized government, invitation to anarchistic action, and aid to seditious propaganda.

During the trial, the state presented some of the materials taken from the camp library. Despite defense objections, prosecutors read excerpts, some of which advocated the use of armed force, to the jury. Stromberg maintained that the library materials had not been presented to the children. However, the district attorney contended that the camp was "conducted as a school of armed revolutionary propaganda" and that the flag was displayed as a symbol of this teaching.

The defense argued that the camp was not a public place because of its limited clientele and its inaccessible location. Stromberg's attorneys contended that the California statute contradicted the Fourteenth Amendment's protection of First Amendment free-speech privileges and immunities of American citizens. They also argued that the law conflicted with the California constitution's protection of freedom of expression.

On October 23, 1929, the jury convicted Yetta Stromberg of violating the Red Flag Law, and it also convicted her and all but one of the other defendants on the conspiracy charge. The custodian committed suicide shortly after the verdict, and the charges against all except Stromberg were dropped when a California court of appeals, in June 1930, affirmed Stromberg's conviction. When the California Supreme Court declined to hear the case in July 1930, Stromberg's attorney, John Beardsley, with help from the International Labor Defense and the American Civil Liberties Union, appealed to the U.S. Supreme Court on Fourteenth Amendment grounds.

The Supreme Court brief on behalf of Stromberg discussed the judicial test of red-flag laws, an area of civil liberties law not previously presented before the High Court. Beardsley distinguished Stromberg's situation from the *Gitlow* and *Whitney* Supreme Court opinions, which had recently upheld convictions under criminal anarchy and criminal syndicalism statutes. He argued that the California

Red Flag Law did not mention force or violence "but is all inclusive in its condemnation of the display of a flag as an emblem of opposition to organized government." In other words, it could be interpreted to outlaw any form of opposition to government, including support of a candidate seeking to defeat an incumbent.

The brief went on to argue that the political teaching was only one aspect of the camp activities and that the state's evidence that the red flag at issue had stood for opposition to organized government came only from the Communist Party literature confiscated from the camp library. This same party, Beardsley pointed out, was on the presidential ballot in 1928 and had polled fifty thousand votes. If the Communist Party could legally field a presidential candidate, why couldn't Yetta Stromberg's camp display the party's red flag?

Beardsley was able to draw upon the experience of attorneys who had practiced in the newly developing field of civil-liberties defense law in the years since World War I. Focusing on constitutionally based arguments, he cited the clear-and-present-danger test developed by Justice Oliver Wendell Holmes Jr. in the interpretation of the federal World War I Espionage and Sedition Acts. In his test, Holmes had maintained that the circumstances under which the alleged violation occurred had to be considered. Beardsley argued that this small camp in rural California could "scarcely be pictured as a menace to the stability and life of the Republic." The brief also cited Harvard Law School professor Zechariah Chafee's scholarship, which had concluded that the First Amendment free-speech clause had abolished the crime of sedition. Beardsley repeated one of his brief's main points and concluded that the California statute was "arbitrary and vague" because it referred inclusively to outlawing a symbol of opposition to organized government, an opposition that included legitimate partisan activity.

California's attorneys countered by insisting that freedom of speech could not be interpreted to be unlimited but was subject to the restrictions of the state's police power to protect the public welfare. They maintained that the law was not uncertain and vague and that the evidence found in the Communist Party literature

"overwhelmingly supports" the conviction. The state concluded that Stromberg was igniting in these children a spark, which might at some time "burst into a great conflagration." According to this analysis, California was justified in restricting Stromberg's speech in order to prevent some possible future opposition to the government.

The justices responded on May 18, 1931, in a 7-2 decision with an opinion written by Chief Justice Charles Evans Hughes. The majority overturned Stromberg's conviction on the grounds that the California verdict was a general one based on all three points in the statute—including banning the red flag as a symbol of opposition to organized government. The Court majority concluded that such a ban was too vague, for it was not specific and could be construed to refer to peaceful and legal political and partisan opposition to a party in power. Curbing such opposition would threaten "new thought and the development of original ideas." Hughes reasoned that because political change is based upon the confrontation of ideas, "peaceful opposition is guaranteed to our people."

As a result of this line of reasoning, Hughes concluded that banning such political speech violated the liberty protected by the Fourteenth Amendment due process clause. Therefore, the Court declared the central portion of the California Red Flag Law unconstitutional. Hughes agreed with precedents that had determined the constitutional mechanism for Fourteenth Amendment protection of free speech but not as an absolute fashion, for he maintained that states could punish "abuse of this freedom."

Chief Justice Hughes's *Stromberg* opinion is often considered in tandem with another of his 1931 civil liberties commentaries, the 5-4 ruling in *Near v. Minnesota*. There, the Court discarded a Minnesota "gag law" as a violation of the First Amendment freedom-of-the-press protections against the use of prior restraint. In each of these opinions, Hughes took the Court beyond using the Fourteenth Amendment simply as a vehicle for free-speech protection. Hughes's opinions extended the concept of nationalization of the Bill of Rights—using the Fourteenth

Amendment to protect basic rights against state encroachment—to protecting the substance of the symbolic speech of flag displays and to shielding freedom of the press from state-imposed restraint. Although Hughes did not directly discuss a clear-and-present test in *Stromberg*, his opinion vindicated the several dissents of Justices Oliver Wendell Holmes and Louis Brandeis, who throughout the 1920s had argued not only for applying the Fourteenth Amendment to protect basic liberties but also for extending the boundaries of protected speech. With the advent of Hughes's leadership, Holmes's and Brandeis's First Amendment views had become part of the opinion of the Court majority.

Selected Bibliography

Chafee, Zechariah, Jr. *Free Speech in the United States*. Cambridge, Massachusetts: Harvard University Press, 1967.

Hildebrand, D. "Free Speech and Constitutional Transformation." *Constitutional Commentary* 10 (Winter 1993): 133–166.

Murphy, Paul L. *The Meaning of Freedom of Speech*. Westport, CT: Greenwood, 1972.

Cold War, Communism, and Free Speech

—◄◦►—

Michal R. Belknap
California Western School of Law

Dennis v. United States, 341 U.S. 494 (1951) [U.S. Supreme Court]

◄◦► THE CASE IN BRIEF ◄◦►

Date
1951

Location
New York
District of Columbia

Court
U.S. Supreme Court

Principal Participants
Eugene Dennis
United States government

Significance of the Case
The Supreme Court struck a severe blow to First Amendment liberties when Cold War fears eclipsed freedom of speech protection in a decision to uphold the conviction of Communist Party leaders.

"We are fighting Communism with blood and money on both sides of the world; now the Supreme Court permits us to fight it at home," the *Los Angeles Times* editorialized on June 6, 1951. It was applauding the Court's decision two days earlier in *Dennis v. United States*, upholding the convictions of eleven top leaders of the Communist Party of the United States (CPUSA) for violation of a sedition statute known as the Smith Act.

Such praise of *Dennis* was predictable. In June 1951, the United States was at war with Communist enemies in Korea, and the anti-Communist hysteria known as McCarthyism was sweeping the country. Unfortunately, while delivering a blow to Communism, the Supreme Court had also injured free speech. Recognizing this, Justice Hugo Black, in a dissenting opinion, expressed the plaintive hope "that in calmer times, when present pressures, passions and fears subside, this or some later Court will restore the First Amendment liberties to the high preferred position where they belong in a free society."

Like *Dennis* itself, the statute whose constitutionality the Supreme Court upheld in that case was a product of times that were anything but calm. The Smith Act became law on June 28, 1940, ten months after German aggression plunged Europe into World War II. The act was an omnibus anti-alien and sedition measure, which, among other things, criminalized the teaching and advocacy of the violent overthrow of the government, as well as membership in any organization that engaged in such conduct. Opponents of the Communist Party had introduced proposals similar to some of its provisions as early as 1935, but they had made little headway. In 1939 and 1940, with events in Europe inspiring fears of subversion by foreigners and foreign ideologies, the Smith Act marched relentlessly through Congress.

The target of the act's sedition sections was the CPUSA, but eight years passed before the government employed the new law against Communists. The reason was the World War II alliance between the United States and the USSR. American officials did not want to offend the Soviets by prosecuting their coadjutors in this country. As the joint Soviet-American struggle against Nazi Germany approached a victorious conclusion, the two allies began to quarrel over the future of Eastern Europe. By 1948, the relationship between them had deteriorated into the bitter international confrontation known as the Cold War. That quarrel was essentially a conflict of interest between two powerful nation-states. In trying to rally the American people behind a policy of containing Soviet expansionism, however, President Harry Truman characterized the conflict as an ideological struggle between democracy and Communism.

Truman thereby created a serious political problem for his own Democratic Party. At least since 1944, Republicans had been trying to discredit Democrats by linking them with Communism. Until the onset of the Cold War, voters displayed little interest in such charges. When the president began insisting that the country must spend millions of dollars to resist Communists abroad, however, the public started to take seriously GOP allegations that his administration was not doing enough to combat Communism at home. Neither the president nor his attorney general, Tom Clark, considered domestic Communism a serious problem. Nevertheless, after Clark was sharply criticized by the Republican-controlled House Committee on Un-American Activities for not doing more about it, he decided to accept a recommendation made earlier by FBI Director J. Edgar Hoover for a Smith Act prosecution of the CPUSA. The U.S. Attorney for the Southern District of New York, John F. X. McGohey, was set to work preparing a case against the Communist Party's leaders, and on July 20, 1948, a federal grand jury in Manhattan indicted all twelve members of its national board.

The grand jury accused these radicals of conspiring with one another, and with persons unknown, to organize the CPUSA. The Communist Party was, the indictment alleged, "a society, group and assembly of persons who teach and advocate the overthrow and destruction of the Government of the United States by force and violence." The grand jury also charged the defendants with conspiring to teach and advocate violent overthrow. Finally, it accused them of membership in an organization that engaged in such teaching and advocacy (a charge on which they were never tried). Contrary to what many people believed, the indictment did *not* accuse the Communist leaders of conspiring to overthrow the government. There was a good reason for this: the Justice Department lawyer who reviewed the huge mass of evidence on the CPUSA assembled by the FBI concluded that prosecutors could not prove the defendants had committed that offense. Hence, the grand jury accused the party leaders not of engaging in, or even plotting, revolutionary action, but merely of preparing to advocate revolutionary ideas.

Throughout most of 1949, all of the indicted Communists, except National Secretary William Z. Foster (whose case was severed from those of his codefendants because of a severe heart condition), stood trial on this charge before Judge Harold Medina in the federal courthouse on New York's Foley Square. According to *Newsweek*, that tumultuous proceeding, which began on January 17 and did not stagger to a conclusion until October 14, was "the longest, dreariest and most controversial" American criminal trial to date. The transcript of its tortious progress stretched to over twenty-thousand pages.

Much of this record chronicled bitter wrangling between Judge Medina and a battery of five defense attorneys. Those lawyers argued loudly, persistently, and with considerable justification that, particularly in his rulings on the admission and exclusion of evidence, Medina favored the prosecution. Their constant attacks convinced the judge that they were plotting to destroy his health and thus bring about a mistrial. Mutual distrust bred animosity, and the level of conflict between Medina and the defense attorneys rose higher and higher as the trial progressed.

Their constant wrangling added fuel to fires ignited by the questionable tactics of the prosecution and defense. The Communists did not believe they could win this trial in any traditional sense; not even their lawyers thought the jury would acquit the defendants. Hence, rather than concentrating on rebutting the prosecution's case, the Communists adopted a "labor defense" strategy. The party organized demonstrations and correspondence campaigns designed to pressure the government into dropping the charges against its leaders. Meanwhile, with the assistance of their attorneys, the Communists sought to employ the courtroom as a propaganda platform. Defense witnesses made political speeches and extolled the party's efforts on behalf of veterans, blacks, organized labor, and other interest groups. The Communists also sought to discredit American government by, for example, attacking the system of jury selection used by the court, which they claimed discriminated against members of racial minorities, supporters of radical political parties, wage workers, and the poor. Judge Medina's efforts to curtail this propagandizing triggered much of the conflict that disrupted the proceedings.

Another source of turmoil was a tactic that the government employed repeatedly to discredit defense witnesses. Again and again, when cross-examining Communists, government lawyers would ask them to identify as members of the CPUSA other persons having little or no connection with the case. As the defendants' attorneys pointed out many times, given the intense hostility toward Communism that was gripping the country, anyone linked to it in this way was likely to suffer loss of government benefits, unemployment, and ostracism. Besides, like many persons associated with the American labor movement, Communists had a deep aversion to becoming stool pigeons. They consistently refused to "name names." The prosecution went right on demanding them anyhow. The results were a great deal of courtroom conflict and the jailing of defendants John Gates, Henry Winston, Gus Hall, and Carl Winter for contempt.

The government's case was as unimpressive as its methods were dubious. Most of the evidence that the prosecution produced had little or nothing to do with the nominal defendants. The prosecution devoted about ten percent of its attention to proving the participation of General Secretary Eugene Dennis and the other members of the national board in the alleged conspiracy, and about ninety percent to building a case against the Communist Party. Because the defendants were alleged to have violated the Smith Act by reconstituting the CPUSA in 1945, after it had dissolved itself temporarily during World War II, the character of the party was an issue. Only if it were an organization of the type prohibited by the Smith Act could the defendants be guilty of violating that law by conspiring to organize it. But the prosecution often acted as if the party itself were the defendant. The theory of its case was that the CPUSA was an instrument that a group of conspirators had created to accomplish their objective of teaching and advocating violent overthrow. Yet, much of its evidence was admissible only if the party was itself the conspiracy.

That evidence consisted largely of articles, pamphlets, and books, many of which, as the defense pointed out, could be found on the shelves of university and public libraries. Most of these works had been written by Communists other than the defendants, and a number of them, such as Marx's The Communist Manifesto (1848) and Lenin's State and Revolution (1917), had been published long before Congress passed the Smith Act. The government presented excerpts from these works, which contained ominous-sounding references to violence. The defense sought to put those passages into what it insisted was a proper context by reading to the jury other parts of the same publications dealing with quite different subjects. Judge Medina, convinced the Communists were stalling again and trying to exploit the trial for propaganda purposes, repeatedly thwarted their efforts. What the jury heard was a disjointed and often incomprehensible collection of quotations that tended to overemphasize the importance of violent revolution in Communist ideology.

The witnesses called by the government were there mainly to identify the publications it wished to use and to satisfy the legal requirements that had to be met to get these admitted into evidence. Some witnesses, such as Herbert Philbrick (an FBI informant who had spent nine years masquerading as a dedicated Communist), told stories that were as dramatic as a spy thriller. But the relevance of their accounts to the charges against the defendants was marginal, and such testimony was not nearly as common as were dull recitations of the allegedly Communist publications a teacher had assigned to his students. The literary evidence was the guts of the prosecution's case. It did not impress the *New Republic,* which observed that the government had "failed to make out the overwhelming case that many people anticipated when the trial began."

Although it failed to impress the *New Republic,* the prosecution's evidence proved sufficient to convict the defendants. After deliberating for seven and one-half hours, the jury returned guilty verdicts against all of them. What convicted the Communist leaders was not the strength of the government's case but the intensity of public hostility toward Communism. Politicians from both major parties applauded the verdicts, as did newspapers of almost every political persuasion throughout the country. Within a month after the trial ended, Medina received fifty thousand congratulatory letters.

The judge, who was transformed by the Communist trial into a sort of folk hero, sentenced ten of the defendants to five years in prison. The only one toward whom Medina showed any mercy was Robert Thompson, a World War II hero to whom he gave only three years. Besides sentencing the Communist lead-

ers to prison, the judge jailed their lawyers. After the jury returned its verdicts, Medina castigated the defense attorneys for conspiring to disrupt the trial, adjudged all five (along with General Secretary Eugene Dennis, who had acted as his own attorney) guilty of multiple counts of contempt, and imprisoned them for periods ranging from thirty days to six months. The U.S. Court of Appeals for the Second Circuit affirmed contempt judgments against the defense attorneys. So did the U.S. Supreme Court.

Appeal proved equally futile for the defendants themselves. The Communist leaders attempted to persuade the Second Circuit that Medina's bias and misconduct had deprived them of a fair trial. The judge had, they insisted, committed numerous reversible errors, particularly in his rulings on the admission and exclusion of evidence and in his instructions to the jury. The leaders of the CPUSA also claimed they had been deprived of an impartial jury and that the trial court had violated a number of their constitutional rights. They argued further that the Smith Act, both on its face and as Medina had construed and applied it, violated the First Amendment's guarantee of freedom of expression.

An amicus curiae brief filed by the American Civil Liberties Union (ACLU) supported that assertion, but the three judges who heard the Communists' appeal rejected it, along with all of their other contentions. Even before oral argument, two of these jurists expressed privately a distinct lack of sympathy for the defendants. The invasion of South Korea by its Communist neighbor, North Korea, while the case was being argued, and the United States' subsequent plunge into a shooting war with Communism in Asia, destroyed whatever slight chance the leaders of the CPUSA had of persuading the Second Circuit to overturn the verdicts against them. On August 1, 1950, the court of appeals unanimously affirmed all of the convictions.

It also upheld the Smith Act, despite the substantial restrictions that law imposed on freedom of expression. In 1950, the generally accepted rule for determining whether speech or writing could be punished without violating the First Amendment was the clear-and-present-danger test, formulated by Supreme Court Justice Oliver Wendell Holmes Jr. just after World War I. Under that test, as it had come to be understood by the time of the *Dennis* trial, expression enjoyed constitutional protection unless it created an immediate danger of some serious evil that the authorities had a right to prohibit. The threat allegedly posed by Communist teaching and advocacy—violent revolution against the U.S. government—was certainly very serious. But the prosecution had failed to prove that such a rebellion was imminent, let alone that, at a time when most Americans would reject out of hand anything urged by the CPUSA, it had any chance of succeeding. In order to uphold the Smith Act, as applied to the *Dennis* defendants, Judge Learned Hand had to alter the clear-and-present-danger test. In each case, he wrote in his opinion for the Second Circuit, courts "must ask whether the gravity of the 'evil,' discounted by its improbability, justifies such invasion of free speech as is necessary to avoid the danger." This reformulation eliminated the time element from the test. Under Hand's version, all that mattered were the gravity of the evil and the possibility that it could occur someday, however far in the future that day might be. As Hand saw it, the CPUSA was a rigidly disciplined band of zealots, committed to the eventual capture of all existing governments and acting in concert with a worldwide movement headed by the Soviet Union, which even then was agitating for control of various countries in Western Europe. "We do not understand how one could ask for a more probable danger, unless we must wait until the actual event of hostilities," he wrote. As far as Hand was concerned, with the United States and the Soviet Union locked in the Cold War, Communists constituted a clear and present danger. For that reason, restrictions on their speech did not violate the First Amendment.

The Supreme Court agreed. After the court of appeals ruled against them, Eugene Dennis and his comrades sought review of their convictions by the high tribunal. It refused even to consider most of the issues they had raised before the Second Circuit. The Communists obtained a hearing only on the question of the constitutionality of the Smith Act.

Before the Supreme Court, they again argued that the Smith Act violated the First Amendment. Attorneys representing the Communist leaders insisted no one could make advocating ideas or exercising the rights of speech, press, and assembly criminal. According to them, even if advocacy were part of an effort to bring about a substantive evil, the First Amendment protected it unless there was a clear and present danger. That the leaders of the CPUSA sympathized with the Soviet Union could not deprive them of the protection of that constitutional provision. Counsel for the Communists attacked Judge Hand for changing the meaning of the clear-and-present-danger rule, which defense attorney Harry Sacher insisted during oral argument was that only an immediately threatening emergency could justify the government in abridging freedom of speech. Because no such danger existed, affirming the convictions of the Foley Square defendants would amount to "a confession of our unwillingness to take the risk of permitting political dissent to be heard," counsel for the Communists contended. That would amount to "suppression of the democratic process itself."

The Justice Department disputed the defense characterization of the case, strenuously denying that this litigation involved freedom of expression. Solicitor General Philip Perlman argued that because Communists would abolish free speech if they gained power, it was not an issue in the *Dennis* case. According to the Justice Department, what the Smith Act punished was not expression at all, but rather the formation of "fifth columns" serving the aggressive purpose of foreign powers. The government conceded that requiring prosecutors to establish the existence of an imminent and immediate danger, even after Congress had explicitly prohibited speech of a particular type, might be appropriate in dealing with unorganized and irresponsible agitators. "Applied to these petitioners and their Communist Party, it would mean that the First Amendment protects their preparations until they are ready to attempt a seizure of power, or to act as a fifth column in time of crisis."

That idea was as unacceptable to most members of the Supreme Court as it was to the

Justice Department. On June 4, 1951, the Court ruled against the Foley Square defendants by a vote of 6-2 (with Tom Clark, now a Supreme Court justice, excusing himself because of his previous involvement in the case). The high tribunal spoke through Chief Justice Fred Vinson, a man convinced that the government had to protect itself from Communists. Vinson entertained no doubts at all about how cases involving members of the CPUSA ought to be resolved. Having held several high-level administrative positions associated with the nation's economic mobilization for World War II, he appeared to have viewed *Dennis* as an opportunity to help mobilize Americans for the Cold War.

In formulating his opinion, Vinson followed the lead of Learned Hand, affirming Hand's conclusion that, as interpreted to the Foley Square jury by Judge Medina, the Smith Act was constitutional. Free speech was not an unlimited and unqualified right, the chief justice asserted, and saving the government from violent overthrow was certainly an interest substantial enough to warrant restricting it. Vinson realized that the clear-and-present-danger test controlled when this could be done, but as far as he was concerned, that rule could not mean that the authorities must wait "until the putsch is about to be executed, the laws have been laid and the signal is awaited." If government learned that a group bent on revolution was indoctrinating members and committing them to act when its leaders thought the time was ripe, then government action was required. What the authorities might do should not depend on the immediacy of the threat or on the likelihood that the rebellion would succeed. Vinson endorsed as "succinct and inclusive" Hand's reformulation of the clear-and-present-danger test. As far as the chief justice was concerned, the requirements of the new version had been met in this case; the formation by the leaders of the CPUSA of a "highly organized conspiracy with rigidly disciplined members" ready to act when they gave the word, together with the "inflammable nature of world conditions" and the tense state of relations between the United States and Communist countries, had created the sort of danger it required.

Justice Felix Frankfurter agreed with Vinson that Eugene Dennis and his comrades had been "properly and constitutionally convicted for violation of the Smith Act," but he did not wish to associate himself with the reasoning of the chief justice. As far as Frankfurter was concerned, suppressing advocacy of the overthrow of the government was an unwise policy. He believed, however, that judges should leave policy making to the legislative branch of the government. Congress had made a decision on this question, and while Frankfurter disagreed with what it had decided, he would defer to its judgment.

Like Frankfurter, Justice Robert Jackson wrote a separate concurring opinion. He thought that the clear-and-present-danger test should not be employed at all in cases involving conspiracies such as Communism. Jackson maintained that what the Foley Square defendants had really been tried and convicted of was conspiring to overthrow the government. To him, conspiracy law seemed well suited to dealing with defendants such as these.

Only Justices Hugo Black and William O. Douglas dissented. Black, who believed that the First Amendment prohibited all restrictions on freedom of expression, condemned the prosecution of the Communist leaders as "a virulent form of prior censorship of speech and press." Douglas did not endorse Black's absolutist position on freedom of expression, but he did believe that the First Amendment had been violated in this case, because the Foley Square jury had not been required to find the existence of a clear and present danger. Considering American Communists "the most beset and least thriving of any fifth column in history," Douglas denied that they posed a threat great enough to justify suppression of their speech. The Foley Square defendants had done nothing more than organize to teach and advocate doctrines that were themselves perfectly legal. They had been adjudged criminals not for what they had done but rather because of who they were.

In 1951, there was general agreement that simply being a Communist was sufficient grounds for condemnation. Hence, the public viewed *Dennis* far more favorably than did Douglas and Black. "The American people in overwhelming majority will rejoice in this judicial affirmation of the nation's right and power," the *New Orleans Times-Picayune* predicted accurately. Few but close associates of the Communist Party objected to the *Dennis* decision. The only independent groups to condemn it were the ACLU, the Trotskyist Socialist Workers Party, and the Congress of Industrial Organizations (CIO). In the entire country, only five major newspapers expressed opposition. Most editorial writers seemed unaware that freedom of speech had even been an issue in the case.

Among legal commentators, who more fully understood all of its implications, *Dennis* did not fare so well. Famed political scientist Edward S. Corwin endorsed the Court's ruling, but a number of other legal scholars, among them Robert McCloskey of Harvard and Eugene V. Rostow of Yale, criticized *Dennis* severely. To Rostow, that the Supreme Court had abandoned the classic version of the clear-and-present-danger test in order to uphold the Smith Act suggested that the country was in the midst of a grave civil-liberties crisis.

Following the *Dennis* decision, the Justice Department launched an all-out war on the CPUSA, prosecuting 132 more Communists on Smith Act charges. By July 1956, it had tried "second string" party leaders in Los Angeles, Baltimore, Honolulu, Pittsburgh, Seattle, Detroit, St. Louis, Philadelphia, Cleveland, Denver, New Haven, and New York for conspiring to violate the 1940 sedition law. The government also secured conspiracy indictments against Communist functionaries in Boston and San Juan, Puerto Rico. In addition, it prosecuted seven party officials for membership in an organization that taught and advocated the violent overthrow of the government.

The Communists lost almost all of these post-*Dennis* cases. Of the 126 men and women indicted for conspiracy, only ten were acquitted. Eighteen were never brought to trial. And a hung jury, three severances because of ill health, and a death terminated five other cases. Thus, of those Communists who actually had their fates decided by a trial court, the vast majority were convicted. Only once (in Cleveland) did a jury free any conspiracy defendants. Every Communist tried on membership charges suf-

fered conviction. Smith Act defendants enjoyed even less success in appellate litigation. During the six years after *Dennis*, courts of appeals affirmed every conviction that came before them. Twice the Supreme Court refused even to review Smith Act cases.

Battered in the courts, the CPUSA also suffered from a loss of leadership. Believing that the country was moving into a reactionary period during which the party would have to function both legally and illegally, its national committee decided that not all of the Foley Square defendants should go to prison. While seven of them reported to begin serving their sentences on July 2, 1951, Gil Green, Robert Thompson, Gus Hall, and Henry Winston went underground, forfeiting eighty thousand dollars in bail. Hall was captured by Mexican police and turned over to the FBI in October, and the bureau apprehended Thompson at a California mountain cabin in August 1952. Winston and Green managed to elude authorities until 1956, when, with their comrades emerging from prison, they surrendered voluntarily.

Neither in hiding nor serving their sentences were Smith Act defendants in a position to provide the CPUSA with guidance and direction. Dennis tried to continue running the party from his cell in the Atlanta penitentiary by passing instructions to his wife in correspondence and during her visits, but prison officials heavily censored his mail and managed to isolate the general secretary from his comrades on the outside. Other imprisoned party leaders experienced similar isolation. By 1953, the FBI considered the national committee "more or less inoperative."

Deprived of direction from much of its leadership, the CPUSA experienced a breakdown of internal discipline. While Thompson was in hiding and in jail, a "young Turk" movement within the New York State organization challenged his policies and plunged that segment of the party into a confrontation with the decimated national office. The ailing William Z. Foster could not control the dissident New Yorkers. Nor could he keep California Communists from defying the national headquarters or a district organizer in Maryland from publicly advocating an unauthorized alteration of the party's "line."

The breakdown of discipline within the CPUSA grew worse as the Smith Act prosecutions spread and second-string leaders followed the Foley Square defendants into prison, the underground, or bth. Those members of the CPUSA who found themselves isolated from their associates in jail or in hiding had time to think, and many of them began to question the policies of an organization to which they had given blind allegiance for years. In 1956 and 1957, the CPUSA figuratively blew apart, and much of its membership walked away. While events abroad, such as Nikita Khrushchev's revelations concerning the crimes of Joseph Stalin and Russia's brutal suppression of the Hungarian Revolution, were the immediate causes of this collapse, they proved as destructive as they did only because the *Dennis* case and subsequent Smith Act prosecutions had badly undermined the party's organizational cohesion.

While the CPUSA was collapsing, the prosecutions that had disrupted it so badly were coming to an end. By 1956, Cold War tensions had eased a good deal. At home, too, the mood was changing. The most dramatic indication of this was the December 1954 vote by the U.S. Senate to censure Wisconsin's senator Joseph R. McCarthy, a once-powerful demagogue whose name had become synonymous with hysterical anticommunism and the abuse of constitutional rights.

The Supreme Court shared the country's decreased fear of Communism and increased concern for civil liberties. In 1956, it reversed the convictions of the Pittsburgh Smith Act defendants on grounds that the convictions might have resulted from the use of perjured testimony. Then, on June 17, 1957, in *Yates v. United States*, the Court overturned the Los Angeles second-string convictions. It also interpreted the Smith Act in a way that severely limited the use of that law as a weapon against the CPUSA. Observing that the existing Communist Party had come into being in 1945 and that the indictment in this case had not been returned until 1951, the Court held that the charge of conspiracy to organize the CPUSA on which the defendants had been convicted was barred by the three-year statute of limitations.

It rejected the government's contention that organization was an ongoing process that included actions such as setting up new units. Its resolution of this issue ensured that no member of the CPUSA could ever again be prosecuted for conspiring to organize. The Court also held that to be subject to punishment under the Smith Act, a person had to advocate not merely ideas but action. Those to whom the advocacy was addressed "must be urged to do something now or in the future, rather than merely to believe in something."

Because the government could not prove Communists did that, the *Yates* decision effectively blocked further legal assault on them. Although the Supreme Court offered the opportunity to retry nine of the fourteen Los Angeles defendants, the Justice Department failed to do so because it lacked evidence of the kind of advocacy it now had to prove. Recognizing the government could not produce this, courts of appeals in four circuits ordered the release of all defendants in pending Smith Act cases. Appellate judges, who reversed convictions obtained in Detroit, St. Louis, Cleveland, Philadelphia, and Pittsburgh on the basis of *Yates*, did authorize the retrial of those cases. But the Justice Department itself terminated them because it could not produce the type of evidence the Supreme Court had demanded. Prosecutors did not even attempt to try the Boston and San Juan groups. Only in Denver were Communists again brought to trial on Smith Act conspiracy charges. The government obtained convictions there, but when the Ninth Circuit Court of Appeals reversed them because of errors in the conduct of the trial, the government dropped the case. Ultimately, the *Yates* evidentiary standards saved from prison all but one of the membership-clause defendants.

While it halted the wave of prosecutions that *Dennis* had initiated, *Yates* did not reverse the 1951 ruling. It was not until the 1960s that the Court finally repaired the damage that *Dennis* had done to the First Amendment. In *Brandenburg v. Ohio* (1968), it adopted a new rule for defining the outer boundaries of constitutionally protected speech that was even more protective of freedom of expression than was the classic version of the clear-and-present-danger test. The Court in *Brandenburg* declared that "the constitutional guarantees of free speech and free press do not permit [government] to forbid or proscribe advocacy of the use of force or law violation except where such advocacy is directed to inciting or producing imminent lawless action and is likely to incite or produce such action." The job of protecting the government from advocacy of anything but the most immediate attacks upon it was left to counter speech.

Yet, while departing from the principles of *Dennis*, the Court in *Brandenburg* did not actually overrule the 1951 decision. Should passions as intense as those that gripped the United States during the early 1950s once more agitate the nation, the Supreme Court could resurrect its doctrine, and *Dennis v. United States* might become again something more than a legal relic of the Cold War.

Selected Bibliography

Belknap, Michal R. "Cold War in the Courtroom" in *American Political Trials*, ed. Michal R. Belknap, 233–262. Westport, CT: Greenwood, 1981.

———. *Cold War Political Justice: The Smith Act, the Communist Party and American Civil Liberties*. Westport, CT: Greenwood, 1977.

Boudin, Louis B. "Seditious Doctrines and the 'Clear and Present Danger' Rule." *Virginia Law Review* 38 (February, April 1952): 143–186, 315–356.

Corwin, Edward S. "Bowing Out Clear and Present Danger." *Notre Dame Lawyer* 27 (Spring 1952): 325–359.

Daniel, Hawthorne. *Judge Medina: A Biography*. New York: Wilfred Funk, 1952.

Mendelson, Wallace. "Clear and Present Danger from *Schenck* to *Dennis*." *Columbia Law Review* 52 (March 1952): 313–333.

Mollan, Robert. "Smith Act Prosecutions: The Effect of the *Dennis* and *Yates* Decisions." *University of Pittsburgh Law Review* 26 (June 1965): 705–748.

Nathanson, Nathaniel L. "The Communist Trial and the Clear and Present Danger Test." *Harvard Law Review* 63 (May 1950): 1167–1175.

Rostow, Eugene V. "The Democratic Character of Judicial Review." *Harvard Law Review* 66 (December 1952): 193–224.

Sabin, Arthur J. *In Calmer Times: The Supreme Court and Red Monday*. Philadelphia: University of Pennsylvania Press, 1999.

Steinberg, Peter L. *The Great Red Menace: United States Prosecution of American Communists 1947–1952*. Westport, CT: Greenwood, 1984.

Wormuth, Francis. "Learned Legerdemain: A Grave But Implausible Hand." *Western Political Quarterly* 6 (September 1953): 543–558.

The Smith Act Narrowed

————◄o►————

Jerold L. Simmons and Karen Bruner

Department of History
University of Nebraska at Omaha

Yates v. United States, 354 U.S. 298 (1957) [U.S. Supreme Court]

◄o► THE CASE IN BRIEF ◄o►

Date
1957

Location
California
District of Columbia

Court
U.S. Supreme Court

Principal Participants
Oleta O'Connor Yates
California Communist Party members
United States Department of Justice

Significance of the Case
With the communist scare softened by political events, Communist Party members' appeals resulted in four sweeping decisions by the Supreme Court, limiting the effects of the Smith Act on a date recalled as Red Monday.

July 26, 1951, began inauspiciously for thirty-seven-year-old West Coast newspaper editor Al Richmond. As usual for a Thursday, he was at his desk before 8:00 A.M. hurriedly finishing an editorial for the newspaper's expanded weekend edition. The column that Richmond was busily composing that day, however, was not destined to be completed, for a few minutes later the hum of activity in the small San Francisco office was abruptly interrupted by the rude arrival of a phalanx of FBI agents, an event that Richmond had been fearfully anticipating for over a month. As he was handcuffed, arrested, and transported to FBI headquarters, Richmond mused about the battle that he knew awaited him and wondered if he would have to face it alone. Little did he suspect that the happenings of that morning were just the beginning of a chain of events that would have extraordinary implications for him personally, and even more momentously for the nation at large.

Al Richmond was no ordinary journalist. Nor was he alone in his predicament. As editor of the U.S. Communist Party's (CPUSA) West

Coast organ, the *Peoples World*, he was one of fourteen California Communists arrested simultaneously that day in San Francisco, Los Angeles, and New York. Among the others arrested were William Schneiderman, the California Communist Party state chairman, and Oleta O'Connor Yates, the state secretary. At the arraignment that afternoon, a majority of the defendants were required to post bail of $75,000, a testament to the seriousness of their crime: violation of the Smith Act.

Adopted by Congress in 1940, the Smith Act made it a crime to knowingly advocate or teach the forcible overthrow of the U.S. government, to organize or become a member of any group dedicated to such purposes, or to conspire to do either. The measure was one of nearly one hundred antiradical proposals considered by Congress in the two years preceding World War II. Like many of the others, its target was the subversive propaganda of both the Fascist right and the Communist left. Its vague wording, especially when set against the First Amendment, made prosecution uncertain, and Franklin Roosevelt's Justice Department proved reluctant to enforce the measure. The postwar atmosphere, however, gave the Smith Act new life. Mounting national frustration over Soviet expansion, coupled with the strident rhetoric of the political right, eventually convinced the Truman administration of the need to embark on its own anticommunist crusade. The Federal Loyalty Program and the infamous Attorney General's List of subversive organizations quickly followed, and in July 1948, the Justice Department brought charges against key members of the Central Committee of the Communist Party of the United States.

A stormy nine-month trial in 1949 culminated in the conviction of the Communist leaders and nearly two years later the Supreme Court both affirmed those convictions and upheld the constitutionality of the Smith Act in *Dennis v. United States* (1951). Chief Justice Vinson's majority opinion avoided discussion of the meaning of such words as "teach" and "advocacy," and concentrated on the conspiratorial nature of the Communist Party. While paying homage to Justice Holmes's "clear and present danger" test, Vinson largely dismissed

its relevance: "Obviously, the words cannot mean that before the Government may act, it must wait until the putsch is about to be executed, the plans have been laid and the signal is awaited." The "gravity of the evil" combined with the party's secrecy thus justified prosecution well before the advocacy became action.

Armed with this new license, the government pursued a strategy of emasculating the Communist Party by incarcerating its leaders. *Dennis* led directly to a roundup of top party functionaries, including editor Richmond and his California colleagues. In the trial of the Californians, which ran from February 1 to August 5, 1952, the defendants chose a strategy markedly different from that used by the *Dennis* group. The *Dennis* defendants had elected to challenge directly prosecution allegations that Communist Party doctrine was seditious. The California Communist leaders chose instead to focus on the constitutional right to advocate abstract political doctrine, no matter its content. Not only did this strategy produce a more decorous proceeding, but it would prove significant five years hence when the Supreme Court ruled on their convictions in *Yates v. United States*. But in the short run, the more restrained tactics notwithstanding, the *Yates* defendants were all found guilty and received the maximum allowable sentences of five years in prison and $10,000 fines.

With little optimism, Yates, Schneiderman, Richmond, and the others embarked on what would be a lengthy appeals process. Their lack of confidence in obtaining a reversal seemed well founded when, in January 1955, the Supreme Court denied petitions to review the convictions of their comrades in New York and Baltimore who had been arrested at the same time and prosecuted on approximately the same charges. Nonetheless, after the circuit court ruled against the *Yates* group the following March, their lawyers dutifully filed for a writ of certiorari. Surprisingly the U.S. Supreme Court granted the writ in October and heard oral arguments one year later.

The years of waiting between initial conviction and the final Supreme Court decision were suspended time for the *Yates* group, with a prison term always a likely eventuality. The rest of the country, however, was undergoing profound changes, particularly with regard to the fear of Communist subversion. Stalin's death in 1953, the Korean armistice, the Geneva Summit, and Khrushchev's startling 1956 speech denouncing the crimes of the Stalin era all seemed to soften the image of communism abroad. At home, four years of Republican prosperity, the absence of new spy scares, and the Senate censure of Joe McCarthy diminished the fear of internal subversion. The startling announcements from the Kremlin, coupled with internal doctrinal disputes within the CPUSA, accelerated the decline in the fortunes of American communism. Not only had the party been deprived of much of its leadership by the Smith Act prosecutions, but squabbling among its current directors also undermined the cogency of its message. The party was in shambles.

It was this milieu that provided the setting for the four startling decisions announced on June 17, 1957. On what became known as "Red Monday," the Court attempted to limit the excesses of the anticommunist crusade. These decisions circumscribed the procedures of congressional investigating committees (*Watkins v. United States*), limited the authority of state investigations (*Sweezy v. United States*), set restraints on executive branch loyalty dismissals (*Service v. Dulles*), and reversed the convictions of the *Yates* defendants.

The majority opinion in *Yates v. United States*, written by Justice John Marshall Harlan, carefully avoided a direct reversal of *Dennis* and focused on two largely semantic issues. Harlan explained that the framers of the Smith Act intended the proscription only against organizing a group that advocated forcible overthrow of the government to apply to the single original act of organizing; it did not apply to the ongoing addition of new units or to the continuing recruitment of new members. The CPUSA had been reorganized in 1945; since the three-year statute of limitations for prosecution had expired in 1948, the *Yates* convictions under the organizing clause of the act were void.

Harlan's second major foundation for reversal involved the implications of the term *advocacy*. In *Dennis*, Chief Justice Vinson accepted the government's contention that the Smith Act

had been "directed at advocacy, not discussion." While the latter was protected by the First Amendment, the former fell within the limits of permissible government action. Although Harlan accepted that distinction, he rejected its fundamental premise—that all advocacy of Marxism represents an incitement to illegal action. Instead he drew another, even narrower, distinction "between advocacy of abstract doctrine and advocacy directed at promoting unlawful action." With that, the central question in *Yates v. United States* became "whether the Smith Act prohibits advocacy and teaching of forcible overthrow as an abstract principle, divorced from any effort to instigate action to that end." The Court held it did not. Since the trial judge failed to note this distinction in his charge to the jury, all the convictions were flawed. Drawing upon his reading of the trial evidence in light of these new standards, Harlan ordered five of the *Yates* defendants, including Richmond, released and the other nine retried.

Faced with having to prove that the Marxism taught by the CPUSA was directly aimed at promoting illegal action, the government ceased all further prosecution under the *advocacy* clause of the Smith Act. Charges against the remaining nine *Yates* defendants were dropped. Charges were also dropped or convictions reversed for another eighty-one Communists in various stages of prosecution. The Smith Act, for all intents and purposes, was dead.

Not unexpectedly the Red Monday decisions generated intense criticism. Conservative opinion was vocal and harsh. David Lawrence, writing in *U.S. News and World Report*, scornfully asserted, "treason as an 'abstract doctrine' has now been legalized by the Supreme Court." The New York *Daily Mirror* characterized June 17 as a "moment for weeping." *Life* declared that "the Court displays the most lamentable virginity about Communism." Leaders of the legal and law enforcement communities likewise criticized the decisions as "an appalling setback" in the maintenance of national security and assailed the national tribunal as too zealous in the protection of individual rights at the expense of national self-preservation.

The loudest protests arose in the halls of Congress. To many conservative congressmen, the Court not only seemed to be giving Communists free reign to subvert American institutions, but it was also deliberately seeking to undermine legislative authority. Most vitriolic of all was Republican Senator William Jenner of Indiana, who, in a speech on the floor of the Senate on July 26, 1957, asserted: "No conceivable combination of votes in Congress could have done as much damage to our legislative barriers against communism and subversion as the Supreme Court of the United States.... There was a time when the Supreme Court conceived its function to be the interpretation of the law. For some time now, the Supreme Court has been making law—substituting its judgment for the judgment of the legislative branch."

Accordingly in 1957 and 1958 a number of anti-Court bills appeared on the floor of both the Senate and the House. Most were aimed at curtailing the High Court's appellate jurisdiction in the areas of antisubversive activities. Four were introduced to reverse the Court's narrow definition of the word *organize* so as to amend the Smith Act and allow prosecution for those activities that expanded and enlarged organizations dedicated to the violent overthrow of the government. None of the bills were enacted, but each generated intense debate. Efforts aimed at clarifying congressional intent concerning "advocacy" also made little headway, largely because Harlan's ruling clearly suggested that any law designed to punish the advocacy of abstract doctrine would be ruled unconstitutional. The strong sentiment voiced in Congress did, however, attract the Court's attention. In several political offender cases decided subsequently, the Court abruptly stepped back from its libertarian stance. In *Barenblatt v. United States* (1959), for example, the High Court sustained the contempt conviction of a college professor who refused to answer questions of the House Un-American Activities Committee concerning his membership in the Communist Party. In *Scales v. United States* (1961), it also upheld that portion of the Smith Act that made it a crime to be a member of an organization that advocates the violent overthrow of the government.

In spite of this retrenchment, the *Yates* ruling did signal a new determination on the part of the Warren Court to stem the excesses of anticommunism. By interpreting the organizing and advocacy clauses very narrowly, Harlan and his colleagues rendered the Smith Act virtually unenforceable and thereby removed a powerful weapon from the arsenal of those who sought to crush political radicalism.

Selected Bibliography

Belknap, Michal R. *Cold War Political Justice: The Smith Act, the Communist Party, and American Civil Liberties.* Westport, CT: Greenwood Press, 1977.

Mollan, Robert. "Smith Act Prosecutions: The Effect of the *Dennis* and *Yates* Decisions." *University of Pittsburgh Law Review* 26 (1965): 705–748.

Murphy, Walter F. *Congress and the Court: A Case Study in the American Political Process.* Chicago: University of Chicago Press, 1962.

Richmond, Al. *A Long View from the Left: Memoirs of an American Revolutionary.* Boston: Houghton Mifflin, 1973.

Sabin, Arthur J. *In Calmer Times: The Supreme Court and Red Monday.* Philadelphia: University of Pennsylvania Press, 1999.

Steinberg, Peter L. *The Great "Red Menace": United States Prosecution of American Communists, 1947–1952.* Westport, CT: Greenwood Press, 1984.

"Breach of Peace" and Group Libel

———— ◄◦► ————

Susan Duffy

Speech Communication Department
California Polytechnic State University

Beauharnais v. People of the State of Illinois, 343 U.S. 250 (1952) [U.S. Supreme Court]

◄◦► THE CASE IN BRIEF ◄◦►

Date
1952

Location
Illinois

Court
U.S. Supreme Court

Principal Participants
Joseph Beauharnais
State of Illinois

Significance of the Case
A white supremacist's right to free speech again tested the constitutionality of a statute and led to a split Court decision, establishing a measure by which First and Fourteenth Amendment rights are still weighed.

On January 6, 1950, Joseph Beauharnais, president of an "all-white" activist group called the White Circle League of America, met with his membership to distribute lithographs and other materials to volunteers for subsequent distribution in Chicago the following day. Under an enlarged and boldfaced heading, his pamphlet proclaimed: "PRESERVE AND PROTECT WHITE NEIGHBORHOODS! FROM THE CONSTANT AND CONTINUOUS INVASION, HARASSMENT AND ENCROACHMENT BY THE NEGROES."

Beauharnais's flyer attempted to accomplish two things:

1. to act as an organizing device for a petition to the mayor and aldermen of Chicago to "halt the further encroachment, harassment and invasion of white people, their property, neighborhoods and persons, by the Negro— through the exercise of the Police Power; of the office of the Mayor of the City of Chicago, and the City Council."

2. to garner new members for the White Circle League, which saw itself as "the only articulate white voice in America being raised in protest against negro aggressions and infiltrations into all white neighborhoods."

Beauharnais's position, and that of the White Circle League outlined in the lithograph, suffered from intolerance and undisguised prejudice, but it was an elaboration of the argument on the flyer that caused Beauharnais to be charged with violating a 1917 Illinois statute prohibiting group libel. In his call for racial unity, Beauharnais claimed on the flyer: "If persuasion and the need to prevent the White race from becoming mongrelized by the negro will not unite us, then the aggressions . . . rapes, robberies, knives, guns and marijuana of the negro, SURELY WILL."

With this claim, Beauharnais found himself charged with violating an Illinois criminal libel statute that stated, "It shall be unlawful for any person, form or corporation to manufacture, sell, or offer for sale, advertise or publish, present or exhibit in any public place . . . any lithograph, moving picture, play, drama or sketch, which publication or exhibition portrays depravity, criminality, unchastity, or lack of virtue of a class of citizens, of any race, color, creed or religion which said publication or exhibition exposes the citizens of any race, color, creed or religion to contempt, derision, or obloquy or which is productive of breach of the peace or riots."

Judge Joseph H. McGarry in the Municipal Court of Chicago found Beauharnais guilty. The defendant appealed to the Illinois Supreme Court, where his conviction was upheld on the basis that Beauharnais did, in fact, "publish" the lithographs in question and that they exposed "citizens of Illinois of the Negro race and color to contempt, derision or obloquy." Beauharnais appealed this decision to the U.S. Supreme Court, claiming that he had been denied due process because he had not been permitted to defend the "truth" of his arguments nor the "good motive" for their publication.

The Supreme Court decision upheld the Illinois court's conviction by a vote of 5-4. Justice Felix Frankfurter's majority opinion reiterated the opinion of the municipal and state courts that Beauharnais's publication of the lithographs was in violation of the Illinois statute, which prohibited portrayal of "depravity, criminality, unchastity or lack of virtue of a class of citizens of any race." Frankfurter elaborated further, claiming that Beauharnais's flyer fell under the "traditional justification for punishing libels criminally, namely their 'tendency to cause breach of the peace.' " The Court found that given heated racial tensions in Chicago and in Illinois generally, the language of the flyer fell readily into the "fighting words" class of speech, which can be prevented and punished without violation of First Amendment rights. In short, the Court supported the position that the flyer could lead to civil disturbances and that it fit the clear-and-present-danger test for libel convictions.

The dissenting opinions of Justices Hugo Black, William Douglas, Stanley Reed, and Robert Jackson articulate clearly the problem areas that split the Court. Justice Black's dissent, without condoning Beauharnais's racist statements, noted that Beauharnais and the White Circle League were making a genuine effort to petition their elected representatives and that it is illegal to prosecute such petitions. Black saw the decision against Beauharnais as one that curbed freedom of expression and dangerously expanded criminal libel laws.

In his dissent, Justice Douglas lamented what he called an "alarming trend" in recent Court decisions that, like this one, placed "in the hands of the legislate branch the right to regulate 'within reasonable limits' the right of free speech." His position, like Black's, saw the expansion of the definition of individual libel to group libel ultimately expanding legislative control over speech. He claimed that "intemperate speech is a distinctive characteristic of man"—one readily known to the framers of the Constitution who chose freedom of speech over restrained speech. It was this choice of liberty, he believed, that should be made, no matter how distasteful the language of Beauharnais's pamphlet.

Justice Jackson's dissent also raised interesting questions about the "concept of ordered liberty" over freedom of expression. He pointed out that "criminality of defamation is predicated upon power either to protect the private right to enjoy integrity of reputation or the public right to tranquility." Beauharnais's conviction was based largely on the potential of his flyer to incite a "breach of peace" in Illinois—although there was never evidence presented that it did, in fact, disturb state peace. There had been no actual violence or injury caused by the flyer. The conviction stood on what Jackson called the "likelihood of evil results." In his mind, this failed the clear-and-present-danger test for suppression of speech.

Justice Jackson also raised the crucial issue of due process, noting that the only defenses in libel cases are the proof of the truth of the statements and that they were published with good motives for justifiable ends. In this case, the judges in the lower courts decided that the statements were criminally libelous and instructed the jury to convict on the basis of whether Beauharnais had published the flyer, a claim that was undisputed in the trial. The trial court refused Beauharnais's attempt to prove the truth of his statements as immaterial, to which Jackson argued, "If the court would not let him try to prove he spoke truth, how could he show that he spoke truth for good ends? . . . [H]is evidence proffered for that purpose, was excluded instead of being received and evaluated."

Finally, the dissenting justices pointed to the all-encompassing language of the Illinois statute, which prohibited any printed matter, moving picture, play, drama or sketch from portraying a class of citizens of any race, color, creed, or religion as lacking in virtue. Justice Black noted wryly "the statute is broad enough to make criminal the publication, sale, presentation or exhibition of many of the world's great classics, both secular and religious."

Reactions by the press were quick and disapproving. The chilling effect of the ruling was not lost on the major publications of the day, and the cry of censorship was loud.

Beauharnais v. Illinois was the first conviction under a group libel statute. It has served as a conservative litmus test by which First and Fourteenth Amendment rights have been measured ever since.

Selected Bibliography

Be Vier, Lillian. "The First Amendment and Political Speech: An Inquiry into the Substance and Limits of Principle." *Stanford Law Review* 30 (1979): 299–358.

Brennan, William J., Jr. "The Supreme Court and the Meikeljohn Interpretation of the First Amendment." *Harvard Law Review* 79 (1965): 1–20.

The Constitution Finds Its Way Inside the Schoolhouse Gate

John W. Johnson
Department of History
University of Northern Iowa

Tinker v. Des Moines Independent Community School District, 393 U.S. 503 (1969) [U.S. Supreme Court]

—◄○► THE CASE IN BRIEF ◄○►—

Date
1969

Location
Iowa

Court
U.S. Supreme Court

Principal Participants
John and Mary Beth Tinker
Christopher Eckhardt
Des Moines Independent Community
 School District

Significance of the Case
The High Court's decision to uphold the freedom of expression, on constitutional grounds, of students who wore black armbands at school to protest the Vietnam War opened the door for students' rights.

November 1965 witnessed the first large-scale American protests against the Vietnam War. Among the approximately twenty-five thousand demonstrators who journeyed to Washington over that Thanksgiving weekend were about fifty Iowans. On the bus ride back to the Hawkeye state, the participants discussed what they could do to make their strong feelings known in their own communities. One suggestion offered was to wear black armbands. Accounts differ as to who first mentioned the armband option, but some of those on the bus attributed the idea to Herbert Hoover, the namesake and distant cousin of the former U.S. president.

Those interested in planning local demonstrations met in early December 1965 at the Des Moines home of Dr. William Eckhardt and Mrs. Margaret Eckhardt. Among the approximately two dozen attendees were the Reverend Leonard Tinker and his wife, Lorena Jeanne Tinker. Like the Eckhardts, the Tinkers were well known in Iowa as civil rights and peace activists. Also at the meeting were a few members of the college protest group Students for a Democratic Society (SDS). At the meeting it was agreed that students in local secondary schools and colleges should, if they were so inclined, wear black armbands to classes on December 16 and 17, 1965. Those who ultimately chose to wear the armbands later maintained they did so for two reasons: to express their sorrow over the casualties in the Vietnam War (Vietnamese as well as American) and to support a truce in the Southeast Asian hostilities so as to encourage peace talks.

Des Moines public school administrators somehow learned of the impending demonstration and attempted to stop it before it began. They passed a resolution banning black armbands in their schools and announced it over the building intercom systems. On the day before the anticipated demonstration, some of the gym teachers at one city high school encouraged students to perform calisthenics to the chant of "Beat the Viet Cong." Also, Christopher Eckhardt, the fifteen-year-old son of the Eckhardts, was told by a group of angry male classmates that if he wore an armband later that week he would find "fists in your face and a foot up your ass."

On the designated days for the protest, only a handful of the eighteen thousand Des Moines public school students defied the school district order and wore armbands to class. Among them were John and Mary Beth Tinker, teenage children of the Reverend and Mrs. Tinker, and Christopher Eckhardt. Two of the Tinkers' younger children also wore armbands to their elementary schools. Eckhardt and the Tinkers were the objects of some not so kind teasing by classmates who objected to the armbands. Eckhardt was also told by his assistant principal that he might receive a "broken nose" if he did not remove his armband. Ultimately, Eckhardt, Mary Beth Tinker, and two other students were suspended when they refused to remove the offending pieces of cloth; John Tinker, although not technically suspended, was asked to leave school.

The armband suspensions quickly became a focus of controversy among Iowans who were beginning to pay attention to the escalating Vietnam War. Scores of editorials, opinion pieces,

and letters to the editor appeared in Iowa newspapers over the 1965–66 holiday period. Radio and television also played up the controversy. Members of the Eckhardt and Tinker families received threats against their persons and property. Ultimately, in the second of two raucous public meetings held on the armbands, the Des Moines School Board voted 5-2 to uphold the suspensions.

Rather than challenging the board decree with further acts of civil disobedience, Christopher Eckhardt and the Tinkers returned to school after the holidays without sporting any symbols of protest. Now represented by Dan Johnston, a volunteer attorney for the Iowa Civil Liberties Union (ICLU), Eckhardt, the two Tinkers, and their fathers as "next friends" challenged the school suspensions in federal court. The principal argument presented by the ICLU was that the students, by wearing armbands to express their feelings about the Vietnam War, were exercising "symbolic speech" as protected by the First Amendment to the U.S. Constitution. They asked for nominal damages and a permanent injunction against the administrative ban on armbands.

The students' case was heard in federal district court in Des Moines in the summer of 1966 before District Judge Roy Stephenson, a decorated World War II veteran and former Republican Party activist. The lead attorney for the Des Moines School Board was Allan Herrick, a veteran of World War I and a staunch conservative. Shortly after the district court hearing, Judge Stephenson issued an opinion that upheld the students' suspensions as a "reasonable" means to maintain order in the classroom. The students and their ICLU attorney, Dan Johnston, appealed the district court ruling to the Eighth Circuit Court of Appeals in St. Louis. In November 1967, without explanation, an equally divided (4-4) en banc panel of the entire circuit affirmed Judge Stephenson's ruling. Almost immediately, Johnston (now assisted by the experienced national legal staff of the American Civil Liberties Union) filed an application for a writ of certiorari to the U.S. Supreme Court.

In early 1968, at about the time that criticism of the Vietnam War forced President Lyndon

Johnson to abandon his campaign for reelection, the High Court agreed to grant a full dress review of the lower court rulings in *Tinker v. Des Moines*. Oral Argument in *Tinker* took place in November 1968, the week following Richard Nixon's election as president. A few days later the case was discussed by the justices at an in-chambers conference, a preliminary vote was taken, and the majority opinion was assigned to Justice Abe Fortas, a liberal appointed to the Court by President Johnson. Ironically, Fortas had earlier voted against granting certiorari in *Tinker*.

While the draft opinions in *Tinker* were being written in the winter of 1968–69, the U.S. commitment of soldiers to the Southeast Asian theater passed five hundred thousand and the American death toll in the war approached thirty thousand. In February 1969 the Supreme Court announced its decision in *Tinker v. Des Moines*. Writing for the seven-person majority, Fortas first stated that the Court accepted the assertion that the wearing of black armbands was a "type of symbolic act that is within the Free Speech Clause of the First Amendment." Then, in language that would frequently be cited by those agreeing with the decision, he submitted that "it can hardly be argued that . . . students or teachers shed their constitutional rights to freedom of speech or expression at the schoolhouse gate." For Fortas and the Court majority, the right to wear armbands needed to be balanced against the right to maintain order in the schools. In applying this classic example of "the balancing test" of free expression versus public order, Fortas concluded that the record of the case did not reveal any disorder or disturbance on the part of the petitioners, nor did the wearing of the armbands interfere with the school's work or collide with the rights of other students.

Having determined that the wearing of the armbands did not cause any actual disruptions in the Des Moines schools, the *Tinker* majority also considered whether the school administration's apprehension of *possible* disruptions could justify a proscription of this form of expression. Here the Court applied a standard taken from two recent Fifth Circuit cases involving buttons worn by members of the Student Nonviolent

Coordinating Committee (SNCC) in Mississippi schools in defiance of an order prohibiting the buttons. The principle emerging from those cases was that the administrative body arguing for a policy restricting expression must demonstrate that exercising the proscribed right would "materially and substantially interfere with the requirements of appropriate discipline in the operation of the school." Justice Fortas concluded that this constitutional standard had not been met by the Des Moines school district in *Tinker*. In his words, the American historical experience bespeaks a "sort of hazardous freedom . . . that is the basis of our national strength." A "mere desire to avoid . . . discomfort and unpleasantness" is not enough to sanction a ban of certain types of conduct.

Fortas's opinion also identified a double standard in the school district's behavior regarding student conduct that had been pointed out by the students in their briefs and the oral argument. On several occasions in the mid-1960s Des Moines students had worn religious or political symbols to school without sanction. To permit such forms of expression for political or religious causes but to proscribe black armbands relating to the conduct of the Vietnam War, appeared inconsistent to Fortas and the Court majority. School officials must grant students a fair and equal treatment under the law. Paraphrasing a statement of Justice William Brennan from a 1967 opinion, the *Tinker* majority held that education works best if it is practiced with "a robust exchange of ideas which discovers truth out of a multitude of tongues, [rather] that through any kind of authoritative selection."

Of the two dissenting opinions in *Tinker*, Justice John Marshall Harlan's was quite brief. Given his usual reluctance to overturn decisions of governmental agencies, Harlan argued that school authorities should be given the benefit of the doubt in actions taken to maintain discipline and order. He proposed that a school administrator's decision should be upheld unless it was clearly established from the factual record that the policy "was motivated by other than legitimate school concerns." Because Harlan found nothing in the record to call into question the good faith of the Des

Moines school administration, he voted to affirm the lower court rulings.

That Justice Hugo Black would file a dissenting opinion was apparent from his hostility to the student litigants at the oral argument. What was surprising was the passion that the Court's senior justice poured into his remarks. Justice Black commenced with guns blazing: "I want it thoroughly known that I disclaim any sentence, any word, any part of what the Court does today." He proceeded to speak extemporaneously for about twenty minutes, emphasizing the horrible consequences that he believed would result from the majority's decision: students running amok in school corridors, children determining their own curricula, and youngsters setting their own standards for evaluation. Black summarized his position by quoting with approval the cliché "children should be seen not heard."

Black's opinion was surprising to many Court watchers because the Alabama justice was one of the High Court's greatest defenders of civil liberties. However, he made an exception in this case because of the context or "forum" for the expression. "It is a myth," Black wrote, "to say that any person has a constitutional right to say what he pleases, where he pleases, and when he pleases." Throughout most of his judicial career, Black had been an "absolutist" regarding "pure speech." But he felt that symbolic speech and political demonstrations that often accompanied it should not be protected by the First Amendment if that expression threatened disruption. Since Black perceived more disruption or potential disruption in the lower court record than did Fortas and the Court's majority, he was more willing to vote to uphold the proscription on armbands.

But, at bottom, what seemed to bother Black the most was the support that the majority opinion would now give to student protests that were running at high tide in 1968–69. He wrote: "One does not need to be a prophet or the son of a prophet to know that after the Court's holding today that some students . . . will be ready, able, and willing to defy their teachers on practically all orders. . . . [G]roups of students all over the land are already running loose, conducting break-ins, sit-ins, lie-

ins, and smash-ins." Black acknowledged that the three student plaintiffs in *Tinker* were expressing only a mild form of protest, but he felt that the consequence of the decision would be to open the floodgates: "This case . . . subjects all the public schools in the country to the whims and caprices of their loudest-mouthed, but maybe not their brightest, students."

Justice Black's opinion notwithstanding, the Supreme Court filed an order directing the Des Moines Independent Community School District to pay the plaintiffs in *Tinker* a grand total of $326.65 for "clerk's costs" and "printing the record." In the larger sense, the ruling in *Tinker* was greeted by legal experts as the Supreme Court's most significant decision to date on the rights of students. For those young people wishing to express political opinions, the holding in *Tinker* provided legal support for symbolic expressions at secondary schools and on college campuses—with the important proviso that the expression must not "materially and substantially" interfere with the operation of a school's normal curriculum. In other words, armbands worn by well-behaved kids in Des Moines were constitutionally permitted, but violent protests—such as those taking place in the late 1960s at campuses in New York City, Madison, Wisconsin, and Berkeley, California—were not.

Although the Supreme Court decision in *Tinker v. Des Moines* saw a small group of teenagers from the nation's heartland successfully obtain some of the protections of the Bill of Rights for the nation's students, that victory was undercut in the last three decades of the twentieth century. Between 1969 and the mid-1980s, *Tinker* served as a precedent in hundreds of student rights cases in the federal and state courts concerning such subjects as hair length, body piercings, student publications, school elections, and, of course, discipline. The *Tinker* standard for student expression requires a case-by-case analysis based on the facts of each particular situation. Not surprisingly, the case holdings have been widely divergent.

The *Tinker* decision was issued in the last term of Chief Justice Earl Warren, at close to the high point of judicial liberalism in U.S. Supreme Court history. In the successor Courts, under the leadership of Chief Justices Warren Burger and William Rehnquist, student rights have generally been held to be secondary to orderly schools. For example, in the 1986 decision of *Fraser v. Bethel School District No. 403*, the Supreme Court ruled that a principal was within his rights for suspending a student who employed sexual innuendos in a speech before a school assembly. Similarly, in the 1988 case of *Hazelwood School District v. Kuhlmeier*, the Court validated a principal's decision to delete two pages from an issue of a student newspaper because that school official felt that the content of the articles—one on the effects of divorce on families and the other on birth control and teenage pregnancy—might offend some students and other readers of the publication.

More recently, the 1999 killings at Columbine High School in Littleton, Colorado—real tragedies but hardly the consequences of student free expression run amok—led numerous schools to clamp down on student speech. After Columbine, the ACLU "intake files" of inquiries about possible threats to student rights increased significantly. One such inquiry involved a young man's request for ACLU assistance in the face of a possible charge of terrorism. His alleged crime was that he wrote "the end is near" in a computer e-mail message. In October 1999, Drake University Law School in Des Moines held a conference titled "Student Rights: Thirty Years After *Tinker v. Des Moines*." The formal presenters, although recognizing the pathbreaking importance of the *Tinker* decision, generally saw the three-decade-old holding as being significantly undercut by recent court decisions and social trends. In the closing words of one of the speakers, "Simply put, thirty years after *Tinker*, students do leave most of their First Amendment rights at the schoolhouse gate."

Selected Bibliography

Denno, Theodore F. "Mary Beth Tinker Takes the Constitution to School." *Fordham Law Review* 38 (October 1969): 35–62.

Geimer, William S. "Juvenileness: A Single-Edged Constitutional Sword." *Georgia Law Review* 22 (Summer 1988): 949–973.

Golub, Shari. "*Tinker* to *Fraser* to *Hazelwood*—Supreme Court's Double Play Combination Defeats High School Students' Rally for First Amendment Rights." *DePaul Law Review* 38 (1989): 487–515.

Johnson, John W. "'Dear Mr. Justice': Public Correspondence with Members of the Supreme Court." *Journal of Supreme Court History* 2 (1997): 101–112.

———. *The Struggle for Student Rights: Tinker v. Des Moines and the 1960s.* Lawrence: University Press of Kansas, 1997.

Nahmod, Seldon H. "Beyond *Tinker*: The High School as an Educational Public Forum." *Harvard Civil Rights and Civil Liberties Law Review* 5 (April 1970): 278–300.

Commercial Speech and the First Amendment

―◦―

Tinsley E. Yarbrough

Department of Political Science
East Carolina University

Virginia State Board of Pharmacy v. Virginia Citizens Consumer Council, Inc.,
425 U.S. 748 (1976) [U.S. Supreme Court]

◦ THE CASE IN BRIEF ◦

Date
1976

Location
Virginia

Court
U.S. Supreme Court

Principal Participants
Virginia State Board of Pharmacy
Virginia Citizens Consumer Council, Inc.

Significance of the Case
A prescription drug advertisement spurred a Court decision recognizing that commercial speech is also guaranteed free-speech protection under the First Amendment.

Fighting words, obscenity, and libel have not been the only forms of expression largely excluded from First Amendment protection. In 1942, the same year that the Supreme Court recognized the fighting words exception to free speech in *Chaplinsky v. New Hampshire*, the justices added "commercial speech" to the categories of proscribable expression. *Valentine v. Chrestensen* (1942) sustained a New York statute prohibiting the distribution of handbills by an enterprising man who printed on one side of a circular an advertisement soliciting customers to tour his submarine, while using the other side to protest the city's refusal to permit him use of a municipal pier for his exhibit. In *Breard v. Alexandria* (1951), moreover, a majority upheld a conviction under an ordinance prohibiting the door-to-door solicitation of magazine subscriptions, distinguishing that case from *Martin v. Struthers* (1943), in which the Court had reversed the conviction of a door-to-door distributor of religious tracts whose activities involved "no element of the commercial."

After *Breard*, the Court never again denied protection to expression purely on the ground that it constituted commercial speech. Justice William O. Douglas, who had joined *Valentine*, observed in a concurrence in *Cammarano v. United States* (1959) that the *Valentine* court's pronouncement "was casual, almost offhand. And it has not survived reflection." Scholarly commentaries were equally critical. In *Pittsburgh Press Company v. Pittsburgh Commission on Human Relations* (1973), a 5-4 majority, speaking through Justice Lewis F. Powell, relied only to a limited degree on the commercial-speech exception to free expression in rejecting a First Amendment attack on an order prohibiting a newspaper from listing certain job advertisements in sex-designated help-wanted columns. Employment discrimination, the justice emphasized, was *illegal* commercial activity under Pittsburgh's human relations ordinance; and "[a]ny First Amendment interest which might be served by advertising an ordinary commercial proposal and which might arguably outweigh the government interest supporting the regulation is altogether absent when the commercial activity itself is illegal and the restriction on advertising is incidental to a valid limitation on economic activity."

The four *Pittsburgh Press* dissenters saw the challenged regulation primarily as an attempt to impose restrictions on a newspaper's editorial judgment. Justice Potter Stewart, joined by Justice Douglas, wrote a strong dissent, for example, declaring that no "government agency— local, state, or federal—can tell a newspaper in advance what it can print and what it cannot." But Justice Douglas filed a brief dissent reiterating his opposition to the commercial-speech exception. Thus, the majority opinion in *Pittsburgh Press* was hardly a reaffirmation of *Valentine*.

Bigelow v. Virginia (1975) further eroded the commercial-speech exception to protected expression. A 7-2 majority overturned a state statute making it a misdemeanor to encourage or prompt abortions through publications, as applied to the managing editor of a Virginia newspaper who ran an advertisement for a legal New York abortion service. The earlier commercial-speech cases, declared Justice Harry A. Blackmun for the Court, had not completely stripped advertisements of all First Amendment protection. An advertisement containing information of potential interest and value to a diverse audience, observed the author of *Roe v. Wade*, the Court's 1973 decision recognizing abortion rights, was constitutionally protected, and the state's interest in shielding Virginians from information about legal (indeed, constitutionally guaranteed) activities outside its borders was entitled to little, if any, weight.

Bigelow involved an advertisement about abortions, a constitutionally protected activity. The Court's ruling thus could be viewed as only a modest departure from *Valentine*. The next year, however, the justices drastically curtailed the authority of government to regulate commercial speech. *Virginia State Board of Pharmacy v. Virginia Citizens Consumer Council* (1976) was a challenge to a state statute that declared it unprofessional conduct for a licensed pharmacist to advertise prescription drug prices. Shortly after that requirement was first added to the standards of professional conduct for Virginia pharmacists in 1968, a drug retailing company and one of its pharmacists filed a suit challenging the ban on First Amendment grounds. On that occasion, a three-judge federal district court sustained the regulation, declaring the dispensing of prescription drugs a matter clearly within the state's power to protect the public's health, safety, and welfare. That decision was not appealed. Later, however, consumers of prescription drugs and associations representing their interests filed a second suit, contending that the First Amendment entitled users of prescription drugs to receive information about drug prices that pharmacists wished to communicate through advertising and other promotional means. In 1974, a three-judge panel unanimously invalidated the challenged regulation.

On May 24, 1976, the Supreme Court, speaking again through Justice Blackmun, affirmed the district court. Citing *Lamont v. Postmaster General* (1965), among other cases embracing a First Amendment right to receive communications, Blackmun concluded in *Virginia State Board of Pharmacy v. Virginia Citizens Consumer Council* that "[i]f there is a right to advertise, there is a reciprocal right to receive the advertising, and it may be asserted by these appellees." He also characterized *Valentine* and *Breard* as "simplistic," and he declared that "the notion of unprotected 'commercial speech' [had] all but passed from the scene" with the *Bigelow* ruling the previous term. Because *Bigelow* had clearly involved an advertisement of public interest, however, he realized that "[s]ome fragment of hope for the continuing validity of a 'commercial speech' exception arguably might have persisted" after *Bigelow*, and that it was thus necessary to administer the doctrine a final, fatal blow.

Clearly, Blackmun reasoned, speech did not lose its First Amendment status merely because it entailed the expenditure of money or was engaged in for profit. Nor could expression be denied protection merely because it addressed a commercial subject. "No one could contend," asserted Blackmun, "that our pharmacist may be prevented from being heard on the subject of whether, in general, pharmaceutical prices should be regulated, or their advertisement forbidden." The First Amendment, moreover, had traditionally covered the presentation of noneditorial, factual material, such as that offered in advertisements. The question before the Court, therefore, was "whether speech which does 'no more than propose a commercial transaction' . . . is [for that reason alone] so removed from [expression traditionally accorded First Amendment protection] . . . that it lacks all protection. Our answer is that it is not."

Turning to the First Amendment interests that might override a regulation of commercial speech, Blackmun assumed that advertisers had a "purely economic" interest in their advertisements, yet concluded that their interest hardly disqualified them from constitutional protection, just as the First Amendment clearly extended to the purely economic interests of participants in a labor dispute. Consumers also had an interest in the free flow of purely commercial information—one, in fact, that "may be as keen, if not keener by far, than his interest in the day's most urgent political debate." Clearly, asserted the justice, the appellees had made such a case. "Those whom the suppression of prescription drug price information hits the hardest are the poor, the sick, and particularly the aged. A disproportionate amount of their income tends to be spent on prescription drugs; yet they are the least able to learn, by shopping from pharmacist to pharmacist, where their scarce dollars are best spent. When drug prices vary as strikingly as they do, information as to who is charging what becomes more than convenience. It could mean the alleviation of physical pain or the enjoyment of basic necessities." Society, in general, also had a "strong interest" in the free flow of commercial information. Indeed, observed Blackmun, in a predominantly free-enterprise economy, private economic decisions largely determined the allocation of resources. "It is a matter of public interest that those decisions, in the aggregate, be intelligent and well informed. To this end, the free flow of commercial information is indispensable," just as such information was critical to the development of intelligent opinions on all issues confronting a political system.

In defending the advertising ban, the pharmacy board had argued that its elimination might lead to aggressive price competition that could threaten the quality of pharmaceutical products and services; in fact, it might even result in higher overall drug prices as a result of increased demand brought on by aggressive marketing. The Court concluded, however, that "on close inspection," the ban worked mainly to benefit certain pharmacists by keeping consumers "in ignorance." After all, the advertising ban did not directly affect professional standards; the pharmacist inclined to cut corners could do so even with the ban. "The only effect the advertising ban has on him is to insulate him from price competition and to open the way for him to make a substantial, and perhaps even excessive, profit in addition to providing an inferior service." The alternative to the "highly paternalistic approach" that the ban reflected, contended Blackmun, was to maintain open channels of communication and permit people to make their own choices. "It is precisely this kind of choice, between the dangers of suppressing information, and the dangers of its misuse if it is freely available, that the First Amendment makes for us."

While recognizing some degree of First Amendment protection for commercial speech, Justice Blackmun also emphasized that certain controls over such expression were clearly permissible. As in other First Amendment fields, commercial speech could be subjected to reasonable regulations of time, place, and manner if they were unrelated to the content of the speech in question, served a significant governmental interest, and left open ample alternative channels of communication. False, deceptive, and misleading advertisements, as well as those making illegal offers, could also be regulated to insure "that the stream of commercial information flow[s] cleanly as well as freely." Blackmun acknowledged, too, that commercial advertisements might enjoy a different degree of constitutional protection than do other sorts of expression, in part because the accuracy of commercial speech might be more easily verifiable than, for example, news reporting or political commentary. Reserved for another day, moreover, were regulations of commercial speech in other fields, such as the medical and legal professions. What the Court had decided, however, asserted the justice, was that states could not "completely suppress the dissemination of concededly truthful [commercial] information about entirely lawful activity, fearful of that information's effect upon its disseminators and its recipients."

In a brief concurrence, Chief Justice Warren Burger stressed that the Court's decision largely dealt with state authority to forbid the advertising of the retail prices of prepackaged prescription drugs. "[Q]uite different factors would govern," declared Burger, "were we faced with a law regulating or even prohibiting advertising by the traditional learned professions of medicine or law. . . . Attorneys and physicians are engaged *primarily* in providing services in which professional judgment is a large component. . . . I think it important to note . . . that the advertisement of professional services carries with it quite different risks from the advertisement of standard products." In Burger's judgment, the Court had wisely reserved such issues for another day.

Concurring separately, Justice Stewart applauded *Valentine*'s demise, but he emphasized the important differences between commercial advertisements and ideological communications, with the latter accorded constitutional protection "whether or not it contains factual representations and even if it includes inaccurate assertions of fact," while "the factual claims contained in commercial price or product advertisements [could] be tested empirically and corrected to reflect the truth without in any manner jeopardizing the free dissemination of thought."

Justice William Rehnquist, the lone dissenter, disputed virtually every element of the majority's rationale, recommending leaving the issue in legislative hands. Because individuals could simply telephone druggists to inquire about their prices, while consumer groups could collect and publish comparative price information, Rehnquist doubted they possessed the requisite standing to sue. "[T]he only group truly restricted by [the] statute, the pharmacists," he added, had "not even troubled to join in this litigation and may well feel that the expense and competition of advertising is not in their interest." Citing the important "societal interest against the promotion of drug use for every ill, real or imaginary," Rehnquist also warned that the Court's apparent restriction of governmental authority to false, deceptive, and misleading advertisements left advertisers free to aggressively promote demand for their products. He feared the consequences of such a stance. A drug advertisement might ask, for example, "Pain getting you down? Insist that your physician prescribe Demerol." Nor could the ruling be limited to price information alone; in Rehnquist's judgment, the Court had also left the way open "for active promotion of prescription drugs, liquor, cigarettes, and other products the use of which it has previously been thought desirable to discourage." Most disturbingly for the justice, perhaps, the Court's inclusion of truthful commercial speech within the First Amendment's scope could not "possibly be confined to pharmacists but must likewise extend to lawyers, doctors, and all other professions."

Rehnquist proved prophetic in 1977, when the Court in *Bates v. State Bar of Arizona* struck down a state bar regulation forbidding all advertising by lawyers. Later, the justices invalidated a rule prohibiting certain types of lawyer advertising not shown to be misleading or fraudulent, but also upheld the disciplining of lawyers who directly and personally solicited clients for financial gain, as well as those whose advertisements misled prospective clients regarding their obligations under contingent-fee arrangements. *Central Hudson Gas v. Public Service Commission* (1980) adopted a three-pronged test under which commercial expression could be regulated if the control at issue promoted a substantial governmental interest, directly advanced that interest, and did so through means narrowly tailored to achieve its objective. Applying the *Central Hudson* standard, the Burger and Rehnquist Courts both sustained and struck down a variety of controls over commercial speech.

Selected Bibliography

Meiklejohn, Donald. "Commercial Speech and the First Amendment." *California Western Law Review* 13 (1977): 480–495.

Free Speech and Legal Ethics:
The Issue of Lawyer Advertising

—◄o►—

Roger D. Hardaway

Department of History
Northwestern Oklahoma State University

Bates v. State Bar of Arizona, 433 U.S. 350 (1977) [U.S. Supreme Court]

◄o► THE CASE IN BRIEF ◄o►

Date
1977

Location
Arizona
District of Columbia

Court
U.S. Supreme Court

Principal Participants
John R. Bates
Van O'Steen
Arizona State Bar Association

Significance of the Case
The Court upheld a lawyer's right to free speech to promote his practice but held that such advertising could be regulated to some degree. In response, the American Bar Association drafted rules of conduct concering lawyer advertising.

Critics charged that it would tarnish the image of the profession. Proponents countered that it would help consumers make informed decisions, make services available to a greater number of people, and lower artificially inflated fees. The issue was advertising by lawyers in traditional commercial outlets such as newspapers. The U.S. Supreme Court addressed the question in 1977.

Attorney disciplinary rules in effect in the United States had traditionally prohibited any form of advertising by lawyers except for brief listings in legal publications and directories. In 1975, the American Bar Association, which makes recommendations to state entities concerning regulation of the legal profession, suggested allowing attorneys to list fees for initial consultations in the yellow pages. Other forms of attorney advertising were generally forbidden by state regulating bodies. John R. Bates and Van O'Steen, two Phoenix attorneys, decided to challenge Arizona's ban on lawyer advertising.

Bates and O'Steen formed a law partnership in 1974, which they termed a "legal clinic." Their plan was simple. They would perform only routine legal matters such as uncontested divorces, adoptions, uncomplicated bankruptcies, and name changes. They would charge modest fees, and count on a heavy volume of business in order to be profitable. They soon realized, however, that they did not have enough clients to make their experiment succeed. To increase business, therefore, Bates and O'Steen placed an advertisement in the *Arizona Republic,* a Phoenix newspaper, in February 1976, listing their fees for several types of legal services.

The president of the state bar of Arizona, to which all licensed Arizona lawyers were required to belong, filed a complaint against the two attorneys. The case was referred to a special disciplinary committee, which recommended that Bates and O'Steen be suspended from practicing law for six months. The state bar association's board of governors, however, reduced the period of suspension to one week because Bates and O'Steen had advertised in the good-faith belief that the disciplinary rule violated their rights of free speech guaranteed by the First Amendment.

The two lawyers next asked the Supreme Court of Arizona to review the bar association's recommendation. The Court, in *Matter of Bates,* upheld the rule prohibiting lawyer advertising, but reduced the attorneys' punishment to censure only—a penalty less harsh than suspension. Undaunted (and unsatisfied), Bates and O'Steen petitioned to have their case heard by the U.S. Supreme Court.

The Supreme Court issued its ruling on the issue in June 1977 in *Bates v. State Bar of Arizona.* The Court's decision, written by Justice Harry A. Blackmun, first rejected the lawyers' argument that the rule in question violated the Sherman Antitrust Act by its "tendency to limit competition." But the Court, in a bare majority of 5-4, held that attorneys have a right under the First Amendment to advertise their fees and services, or to engage in what the justices called "commercial speech."

"Commercial speech," Blackmun asserted, "serves to inform the public of the availability, nature, and prices of products and services, and thus performs an indispensable role in the allocation of resources in a free enterprise system. . . . In short, such speech serves individual and societal interests in assuring informed and reliable decisionmaking." Moreover, Blackmun reasoned, the Arizona rule prohibiting attorney advertising "serves to inhibit the free flow of commercial information and to keep the public in ignorance." The justice further noted that studies had shown that commercial advertising reduced the prices of consumer goods, and suggested that the same would be true of services offered by attorneys.

The Court's majority was careful to declare, however, that while attorney advertising was protected by the First Amendment's guarantee of free speech, it could nevertheless be regulated to some degree. Specifically, Blackmun instructed the legal community to promulgate rules that would outlaw "advertising that is false, deceptive, or misleading," as well as that "concerning transactions that are themselves illegal." In addition, disciplinary rules could put "reasonable restrictions on the time, place, and manner of advertising."

The dissenting Court members, led by Justice Lewis F. Powell Jr., argued that attorney advertising was not protected by the First Amendment and was not in the public interest. Powell noted that it was more difficult to estimate the value of professional services than it was of "tangible products." Moreover, Powell contended that unethical lawyers could use ads to mislead the public because legal "services are individualized with respect to content and quality and because the law consumer of legal services usually does not know in advance the precise nature and scope of the services he requires."

After the Supreme Court's decision was issued, the American Bar Association (which had opposed the Bates and O'Steen ad) drafted some proposed rules concerning lawyer advertising. Today, these regulations, embodied in the *Model Rules of Professional Conduct,* permit ads not only in newspapers, legal periodicals, and telephone directories, but also on television, radio, outdoor signs, and in mass mailings to the general public. Each state's legal establishment, however, is free to adopt, reject, or modify the ABA proposals. Consequently, there currently exists no uniform national standard of conduct for attorneys wishing to advertise their services.

Despite the *Bates* decision, many attorneys remain reluctant to advertise. This is perhaps due to fear of appearing "unprofessional" in the eyes of their peers or simply because of custom. Surveys have shown that the majority of those who do advertise restrict their activity in this regard to the yellow pages of their local telephone books. Other lawyers, however, have not been afraid to advertise in the mass media, and this has apparently been beneficial to consumers. In recent years, the number of legal clinics in the United States has increased steadily, delivering legal services to consumers, in most instances, at reduced prices. This is exactly what John R. Bates and Van O'Steen had in mind when they fought traditional notions of ethical legal conduct—and won.

Selected Bibliography

Bowers, Gregory H., and Otis H. Stephens Jr. "Attorney Advertising and the First Amendment: The Development and Impact of a Constitutional Standard." *Memphis State University Law Review* 17 (Winter 1987): 221–262.

Whitman, Douglas, and Clyde D. Stoltenberg. "Evolving Concepts of Lawyer Advertising: The Supreme Court's Latest Clarification." *Indiana Law Review* 19 (Spring 1986): 497–560.

Flag Burning and the Constitution

—◀◎▶—

Paul Finkelman
College of Law
University of Tulsa

Texas v. Johnson, 491 U.S. 397 (1989), and *Eichman v. United States*,
496 U.S. 310 (1990) [U.S. Supreme Court]

◀◎▶ THE CASE IN BRIEF ◀◎▶

Date
1989

Location
Texas

Court
U.S. Supreme Court

Principal Participants
Gregory Lee Johnson; State of Texas

Significance of the Case
In defiance of an act of Congress, a protester won the right, under the First Amendment, to burn an American flag. A few years later there was a push headed by President George Bush for an amendment to the Constitution making it a crime to burn the American flag. The amendment died when it failed to receive the necessary two-thirds needed in Congress.

Texas v. Johnson ought to have been a relatively simple case involving freedom of expression. Instead, it sparked a highly emotional response that led to the adoption of a federal statute prohibiting the desecration of the flag and calls for a constitutional amendment on the subject.

During the 1984 Republican National Convention in Dallas, Texas, Gregory Lee Johnson was one of about one hundred demonstrators who participated in a march protesting policies of the administration of Ronald Reagan and certain Dallas-based corporations. The march ended at city hall, where Johnson burned an American flag in symbolic protest. No riot or violence occurred, and no one was hurt during the demonstration, although some observers later testified that they "had been seriously offended by the flag-burning."

Johnson was the only person arrested. He was charged under a Texas law that made it a crime to desecrate "a venerated object." At trial, he was convicted and sentenced to a year in prison and fined two thousand dollars. His conviction was later reversed by the Texas Court of

A protestor burns an American flag in Seattle a few months after a federal law went into effect making it illegal to burn the flag. *AP/Wide World Photos.*

Criminal Appeals, which found that the statue violated the right to freedom of expression found in the federal Constitution. The Texas court based part of its decision on the reasoning in the 1943 case of *West Virginia Board of Education v. Barnette,* where the U.S. Supreme Court had "recogniz[ed] that the right to differ is the centerpiece of our First Amendment freedoms." Further drawing from *Barnette,* the Texas court found that the burning of a single flag did not place the national flag in "grave and immediate danger" of losing its symbolic value. Indeed, although the Texas Court did not make this point, the fact that Gregory Lee Johnson chose to burn the flag as an act of protest underscores the continuing viability of the flag as a national symbol, even to protesters.

Speaking for a sharply, and oddly, divided Court, Justice William J. Brennan Jr. upheld the Texas court, which had overturned Johnson's conviction. That the Court split 5-4 on this case is not itself surprising, since many of the Court's important 1988–1989 decisions were decided by one vote. For example, at about the same time it revealed its decision, the Court also announced its decision in an important establishment clause case involving the display of a Christmas tree, menorah, and a cross on public buildings in Pittsburgh and in Allegheny County. In that case, the Court was divided 4-1-4, with Justice Sandra Day O'Connor holding that one form of display was permissible, but another form was not. What was surprising in all these cases was the alignment of the Court.

Siding with Justice Brennan were two consistent liberals, Harry Blackmun and Thurgood Marshall, and two consistent conservatives, Antonin Scalia and Anthony Kennedy. On the other hand, Justice John Paul Stevens, who is often a liberal on free-speech matters, wrote an emotional dissent.

In the majority opinion, Justice Brennan offered a straightforward liberal analysis, deeply rooted in First Amendment law. He acknowledged that the government had "a freer hand in restricting expressive conduct than it has in restricting the written or spoken word." But, he also noted that any restriction of such symbolic speech turned on "the governmental interest at stake." Brennan asserted that the conviction could be sustained only if the state could show that "Johnson's conviction . . . is unrelated to the suppression of expression." But this was clearly impossible. There had been no violence or threat to the peace from Johnson's act. Therefore, the prosecution could only be interpreted as a judicial assault on the content of Johnson's expression. Indeed, in oral arguments, the attorney for Texas argued that the state had an interest in protecting the flag as a symbol—which of course implies that it was the political content of burning the flag that Texas sought to prevent. Thus, Brennan concluded that "Johnson was not . . . prosecuted for the expression of just any idea; he was prosecuted for his expression of dissatisfaction with the policies of this country, expression situated at the core of our First Amendment values." All parties to the case agreed that Johnson burned the flag "because he knew that his politically charged expression would cause 'serious offence.'" But Justice Brennan noted, "If there is a bedrock principle underlying the First Amendment, it is that the Government may not prohibit the expression of an idea simply because society finds the idea itself offensive or disagreeable." To find for Texas, Brennan reasoned, the Court would have to hold "that the Government may ensure that a symbol be used to express only one view of that symbol or its referents." But, such a conclusion would lead the Court "to enter territory having no discernible or defensible boundaries," and the justices would be "forced to consult our own political preferences, and impose them on the citizenry, in the very way that the First Amendment forbids us to do."

Brennan concluded by arguing that through this decision "the flag's deservedly cherished place in our community will be strengthened, not weakened," because the decision is a "reaffirmation of the principles of freedom and inclusiveness that the flag best reflects, and of the conviction that our toleration of criticism such as Johnson's is a sign and source of our strength." He warned that "we do not consecrate the flag by punishing its desecration, for in doing so we dilute the freedom that this cherished emblem represents."

Justice Anthony Kennedy, a conservative Republican and the most recent appointee to the Court, concurred with Brennan: "The hard fact is that sometimes we must make decisions we do not like. We make them because they are right, right in the sense that the law and the Constitution, as we see them, compel the result" even when that result is one that is "painful."

In dissent, Chief Justice William Rehnquist quoted numerous poems, slogans, and songs about the flag. He mentioned images of soldiers dying in foreign wars, as well as Iwo Jima, where "United States Marines fought hand-to-hand against thousands of Japanese" and they "raised a piece of pipe upright and from one end fluttered a flag." He pointed out that the flag was on all cartons and containers involved in lend-lease during World War II, and that it is flown at half-mast at the death of a president. In a separate dissent, Justice John Paul Stevens concluded: "The ideas of liberty and equality have been an irresistible force in motivating leaders like Patrick Henry, Susan B. Anthony, and Abra-

ham Lincoln, schoolteachers like Nathan Hale and Booker T. Washington, the Philippine Scouts who fought at Bataan, and the soldiers who scaled the bluff at Omaha Beach." If those ideas are worth fighting for—and our history demonstrates that they are—it cannot be true that the flag that uniquely symbolizes their power is not itself worthy of protection from unnecessary desecration."

Although stirring paeans to patriotism and history, the two dissents did not confront the constitutional issue: the meaning of freedom of expression. Indeed, their very emotional content underscored the power of Brennan's analysis: precisely because a flag burning generated such strong *political* feelings, it deserved the protection of the First Amendment. Significantly, conservatives like Scalia and Kennedy, as well as liberals like Marshall and Blackmun, joined Brennan.

Immediately after the decision, President George Bush called for a constitutional amendment to overturn the holding. Initially, there was great public support for this idea, but by the end of the summer most opinion polls showed that a majority of Americans did not want to see an amendment to the Bill of Rights. Many newspapers, especially conservative papers in the South and Midwest, argued that however bad flag burning might be, amending the Bill of Rights was worse.

In October 1989, Congress passed a law making it a federal crime to desecrate the flag. Some Republicans loyal to President Bush argued against the statute, on the grounds that it would violate the Constitution as interpreted in *Texas v. Johnson*. These congressmen and senators also thought they could use the flag issue—and the demand for a protective amendment—as a political weapon in future elections. Ultimately, though, most members of Congress supported the bill. President Bush allowed the bill to become law without his signature, because he was holding out for a constitutional amendment.

On October 19, 1989, the Senate voted 51-48 in favor of a constitutional amendment to restrict flag burning. This was far short of the two-thirds majority needed to send an amendment on to the states, and so the amendment died. Opponents of the amendment included over eleven Republicans, who broke with the president on this issue. Some had initially favored an amendment, but changed their minds as opposition to amending the Bill of Rights grew. Senator John Danforth, a Missouri Republican who had previously supported an amendment, now argued against it. He warned that those who voted for the amendment should not turn it into a political issue in a future election. They might castigate those who opposed the amendment for being "soft" on the flag, but, he warned, opponents of the amendment would successfully argue that they had in fact stood up for the Constitution.

The initial political response to the issue of flag burning is significant for an understanding of the Bill of Rights and American culture. A popular president took a strong position in favor of amending the Bill of Rights because of his own emotional response to the decision. Many politicians initially hedged on the issue, but when brought to a vote, nearly a majority of the Senate opposed tinkering with America's basic freedoms. More significantly, a majority of Americans rejected the simplistic patriotic appeal of the flag for the more intellectually and politically complex view that freedom of speech and the First Amendment are even more important than the symbol of the flag. Most Americans agreed that what Johnson did was reprehensible, but that freedom of expression was too valuable to risk, even for such an offensive act as burning the flag.

Instead of amending the Constitution, Congress wrote a new statute, designed to protect the flag from desecration. Immediately, a number of Americans challenged this law by actually burning the flag. In *United States v. Eichman* (1990), the Supreme Court reaffirmed its original flag-burning ruling by the same 5-4 vote. A new movement to amend the Constitution began. Opponents of an amendment immediately reconstituted the Emergency Committee to Defend the First Amendment, which was led by an unusual coalition of civil libertarians and conservatives. The three co-chairs of the committee were New York University professor Norman Dorsen, the president of the American Civil Liberties Union; Harvard Law professor

Charles Fried, who had been solicitor general under President Ronald Reagan; and President Richard Nixon's former solicitor general, Erwin Griswold. Other opponents of the amendment included three former presidents of the American Bar Association. After much heated debate, a majority of the House of Representatives voted for an amendment, but this majority was far short of the two-thirds needed to send the amendment on to the Senate and then to the states. Thus, as of June 1990, the flag-burning amendment was dead. With little public support for the amendment, and a great deal of opposition from the entire political spectrum, the amendment failed, despite attempts by President Bush and the Republican minority in the House to make this a litmus test of patriotism for members of Congress running for reelection. Particularly significant was the opposition to the amendment from a number of Democratic congressmen and senators who had served in Vietnam with great distinction, and who had no doubt that the electorate understood the difference between flag-waving and what they conceived to be a patriotic duty to protect the basic fabric of liberty guaranteed by the Bill of Rights.

Throughout the 1990s, occasional efforts to reintroduce an anti–flag-burning amendment were mounted in Congress. These efforts failed to generate sufficient political support, and they appear unlikely to do so in the early twenty-first century.

Selected Bibliography

Bloom, Lackland H., Jr. "*Barnette* and *Johnson*: A Tale of Two Opinions." *Iowa Law Review* 75 (January 1990): 417–432.

Comment. "Flag Burning Yes, Loud Music No: What's the Catch?" *University of Miami Law Review* 44 (March 1990): 1033–1074.

Goldstein, Robert J. *Flag Burning and Free Speech: The Case of* Texas v. Johnson. Lawrence: University Press of Kansas, 2000.

Kmiec, D. W. "In the Aftermath of *Johnson* and *Eichman*: The Constitution Need Not Be Mutilated to Preserve the Government's Speech and Property." *Brigham Young University Law Review* (1990): 577–638.

Reigniting the "Fighting Words"/ "Symbolic Speech" Debate: Cross Burning and the Constitution

—◄○►—

Tinsley E. Yarbrough
Department of Political Science
East Carolina University

R.A.V. v. City of St. Paul, Minnesota, 505 U.S. 377 (1992) [U.S. Supreme Court]

◄○► THE CASE IN BRIEF ◄○►

Date
1992

Location
Minnesota

Court
U.S. Supreme Court

Principal Participants
"R.A.V.," a teenager
City of St. Paul

Significance of the Case
A city ordinance that included a ban on flag burning was overturned by the Supreme Court, which ruled it to be too broad in its scope.

Not all speech enjoys First Amendment protection. In *Chaplinsky v. New Hampshire* (1942), the U.S. Supreme Court upheld the conviction of a Jehovah's Witness who cursed a town marshal and was prosecuted under a statute the state supreme court had construed to forbid "fighting words." Such face-to-face verbal assaults were so lacking in social value and so likely to provoke violence, declared Justice Frank Murphy in the *Chaplinsky* ruling, that they simply were not entitled to constitutional protection.

Since *Schenck v. United States* (1919), speech creating a clear-and-present-danger of riot, revolution, or other conduct that is clearly within the power of government to prevent has also been held subject to regulation. But in *Brandenburg v. Ohio* (1969), the Warren court struck down a state criminal syndicalism statute broadly forbidding the advocacy of violence or other illegal means for promoting political and social change.

Only incitement of imminent lawless action very likely to occur as a result of the speech at issue, the Court cautioned, could be criminally prosecuted. Expression could not be proscribed merely because others found it provocative, offensive, or contrary to prevailing opinion.

Furthermore, the Supreme Court has held that the constitutional protection guaranteed to freedom of speech extends not only to verbal and printed expression, but also to "symbolic speech," or conduct intended to communicate ideas or feelings. Only compelling governmental interests unrelated to the suppression of ideas are sufficient, moreover, to justify infringements upon symbolic speech. Therefore, laws restricting expression—pure or symbolic—on the basis of its content or viewpoint bear a particularly heavy burden of justification.

Finally, regulations of speech-related conduct that are so vague or substantially "overbroad" in their scope that they can be used to restrict many protected as well as unprotected activities are considered unconstitutional on their face and cannot be enforced, not even against conduct subject to governmental control under a narrowly and clearly drafted law.

A number of cases confronting the Supreme Court under Chief Justice William Rehnquist have involved content-based regulations of symbolic speech, defended as controls over fighting words or protections against lawless action. For example, in *Texas v. Johnson* (1989) and *United States v. Eichman* (1990), the Supreme Court included flag burning within the scope of symbolic speech protected by the First Amendment, and it rejected claims that flag burning, by its very nature, amounted to an incitement of imminent lawless action or constituted fighting words. Writing for the five-member *Johnson* majority, Justice William J. Brennan concluded that Government could not simply assume that a particular form of expression would inevitably cause a riot, but instead was obliged to examine the circumstances of each incident to determine whether the speech at issue had actually incited imminent illegal conduct. Yet, the flag-burning for which Gregory Lee Johnson was convicted had neither caused nor threatened a breach of the peace. Nor could the state equate the mere burning of a flag with fighting words. That ex-

ception to protected expression, declared Brennan, had consistently been limited to face-to-face verbal assaults inherently likely to provoke violent retaliation. According to Brennan, "no reasonable onlooker would have regarded [the flag-burning at issue in *Johnson*] . . . as a direct personal insult or an invitation to exchange fisticuffs." Moreover, no form of expression could be presumed so inherently inflammatory as to provoke a violent reaction, whatever the circumstances.

The flag-burning cases were not the only Rehnquist court decisions igniting intense debate among the justices about the scope of symbolic speech and the fighting-words exception to protected expression. In the predawn hours of June 21, 1990, several white teenagers in St. Paul, Minnesota, taped broken chair legs together in the shape of a cross and set it ablaze inside the fenced yard of a black family who lived across the street from one of the youths, known as "R.A.V." The victims were the only blacks living in the neighborhood. Although the teenager's conduct could have been punished under laws forbidding terrorist threats, arson, and criminal damage to property, R.A.V. was charged with violating a state statute forbidding racially motivated assaults. He was also charged with violating St. Paul's bias-motivated, disorderly conduct ordinance: "Whoever places on public or private property a symbol, object, appellation, characterization or graffiti, including, but not limited to, a burning cross or Nazi swastika, which one knows or has reasonable grounds to know arouses anger, alarm or resentment in others on the basis of race, color, creed, religion or gender commits disorderly conduct and shall be guilty of a misdemeanor."

R.A.V.'s counsel, while not challenging the racially motivated assault charge, moved to dismiss the bias-motivated disorderly conduct count on the grounds that the St. Paul ordinance was overbroad and that it imposed a forbidden, content-based restriction on expression. The trial court granted that motion, but a unanimous Minnesota Supreme Court, sitting *en banc*, (i.e., in full court) with one justice not participating, reversed it. Citing Minnesota precedents limiting the challenged ordinance to fighting words, the state high court left no doubt that it found that the reprehensible symbolic action for which R.A.V. was charged fell within that exception to protected expression. "Burning a cross in the yard of an African-American family's home is deplorable conduct that the City of St. Paul may without question prohibit. The burning cross is itself an unmistakable symbol of violence and hatred based on virulent notions of racial supremacy. It is the responsibility, even the obligation, of diverse communities to confront such notions in whatever form they appear."

R.A.V. readily conceded that the city could prosecute his alleged conduct under a narrow law that did not also sweep within its scope constitutionally protected activities. His counsel had contended, however, that the St. Paul ordinance was so broad in its reach that it imposed a chilling effect on those wishing to engage in many forms of protected expression, and thus it should be declared unconstitutionally broad on its face. The Minnesota high court countered, however, that declaring a statute invalid on its face, thereby completely forbidding its future enforcement, was "strong medicine" that courts should "not hastily prescribe." Citing U.S. Supreme Court precedents, the state justices declared that such rulings were limited to cases involving statutes that were substantially overbroad in their reach and not susceptible to a sufficiently narrowing judicial interpretation. Because the city's bias-motivated, disorderly conduct ordinance had been narrowly construed to reach only unprotected fighting words, it could not be invalidated on what the court termed "facial overbreadth grounds." The state court observed that "the ordinance is a narrowly tailored means toward accomplishing the compelling governmental interest in protecting the community against bias-motivated threats to public safety and order." It was thus distinguishable from the flag-desecration statute struck down in *Texas v. Johnson*, which had rested on an assumption that the mere presence of a particular form of expression would invariably incite a riot or constitute fighting words, whatever the circumstances.

During oral arguments before the U.S. Supreme Court on December 4, 1991, counsel for the city of St. Paul assumed essentially the same stance, contending that the municipal ordinance applied only to fighting words and conduct likely to provoke imminent lawless action. Edward J. Cleary, counsel for R.A.V., contended, on the other hand, that the ordinance was overly broad and vague, even as construed in the state courts. In response to a question from Chief Justice William H. Rehnquist, Cleary agreed that the ordinance violated the First Amendment by singling out certain fighting words, but not others, for regulation. The danger inherent in such a law, he asserted, was that it was viewpoint-discriminatory and thus susceptible to selective enforcement.

Such a rationale furnished the basis for Justice Antonin Scalia's opinion of the Court that invalidated the challenged ordinance on the ground that it was, on its face, infringement of First Amendment rights. Rather than holding the antibias statute substantially overbroad, Justice Scalia ruled that the ordinance unconstitutionally restricted speech on the basis of content and viewpoint. He agreed that fighting words and certain other recognized categories of expression could be regulated on the basis of their content, but he rejected the traditional view that such forms of speech were completely excluded from constitutional protection. Such speech could not be regulated, he asserted, on the basis of government hostility or sympathy for the messages it delivered. Under that standard, the St. Paul ordinance was unconstitutional on its face because it imposed special burdens on speech relating to the disfavored subjects of "race, color, creed, religion or gender," while permitting other forms of invective. "In practical operation," declared Scalia, "the ordinance goes even beyond mere content discrimination, to actual viewpoint discrimination. Displays containing some words—odious racial epithets, for example—would be prohibited to proponents of all views. But 'fighting words' that do not themselves invoke race, color, creed, religion, or gender—aspersions upon a person's mother, for example—would seemingly be usable *ad libitum* in the placards of those arguing *in favor* of racial, color, etc. tolerance and equality, but could not be used by that speaker's opponents. . . . St. Paul has no such authority to license one side of a debate to fight freestyle, while requiring the other to follow Marquis of Queensbury Rules."

Justice Byron R. White, joined by Justices Harry A. Blackmun and Sandra Day O'Connor and, in part, by Justice John Paul Stevens, filed an opinion concurring in the judgment on the ground that the St. Paul ordinance was overbroad on its face. White, however, resisted Justice Scalia's contention that, under certain circumstances, fighting words were entitled to constitutional protection. At the same time, he agreed that the challenged ordinance, even as construed by the Minnesota Supreme Court, reached beyond fighting words to a substantial amount of expression that—however repugnant—was protected by the First Amendment. The state court had interpreted the statute to prohibit expression that "by its utterance" caused "anger, alarm, or resentment." Yet, declared White, the Court's fighting-words precedents had made clear "that such generalized reactions [were] not sufficient to strip expression of its constitutional protection." Because St. Paul's ordinance covered much of such protected speech, as well as expression subject to government's control, asserted Justice White, it was fatally overbroad.

In a brief concurrence, Justice Blackmun joined White's conclusion that the antibias measure was void for overbreadth. But he also expressed concern about the possible impact on First Amendment law of Justice Scalia's suggestion, in Blackmun's words, that "a State cannot regulate speech that causes great harm unless it also regulates speech that does not (setting law and logic on their heads)." Blackmun saw no compromise of First Amendment values in a law "that prohibits hoodlums from driving minorities out of their homes by burning crosses on their lawns," but saw "great harm in preventing the people of Saint Paul from specifically punishing the race-based fighting words that so prejudice their community." Under a narrowly written law, in Blackmun's judgment, government clearly possessed the power to single out those categories of fighting words it considered of greatest danger to the community's welfare. The key was simply to draft a law that reached only fighting words and not protected expression as well.

Justice Stevens also concurred in the Court's judgment, but criticized both the Scalia and White opinions for yielding to "the allure of absolute principles." Justice Scalia, asserted Stevens, had rejected the traditional view denying fighting words virtually all constitutional protection, yet he had embraced a "near-absolute ban on content-based regulation of" such expression. Within a particular category of expression, government was obliged under Scalia's approach to "either proscribe *all* speech or no speech at all." By reaffirming the traditional notion that fighting words are devoid of First Amendment coverage, on the other hand, Justice White had embraced another absolute. Stevens rejected both approaches. Instead, he contended, the Court's precedents had established "a more complex and subtle analysis . . . that considers the content and context of the regulated speech, and the nature and scope of the restriction on speech." Applying that more flexible approach to the St. Paul ordinance, Stevens concluded that, were the measure not overbroad, "such a selective, subject-matter regulation on proscribable speech [would be] constitutional." In short, he submitted, "[c]onduct that create[d] special risks or special harms [could] be prohibited by special rules." Furthermore, he intoned, there were "legitimate, reasonable, and neutral justifications" for permitting government to subject cross burning to such special rules, albeit under more narrowly drawn regulations than the St. Paul ordinance imposed.

Selected Bibliography

Cleary, Edward J. *Beyond the Burning Cross: A Landmark Case of Race Censorship, and the First Amendment.* New York: Random House, 1995.

Kagan, Elena. "Regulation of Hate Speech and Pornography after *R.A.V.*" *University of Chicago Law Review* 60 (1993): 873–902.

Freedom of the Press

Myth and Reality: The Case of John Peter Zenger

—◄◦►—

William F. Steirer Jr.
Department of History
Clemson University

Rex v. John Peter Zenger, (1735) [New York colonial court]

◄◦► THE CASE IN BRIEF ◄◦►

Date
1735

Location
New York

Court
New York colonial court

Principal Participants
John Peter Zenger
Andrew Hamilton

Significance of the Case
This case of libel in colonial America is widely believed to have established a precedent for freedom of the press. Yet the decision was ignored by most courts and had little practical effect in law.

Few court proceedings have contributed more to the mythology of the American libertarian tradition than has the case of John Peter Zenger in 1735. As recently as January 1989, a South Carolina assemblyman, Joe Wilder, justified his attack on the state's criminal libel law by referring to John Peter Zenger. Wilder noted that the Zenger case had established a principle that South Carolina was overdue in embracing.

In reality, the case was an interesting one with surprising twists and turns. Zenger was a poorly educated and poorly trained printer whose place in the drama that unfolded in New York during 1734 and 1735 was more coincidental than intentional. Political foes of Governor William Cosby attracted Zenger to New York in 1733 to publish the *New York Weekly Journal* for them.

Zenger was "free" to print only items that Cosby's foes wished published. These individuals included James Alexander and William

897

Smith, men who would later serve as Zenger's first lawyers in the famous case.

The so-called popular party had opposed Cosby's policies from the moment that Cosby had landed in New York on August 1, 1732. One member lamented, "If the Hand of Providence does not arrest and give us some relief very quickly, I cannot see that any one Man of Honor and Honesty can remain in this Province without falling a sacrifice to the basest and vilest of villains." Historians have universally accepted the popular party version of events during the three years of Cosby's administration, citing the avariciousness and arbitrariness of the governor.

Prior to his position at the *New York Weekly Journal*, Zenger had done little to distinguish himself in the printing business. Born in Germany in 1697, he reached New York in 1710 and was an apprentice to William Bradford, Governor Cosby's printer. Finishing his apprenticeship in 1719, Zenger moved to Maryland, but he returned to New York in 1722 where eventually he was hired to print the newspaper that would expose Cosby's "villainies." He was available, lacked better prospects, and apparently was politically naive and unaware. James Alexander actually decided what to print of a politically sensitive nature.

From the beginning, the *New York Weekly Journal* added much spice to the political life of the colony, being filled with articles critical of Cosby and his supporters. The legal battle began with Chief Justice James Delancey opening court on January 15, 1734, by directing the grand jury to indict Zenger for seditious libel. This effort to indict failed, as did another grand jury charge on October 15, 1734. On October 17, the governor's council asked the assembly to join with the council in having the common hangman burn numbers 7, 47, 48, and 49 of Zenger's paper and in prosecuting the printer. After the assembly refused to cooperate, the court of quarter sessions was then asked to authorize burning the papers. On November 6, that court, too, filled with foes of Cosby, refused to comply. The sheriff then ordered his own slave to burn the four "condemned" copies.

Zenger was arrested on November 17, 1734, by a council warrant that was probably illegal.

In theory, the council could act with the governor only as a court for the correction of errors and appeals and should legally have extended Zenger a prior opportunity to defend himself. Chief Justice Delancey refused Zenger reasonable bail, so the hapless printer remained in jail for 260 days. Meanwhile, James Alexander and William Smith challenged the commissions of Judge Delancey and another jurist, but succeeded only in getting themselves disbarred. Instead of using an inexperienced replacement, who would have to deal with two implacable judicial enemies, Alexander hired the distinguished Philadelphia attorney Andrew Hamilton to take over Zenger's defense.

Together, Alexander and Hamilton produced the defense that eventually proved victorious at the trial on August 4, 1735. That defense was blessed with a jury that looked to be favorably disposed toward the popular party. Furthermore, the prosecution had drawn a poorly worded charge that read, "printing and publishing a false, scandalous and seditious libel." The defense strategy was simple: admit that Zenger had printed the newspapers in question, but argue that a true statement could not be libelous and that the jury should decide the law as well as the facts in the case. The charge that Zenger had printed "a false . . . libel" made it easier to accomplish both tasks because the jury seemed primed to believe that Zenger had printed only "true" stories.

Never did the attorney general deny that the newspaper stories were accurate. He relied upon the common-law rule that mere publication constituted a libelous action and that a truthful story actually represented a greater threat to good order than did a false story. Why he included the superfluous word *false* in his charge, he never explained. Its inclusion was almost unheard of in the history of libel prosecutions and seems to have resulted from the incompetence of an officeholder chosen more for his loyalty to "friends" than for his legal skills.

The Alexander-Hamilton strategy worked precisely because their argument that the jury should determine whether the statements were true met with the jury's approval. Hamilton noted that men are free to say anything about

God without punishment, "I think it is pretty clear that in New York a man may make very free with his God, but he must take special care what he says of his governor." Hamilton questioned whether this law was appropriate for a free society.

Hamilton argued further that the notion that a true statement would provoke vengeance, thereby breaching the peace, was absurd. That truth constituted a worse offense than falsehood harkened back to star-chamber days and, said Hamilton, had no place in a free society. Few charges that Hamilton hurled at the prosecution could have possessed more power than this one. For modern Americans, *star chamber* has little meaning, but for provincial New Yorkers in the 1730s, who revered the movement that had culminated in parliamentary sovereignty and the notion that law in Britain should be public and impartial, the term possessed great meaning.

After innumerable citations and pages filled with arguments, the king's attorney concluded his case by demanding that Zenger, having confessed to printing "two scandalous libels," must be found guilty. Chief Justice Delancey's charge to the jury emphasized that, as a matter of law, they must declare Zenger guilty of libel. The jury rebuffed both men and quickly returned a verdict of not guilty.

The Zenger case was never cited seriously in an English court of law during the eighteenth century, and it was never a factor in the evolution of English law on seditious libel. As hard as it may be to believe in view of the Zenger trial's reputation, that is also the situation in American law.

The mythologizing process began almost immediately, with the Corporation of the City of New York honoring Andrew Hamilton for "his learned and generous defense of the rights of mankind, and the liberty of the press." Between 1735 and 1737, the news percolated slowly through the British Empire, with Hamilton receiving generally enthusiastic accolades, but nowhere did the case establish a legal precedent. In the empire, people became aware of developing notions of free speech and free press, but that awareness did not translate into any fundamental changes. The frequent arguments

that the Zenger case accomplished fundamental changes in thinking are done, as Leonard Levy so cogently put it, in "anticipation of the past." Too many scholars, even those as competent as Zechariah Chaffee, instead of observing what did happen, have read back into the past what they wanted to happen. Levy observes further, "The American contribution to libertarian theory on freedom of speech and press, so strikingly absent prior to the Zenger case of 1735, was inconspicuous for long after."

Mythmaking must fill a need, and in this case the need was to find answers to the question, "How did the libertarian notion of a free press begin and develop?" To place the beginnings of that notion two generations before the American Revolution and five generations before the principle became securely fixed in America law is clearly bad history.

The Zenger case is representative of another facet of American law—the careful designing of a strategy that relies upon popular feelings rather than upon legal craft. What Alexander and Hamilton did was attack an unpopular governor who presented an oppressive, tyrannical face to the world and appeal to the prejudices of a particular jury in order to gain sympathy for the unfortunate Zenger. All that the two successful lawyers proved, however, was that juries could be susceptible to prevailing prejudices—as readily swayed by emotion or interest or ignorance as were judges.

Once the Zenger case was finished, three factors hampered its use as a precedent. One lay in the difficulty of relying upon jury verdicts to provide definitions of law. The jury's verdict may represent one view of law. But what law? And how predictable? And who applies or interprets it? Because two separate groups of twelve people would not necessarily look at any situation in the same way, the Zenger case might just as easily have turned out differently if argued before another jury. Law in such circumstances is whimsical and capricious. Precedents do not get established on such a basis.

A second difficulty arose out of what was actually one of the strengths of the Zenger verdict. The fundamental premise of Zenger is that truth could not be considered a libel—that truth marks how far men may go in writing, publishing, or speaking about authority. But truth, in many cases, cannot be either proven or disproven. Truth is usually a matter of opinion, and one man's truth is not everyone's. Truth in the Zenger case was dependent upon one jury's acquiescence in a definition of truth founded in a particular situation.

Third, Alexander and Hamilton were themselves acutely aware of the need for order, admitting that "to infuse into the minds of the people an ill opinion of a just administration, is a crime that deserves no mercy." This belief qualified their victory for "individual freedom" in the Zenger case. For eighteenth-century Anglo-Americans, the value of order generally surpassed the value of justice.

So, for these reasons, the Zenger decision had little practical effect in law. Following the Zenger decision, while governors no longer could get away with prosecuting printers for libel, popularly elected assemblies could and did. They did so throughout the remainder of the eighteenth century and into the nineteenth, bothering not at all to go into court after printers, but dragging errant printers before legislative assemblies where truth proved to be no defense.

Truth proved not to be a defense in libel cases until the passage of a New York Sedition Act and its interpretation in an 1864 New York case. Although far less famous than the Zenger case, *People v. Croswell* nonetheless proved more significant in advancing the legal concept of a free press, for it was in the very next year that the New York legislature accepted the doctrine that truth is a defense in libel cases. Victory was not immediately complete, but the process begun haltingly and reluctantly in the Zenger case was on its triumphant way to final success.

Selected Bibliography

Finkelman, Paul, ed. *A Brief Narrative of the Case and Tryal of John Peter Zenger.* St. James, NY: Brandywine, 1977.

Levy, Leonard W. *Emergence of a Free Press.* New York: Oxford University Press, 1985.

———. *Freedom of Speech and Press in Early American History: Legacy of Suppression.* New York: Harper & Row, 1963.

Rutherford, Livingston. *John Peter Zenger, His Press, His Trial and a Bibliography of Zenger Imprints.* New York: Peter Smith, 1941.

Salmon, Lucy M. *The Newspaper and Authority.* New York: Octagon, 1976.

The Sedition Act and the Price of a Free Press

———⋖○⋗———

Mary K. Bonsteel Tachau
Deceased Professor of History
University of Louisville

United States v. Callender, 25 Fed. Cas. 239 (1800) [U.S. Circuit Court]

⋖○⋗ THE CASE IN BRIEF ⋖○⋗

Date
1800

Location
Virginia

Court
U.S. Circuit Court

Principal Participants
James Thomson Callender
Associate Justice Samuel Chase

Significance of the Case
An indignant Federalist judge overstepped his bounds to convict a muckraking journalist in opposition to the First Amendment's guarantee of freedom of the press. This was an example of how the Sedition Act denied constitutional rights to those who opposed the government or, in this case, a particular elected official.

James Thomson Callender was a journalist whose scandalmongering made him notable even in an era of sensationalists. During his remarkable career, his wide swath humiliated Alexander Hamilton, infuriated John Adams, contributed to the impeachment of Samuel Chase, clouded the reputation of Thomas Jefferson, and led to his own conviction and imprisonment.

Callender's career as a critic of government and of government officials began in Scotland. In 1793, he ran afoul of the British law of seditious libel, which held that government was profoundly injured by criticism, especially if it was true. His book *The Political Progress of Great Britain*, published the year before, led to his indictment. He fled to the United States to escape trial.

By 1796, Callender felt sufficiently knowledgeable about the United States that he published *History of the United States for 1796*, which brought him a well-deserved reputation as a muckraker. Among other revelations in the book was that in 1791, Alexander Hamilton had

had an affair with the wife of James Reynolds, a well-known speculator in securities issued during the American Revolution. Hamilton responded by writing a book in which he admitted to the affair, but denied he had conspired with Reynolds to buy up certificates that, with his funding program, were redeemable at face value (which was probably also true). Callender also reported that as a bachelor, Thomas Jefferson had tried to seduce a married woman. Vice President Jefferson, too, confessed to his indiscretion. The acknowledged truth of Callender's assertions added to his stature.

By 1798, Callender had settled in Philadelphia, where he made common cause with Benjamin Franklin Bache and William Duane of the Republican newspaper *Aurora*. Callender soon joined in contributing to their anti-Federalist columns and sometimes edited the paper during Bache's absence.

Meanwhile, the wars of the French Revolution continued in Europe. Hoping to bring an end to French attacks on American shipping, President John Adams had sent John Marshall and Elbridge Gerry to join Charles Cotesworth Pinckney to negotiate a treaty of amity and commerce with France. After some months, French envoys (called Messieurs X, Y, and Z in the Americans' dispatches) agreed to meet, but only if the Americans met conditions that were unacceptable and humiliating. News of what was called "The XYZ Affair" set off a torrent of indignation throughout the United States.

The Federalist-controlled Congress responded by providing for a new standing army, a small navy, and the arming of American merchant ships. More ominously, it also moved against a perceived threat from within the nation by passing four measures directed at aliens and critics of the government. The three statutes affecting aliens tripled the time required for naturalization, gave the president authority in time of peace to deport aliens he believed dangerous, and gave him power in time of war to imprison them.

The fourth statute was the Sedition Act, which made it a high misdemeanor punishable by up to two years in prison and a fine of two thousand dollars to combine or conspire with intent to oppose any measures of the government. It also made it a crime for anyone to "write, print, utter or publish . . . any false, scandalous and malicious writing . . . against the government of the United States, or either house of the Congress . . . or the President . . . with intent to defame . . . or to bring them, or any of them, into contempt or disrepute." The vice president, against whom the statute was aimed, was conspicuously omitted from its proscriptions.

The Sedition Act violated the free-speech and free-press provisions of the First Amendment, whose unequivocal command was that "Congress shall make no law . . . abridging the freedom of speech, or of the press." Yet, fewer than seven years after the amendment had been ratified, Congress passed just such a law. Its supporters noted that, unlike the common-law crime of seditious libel, it provided for truth as a defense and gave juries the right to determine the law as well as the facts. Nevertheless, it was clearly intended to silence domestic opponents and to cripple the opposition party: it was to expire on March 3, 1801, the day that the winner of the election of 1800 would take office. But when it was signed by Adams on July 14, 1798, it became the law of the land for two and one-half years. Presumed violators of the statute, passed by a Federalist Congress and signed by a Federalist president, would be tried in courts before Federalist judges. Critics of the government rightly feared its consequences. After a series of prosecutions and convictions of Republicans in Vermont, Massachusetts, New Jersey, Pennsylvania, and New York, the Sedition Act provided the occasion for a confrontation between Associate Justice of the Supreme Court Samuel Chase and James Thomson Callender.

As it happened, Chase, who had once championed the anti-Federalist cause in Maryland but who had since become an ultra-Federalist, had agreed to take the middle circuit for the spring of 1800. His progress through those states could be measured by the gasps of indignation that accompanied his management of their dockets. Chase was on the warpath against anyone he perceived to be a threat to Federalism and order. At the Sedition Act trial of Thomas Cooper in New York, Chase shifted the burden of proof to the defendant, requiring him to prove his innocence (instead of the prosecutor proving his guilt). In Pennsylvania, Chase presided over the second treason trial of John Fries for his participation in the insurrection of the Northampton Insurgents (the so-called Fries Rebellion). There he issued the opinion of the court before the trial began, which led to the defense lawyers' refusal to continue in the case. Chase then stormed into Delaware, and when neither the federal attorney or the grand jury proffered victims, he referred them to Wilmington to get an indictment against a printer whom he believed to be seditious. Frustrated by their refusal to cooperate, Chase moved into Virginia, where, he promised, he would teach the lawyers the difference between liberty and licentiousness of the press—if a jury of honest men could be found there. He carried with him a copy of Callender's latest political pamphlet, *The Prospect before Us,* with offensive passages carefully underlined.

By this time, James Thomas Callender had become a citizen and, leaving his children behind, moved to Petersburg. Believing that no judge in the Republican stronghold of Virginia would attempt to enforce the Sedition Act, he soon found compatible work on the Richmond *Examiner.* He had, however, underrated Secretary of State Timothy Pickering. Determined to silence the Republican press before the election of 1800, Pickering had instructed the federal attorney for the district to scrutinize the *Examiner* and prosecute the perpetrators of "any libelous matter against the government or its officers."

The attorney had not only the newspaper as grist for his mill, but he also had Callender's pamphlet, which gave the public, as its author had promised, "such a Tornado as no Govt ever got before." In it, Callender described *The Prospect before Us* as a choice between Thomas Jefferson ("that man whose life is unspotted by crime") and John Adams ("that hoary headed incendiary," "whose hands are reeking with . . . blood").

A grand jury, allegedly packed with Federalists, promptly responded to Chase's charge and brought a presentment against Callender as an offender against the sedition law, and the Federalist federal attorney drew up an indictment.

Yet Callender was not without friends. The citizens of Caroline County contributed a hundred dollars for the support of his children, and three prominent Virginians contributed their services as defense counsel: the attorney general, the governor's son-in-law, and the clerk of the House of Delegates. They asked for a continuance until November so that they might secure witnesses and documents, but Chase denied it on the grounds that anyone who published an alleged libel ought always to have the documents that would prove its truthfulness on hand.

The trial, which began on June 3, 1800, was marked by what had become Chase's trademarks and would become charges in his later impeachment. Justice Chase repeatedly overruled the defense counsel and proclaimed that Callender's book was false and his intent obvious. He upheld the prosecution's assertions that Callender had to prove his own innocence and, despite the wording of the statute, that truth was not a defense. The judge admitted the book as evidence, although it was not mentioned in the indictment. He refused to let a defense witness testify on the grounds that, unless he could disprove all of the charges, his evidence on one was inadmissible. He denied the right of the jury to consider the constitutionality of the Sedition Act. He declared that it was his duty (not that of the executive branch) to execute the laws. Finally, his behavior caused Callender's attorneys, like Fries's, to withdraw from the case.

Whether the petit jury was packed cannot be proved, but all of its members were Federalists, and after only two hours, they returned a verdict of guilty. Chase congratulated them because they had shown that federal laws could be enforced in Virginia, "the principal object of this prosecution." He proceeded to lecture Callender for his "ungenerous" behavior as a foreigner who presumed to criticize the president and who disobeyed the laws of his adopted country. Callender was sentenced to nine months in prison, was fined $200, and was required to post a $1,200 bond guaranteeing his good behavior for two years.

Unrepentant and unsilenced, Callender wrote a second volume of *The Prospect before Us* while in prison. To his list of despised Federalists, he now added Chase: "the most detestable and detested rascal in the state of Maryland." Far from discrediting him, Callender's conviction brought him an even wider audience, and his writings and the accounts of his trial circulated as campaign documents in the election of 1800.

Callender served his sentence until Jefferson became president in March 1801. One of his first acts was to pardon Callender and the four others still imprisoned under the Sedition Act and to order compensation for the fines they had paid. But this was not enough for Callender, who asked the president to appoint him postmaster in Richmond. When Jefferson refused, Callender fought back. In September 1802, as editor of the Federalist Richmond *Recorder*, he published the most sensational story of his notorious career, alleging that the president "for many years past has kept, as his concubine, one of his own slaves . . . [whose] name is SALLY" and that he had several children with her.

Although impossible to prove at the time, the charge was also impossible to disprove.

Nineteenth-century British travelers who were critics of the American experiment in democratic government spread and extended Callender's allegation: it suited their purpose to believe that the author of the Declaration of Independence was a hypocrite. Two hundred years after they achieved notoriety, Chase, Callender, and even the Sedition Act are footnotes to history. But the Jefferson miscegenation allegations persisted and were, in fact, confirmed by scientific DNA testing in 1999.

Selected Bibliography

Ellis, Richard E. *The Jeffersonian Crisis: Courts and Politics in the Young Republic.* New York: Norton, 1971.

Miller, John C. *The Federalist Era, 1789–1801.* New York: Harper & Row, 1960.

Moss, Sidney P., and Carolyn Moss. "The Jefferson Miscegenation Legend in British Travel Books." *Journal of the Early Republic* 7 (Fall 1987): 253–274.

Smith, James Morton. *Freedom's Fetters: The Alien and Sedition Laws and American Civil Liberties.* Ithaca, NY: Cornell University Press, 1956.

The Limits of Prior Restraint

—◄○►—

Paul L. Murphy

Deceased Professor of History
University of Minnesota

Near v. Minnesota, 283 U.S. 697 (1931) [U.S. Supreme Court]

◄○► THE CASE IN BRIEF ◄○►

Date
1931

Location
Minnesota

Court
U.S. Supreme Court

Principal Participants
Jay M. Near
Howard Guilford
State of Minnesota

Significance of the Case
A journalist's writing in a scandal sheet had the Supreme Court rule for the first time that the First Amendment's freedom of the press clause should also be applied to states.

When the decision in *Near v. Minnesota* was handed down in June 1931, one legal expert promptly called it "the most important decision rendered since the adoption of the first amendment." Significantly, it was the first case in which the U.S. Supreme Court held that the freedom-of-the-press provision of the First Amendment should be applied to the states. The case involved a Minneapolis scandal sheet and a state nuisance law passed to close down such publications. In ruling that state law unconstitutional, Chief Justice Charles Evans Hughes found, in the "general conception" of liberty of the press, as adapted by the Constitution, the essential attribute of freedom from prior restraint, which the five-man majority was convinced the state had violated. Thus, freedom from prior restraint, a concept embraced by William Blackstone in the eighteenth century, finally gained formal constitutional status in the fourth decade of the twentieth, opening a new area of permissible press expression and criticism.

The background of the case was both legally and historically significant. In 1925, the Minnesota legislation had passed a public nuisance law, called a "gag law" by its critics, for one purpose—to close down John Morison's Duluth *Rip-Saw,* a newspaper notorious for its vicious attack on public officials, both in that city and in the state at large. The law permitted a single judge, acting without a jury, to stop the publication by injunction of a newspaper or magazine, if he found it "obscene, lewd, and lascivious . . . or malicious, scandalous and defamatory." More broadly at issue, however, was the question of how much the public, through the media, had a right to know about the actions of its governing officials, the policy they intended to follow, and the methods they planned to use in that pursuit, as well as the degree to which they indulged their own human venality. Questions were also raised about the proper use of press freedom and the responsibility of both government officials and media decision makers to the public and to the general welfare of the nation. The steps leading up to the case's final adjudication tell an interesting story of attempts to answer such questions.

In 1927, Jay M. Near and Howard Guilford had established the *Saturday Press* in Minneapolis. Near, an experienced journalist, was known for his bigotry against Catholics, blacks, Jews, and organized labor. Guilford had run scandal sheets before in other cities. These were generally focused on exposing gambling, prostitution, and the sexual adventures of the local elite. Both, however, specialized in reporting scandals in a sensational manner. From its first issue, the *Saturday Press* hammered away at supposed ties between gangsters and police. In a series of florid stories, the *Press* elicited not only verbal hostility and denunciation, but it also provoked a gangland attempt to kill Guilford on his way home from work (with assailants pumping four bullets into his car and hitting him). Guilford recovered and went on to expose city and county officials, attacking not only Minneapolis police chief Frank Brunskill, but also the future governor of Minnesota, then county prosecutor Floyd B. Olson, for ties to the Minneapolis Jewish underworld.

Near and Guilford wrote: "Practically every vendor of vile hooch, every owner of a moonshine still, every snake-faced gangster and embryonic yegg in the Twin Cities is a JEW." Specifically, the paper accused Olson of being a Jew-lover and dragging his feet in the investigation of gangland pursuits. Olson was enraged, and on November 21, 1927, he filed a complaint under the state nuisance law with Hennepin County District Judge Mathias Baldwin, charging that the *Saturday Press* had defamed Mayor George Leach, Police Chief Brunskill, and Charles G. Davis, head of the Law Enforcement League, as well as the *Minneapolis Tribune,* the *Minneapolis Journal,* the Hennepin County Grand Jury, Olson himself, and the entire Jewish community. He went on to argue that continued publication of the paper was harmful to the community at large and that the public should be protected against it. The judge issued a temporary restraining order closing down the paper. Near and Guilford promptly demurred, arguing that the statute authorizing such a "padlock injunction" was unconstitutional. They in turn pointed to a clear statement in the Minnesota constitution that "the liberty of the press shall forever remain inviolate, and all persons may freely speak, write, and publish their sentiments on all subjects." The judge, conscious of this guarantee, certified an appeal in the case to the Minnesota Supreme Court, leaving to it the question of the law's constitutionality.

The removal of the *Saturday Press* from the streets was popular in the Twin Cities. Many people praised Floyd B. Olson's actions and those of the judge who issued the restraining order. But its removal did little to hinder ongoing criminal action. In fact, shortly after the ban, a county grand jury began probing various charges of misconduct against Police Chief Brunskill, a number of which had been first lodged against him in the *Saturday Press.* County prosecutor Olson called seventeen witnesses (including Howard Guilford), and the grand jury listened to charges ranging from political impropriety to allegations of covering up criminal behavior.

In the Minnesota Supreme Court, Near's attorney, Thomas Latimer, a talented Minneapolis lawyer who later became mayor, raised the constitutional issue. The law was, he contended, a violation of the state constitution. It was also null, void, and invalid because it was in violation of the Fourteenth Amendment of the U.S. Constitution. Latimer also stressed the denial of a jury trial, guaranteed by the Sixth Amendment, and contended that the entire concept of freedom of the press, guaranteed by the First Amendment, had been breached. He further argued that the due process clause of the Fifth Amendment, which had been made applicable to the states by the passage of the Fourteenth, had been violated.

The Minnesota Supreme Court was unimpressed. Speaking through its chief justice, Samuel B. Wilson, it ruled unanimously to uphold the state law. Comparing the *Saturday Press* to houses of prostitution, noxious weeds, itinerant carnivals, saloons, lotteries, and malicious fences, Wilson asserted that the legislature had the power to do away with such nuisances. In Minnesota, he argued, no one could stifle the truthful voice of the press, but the constitution's drafters never intended for it to protect malice, scandal, and defamation.

By this time, the case had drawn national attention, not only in the legal community but even more broadly. The law was being seen as a model . . . a "wise and desirable remedy" for the evils of yellow journalism. The national student debate topic for 1930 was: "Resolved: That the Minnesota Nuisance Law Should Be Adopted by Every State in the Union." Other states were being urged to use their local police power in similar fashion.

Arguments supporting the law were persuasive to many. However, the complications of ordinary censorship, or of prior restraint, made such censorship impractical. It would be impossible to have government censors read every magazine and delete every falsehood, exaggeration, indecency, or obscenity. Censorship would require an enormous, highly trained staff and would therefore be expensive and unworkable. Legal actions against undesirable publications would also fail completely. Prosecutions under the criminal libel statutes would not result in effective repression of such literature. Further,

civil actions for damages could not prevent the harm done and did not guarantee against a repetition of the offenses.

The publicity given to trials sometimes does more harm than good. In addition, the expense of trials and appeals puts these remedies out of the reach of all except the wealthy. Supporters also argued that the Minnesota law could be applied promptly and could stop obscenity, indecency, falsehood, and defamation, as well as end the publication of scandal sheets completely. It could, in other words, make the journalistic profession responsible again, intimidate the criminal element among writers and publishers, and encourage reputable newspapers and magazines. Freedom of the press would not be impaired—it never meant a license to publish scandalous, malicious, obscene, or indecent matters. Finally, gag-law advocates contended that the First Amendment did not limit the power of the state governments; it merely limited Congress. Each state could properly regulate its own newspapers, magazines, and news agencies under its police power.

Clearly, the law established positive regulatory overtones. It sought to protect the property rights of certain individuals against blackmailers and scandalmongers who might damage their reputation and standing in the community, injuring them financially. The purpose of the law placed the public welfare above any First Amendment rights that people might claim. To the extent that it protected "liberty," the law saw liberty as the citizen's freedom from the evil impacts of this new journalistic development; certainly, it was not the liberty of members of the fourth estate to publish freely what they wanted.

But civil libertarians, including responsible publishers, were alarmed by this cavalier attitude toward a basic constitutional right. In both New York and Chicago, the Minnesota gag order was being viewed with particular alarm. The American Civil Liberties Union sent money from New York for Near's legal defense, and ACLU lawyers focused on the doctrine of prior restraint. Heretofore, the only control of the press had been through prosecution for criminal or libelous matter after the material had been printed. "We see in this new device for previous restraint of publication a menace to the whole principle of the freedom of the press," the ACLU stated. It also saw the public nuisance law as a dangerous model. "If the Minnesota law is unconstitutional, then the Fourteenth Amendment and inferentially the First Amendment no longer protects the press against prior restraint."

Minnesota newspaper editors scoffed at the fears of the ACLU. But the editor of the *Chicago Tribune* was not nearly as myopic. Colonel Robert Rutherford "Bertie" McCormick admired Near for his guts. Ultraconservative in his politics, McCormick disliked blacks, Jews, and other minorities, to say nothing of labor unions, and he had fought many legal battles over exposés published in his newspaper and particularly aimed at public officials. He, thus, agreed to provide extensive legal counsel in the case and ultimately succeeded in drawing behind Near's cause the American Newspaper Publishers Association— that body contending that Minnesota's action rendered all guarantees of free speech valueless in the state, and choked off thought and expression that should be constitutionally protected. The *New York Times* also deplored the Minnesota statute as a "vicious law." Many other national newspapers followed suit.

The case was appealed to the U.S. Supreme Court, and the Court for the first time heard a freedom-of-the-press case involving the role of the states and the vital and ancient principle of prior restraint. It also returned to consideration of a dilemma that had bothered the leading "father" of the First Amendment, James Madison.

Madison, in his concern for the potential abuse of governmental power, had been convinced that the Constitution should forbid not only Congress but the executive and judicial branches from limiting the guarantees to be placed in the First Amendment. Further, Madison had wanted more. Possibly anticipating a situation such as the one in *Near v. Minnesota,* and clearly responding to the repressive behavior of some of the states during the confederation period, he advocated an amendment that he considered "the most valuable in the whole list." It stated that "no State shall violate the equal right of conscience, (or of the) freedom of the press . . . because it is proper that every

Government should be disarmed of powers which trench upon those particular rights." "I cannot see any reason," he said, "against obtaining even a double security on these points. . . . It must be admitted, on all hands, that the State Governments are as liable to attack these invaluable privileges as is the General Government, and therefore ought to be as cautiously guarded against." Madison failed. Neither proposal was adopted. Only Congress was initially to be limited by the First Amendment and the states' role was left undesignated. This was done despite Madison's strong plea that the power of censorship should be exercised by the people over the government, and not by the government over the people.

In the argument before the Supreme Court, subsequent and recent history was on Near's side. Louis D. Brandeis, the most eloquent justice on this issue, had been steering the Court for a decade toward protecting free speech and press against state legislation by stressing the term *liberty* in the due process clause of the Fourteenth Amendment. "I cannot believe," he had argued in *Gilbert v. Minnesota* in 1920, that "the liberty guaranteed by the Fourteenth Amendment includes only liberty to acquire and enjoy property." Further, he had strongly supported the Court's first steps in the mid-1920s to apply the First Amendment protections of speech and press against the states.

Brandeis had prepared himself assiduously for the *Near* appeal, even probing into the ousting of Police Chief Brunskill, an action that was not unrelated to the attacks on that official by the *Saturday Press* itself. Thus, when the *Chicago Tribune's* attorney, Weymouth Kirkland, contended that the injunction closing the *Saturday Press* was a prior restraint, violating the First and Fourteenth Amendments, Brandeis was clearly in agreement. The *Saturday Press* articles, Kirkland had argued, were defamatory. But "so long as men do evil, so long will newspapers publish defamation. Every person does have a constitutional right to publish malicious, scandalous, and defamatory materials, though untrue, and with bad motives, and for unjustifiable ends." Such persons could always be punished afterward. But the remedy was not prior censorship of the offending newspaper. Rather, the state should bring specific criminal charges against such a newspaper after it has published the material.

The counsel for Minnesota was Deputy State Attorney General James F. Markham, along with William C. Larson, and Arthur I. Markve, representing the Hennepin County prosecutor's office, which had brought the original injunction. Markham argued that the law was constitutional and that the injunction was not a prior restraint. The public nuisance law was well within the police powers of the state. It was the responsibility of the state to interpret the provisions of the state constitution. The state court had done so, and it had done so properly.

Brandeis, in a questioning role, however, probed further. How, he asked Markham, can a community secure protection from combinations between criminals and public officials, if people are not allowed to engage in free discussion of such matters? "You cannot disclose evil," he observed, "without naming the doers of evil. It is difficult to see how one can have a free press and the protection that it affords in the democratic community without the privilege this act seems to limit." This question, he went on, is of prime interest to every American citizen and should be privileged communication. "Assuming it to be true . . ." Markham countered. "No," Brandeis snapped. "Even if it was not true, a malicious and scandalous statement could not be restrained before publication. A newspaper cannot always wait until it gets the judgment of the court." Sometimes it must invite suits for criminal libel in order to inform the public.

In the secret conference among the justices that followed the oral arguments, Chief Justice Hughes elicited from a majority of the conferees the view that the nuisance law was a suppression, not just of defamatory material, but of any future publication and thereby a clear violation of the guarantee of no prior restraint. This view was strongly denounced by Justice Pierce Butler, the one Minnesota member of the Supreme Court, who could not understand how Justices Hughes, Brandeis, and Oliver Wendell Holmes, could give First Amendment protection to scoundrels such as Near and Guilford.

The public nuisance law, he argued, was not suppression, but punishment for an injustice already committed.

But the Hughes view prevailed, and the chief justice assigned himself the task of writing the majority opinion. Setting the case in broad national context, he argued: "The administration of government has become more complex, the opportunities for malfeasance and corruption have multiplied, crime has grown to most serious proportions, and the danger of its protection by unfaithful officials and of the impairment of the fundamental security of life and property by criminal alliances and official neglect, emphasize the need of a vigilant and courageous press, especially in great cities. The fact that liberty of the press may be abused by miscreant purveyors of scandal does not make any less necessary the immunity of the press from prior restraint in dealing with official misconduct."

Regarding the limits of public criticism and exposure of officials, Hughes quoted Madison, pointing out that statesman's role as a leading spirit in the preparation of the First Amendment. The chief justice stated: "Some degree of abuse is inseparable from the power use of everything, and in no instances is this more true than in that of the press. It has accordingly been decided by the practice of the states that it is better to leave a few of its noxious branches to this luxurious growth than, by pruning them away, to injure the vigour of those yielding the proper fruits." But Hughes also understood Madison in another way as well, and his *Near* opinion finally made concrete the Virginian's desired safeguard in protecting the press freedom from state encroachment. Thus, finding the Minnesota law to be an unconstitutional infringement of freedom of the press, safeguarded by the due process clause of the Fourteenth Amendment, was a latter-day vindication for the First Amendment's initial sponsor.

But there were limits to what the broad prohibition against prior restraint could protect. Minor exceptions did exist. The four suggested exceptions were publication of critical war information ("no one would question but that a government might prevent actual obstruction to its recruiting service or the publication of the sailing dates of transports or the number and location of troops"); obscenity; publication inciting acts of violence against the community or violent overthrow of the government; and publications invading private rights. Contemporary commentators viewed the exceptions as insignificant and hypothetical. Ironically, however, *Near* was to become the doctrinal starting point for most defenses of prior restraint as the legitimacy of those exceptions was later developed. Contemporaneously, it was the broader implications of the majority opinion that gave the decision its historical significance as a turning point in American law and public policy.

Pierce Butler, speaking for four dissenters, deplored the ruling. Near and Guilford, he was convinced, were threatening the morals, peace, and good order of the state. Their behavior was a nuisance. Any way that such a nuisance could be legally suppressed appeared to be condonable in his eyes.

The immediate reaction to the decision was overwhelmingly positive. The nation's press was generally gratified and relieved. Many newspapers quoted Colonel McCormick's statement that "the decision of Chief Justice Hughes will go down in history as one of the greatest triumphs for free thought." The irrepressible colonel even wrote a letter to Chief Justice Hughes: "I think your decision in the Gag Law case will forever remain one of the buttresses of free government." The *Chicago Times,* competitor to the *Tribune,* graciously praised the latter for performing "a public service of high order when it carried the Minnesota case to the Supreme Court." The *New York Times* called the decision "weighty and conclusive," although it added a note of caution: "Freedom of the press, now again happily vindicated and affirmed, is not freedom to be a 'chartered libertine.'" The *New York Herald Tribune* observed that "the very fact the exercise of liberty of the press in this momentous case came before the Supreme Court in the least favorable light adds a buttress of steel to the constitutional guarantee."

The long-range implications of the ruling were many. It brought to a significant new stage Brandeis's long crusade to redefine *liberty* in human-rights rather than property-rights terms. By actually using that concept to strike down a state

law, the decision logically extended the incorporation theory as it related to freedom of the press. It also shifted the presumptions regarding the constitutionality of state laws. Laws restricting personal liberties now demanded new and vigorous justification, while laws restricting property rights were to be given the judicial benefit of the doubt. Thus, the ruling culminated more than sixty years of struggle over the proper relationship among the federal government, the states, and the citizens regarding First Amendment issues. The press now joined speech in being protected not only from formal federal-government restraint, but also from state restraint and more subtle forms of local restraint such as those authorized by the Minnesota law.

The ruling was also a reflection of marketplace theory. It strongly stressed the importance in a democratic society of the press being free to carry out its proper function of informing the electorate, particularly about the behavior of public officials. The behavior of the editors of the *Saturday Press* obviously troubled the chief justice. For him, the type of exposé writing they pursued was clearly designed to arouse passion rather than to dispense information. His opinion, however, in some ways blurred this distinction, stressing instead the importance of editors being able to criticize public officials and downplaying any illicit motives they might have. Hughes focused upon what was defensible about Near's operation, rather than what was indefensible. In this regard, the opinion came directly to terms with the changing and modernizing conditions that produced much of the new exposé journalism.

Near's subsequent history as a precedent is impressive. The list of cases in which it has been cited takes up many pages of *Shepard's U.S. Citations* and includes Supreme Court cases, lower federal court cases, and cases in the supreme courts of many states. Its most famous usage came in the *Pentagon Papers Case* (1971) involving the Nixon administration's effort to prevent publication of a forty-seven–volume secret history of the Vietnam War and detailing aspects of the reasons behind American involvement. There, attorneys for both sides cited the *Near* decision. The opponents of the government's injunction against publication using the

Near argument for prior restraint; attorneys for the government focused on the *Near* exception and stressed the need for the government to restrain publication of information covering a broad range of national defense activities. The Court victory of the *New York Times* and the *Washington Post* was a latter-day victory for Hughes's view, and for the view of federal judge Murray I. Gerfein who, in following *Near,* stated "there is no greater safety valve for discontent and cynicism about the affairs of government than freedom of expression in any form." Thus, Jay M. Near, although clearly a "miscreant purveyor of scandal," was a catalyst for redefining and extending one of the most basic freedoms of the Bill of Rights.

Selected Bibliography

Blasi, Vincent. "Toward a Theory of Prior Restraint: The Central Linkage." *Minnesota Law Review* 66 (1981): 11–93.

Emerson, Thomas I. "The Doctrine of Prior Restraint." *Law and Contemporary Problems* 20 (1955): 648–671.

———. *The System of Freedom of Expression.* New York: Random House, 1981.

Friendly, Fred W. *Minnesota Rag: The Dramatic Story of the Landmark Supreme Court Case That Gave New Meaning to Freedom of the Press.* New York: Random House, 1981.

Haiman, Franklyn S. *Speech and Law in a Free Society.* Chicago: University of Chicago Press, 1981.

Knoll, Erwin. "National Security: The Ultimate Threat to the First Amendment." *Minnesota Law Review* 66 (1981): 161–170.

Linde, Hans A. "Courts and Censorship." *Minnesota Law Review* 66 (1981): 171–208.

Murphy, Paul L. "Near v. Minnesota in the Context of Historical Development." *Minnesota Law Review* 66 (1981): 95–160.

Public Officials, Libel, and a Free Press

---◄○►---

Susan Duffy

Speech Communication Department
California Polytechnic State University

New York Times Company v. L. B. Sullivan, 367 U.S. 254 (1964) [U.S. Supreme Court]

◄○► THE CASE IN BRIEF ◄○►

Date
1964

Location
New York
Alabama

Court
U.S. Supreme Court

Principal Participants
The New York Times Company;
L. B. Sullivan, Montgomery police
commissioner; Justice William Brennan

Significance of the Case
The High Court overturned the state
court's decision that a public official was
harmed by some erroneous statements in
a newspaper advertisement by a civil
rights group, thus reaffirming the rights of
both the people and the press to criticize
government and its officials.

On Tuesday, March 29, 1960, as the civil-rights movement was struggling for recognition, the *New York Times* ran a full-page advertisement, paid for by the Committee to Defend Martin Luther King, Jr., and the Struggle for Freedom in the South. Over the names of sixty-four prominent Americans, with an addended list of twenty southern clergy and civil-rights activists, the advertisement outlined a litany of abuses directed against blacks in the South. Racial incidents in Orangeburg, South Carolina, and Montgomery, Alabama, were outlined specifically, while confrontations in Tallahassee, Atlanta, Nashville, Savannah, Greensboro, Memphis, Richmond, and Charlotte were alluded to in passing. It was the eight-line description of events in Montgomery that rankled L. B. Sullivan, a public official in that city, and prompted him to initiate litigation that would lead to this landmark decision supporting freedom of the press.

The offending lines in the ad read: "In Montgomery, Alabama after students sang 'My Country Tis of Thee' on the state capitol steps, their leaders were expelled from school, and truck-

912

loads of police armed with shotguns and tear gas ringed the Alabama State College campus. When the entire student body protested to state authorities by refusing to re-register, their dining hall was padlocked in an attempt to starve them into submission." Three paragraphs later, the ad claimed: "Again and again the Southern violators have answered Dr. King's peaceful protest with intimidation and violence. They have bombed his home almost killing his wife and child. They have assaulted his person. They have arrested him seven times—for speeding, loitering and similar offenses."

More than being hyperbolic, these lines contained factual errors, which, most probably, influenced the trial court's finding in favor of Sullivan. However, Sullivan's suit against the *New York Times* and four black Alabama clergymen whose names appeared in the ad published by the *Times* did not rest on the inaccuracy of the details. He claimed that he had been defamed in the ad through the explicit use of the word *police* and in the implied activity of the police in the arrests of Martin Luther King. Sullivan contended that, as the Montgomery commissioner who supervised the police department, he was considered directly responsible for the actions of that department. His claim essentially was that as commissioner, he was synonymous with *police*. He therefore claimed that he was the one accused of ringing Alabama State College's campus with police—an inaccurate statement because the campus was not surrounded—and that the references to the seven arrests of King (an inflated number) referred to him because arrests were obviously made by the police. That Sullivan was never mentioned by name in the ad did not seem to be a salient issue in the circuit court of Montgomery County. It found in favor of Sullivan and awarded him an unprecedented half-million dollars in damages. This was a thousand times higher than the five-hundred-dollar penalty provided for under Alabama defamation law.

The Alabama Supreme Court upheld the decision. However, when the case reached the U.S. Supreme Court in January 1964, the end result was a striking and total repudiation of the lower court. In a 9-0 vote, the Court reversed the decision and remanded it back to the state

courts for further proceedings. Justice William Brennan delivered the opinion of the Court. In it, he clearly outlined the constitutional deficiencies in the Alabama libel law that empowered states to award damages to public officials when their official conduct had been the target of criticism. Comparing it to the notorious Sedition Act of 1798, which prohibited criticism of the government and elected officials, Brennan argued that the Alabama law directly threatened First Amendment freedoms by "raising . . . the possibility that a good-faith critic of government will be penalized for his criticism." Brennan continued: "[T]he Constitution delimits a State's power to award damages for libel in actions brought by public officials against their official conduct." He maintained that impersonal attacks on government operations could not be construed to be libelous statements directed maliciously against the individual official responsible for those operations.

The justices discounted Sullivan's claim that his reputation was damaged by the ad even though it did not mention him by name. Brennan noted that Sullivan made no effort to prove that he had suffered any real financial loss as a result of the "libelous" statements. An interesting footnote in Brennan's opinion further undermines Sullivan's claim by noting that of the 650,000 copies of the *Times* distributed that day, only 394 copies containing the ad were circulated in all of Alabama, and only 35 of those in Montgomery County. The likelihood of Sullivan suffering great loss was substantially reduced when one considered how few people would have seen the ad, read it in its entirety, and then concluded that Sullivan was the one being singled out for blame. Brennan reiterated the position taken in earlier decisions that criticism of public officials is not merely a right, but also a duty that must not be stifled.

Justice Hugo Black, adding a separate opinion with Justice William O. Douglas concurring, said that, unlike the Court opinion, which rested on a myriad of issues, his vote rested exclusively on the *Times* and the individual clergyman's "absolute, unconditional constitutional right" to publish criticism of the Montgomery agencies and officials handling the incidents recounted. Black maintained that the "factual background" to this case underscored the enormous threat posed by state libel laws to a free press. As a native Alabamian, Black's assessment of the facts of the case came very close to leveling charges of bigotry at the decisions of his state's trial courts. He wrote that despite several decisions of the Supreme Court forbidding segregation in public schools, Montgomery had manifested "widespread hostility" toward desegregation, and this hostility had been extended by labeling those in favor of desegregation as "outside agitators." This appellation, he pointed out, could readily be applied to the *New York Times*. Black maintained no proof had been presented that Sullivan had suffered any damages. In fact, Black commented that a realistic appraisal of the record could lead one to infer that Sullivan's "political, social and financial" prestige had been enhanced rather than hurt by the ad.

New York Times Company v. Sullivan reaffirmed the rights of citizens and the press to criticize the government. For Sullivan to have won, the Court required proof of "actual malice" on the part of the *New York Times*. The decision to reverse and remand was one that worked to eliminate the chilling effect that could potentially paralyze the nation's press in its coverage of political issues and figures. Despite criticisms of the decision, which claimed that the Court established two separate standards for libel—one for private citizens and one for public figures—the decision of the Court is one against which libel cases have been measured for the last three and one-half decades.

Selected Bibliography

Del Russo, Alexander D. "Freedom of the Press and Defamation: Attacking the Bastion of *New York Times Co. v. Sullivan*." *St. Louis University Law Journal* 25 (1981): 501–541.

Elder, David. "Defamation, Public Officialdom and the 'Rosenbaltt v Baer' Criteria—A Proposal for Revivification: Two Decades after *New York Times Co. v. Sullivan*." *Buffalo Law Review* 33 (Fall 1984): 579–680.

Public Personalities and the Right to Privacy

—◦—

Susan Duffy

Speech Communication Department
California Polytechnic State University

Time Inc. v. James J. Hill, 385 U.S. 374 (1967) [U.S. Supreme Court]

◦ THE CASE IN BRIEF ◦

Date
1967

Location
Pennsylvania

Court
U.S. Supreme Court

Principal Participants
James J. Hill
Time Inc.
Justice William Brennan

Significance of the Case
A former hostage sued a magazine alleging privacy infringement over an article identifying his trauma, but on appeal the Supreme Court found the rights of the press outweighed a citizen's right to privacy.

The experience of hostage-taking is not new in American history. Today, however, the exploitation of the hostage situation by the media arouses controversy. The lives of private citizens are dramatically altered when, as hostages, they, their families, and their friends become public personae. Even after the ordeal ends, public interest often persists, and the victims are faced with living in the glare of media scrutiny for weeks, months, and even years. The issue of the private citizen becoming the unwilling target of public attention was central when James J. Hill sued Time Inc. for invasion of privacy.

In 1952, Hill's family was held hostage for nineteen hours in their suburban Philadelphia home by three escaped prisoners. When released unharmed on September 12, 1952, the family's ordeal was covered extensively by the national press. The Hills stressed that they had been treated courteously by the convicts, and that there had been no violence, molestation, or abuse directed toward them. In an effort to regain normalcy in their lives, the Hills moved to Connecticut and subsequently rejected efforts by both the print and broadcast media to tell their story. They assiduously avoided the notoriety of becoming a public commodity.

The following year, Joseph Hayes wrote and published *The Desperate Hours*, a novel that depicted a family of four being held hostage in their suburban home. As a novelist, Hayes had an interest in writing about actual crimes. He had for years prior to the Hill incident maintained a clippings file of articles about hostages. The Hills' ordeal ultimately proved the impetus for Hayes to write *The Desperate Hours*, but the novel was factually different. Still, the public associated the novel with the actual situation. There is no evidence to suggest that this was troublesome to James Hill. Hayes adapted his novel to a script for a Broadway play and later sold it as a screenplay: all bore the same title. Even with this, the Hills were acquiescent.

The problem, and ultimately the legal action, resulted from an article about the play in *Life* in February 1955. It was on the pages of *Life* that an overt reference to the Hills appeared in an article showcasing the opening of *The Desperate Hours* in Philadelphia. *Life* included photographs of the play, as well as photographs of actors at the former Hill home reenacting scenes of physical confrontation, something the Hills maintained never happened. These pictures, coupled with the text, prompted James Hill to sue Time Inc. because he believed (1) the *Life* article portrayed the play falsely and irresponsibly as being a "reenactment of the Hill's experiences" and (2) it included statements that were knowingly false.

The issue in the trial court focused on the truth of the article. A secondary issue was whether *Life*, in an attempt to increase circulation, exploited the Hills' situation by using the sensational headline, "True Crime Inspires Tense Play," and knowingly allowed the article to run with factual errors. The trial court held *Life* liable. On appeal, the case eventually reached the U.S. Supreme Court, which considered it on the constitutional question of freedom of speech and press. Harold R. Medina Jr. argued the case for Time Inc., while former vice president and soon-to-be president Richard M. Nixon argued for James J. Hill.

Reversing the judgment of the lower courts, the Supreme Court remanded the case for further proceedings consistent with the Court's 1964 ruling in *New York v. Sullivan*. Justice William Brennan wrote the opinion of the Court, but Justice William O. Douglas's concurring opinion explains the decision compactly: "[A] private person is catapulted into the news by events over which he has no control. He and his activities are then in the public domain as fully as the matters at issue in *New York Times Company v. Sullivan*." The Court's preservation of the rights of freedom of speech and press was the overriding concern.

Acknowledging that private citizens inadvertently may become individuals of public interest, and that reportage and debate about a situation of public interest may contain some error, the Court held the press still has a constitutional right to print such stories, provided they do not contain maliciously calculated false statements or statements made with reckless disregard for the truth. Essentially, the Court held that once a citizen becomes the subject of public interest, the press has a right to print stories about the individual; "inevitably" these stories will contain some factual errors or distortions, but the citizen cannot claim a violation of his or her "right to privacy," stop publication, or receive damages for publication. To the Court, such actions would be tantamount to censorship, and the rights of the press outweighed the rights of the citizen to privacy.

The dissenting opinion, penned by Justice Abe Fortas with Chief Justice Earl Warren and Justice Tom Clark concurring, outlined several problematic areas. They believed that private citizens did have a right to be protected from untrue printed statements and that the First Amendment did not preclude "effective protection of the right of privacy." They cited the landmark 1890 article, "The Right to Privacy," by Charles Warren and Louis Brandeis, in which it is argued that " 'excesses of the press in overstepping . . . the obvious bounds of propriety and decency' made it essential that the law recognize a right to privacy, distinct from traditional remedies of defamation, to protect private individuals against the unjustifiable infliction of mental pain and distress."

The justices in dissent noted that "political personalities" should be governed by the judgment of *New York Times v. Sullivan*, but that a distinction was called for concerning private citizens. Implicit in this line of reasoning is that public officials seek public office and are, therefore, rightfully subject to continual public scrutiny and analysis in the press, whereas the private citizen thrown involuntarily into the public arena should be protected from the press. The dissenters felt that the decision of the Court totally "immunized the press."

Selected Bibliography

Becker, Martin S. "Torts—Privacy—Actual Malice Required for Redress of False Reports of Matters of Public Interest—*Time Inc. v. Hill.*" *American University Law Review* 16 (June 1967): 442–449.

Braun, Richard A. "Discussion of Recent Decisions." *Chicago-Kent Law Review* 44 (Spring 1967): 58–63.

Carl, William J. "Right of Privacy: Knowing or Reckless Falsity in Publication Required to Sustain Liability under New York Right of Privacy Statute." *Montana Law Review* 28 (Spring 1967): 243–249.

Kellogg, Philip L. "Constitutional Law: State Cannot Award Damages for Invasion of Privacy without Proof of Malice." *North Carolina Law Review* 45 (April 1967): 740–747.

The Pentagon Papers

—◄◦►—

Edwin E. Moise
Department of History
Clemson University

New York Times Company v. U.S., 403 U.S. 713 (1971) [U.S. Supreme Court]

◄◦► THE CASE IN BRIEF ◄◦►

Date
1971

Location
New York
District of Columbia

Court
U.S. Supreme Court

Principal Participants
Dr. Daniel Ellsberg; The New York Times
Company; The Washington Post

Significance of the Case
The Justice Department's effort to stop
two newspapers from publishing stories
that uncovered an extensive Defense
Department report on the Vietnam War
was rebuffed by the High Court. The
key to the outcome was the belief that
Congress had not intended to censor the
press with the Espionage Act.

American participation in the Vietnam War was winding down by 1971, but public debate over the war was escalating. It was in this situation that the *New York Times* began to publish excerpts and summaries from a heavily documented history of U.S. policy toward Vietnam, originally compiled within the Department of Defense. Formally titled *United States–Vietnam Relations, 1945–1967,* it is commonly referred to as "The Pentagon Papers."

The decision to compile such a history had been taken by Secretary of Defense Robert McNamara on June 17, 1967. A "Task Force" headed by Leslie Gelb was established within the International Security Affairs section of the Department of Defense. Members of the Task Force were recruited from various places, both within and outside the Department of Defense. Few were able to remain on the Task Force for the entire duration of the project; Gelb estimated that the thirty-six professionals who worked on the project did so for an average of four months each.

The Task Force conducted no interviews; its work was based entirely on written materials, mostly government files. It collected documents on U.S. policy toward Vietnam not only from the files of the Department of Defense but also from the Department of State and the Central Intelligence Agency. Some of its members had a limited and informal access to White House files. The task of synthesizing the documents to produce a history was carried out collectively; most chapters had more than one author, and the final version does not carry the authors' names.

The end product was a history accompanied by the original texts of many of the documents on which it had been based. Narrative and documents totaled well over seven thousand pages, arranged in forty-seven volumes. The writing was declared complete on January 15, 1969; retyping and reproduction took additional time. Fifteen copies were finally available for distribution—seven within the Department of Defense and eight elsewhere—in June 1969.

Dr. Daniel Ellsberg, a researcher with the Rand Corporation (a think tank devoted to national defense issues), had been a minor participant in the writing of the Pentagon Papers. After the project was completed, however, he studied the whole manuscript carefully. Having already developed doubts about the U.S. role in Southeast Asia, his close reading of the Pentagon Papers turned him strongly against the war. He decided that the U.S. involvement in Vietnam had been fundamentally immoral and should be ended immediately. He believed that the evidence that convinced him of this should be made available to the Congress and the public.

The Rand Corporation had been given two of the fifteen complete sets of the Pentagon Papers. Ellsberg began systematically photocopying one of these late in 1969. He then searched for a way to get this material released to the public. In March 1971, after failing to persuade several U.S. senators to make the study public, he delivered a large portion of the Pentagon Papers to Neil Sheehan of the New York Times. The Times did not receive the four volumes of the study devoted to U.S. efforts, conducted through intermediaries, to negotiate an end to the war. Ellsberg later explained, "I didn't want to get in the way of the diplomacy."

Sheehan and others at the Times, working in extreme secrecy, produced a series intended for publication on ten consecutive days. Each daily installment was made up of a long article, plus the original texts of some of the most important supporting documents. The articles were not abridged versions of the corresponding sections of the narrative that had been written by the Task Force in the Department of Defense; they were written by reporters of the New York Times, using information from both the narrative and the documents in the Defense Department version. On the average, about half of each installment was narrative and half was composed of texts of original documents. The first installment was published Sunday, June 13, 1971.

On the evening of June 14, at which point two installments had been published and the third was about to go to press, Attorney General John Mitchell informed the Times that "publication of this information is directly prohibited by the provisions of the Espionage Law, Title 18, United States Code, Section 793. Moreover, further publication of information of this character will cause irreparable injury to the defense interests of the United States. Accordingly, I respectfully request that you publish no further information of this character and advise me that you have made arrangements for the return of these documents to the Department of Defense." The newspaper rejected Mitchell's request.

On June 15, the Justice Department asked for an injunction forbidding the publication of further installments. Judge Murray I. Gurfein of the Southern District of New York issued a restraining order, preventing the publication of any further installments for four days, to allow time for the case to be argued. This set an important precedent. It was the first time that an American court had restrained a newspaper, in advance, from publishing a specific article.

That there was no precedent for such an action helps to explain the extraordinary speed with which the case moved through the courts. The Justice Department had obtained the restraining order without first proving to Judge Gurfein's satisfaction that such restraint was either necessary or legal. All of the courts that became involved in the case were in agreement that such a situation could not be allowed to persist for the length of time usually required for the U.S. court system to decide anything important.

Judge Gurfein heard arguments from both sides June 18. The hearing included a closed session during which classified information was considered; Judge Gurfein excluded from the court all but two members of the New York Times's defense team, over the objections of the Times's attorneys. On June 19, he handed down a decision in favor of the Times. He cited principles of freedom of the press, and a lack of evidence that publication of the Pentagon Papers posed a serious danger to the nation. He extended his restraining order, however, to allow the Justice Department time to appeal.

Immediately after the first restraining order was issued against the New York Times, Daniel Ellsberg provided a substantial portion of the Pentagon Papers to the Washington Post. The Post decided not to publish the texts of original documents, as the Times had done, but published on June 18, in some editions, the first of a series of articles written by Post reporters based on the Pentagon Papers.

The Justice Department made the same legal moves as in the case of the Times, but more quickly. The attorney general's request that the newspaper cease publication of the series, the newspaper's refusal, and the filing of a suit in U.S. District Court for the District of Columbia all occurred on June 18. District Judge Gerhard A. Gesell asked the Post to withhold publication voluntarily, for a brief period, to allow time for consideration of the case. The Post refused. Gesell then ruled in favor of the newspaper, citing the First Amendment principle of freedom of the press; the fact that the Espionage Act, which the Justice Department used as the legal foundation of its suit, contained no provision for restraint or censorship of the press; and the fact that "the Court has before it no precise information suggesting in what respects, if any, the publication of this information will injure the United States."

The Justice Department proceeded immediately to the U.S. court of appeals, which voted 2-1 to reverse Gesell's decision. The court of appeals temporarily restrained publication of the

series in the Post and ordered Judge Gesell to hold a further hearing June 21, at which the Justice Department would have a further opportunity to prove that publication of the series in the Post would cause such harm to the United States as to justify a prior restraint on publication.

At this June 21 hearing, as at the one June 18 before Judge Gurfein, there were several hours of secret testimony from which the public was excluded. Judge Gesell, however, allowed the full defense team of the Post to remain in the courtroom during this testimony. At the end of the day, Judge Gesell ruled that the government had provided no proof that publication of the Pentagon Papers would cause disastrous harm to the country. He concluded: "The First Amendment remains supreme."

The Justice Department appealed the rulings by Judge Gurfein and Judge Gesell; the appeal in each case was heard June 22 and produced a decision June 23. The Second Circuit Court of Appeals ordered that the case against the New York Times be sent back to Judge Gurfein, for him to hold yet another hearing, at which time the Justice Department would have the opportunity to present additional evidence that publication of the Pentagon Papers would harm national security. The U.S. Court of Appeals for the District of Columbia upheld Judge Gesell's ruling in favor of the Post, but extended the restraining order against the Post to allow time for the Justice Department to appeal to the Supreme Court.

On June 24, the Times appealed the ruling of the Second Circuit to the U.S. Supreme Court. The Department of Justice, after an unsuccessful effort to win another hearing before the District of Columbia Circuit, also appealed the decision of that court to the Supreme Court. Four justices voted to reject the appeal by the Department of Justice without a hearing, and allow the newspapers to proceed with publication forthwith. The majority, however, voted to combine the two cases and hear them on June 26.

When the Supreme Court agreed to hear the two cases, it also narrowed the restraining orders then in effect against the two newspapers to cover only a limited amount of material from the Pentagon Papers that the government had designated as exceptionally sensitive. The newspapers did not take immediate advantage of this, however, one of the reasons being that the list of documents the publication of which was still forbidden was itself a secret document, which could not legally be shown to the editor of either newspaper. The government did not want to give the newspapers information they might not already have about highly sensitive documents.

The two newspapers had refused, as a matter of principle, to tell the government what information they intended to publish, or even what portions of the Pentagon Papers they had in their possession. This was a serious handicap to them in court. It allowed the Justice Department to search through the whole of the Pentagon Papers, not just the sections the newspapers were actually planning to publish, for material the disclosure of which would harm the national interest.

The last four volumes of the original study, the disclosure of which seemed to the government extremely undesirable, had never been given to either newspaper because Daniel Ellsberg shared the government's view in this instance. In regard to the material that Ellsberg *did* furnish, the *Times* exercised some restraint in avoiding the publication of information about which the newspaper felt there might be legitimate national security concerns. The *Post* exercised a considerably greater degree of restraint, avoiding the publication of the full texts of any of the documents from the Pentagon Papers. Had the newspapers been less secretive about their own publication plans, court proceedings might have centered on the articles that the two newspapers were planning to publish, rather than on the original text of the Pentagon Papers, and the Justice Department would less often have been able to cite specific passages the publication of which could plausibly be described as imperiling national security.

The decision whether to publish such material at all had been hotly debated at both newspapers; in each case the publishers were caught between news personnel who urged publication and a vigorous assertion of freedom of the press, and attorneys who urged a much more conservative attitude. The *New York Times*'s law

firm, Lord, Day, and Lord, had strongly advised against publication. This advice having been rejected, Lord, Day, and Lord declined to represent the newspaper when its legal battle with the government began on June 15. Alexander M. Bickel, a Yale law professor and noted constitutional expert, agreed to represent the *Times* only a few hours before the first court hearing June 16.

The withdrawal of the firm that the *New York Times* had consulted before publication left all the parties in the ensuing battles—the Justice Department and both newspapers—represented in court by attorneys who had known nothing whatever about the Pentagon Papers until the *Times* began publication of its series June 13. They did not have a reasonable opportunity to familiarize themselves with this mass of material in the brief interval before the case reached the Supreme Court.

The fact that the attorneys had not had adequate time to prepare may help to explain the frequency with which the government, when asked before lower courts to cite particular items in the Pentagon Papers the disclosure of which would seriously harm national security, had picked items that the newspapers were able to prove had already been published elsewhere, long before the *Times* began its series.

The Supreme Court heard arguments June 26. The whole of the hearing was public; the Court had rejected, 6-3, a request by the Justice Department that there be a closed session for discussion of secret material. Such material was discussed in secret briefs filed by both sides.

The Justice Department, by this time, had shifted the legal basis of its case from the Espionage Act, under which its suits against the two newspapers had originally been brought, to the inherent powers of the presidency. Solicitor General Erwin Griswold argued that the president's responsibility for the conduct of foreign policy, and his role as commander in chief of the armed forces, required that he have the ability to forbid the publication of military secrets.

The Court handed down its decision June 30, finding for the newspapers 6-3. Justices Hugo Black, William Brennan, William Douglas, Thurgood Marshall, Potter Stewart, and Byron White were able to agree on a very short statement, the core of which was: "Any system of prior restraints of expression comes to this Court bearing a heavy presumption against its constitutional validity." The government "thus carries a heavy burden of showing justification for the enforcement of such a restraint. The District Court for the Southern District of New York in the *New York Times* case and the District Court for the District of Columbia and the Court of Appeals for the District of Columbia Circuit in the *Washington Post* case held that the Government had not met that burden. We agree."

Each of the six, however, wrote a separate concurring opinion; Black and Douglas each joined in the other's opinion, and Stewart and White likewise. No common thread unites all six concurring opinions. Themes touched in some of the opinions include assertions that a free press plays a vital role and must be protected; Congress had passed no law, and indeed had repeatedly rejected proposed laws, under which the government could enjoin publication of government secrets by the press; and the government had failed to prove that publication of the Pentagon Papers would cause such dire harm as to justify making an exception to the general principles of the First Amendment.

The key to the outcome lay with Stewart and White, the two justices who had not been willing to find for the newspapers on June 25 without a hearing, but who did find for them on June 30. They believed that Congress had not intended that the Espionage Act be used as a basis for restraints on the press. They said that publication of the Pentagon Papers would cause significant harm to the nation but that the government had not proven that publication would cause such great harm as to justify prior restraint. They rejected Solicitor General Griswold's arguments regarding the inherent powers of the presidency. As Justice White put it, with Justice Stewart joining him, "The Government's position is simply stated: The responsibility of the Executive for the conduct of foreign affairs and for the security of the Nation is so basic that the President is entitled to an injunction against publication of a newspaper story whenever he can convince a court that the information to be revealed threatens 'grave and irreparable' injury to the public interest; and the injunction should issue whether

or not the material to be published is classified, whether or not publication would be lawful under relevant criminal statutes enacted by Congress, and regardless of the circumstances by which the newspaper came into possession of the information. At least in the absence of legislation by Congress, based on its own investigations and findings, I am quite unable to agree that the inherent powers of the Executive and the courts reach so far as to authorize remedies having such sweeping potential for inhibiting publications by the press."

The minority—Chief Justice Warren Burger, and Justices Harry Blackmun and John Marshall Harlan—produced three dissenting opinions, but the three were in close agreement; Burger and Blackmun both joined in Harlan's opinion. By and large, they discussed entirely different questions from those analyzed in the opinions of the majority, rather than taking opposite sides on the same questions. They did not believe that restraints on publication of government secrets had to be based on legislation passed by the Congress, and in the realm of foreign affairs they were willing to grant the executive branch almost unfettered authority to decide which government secrets the press should be forbidden to publish. Also, they did not claim that the government had proved that publication of the Pentagon Papers would cause such dire harm to the nation as would justify an exception to the First Amendment; the closest any of them came was Justice Blackmun's statement that the evidence provided a "possible foundation" for such a claim. Finally, they did not feel that the government should have been required to provide such proof. Harlan, indeed, appeared to take seriously the possibility that it would be legal to enjoin publication of a top secret document, the actual contents of which were innocuous, on the theory that "harm enough results simply from the demonstration of such a breach of secrecy."

Justice Harlan, with Burger and Blackmun joining him, argued that the decision as to whether the Pentagon Papers could be published without harm to the national interest was a decision that only the executive branch was qualified to make, and that it would be a violation of the separation of powers for the judiciary to enquire too closely about the rationale for the decision of the executive branch, before enforcing it upon the press: "in performance of its duty to protect the values of the First Amendment against political pressures, the judiciary must review the initial Executive determination to the point of satisfying itself that the subject matter of the dispute does lie within the proper compass of the President's foreign relations power. Constitutional considerations forbid a complete abandonment of judicial control. . . . Moreover, the judiciary may properly insist that the determination that disclosure of the subject matter would irreparably impair the national security be made by the head of the Executive Department concerned—here the Secretary of State or the Secretary of Defense—after actual personal consideration by that officer. . . . But in my judgment the judiciary may not properly go beyond these two inquiries and redetermine for itself the probable impact of disclosure on national security."

The case did not seem, on its face, an overwhelming victory for freedom of the press. The barrier against prior restraint of publication had been breached, and attorneys for both the *Times* and the *Post* had conceded, in arguments before the Supreme Court, that the breach was to an important degree legitimate—that the government could legally forbid publication of an article if it could prove that publication would cause sufficient harm. Of the six justices making up the majority, three—Brennan, Stewart, and White—suggested that prior restraint of publication would be acceptable if the government proved that what Stewart called "direct, immediate, and irreparable damage" would follow from publication. They found in favor of the newspapers because the government had failed to meet such a standard of proof.

Furthermore, the precedent had been set that a temporary restraining order could be issued in anticipation of the government's proof that serious harm would result from publication. Only three justices—Black, Douglas, and Brennan—opposed the use of such restraining orders in their opinions. At the other extreme, the three justices in the minority argued that the government should be permitted to enjoin publication for an extended period, much longer than had been done in this case, to allow time for a proper

evaluation of the Pentagon Papers. Chief Justice Burger suggested that something clearly warranting prior restraint of publication, analogous to Justice Holmes's famous example of shouting "fire" in a crowded theater, "may be lurking in these cases and would have been flushed had they been properly considered in the trial courts, free from unwarranted deadlines and frenetic pressures."

Neither of these precedents has had an important impact since 1971, however, because they apply only in cases where the issue is prior restraint. The government can seldom learn, in advance, that a particular newspaper is about to publish government secrets. The newspapers had won on several issues that potentially had broader implications.

First, the Justice Department had attempted to establish a theory that the fact that documents were classified "Top Secret" created a presumption that their disclosure would harm the nation seriously enough to justify prior restraint on publication. As the Justice Department's brief in the Second Circuit Court of Appeals had put it, "the government does not have the burden of supporting a Top Secret classification." This theory had been rejected. Second, the courts had rejected the theory that the Espionage Act applied to publication of secret material in the U.S. press. Finally, the Court had rejected the Justice Department's claim for the inherent powers of the presidency.

Although the Supreme Court had rejected prior restraint of publication in this case, Justices Stewart and White, the swing votes, suggested that the appropriate way for the government to protect its secrets was the deterrent effect of criminal prosecution, rather than prior restraint of publication. The Justice Department did not attempt criminal action against the newspapers, but it did obtain indictments against Daniel Ellsberg for conspiracy, theft of government property, and violation of the Espionage Act.

The trial of Ellsberg and an alleged coconspirator, Anthony Russo, began January 3, 1973, in Los Angeles. Its verdict might have clarified some of the issues that had been left unresolved by the plethora of opinions in *New York Times v. United States*, but the judge dismissed the charges on May 11, citing a pattern of government misconduct including the facts that the government repeatedly failed to make timely disclosure of exculpatory information to the defense; some of Dr. Ellsberg's telephone conversations had been overheard by a government wiretap, but the records of this wiretap (including both the authorizations for it and the logs that would have revealed what conversations had been overheard) were missing from Justice Department files; and the White House "plumbers," whose activities were beginning to be revealed in connection with the Watergate affair, had burglarized the office of Ellsberg's psychiatrist in search of evidence against Ellsberg.

Some of the issues in the Pentagon Papers case were revisited in August 1984 when *Jane's Defence Weekly* published U.S. satellite photographs of a Soviet aircraft carrier. *Jane's*, a British publication, was less committed to protecting its sources than a similar U.S. publication might have been, and quickly furnished investigators proof that the photographs had come from Samuel L. Morison, an intelligence analyst working for the U.S. navy. Morison was arrested October 1, 1984, and charged with espionage and theft of government property, in regard to the photographs and also some other classified information he had given to *Jane's*.

From the government viewpoint, this was a perfect case to test the theory that giving classified information to the press can be a violation of the Espionage Act, since prosecutors could plausibly claim that Morison had been motivated by money. He had been hoping to obtain a full-time job with *Jane's*, and he had actually been paid a small amount for some of the information he had given the magazine.

United States v. Morison moved through the courts at a more normal speed than the Pentagon Papers case. Morison was convicted in October 1985. He was given a two-year sentence, of which he eventually served slightly fewer than eight months before being paroled. His appeal was rejected by the Fourth Circuit Court of Appeals in April 1988. On October 17, 1988, the Supreme Court announced its refusal to hear the case.

United States v. Morison established a precedent that the Espionage Act can apply to government employees who give classified information to the press. It remains to be seen whether this will reopen the question of whether the Espionage Act can be used against the press itself in cases of publication of classified information.

Selected Bibliography

The Pentagon Papers, as Published by The New York Times. New York: Bantam Books, 1971.

The Pentagon Papers: The Defense Department History of United States Decisionmaking on Vietnam. 5 vols. Boston: Beacon Press, 1971–72.

Rudenstein, D. *The Day the Presses Stopped: A History of the Pentagon Papers Case*. Berkeley: University of California Press, 1996.

Schrag, Peter. *Test of Loyalty: Daniel Ellsberg and the Rituals of Secret Government*. New York: Simon and Schuster, 1974.

Ungar, Sanford J. *The Papers & The Papers: An Account of the Legal and Political Battle over the Pentagon Papers*. New York: Dutton, 1972.

United States–Vietnam Relations, 1945–1967: Study Prepared by the Department of Defense. 12 vols. Washington, D.C.: U.S. Government Printing Office, 1971.

Public Disclosure of Private Facts

Susan Duffy

Speech Communication Department
California Polytechnic State University

Cox Broadcasting Corporation v. Martin Cohn, 420 U.S. 469 (1975) [U.S. Supreme Court]

◦ THE CASE IN BRIEF ◦

Date
1975

Location
Georgia

Court
U.S. Supreme Court

Principal Participants
Cox Broadcasting Corporation
Martin Cohn
Justice Byron White

Significance of the Case
After the father of a rape victim won his suit against a television station for identifying his daughter in a broadcast, the Supreme Court overturned the decision finding that the documents of a trial are a matter of public record.

In August 1971, Cynthia Cohn, a seventeen-year-old high-school student, was raped and murdered by six youths in Sandy Springs, Georgia. The trial, held in April 1972, was the source of intense media coverage. As part of this coverage, Tom Wassell, a reporter for WSB-TV, attended the trial. In the course of preparing his story, he asked to see the rape and murder indictments, which were given to him freely by the clerk of courts. Wassell subsequently broadcast a report of the trial on the evening news in which he mentioned the name of the victim.

Martin Cohn, the victim's father, sued Cox Broadcasting for invasion of privacy. Under a Georgia statute that made it a misdemeanor to publish or broadcast the name of a rape victim, Cohn won the case. In its written opinion, the Georgia Supreme Court asserted: "The surviving father . . . contends that the public disclosure of the identity and involvement of his daughter eight months after the fact invaded his right to privacy and intruded upon his right to be left alone, free from and unconnected with the sad and unpleasant events that had

925

previously occurred." Along with the Georgia law making it a misdemeanor to reveal the name of a rape victim, Cohn's arguments relied on the contention that the private matter disclosed must be one which would be "offensive and objectionable to a reasonable man of ordinary sensibilities."

Cox Broadcasting maintained that their reporter had obtained information from a public trial and a public document open to investigation by any interested citizen. The report aired contained no distortion of fact. Thus, Cox Broadcasting concluded that the Georgia statute under which the company was held liable was a violation of the First and Fourteenth Amendments. The Georgia Supreme Court upheld the state's "tort for public disclosure" in ruling for Cohn when it found "no public interest or general concern about the identity of the victim of such a crime . . . will make the right to disclose the identity of the victim rise to the level of First Amendment protection."

Cox Broadcasting appealed the decision. In the U.S. Supreme Court, the Georgia decision was overturned in favor of the rights of a free press. Justice Byron White delivered the opinion of the Court on behalf of himself, and Justices William Brennan, Potter Stewart, Thurgood Marshall, Harry Blackmun, and Lewis Powell. Warren Burger and William O. Douglas concurred in the judgment, while Justice Rehnquist filed the sole dissent. The heart of the issue rested on the clash between the individual's right to privacy and the press's right to print the truth.

The Court stepped carefully in its decision, recognizing the dilemma posed by the "collision between claims of privacy and those of the free press." White took three pages in the decision to outline the historical precedents and arguments. He noted that this issue was not unlike the issue central to the famous 1890 article on "The Right of Privacy," written by Charles Warren and Louis Brandeis. And he acknowledged that in the twentieth century, there was a "strong tide running in favor of the so-called right of privacy." However, White cited favorable language from a 1947 opinion of Justice Douglas: "A trial is a public event. What transpires in the court room is public property. If the transcript of the court proceedings had been published, we suppose none would claim that the judge could punish the publisher for contempt. . . . Those who see and hear what transpired can report it with impunity. There is no special perquisite of the judiciary which enables it, as distinguished from other institutions of democratic government, to suppress, edit, or censor events which transpire in proceedings before it." With this in mind, the Court voted to reverse the state court's decision, concluding, "Under these circumstances, the protection of freedom of the press provided by the First and Fourteenth Amendments bars the State of Georgia from making appellants' broadcast the basis of civil liability."

Most of the criticism leveled at this decision focused on the argument that the "name" or identity of the victim in no way served the public interest and that there was little, if anything, to be gained from knowing the name of a rape victim. That such a revelation would cause pain and emotional distress within a victim's family, and that it would indeed be an invasion of privacy, were important in the counterarguments. These considerations were overridden, however, by the Court's position that the identity of the victim was already a matter of public record and that, under the First Amendment, this was information available to the public and press alike. The Court advised that to protect the right of privacy, states must move to keep names out of the public record.

White noted also that the Court's failure to decide the question would "leave the press in Georgia operating in the shadow of the civil and criminal sanctions of a rule of law and a statute the constitutionality of which is in serious doubt." The Court's decision reinforced other landmark free-press decisions in this century that allowed the rights of the press to outweigh those of the individual citizen. Yet, as one law-review article written in the wake of the decision noted, "In *Cox Broadcasting Corp. v. Cohn* the Court encountered for the first time the tension between the First Amendment and a privacy action based on public disclosure of wholly accurate information." The *Cox* decision may have freed the press from certain censorious overtures by states, yet it placed on the press a greater responsibility for self-restraint.

Selected Bibliography

Baer, Robert L. "Constitutional Law—Right to Report Judicial Records." *Washburn Law Journal* 15 (Winter 1976): 163–167.

Blackmun, Sally A. "Constitutional Law—Right of Privacy Versus Freedom of the Press—The Press Cannot Be Restrained from Reporting Facts Contained in Official Court Records." *Emory Law Journal* 24 (Fall 1975): 1205–1228.

Martin, Jeffrey C. "First Amendment Limitations on Public Disclosure Actions." *University of Chicago Law Review* 45 (Fall 1977): 180–217.

McGinnis, Patrick Edward. "Civil Procedure—New Insight on Finality of State Court Judgments." *Arizona State Law Journal* (1975): 627–645.

McKeever, Joyce. "Recent Decisions." *Duquesne Law Review.* 14 (Spring 1976): 507–520.

"Recent Decisions." *Georgia Law Review* 9 (Summer 1975): 963–979.

Did CBS Libel General Westmoreland?

Edwin E. Moise

Department of History
Clemson University

William Westmoreland v. Columbia Broadcasting System, Inc., et al.,
596 F. Supp. 1170 (1984) [U.S. Federal District Court]

◄◦► THE CASE IN BRIEF ◄◦►

Date
1985

Location
New York

Court
U.S. Federal District Court

Principal Participants
General William Westmoreland
George Crile
Mike Wallace
Samuel Adams
Columbia Broadcasting System, Inc.

Significance of the Case
Claims of inflated war-report figures and a military officer's honor were at stake when General Westmoreland sued a television network for libel. When two witnesses were called that threatened his case, Westmoreland withdrew his suit.

On January 23, 1982, the Columbia Broadcasting System (CBS) presented a documentary titled *The Uncounted Enemy: A Vietnam Deception.* It argued, that during 1967, U.S. intelligence estimates in Vietnam had been formulated with deliberate and knowing dishonesty. Intelligence officers at Military Assistance Command, Vietnam (MACV), under pressure from their superiors to show progress in the war, had seriously underestimated enemy strength. These underestimates had left the United States unprepared for the strength of the Tet offensive of January 1968. The program indicated that General William Westmoreland, American commander in Vietnam from 1964 to 1968, was to a significant extent responsible for this deception.

The United States had sent ground troops into Vietnam in 1965 without having adequate intelligence on the Communist forces its troops were to fight. When MACV began to issue monthly reports on the organization and strength of the Communists in South Vietnam, the order of battle, the figures were at first very incomplete.

As intelligence improved during 1966, the figures for the Communists' regular combat units came to be reasonably accurate. The order of battle reports also, however, contained figures for three other types of Communist personnel: (1) "combat support" or "administrative services" (the people who provided transport, medical care, and other services for the enemy forces); (2) "political cadres" or "political infrastructure" (most of the people in this category were local administrative personnel—village administrators, tax collectors, police—of the areas of South Vietnam that were partially or wholly under Communist rule); (3) "irregulars" or "militia" (a variety of guerrilla and militia organizations, of varying capabilities, of which two would eventually become the subject of particular attention in the case, the "self-defense" militia [SD] in Communist-controlled villages and the "secret self-defense" militia [SSD] in government-controlled villages).

Most of the Communist personnel in South Vietnam fell in these three categories, but the figures for them in the order of battle reports had little foundation. The officers responsible had no idea how many personnel were actually in these categories, but bureaucratic inertia dictated that, for lack of anything better, they repeat each month the unfounded estimate in the previous month's report.

By the first half of 1967, enough information was becoming available to make realistic estimates possible for all categories. This created a major problem. The new estimates, especially for the administrative services and irregulars, were enormously higher than the old ones. Because public support for the war was already becoming shaky in the United States, if the official estimate of total enemy personnel in South Vietnam suddenly increased, perhaps even doubled, there could have been serious repercussions.

There followed a series of acrimonious conferences at which the CIA argued for comparatively high estimates of Communist personnel and MACV intelligence argued for much lower estimates. In September 1967, an agreement was worked out under which the definitions used in compiling the estimates were drastically changed. U.S. intelligence simply stopped estimating the numbers of people in the SD and SSD militias. Estimates of the number of political cadres continued to be compiled but were

no longer treated as part of the military order of battle. Having dropped these categories, MACV accepted higher estimates of some others (though not as high as CIA estimates) without **any** increase in the overall total.

Samuel Adams, a CIA analyst of order of battle issues, had been one of the CIA negotiators at the 1967 conferences. He believed that the estimates agreed upon at the September conference were grossly dishonest—incomplete and inaccurate to an extent that would seriously interfere with the war effort against the Communists. He made his view public in May 1975, in an article in *Harper's* magazine titled "Vietnam Cover-up: Playing War with Numbers." Years later, George Crile, the editor who had handled the article in *Harper's*, took a position at CBS, and he decided that the story would make a good television documentary.

Crile began work on the project late in 1980; the ninety-minute program was ready for broadcast at the beginning of 1982. Despite rather melodramatic publicity, which used the word "conspiracy" far more than the actual documentary did and later formed part of the basis for Westmoreland's libel suit, relatively few people watched the show.

When General Westmoreland began to consider legal action, the prospects seemed poor. But after *TV Guide* conspicuously labeled the program a "smear" against him, and Dan M. Burt, head of the Capitol Legal Foundation, offered to have the foundation represent him without charge, the general filed suit for $120 million. The defendants were CBS, Samuel Adams, George Crile, Mike Wallace (chief correspondent for the program) and Van Gordon Sauter (president of CBS News).

Westmoreland and Burt began the case with a crucial error. They could have filed their suit in the city where Westmoreland lived, military-oriented and politically conservative Charleston, South Carolina, where they would have had an excellent chance of victory. Instead they went two hundred miles northwest and filed in Greenville, South Carolina. Possibly they were hoping to benefit from the support of the local CBS station, WSPA-TV. WSPA had not broadcast *The Uncounted Enemy*, had given Westmoreland half an hour of prime time to respond to the program it had not broadcast, and had taken his side against the network in a broadcast editorial.

The defendants failed to get the case dismissed on the jurisdictional ground that none of the actions of which the defendants were accused had occurred in South Carolina. The defendants, however, asked for a change of venue, either to New York or to Washington, DC, on the grounds that Greenville was not a convenient location for the plaintiff, the defendants, or any important witness for either party. General Westmoreland said, "It would be a great personal hardship to me to be forced to litigate this case away from home. The expense of hotels, travel and retaining local counsel elsewhere would be a serious burden." As an argument for trying the case in Charleston, this might have been decisive. But when it was presented as a reason the case should be tried in Greenville, it was less compelling. The case was transferred to New York, where it came before Federal District Judge Pierre N. Laval.

Just before the trial began, Westmoreland dropped from his suit claims that CBS had libeled him by broadcasting that he had conspired to deceive the press, the Congress, and the public. He narrowed his suit to the claim that CBS had libeled him by accusing him of conspiring to deceive his superiors in the military chain of command.

Some variations from usual trial procedure were made to help the jury cope with the complexity of the issues in the case. Judge Laval allowed attorneys for both sides to make interim summations to the jury at intervals during the case instead of reserving the summations for the end of the trial. Each side was allowed a total of two hours for interim summations. Judge Laval also encouraged the jurors to take written notes during testimony. Some witnesses, who lived very far from New York, were allowed to present testimony without being physically present in the court. Before the trial, all witnesses had been questioned under oath by attorneys for both sides. Judge Laval, in some instances, permitted the transcripts of these interrogations to be read from the witness stand by attorneys for the two parties, and he treated them as if the witnesses themselves had been on the stand presenting testimony.

General Westmoreland's avowed primary concern was to maintain his reputation in the press and before the public. The libel suit, he maintained, was a means to make his case heard, not an effort to win money (he said he would give away any monetary award if he won the case). He did very well in the struggle for public opinion, at least up to the time the trial began, in October 1984. CBS was forced to admit having made factual errors in *The Uncounted Enemy*, having violated proper journalistic procedures by failing to interview several crucial witnesses, having used excerpts from filmed interviews out of context, having filmed one interview twice when the first version proved unsatisfactory, and having allowed one subject to view the film of an interview with another subject before the filming of his own interview.

Once the trial began, however, on October 9, 1984, these issues became less relevant. Compliance with proper journalistic procedures is not a legal obligation. After the defense case began on January 8, 1985, CBS was able to show credible evidence for the central thesis of its program: that military intelligence officers under General Westmoreland's command had been pressured by their superiors to report fewer Communist personnel in South Vietnam than they believed were actually there.

General Westmoreland and his supporters have tended to describe the intelligence debate of 1967 as having pitted the CIA against MACV and having been fully reported to the White House. At the trial, however, another division was made visible, this one within MACV intelligence.

On one side there had been intelligence officers, mostly of higher rank, who did not regard order of battle work—the production of estimates of the overall structure and strength of the enemy forces—as very interesting or important. They did such work on a part-time basis if at all, and they had little respect for the officers who worked on it full time. Several of them appeared as witnesses for Westmoreland. They supported the relatively low estimates of overall enemy strength that had represented the official MACV position in 1967.

On the other side were officers, mostly of lower rank, who had been assigned full-time to order of battle work during 1967. Several of them testified, as witnesses for CBS, that they had been ordered by their superiors to issue estimates that they believed seriously understated the level of enemy strength.

Colonel Gains Hawkins, the man directly responsible for MACV's overall estimates of enemy strength, testified that, under pressure from his own superiors, he had ordered his subordinates to lower their estimates in mid-1967. He was not aware of any evidence justifying lower estimates; he said that the evidence suggested that the estimates were already too low. On the witness stand, he described the estimates that MACV had presented to other intelligence agencies in August 1967 as "crap."

For the most part, General Westmoreland had not been directly involved; his immediate subordinates had passed down the chain of command what they believed to be his wishes, without necessarily consulting him in detail. General Phillip Davidson, chief of intelligence for MACV from mid-1967 onward, once stated in a directive to his officers: "in view of General Westmoreland's conversations, all of which you have heard, I am sure that this headquarters will not accept a figure in excess of the current strength figure carried by the press. . . . Let me make it clear that this is my view of General Westmoreland's sentiments. I have not discussed this directly with him but I am 100 percent sure of his reaction."

CBS was able to present two witnesses, however—General Joseph McChristian, former chief of MACV intelligence, and Colonel Hawkins—who in May 1967 had presented more accurate figures to substitute for the underestimates in the order of battle directly to Westmoreland.

Westmoreland had to convince the jury of two things: that the accusations made in the CBS program had been false, and that they had been made in reckless disregard of the evidence available to CBS. The testimony of McChristian and Hawkins left him little chance to accomplish the second, and in serious danger of failing with the first. On February 18, 1985, it was announced that he was withdrawing his suit.

The terms, less favorable than those CBS had offered a few months before, included carefully worded statements by CBS. CBS said that it stood by its broadcast, but also said that it "never intended to assert, and does not believe, that General Westmoreland was unpatriotic or disloyal in performing his duties as he saw them." General Westmoreland interpreted this as an apology; a more realistic interpretation would be that CBS was saying General Westmoreland had believed it was his duty to distort intelligence estimates, in order to keep the American public from becoming discouraged about the war.

Selected Bibliography

Adams, Samuel. *War of Numbers: An Intelligence Memoir.* South Royalton, VT: Steerforth, 1994.

Brewin, Bob, and Sydney Shaw. *Vietnam on Trial: Westmoreland vs. CBS.* New York: Atheneum, 1987.

The "Preacher" and the "Smut Merchant"

Donald E. Boles

Professor of Political Science, Emeritus
Iowa State University

Hustler Magazine and Larry C. Flynt v. Jerry Falwell, 485 U.S. 46 (1988) [U.S. Supreme Court]

‹○› THE CASE IN BRIEF ‹○›

Date
1988

Location
Virginia

Court
U.S. Supreme Court

Principal Participants
Reverend Jerry Falwell
Larry Flynt
Chief Justice William Rehnquist

Significance of the Case
A case involving a political cartoon published in a controversial magazine allowed the Supreme Court to apply a broad interpretation of First Amendment protection to political speech and expression.

Seldom in Supreme Court history have representatives of two more diametrically opposed social forces collided than in this case: the Reverend Jerry Falwell, a leader in the right-wing Evangelical movement, sued Larry Flynt, the publisher of *Hustler,* one of the more vulgar national "girlie magazines." At issue was the question of whether political cartooning was to remain constitutionally protected and unfettered by legal constraints even if it was *outrageous* and was intended to cause *emotional distress* to the party being caricatured.

The magazine had published an advertisement "parody" that, among other things, portrayed the Reverend Falwell as having engaged in a drunken, incestuous rendezvous with his mother in an outhouse. Following the appearance of the issue carrying the advertisement, Falwell brought a damage action against the magazine for libel, invasion of privacy, and intentional infliction of emotional distress. To exacerbate matters, while the case was still pending, the ad parody was published in *Hustler* a second time.

Pivotal to an understanding of the case is the fact, that throughout the litigation, it was accepted by all parties that the Reverend Falwell was a "public figure." It is much more difficult for a public figure to prove libel or damage to his or her reputation than it is for the average person. The U.S. Supreme Court, since the 1964 case of *New York Times v. Sullivan,* has held that not all speech about public figures is immune from legal sanctions. But, to be successful in such litigation, the public figure must demonstrate that the offending statement was made "with knowledge that it was false or with reckless disregard of whether it was false or not."

Counsel for Reverend Falwell argued, however, that a different standard should apply in this case, because here the state sought to prevent not reputational damage, but severe emotional distress suffered by the person who is the subject of an offensive publication. According to this view, so long as the utterance that was intended to inflict emotional distress was outrageous and did in fact inflict serious emotional distress, it was of no constitutional importance whether the statement was a fact or an opinion—or, for that matter, whether it was true or false. The key, as they saw it, was the intent to cause injury. Moreover, Falwell's attorney argued, the state's interest in preventing emotional harm simply outweighed whatever interest a speaker might have in speech of this type.

At trial, the Federal District Court threw out the invasion of privacy claim. The jury also ruled against Reverend Falwell on the libel claim, specifically finding that the ad parody could not "reasonably be understood as describing actual facts about [the Reverend] or actual events in which [he] participated." On the other hand, the jury found for Falwell on the claim of intentional infliction of emotional distress and awarded him $100,000 in compensatory damages, as well as $50,000 in punitive damages.

Flynt appealed the decision to the U.S. Court of Appeals for the Fourth Circuit. This court not only affirmed the judgment against Flynt but seemed to go farther in forging an important exception to the "public figure" doctrine of *Times v. Sullivan.* The court here rejected Flynt's argument that the "actual malice" standard of the *Sullivan* case must be met before Falwell could recover for "emotional distress." It went on to reject the contention that because the jury found

that the ad parody did not describe actual facts about Falwell, the ad was an opinion that is protected by the First Amendment. As the Court of Appeals put it, this was "irrelevant," because the real issue, as it saw it, was "whether [the ad's] publication was sufficiently *outrageous* [emphasis added] to constitute intentional infliction of emotional distress."

On further appeal, the U.S. Supreme Court began by reviewing in detail the fact situation. It noted that the inside front cover of the November 1983 issue of *Hustler* magazine featured a "parody" of an advertisement for Campari liqueur that contained the name and picture of Falwell and was entitled "Jerry Falwell talks about his first time." This parody was modeled after actual Campari ads that included interviews with various celebrities about their "first time." In the Court's words, "Although it was apparent by the end of each interview that this meant the first time they sampled Campari, the ads clearly played on the sexual double entendre of the general subject of 'first times.' "

Copying the form and layout of these Campari ads, *Hustler*'s editors chose Falwell as the featured celebrity and drafted an alleged "interview" with him in which he stated that his "first time" was during a drunken, incestuous rendezvous with his mother in an outhouse. As the Court explained it, "The *Hustler* parody portrays respondent and his mother as drunk and immoral and suggest that [he] is a hypocrite who preaches only when he is drunk." In an attempt to protect the magazine from legal action, in small print, at the bottom of the page, the ad contained the disclaimer "ad parody—not to be taken seriously." The magazine's table of contents also listed the ad as "Fiction; Ad and Personality Parody."

It was clear from the outset that the Court's majority recognized that the issues of this case far transcended the immediate battle between Falwell and Flynt. The novel question in the case, as Chief Justice William Rehnquist saw it, was whether a public figure could recover damages for *emotional harm* caused by the publication of an ad parody offensive to him and "doubtless gross and repugnant in the eyes of most."

Moreover, in the justices' view, Falwell sought to have the Court find that a "State's interest in

Hustler Magazine publisher Larry Flynt signs a copy of "The People Vs. Larry Flynt," a movie based on his life. The movie depicts events from Flynt's life including his legal battle with the Rev. Jerry Falwell. *AP Photo/Tom Uhlman.*

protecting public figures from *emotional distress* is sufficient to deny First Amendment protection to speech that is patently offensive and is *intended* to inflict *emotional injury*" [emphasis added]. The Court was asked to arrive at this conclusion even though "the speech could not reasonably have been interpreted as stating actual facts about the public figure involved."

Then, to the surprise of some Court watchers, Chief Justice Rehnquist, long the leader of right-wing forces on the Court, launched a ringing defense of freedom of speech, press, and expression. He noted that "At the heart of the First Amendment is the recognition of the fundamental importance of the free flow of ideas and opinions on matters of public interest . . . [and] 'is essential to the common quest for truth and the vitality of society as a whole.' "

He emphasized that "The First Amendment recognizes no such thing as a 'false' idea." To support this sometimes forgotten point, he quoted Justice Oliver Wendell Holmes's famous lines from his dissenting opinion in the 1919 case of *Abrams v. United States*: "[W]hen men have realized that time has upset many fighting faiths, they may come to believe even more than they believe the very foundations of their own conduct that the ultimate good desired is better reached by free trade in ideas—

that the best test of truth is the power of the thought to get itself accepted in the competition of the market."

Furthermore, Rehnquist explained that in the real world "robust political debate . . . is bound to produce speech that is critical of those who hold public office." Indeed, "[o]ne of the prerogatives of American citizenship is the right to criticize public men," and some of such commentary will be "vehement, caustic and sometimes unpleasantly sharp." However, the chief justice emphasized, because of the critical importance of free expression to the maintenance of a free society, the Court has held that a speaker can be held liable for damage to the reputation of a public figure only if the statement was made with "knowledge that it was false or with reckless disregard of whether it was false or not."

The Court summarily rejected Falwell's contention that a different standard should apply to this case because the law seeks to prevent not reputational damage but *severe emotional distress* to the public figure. As Rehnquist drolly explained it, "Generally speaking the law does not regard the intent to inflict emotional distress as one which should receive much solicitude." The Court had previously recognized that in the world of political debate, "many things done with motives that are less than admirable are protected by the First Amendment." Indeed, in the arena of public affairs, the Court had held that "even when a speaker or writer is motivated by hatred or ill-will his expression was protected by the First Amendment."

Then, getting to the case's real significance in today's politics, Rehnquist noted that using *bad motive* as a criterion for limiting public debate would effectively subject political cartoonists and satirists to damage awards without any demonstration that their work *falsely defamed* its subject. After all, he explained, "The appeal of the political cartoon or caricature is often based on exploration of unfortunate physical traits or politically embarrassing events . . . often calculated to injure the feelings of the subject." The cartoonist's work, as the chief justice saw it, typically is not "reasoned or evenhanded, but slashing and one sided." After reviewing the role of the political cartoon in our political history, Rehnquist stressed that our "political discourse would have been considerably poorer without them."

Reverend Falwell contended, however, that the caricature in question was so *outrageous* as to distinguish it from more traditional political cartoons, and thus it should not receive the same First Amendment protections. Acknowledging that the *Hustler* parody in question was "at best a distant cousin of the political cartoon," the Court nonetheless recognized that a workable legal standard distinguishing between the two did not exist. More important, Rehnquist emphasized, the "pejorative description 'outrageous' does not supply" such a standard. "Outrageousness" as a standard would permit individual jurors to use their personal tastes or views to find a cartoonist guilty simply because the cartoonist's views did not conform to those of the jurors.

To prevent any misconceptions as to the scope of this decision, Rehnquist went on to emphasize that limitations previously imposed by the Court on freedom of expression continued to be applicable. Speech that is "vulgar," "offensive," and "shocking" is "not entitled to absolute constitutional protection under all circumstances," he noted. Nor do First Amendment protections apply to "fighting words," which by their very utterance inflict injury or tend to incite an immediate breach of peace, explained the chief justice, referring to a 1942 case, *Chaplinsky v. New Hampshire*. But, he went on, the type of expression in the *Hustler* ad clearly was not governed by these exceptions to First Amendment rights.

Thus, the Court concluded that public figures may not recover damages for the "intentional infliction of emotional distress" in car-

toons or ads such as this without showing that the publication contains a "false statement of fact which was made with actual malice, i.e., with knowledge that the statement was false or with reckless disregard to whether or not it was true." This standard, the Court argued, "is necessary to give adequate 'breathing space' to the freedoms protected by the First Amendment."

Political satirists and cartoonists, such as the author of "Doonesbury," and their devoted followers (as well as Larry Flynt), can heave a collective sigh of relief at this decision. The case also demonstrates an adage in civil liberties law: that our rights are frequently protected by litigants with whom we may not agree, or whom we might not be comfortable having as our next-door neighbors. It also demonstrates what careful Rehnquist watchers already know: that the chief justice, although normally supporting the power of the government over individual rights, marches to a different drummer in the area of *political* speech or expression. On that subject, he frequently supports a broad application of First Amendment protections.

Selected Bibliography

Note. "Did Falwell Hustle *Hustler*: Allowing Public Figures to Recover Emotional Distress Damages for Nonlibellous Satire." *Washington and Lee Law Review* 44 (1987): 1381–1414.

Note. "Free Speech and Emotional Distress—*Hustler Magazine v. Falwell*." *Harvard Journal of Law and Public Policy* 11 (1988): 843–849.

Stone, R. "Intentional Contempt and Press Freedom." *New Law Journal* 138 (1988): 423–424.

Wright, R. G. "*Hustler Magazine v. Falwell*." *Cumberland Law Review* 19 (1988): 19–42.

Freedom of Religion

Religion, Cultural Pluralism, and the Constitution: Mormonism and Polygamy

—◄○►—

Gordon Morris Bakken
Department of History
California State University, Fullerton

Reynolds v. United States, 98 U.S. 145 (1879) and *Davis v. Beason,*
133 U.S. 33 (1889) [U.S. Supreme Court]

◄○► THE CASE IN BRIEF ◄○►

Date
1879, 1890

Location
Utah
Idaho
District of Columbia

Court
U.S. Supreme Court

Principal Participants
The Church of Jesus Christ of the Latter-Day Saints; George Reynolds; Samuel D. Davis

Significance of the Case
National efforts to eradicate polygamy generated both constitutional law arguments and political rhetoric during the Grant administration, and two Supreme Court decisions effectively banned polygamy under United States law.

The national efforts to eradicate polygamy generated a great deal of constitutional law and political rhetoric in the period 1862–1890. Lawmakers in Washington and in the territories attacked behaviors of members of the Church of Jesus Christ of Latter-Day Saints, generally known as Mormons, found odious to the general moral and political culture of the period. Mainstream American culture, of course, found the religious practice of polygamy to be immoral. In addition, the Mormon political behavior of bloc voting deeply upset local politicians. The legal assault to end polygamy in federal and territorial law included both criminal sanctions and limitations on the franchise.

In *Reynolds v. United States* (1879), the U.S. Supreme Court decided that the First Amendment protections of religious liberty did not extend to religious practices that impaired the public interest. The issue before the Court was whether polygamy, declared by Mormon doctrine to be a religious practice but designated by federal law to be a crime, was a protected liberty to the extent that a bigamy conviction should be overturned. Chief Justice Morrison

R. Waite, for a unanimous Court, declared that a federal statute could constitutionally punish criminal activity, regardless of religious belief. Although the government could not punish religious beliefs, the government could punish activities that were declared to be crimes. To hold otherwise would undermine the foundations of government and make religion superior to law.

The national effort to eradicate polygamy had antebellum roots but no statutory support until the passage of an antibigamy act in 1862. The Mormon hierarchy put George Reynolds forward to test the statute. Reynolds was secretary to Brigham Young, the spiritual leader of the Mormons. He was also a faithful polygamist. First convicted in the territorial district court, Reynolds had his conviction sustained in the Utah Supreme Court in 1876. He then appealed to the U.S. Supreme Court. Anti-Mormon forces welcomed the test case.

Several years prior to the *Reynolds* case, the Grant administration—believing that polygamy was a relic of barbarism—attacked the surviving practice with gusto. Grant appointed James B. McKean as Utah's territorial supreme court chief justice and General J. Wilson Shaffer as territorial governor to root out the vestiges of polygamy. McKean used U.S. marshals to round up polygamists and to select juries. This resulted in numerous indictments, convictions, and imprisonments. The Mormons appealed these convictions, based upon procedural error in the jury selection process, and in 1872 won a favorable U.S. Supreme Court ruling which quashed 130 indictments and released scores from incarceration.

In Congress, anti-Mormon forces threw their support to legislation known as the Cullom Bill, which enlarged the appointive powers of the territorial governor to include local judges and law enforcement personnel, limited the jurisdiction of Mormon-controlled probate courts, excluded polygamists from juries, and made polygamy convictions easier to obtain. The bill even authorized the president of the United States to use military force in the enforcement of the statute. The Cullom Bill never reached the president's desk. But in 1874 another statute, called the Poland Bill, did become law. This statute revised the territorial court structure and jurisdictions to limit the probate courts. Further, the law revised the jury selection process to attempt to balance Mormon and Gentile representation. Anti-Mormons thought the Poland Act insufficient, and looked to the *Reynolds* as a means of attacking the moral menace in Salt Lake City.

In reaching the nation's highest tribunal, anti-Mormon forces branded polygamy as socially destructive and characterized Mormons as enemy deviants. Mormons countered by submitting that religious freedom of belief was inviolate under the Constitution and that polygamy was not bigamy. Further, they argued that plural marriage, as practiced by Mormons, was not destructive of any social interest or the public peace. Quite the contrary, Mormons maintained that plural marriage was supportive of the family, family values, and spiritual growth. Polygamy was religious in nature and not harmful to society in any way. The 1879 Supreme Court, however, did not see the same social utility the Mormons did.

In the aftermath of the *Reynolds* case, anti-Mormonism in Idaho territory produced yet another U.S. Supreme Court ruling on anti-Mormon legislation. Mormons settled southeastern Idaho before the creation of the territory. Mormon affiliation with the Democratic Party in 1872 marked the beginning of organized anti-Mormon activity. By 1882 anti-Mormonism had become a territorial political issue and a Republican Party initiative. Idaho Republicans used the Mormon menace to elect a territorial delegate to Congress. But, once in Washington, national Republicans denied the territorial delegate his seat and passed the Edmunds Anti-Polygamy Act of 1882. The Edmunds Act effectively disfranchised the Mormons in Utah and Idaho territories. With the franchise denied, anti-Mormon forces imposed the requirement of a test oath to disqualify Mormon legislators from sitting in 1884 or from holding county offices. The territorial legislature subsequently amended the test oath statute to exclude Mormons from office, from voting, and from jury service if they had been Mormons on January 1, 1888. The governor signed the amendatory legislation despite constitutional doubts about its retroactivity. The doubts about the constitutionality of the Idaho test oath were resolved by the U.S. Supreme Court in *Davis v. Beason* (1889).

The facts of the *Davis* case were fairly simple. In April 1889, Samuel D. Davis was indicted in the Third Judicial District of Idaho Territory, in the county of Oneida, for conspiracy to obstruct the administration of the law and unlawfully attempting to register to vote. The legal issue was the constitutionality of the test oath statute. Davis's attorney argued that Idaho could not refuse registration based solely upon church membership, because such membership had not been declared to be a crime. Further, he argued that the statute was unconstitutional because it prohibited the free exercise of religion. The statute, Davis's attorney argued, also violated the Fourteenth Amendment as well as the Article VI of the U.S. Constitution. The latter specifically stated that "no religious Test shall ever be required as a Qualification to any Office or Public Trust under the United States." Finally, the lawyer urged that the Edmunds Act had preempted the field and that the Idaho legislature was without authority to legislate on the subject matter. Justice Stephen J. Field wrote the opinion for a unanimous Court, rebutting every claim.

Field stressed the jurisdictional issues in his opinion, but he also used the case to condemn polygamy. The issue that required legal attention was the jurisdiction of the territorial court. Polygamy and bigamy were clearly criminal. "They tend to destroy the purity of the marriage relation, to disturb the peace of families, to degrade woman and to debase man," Field maintained. Further, "few crimes are more pernicious to the best interests of society and receive more general or more deserved pun-ishment." Finally, "to extend exemption from punishment for such crimes would be to shock the moral judgment of the community." To meet the "free exercise" argument, Field observed that the "laws are made for the government of actions, and while they cannot interfere with mere religious belief and opinions, they may with practices." From this it was clear that the territory had authority to make law because the federal statute had not dealt with the teaching, advising, or counseling of the practices of bigamy and polygamy, thereby leaving open the regulation of these elements of behavior for the territorial government.

Justice Field's *Davis* opinion contained a footnote documenting the long-standing position of the nation regarding the extent of religious freedom. The centerpiece of the note was the New York Constitution of 1777, which declared that "liberty of conscience . . . shall not be so construed as to excuse acts of licentiousness, or justify practices inconsistent with the peace or safety of this state." The Court listed numerous other examples of state constitutional condemnation of Mormon practices, indicating that the constitutional door was now completely closed to pro-polygamy arguments.

Selected Bibliography

Firmage, Edwin Brown, and Richard Collin Mangrum. *Zion in the Courts: A Legal History of the Church of Jesus Christ of Latter-day Saints, 1830–1900.* Urbana: University of Illinois Press, 1988.

Hardy, B. C. *Solemn Covenant: The Mormon Polygamous Passage.* Urbana: University of Illinois Press, 1992.

Wells, Merle W. *Anti-Mormonism in Idaho, 1872–92.* Provo, UT: Brigham Young University Press, 1978.

The Scopes Trial: A Collision of Cultures

—◄o►—

Bernard K. Duffy

Speech Communication Department
California Polytechnic State University

State of Tennessee v. John Thomas Scopes, (1925) [State court of Tennessee]

◄o► THE CASE IN BRIEF ◄o►

Date
1925

Location
Tennessee

Court
Tennessee Supreme Court

Principal Participants
John Thomas Scopes; Clarence Darrow;
William Jennings Bryan

Significance of the Case
John T. Scopes, a Tennessee physics
teacher, along with the American Civil
Liberties Union challenged the Butler
Act, a law that made it illegal to teach
evolution in public schools. The trial and
its result were merely a sidebar to a major
battle between science and Christian
Fundamentalism.

The Scopes trial, a small, white-hot fire fed by the swirling ethers of religious fundamentalism and science, was ignited by partisans who wished to illuminate unresolved differences of culture and faith that divided the technological North from the agrarian South. Dayton, Tennessee, where the Scopes trial took place, became the crucible of a controversy that led the nation to recognize the existence of two national cultures, one steeped in the small-town values and mores learned at the hearth and in the pew, and the other based upon beliefs learned in the laboratory and the lecture hall.

The anti-evolution Butler Act, approved by the Tennessee state legislature and the Governor in 1925, was not intended to create controversy. As Ray Ginger observed, "The Butler Act was a stump speech; it was each legislator telling his constituents that he very much wanted to be re-elected." The Butler Act prohibited the teaching of evolution in the public schools, universities, and normal schools. Despite its far-reaching implications, public universities ignored the bill, and the Governor, whom some expected would veto it, signed it into law but expressed the opinion that it would not be enforced. He understood it for what it was, a symbolic protest against the undermining of religion by science.

Opportunism brought the Butler Act to a test that neither its author, the state legislature, nor the Governor had anticipated. The city of Chattanooga was first to attempt to arrange a test case. The American Civil Liberties Union (ACLU) stood ready to bankroll the defense, but Chattanooga's plans fell through. In Dayton, however, a local mining engineer originally from New York, George Rappalyea, was successful in putting a sleepy Southern town on the map by setting in motion events that would lead to a trial. A drugstore discussion with John T. Scopes, the local physics teacher and an occasional substitute in the biology class, resulted in an agreement that would put Scopes on trial for teaching the pernicious doctrine of evolution. Scopes obligingly asked the biology class to copy a diagram from a biology text and was, accordingly, arrested for violating the Butler Act. Ironically, the text had been approved by the state—presumably prior to the passage of the Butler Act.

Rappalyea had presciently foreseen the possibility of bringing to Dayton well-known scientific experts and fundamentalist leaders. It was an occasion for civic pride that such gladiators as the three-time presidential candidate and leading spokesman for religious fundamentalism, William Jennings Bryan, and the celebrated but controversial "attorney for the damned," Clarence Darrow, offered to meet in rhetorical combat. Bryan would serve as the state prosecutor pro tempore, and Darrow would serve on the defense team. Other attorneys who represented Scopes were Arthur Garfield Hays (a leading ACLU attorney), John Randolph Neal (a Tennessean expert in constitutional law, who led the defense team), and Dudley Field Malone (a brilliant defense counsel who delivered some of the most incisive and eloquent speeches in the trial). The ACLU, advised by such astute legal minds as Felix Frankfurter, was concerned that Malone, a divorced man, and Darrow, an agnostic, would hinder Scopes's defense before a jury composed of Dayton townsfolk.

Darrow proposed to stop the Scopes trial and challenge the constitutionality of the law in federal court; Scopes agreed. Neal vetoed Darrow's plan, much to the relief of Daytonians, who feared that their day in the sun would be denied them. Darrow was rightly concerned that the trial judge, John Raulston, would rule evidence of the statute's absurdity inadmissible. Indeed, Bryan had already noted that the prosecution could win its case quickly if the only issue became whether or not Scopes had taught evolution.

The days preceding the opening of the trial were marked by an influx and milling about of reporters, newsreel camera crews, revivalists, rusticating urbanites, farmers gawking at the city slickers, and hucksters selling everything from biology texts and religious treatises to hot dogs and lemonade. There were a hundred or more newspapermen, and Western Union was kept busy even with the twenty-one operators who worked at telegraphs installed in a makeshift office. Among the reporters was H. L. Mencken, the sage of Baltimore, for whose caustic wit the prejudices of what he dubbed the "Bible Belt" were an easy target. It was an unpleasantly hot July, and the cast of characters tried to gain relief from the suffocating heat as best they could. Bryan strolled around town wearing a short sleeve pongee shirt and pith helmet, fanning himself with a palm frond and eating a bunch of radishes. The national press described Dayton as if it were a stage set for a comic opera, and indeed the scene did belie the seriousness of the issues that were to be brought before the bar.

Judge Raulston set the tone for the proceedings by conferring upon the attorneys present the honorific titles of General, Colonel, or Captain. He also did not hide the fact that his sentiments lay with the God-fearing Tennesseans who would vote on his reelection the following year. The court proceedings were opened with a lengthy invocation, punctuated with "amens." The atmosphere of the trial was an extension of the one that had been established outside the courthouse. Judge Raulston and the trial's cast of characters were aware that they were on stage, and what was said at the trial would shape a perception of fundamentalism and the rural South as much as it would reflect upon Northern urban industrialism, modernist religious views, and faith in science.

From the beginning, the defense and the prosecution, though agreed on the dramatic potential of the trial, had quite different interpretations of the case. The prosecution insisted that the reasonableness of the law and the truth or falsehood of evolutionary theory were irrelevant. The state of Tennessee had exercised its right to regulate the nature of public education; the legislature and Governor had spoken on behalf of the people; and it was not for science or the federal government to interfere. Essentially, the prosecution asserted the right of a state to cultural autonomy. It was for the legislature to decide what was good or bad for the students of Tennessee's public schools and colleges. The defense, on the other hand, wished to show that the law not only was unconstitutional, but also flew in the face of accepted scientific knowledge. Therefore, the defense brought to Dayton a battery of witnesses who were to testify to the objective truth of evolutionary doctrine. The defense would also play heavily on the theme that religious prejudice and fear, rather than concern for the welfare of the state's youth, underlay the passage of the Butler Act.

John Neal argued for the defense that the statute violated the Fourteenth Amendment's protection against the establishment of religion. Ben McKenzie, one of the prosecuting attorneys, responded that the Butler Act protected the people from the establishment of religion, because it disallowed teaching a doctrine that was antithetical to religion. "We cannot teach any religion in the schools, therefore you cannot teach any evolution, or any doctrine that conflicts with the Bible." But why, asked Neal of the prosecution's "General" Stewart, did the act prefer the Bible to the Koran? Because "We are not living in a heathen country," came McKenzie's confident response.

When Darrow rose to speak, it was to establish the philosophy of the defense with the verbal pyrotechnics for which he had become famous. He quickly warmed to his task and concluded with an emotional peroration in which he predicted that the Butler Act would

be followed by more "ignorance and fanaticism." "After a while, your Honor, it is the setting of man against man and creed against creed, until with flying banners and beating drums we are marching backward to the glorious ages of the sixteenth century, when bigots lighted fagots to burn the men who dared to bring any intelligence and enlightenment and culture to the human mind."

The defense had brought to Dayton an array of experts to affirm the validity of evolutionary doctrine. The prosecution was immediately opposed to the idea; it saw the damage it could do, if not to their case against Scopes, then certainly to the public perception of the broader contest between religion and science. Argued Bryan: "It is not a mock trial; this is not a convocation brought here to allow men to come and stand for a time in the limelight and to speak to the world from the platform at Dayton." Scientific fact, the prosecution maintained, could not overturn the legislature's judgment that evolutionary theory would adversely affect the piety of the state's youth. The belief in an inerrant Bible belonged to an entirely different order of knowledge; more than a religious doctrine, it was a basis of cultural conservatism, communicated and supported by the families and communities of the rural South. If anyone doubted that a child's schooling might affect his moral judgment, Bryan reminded the jury of Darrow's recent defense of Leopold and Loeb, the Chicago youths responsible for the brutal and irrational murder of another youth in Chicago. In pleading that the convicted murderers' lives be spared, Darrow had argued that Leopold's study of Nietzsche's nihilistic philosophy had numbed his moral sensibilities. If education can so affect one, should not the state of Tennessee have the right to legislate against education it believes will adversely affect its citizens?

From the defense's point of view, calling witnesses to testify to the scientific validity of evolutionary fact and theory was crucial, for if evolution is a legitimate scientific finding, it should unquestionably be taught. This is, however, a very difficult position to defend in a court of law, unless there is some prior agreement on the role of science. Without such agreement, the defense needed to argue what was by the 1920s a

Clarence Darrow, left, and William Jennings Bryan chat during the Scopes Trial in Dayton, Tennessee. The famous 1925 trial was a stage for controversy as scientific law was pitted against the law of the Bible. *Associated Press.*

foregone conclusion to most of the developed world: that the dissemination of scientific fact and theory is of the utmost cultural value. Malone articulated this value with an encomium of truth, which the audience rewarded with sustained applause: "There is never a duel with the truth. The truth always wins and we are not afraid of it. The truth is no coward. The truth does not need the law. The truth does not need the forces of government. The truth does not need Mr. Bryan. The truth is imperishable, eternal and immortal and needs no human agency to support it. We are ready to tell the truth as we understand it and we do not fear all the truth that they can present as facts. We are ready. We are ready. We feel we stand with progress. We feel we stand with science. We feel we stand with intelligence. We feel we stand with funda-

mental freedom in America." (Malone's fervent pronouncements were cheered by Dayton's citizens, and the usually silent reporters gave him a standing ovation.) Despite his impassioned appeal, the judge ruled against the defense, which nevertheless managed to persuade the prosecution to allow the written statements of their experts to be entered into the trial transcript, so that they might be used on appeal.

The climax of the trial is well remembered, not only because of the reporting of journalists like Mencken but also because of the trial's fictional representation in *Inherit the Wind*, a successful Broadway play and movie about the trial. Frustrated that he could not introduce the witnesses he had assembled on behalf of evolution, Darrow cagily called Bryan to the stand. What followed was a humiliating exercise for Bryan, who was ill-prepared for Darrow's adroit cross-examination. (Bryan expected to reveal the inadequacies of Darwinism; instead, Darrow cast him in the role of apologist for biblical literalism, a doctrine that Bryan himself questioned.) The effect of the questioning was cumulative. To show the unreasonableness of Bryan's commitment to the idea that the Bible was the revealed word of God, Darrow challenged Bryan to defend the literal truth of one biblical parable after the next. Darrow questioned Bryan about the story of Jonah and the whale; about Joshua, said to make the sun stand still; about the date of the Great Flood; about the Tower of Babel; about the story of creation; and about Adam and Eve.

The cross-examination was frequently acrimonious on both sides. At one point, Darrow referred to Bryan's "fool religion," and later stated flatly that the purpose of the defense was to prevent "bigots and ignoramuses from controlling the education of the United States," while Bryan declared that his purpose was "to protect the Word of God against the greatest atheist or agnostic in the United States." On the next day the judge expunged Bryan's testimony from the record; he concluded that, like the testimony of scientific experts to the truth of evolutionary theory, Bryan's testimony regarding the validity of the Bible was not relevant. Although Judge Raulston's decision to expunge Bryan's testimony made it impossible for Bryan to question Darrow in court, as was originally planned, a brief but pointless cross-examination occurred after the trial for the benefit of the press. Bryan simply established for the record what everyone already knew: Darrow was an agnostic. Bryan did not succeed in reclaiming his lost pride. Shaken by his embarrassment at the trial, he died a few days later.

The defense wished to see the case come before a Tennessee appellate court and, with luck, the U.S. Supreme Court, so there was no objection to the jury's guilty verdict. A year elapsed, briefs were filed, and finally Darrow and other defense lawyers presented oral arguments for the appeal before the Tennessee Supreme Court. A majority of that court upheld the Butler Act, reversed the decision of the lower court on a technicality, and proposed that the indictment be dropped. The result was that Scopes was not retried, and the defense lost the basis for a further appeal to the U.S. Supreme Court.

Dayton, Tennessee, was the site of William Jennings Bryan's last hurrah and, despite his failure to win a victory for religious fundamentalism, it is probable that his performance, and indeed his suffering, helped deepen the commitments of many religious fundamentalists. On the other hand, those who did not accept fundamentalism had been confirmed in their belief that the claims of biblical literalists were irreconcilable with the scientific and technological culture that the government had tried to legislate out of existence.

Selected Bibliography

Conkin, P. J. *When All the Gods Trembled: Darwinism, Scopes and American Intellectuals*. Lanham, MD: Rowan & Littlefield, 1998.

Gilbert, J. *Redeeming Culture: American Religion in an Age of Science*. Chicago, IL: University of Chicago Press, 1997.

Ginger, R. *Six Days or Forever*. Boston, MA: Beacon Press, 1958.

Hofstadter, R. *Anti-Intellectualism in American Life*. New York, NY: Alfred Knopf, 1962.

Larson, E. J. *Summer for the Gods: The Scopes Trial*. New York, NY: Basic Books, 1997.

The Flag Salute Cases

—◄○►—

Paul Finkelman
College of Law
University of Tulsa

Minersville School District Board of Education, et al. v. Gobitis et al., 310 U.S. 586 (1940)
and *West Virginia State Board of Education, etc. et al., Appellants v. Walter Barnette,*
Paul Stull and Lucy McClure, 319 U.S. 624 (1943) [U.S. Supreme Court]

◄○► THE CASE IN BRIEF ◄○►

Date
1940, 1943

Location
Pennsylvania; West Virginia

Court
U.S. Supreme Court

Principal Participants
Lillian and William Gobitis; Walter Barnette; Paul Stull; Lucy McClure

Significance of the Cases
The constitutionality of a state requirement of public school students to salute the flag was tested in two Supreme Court cases. One decision upheld a school district's right to force children to salute the flag, and the other overruled the state's right to do so, citing obstruction of personal liberties.

These cases, commonly referred to as the Flag Salute Cases, are among the most peculiar in American constitutional history. At issue in both cases was the right of a state to require public school students to salute the flag and say the Pledge of Allegiance. The plaintiffs in both cases were Jehovah's Witnesses who refused to participate in flag ceremonies because such acts violated their religious precepts. In the first case, *Minersville School District v. Gobitis* (1940), the Supreme Court upheld the school district's attempt to force students to salute the flag. In *West Virginia State Board of Education v. Barnette* (1943) the Court reversed course, siding with the claims of religious freedom made by the Jehovah's Witnesses.

These cases must be understood in the light of the evolution of the Jehovah's Witness faith, the emergence of a "Roosevelt Court," and the issues of patriotism and national unity surrounding American entrance into World War II.

The origins of the Jehovah's Witnesses are found in the Adventist bodies and ideas of the mid-nineteenth century. The Jehovah's Witness movement (members of the faith are emphatic

947

that it is not a "church") began in the 1870s under the leadership of Charles Taze Russell, but did not become widespread until the 1920s and 1930s, when Joseph F. Rutherford was the head of the movement. Rutherford organized a proselytizing movement which was aggressively millennial in outlook. The Jehovah's Witnesses publicly bear "witness" against what they believe are the three major allies of Satan: the "false" teachings of most other churches and the Catholic Church in particular, human government, and capitalism and business.

The proselytizing of the Jehovah's Witnesses, and their anti-Catholic rhetoric, first brought members of the faith before the Supreme Court in *Cantwell v. Connecticut* (1940). There the Court affirmed the right of the Jehovah's Witnesses to publicly proselytize, even though their actions bothered many people in a particular neighborhood. However, in subsequent cases the Supreme Court upheld the right of localities to require permits and licenses for Witnesses who held public marches or distributed or sold religious literature.

In addition to denouncing "false" churches, members of the faith denounce patriotic exercises. Starting in 1935, Jehovah's Witnesses in the United States refused to salute the flag, asserting that it violated the biblical injunction against worshiping graven images. This meant that Jehovah's Witnesses' children refused to salute the flag in public schools.

Their aggressive proselytizing, their heated denunciations of other faiths, and their uncompromising stands on scriptural interpretation made the Jehovah's Witnesses one of the most unpopular religious minorities in the nation. Their hostility to political authority and their refusal to salute the flag further alienated them from mainstream America and from political and police officials. This set the stage for the Flag Salute Cases.

The first case, *Minersville School District v. Gobitis*, resulted from the refusal of twelve-year-old Lillian Gobitis and her ten-year-old brother William to say the Pledge of Allegiance in the public schools of Minersville, Pennsylvania. Their father, Walter Gobitis, had grown up in Minersville, was raised in a Roman Catholic family, and, of course, saluted the flag as a child.

In 1931, Gobitis became a Jehovah's Witness. At the time, Lillian was eight and William was six. The Gobitis children continued to salute the flag until November 1935. In 1935 Jehovah's Witnesses in Germany refused to salute the Nazi flag. Ultimately, more than ten thousand German Jehovah's Witnesses would be sent to concentration camps for their affront to Nazi authorities. In 1935 the leader of the Jehovah's Witnesses in America declared that followers of the faith "do not 'Heil Hitler' nor any other creature." After this speech American Jehovah's Witnesses refused to take part in saluting the flag.

In a more cosmopolitan community, the refusal of the Gobitis children to salute the flag might have gone unnoticed. But neither Gobitis nor his faith was popular in Minersville, where 80 percent of the population was Roman Catholic. Rather than ignoring what was neither an act of defiance nor a disruption in the schools, School Superintendent Charles E. Roudabush took actions which eventually brought the school board and the Gobitis family before the Supreme Court.

After consulting the Pennsylvania Department of Public Instruction, the school board adopted a regulation allowing for the expulsion of any students who would not salute the flag. Superintendent Roudabush immediately expelled the Gobitis children and one other sixth grader who was a Jehovah's Witness. Gobitis then sent his children to a private Jehovah's Witness school.

Eighteen months later Gobitis filed a suit against the school district in federal district court. The case was first heard by Judge Albert B. Maris, a recent Roosevelt appointee to the federal court. As a Quaker, Maris was probably more sympathetic to the Jehovah's Witnesses than most Americans. Although he had a distinguished military record during World War I, as a member of a faith long persecuted for its pacifism, Maris doubtless understood the nature of prejudice and religious persecution that the Jehovah's Witnesses faced.

During the trial Superintendent Roudabush was openly hostile toward the Gobitis children and the Jehovah's Witnesses. He asserted that the children were "indoctrinated," thereby implying that their actions were not based on sincerely held religious beliefs. Judge Maris rejected Roudabush's contentions, asserting that "To permit public officers to determine whether the views of individuals sincerely held and their acts sincerely undertaken on religious grounds are in fact based on convictions religious in character would sound the death knell of religious liberty." Maris refused to sustain "such a pernicious and alien doctrine." He reminded the school officials that Pennsylvania itself had been founded "as a haven for all those persecuted for conscience' sake."

Judge Maris believed that the acts of these children "could not in any way prejudice or imperil the safety, health or morals, or the property or personal rights" of the other students in Minersville. After Roudabush's hostile testimony, Maris found that "although undoubtedly adopted from patriotic motives," the flag salute requirement "appears to have become in this case a means for the persecution of children for conscience' sake." Such persecution, the judge stated, is not permissible in a free society.

Finally, Maris noted that "religious intolerance is again rearing its ugly head in other parts of the world," and thus it was of "utmost importance that the liberties guaranteed to our citizens by the fundamental law be preserved from all encroachment." Though not central to his decision, Maris's point placed the controversy over the Jehovah's Witnesses in the context of the rise of Nazism, preparation for World War II, and eventually American involvement in the war. In part, the cases involving the Jehovah's Witnesses raised important questions about how much dissent a democracy can allow at a time of crisis and international conflict. Maris took the position that such dissent was vital to the democracy and part of its ultimate strength. The Minersville school board took the position that national unity required submission to the will of the majority, especially on issues involving outward displays of patriotism. This argument would reemerge among the justices of the Supreme Court in both *Gobitis* and *Barnette*.

Having concluded that the flag salute requirement was motivated by a desire to provide "a means for the persecution of children

for conscience' sake," Judge Maris ordered the children readmitted to the public schools, but then stayed the order pending an appeal to the U.S. Court of Appeals. Eighteen months later a unanimous three-judge panel upheld Maris. By this time many other states had begun to prosecute Jehovah's Witnesses for their refusal to salute the flag. In his opinion, Court of Appeals Judge William S. Clark denounced the "eighteen big states" which "have seen fit to exert their power over a number (at least 120 nationwide) of little children" who sought to worship God in their own way and also to attend the public schools. Judge Clark also tied the controversy to the war against Nazism in Europe by quoting, in a footnote, Adolf Hitler's 1935 declaration dissolving the Jehovah's Witnesses in Germany and confiscating their property. Clark also argued that refusing to salute the flag created no "clear and present danger" to the government, and thus the religious freedom of the children should be protected.

Initially the Minersville school officials did not plan to appeal to the Supreme Court. Such an appeal cost more than this rural school district cared to spend. But patriotic groups, including the American Legion, stepped in to help finance the appeal. Before the Supreme Court, Harvard Law School professor George K. Gardner argued Gobitis's case on behalf of the American Civil Liberties Union. He was joined by the national leader of the Jehovah's Witnesses, Joseph Rutherford, who was also an attorney and had once been a judge in Missouri. Joseph W. Henderson, a Philadelphia lawyer, represented the school board, as he had in the lower courts.

In an 8-1 decision, the Supreme Court reversed the two lower court decisions and upheld the right of the Minersville School District to require that students salute the flag. Writing for the Court was Justice Felix Frankfurter, a former Harvard Law School professor and liberal activist recently appointed by President Roosevelt. Frankfurter was a Jewish immigrant from Austria. From his background one might assume that he would have responded favorably to those who were persecuted for their religious beliefs and who, at that very moment, were facing death alongside the Jews in

Germany, Austria, and elsewhere in Europe. However, when Frankfurter joined the Court, he adopted the credo of a self-restrainer and put aside many of his liberal sympathies and sensitivities to the plight of minorities.

Frankfurter conceded that "the affirmative pursuit of one's convictions about the ultimate mystery of the universe and man's relation to it is placed beyond the reach of law. Government may not interfere with organized or individual expression of belief or disbelief." However, Frankfurter noted that there were no absolute guarantees of religious freedom. He found that the task of the Court was to "reconcile two rights in order to prevent either from destroying the other." He found that "conscientious scruples have not, in the course of the long struggle for religious toleration, relieved the individual from obedience to a general law not aimed at the promotion or restriction of religious beliefs. The mere possession of religious convictions which contradict the relevant concerns of a political society does not relieve the citizen from a discharge of political responsibilities." Put simply, Frankfurter was arguing that the First Amendment's guarantee of religious freedom extended only to protection from laws that were overtly religious in nature. He rejected the findings of the lower court that the enforcement of the pledge was overt religious discrimination.

In an analogy, Frankfurter compared the dilemma of the Jehovah's Witnesses to that of Lincoln's query during the Civil War: "Must a government of necessity be too *strong* for the liberties of its people, or too *weak* to maintain its own existence?" Frankfurter argued that the flag was a "symbol of national unity, transcending all internal differences" and implied that, as such, failure to salute it somehow threatened the existence of the nation.

He further argued that the states should be given great latitude in determining how best to instill patriotism in children. He argued that the state was doing no more than "asserting . . . the right to awaken in the child's mind considerations as to the significance of the flag contrary to those implanted by the parent." This, he thought, was constitutionally permissible. He ended by noting that judicial review was "a limitation on popular government" which

should be used sparingly. He urged that issues of liberty be fought out in the state legislatures and "in the forum of public opinion" in order to "vindicate the self-confidence of a free people."

Justice Harlan Fiske Stone dissented, asserting that "by this law the state seeks to coerce these children to express a sentiment which, as they interpret it, they do not entertain, and which violates their deepest religious convictions." Stone dismissed Frankfurter's appeals to patriotism and his suggestion that the issue be decided "in the forum of public opinion" by appeals to the wisdom of the legislature. Stone pointed out that "History teaches us that there have been but few infringements of personal liberty by the state which have not been justified, as they are here, in the name of righteousness and the public good, and few which have not been directed, as they are now, at politically helpless minorities." Finally, Stone argued that the Constitution was more than just an outline for majoritarian government; it was "also an expression of faith and a command that freedom of mind and spirit must be preserved, which government must obey, if it is to adhere to that justice and moderation without which no free government can exist."

Stone understood the value of instilling patriotism in future citizens. He declared that the state might "require teaching by instruction and study of all in our history and in the structure and organization of our government, including the guarantee of civil liberty, which tend to inspire patriotism and love of country." But forcing children to violate their religious precepts was, in Stone's mind, not the way to teach patriotic values. He thought it far better that the schools find "some sensible adjustment of school discipline in order that the religious convictions of these children may be spared" than to approve "legislation which operates to repress the religious freedom of small minorities."

The *Gobitis* decision helped unleash a wave of political, legal, and physical attacks on Jehovah's Witnesses. Immediately following the decision there were hundreds of assaults on Jehovah's Witnesses and their property. In Kennebunk, Maine, a Jehovah's Witnesses temple was burned; in Maryland the police helped a mob break up a Jehovah's Witnesses meeting; in Illinois, Texas, Arkansas, West Virginia, Wyoming, Oregon, Kentucky, New Hampshire, New Jersey, Pennsylvania, Mississippi, Louisiana, and Nebraska, Jehovah's Witnesses were beaten, mobbed, and kidnapped. Their attackers often included police officials. In Odessa, Texas, for example, seventy Jehovah's Witnesses were arrested for their own "protection," held without charges when they refused to salute the flag, and then released to a mob of over a thousand people which chased them for five miles, throwing stones at them. In Wyoming some Jehovah's Witnesses were tarred and feathered, in Arkansas some were shot, and in Nebraska one Jehovah's Witness was castrated.

Besides mob violence, the Jehovah's Witnesses faced official violence and persecution. Throughout the country Jehovah's Witnesses were arrested and incarcerated without charges or on bogus charges. Sometimes the police tortured them. In Richwood, West Virginia, the police arrested a group of Jehovah's Witnesses who sought police protection, forced them to drink large amounts of castor oil, tied them up, and paraded them through the town.

The nation's legislatures and school boards responded to *Gobitis* by adopting strict flag salute requirements. By 1943 over two thousand Jehovah's Witnesses had been expelled from schools in all forty-eight states. This was the nationwide answer to Justice Frankfurter's suggestion that the Jehovah's Witnesses appeal to the state legislatures for relief.

The nation's intellectual community responded to *Gobitis* in quite a different way. Overwhelmingly, law review articles condemned the decision. The law reviews at Catholic universities, such as Fordham, Georgetown, and Notre Dame, were unanimous in their opposition to *Gobitis,* even though the Jehovah's Witnesses had traditionally vilified the Roman Catholic Church. But the issue here was civil liberties, not theology, as Catholic scholars clearly understood.

Members of the Supreme Court soon came to doubt the wisdom of *Gobitis.* In *Jones v. Opelika* (1942), the Court affirmed the convictions of Jehovah's Witnesses for distributing their pamphlets without proper licenses from towns in Alabama, Arkansas, and Arizona. The laws in question were similar to other repressive laws passed in the wake of *Gobitis.* Significantly, however, this decision was not decided by the overwhelming 8-1 vote of *Gobitis.* In this case four justices dissented, arguing that the statutes unconstitutionally restricted freedom of the press, freedom of speech, and the free exercise of religion. One of the dissenters was Justice Stone, recently promoted to Chief Justice. Also dissenting were three members of the *Gobitis* majority: Justices Frank Murphy, William O. Douglas, and Hugo Black. They specifically concurred in Stone's dissent and in a longer dissent written by Murphy. Finally, they concurred in an exceedingly short dissent by Black, which was designed to make only one simple point. Black wrote: "Since we joined in the opinion in the *Gobitis* Case, we think this is an appropriate occasion to state that we now believe that it was also wrongly decided. Certainly our democratic form of government functioning under the historic Bill of Rights has a high responsibility to accommodate itself to the religious views of minorities however unpopular and unorthodox those views may be. The First Amendment does not put the right freely to exercise religion in a subordinate position. We fear, however, that the opinions in these [*Jones v. Opelika* and its two companion cases] and in the Gobitis Case do exactly that."

Equally important, the majority opinion in *Jones v. Opelika* conspicuously failed to rely on *Gobitis* for its result. This was probably because the recently appointed Justice Robert Jackson, one of the majority justices, did not disagree with the reasoning and result in *Gobitis.* Just as *Gobitis* has served as an invitation for the states to suppress the Jehovah's Witnesses, so the dissents in *Jones v. Opelika,* combined with the failure of the majority to cite *Gobitis,* served as an invitation for a challenge to that recent precedent.

The final step before a reversal of *Gobitis* was a change in the membership of the Court. In October 1942 Justice James F. Byrnes, one of the majority in *Opelika,* resigned. In February 1943, District Judge Wiley Rutledge, a former dean of the Iowa State University Law School, joined the Court. On the district court Rutledge had dissented in a case very similar to *Opelika*. His dissent there seemed to indicate that he would favor overturning *Gobitis*. It now appeared that a majority of the Court—either five or six judges—wished to overturn *Gobitis*. All that was lacking was a test case to bring the issue back to the Supreme Court.

That case emerged quickly. In January 1942 the West Virginia State School Board adopted a strict flag salute requirement. The board's resolution, which had the authority of a statute, began with a long preamble which quoted at length portions of Frankfurter's *Gobitis* opinion. The resolution ended by declaring "that refusal to salute the Flag [shall] be regarded as an act of insubordination, and shall be dealt with accordingly." Shortly after the adoption of this resolution, school officials in Charleston expelled a number of Jehovah's Witnesses, including the children of Walter Barnette.

In August 1942, two months after the decision in *Jones v. Opelika*, attorneys for Barnette and other Jehovah's Witnesses asked the district court to convene a three-judge panel to permanently enjoin state school officials from requiring Jehovah's Witnesses to salute the flag.

Writing for a unanimous court, Judge John J. Parker, of the Fourth Circuit Court of Appeals, granted the injunction. Parker acknowledged that "ordinarily" the lower court would "feel constrained to follow an unreversed decision of the Supreme Court of the United States, whether we agreed with it or not." Indeed, not to do so threatened "the orderly administration of justice." However, in the light of the dissents in *Opelika*, Parker expressed doubt that *Gobitis* was still binding. He noted that three justices had explicitly announced their disagreement with *Gobitis* and also that the majority opinion "thought it worth while to distinguish the decision in the *Gobitis* case, instead of relying upon it as supporting authority." Because the three-judge panel believed that the West Virginia flag salute requirement was "violative of religious liberty when required of persons holding the religious views of the plaintiffs," Parker declared that the panel members would be "recreant to our duty as judges, if through a blind following of a decision which the Supreme Court itself has thus impaired as an authority, we should deny pro-

tection to rights which we regard as among the most sacred of those protected by constitutional guaranties."

In the rest of his opinion Parker made three important points. First, he noted that the flag salute controversy had become another episode in the history of religious persecution, and those who defended it differed little from past persecutors: "There is not a religious persecution in history that was not justified in the eyes of those engaging in it on the ground that it was reasonable and right and that the persons whose practices were suppressed were guilty of stubborn folly hurtful of the general welfare."

Second, he noted that religious freedom had its limits. "He (who belongs to the minority religion) must render to Caesar the things that are Caesar's as well as to God the things that are God's. He may not refuse to bear arms or pay taxes because of religious scruples, nor may he engage in polygamy or any other practice directly hurtful to the safety, morals, health or general welfare of the community."

Finally, he answered Frankfurter's point in his *Gobitis* opinion that the courts should show deference to the state legislatures. He argued that the "suggestion that the courts are precluded by the action of state legislative authorities in deciding when rights of religious freedom must yield to the exercise of a police power would of course nullify the constitutional guarantee." Indeed, the guarantee of religious freedom "would not be worth the paper it is written on if no legislature or school board were bound to respect it except in so far as it might . . . choose" to respect it. If the courts were "to abdicate the most important duty which rests on them," then the "tyranny of majorities over the rights of individuals or helpless minorities" would continue to be "one of the great dangers of popular government."

The appeals court found that to "force" someone to salute the flag "is petty tyranny unworthy of the spirit of this Republic." It was a spirit the three-judge panel would not support; thus the judges granted the injunction and, for the most part, West Virginia authorities obeyed. No more Jehovah's Witnesses were expelled from the schools, and the children of Walter Barnette returned to their classes. Meanwhile, the West Virginia Board of Education voted to appeal the case over the advice of their attorney, Ira J. Partlow. By the time the case reached the Supreme Court, Partlow had become the state's acting attorney general. He refused to argue the appeal, and could find no one in his office willing to take the case. Ultimately Partlow brought in outside counsel.

Before the Supreme Court the attorney for the West Virginia Board of Education offered an unimaginative argument that relied almost entirely on *Gobitis*. His brief was supported by a weak amicus curiae brief from the American Legion. Attorneys for Barnette attacked *Gobitis*, comparing it to the *Dred Scott* decision of 1857. Amicus briefs for Barnette came from the American Civil Liberties Union, written by Osmond K. Fraenkel and Arthur Garfield Hays, and the American Bar Association's Committee on the Bill of Rights, written by Harvard Law professor Zechariah Chafee, Jr.

On June 14, 1943, Flag Day, the Court announced its opinion, upholding the lower court and reversing the precedent in *Gobitis*. Justice Jackson wrote for the six judge-majority, and Justice Frankfurter wrote a bitter dissent.

Though the Flag Salute Cases are generally seen as involving freedom of religion, that issue is virtually absent from Jackson's majority opinion. He accepted, without question, that the Jehovah's Witnesses sincerely held beliefs which made it impossible for them to conscientiously salute the flag. But Jackson did not offer any analysis of the importance of that belief or even of the role of religious freedom in striking down the mandatory flag salute. Instead, he linked the freedom to worship with other Bill of Rights protections, noting that the "right to life, liberty, and property, to free speech, a free press, freedom of worship and assembly, and other fundamental rights may not be submitted to vote; they depend on the outcome of no elections." He found that the "freedoms of speech and of press, of assembly, and of worship may not be infringed" on "slender grounds."

Rather than grounding his opinion in terms of freedom of religion, Jackson analyzed the case as one of freedom of speech and expression. He argued that the flag salute—or the refusal to salute the flag—was "a form of utter-

ance," and thus subject to standard free speech analysis. He noted that the flag was a political symbol and, naturally, saluting that symbol was symbolic speech: "Symbolism is a primitive but effective way of communicating ideas. The use of an emblem or flag to symbolize some system, idea, institution, or personality, is a short cut from mind to mind. Causes and nations, political parties, lodges and ecclesiastical groups seek to knit the loyalty of their followings to a flag or banner, a color or design. The State announces rank, function, and authority through crowns and maces, uniforms and black robes; the church speaks through the Cross, the Crucifix, the altar and shrine, and clerical raiment. Symbols of the State often convey political ideas just as religious symbols come to convey theological ones."

The question for Jackson was rather simple: Did the "speech" of the Jehovah's Witnesses threaten the rights of any individuals or the peace and stability of the government? If the answer to either question was yes, then Jackson might have allowed the mandatory flag salute. But if they did not threaten the rights of others or threaten the government, then there was no valid reason to suppress their expression.

Jackson noted that the conduct of the Jehovah's Witnesses "did not bring them into collision with rights asserted by any other individuals." The Court was not being asked "to determine where the rights of one end and another begin." It was, rather, a conflict "between (governmental) authority and rights of the individual."

Jackson compared the forced flag salute to *Stromberg v. California*, the Supreme Court's 1931 decision which had allowed protestors to raise a red flag. This case and others supported the "commonplace" standard in free speech cases "that censorship or suppression of expression of opinion is tolerated by our Constitution only when the expression presents a clear and present danger of action of a kind the state is empowered to prevent and publish. It would seem that involuntary affirmation could be commanded only on even more immediate and urgent grounds than silence." But were there such grounds? No one claimed that the silence of the children "during a flag salute ritual creates a clear and present danger that would justify an effort even to muffle expression." Jackson pointed out the irony of the flag salute requirement, in light of the expanded freedom of speech found in recent decisions: "To sustain the compulsory flag salute we are required to say that a Bill of Rights which guards the individual's right to speak his own mind, left it open to public authorities to compel him to utter what is not in his mind."

Jackson's shrewd analysis had turned the case inside out. It was no longer one of freedom of religion, but one that in part took the form of an establishment of religion on the part of the government through its "flag salute ritual." Jackson correctly saw that the Jehovah's Witnesses were not trying to force their views on anyone else, but rather, that the government was trying to force its views and beliefs on the Jehovah's Witnesses. He noted that in *Gobitis* the Court had "only examined and rejected a claim based on religious beliefs of immunity from general rule." But, Jackson pointed out, this was not the correct question to ask. Indeed, Jackson noted that people who did not hold the religious views of the Jehovah's Witnesses might still find "such a compulsory rite to infringe constitutional liberty of the individual." For Jackson the correct question was "whether such a ceremony so touching matters of opinion and political attitude may be imposed upon the individual by official authority . . . under the Constitution." In other words, did the government have the power to force anyone, regardless of his or her religious beliefs, to participate in any ceremony or "ritual"? What Jackson asked was whether the Constitution allowed for the establishment of a secular national religion with the flag as the chief icon. This led him to a discussion, and refutation, of various points in *Gobitis*.

In *Gobitis*, Frankfurter had quoted Lincoln's "memorable dilemma" of choosing between civil liberties and maintaining a free society. Jackson had little patience for "such oversimplification, so handy in political debate." He "doubted whether Mr. Lincoln would have thought that the strength of government to maintain itself would be impressively vindicated by our confirming power of the state to expel a handful of children from school." Here Jackson revealed the fundamental weakness of Frankfurter's assertion in *Gobitis*: that somehow the safety of the nation depended on whether Jehovah's Witnesses were forced to salute the flag in the public schools.

Along this line Jackson noted that Congress had made the flag salute optional for soldiers who had religious scruples against such ceremonies. This act, "respecting the conscience of the objector in a matter so vital as raising the Army," contrasted "sharply with these local regulations in matters relatively trivial to the welfare of the nation."

This led Jackson to the national security issue raised by Frankfurter in *Gobitis*. At the time of *Gobitis* the nation was not at war, but war seemed imminent. By the time of *Barnette* the nation had been at war for over a year. Jackson agreed that in wartime "national unity" was necessary and something the government should "foster by persuasion and example." But could the government gain national unity by force? Jackson made references to the suppression of the early Christians in Rome, the Inquisition, "the Siberian exiles as a means of Russian unity," and the "fast failing efforts of our present totalitarian enemies." He warned that "those who begin coercive elimination of dissent soon find themselves exterminating the dissenters. Compulsory unification of opinion achieves only the unanimity of the graveyard." During a war against Nazism, Jackson's opinion was a plea for the nation to avoid becoming like its enemies.

Jackson ended his opinion by reminding Americans that the patriotism in a free country could not be instilled by force. Indeed, he argued that those who thought otherwise "make an unflattering estimate of the appeal of our institutions to free minds." America's strength, he stated, was found in diversity. The test of freedom was "the right to differ as to things that touch the heart of the existing order." This led Jackson to a ringing defense of individual liberty: "If there is any fixed star in our constitutional constellation, it is that no official, high or petty, can prescribe what shall be orthodox in politics, nationalism, religion, or other matters of opinion or force citizens to confess by word or act their faith therein."

Justice Felix Frankfurter was unmoved by Jackson's powerful defense of individual liberty and his condemnation of oppressive "village tyrants" who expelled small children from school because of their religious beliefs.

At a time when millions of Jews (and thousands of Jehovah's Witnesses) were perishing in German death camps, Frankfurter used his ethnicity to justify his support for the suppression of a religious minority in the United States. He began: "One who belongs to the most vilified and persecuted minority in history is not likely to be insensible to the freedoms guaranteed by our Constitution." But he argued that he could not bring his personal beliefs to the Court because "as judges we are neither Jew nor Gentile, neither Catholic nor agnostic." He then defended judicial self-restraint and recapitulated and elaborated on his *Gobitis* opinion.

Frankfurter argued that "saluting the flag suppresses no belief nor curbs it" because those saluting it were still free to "believe what they please, avow their belief and practice it." In making this point Frankfurter failed to explain how one could "practice a belief" by doing what that belief prohibited. Nor did he explain how forcing children to say and do one thing, while encouraging them to secretly believe that what they were doing was a violation of God's commandments, would inspire patriotism in them.

Frankfurter conceded that the flag salute law "may be a foolish measure," and that "patriotism cannot be enforced by the flag salute." But he argued that the Court had no business interfering with laws made by democratically elected legislatures. Because a total of thirteen justices had found the flag salute laws to be constitutional, the state laws "can not be deemed unreasonable." Because the state legislators had relied upon the recent decision in *Gobitis*, Frankfurter felt it unfair to strike down their legislation.

Frankfurter condemned "our constant preoccupation with the constitutionality of legislation rather than with its wisdom." Yet he refused to strike down the West Virginia law, which he conceded was unwise, not because it

passed all constitutional tests but because of judicial restraint and respect for stare decisis ("let the decision stand"). He argued that the "most precious interests of civilization" were to be "found outside of their vindication in courts of law," and thus urged that the Court not interfere in the democratic process but wait for a "positive translation of the faith of a free society into the convictions and habits and actions of the community." What would happen to the Jehovah's Witnesses in the meantime seemed to be of little concern to Frankfurter.

There was minor resistance to *Barnette* in a few localities. The Supreme Court heard a few cases in which various local decisions were overturned. For instance, on the same day it handed down *Barnette*, the Court unanimously overturned a conviction for sedition in *Taylor v. Mississippi* (1943). The Jehovah's Witnesses in that case had been convicted of "violating a statute making it an offense to preach, teach or disseminate any doctrine which reasonably tends to create an attitude of stubborn refusal to salute, honor, or respect the Government of the United States or the State of Mississippi." The defendants had been sentenced to remain in jail until the end of the war or for ten years, whichever came first. The Court found that the act abridged freedom of speech and press, and was "so vague, indefinite, and uncertain as to furnish no reasonably ascertainable standard of guilt." The Mississippi law, and the prosecutions under it, illustrate the extent of official persecution of the Jehovah's Witnesses.

After 1946 the Court heard no more cases on the flag salute issue. *Barnette* became an important precedent for other free speech and freedom of religion cases. However, in 1988 the flag salute issue arose in a new way.

As governor of Massachusetts, Michael Dukakis had vetoed a mandatory flag salute law for public school teachers. In 1988 Dukakis was the Democratic nominee for President. His opponent, George Bush, raised the flag salute veto throughout the campaign, in an attempt to imply that Dukakis was not a true patriot. Initially Dukakis did not respond to Bush's attack. When he did respond, Dukakis did not give a ringing defense of freedom of religion. Instead, he said that he vetoed the bill because the Supreme Judicial Court of Massachusetts, relying on *Barnette* in an advisory opinion, had said the law would be unconstitutional. This answer was legally precise but politically unsatisfactory. And the flag salute issue probably contributed to Dukakis's defeat. During the campaign Bush and his running mate, Dan Quayle, often started campaign rallies with the Pledge of Allegiance. Shortly after Bush and Quayle assumed office, they stopped saluting the flag at all public events.

Selected Bibliography

Irons, Peter. *The Courage of Their Convictions.* New York: The Free Press, 1988.

Manwaring, David. *Render unto Caesar: The Flag Salute Controversy.* Chicago: University of Chicago Press, 1962.

Roenme, Victor W., and G. F. Folsom, Jr. "Recent Restrictions upon Religious Liberty." *American Political Science Review* 36 (1942): 1053–1068.

Religion in the Public School Day: The Released Time Cases

—◄o►—

Frank J. Sorauf

Emeritus Professor of Political Science
University of Minnesota

McCollum v. Board of Education, 333 U.S. 203 (1948) and *Zorach v. Clauson,*
343 U.S. 306 (1952) [U.S. Supreme Court]

◄o► THE CASE IN BRIEF ◄o►

Date
1948, 1952

Location
Illinois
New York

Court
U.S. Supreme Court

Principal Participants
Vashti and James Terry McCollum; Tessim Zorach; Esta Gluck; Champaign Board of Education; Board of Education of the City of New York

Significance of the Cases
Through a series of rapid-fire decisions that set precedents in the constitutional law of church-state relationships, these two cases were landmarks in the Court's rulings on the separation of church and state in public schools.

Supreme Court decisions often outlive the policies and controversies that give rise to them. The Court's decisions in the Released Time Cases, for one example, remain landmark precedents in the constitutional law of church-state relationships even though the released time programs themselves are far less common than they once were.

In many parts of the United States in the years between World War I and World War II, released time programs seemed to many religious groups, primarily Protestants, the answer to an absence of religious training in the country's public schools. The Roman Catholics had their flourishing, full-time parish schools, a system that was the envy of the world's Catholics, but there were relatively few non-Catholic elementary or secondary schools in the United States. For most Protestant and Jewish groups, the Sunday or Sabbath schools were the major vehicles for teaching their young. Released time programs—also called weekday religious education—supplemented those schools; they also integrated religious teaching into the public school week as it was defined by compulsory school attendance laws. Students choosing religious classes were "released" during the regular school day of the public schools to go to religious classes; other students remained in the school.

In virtually all released time programs the religious teaching was done by representatives of the respective religious groups. The religious classes generally lasted approximately an hour a week. Otherwise the programs varied greatly. Some were held in the public schools, whereas others convened in nearby churches or other church buildings. In some the programs were promoted, even urged, by the public school teachers or systems; in others a scrupulous detachment prevailed. In some the apparatus of the public schools administered the programs, whereas in others the religious groups bore the administrative expenses and burdens.

The variety within the released time movement doubtless reflected adaptation to local circumstances and expectations—and thereby helped assure its growth. By the early 1930s released time programs enrolled some 250,000 students, and by the early 1940s enrollment had jumped, according to its supporters, to a million and a half in at least forty states.

Just as the released time movement reached its zenith in the 1940s, the U.S. Supreme Court was beginning its first extended attempt to define the constitutional law of church-state relationships. Under the long-standing doctrine that the Bill of Rights applied only to acts of Congress (a position set down in the 1833 case of *Barron v. Baltimore*), the Court had decided very few church-state cases. Most of the close relationships between church and state that occasioned objections involved state and local governments, and under *Barron* only the state constitutions might limit them. But gradually, in the twentieth century, the Court began to interpret the due process clause of the Fourteenth Amendment to include the various protections of the Bill of Rights, thus applying them against actions by the states. That process of "incorporating" (or "nationalizing") the Bill of Rights reached the two freedom of religion clauses of the First Amendment in 1940 in a case involving local attempts to control proselytizing by the Jehovah's Witnesses, *Cantwell v. Connecticut*.

Cantwell was a general invitation, welcoming issues of the relationship between religion and government to the federal courts. Just seven years later, in a case from New Jersey, *Everson v. Board of Education*, the Court decided its first post-incorporation case involving the First Amendment clause forbidding any law "respecting the establishment of religion." Because it dealt with relationships of help and support for religion by government—rather than with restrictions on religious practices—the establishment clause was the one on which the separation between church and state rested. *Everson* involved New Jersey legislation permitting local school boards to reimburse parents of children attending private schools, including religious schools, for the cost of bus transportation to and from their schools. Ewing Township chose to do so, and several plaintiffs challenged those reimbursements on the grounds that they violated the separation between church and state mandated by the First and the Fourteenth Amendments.

In a 5-4 decision, the Court in *Everson* upheld the reimbursements for bus transportation to religious schools in New Jersey, treating it as a public or social service, much like police or fire protection. The aid went not to religious groups or schools, the majority reasoned, but to the children and their parents. The distinction was quickly tabbed the "child benefit theory." Although ruling in favor of the parents in the case, the majority spelled out a commitment to the separation of church and state couched in absolute language. Interpreting the establishment clause for the first time in the Supreme Court's history, Justice Hugo Black wrote: "Neither a state nor the Federal Government can set up a church. Neither can pass laws which aid one religion, aid all religions, or prefer one religion over another.... No tax in any amount, large or small, can be levied to support any religious activities or institutions, whatever they may be called, or whatever form they may adopt to teach or practice religion.... In the words of Jefferson, the clause against establishment of religion by law was intended to erect a 'wall of separation between Church and State.'... That wall must be kept high and impregnable. We could not approve the slightest breach. New

Jersey has not breached it here." The four-justice minority in the case rejected the distinction between aid to the child and aid to the religious school. Justice Robert Jackson, speaking for the dissenters, had only ridicule for the gulf between the rhetoric and the outcome in the case. The majority reminded him of Byron's feckless Julia, who "whispering 'I will ne'er consent'—consented."

Before the decision in *Everson*, however, a mother of no religious sympathies, Vashti McCollum, rebelled against the released time program in the local schools of Champaign, Illinois. It was, to be sure, a released time program in which the cooperation between the public schools and the religious groups running the classes was particularly close. Schoolteachers and other personnel administered a good deal of the program, and school buildings were used for the religious classes. Moreover, Mrs. McCollum believed her son was under an assortment of pressures to participate in the program, pressures that ranged from a fourth grader's desire to conform to a teacher's campaign to get 100 percent participation in her class. Her resolve to challenge the program, she later wrote, crystallized on the day her son was banished to the school hallway during the religious classes because he was the only student in his grade not attending them.

So, in June of 1945—more than a year and a half before the decision in the New Jersey bus case—Vashti McCollum brought suit to stop released time classes in the local schools of Champaign. The popularity of released time programs was at an all-time high in the nation—about two million students were enrolled—and the beginnings of what became a postwar religious renaissance were increasingly evident. At the same time, of course, the Supreme Court was confronting for the first time the task of giving systematic meaning to the establishment clause of the First Amendment. The religious moment, an emerging jurisprudence, and a determined individual came together to produce a momentous case and precedent.

Except for an attorney provided by several Chicago separationist groups and for the advice and support of the local Unitarian minister, Vashti McCollum's battle in the local com-munity was a lonely one. It was also a difficult and trying one. Popular outcry and harassment of the McCollums reached a peak about the time of the long trial before a three-judge panel in the local circuit court, a trial that included four hours of testimony by the fourth grader in the case, James Terry McCollum, on the pressures and harassment he reported. In January 1946 the three judges upheld the released time program in Champaign. In so deciding, the court relied on a lower court decision in Chicago upholding that city's released time program, even though the schools' cooperation with religious groups there was less close than it was in Champaign.

After the initial loss, Mrs. McCollum hired her own lawyer, Walter F. Dodd, a distinguished constitutional scholar and author, and a former professor of law at Yale University. The appeal went forward to the Illinois Supreme Court, and that court, after first deciding in favor of the Chicago program, unanimously upheld the Champaign plan. This was in late January 1947. Just two weeks later the U.S. Supreme Court announced its decision in *Everson*, the school bus case from New Jersey. Then, less than four months after the *Everson* opinion came down, the Supreme Court noted probable jurisdiction in the McCollum case. The new jurisprudence of church-state relations unfolded with unexpected rapidity.

In appealing her case to the Supreme Court, Mrs. McCollum attracted support from many amici curiae, among them Baptist groups, the Synagogue Council of America, the American Civil Liberties Union, Seventh Day Adventists, the American Unitarian Association, and the American Ethical Union. After oral arguments in late 1947, the Supreme Court handed down its decision on March 8, 1948. With only one justice dissenting, the Court held the released time program of Champaign County in violation of the "no establishment" clause as it was applied to the states via the Fourteenth Amendment. Justice Black again wrote for the majority. Even leaving aside the disputed facts, he concluded, the undisputed facts of the released time program in Champaign "show the use of tax-supported property for religious instruction and the close cooperation between the school

authorities and the religious council in promoting religious education. The operation of
the State's compulsory education system thus
assists and is integrated with the program of
religious instruction carried on by separate religious sects. Pupils compelled by law to go to
school for secular education are released in part
from their legal duty upon the condition that
they attend religious classes. This is beyond all
question a utilization of the tax-established and
tax-supported public school system to aid religious groups to spread their faith. And it falls
squarely under the ban of the First Amendment
(made applicable to the states by the Fourteenth)." In concluding, the Court explicitly
rejected the state's contention that the First
Amendment banned only aid to one or a small
number of religious groups and that, consequently, the program in Champaign was permissible because it assisted any and all religious
faiths. In the words of the concurring opinion
written by Justice Felix Frankfurter, "Separation
is a requirement to abstain from fusing functions of Government and of religious sects, not
to treat them all equally."

Justice Stanley Reed, the sole dissenter,
rested his position primarily on the traditional
and historic closeness between church and
state in American history. After noting such
long-established practices as chaplains in the
Congress and the armed services, Bible reading in the schools of the District of Columbia, and religious activities at West Point
and the Naval Academy, Reed concluded that
"past practice shows cooperation between the
schools and a non-ecclesiastical body is not
forbidden by the First Amendment." And in
conclusion, the "prohibition of enactments respecting the establishment of religion do not
bar every friendly gesture between church
and state. It is not an absolute prohibition
against every conceivable situation where the
two may work together, any more than the
other provisions of the First Amendment—free
speech, free press—are absolutes."

The reaction to *McCollum* was both mixed
and vocal. The decision realized the worst fears
of some religious groups and leaders; what had
been merely absolutist rhetoric in *Everson* was
actual outcome in *McCollum*. Criticism of the

Court surfaced quickly in the media and pul-
pits of the nation; the Court was variously accused of reading secularism or atheism into
the Constitution or, worse, of being unwitting
dupes of godless international communism.
Indeed, in his dissent in the 1952 *Zorach* case,
Justice Black would take official, and unusual,
note of the criticism: "I am aware that our
McCollum decision on separation of Church
and State has been subjected to a most searching examination throughout the country. Probably few opinions from this Court in recent
years have attracted more attention or stirred
wider debate." Above all, it seemed ironic, perhaps even incredible, that a doctrine of seemingly absolute separation should emerge at the
very time of the rising visibility and importance of religion in American life.

On just the question of released time programs, however, *McCollum* left unanswered the
question of whether all or only some released
time programs were doomed. On the one hand,
the majority emphasized the use of the state's
compulsory school attendance laws as an integral part of released time programs, and that
observation pointed to the invalidation of all
programs. Yet, on the other hand, as the concurring opinion of Justice Felix Frankfurter underscored, the Court had before it only one
program presenting one set of facts, and its decision applied only to that and identical released time programs.

Indeed, the role of the compulsory school
attendance laws—and the school day, school
week, and school year they defined and
enforced—were at the very nub of the matter.
The whole issue could have been put to rest
with programs scheduled "after school" or,
very likely, with the slight accommodation
of an early closing of schools one day in the
week (the "dismissed time" option). But released time programs are defined by the fact
that they go on during the school day. Their
advocates want it so for a number of reasons.
They seek the legitimacy of including religious education in the regular school day and
week. They prefer released time to dismissed
time because it offers more flexible schedul-
ing over different hours of the week. And—
and a large "and" it is—they are not anxious

to compete with students' leisure time pursuits after the end of the school day.

That same uncertainty about the scope of the *McCollum* decision explains at least part of its mixed impact on existing released time programs. Those in which the classes were held off school premises generally continued without change, on the assumption that the use of public school classrooms was the salient characteristic of the unacceptable program in Champaign. In those with classes in the schools, the future was varied. In Champaign itself, released time became an after-school program and declined into collapse by 1950. Similar programs shifted to off-premises classes or dismissed time programs, often resulting in a decline in participation. Still others continued in the public schools with few if any changes, either out of defiance and noncompliance or out of a conviction that other differences from the Champaign program distinguished them. Overall, however, released time enrollments declined after *McCollum*. Just how much of a decline there was in the nation as a whole is a matter of dispute, but all observers agree that released time never regained its pre-*McCollum* enrollments.

Support for the Court's decision in *McCollum* was active, if less visibly so than the opposition. Traditional separationist groups were pleased—the American Civil Liberties Union, Protestants and Other Americans United, the American Jewish Congress, various Baptist and Masonic groups among them. Some of them sought other test cases to clarify and extend the application of the *McCollum* precedent. One of those actions challenged the New York City program. It was not an easy target, for, unlike the Champaign plan, the one in New York involved classes in private buildings, administration by the religious groups, and a stated policy by public school authorities to make no comments on the program and to handle none of its administration. In New York there was, in other words, little more public aid to the program than the excusing of students from classes during the regular school day—little more, that is, than the leverage of required student attendance during the school day.

Actually the case of *Zorach v. Clauson* was the second challenge to New York City's released time program. Joseph Lewis, an organizer and publicist for militant atheism, quickly brought suit unsuccessfully after *McCollum* to direct the state Commissioner of Education to stop released time programs in New York and other cities of the state. Experienced litigating groups in the separationist camp, especially the American Civil Liberties Union (ACLU) and the American Jewish Congress (AJC), viewed the Lewis suit with apprehension. Lewis was widely identified as an enemy of religion in any form, and he was not a resident of New York City; moreover, they thought, his suit was hastily prepared and bereft of the facts of the city program as it actually operated. Their apprehension changed to distress when they found that Lewis had appealed his loss to the state's highest court, the Court of Appeals. Despite their reservations about bringing their own challenge in the heated aftermath of *McCollum*, the ACLU and AJC agreed to do so when negotiations with Lewis made it clear that he would drop his appeal only if they agreed to bring their own suit. Thus was born the case of *Zorach v. Clauson*.

In this group organized case, the plaintiffs played a far less active and prominent role than Vashti McCollum had played in hers. Tessim Zorach and Esta Gluck were in fact recruited by the groups as ideal plaintiffs—respected and religious members of the community who were willing to leave the decisions in the case to the sponsoring groups. Zorach, a food broker and son of the noted American sculptor William Zorach, was an Episcopalian who lived in fashionable Brooklyn Heights. Mrs. Gluck, president of the local public school PTA, belonged to a local synagogue and was the mother of children who received religious instruction in the synagogue after the public school day was over. The major decisions in their case were in the hands of their lawyers, Kenneth Greenawalt for the ACLU and Leo Pfeffer for the AJC. Greenawalt was a member of a prestigious New York law firm, and Pfeffer was both an AJC official and a distinguished scholar of church-state relations who had written articles and an authoritative book, *Church, State and Freedom*.

The suit to replace the one of Joseph Lewis was filed in June 1948, a little more than three months after the Supreme Court's decision in

McCollum. Preliminary skirmishing occupied much of the next two years, in the course of which three defendants were specified: the Board of Education of the City of New York (Clauson et al.), the state Commissioner of Education, and the Greater New York Coordinating Committee on Released Time of Jews, Protestants, and Roman Catholics, the umbrella group organizing the released time classes. Finally, in 1950 a New York trial court held that the New York program was constitutional after denying an ACLU-AJC request for a trial on the facts. On appeal, the Appellate Division of the Supreme Court upheld the trial court by a 3-2 margin. Finally, on July 11 the state's highest court, the Court of Appeals, affirmed the lower court decisions by a 6-1 vote.

Within a short span of time, therefore, thirteen New York state judges had wrestled with the constitutionality of the New York City released time program and, indirectly, with the question of whether *McCollum* had ended all released time programs. Of the thirteen, all five Catholics voted in favor of released time, and both Jews voted against it; the remaining six Protestants broke 5-1, the one being a Congregationalist. Interestingly, all thirteen took the same positions on the issue that their organized denominations had taken on released time legislation in the state.

The judicial reasons for decision in the New York courts were also symmetrical. The majority judges all cited the differences between the Champaign and New York programs, and all argued for a separation that would not end all friendliness and accommodation between church and state. The dissenters all argued that released time's use of the state's compulsory education system to secure its pupils was its central fact and its fatal flaw.

In a significant way, the *Zorach* outcomes in the New York courts were foreordained by the facts that were considered. The separationist sponsors of the suit hoped that a trial would permit them to show that even in the New York plan there was substantial public school aid and involvement, and that there were strong pressures on children to participate. Moreover, they wanted to show that released time programs intrinsically violated the separation of

church and state. Their statement of charges read: "Administration of the system necessarily entails use of the public school machinery and time of public school principals, teachers, and administrative staff.... Operation of the released time program has resulted and inevitably results in the exercise of pressure and coercion upon parents and children to secure attendance ... [and] has resulted and inevitably will result in divisiveness because of difference in religious beliefs and disbeliefs." The defendants opposed a trial, and the trial court judge agreed. Thus, the "facts" in the case remained the formal statements of state and city public school policy on released time programs. Had there been violations of those policies in the operation of released time, the New York courts ruled, there were remedies available to bring administration into line with policy.

Following the loss in the New York Court of Appeals, the ACLU and the AJC immediately took the case on appeal to the U.S. Supreme Court. The Court granted appeal and heard oral arguments in early 1952. The principal participants remained as they had been in the New York courts. Greenawalt argued the case and Pfeffer joined him on the petitioners' brief. Strategy and argument for the respondent were largely in the hands of Michael Castaldi, attorney for the Board of Education, and Charles Tuttle, a Wall Street lawyer, counsel for the National Council of Churches, and both chairman and attorney for the Coordinating Committee, which ran the released time program. Eight states (California, Indiana, Kentucky, Maine, Massachusetts, Oregon, Pennsylvania, and West Virginia) filed as amici curiae urging the constitutionality of the New York plan.

The Supreme Court announced its decision on April 28, 1952. A 6-3 majority upheld the New York courts and the New York City plan. After dismissing the contention that students had been coerced to choose religious instruction, Justice William Douglas, writing for the majority, set out an understanding of the wall of separation quite different from the absolutism of *Everson* and its reaffirmation in *McCollum.* "The First Amendment ... does not say that in every and all respects, there shall be a separation of Church and State. Rather, it studiously defines the manner, the specific ways, in which there shall be no concert or union or dependency one on the other. That is the common sense of the matter. Otherwise the state and religion would be aliens to each other—hostile, suspicious, and even unfriendly. Churches could not be required to pay even property taxes. Municipalities would not be permitted to render police or fire protection to religious groups. Police who helped parishioners into their places of worship would violate the Constitution." To support such a less demanding view of the separation, Douglas (as had Reed in *McCollum*) drew on examples of a traditional alliance between religion and the state: prayers in legislatures, the use of "so help me God" in courtrooms, the making of Thanksgiving a holiday, and even the "supplication" opening the sessions of the Supreme Court: "God save the United States and this Honorable Court."

After equating released time programs with excusing students for worship on religious holidays—whether the teacher excuses absences for "a few students, regularly for one, or pursuant to a systematized program designed to further the religious needs of all the students does not alter the character of the act"—Douglas formulated the most widely quoted dictum in the majority opinion: "We are a religious people whose institutions presuppose a Supreme Being. . . . When the state encourages religious instruction or cooperates with religious authorities by adjusting the schedule of public events to sectarian needs, it follows the best of our traditions. For it then respects the religious nature of our people and accommodates the public service to their spiritual needs. To hold that it may not would be to find in the Constitution a requirement that the government show a callous indifference to religious groups. That would be preferring those who believe in no religion over those who do believe." Government may not force its citizens into religious activity or observance, wrote Douglas, but it may "close its doors or suspend its operations as to those who want to repair to their religious sanctuary for worship or instruction. No more than that is undertaken here." To extend the *McCollum* precedent to cover the New York program, the majority concluded, would be to

read into the Bill of Rights a "philosophy of hostility to religion."

Justices Black, Frankfurter, and Jackson dissented, each writing a separate opinion that sounded a personal variation on the single theme of coercion. Black, the author of the majority opinion in *McCollum,* defined the "sole question" as "whether New York can use its compulsory education laws to help religious sects get attendants presumably too unenthusiastic to go unless moved to do so by the pressure of this state machinery. . . . New York is manipulating its compulsory education laws to help religious sects get pupils. This is not separation but combination of Church and State." Frankfurter reminded the majority that, contrary to its words, New York was not closing its school doors during released time classes and that "[T]here is all the difference in the world between letting the children out of school and letting some of them out of school into religious classes." He also regretted that the petitioners were not permitted the chance to prove their allegations about the operation of the New York program in a trial.

Justice Jackson wrote another of the biting and witty dissents that endeared him to the media, if not to his colleagues. The very effectiveness of released time programs, compared with after-school classes, he wrote, "is due to the truant officer who, if the youngster fails to go to the Church school, dogs him back to the public schoolroom. Here schooling is more or less suspended during the "released time" so the nonreligious attendants will not forge ahead of the churchgoing absentees. But it serves as a temporary jail for a pupil who will not go to Church." After scorning the Douglas majority opinion as "epithetical jurisprudence" and "today's passionate dialectics," Jackson concluded in a final sally that the majority's judgment "will be more interesting to students of psychology and of the judicial processes than to students of constitutional law."

At a time of a ripening religious revival, *Zorach* became the symbol of a new constitutional tolerance of governmental friendliness to organized religion. The Douglas dicta were widely repeated and widely cited as authorization for new forms of public support for religion. For many, the rhetoric was comforting, and *Zorach* became a symbol and beacon far beyond its circumscribed power as a constitutional precedent.

The *Zorach* decision signaled the Court's entry into a national debate over the place of religion and religious values in public life, and, as such, it altered the terms of that debate. It appeared to many people to be a turning point, a departure from the rigid separationist position of *Everson*'s words and *McCollum*'s outcome. A number of state and local courts began to cite its doctrine of friendliness between church and state as they tried to decide new church-state issues.

Very quickly, however, the Supreme Court left both the issue and the rhetoric of *Zorach* behind. There was a hiatus of some years after that decision in 1952 until the Court once again tackled the role of religion in public education—but when it did, the stakes were raised considerably. In the years between 1962 and 1964 the Court decided four cases of religious influences in public schools, all of them involving more substantial forms of cooperation between church and state than released time programs, and all were decided on the side of separationism. It held a nondenominational prayer in New York schools unconstitutional (*Engel v. Vitale* [1962]); it struck down the saying of the Lord's Prayer in the schools of Baltimore (*Murray v. Curlett* [1963]); it declared invalid the compulsory reading of the Bible in Philadelphia's schools (*Schempp v. Abington School District* [1963]); and it applied those precedents to a broader set of religious practices in the public schools of Miami (*Chamberlin v. Dade County* [1964]). In short, the Court moved beyond the question of released time and beyond the words and precedent of *Zorach* as its understanding of the separation of church and state matured in the 1960s.

The two Released Time Cases come from the first, tentative attempts of the Supreme Court to piece together a viable interpretation of the establishment clause. In retrospect, the Court's position in *McCollum* (reflecting that in *Everson*) seems more separationist than its subsequent position; its position in *Zorach* seems much less so. One may see the two cases as early and inexperienced attempts to spell out a doctrine of separation that would be both juridically defensible and socially and politically acceptable. Alternatively, one can see them as a two-part sequence of probing and testing by the Court—a staking out of a strong (even absolutist) position and then a retreating from it in recognition of specific criticism and of a more general context of growing religious enthusiasm in the country. Whatever the explanation, the Court settled down to a more consistent and predictable outlook on church-state separation in the cases of the 1960s and 1970s.

And what of released time itself? Its proponents (and most optimistic estimators) reckoned that it made some comeback after the favorable *Zorach* decision and reached some three million public school pupils by the late 1950s. The trend reversed within a decade or so, however. Practically, released time programs assumed the neighborhood school from which students could easily get to local churches and then back to school again. Busing and school choice, especially in larger cities, ended the ease of those logistics. And philosophically, released time began to lose ground. Many public educators had never favored it, and the mainline Protestant religious groups increasingly turned away from it. Some saw its brief weekly classes as theologically compromised or pedagogically ineffective. Various groups moved on to other options—expanded religious schools, shared time programs, or teaching "about" religion or morality and ethics in the public school curricula.

Selected Bibliography

Fraser, J. W. *Between Church and State: Religion and Public Education in a Multicultural America.* New York: St. Martin's Press, 1999.

McCollum, Vashti C. *One Woman's Fight.* New York: Doubleday, 1951.

Patric, Gordon. "The Impact of a Court Decision: Aftermath of the McCollum Case." *Journal of Public Law* 6 (Fall 1957): 455–464.

Pfeffer, Leo. *Church, State and Freedom.* Rev. ed. Boston: Beacon Press, 1967.

Shaver, Erwin L. *The Weekday Church School.* Boston: Pilgrim Press, 1956.

Sorauf, Frank J. "*Zorach v. Clauson*: The Impact of a Supreme Court Decision." *American Political Science Review* 53 (September 1959): 777–791.

Sorauf, Frank J. "The Released Time Case." In *The Third Branch of Government.* Ed. C. Herman Pritchett and Alan Westin. New York: Harcourt, Brace, 1963.

To Pray or Not to Pray: The Supreme Court Says No to Prayer in the Public Schools

—◄◦►—

Paul L. Murphy
Deceased Professor of History
University of Minnesota

Engel v. Vitale, 370 U.S. 421 (1962) [U.S. Supreme Court]

◄◦► THE CASE IN BRIEF ◄◦►

Date
1962

Location
New York
District of Columbia

Court
U.S. Supreme Court

Principal Participants
Parents of ten public-school students
New York Board of Regents

Significance of the Case
The Court banned prayer in public schools as a violation of the establishment clause of the First Amendment. The Court stood firm against an outcry of public and political protests.

One of the most controversial decisions ever made by the U.S. Supreme Court was handed down in June 1962. In *Engel v. Vitale*, the Court banned prayer as part of public school exercises, as a violation of the establishment clause of the First Amendment. The *Engel* decision engendered a firestorm of public protest because prayer in the public schools had been a common practice in many parts of the nation for years. The outpouring of criticism of the Supreme Court after *Engel* was thought by some to exceed the venomous attacks made on the Court after its famous desegregation decisions in 1954.

The controversy began when the Engels and other parents, representing a total of ten children enrolled in School District Number 9 of New Hyde Park, New York, brought suit against the school board and the state for the inclusion of a prayer in the opening exercises of the schools. The prayer had been adopted by the school board following the recommendation of the New York State Board of Regents that the prayer should be read in the schools. The prayer was composed by the Regents themselves and was intended to be nondenominational in content. It read: "Almighty God, we acknowledge our dependence upon thee, and we beg thy blessings upon us, our parents, our teachers and our country." The prayer was intended to be optional for both the local school boards and for individual students. Although the prayer was supposed to be voluntary, the New Hyde Park school board initially had made no provision for excusing students who did not wish to participate from the classroom.

The parents who brought suit represented various creeds, including Judaism, Unitarianism, atheism, and the Ethical Culture Society. They protested that the so-called nondenominational prayer violated their religious beliefs, that the school had coerced their children into participating in a religious exercise, and that the state's authorization of the prayer was a violation of the First Amendment. The parents lost their case in the trial court of Nassau County, New York. The judge decided that the parents had no valid constitutional objection as long as the prayer was voluntary and students could be excused from participating. The judge based his decision on the long history of prayer in the state's classrooms and argued that prayer "is an integral part of our national heritage." He could not believe that the establishment clause of the First Amendment was ever intended to outlaw prayer in the public schools.

The trial court decision was affirmed by the intermediate appellate court of New York and went on appeal to the state's highest judicial body. In July 1961, the Court of Appeals of the State of New York upheld the two lower court decisions by a 5-2 vote. The opinion of the court was that prayer was neither a form of religious education nor the establishment of religion in any "reasonable meaning" of the First Amendment phrase. The court contended that the Founding Fathers had not meant to prohibit "mere professions of belief in God," but only any "official adoption of a religion by the government" when they wrote the First Amendment. To hold this prayer unconstitutional, the court said, "would destroy a part of the essential foundations of the American governmental structure," and would go against American history. The dissenters pointed out that Supreme Court decisions of the past had shown that the line between church and state may not be overstepped, and asserted that the prayer was a form of state-sponsored religious education. Moreover, the dissenters argued that even though the prayer was voluntary, a type of compulsion still existed because children felt pressure to conform to the activities of their classmates.

Engel v. Vitale was the first case dealing specifically with the issue of prayer in the public schools to reach the U.S. Supreme Court. However, there had been several precedents pertaining to the establishment clause of the First Amendment which gave some indication of the position the Court would take in *Engel*. In 1947 the Court, in *Everson v. Board of Education*, upheld a state program providing for the reimbursement of parents of public and private school students for their children's bus transportation to and from school, on the grounds that the purpose of the law was secular, not religious, and it provided benefits for all students, not just some. In his opinion for the Court, Justice Hugo Black explained the requirements of the establishment clause as follows: "Neither a state nor the Federal Government can set up a church. Neither can pass laws which aid one religion, aid all religions, or prefer one religion over another. Neither can force nor influence a person to go to or to remain away from church against his will or force him to profess belief or disbelief in any religion. No person can be punished for entertaining or professing religious beliefs, for church attendance or non-attendance. No tax in any amount, large or small, can be levied to support any religious activities or institutions . . . whatever form they may adopt to teach or practice religion. Neither a state nor the Federal Government can, openly or secretly, participate in the affairs of any religious organizations or groups and vice versa. In the words of Jefferson, the clause against establishment of religion by law was intended to erect 'a wall of separation between Church and State.' "

A year later, in *McCollum v. Board of Education*, the Supreme Court struck down a state program of religious education which allowed for "released time" during the regular school day. The program provided public school classrooms for various denominations to teach students religion and required that the instructors take attendance. Eight of the Court's justices found this "released time" practice a clear violation of the separation of church and state. The establishment clause had been breached by the use of tax-supported public school buildings for religious instruction and by the fact that the state's compulsory school attendance law was being used to provide students for religious classes. In a 1952 case challenging another "released time" program, *Zorach v. Clauson,* the Court upheld the plan on the basis that students were allowed to leave the public school grounds to attend religious instruction elsewhere, and therefore tax dollars were not being used to support religious instruction.

The Supreme Court decided in *Engel v. Vitale* (Justices Felix Frankfurter and Byron White did not participate.) that the New York Board of Regents' prayer was unconstitutional by a majority of 6-1. Speaking for the Court, Justice Black said that using the public school system to encourage recitation of the prayer was "a practice wholly inconsistent with the Establishment Clause." Contrary to the ruling of the Court of Appeals of the State of New York, the Supreme Court said there could be no doubt that the New York program of daily prayer in the classroom was indeed a religious activity, and therefore subject to the prohibitions of the First Amendment. The Court agreed with the parents that a prayer composed by government officials, in this case the Board of Regents, breached the "Constitutional wall of separation between Church and State." As Justice Black put it, "the constitutional prohibition against laws respecting an establishment of religion must at least mean that in this country it is no part of the business of government to compose official prayers for any group of the American people to recite as part of a religious program carried on by government."

Justice Black went on to point out that the fact that the prayer was both "nondenominational"

and voluntary in nature was irrelevant to the Court's decision in *Engel.* Neither characteristic could "serve to free it from the limitations of the Establishment Clause." It was not necessary to show direct government compulsion, Black argued, in order to find that the establishment clause had been violated: "When the power, prestige and financial support of government [*sic*] is placed behind a particular religious belief, the indirect coercive pressure upon religious minorities to conform to the prevailing officially approved religion is plain. But the purposes underlying the Establishment Clause go much further than that. Its first and most immediate purpose rested on the belief that a union of government and religion tends to destroy government and to degrade religion. The history of governmentally established religion, both in England and this country, showed that whenever government had allied itself with one particular religion, the inevitable result had been that it had incurred the hatred, disrespect, and even contempt of those who held contrary beliefs. That same history showed that many people had lost their respect for any religion that had relied upon support of government to spread its faith. The Establishment Clause thus stands as an expression of principle on the part of the Founders of our Constitution that religion is too personal, too sacred, too holy, to permit its 'unhallowed perversion' by a civil magistrate. Another purpose of the Establishment Clause rested upon awareness of the historical fact that governmentally established religions and religious persecutions go hand in hand."

Justice William O. Douglas, in a concurring opinion, argued that the primary factor making the New York prayer unconstitutional was the fact that it represented a governmentally financed religious exercise. He believed the First Amendment requires that the government be neutral with regard to religion in order to better serve all religious interests. In Douglas's words: "The philosophy is that the atheist or agnostic—the non-believer—is entitled to go his own way. The philosophy is that if government interferes in matters spiritual, it will be a divisive force."

The lone dissenter from the Court's opinion in *Engel,* Justice Potter Stewart, contended that the recitation of the prayer in the public schools did not constitute an establishment of an official religion within the meaning of the First Amendment. Justice Stewart felt that "to deny the wish of these school children to join in reciting this prayer" was "to deny them the opportunity of sharing the spiritual heritage of our Nation." He argued that because the prayer was so brief and nonsectarian in nature, it could not be considered unconstitutional. Furthermore, Stewart criticized Justice Black's reliance on English history to make his case as irrelevant to the question of prayer in American schools.

The practice of incorporating certain kinds of religious activities which were by and large Christian in nature into public school programs had been widespread up to the time the *Engel* decision was announced. It was not surprising, therefore, that public reaction to the Supreme Court's decision was both vociferous and negative. Politicians, church leaders, and celebrities immediately jumped on the bandwagon to decry the Justices and their decision. Former President Herbert Hoover claimed that *Engel* represented "a disintegration of a sacred American heritage." Former President Dwight Eisenhower and former Vice President Richard Nixon also publicly criticized the decision, the latter calling for a constitutional amendment to reverse *Engel* and allow nonsectarian prayers in the schools. Democratic politicians, unless they were Southerners, tended at least to be supportive of the Supreme Court's authority to interpret the Constitution in this area, even if they were not enthusiastic about the decision itself. Former President Harry Truman stated that the Supreme Court was the best interpreter of the Constitution, and President John F. Kennedy advocated obedience to *Engel*, pointing out that the church and the home were the proper places for prayer.

Southern Democrats (Dixiecrats) led the attack on the Supreme Court in Congress, but criticism of *Engel* was common among politicians in both the House and Senate. Dixiecrats were most vicious in their censure because they had hated the Warren court since its 1954 desegregation decision. The "Impeach Earl Warren" signs that had appeared on Southern highways after *Brown v. Board of Education* were updated with the phrases "Save Prayer" and "Save America." Senator Strom Thurmond of South Carolina was the most long-winded critic in the *Congressional Record*, inserting negative comments about the Court and *Engel* for two and a half months after the decision. Senator Herman Talmadge of Georgia charged that "the Supreme Court had set up atheism as a new religion." Many Southern politicians shared the view that the Fourteenth Amendment, which the Court had employed to apply the First Amendment to state law (because the Bill of Rights, in and of itself, applies only to the federal government), had never been legally adopted, and therefore the limitations of the First Amendment could not be imposed on the states. They charged the Supreme Court with the unconstitutional usurpation of state power. Congressman George Andrews summed up the Southern position with regard to the Warren Court in his criticism that the justices had "put the Negroes in the schools" and had "driven God out." Comments by other unhappy Congressmen included the assertion by Representative Mendel Rivers that the decision provided "aid and comfort to Moscow" and Representative Alvin O'Konski's statement that "these men in robes are doing everything possible to help Khrushchev to bury us. . . . We ought to impeach these men in robes who put themselves above God." Congressman Frank Becker found *Engel* to be the most "tragic" decision ever made in the history of the nation.

Several congressmen proposed legislative action in an attempt to circumvent the Court's ban on prayer in the public schools. Fifty-three representatives and twenty-two senators joined in introducing constitutional amendments to overturn *Engel* in their respective houses. The Senate Judiciary Committee held hearings to consider proposed amendments to allow nondenominational prayer in schools. One Senator, Kenneth Keating of New York, appeared before the committee with a proposal to impeach the justices.

Although attempts to amend the Constitution continued for years after June 1962, none of them succeeded. This was due mainly to the vigorous defense of *Engel* by key Northern congressional leaders and by the gradual dissipation of the emotional atmosphere which had inundated Congress and the nation when the decision was first announced. Eventually cooler heads prevailed in Congress, and a reasonable assessment of the ruling led many congressmen to find *Engel* consistent with the precedent and the spirit of the First Amendment. The Becker Amendment, introduced as House Joint Resolution 693 in September 1963, was perhaps the most notable failed attempt to contravene the Court. At the time the House Judicial Committee held hearings to consider the amendment, congressmen testified that they were receiving more negative mail about the *Engel* decision than had been produced by the civil rights controversy. The Becker Amendment passed the House but was defeated in the Senate. The opposition of thirty-seven senators denied the joint resolution the two-thirds majority required for the passage of a constitutional amendment. Much of the credit for the defeat of Becker's proposal went to several grassroots organizations representing civil libertarians, Jews, and some Protestant denominations which organized meetings, speakers, and a letter-writing campaign to influence the vote of congressmen. The efforts of these groups resulted in the shift in the mail on the Becker Amendment from support to opposition. A few prominent theologians were joined by numerous constitutional lawyers and a variety of interest groups in testifying against the amendment at the committee hearings. A drive for the passage of a similar amendment was mounted a few years later in the Senate under the leadership of Senator Everett Dirksen of Illinois, but it failed, too, as did scores of other such proposals. Interest in prayer amendments in Congress waned significantly beginning in 1965, and subsequently such action has not proved to have significant support.

The response to *Engel* among religious leaders was mixed. Francis Cardinal Spellman of New York City attacked the decision vehemently and attempted to stir up Catholic opinion against the Court. Few prominent Catholics supported *Engel*, despite President Kennedy's position. The response from Protestant church leaders ran the gamut from the view of Episcopal Bishop James Pike, who asserted that the Court had "deconsecrated the nation," to vigorous support for the decision. In general, Unitarians, non-Southern Baptists, and Presbyterians supported the Court, and Methodists were divided on the issue. Although it was slow to make an official response, the National Council of Churches, which represented many of the mainstream Protestant denominations, eventually voiced support of *Engel* as a protector of religious liberty.

Jews were the most outspoken in their support of the decision because they had worked for years to eradicate the promotion of Christianity in the public schools. Most Jews viewed *Engel* as a long-awaited legal victory in their fight against discriminatory religious practices. The American Jewish Congress, the American Jewish Committee, and the Anti-Defamation League of B'nai B'rith had all filed amicus curiae briefs in *Engel* in support of the petitioners. The counsel of the American Jewish Congress, Leo Pfeffer, organized 132 law school deans and professors of law and political science of various religious faiths from colleges and universities throughout the nation. This group issued a defense of the *Engel* decision and sent it to the Senate Judiciary Committee as it met to consider the proposed constitutional amendments to put prayer back in the schools. In their influential statement to the committee, these legal experts argued that "the intrusion of religion upon the public school system both threatens the separation of church and state and challenges the traditional integrity of the public schools. That intrusion, if permitted, will greatly endanger the institutions which have preserved religious and political freedom in the United States."

Although thousands of negative telegrams and letters were delivered to the Supreme Court within twenty-four hours of the *Engel* decision, the Court had many supporters as well. Leading newspapers favored the decision, including the *New York Times*, the *New York Herald Tribune*, the *New York Post*, the *Washington Post*, the *St. Louis Post-Dispatch*, and the *Christian Science Monitor*. So did *Time* magazine. Positive editorials in these publications were influential in shifting public opinion toward support for the Court's decision by the autumn of 1962. The *Engel* case was also evaluated in more than twenty-four legal periodicals. Slightly over half of the articles written were unfavorable. Some of the legal critics argued, among other things, that the decision institutionalized agnosticism as the official public religion, that it discriminated against the majority, that it was not the role of the Supreme Court to decide religious controversies, and that the decision was based too much on history and ignored contemporary issues.

The reaction among educators was varied as well. A poll taken several months after the decision showed that 51 percent of public school administrators disagreed with the Court and 46 percent viewed the decision positively. Another poll taken in 1963 and 1964 revealed that only 38 percent of the nation's high school principals supported banning prayer from the schools. This survey also demonstrated a striking difference in opinions on the issue, depending on regional location. Principals in Southern and border states were the least likely to support the Court (only 29 percent and 27 percent), whereas principals in the Pacific and Mountain states were most likely to support the Court (52 percent and 41 percent).

Although *Engel* prohibited prayer in the public schools, surveys taken during the 1960s revealed that many schools and school administrators had chosen to ignore the law of the land by continuing to have prayer in school. A 1965 poll of school superintendents in the South showed that in 26 percent of the school districts, prayers were said in all of the schools and in 35 percent of the districts, prayers were said in some of the schools. Nationwide, 10.7 percent of superintendents reported that prayers continued to be said in some of their schools. A 1969 *New York Times* poll demonstrated that 13 percent of the nation's schools and 50 percent of Southern schools used some type of religious reading in their school exercises. This was despite two 1963 Supreme Court rulings which had outlawed Bible reading and the use of the Lord's Prayer in the public schools. Many school officials chose to ignore the law with regard to religion in the schools in order to avoid conflict with parents in their school districts. Because the Supreme Court relies on government officials to execute its decisions, compliance with *Engel* and related decisions was dependent on the willingness of local officials to enforce the law.

A first-grade class in South Carolina begins their day with a moment of silent prayer. *Bettmann/CORBIS.*

Despite efforts to resist, the decisions in *Engel* and related cases still had a great impact on the nation's schools. A 1960 survey revealed that 42 percent of the school districts in the continental United States had Bible reading in their schools and 50 percent had prayers. A 1965 survey demonstrated that Bible reading was practiced in only 19.5 percent of the schools and prayers were said in only 14 percent. These figures clearly indicate that the Supreme Court's decisions were effective, albeit not completely. Another effect of the *Engel* decisions was to void laws in eleven states which had required religious exercises in the public schools.

Since the *Engel* precedent was established, the Supreme Court has been fairly consistent in maintaining a separation of church and state in the nation's public schools. For example, in a 1987 decision, *Edwards v. Aguillard*, the Court struck down a Louisiana law requiring the teaching of creationism (a religious explanation of the creation of the world based upon a literal reading of the Bible). In *Lee v. Weisman* (1992), the Court ruled that a prayer delivered by a rabbi at a graduation ceremony violated the First Amendment's establishment clause. In 1998, an attempt to pass a constitutional amendment overturning *Engel* failed to survive a vote of the U.S. Senate. And in 2000, in *Santa Fe Independent School District v. Jane Doe*, the High Court ruled that a school district policy permitting student-led prayers at football games violated the establishment clause. However, in *Board of Education v. Mergens* (1990), the Court ruled that student-led religious groups could conduct prayer sessions for their own members on school property before or after classes.

Selected Bibliography

Blanshard, Paul. *Religion and the Schools*. Boston, Mass.: Beacon Press, 1963.

Boles, Donald. *The Two Swords*. Ames: Iowa State University Press, 1967.

Dolbeare, Kenneth, and Phillip Hammond. *The School Prayer Decisions*. Chicago: University of Chicago Press, 1971.

Duker, Sam. *The Public Schools and Religion*. New York: Harper & Row, 1966.

Freund, Paul, and Robert Ulich. *Religion and the Public Schools*. Cambridge: Harvard University Press, 1965.

Hudgins, H. C. *The Warren Court and the Public Schools*. Danville, IL: Interstate Printers and Publishers, 1970.

Johnson, Richard. *The Dynamics of Compliance*. Evanston: Northwestern University Press, 1967.

Laubach, John. *School Prayers*. Washington, DC: Public Affairs Press, 1969.

McMillan, Richard. *Religion in the Public Schools*. Macon, GA: Mercer University Press, 1984.

Muir, William. *Prayer in the Public Schools*. Chicago: University of Chicago Press, 1967.

Conscientious Objection:
A Right or a Privilege?

—◄◦►—

Delane Ramsey

Taylors, South Carolina

United States v. Seeger, 380 U.S. 163 (1965) [U.S. Supreme Court]

◄◦► THE CASE IN BRIEF ◄◦►

Date
1965

Location
New York; District of Columbia

Court
U.S. Supreme Court

Principal Participants
Daniel Seeger; Arno Jakobson; Forest Britt Peter; United States government

Significance of the Case
Three cases involving conscientious objectors were combined by the Supreme Court to consider challenges to the religious requirement for deferment from military service prior to the draft's demise in 1973. The Court eased the burden of proof on young men asserting a moral or philosophical opposition to fighting in a war.

Teachers often have trouble defining "democracy." "Rule by the people" doesn't hold up because it ignores the dynamics, tensions, and compromises characteristic of democracy. A better definition acknowledges the balancing among competing interests that typify democracy: "rule by the majority, while protecting the rights of minorities." Among the competing interests that give democracy its dynamic is the power of the state and the rights of citizens. Competition between these two interests often leads to political and philosophical conflict within democratic societies. Controversies over zoning, discrimination, privacy, and expression are just some examples of the conflict between state interest and citizen's rights.

The competition between state and citizen can reach its most extreme form when the deepest-held values of each conflict. For the state, the greatest value is its own survival. Thus, war is a state's greatest threat. For many citizens, their strongest value is religion. One of the most serious philosophical and, therefore, political problems a state must solve is the conflict between these two strongest values. Can a state compel a citizen to fight in its defense if the citizen is conscientiously opposed to war on religious grounds?

Religious objection to war has a long history in America. The beliefs of the peace churches—including Quakers, Mennonites, and Moravians—were well known and generally respected during the colonial period. Colonial and early state legislatures allowed exemptions from militia duty on religious grounds. These religious exemptions were continued by the Federal Militia and Draft Acts of 1863 and 1864. In addition to religious exemptions, commutation and substitute provisions made it possible for a federal conscript to buy his way out of service if he did not qualify for a religious exemption.

The philosophical basis for exempting conscientious objectors from military service was succinctly stated by Chief Justice Charles Evans Hughes in 1931: "[i]n the forum of conscience, duty to a moral power higher than the State has always been maintained." In the American experience, this "higher moral power" had been consistently and explicitly predicated on religion since only a religious objection to military service was permitted. The Draft Act of 1917 continued the religious requirement for exemption that was offered to those from "a well-recognized religious sect, . . . whose principles forbade participation in war." An executive order soon expanded the exemption to those with "personal scruples against war," because of problems in identifying these sects and their members. This executive order effectively postponed having to solve the problem of nonreligious objection to war. As early as 1919 Harlan Fiske Stone, later a Supreme Court justice, recognized that conscience "may be disassociated from what is commonly recognized as religious." Most legal questions dealing with conflict between the religious and the nonreligious eventually became constitutional questions falling under the establishment and free exercise clauses of the First Amendment. However, in *United States v. Macintosh* (1931), the U.S. Supreme Court ruled that conscientious objection was a privilege subject to congressional action, not a constitutional question, thus apparently ending the constitutional debate.

In the 1940 Draft Act, Congress again established a religious requirement. Conscientious objector status was granted to those whose opposition to war was based on "religious training and belief." The test was now a personal religious belief, not membership in a recognized sect. The Selective Service Act of 1948 further defined religious training and belief as an "individual's belief in a Supreme Being involving duties superior to those arising from any human relation." Exemption was specifically refused on the basis of political, sociological, or philosophical views, or on the basis of a personal moral code.

In 1958, three challenges to the religious requirement for conscientious objector status began working their way through the federal court system. Daniel Seeger wanted exemption because of his belief in "goodness and virtue for their own sakes and a religious faith in a purely ethical creed" and admitted "skepticism in the existence of God." Another such claimant, Arno Jakobson, claimed conscientious objector status on the basis of his belief in "Godness" and that his "most important religious law was that no man ought ever to willfully sacrifice another man's life as a means to any other end." The third, Forest Britt Peter, claimed conscientious objector status because the taking of human life violated his moral code. He explained, "You could call that a belief in a Supreme Being or God. These just do not happen to be the words I use." All three were convicted for failure to report for induction. The court of appeals reversed the Seeger and Jakobson convictions, and the U.S. attorney appealed them to the Supreme Court itself. Peter's conviction was upheld by the court of appeals; he then appealed to the U.S. Supreme Court. Because of their similarity, the Court combined all three cases for argument in November 1964, and considered them together.

Court watchers expected the ruling to be on constitutional grounds, possibly reversing *Macintosh*. The constitutional questions were based on the establishment and free exercise clauses of the First Amendment and the Fifth Amendment's due process clause. The court of appeals had, in fact, reversed Seeger's conviction on the constitutional due process grounds that the religious requirement for exemption created an impermissible classification by treating religious and nonreligious citizens differently. The Supreme Court moved in a different direction, however, and sidestepped the constitutional questions.

The Court's decision in the three combined cases, decided collectively as *United States v. Seeger* (1965), followed the judicial practice of narrow construction. Rather than deciding the cases and resolving the issue on broad constitutional grounds, the Court treated the matter in purely statutory terms: the Court redefined the key term "Supreme Being" in the 1948 law. In reducing a Solomonic legal question to a lexicographer's task, the Court ruled that "religious belief within the meaning of the exemption . . . is whether it is sincere and meaningful belief occupying in the life of its possessor a place parallel to that filled by the God of those admittedly qualified for the exemption." The Court went on to state that the exemption does not cover "political, sociological, or economic considerations rather than religious belief." In an additional attempt to avoid the constitutional issue of the establishment clause, the decision stated: "There is no issue here of atheistic beliefs and accordingly the decision does not deal with that question." By redefining "Supreme Being" as a sincere, meaningful substitute for religious feeling or belief, the Court effectively left sincerity as the only requirement for the conscientious objector exemption. The burden of proof remained on the claimant, but his proof no longer had to include a specific religious component.

The thrust of the *Seeger* decision had been expected, even if on unexpected grounds. Some criticism came from the legal community, taking the Court to task for avoiding the constitutional question. Popular reaction, however, was rather muted. The Court was already unpopular among conservatives; this decision was just additional grist for their mill.

Contrary to popular expectations, mainstream clergy supported both the concept of conscientious objection and the *Seeger* decision. Several denominations had been counseling conscientious objector claimants even before the decision was announced. Following the decision, clergyman now suggested additional activism, saying "the churches should either cease producing such young men or cease neglecting them."

Throughout the Vietnam War, during the late sixties and early seventies, the *Seeger* decision was a staple part of the litany of young men seeking to avoid military service in a war they felt was unjust. In 1966, for example, heavyweight boxing champion Muhammad Ali claimed the exemption as a Muslim. His Selective Service board denied his claim, leading to his arrest and conviction. The board questioned his sincerity, because he had only recently converted to Islam. The Supreme Court reversed his conviction in 1970.

The conscientious objector controversy abated with the end of the draft in 1973. And constitutional issues involving religious and quasi-religious exemptions in the Selective Service System remain unresolved.

Selected Bibliography

Brodie, Abner, and Harold P. Southerland. "Conscience, the Constitution, and the Supreme Court: The Riddle of *United States v. Seeger.*" *Wisconsin Law Review* 1966 (Spring 1966): 306–329.

"Do Pacifists Embarrass the Churches?" *Christian Century* 82 (November 17, 1965): 1404–1405.

Lemon Test, Not So Pretty

—◄◦►—

William Lasser

Department of Political Science
Clemson University

Lemon v. Kurtzman, 403 U.S. 602 (1971) [U.S. Supreme Court]

┌─────────────────────────────────┐

◄◦► THE CASE IN BRIEF ◄◦►

Date
  1971

Location
  Pennsylvania
  Rhode Island

Court
  U.S. Supreme Court

Principal Participants
  Alton J. Lemon; David H. Kurtzman;
  Chief Justice Warren Burger

Significance of the Case
  Two cases concerning public money for
  private and parochial schools led the
  Court to create a formula, the "Lemon
  test," under the First Amendment's
  establishment clause in cases regarding
  religious freedoms. The test specified three
  criteria that, if met, would determine the
  case in favor of religious freedom.

└─────────────────────────────────┘

Some cases are notable because they resolve important questions of law. Some are famous because of the story they tell, or because they embody tragedy, pathos, or high drama. Still others are known primarily for the judges' clarity of thought, elegance of expression, or sense of moral purpose. *Lemon v. Kurtzman*, a 1971 U.S. Supreme Court case which invalidated two state laws authorizing public funding for parochial schools, is remembered for none of these reasons. It is recalled, instead, for the legal "test" which it espoused, a test which sought, albeit vainly, to clarify the jurisprudence swirling around the Court's First Amendment establishment clause.

The plaintiffs in the two cases decided under the heading of *Lemon v. Kurtzman* were citizens and taxpayers of Rhode Island and Pennsylvania. Both states had adopted programs designed to funnel public money to private schools, including parochial schools. The Rhode Island scheme authorized the state to provide up to a 15 percent salary supplement to private school teachers involved in teaching courses offered in the public schools. The Pennsylvania law allowed the government to "purchase" certain educational services from private schools, in effect paying the schools to teach children who, without such subsidy, might otherwise be in the public school system.

Chief Justice Warren Burger, writing for the Court, found both statutes unconstitutional. In the course of his brief opinion, Burger stated what quickly became known as the "Lemon test," a shorthand formula for resolving establishment clause questions. The test, as stated by Burger, contained three parts: "First, the statute must have a secular legislative purpose; second, its principal or primary effect must be one that neither advances nor inhibits religion; . . . finally, the statute must not foster "an excessive government entanglement with religion."

Although Burger admitted that earlier cases had allowed the Court to "only dimly perceive the lines of demarcation in this extraordinarily sensitive area of constitutional law," he nonetheless put forward the Lemon test as a method for the Court to "draw lines with reference to the three main evils against which the Establishment Clause was intended to afford protection." In the 1971 cases, Burger ruled for the Court's eight-person majority that the Rhode Island and Pennsylvania school funding statutes violated the third, or excessive entanglement, prong of the Lemon test.

The Lemon decision was quickly and vigorously attacked by supporters of government "accommodation" of religious interests. The Wall Street Journal and other newspapers predicted that the decision "may have a greater impact on American education than any high court ruling since the 1954 decision banning racial segregation in public schools." Legal analysts declared that the justices had set up "an overwhelming barrier in the path of those who have sought for decades to provide state aid to parochial schools."

But these comments and criticisms were nothing compared to the attacks on Lemon by a generation of legal scholars and, in subsequent cases, by members of the Supreme Court on both ends of the political spectrum. When the Court used the test in Lynch v. Donnelly (1984) to uphold a publicly sponsored nativity scene in a Pawtucket, Rhode Island, Christmas dis-

play, for example, liberals charged that the test allowed too great an accommodation between church and state. But when the Court invoked the Lemon test in a 1993 case involving the after-hours use of public school facilities by church groups, the conservative Justice Antonin Scalia likened the test to "some ghoul in a late-night horror movie that repeatedly sits up in its grave and shuffles abroad after being repeatedly killed and buried." The main problem with the test, Scalia charged, is that its purpose and effect prongs are inconsistent with the Framers' view of the establishment clause.

In fact, the problem with the Lemon test stemmed at least partly from the way the Lemon test was interpreted in later cases by Burger and his fellow justices. To begin with, the Lemon test was not a test at all; it was a package of three criteria, each of which had been used in one or more earlier cases to invalidate state aid to or involvement with religion. If a state law or policy violated any one of the these criteria, it could be declared unconstitutional. But it did not follow that the three criteria stated in Lemon comprised an exhaustive list—a law or program might satisfy all three of the Lemon criteria, yet run afoul of the establishment clause for some other reason. The Court upheld the Pawtucket nativity scene, for example, because it embodied several secular purposes (including depicting the origins of the Christmas holiday); offered only an incidental and remote benefit to one religion or to religion in general; and did not foster an excessive entanglement with religion. But critics charged that the nativity scene violated the Constitution because it embodied the state's "endorsement" of religion, a criterion not explicitly mentioned in Lemon.

In any event, the Lemon test did not produce the predictable or consistent results that Chief Justice Burger had sought. In subsequent years the Court was all over the map in establishment clause cases. Even in the area of parochial school aid, the Court upheld some programs and struck down others, at times seemingly at random. At last the Court, led by Justice Sandra Day O'Connor, began to move toward a different approach, focusing on whether a particular law or program constituted a governmental entanglement with religion or government "endorsement or disapproval" of religion. Although O'Connor's test was originally offered as a clarification of *Lemon*, by 1989, in *County of Allegheny v. ACLU*, a bare majority of the Court adopted the new approach, invalidating a Pittsburgh, Pennsylvania, holiday display of a freestanding nativity scene in a courthouse as an unconstitutional "endorsement" of religion. Although the *Lemon* test continually resurfaces (as suggested by Justice Scalia's colorful metaphor), its usefulness in helping the Court decide difficult establishment clause cases is, at best, doubtful.

Selected Bibliography

Abraham, Henry J., and Barbara A. Perry. *Freedom and the Court: Civil Rights and Liberties in the United States*, 6th ed. New York: Oxford University Press, 1994.

Marks, Thomas C., Jr. "*Lemon* Is a Lemon: Toward a Rational Interpretation of the Establishment Clause." *Brigham Young Journal of Public Law* 12 (1997): 1–69.

Expanded Exercise: The Amish, Compulsory Education, and Religious Freedom

—◄○►—

Steven D. Reschly
Department of History
Truman State University

Wisconsin v. Yoder, 406 U.S. 205 (1972) [U.S. Supreme Court]

◄○► THE CASE IN BRIEF ◄○►

Date
1972

Location
Wisconsin

Court
U.S. Supreme Court

Principal Participants
Jonas Yoder; Wallace Miller; Adin Yutzy; State of Wisconsin; Chief Justice Warren Burger

Significance of the Case
The Supreme Court ruled in favor of Amish parents who had challenged a state compulsory education law by keeping their children out of high school. The Court cited the free exercise clause of the First Amendment and called for a balance between state and parental interest of children.

Early in 1966, Adin Yutzy, an adherent of the Old Order Amish religion, sold his farm in Iowa and moved his family to Green County, Wisconsin, "to get away from all the trouble." The "trouble" Yutzy sought to escape occurred in Buchanan County, Iowa, in 1965 and involved Amish resistance to state compulsory education laws. The dispute in Iowa produced a dramatic photo of Amish children dashing into a cornfield to avoid a forced bus trip to high school, intervention by Governor Harold Hughes, and a statutory exemption to the state's minimum educational standards law granted by the Iowa legislature. Similar compromise solutions had been reached in Pennsylvania and Indiana, where Amish children attended Amish-run vocational schools between completing eighth grade and reaching age sixteen.

Only two years later, Yutzy and two other Amish fathers were arrested near New Glarus, Wisconsin, for failing to enroll their three children in high school. Frieda Yoder and Barbara Miller, both aged fifteen, and Vernon Yutzy, aged fourteen, all had completed the eighth grade in public schools. On complaint of the local school administrator, Jonas Yoder, Wallace Miller, and Adin Yutzy were arrested in November 1968 for violating the Wisconsin compulsory attendance law, which required schooling until a child's sixteenth birthday. As in most states, parents were held responsible for attendance. The three parents were charged, tried, and convicted in Green County Court, and were fined $5 each. However, before the trial began in March 1969, Yutzy moved once again, to southern Missouri, still seeking relief from compulsory education laws.

Why did consolidated schools and compulsory education beyond eighth grade violate Amish religion? The Amish trace their historical and spiritual roots to the Radical Reformation of sixteenth-century Europe. The Amish branch of the Anabaptists separated from the main body of Swiss Brethren and Mennonites in Switzerland and Alsace in the 1690s. Led by Jacob Amman, an elder in the Swiss Brethren congregation at Markirch in Alsace, the Amish emphasized keeping the church pure through strict discipline and visible separation from the world. Biblical texts such as "Be not conformed to this world" (Romans 12:2) and "Do not be unequally yoked with unbelievers" (II Corinthians 6:14), combined with the historical experience of intense persecution and isolation, contributed to strong Amish values of differentiation from mainstream society.

Migration to America began in the 1730s, and the Amish established viable communities in Pennsylvania along with other German minority religions. By the early nineteenth century, the increasing pace of industrialization and urbanization led to stronger efforts by Amish leaders to maintain separate and distinct communities. The Amish built a "spiritual fence" to protect themselves against the encroachments of the world by developing comprehensive regulation and guidance of life, such as clothing, hair styles, decoration of homes, retention of German, and many other aspects of behavior; this containment became known as *Ordnung*, or "order," and separation from "pride" and anything "worldly" became overriding principles in Amish life.

In the nineteenth century, Amish children attended local public schools and Amish parents often helped establish schools and served on school boards. By the early twentieth century, consolidation and, especially, the high school movement began to threaten the carefully constructed fence protecting the Amish community from external forces. Consolidation weakened parental authority over children, and expanding the horizons of adolescents in high school endangered their loyalty to the Amish community. Both imperiled the efforts of Amish parents to retain their children within an agrarian religious tradition. At the same time, compulsory education laws, often tied to child labor legislation, required parents to enroll their children in school until a certain age, generally age sixteen, or about two years of high school. Conflict with public officials occurred when the Amish refused to honor compulsory attendance laws which required high school attendance.

An Amish writer and teacher summarized the essential conflict in 1965: "The public schools are not striving for the same goal Christian parents are. We are not interested in building missiles and jet aircraft. They are not interested in building Christians. We must go separate ways." The first recorded conflict occurred in Geauga County, Ohio, in 1914, coinciding with the reorganization of the Ohio public school system. Three Amish men were fined because they kept their children out of school in violation of the new school statutes. Amish frequently suffered fines and jail sentences during the 1920s and 1930s, but were slow to establish parochial schools because the point of controversy was high school attendance. With the exception of one case in Pennsylvania in 1949, all court decisions went against the Amish. In 1966, the Kansas Supreme Court adopted a distinction between the right to believe and the right to act in upholding the Kansas compulsory education law against an Amish man, LeRoy Garber; the U.S. Supreme Court denied review of the case.

The Amish traditionally refuse to pursue litigation and are reluctant to allow others to litigate in their behalf, often preferring migration in pursuit of less restrictive conditions, the very solution attempted by Adin Yutzy. The Supreme Court case which decided the Amish education controversy arose from an unlikely location: a tiny, recent Amish settlement in southern Wisconsin. Begun in 1963 and consisting of only twenty-four families in 1968, New Glarus took temporary priority over the larger and more visible Amish communities in Lancaster County, Pennsylvania, Holmes County, Ohio, and Lagrange County, Indiana. The National Committee for Amish Religious Freedom, organized by the Lutheran pastor William C. Lindholm in 1966, took the lead in organizing the legal defense of the three Amish parents from New Glarus, and succeeded in gaining their cooperation and consent in appealing the case to higher courts. Attorney William Ball of Harrisburg, Pennsylvania, represented the Amish all the way from Green County to the U.S. Supreme Court.

One defendant in the local trial, Wallace Miller, was a Conservative Amish Mennonite, whereas Jonas Yoder and Adin Yutzy were Old Order Amish. The county court took note of the difference, and acknowledged that Miller belonged to a related Amish group and could take part in the defense. Thereafter all parties referred to the parents as "Amish." Ball used expert testimony from the sociologist John A. Hostetler, the educator Donald A. Erickson, and local law enforcement and welfare officials to establish the intimate ties of Amish faith with life, the critical and successful role of education in maintaining the Amish community, and the complete lack of burden placed upon local legal and welfare systems by Amish customs.

The state did not contest the severe restriction placed upon Amish religious practice by compulsory high school attendance, but instead argued that "the state's compelling interest in an informed citizenry to support a democratic society" was sufficient to justify infringement of the free exercise clause of the First Amendment. At one point in the testimony, the state's prosecutor cross-examined Dr. Hostetler regarding education: "Now, Doctor, let's talk about education. What's the point of education? Isn't it to get ahead in the world?" Hostetler replied, "It all depends on which world," referring to the Amish view that education is preparation for salvation rather than for secular success. Erickson testified that learning by doing represented an "ideal system of education" which fully prepared Amish children for productive membership in their community. Higher courts repeat-

edly turned to the testimony of Hostetler and Erickson for guidance.

Following the pattern of most court cases, dating as far back as 1927, the Green County and Wisconsin circuit courts ruled against the Amish. Despite the trial court's finding that the compulsory education law infringed upon the free exercise of religion by the defendants, the courts held that the state's compelling interest in educating its citizens must overcome any violation of the Amish religion. However, the Wisconsin Supreme Court, in an elegantly written opinion by Chief Justice Hallows, reversed and ruled in favor of the Amish on January 8, 1971. The First Amendment, made applicable to the states by the Fourteenth Amendment, prevented Wisconsin from compelling Amish parents to enroll their children in public high school. Hallows wrote that, beyond the danger of exterminating the Amish community, "There is another impact on the Amish children themselves if they are required to go to high school. They would experience a useless anguish of living in two worlds. Either the education they receive in the public school is irrelevant to their lives as members of the Old Order Amish or these secondary school values will make life as Amish impossible." Basing the decision on the religious liberty of Amish parents to rear their children in their religion, the court denied any harmful impact of an exception from compulsory education for the Amish, because such an exemption "will do no more to the ultimate goal of education than to dent the symmetry of the design of enforcement." Further, the court denied any use of a belief-action distinction despite the precedent of Mormon polygamy rulings. For the Amish, "[t]heir life style is dictated rather than motivated by their religion."

In a move that surprised attorney Ball, the state of Wisconsin decided to appeal its case to the U.S. Supreme Court. Bearded Amish leaders ascended the Supreme Court steps on December 8, 1971, to observe oral argument in the case and to seek protection for their way of life. Assistant Attorney General John W. Calhoun argued the case for Wisconsin, and Ball represented the Amish. Briefs of amici curiae urging affirmation were submitted by such diverse groups as the Mennonite Central Committee, the Seventh-Day Adventists, the National Council of Churches,

Amish children from Lancaster, Pennsylvania, ride in the back of a horse-drawn buggy. *AP Photo/Rusty Kennedy.*

the National Jewish Commission on Law and Public Affairs, and the Synagogue Council of America.

In a 7-0 vote, delivered by Chief Justice Warren Burger on May 15, 1972 (Justices Lewis Powell and William Rehnquist took no part in the case), the Supreme Court affirmed the Wisconsin decision and freed the Amish from compulsory high school attendance. The High Court followed the Wisconsin Supreme Court for the most part, with the critical conceptual addition of a "balancing process" to resolve the conflict of interest between state and parents. The Court recognized the high responsibility of the state for education of its citizens. However, Burger wrote, "[A] State's interest in universal education, however highly we rank it, is not totally free from a balancing process when it impinges on fundamental rights and interests, such as those specifically protected by the free exercise clause of the First Amendment, and the traditional interest of parents with respect to the religious upbringing of their children." Burger utilized a two-part test for analyzing free exercise claims. For Wisconsin to require school attendance beyond the eighth grade, "it must appear either that the State does not deny the free exercise of religious belief by its requirement, or that there is a state interest of sufficient magnitude to override the interest claiming protection under the Free Exercise Clause." The Court proceeded to make proving sufficient state interest extremely difficult, because "only those interests of the highest order

and those not otherwise served can overbalance legitimate claims to the free exercise of religion."

After confirming that compulsory high school education did indeed pose a genuine threat to Amish religious practice and articulating the principle of balancing state and parental interests, the Court proceeded to evaluate Wisconsin's claim to compelling interest. Wisconsin advanced Jeffersonian arguments that education prepares citizens for political participation and prepares individuals to be self-reliant and self-sufficient members of society. Wisconsin also argued that compulsory education is necessary to protect children from ignorance, to allow for the possibility that some Amish children will leave the community and must be prepared for secular life, and that the common-law doctrine of *parens patriae* (state as parent) constituted a substantive right of the Amish child to a secondary education because the state could extend that benefit to children regardless of the wishes of their parents. The Court rejected these arguments, noting that Amish children were exceptionally well prepared for life in Amish communities; that the Amish were not opposed to all education beyond the eighth grade, only to conventional formal education; and that Amish values of reliability, self-reliance, and dedication to work would hardly place an individual at a disadvantage if that person decided to leave the community. In fact, Jefferson's ideal of the "sturdy yeoman" who would serve as the basis for democratic society may find its most complete contemporary fulfillment in the Amish. The Court denied any sweeping power of the state to intervene on behalf of children at the expense of parents' wishes.

Wisconsin failed to prove that forcing Amish children to attend public high school for one or two years beyond the eighth grade would serve any compelling state interest. In fact, by inhibiting the adolescent's integration into the community, compulsory education imposed a severe burden on the parents' religious practices. Therefore, the U.S. Supreme Court affirmed the Supreme Court of Wisconsin in holding that "the First and Fourteenth Amendments prevent the State from compelling respondents to cause their children to attend formal high school to age 16."

However, the Court also carefully circumscribed the decision: "Nothing we hold is intended to undermine the general applicability of the State's compulsory school-attendance statutes or to limit the power of the State to promulgate reasonable standards that, while not impairing the free exercise of religion, provide for continuing agricultural vocational education under parental and church guidance by the Old Order Amish or others similarly situated."

The doctrine of balancing parental and state interests drew a partial dissent from Justice William O. Douglas. In assessing the threat to free exercise, the Court conflated the interests of Amish parent and child, on the grounds that the parents were the ones at risk of punishment. Douglas argued that the balancing process neglected the interests of children, who "themselves have constitutionally protectible interests." Douglas also expressed concern that the decision "opens the way to give organized religion a broader base than it has ever enjoyed." He seemed to miss the point, however, by proclaiming, "Religion is an individual experience." For the Amish, religion is a communal experience.

The landmark First Amendment ruling, *Wisconsin v. Yoder*, provided relief for Adin Yutzy and other Amish parents. The opinion also expanded the purview of the free exercise clause of the First Amendment. However, attempts to apply *Yoder* to other arenas, such as home schooling and preservation of Native American religious sites, have generally not met with success. Religious fundamentalists do not intend to isolate themselves entirely from the rest of society, and the "threshold tests" for evaluating free exercise claims have not transferred easily to non-Christian religions or individual conscience. The chronically ambiguous relationship of church and state continues. In *Yoder*, free exercise seems to mean, above all, the right to be left alone in educational policy.

Schools play a critical role in the reproduction of an established social order, in both dominant and minority cultures. Wisconsin argued that uniform schooling is essential to preserve a democratic political system, to prevent individuals from becoming an economic burden on society, and to socialize children into a common value system acceptable to the majority. The Amish sought the right to direct a nonconformist process of social reproduction, in order to foster cultural values at variance with the dominant society. Cultural pluralism won out over standardization in *Wisconsin v. Yoder*.

On hearing that the Supreme Court had upheld the Amish, defendant Jonas Yoder choked with deep emotion, then remarked, "I'm not one for making words, but it is a miracle from God. It's wonderful that a small people like us can still make a law in Washington. Now I just want to go back to farming."

Selected Bibliography

Erickson, Donald A., ed. *Public Controls for Nonpublic Schools*. Chicago: University of Chicago Press, 1969.

Hostetler, John A. *Amish Society*. 4th ed. Baltimore: Johns Hopkins University Press, 1993.

Hostetler, John A., and Gertrude Enders Huntington. *Amish Children: Education in the Family, School, and Community*. New York: Harcourt Brace Jovanovich, 1992.

Keim, Albert N., ed. *Compulsory Education and the Amish: The Right Not to Be Modern*. Boston: Beacon Press, 1975.

Kraybill, Donald B. *The Riddle of Amish Culture*. Baltimore: Johns Hopkins University Press, 1989.

McVicker, Debra D. "The Interest of the Child in the Home Education Question: *Wisconsin v. Yoder* Reexamined." *Indiana Law Review* 18 (Summer 1985): 711–729.

Riga, Peter J. "Yoder and Free Exercise." *Journal of Law and Education* 6 (October 1977): 449–472.

Sher, Jonathan P., ed. *Education in Rural America: A Reassessment of Conventional Wisdom*. Boulder, CO: Westview Press, 1977.

Thompson, Scott E. "The Demise of Free Exercise: An Historical Analysis of Where We Are, and How We Got There." *Regent University Law Review* 11 (1998): 169–192.

The Pieties of Silence

—◁◦▷—

Frank J. Sorauf

Emeritus Professor of Political Science
University of Minnesota

Wallace, Governor of Alabama, et al. v. Jaffree, 472 U.S. 38 (1985) [U.S. Supreme Court]

◁◦▷ THE CASE IN BRIEF ◁◦▷

Date
1985

Location
Alabama

Court
U.S. Supreme Court

Principal Participants
Alabama Governor George C. Wallace
Ishmael Jaffree

Significance of the Case
The Supreme Court invalidated a state's statute authorizing meditation and voluntary prayer in public schools. The Court found that the law did not have a secular purpose as set forth in the "Lemon test."

When the Supreme Court suddenly ended prayer and Bible reading in the public schools in the early 1960s, there was bound to be a major reaction. In a number of parts of the country the religious practices went on as before, especially in smaller or homogeneous communities in which no one disapproved or no one was prepared to pay the price of disapproving. Other proponents of prayer framed a constitutional amendment to overturn the Court's decisions; however, it never got the necessary two-thirds vote in the two houses of Congress. Simultaneously, a number of state legislatures and local school districts cast about for alternatives to prayer that the Court would accept—prayerful verses of "America," Bible studies before and after school, and, in about half of the states, a "moment of silence."

The Alabama legislature approached the problem in three stages, each increasingly hostile to the Court's rulings. In 1978 it authorized a one-minute period of silence in the schools "for meditation"; in 1981 it approved a period of silence for "meditation or voluntary prayer"; and a year later it authorized teachers to lead "willing students" in a prescribed prayer. As things turned out, it was only the second of the three statutes—silence for "meditation or voluntary prayer"—that was at issue in *Wallace v. Jaffree*. That statute provided that the moment of silence not exceed a minute, that it be held at the beginning of the day, and that no other activities be undertaken during the silent moment.

In 1982 Ishmael Jaffree, an agnostic and an attorney with the Legal Services Corporation, filed suit against the school board of Mobile County challenging both the second and the third of the Alabama statutes. His suit followed the complaints of his three children that their teachers led prayers in school. It was, as most such suits are, an unpopular one. Jaffree was quoted in the *New York Times* about the effects of the suit. He had become, he said, "sort of *persona non grata* in the black community now, but the black community doesn't understand: I was never opposed to religion." As for his youngsters, "I'm still sorry for my children. They have told me they wish I'd never filed the suit. They said they have lost friends over it." Jaffree's suit never challenged the first Alabama statute, the one simply authorizing a period of meditation; his attorney, in fact, freely conceded its constitutionality throughout the case.

The decision of the federal district court went against Jaffree in a opinion the U.S. Supreme Court was later to characterize as "remarkable." Judge William Hand upheld the two Alabama statutes by ruling that the First Amendment and its establishment clause did not apply to the states, thus ignoring some fifty years of Supreme Court precedents and the entire process of incorporating the First Amendment into the due process clause of the Fourteenth Amendment. The Court of Appeals for the Eleventh Circuit overruled, and held the statutes in violation of the Fourteenth Amendment's application of the separation of church and state to the states. On appeal, the U.S. Supreme Court upheld the Court of Appeals summarily on the question of the 1982 statute (the one permitting prayer) and scheduled full oral argument on the questions raised by the 1981 statute—the second one—

authorizing the moment of silence for "meditation or prayer."

In a 6-3 decision, the Supreme Court invalidated that statute because of the legislature's religious purpose and intentions. The testimony of the bill's sponsor in district court was unequivocal; when asked if his bill had any purpose other than the encouragement of prayer in the schools, he replied, "No, I did not have no other purpose in mind." Justice John Paul Stevens, writing for the majority, also relied on the logic of passing the 1981 statute after having passed one in 1978 simply setting up time for meditation. One of the dissenters, however, observed that the words "meditation or prayer" in 1981 might only have been there to make clear that prayer was a legitimate activity during the silence. (Nonetheless, the Court ruled that Alabama's law had failed to meet its requirement that legislation on religion have a "secular purpose," as set forth in *Lemon v. Kurtzman* [1971].)

All three dissenters—Chief Justice Warren Burger and Justices Byron White and William Rehnquist—wrote opinions. It was Rehnquist's that was the most dramatic. Arguing for a completely new interpretation of the establishment clause, he spurned both the "wall of separation" metaphor and the Court's contemporary three-part test for violations of the separation. Rehnquist's case for beginning anew on church-state relationships rested primarily on his conviction that the framers of the First Amendment had intended only to prevent the favoring of one religion or sect over others.

Only fellow dissenter Byron White answered Rehnquist's call to arms. The *Jaffree* case thus extended the Court's commitment to a view of church-state separation that originated with *Everson v. Board of Education* some thirty-eight years earlier. As such, it was a loss for conservatives generally, for the Republican party, and for the Reagan administration, all of whom had hoped that the Court would retreat from its insistence on strict separation. The administration had urged the Court to do so in a brief of amicus curiae, and Deputy Solicitor General Paul Bator had supported that position in oral argument.

In broad doctrinal terms, therefore, *Jaffree*'s importance rests, in part, on what the Court did *not* decide. The same could be said for the outcome on the facts of "silence." It was clearly a narrow decision that hinged on the intention of the Alabama legislature to encourage prayer in the public schools. Though the Court did not rule specifically on moments of silence without encouragements to prayer, a number of the opinions in the case were at pains to indicate that moments without a religious agenda would pass muster.

Unless it is explicitly intended for prayer by school or public officials, the period of silence remains an option for schools wanting to assist student prayer in the schools. About half of the states permit school districts to adopt it, and an unknown number have done so. However, it does not satisfy many advocates of school prayer. They often prefer student-led religious organizations or prayer sessions in the school before or after classes, an option the Supreme Court validated in 1990 in *Board of Education v. Mergens*. Many also hope for an amendment to the U.S. Constitution permitting school prayer, one version of which the House of Representatives, but not the Senate, approved in 1998.

Selected Bibliography

Dellinger, Walter. "The Sound of Silence: An Epistle on Prayer and the Constitution." *Yale Law Review* 95 (July 1986): 1631–1646.

Note. "The Supreme Court: Leading Cases." *Harvard Law Review* 99 (November 1985): 183–193.

Religious Practices and the First Amendment: The Peyote Case

———◦———

Tinsley E. Yarbrough
Department of Political Science
East Carolina University

Employment Division v. Smith, 494 U.S. 872 (1990) [U.S. Supreme Court]

◦ THE CASE IN BRIEF ◦

Date
1990

Location
Oregon

Court
U.S. Supreme Court

Principal Participants
Alfred Smith; Galen Black; State of Oregon

Significance of the Case
The Supreme Court, by upholding a state's denial of benefits to two Native Americans due to their sacramental use of peyote, placed a larger burden on free exercise claims of religious conduct under the First Amendment. One of the later ramifications of the *Smith* decision was the passing of the Religious Freedom Restoration Act in 1993.

The initial U.S. Supreme Court case construing the First Amendment's ban on laws "prohibiting the free exercise [of religion]," *Reynolds v. United States* (1879), drew a clear-cut distinction between religious beliefs and religious practices, holding that the latter were subject to broad governmental control. In *Sherbert v. Verner* (1963), however, a Warren court majority held that government regulations affecting religious practices were contrary to the free exercise guarantee unless they furthered compelling governmental interests through means least restrictive of religious liberty. Invoking that balancing approach, the *Sherbert* decision overturned a state's denial of unemployment compensation to a Seventh-Day Adventist who was unable to keep or find a job not requiring work on Saturday, her day of worship. Emphasizing the grave burdens that Saturday labor imposed on her religious scruples, the Court concluded that the state's interest in preventing fraudulent claims and preserving the integrity of its treasury could be satisfied through means less restrictive of the claimant's freedom. In *Thomas v. Review Board* (1981), the Burger court reaffirmed *Sherbert* in sustaining the right to unemployment benefits of a Jehovah's Witness who quit his industrial job when he was transferred to a department manufacturing weaponry. The Court also extended *Sherbert* to other contexts, holding in *Wisconsin v. Yoder* (1972), for example, that a state had no compelling interest justifying compulsory high school attendance for Amish children in violation of their parents' religious beliefs. Early in William H. Rehnquist's tenure as Chief Justice, however, the Court confined *Sherbert* and its progeny largely to their facts, revived *Reynolds,* and held religious practices to be subject to neutral, generally applicable laws, whether or not the regulations at issue satisfied the compelling interest standard.

In the 1980s Alfred Smith and Galen Black were drug counselors at a private alcohol and drug abuse prevention center in an Oregon county. Both were also members of the Native American Church, which included the ingesting of peyote, a hallucinogenic substance, in its religious rituals. On learning of their use of peyote, the agency that ran the school discharged both men and the state denied them unemployment benefits on the ground that their discharge was for misconduct. Following hearings, a referee concluded in each case that the state had shown no significant interest justifying the denial of benefits. The Oregon Employment Appeals Board reversed, concluding that Oregon's interest in prohibiting the use of illegal drugs was an adequate basis for the state's action. The Oregon Court of Appeals then reversed the board. If the claimants' use of peyote was religiously based, the appeals court ruled, the state's denial of unemployment compensation had imposed a substantial burden upon their free exercise rights. The state's interest in protecting its unemployment compensation fund fell far short of the "compelling interest" standard, the court concluded. Furthermore, the Oregon Court of Appeals ruled, the state's interest in drug control, albeit important, was irrelevant to a resolution of the dispute because the claimants had not been terminated for breaking Oregon's drug laws, but for violating a private agency's personnel rule forbidding employee drug use. The Court of Appeals remanded the case to the Employment Appeals Board, however, for a determination as to whether the claimants' use of peyote constituted a religious act.

Although finding no violation of religious liberty guarantees in the Oregon constitution, the Oregon Supreme Court, citing *Sherbert v. Verner,* agreed that the state's action violated the free exercise clause of the First Amendment. The court noted that the state's financial interest in its unemployment fund, not the weightier commitment to effective drug enforcement, had been cited as the principal justification for the denial of benefits. This financial interest, the Oregon court concluded, hardly overrode the claimants' free exercise rights. Convinced, unlike the appeals court, that the claimants' ingesting of peyote was based upon their sincere religious beliefs, the Oregon Supreme Court saw no need to remand the case to the Employment Appeals Board for further proceedings on that issue.

When the case first went to the U.S. Supreme Court on a writ of certiorari, the justices in 1988 (*Smith I*) remanded the matter to the Oregon Supreme Court for a determination as to whether the sacramental use of peyote was in fact proscribed by Oregon's controlled substance statute. After the Oregon high court ruled that Oregon's drug law made no exception for religious peyote use, the U.S. Supreme Court in 1990 (*Smith II*) upheld the state's denial of benefits and rejected the claimants' free exercise challenge.

Near the end of Chief Justice Warren Burger's tenure, Justice John Paul Stevens had questioned the propriety of applying the *Sherbert* compelling interest standard in cases involving religiously neutral laws of general application. In *United States v. Lee* (1982), the chief justice purported to apply a version of the compelling interest formula in subjecting Amish workers and their employers to Social Security taxes. In a brief *Lee* concurrence, Justice Stevens, a frequent critic of dogmatic constitutional doctrines in a variety of fields, observed, "That [compelling interest] formulation of the constitutional standard suggests that the Government always bears a heavy burden of justifying the application of religiously neutral laws to individual conscientious objectors. In my opinion, it is the objector who must shoulder the burden of demonstrating that there is a unique reason for allowing him a special exemption from a valid law of general applicability." Congress, Stevens reasoned, had already exempted self-employed members of religious groups from any obligation to pay Social Security taxes; and lost revenue created by extension of the exemption to Amish employed by others would be more than offset by their elimination from the Social Security rolls. Given the demonstrated Amish capacity for self-sufficiency, on the other hand, the social impact on the group would be minimal. Stevens thus could not agree that the government had established an overriding interest in requiring Amish employees and their employers to pay Social Security taxes. Yet, in his view, the requirement did not infringe upon their First Amendment rights. What was needed, Stevens contended, was a flexible constitutional standard, deferential to legitimate government interests.

Speaking for a 6-3 majority in the peyote case, Justice Antonin Scalia probably went further than Justice Stevens would have preferred. Although his opinion did not overrule *Sherbert* and other cases subjecting laws that affected religious practices to the strict, compelling interest standard of review, it did distinguish those precedents and held that the application of religiously neutral, generally applicable laws to religious practices was exempt from virtually all judicial scrutiny under the free exercise guarantee. The regulations at issue in *Wisconsin v. Yoder* and other cases not involving unemployment compensation claims had been accorded strict review, Scalia reasoned, only because they involved "not the Free Exercise Clause alone, but the Free Exercise Clause in conjunction with other constitutional protections, such as freedom of speech and of the press . . . or the right of parents . . . to direct the education of their children." The peyote dispute presented no such "hybrid situation." Justice Scalia appeared to concede that *Sherbert* and other unemployment compensation cases raised only free exercise claims. He emphasized, however, that the law relating to unemployment benefits was characterized by an extensive network of exemptions and individualized official judgments with considerable potential for abuse. Hence, following its reading of *Sherbert,* the Court concluded that a state, in order to further a compelling interest, could deny benefits to those unable to find work for religious reasons. But *Sherbert* had "nothing to do with an across-the-board prohibition on a particular form of conduct." Indeed, to hold such regulations subject to strict judicial scrutiny whenever they reached conduct based on religious beliefs would make the individual, declared Scalia, quoting *Reynolds,* "a law unto himself."

Justice Sandra Day O'Connor concurred only in the Court's judgment. O'Connor favored retention of the compelling interest standard for all cases involving free exercise claims, but concluded that Oregon's interest in the effective enforcement of its drug laws met that demanding standard. Justice Harry A. Blackmun, joined by Justices William J. Brennan and Thurgood Marshall, agreed with O'Connor that the state's denial of unemployment benefits based on ritual peyote use was subject to strict scrutiny, but rejected her application of the standard in the case. The governmental interest at stake in the suit, Blackmun argued, was not the state's broad interest in effective drug enforcement, but its limited interest in refusing to create an exception for the religious, ceremonial use of peyote. In Blackmun's view, that latter interest in no way satisfied the demands of strict review. Characterizing peyote as a distasteful, hardly addictive drug, the religious use of which was not even remotely related to "the vast and violent traffic in illegal narcotics that plagues this country," Blackmun also termed "purely speculative" the state's concern that recognition of the peyote exemption would lead to a flood of similar religious claims. After all, Blackmun observed, nearly half the states and the federal government had exempted sacramental peyote use for many years, without confronting an overwhelming number of similar claims.

In the wake of the Supreme Court's decision in *Smith,* a broad and politically diverse coalition of interest groups lobbied Congress to enact legislation restoring a variety of religious exemptions and application of the *Sherbert* standard to all laws affecting religious practices. In

1993, Congress overwhelmingly adopted, and President Bill Clinton signed into law, the Religious Freedom Restoration Act (RFRA). The statute contained formal findings that the *Smith* decision had all but eliminated constitutional protection from laws neutral toward religion that nevertheless imposed significant burdens on the free exercise of religion. Operative RFRA provisions stipulated that laws substantially burdening the free exercise of religion, even if the burden resulted from a rule of general applicability, were unconstitutional unless they furthered a compelling interest through means least restrictive of free exercise rights.

A majority on the Supreme Court remained firmly committed, however, to its *Smith* stance. When a Texas community relied on its historic preservation ordinance in denying a permit to enlarge a local Roman Catholic church, the area archbishop filed suit under RFRA. In *City of Boerne v. Flores* (1997), a 6-3 majority, speaking this time through Justice Anthony Kennedy, invalidated RFRA and its application in the Texas case. Kennedy agreed that Congress was entitled to broad discretion in choosing the means for enforcing the provisions of the Fourteenth Amendment, through which the free exercise guarantee had been extended to the states. He emphasized, however, that ultimate power to determine the substantive scope of constitutional guarantees lay with the courts, not Congress, and declared the RFRA an unconstitutional usurpation of judicial authority. In separate dissents, Justices O'Connor, David H. Souter, and Stephen Breyer recommended a full reexamination of *Smith*. But the majority obviously was not so inclined.

As the broad nature of the coalition of interest groups supporting RFRA's adoption demonstrated, *Smith* is clearly a source of concern for all religious groups. It impinges most heavily, however, upon unorthodox religious groups and their practices rather than on mainstream sects. Justice Scalia conceded as much in his *Smith*

opinion when he observed that "[i]t may fairly be said that leaving accommodation [of claims to religious exemptions from general laws] to the political process will place at a relative disadvantage those religious practices that are not widely engaged in." The rituals of mainstream groups, by contrast, are part of the nation's dominant traditions and, thus, either infringe no criminal law or enjoy special exemption from "neutral" regulations (sacramental consumption of wine, for example). Read together, the *Smith* rationale and the Court's growing willingness, in such cases as *Agostini v. Felton* (1997), to support government accommodation of orthodox religious groups arguably reflect acceptance of an inherently discriminatory approach to the religious issues in constitutional law. On the one hand, *Smith* offers little or no protection to the religious liberty claims of unorthodox groups, except in those rare situations in which a sect's practices are singled out for special restrictions—as, for example, in *Church of Lukumi v. City of Hialeah* (1993), when a community forbade ritual sacrifice of animals while permitting virtually every other form of animal slaughter. On the other hand, the Rehnquist Court's flexible approach to religious establishment issues enables government increasingly to accommodate public policy to mainstream religious traditions and needs. For those committed to a broad reading of both the First Amendment's religion provisions, the Court's developing stance is indeed alarming.

Selected Bibliography

Marshall, W. "The Case Against the Constitutionally Compelled Free Exercise Exemption." *Case Western Reserve Law Review* 40 (1990): 357–412.

Long, Carolyn N. *Religious Freedom and Indian Rights: The Case of* Oregon v. Smith. Lawrence: University Press of Kansas, 2000.

Yarbrough, Tinsley E. *The Rehnquist Court and the Constitution.* New York: Oxford University Press, 2000.

Obscenity and Pornography

Obscenity: "I Know It When I See It!"

—◄◦►—

Elizabeth E. Traxler

Department of Social Sciences
Greenville Technical College

Roth v. United States, 354 U.S. 473 (1957) [U.S. Supreme Court]

◄◦► THE CASE IN BRIEF ◄◦►

Date
1957

Location
New York
District of Columbia

Court
U.S. Court of Appeals
U.S. Supreme Court

Principal Participants
Samuel Roth
United States government

Significance of the Case
The Supreme Court ruled that obscenity is a form of speech or expression that is an exception to the seemingly absolute prohibition of Congress's ability to make laws governing free speech or expression. However, the question of what constitutes obscenity is still open to debate.

"Congress shall make no law . . . abridging the freedom of speech, or of the press. . . ." Of all the civil liberties given in the Bill of Rights, this grant of freedom of expression is one Americans hold most dear. And unlike other much-litigated phrases of the Constitution, such as "equal protection" and "due process," its meaning appears to be quite straightforward, in need of little interpretation. In fact, this First Amendment freedom could be understood as an absolute, allowing for no exceptions to the rule. It does not say, for instance, "Congress shall not make most laws" or "Congress shall make only acceptable laws," but says Congress shall make *no* law. Yet the courts have struggled with it through the years when confronted with situations seeming to require that exceptions be found to its apparently absolute prohibition.

As Samuel Roth learned with his conviction for engaging in the distribution of obscene works and his subsequent loss on appeal, "obscenity" has been identified as one such exception. The Supreme Court decision in *Roth v. United States*, handed down in 1957, stands today as the landmark case governing the relationship of obscenity to the protection offered speech by the U.S. Constitution.

Samuel Roth and the publications he sought to distribute were perhaps unlikely warriors to wage a defense of such a cherished civil liberty. A Polish immigrant, Roth had established a successful mail order business in New York City dealing in erotica and obscene works. His first brush with obscenity statutes had come with his unsuccessful efforts in the 1930s to distribute James Joyce's *Ulysses*. But the publications which led to his arrest in 1955 were hardly such works of literary merit. *Photo and Body* and *American Aphrodite Number Thirteen* have not emerged as classics in the field of literature. It was over such works, rather than ones of clear literary merit, that the U.S. Supreme Court would be asked to decide whether obscenity statutes were unconstitutional restrictions on First Amendment freedoms.

When arrested by federal authorities in 1955, Roth had been using the U.S. postal service to mail circulars advertising his merchandise to unsuspecting individuals. Several of these individuals complained, leading postal authorities to establish fictitious names and addresses from which orders were placed in order to ensnare Roth. Indictments charging Roth with twenty-six counts of violating the federal statute known as the Comstock Act followed. This act, which dated back to 1872, provided for criminal prosecution of anyone mailing obscene works or advertisements for them. Conviction could bring a maximum of five years in prison and/or a fine of up to $5,000. In 1956, found guilty on four counts by a jury in the U.S. District Court in New York, Roth received the maximum sentence. Though he had been convicted of similar offenses on two previous occasions, this was by far the longest sentence he had received. Not surprisingly, an appeal followed. On appeal to the U.S. Court of Appeals for the Second Circuit, Roth's lawyers questioned the constitutionality of the statute.

Roth's attorneys did not argue that the First Amendment absolutely prohibited restrictions on freedom of speech and press. After all, our government is founded on the belief that individuals have certain rights or liberties which ex-

isted prior to the creation of governments. The duty of government is to provide the order necessary for us to enjoy these liberties, until they come in conflict with others' rights. The difficulty, of course, is in determining the point at which government may step in to prevent an individual's liberties from infringing on the rights of others. The Supreme Court had grappled with an effort to demarcate this line in other First Amendment cases where obscenity was not at issue. The clear-and-present-danger test as elaborated by Justice Oliver Wendell Holmes was one result. At its most basic, this test held that the government could deny or restrict freedom of speech if it could be shown that such speech would likely result in illegal or antisocial acts shortly after the speech was uttered. By the time of the *Roth* case, this test had been revised somewhat to allow greater latitude for the government to restrict freedom of expression. However, suppression of freedom of speech still turned on the presence of unacceptable overt action, not mere thoughts following the speech. It was on this basis that Roth's attorneys, arguing that there was no evidence of a clear and present danger (of an overt act) resulting from exposure to obscene works, cast their appeal to the Second Circuit Court of Appeals.

The majority of that court was not swayed by this line of reasoning; it upheld Roth's conviction. Though the U.S. Supreme Court had not yet squarely addressed the constitutionality of obscenity legislation, the Court of Appeals relied on opinions from the High Court and from lower courts in asserting that regulation of obscenity had been presumed constitutional. Thus, the appellate court opinion maintained that it was not up to a lower court, but to the U.S. Supreme Court, to reopen the question. Though this absolved the appeals court from applying the clear-and-present-danger test, the opinion suggested that evidence seemed to point to a link between juvenile delinquency and such works. If true, this would render obscenity statutes acceptable under the clear-and-present-danger test.

The most interesting aspect of the Circuit Court's decision was the separate concurring opinion filed by Judge Jerome Frank. Despite voting with the majority to uphold Roth's conviction, Frank's opinion is better read as a dissent. He, too, maintained that it was up to the Supreme Court to rule on the constitutionality of the statute, but he attached an appendix to his opinion reviewing research evaluating the linkage between obscenity and antisocial conduct, and found it insufficient to meet the clear-and-present-danger test. Judge Frank's effort to provide the Supreme Court with the argument and evidence for use in rendering obscenity statutes unconstitutional proved unsuccessful, however.

Roth and his attorneys held out hope for a reversal of the appeals court decision when the Supreme Court agreed to hear the case and rule on the constitutionality of obscenity statutes. An attempt by the Supreme Court in 1947 to issue such an opinion had fallen short. As a friend of the author whose work was in question, Justice Felix Frankfurter felt obliged to disqualify himself, and the remaining eight justices split evenly on the decision. With no majority, the Court could not issue an opinion in the case. In the following ten years a number of lower court decisions treating this issue did not find obscenity statutes unconstitutional, but instead discussed the test to be used to determine whether a work fell into the obscene category.

When the Supreme Court justices read the briefs and heard oral arguments in *Roth* in April 1957, they were confronted with opposing views on the protection afforded obscenity by the First Amendment. The briefs of Roth's attorneys and a number of amici curiae, filed by organizations such as the American Civil Liberties Union and the Authors League of America, relied upon the clear-and-present-danger test. Because there was no agreement that reading obscene works produced illegal or antisocial conduct, the only "evil" which could result would be thoughts, not actions. The government, they argued, had no business regulating thoughts and, therefore, the statutes must be held unconstitutional.

The government, on the other hand, argued that not all speech was equally protected by the First Amendment; that some expression, such as speech concerning political issues, was due the greatest protection; and that other types of expression, such as obscenity, should receive the least protection. Thus, they attempted to establish a continuum of protection with various categories of speech arrayed along it. As one moved along the continuum toward obscenity, the evidence of dangerous acts resulting from the speech in question could be less specific and less documented.

The government's attorneys also sought to weaken the other side's contention that the banning of *American Aphrodite* might lead to the suppression of a literary masterpiece tomorrow. In an unusual departure from the norm, they provided the justices with a large sample of obscene works which had been seized by the postal service. The samples included only hardcore pornography of the worst variety, and this, they argued, was typical of the vast majority of materials covered by this law. Roth's attorneys were not permitted to view the samples, and to this day the influence the exhibit may have had on the Court's decision is unknown.

What is certain is that the majority of the Court refused both Roth's and the government's arguments which relied on the degree to which this statute met the clear-and-present-danger test. The ruling, which remains the core of the Court's position on obscenity, held that obscene works do not fall under the protection of the First Amendment. In his majority opinion, Justice William Brennan reviewed bills of rights in the states at the time of the Constitution's adoption, the history of state statutes governing obscenity, international agreements on obscenity, and various court cases. He concluded that not all speech, and in particular not obscenity, is to be afforded First Amendment protection. He maintained that obscenity fell into the same category of speech as libel. Five years earlier, in *Beauharnais v. Illinois* (1952), the Supreme Court had ruled that "group libel" was not speech under the meaning of the First Amendment. If there was no First Amendment protection, then the issue of whether suppression of obscenity met the clear-and-present-danger test was irrelevant.

Justice Brennan also ventured the opinion that, unlike speech afforded constitutional protection, obscenity was "utterly without redeeming social importance." Thus, if an expression contained social value, it fell under the First Amendment; if without such value, it stood alone and thus could be restricted or suppressed. Though *Roth* is often cited as the case in which this element became part of the test for obscenity, in fact it was not until the *Fanny Hill* decision several years later that Justice Brennan specifically added this language to the standards for scrutinizing allegedly obscene works.

The case's continuing importance also stemmed from Justice Brennan's efforts to define obscenity. If obscene utterances were not protected by the Constitution, a test would have to be devised to pinpoint obscenity. Justice Brennan's test for obscenity found in *Roth* included several elements: "whether to the average person, applying contemporary community standards, the dominant theme of the material appeals to prurient interest." The Court wished to devise a test which, on the one hand, would not permit a work such as the Bible to be labeled obscene and yet, on the other hand, would not open the floodgates to a tidal wave of hard-core pornography.

Samuel Roth, then, was not able to avoid conviction for mailing obscene works, nor was he able to convince the U.S. Supreme Court of the unconstitutionality of such laws. He did, however, lend his name to a decision which governed the law of obscenity for sixteen years. The fundamental difficulty underlying the issue remained unresolved. If the justices had accepted obscenity as within the protection of the First Amendment, they would have faced a dilemma of considerable magnitude. Without clear evidence that exposure to obscenity results in undesirable acts, how could its suppression be justified? If the relevant authorities agreed that obscenity could lead a person to engage in antisocial acts, the clear-and-present-danger test could be met. Short of this, the Court seemed to be faced with either a wholesale acceptance of obscenity, as argued by Roth and other civil libertarians, or the decision it actually reached. Categorizing obscenity as utterances outside constitutional protection presented even more difficulty by requiring its definition (i.e., when is speech obscene and when is it not?). The definition of obscenity, despite Justice Brennan's efforts in *Roth*, proved so elusive over the years

that the justices eventually agreed to follow their own separate paths. Ultimately, it came down to Justice Potter Stewart's famous admission in *Jacobellis v. Ohio* (1964): "I know it when I see it."

A Supreme Court with a number of new faces attempted to resolve this difficulty in 1973. Chief Justice Warren Burger, in *Miller v. California* (1973), devised yet another test for obscenity. Despite his revisions, no change occurred in the central holding of *Roth v. United States*—that certain speech, including obscenity, falls completely outside the protection afforded by the First Amendment. Even "Internet porn cases," such as *United States v. Thomas* (1996), have not deviated from this aspect of *Roth*.

Selected Bibliography

Doggett, Robert I. "Recent Decisions Approve Decency Statutes." *University of Cincinnati Law Review* 27 (Winter 1958): 61–75.

Ernest, Morris L., and Alan U. Schwartz. *Censorship: The Search for the Obscene.* New York: Macmillan, 1964.

Fahringer, Herald Price, and Michael J. Brown. "The Rise and Fall of *Roth*—A Critique of the Recent Supreme Court Obscenity Decisions." *Criminal Law Bulletin* 10 (November 1974): 785–826.

Gaede, Donovan W. "Constitutional Law-Policing the Obscene: Modern Obscenity Doctrine Reevaluated." *Southern Illinois University Law Journal* 18 (Winter 1994): 439–451.

Michael, Jennifer K. "Where's 'the Nastiest Place on Earth'? From *Roth* to Cyberspace of Whose Community Is It, Anyway? The US Court of Appeals for the Sixth Circuit Addresses Local Community Standards in *US v. Thomas.*" *Creighton Law Review* 30 (June 1997): 1405–1459.

Rembar, Charles. *The End of Obscenity.* New York: Random House, 1968.

Roberts, Simon. "The Obscenity Exception: Abusing the First Amendment." *Cardozo Law Review* 10 (February 1989): 677–728.

Schauer, Frederick F. *The Law of Obscenity.* Washington, DC: Bureau of National Affairs, 1976.

Schmidt, Godfrey P. "A Justification of Statutes Barring Pornography from the Mail." *Fordham Law Review* 26 (Spring 1957): 70–97.

A Book Named *Fanny Hill*

—◁o▷—

William Lasser

Department of Political Science
Clemson University

A Book Named "John Cleland's Memoirs of a Woman of Pleasure" et al. v.
Attorney General of Massachusetts, 383 U.S. 413 (1966) [U.S. Supreme Court]

◁o▷ THE CASE IN BRIEF ◁o▷

Date
 1966

Location
 Massachusetts

Court
 U.S. Supreme Court

Principal Participants
 Massachusetts attorney general
 Publisher
 Associate Justice William Brennan
 Associate Justices

Significance of the Case
 The Supreme Court set a three-element test for obscenity when a controversial book first published in the 1700s was declared not obscene.

The first reported obscenity case in the United States was an 1821 Massachusetts decision involving John Cleland's book *Memoirs of a Woman of Pleasure,* (published circa 1750), commonly known as *Fanny Hill.* It was therefore fitting that the most important obscenity case of the 1960s should also involve *Fanny Hill* and should also arise out of Massachusetts.

The 1966 Supreme Court case, generally known as *Memoirs v. Massachusetts,* began when the attorney general of Massachusetts brought a civil suit asking the courts of Massachusetts to declare *Fanny Hill* legally obscene. The Massachusetts procedure was designed to allow the courts to determine the legal status of an allegedly obscene book without the risk of criminal penalties against any interested party.

The legal status of obscenity in the United States was unsettled in the mid-1960s. The 1957 Supreme Court case *Roth v. United States* had determined that obscenity was not protected under the First Amendment and had made a first stab at defining that term under the law. Material could be declared obscene under *Roth* only if "the average person, applying contemporary community standards" would find that "the dominant theme of the material taken as a whole appeals to the prurient interest." The *Roth* formulation raised as many questions as it answered, and it sparked a rash of lawsuits and legal analyses.

Central to the *Roth* Court's classification of obscenity as unprotected speech was its finding that obscene speech was "utterly without redeeming social importance." "All ideas having even the slightest redeeming social importance—unorthodox ideas, controversial ideas, even ideas hateful to the prevailing climate of opinion—have the full protection of the guaranties" of the First Amendment, wrote Justice William Brennan for the Court. Obscenity, however, lacked even the slightest social importance, and was, therefore, outside the protections of the Constitution.

One of the issues left unclear by *Roth* was whether the Court's comments about "redeeming social importance" constituted an independent test for determining whether material was obscene, or were simply directed toward establishing the underlying basis for leaving obscenity outside the confines of the First Amendment. Put another way, the question was whether allegedly obscene material had to be shown not only to appeal to the prurient interest but also to be without redeeming social value; or, conversely, whether the showing of prurient interest carried with it the implication of a lack of social importance. The distinction was critical: if those who sought to ban publication of a book or to punish its distribution had to show that the material appealed to the prurient interest *and* was "without redeeming social importance," their burden would be far greater than if they had to satisfy the prurient interest test alone.

In 1964, in *Jacobellis v. Ohio*, Justices Brennan and Arthur Goldberg had suggested that the "social value test" was indeed separate and independent. *Memoirs* thus presented a perfect opportunity to allow the Court to clarify the meaning of *Roth* and to try to convince the entire Court that the social value test should be given independent weight. *Fanny Hill* was admittedly an erotic novel but, unlike much of the mate-

rial challenged as obscene in American courts, it was also recognized as literature. At the trial, several university professors testified as to the book's status as a literary document, describing the book as a minor "work of art" having "literary merit." It was placed squarely in the eighteenth-century English literary tradition of Samuel Richardson and Henry Fielding.

In the Supreme Court, counsel for *Fanny Hill* made the social value test explicit. The record in this case, the justices were told, contains "an overwhelming demonstration of the kind of value that all counsel here today agree invokes the protection of the First Amendment." Relying on Justice Brennan's argument in *Roth*, counsel urged that "under the decisions of this Court, if it has value, literary value or some other type of value, then it cannot be obscenity. Obscenity is worthless trash. That is its definition constitutionally."

The plurality decision in *Memoirs* accepted these contentions. Written by Justice Brennan and joined by Justice Abe Fortas and Chief Justice Earl Warren, it formally split the legal test for obscenity into three parts. For a work to be declared obscene, wrote Brennan, "three elements must coalesce: it must be established that (a) the dominant theme of the material taken as a whole appeals to a prurient interest in sex; (b) the material is patently offensive because it affronts contemporary community standards relating to the description or representation of sexual matters; and (c) the material is utterly without redeeming social value." Moreover, each of these tests had to be "applied independently; the social value of the book can neither be weighed against nor canceled by its prurient appeal or patent offensiveness." Under such a test, *Memoirs of a Woman of Pleasure* could not be declared obscene, for even the Massachusetts court below conceded that the book has "a modicum of literary and historical value."

Although Brennan's opinion carried the votes of only three justices, the concurring opinions of Justices Hugo Black and William O. Douglas made it clear that a majority of the Court supported at least the level of constitutional protection recognized by the plurality opinion. Justice Potter Stewart stuck by his view that the Constitution protects all but "hard-core" pornography, though he found it unnecessary to define that term. Justices Tom Clark, John Marshall Harlan, and Byron White dissented.

The *Memoirs* standard, never formally endorsed by a majority of the Court, lasted only seven years. In 1973, in *Miller v. California,* the Court modified it by refining the meaning of "community standards" and by removing the word "utterly" from the social value test. Henceforth, material could be classified as obscene if it lacked "serious literary, artistic, political or scientific value." Nevertheless, *Memoirs v. Mass-* *achusetts* remains a landmark on the Supreme Court's tortuous road toward developing a constitutional standard for obscenity.

Selected Bibliography

Fahringer, Herald Price, and Michael J. Brown. "The Rise and Fall of *Roth*—A Critique of the Recent Supreme Court Obscenity Decision." *Criminal Law Bulletin* 10 (November 1974): 785–826.

Rembar, Charles. *The End of Obscenity.* New York: Random House, 1968.

The Triumph of "Community Standards"

William Lasser
Department of Political Science
Clemson University

Miller v. California, 413 U.S. 15 (1973) and
Paris Adult Theatre I et al. v. Slaton, 413 U.S. 49 (1973) [U.S. Supreme Court]

◄○► THE CASE IN BRIEF ◄○►

Date
1973

Location
California
Georgia

Court
U.S. Supreme Court

Principal Participants
State of California
Paris Adult Theatre
Marvin Miller
Atlanta District Attorney Slaton

Significance of the Case
After struggling with many cases on obscenity issues, the Supreme Court focused on the definition of obscenity and rewrote the rules for two cases by shifting the burden of proof to local communities.

The Supreme Court of the United States struggled to define "obscenity" in legal terms from the late 1950s throughout the 1960s and early 1970s. In the 1960s the Court became the butt of jokes and ridicule because of the justices' habit of viewing allegedly obscene films on a case-by-case basis to determine their legal status. Moreover, the legal definition of obscenity was broadened and narrowed over and over again. At last, in 1973, the Supreme Court handed down a pair of decisions intended, at least in part, to ease the burden that these countless obscenity cases were placing on the Court. To some extent the Court succeeded in doing so.

In order to understand the significance of the *Miller* and *Paris* decisions, a brief review of the Court's struggles with the obscenity question is necessary. As early as 1942, the Court held in dicta that "There are certain well-defined and narrowly limited classes of speech, the prevention and punishment of which have never been thought to raise any Constitutional problem. These include the lewd and obscene." In all the obscenity cases which have followed, the Court has never once challenged this basic proposition; in fact, it has hardly even seen fit to defend or justify it. Instead, all of the Court's obscenity decisions have focused on the *definition* of obscenity. Given that obscenity is unprotected by the First Amendment, the question has been reduced to determining precisely what constitutes obscenity.

The Court's first attempt to deal with the definitional question was in *Roth v. United States* and *Alberts v. California*, decided together in 1957. Justice William Brennan, writing for the Court, held that "sex and obscenity are not synonymous. Obscenity is material which deals with sex in a manner appealing to prurient interest. The portrayal of sex, e.g. in art, literature and scientific works, is not itself sufficient reason to deny the material the constitutional protection of freedom of speech and press." Brennan went on to specify the first of many "tests" used by the Court to define obscenity: "whether to the average person, applying contemporary community standards, the dominant theme of the material taken as a whole appeals to the prurient interest." In doing so, Brennan rejected the "Hicklin" test, which judged allegedly obscene material by the effect of an "isolated excerpt upon particularly sensitive persons." Brennan's requirements that the work be judged as a whole and that it be judged according to the standards of the average person, together with his specific exemption of works judged scientific, literary, or artistic, were a victory of sorts for free speech advocates.

The *Roth* standard soon proved difficult to apply in practice. Though the Court held to the *Roth* standard or to a variant thereof throughout the 1960s, it was readily apparent that agreement on such a theoretical standard did not translate into agreement on the merits of any particular case. The Court soon split into distinct camps: at one extreme, Justices Hugo Black and William O. Douglas seemed to reject any attempt by government to regulate obscenity; at the other, Justice John Marshall Harlan expressed the belief that the states could ban any material that treated sex "in a fundamentally offensive manner." Justice Potter Stewart would have limited the government's power to banning "hard-core" pornography, but not soft-core, a standard which Harlan

would have applied at the federal level. The Court's frustration in dealing with the obscenity problem is best symbolized by Justice Stewart's oft-quoted remark, in *Jacobellis v. Ohio* (1964), that, although unable to define hard-core pornography, "I know it when I see it."

In the Court's center, a consensus view was being built. In the 1966 case of *Memoirs v. Massachusetts*, Justice Brennan wrote for himself, Chief Justice Warren, and Justice Abe Fortas, enunciating a three-part formula derived from *Roth.* The state and federal governments could ban allegedly obscene material only if it was established that "(a) the dominant theme of the material taken as a whole appeals to a prurient interest in sex; (b) the material is patently offensive because it affronts contemporary community standards relating to the description or representation of sexual matters; and (c) the material is utterly without redeeming social value." This standard, though more precise than previous formulations, still had its problems. For one thing, it did not command a majority of the Court. For another, it masked serious questions of emphasis and interpretation which would continue to haunt the Court in later years.

In the years after *Memoirs*, the Court fell back on the practice of deciding obscenity cases using short, per curiam opinions reversing convictions in cases where a majority of the Court believed the material in question to be protected under the Constitution. This type of apparently standardless jurisprudence (which, in fact, represented a number of different and unexpressed standards) was initiated in *Redrup v. New York* in 1967, and was used, according to Justice Brennan, no fewer than thirty-one times. This was clearly an untenable situation for a Court that prided itself on principled decision-making, and in 1973 the Court finally tried to find a way out of the difficulties it had made for itself.

The Court that decided *Miller* was a different Court than the one which had struggled with the obscenity problem down through the 1960s. At its head was Chief Justice Warren Burger, who had replaced Earl Warren in the center seat in 1969. Also new to the Court were the three other Richard Nixon appointees: Harry Blackmun, Lewis Powell, and William Rehnquist. They replaced Abe Fortas, Hugo Black, and John Marshall Harlan. The only justices left from the *Memoirs* Court were Brennan, William O. Douglas, Byron White, and Potter Stewart.

Miller, Chief Justice Burger began for the Court, called for "a re-examination of standards enunciated in earlier cases involving what Mr. Justice Harlan called 'the intractable obscenity problem.'" In an effort to make sense of this difficult question, Burger both recast the *Roth-Memoirs* test and greatly changed its emphasis. Under the new *Miller* standard, works could not be judged legally obscene unless "(a) 'the average person, applying contemporary community standards', would find that the work, taken as a whole, appeals to the prurient interest . . . ; (b) . . . the work depicts or describes, in a patently offensive way, sexual conduct specifically defined by the applicable state law; and (c) . . . the work, taken as a whole, lacks serious literary, artistic, political, or scientific value."

Burger's new formulation fine-tuned the *Memoirs* test in three ways. First, obscenity laws were now restricted to depictions or descriptions of sexual conduct as opposed to sexual expression. Second, state obscenity statutes were now required to be quite specific in their description of the sexual conduct banned. Finally, and perhaps most important, works no longer had to be "utterly" without redeeming social value to be judged obscene; they could be so judged if found to be without "serious" literary, artistic, political, or scientific value. No longer could "a quotation from Voltaire in the flyleaf of a book" protect "an otherwise obscene publication," Burger wrote.

Throughout his opinion, Burger held to his view that *Memoirs* never commanded the support of more than three justices. Although it is true that only two justices joined Brennan's *Memoirs* opinion, two more—Black and Douglas—took an even more expansive view of the First Amendment. It is clear, at the least, that the *Miller* formulation would have been unacceptable to a majority of the *Memoirs* Court.

What was even more significant than these tinkerings with the *Memoirs* approach was the Court's decision to shift the burden of responsibility for the determination of obscenity from

the judges to the local communities—as represented by the juries in criminal obscenity cases. Moreover, Chief Justice Burger gave up on any attempt to develop or impose "national standards," by which to judge obscenity. Instead, jurors would be asked to determine how "the average person, applying contemporary community standards," would react to the material in question. As representatives of a cross section of their community, jurors would seem particularly well placed to make such a determination. "The adversary system, with lay jurors as the usual ultimate fact finders in criminal prosecutions, has historically permitted triers of fact to draw on the standards of their community, guided always by limiting instructions on the law," Burger wrote. In a nation as large and as vast as the United States, it would be "futile" to ask jurors to determine national standards; and besides, "it is neither realistic nor constitutionally sound to read the First Amendment as requiring that the people of Maine or Mississippi accept public depiction of conduct found tolerable in Las Vegas, or New York City."

In the companion case of *Paris Adult Theatre v. Slaton*, the Court rejected the argument that the right to privacy extends to the commercial exhibition of obscene material in a theater closed to the unconsenting public. An earlier case, *Stanley v. Georgia* (1969), had held that individuals have an absolute right to view obscene materials in the privacy of their own homes, but Chief Justice Burger, again writing for the Court, held that there are "legitimate state interests at stake in stemming the tide of commercialized obscenity," including "the interest of the public in the quality of life and the total community environment, the tone of commerce in the great city centers, and, possibly, the public safety itself."

The majority in both *Miller* and *Paris* was the narrowest possible: 5-4. Justice Douglas wrote a dissent to each case, as did Justice Brennan, who was joined by Justices Marshall and Stewart. Douglas repeated his long-held view that obscene speech is protected by the First Amendment, and argued that, in any event, no one should be convicted on an obscenity charge unless the material in question has been declared obscene in a civil proceeding. Brennan, after a long review of the precedents, concluded that it was impossible to define obscenity with sufficient precision and predictability, and warned that the Court's decision would have a "chilling effect" on freedom of expression in the United States. Therefore, he concluded, "in the absence of distribution to juveniles or obtrusive exposure to unconsenting adults," the states were prohibited from attempting wholly to suppress allegedly obscene material on the basis of content.

Miller was vociferously criticized in the years after it was handed down. The *Miller* standard, however difficult to apply at the margins, has at least narrowed the definition of obscenity to "hard-core" material. Properly applied, it would probably have little, if any, chilling effect on serious literary, artistic, scientific, or political expression. But the *Miller* test has failed to achieve its stated objectives in at least two ways. First, the Court has found it impossible to rely on juries for the determination of obscenity questions, because the question of whether specific material is obscene involves questions not only of fact but also of law, and because the facts themselves are subject to appellate review. In one case, for example, the Court had to intercede when a Georgia jury decided that the fea-

ture film *Carnal Knowledge* violated community standards; even so, wrote Justice Rehnquist for the Court, that film could in no way be seen as depicting "sexual conduct in a patently offensive way." (Similarly, the Court held in *Pope v. Illinois* [1987] that the third prong of the *Miller* test, dealing with the "value" of the work in question, must be judged not by community standards but by a national standard.) Second, the *Miller* test has done nothing to clarify the meaning of obscenity where great uncertainty still exists. Thus, national publications or films may be judged by the standards of the most restrictive communities in the nation, and local communities have the latitude to make sweeping attacks on alleged obscenity—at times to the detriment of the free exchange of ideas.

Miller has fulfilled its major purpose, however. The Court may still sit as the final arbiter in obscenity cases, but it does it far less frequently, and with far less embarrassment to the Court and the justices.

Selected Bibliography

Schauer, Frederick F. *The Law of Obscenity.* Washington, D.C.: Bureau of National Affairs, 1976.

Pornography, Feminism, and Free Speech

—◄o►—

Stephen Lowe
Greenville, South Carolina

American Booksellers Association, Inc. v. William H. Hudnut, 771 F 2d 323 (1985);
Andrea Dworkin v. Hustler Magazine, Inc., 867 F. 2d 1188 (1989) [U.S. Circuit Courts of Appeals]

◄o► THE CASE IN BRIEF ◄o►

Date
1985, 1989

Location
Indiana; Wyoming; California

Court
U.S. Court of Appeals
California District Court

Principal Participants
Andrea Dworkin; Catherine MacKinnon;
Larry Flynt

Significance of the Case
An anti-pornography ordinance in Indianapolis written by two feminists was deemed unconstitutional in court. After being ridiculed by *Hustler* magazine, one of the women sued the publisher but lost her bid when the court found that her claims lacked sufficient constitutional merit and violated the First Amendment.

During the mid-1980s, the United States witnessed a renewed attack on pornography. The President's Commission on Pornography, chaired by Attorney General Edwin Meese, issued a controversial report in 1986, and court cases throughout the decade probed various First Amendment issues raised by allegedly pornographic representations. For example, the U.S. Supreme Court's decision in *Hustler Magazine v. Falwell* (1988) allowed Larry Flynt, the publisher of *Hustler* Magazine, to print scurrilous diatribes against his targets—people who spoke out vigorously against Flynt's magazine and its pornographic content.

Overwhelmed by what many perceived as the sleaze marketed by the pornography industry, various American cities in the 1980s passed laws to limit the rights of pornographers to sell their wares. Indianapolis, Indiana, was one such city. In adopting a model anti-porn law drafted by Andrea Dworkin and Catherine MacKinnon, Indianapolis opened itself up for an attack by purveyors and consumers of pornography. Dworkin is a feminist writer and crusader against pornography; MacKinnon is a professor at the University of Michigan Law School. Each had been active in the campaign against pornography for several years. Together, Dworkin and MacKinnon represent a faction of the feminist movement that opposes pornography in all its forms because of the genre's supposed "paternalistic representations of the subjugation of women." According to Dworkin and MacKinnon, pornography, by definition, demeans and subjugates women.

Indianapolis's anti-pornography ordinance proscribed "the graphic sexually explicit subordination of women, whether in pictures or in words" that involved descriptions of humiliation, degradation, pain, or domination. Departing from constitutionally accepted criteria for obscenity, the ordinance did not refer to "prurient interest," "offensiveness," or even to "community standards." Redeeming value was irrelevant under the terms of the ordinance. According to Judge Frank Easterbrook, in his opinion for the Seventh Circuit Court of Appeals in *American Booksellers Association, Inc. v. Hudnut*, the Indianapolis ordinance created a set of "ordained preferred viewpoints" that, in effect, gave the state the right "to declare one perspective right and silence opponents." Graphic sexual speech was pornography based solely on the perspective of the author. No matter how offensive the material, if women were portrayed in positions of sexual equality, the material would be permitted. No matter how significant the material from an artistic, literary, or political perspective, if women were portrayed in "subordinate" positions, the material would be forbidden.

The ordinance also entitled an individual woman to file a complaint against "trafficking" in pornography, "as a woman acting against the subordi nation of women." The district court held that that part of the ordinance constituted a prior restraint on freedom of the press, and Judge Easterbrook agreed. However, Easterbrook did admit that there was something in the underlying arguments made in support of the legislation. "Words and images," he wrote, "act at the level of the subconscious before they persuade at the level of the conscious." The court accepted those basic ideas, and agreed that "depictions of subordination tend to perpetuate subordination." A

concurring judge saw this aspect of the decision as unnecessary, arguing that whether pornography affects behavior or not, the ordinance would be unconstitutional.

The court, however, while granting that the influence of pornography may be substantial, rejected the argument that such effects would be enough to justify the legislation constitutionally. "If the fact that speech plays a role in a process of conditioning were enough to permit govern mental regulation," the court ruled, "that would be the end of freedom of speech." One of the fundamental foundations of free speech doctrine has been the notion of the "marketplace of ideas," yet the city of Indianapolis argued that pornography was "unanswerable," meaning that the marketplace metaphor did not apply. The court rejected that argument as well: in effect, the ordinance characterized pornography as bad, or "low-value," speech, and declared that the truth was not likely to prevail in a marketplace dominated by pornographic speech. The court replied that such an assertion amounted to the power to declare truth, which was unconstitutional on its face.

The Dworkin-MacKinnon law in Indianapolis was held unconstitutional in 1985, but the efforts to rid the American landscape of pornographic speech did not abate. Andrea Dworkin became, like Reverend Jerry Falwell, a target of Larry Flynt's *Hustler* magazine in the mid-1980s. *Hustler*'s scatological attack on Falwell brought to the fore the issue of how far a magazine can go in attacking individuals who disagree with the magazine's publishing philosophy. A few months following the attack on Falwell, *Hustler* began publishing a series of attacks on Andrea Dworkin. In three 1984 issues of the magazine, Dworkin was subjected to ridicule of a sexually explicit and offensive nature, and she replied to the attacks by suing the magazine, Larry Flynt, and others associated with the production and distribution of the magazine.

The Ninth Circuit Court of Appeals heard the case of *Andrea Dworkin v. Hustler Magazine, Inc.* (1989) on appeal from the Central District of California, though the case had originated in Wyoming. The defendants associated with

Hustler requested a transfer of venue, which was granted. The federal district court in California, acting on a motion for summary judgment that was still pending when the case was transferred, dismissed the case and ruled in *Hustler*'s favor on all the remaining issues. In light of the *Falwell* decision that the Supreme Court had issued while *Dworkin* was making its way through the courts, the entire claim made by Dworkin that *Hustler* had libeled her was insufficient to merit constitutional review.

Also significant in *Dworkin* was the argument put forth by the co-plaintiffs, representatives of the Wyoming and Jackson chapters of the National Organization for Women. They argued that "a new category of expressive activity—non-obscene 'pornography'—that is 'not entitled to constitutional protection' " should be created. The court expressly refused to entertain that possibility: "to do so would require us to flout the fundamental principle that the First Amendment is designed to foster robust public debate on such matters."

Finally, the appellants claimed that the attacks by *Hustler* against Dworkin and other pornography foes were violative of their free speech rights. If they spoke out, they argued, they became subject to the kind of vile attacks that Falwell and Dworkin suffered. Unfortunately, the court found that their argument was "virtually incoherent, [consisting] . . . of little more than the unsupported assertion" that someone can violate the First Amendment if he or she says something that harms the ability of others to speak out. The court decided that this argument amounted to a group libel claim, which required state action rather than private action.

Pornography is a touchy issue. Whether it does or does not have an impact on behavior or attitudes is a matter that social scientists continue to debate. The courts, however, have spoken. Although obscenity still cannot receive constitutional protection, the right of individuals to engage in the production or sale of pornography, or to attack—even vilify—their political opponents through the use of pornographic speech, is protected under the First Amendment.

Selected Bibliography

Dworkin, Andrea. "Against the Male Flood: Censorship, Pornography, and Equality." *Harvard Women's Law Journal* 8 (1985): 1–30.

Dworkin, Andrea. *Pornography: Men Possessing Women.* New York: Plume, 1989.

Strossen, Nadine. *Defending Pornography: Free Speech, Sex, and the Fight for Women's Rights.* New York: Scribner's, 1995.

Ulmschneider, Georgia Wralstad. "The Supreme Court, the First Amendment, and Anti-Sex-Discrimination Legislation: Putting *American Booksellers Association, Inc. v. Hudnut* in Perspective." *Duquesne Law Review* 32 (Winter 1994): 187–218.

"Cyberporn" and the Constitution

—◄◦►—

Tinsley E. Yarbrough
Department of Political Science
East Carolina University

Reno v. American Civil Liberties Union, 521 U.S. 844 (1997) [U.S. Supreme Court]

◄◦► THE CASE IN BRIEF ◄◦►

Date
  1997

Location
  Pennsylvania; District of Columbia

Court
  U.S. Supreme Court

Principal Participants
  U.S. Attorney General Janet Reno;
  American Civil Liberties Union; American
  Library Association; Various Internet
  providers

Significance of the Case
  An amendment to the Communications
  Decency Act of 1996 that attempted to
  prevent the transmission of offensive
  messages to minors over the Internet was
  deemed too broad and, therefore,
  unconstitutional.

Even during the tenure of Chief Justice Earl Warren, the U.S. Supreme Court recognized relatively broad authority for government to protect minors from exposure to erotica that would not be considered obscene for adults. *Roth v. United States* (1957) had limited obscenity to material that appealed to the prurient interest of the "average person." In *Mishkin v. New York* (1966), however, the Court rejected the argument that publications tailored for a sexually deviant audience could not be regulated as obscenity since they would not stimulate average persons to prurient thoughts. Instead, the justices held that the decision whether a particular work was obscene would depend on the context in which it was presented. Applying this "variable obscenity" approach in *Ginsberg v. New York* (1968), a case involving a man who sold two "girlie" magazines to a sixteen-year-old, the Court upheld a state statute forbidding the sale of obscenity to persons under age seventeen. Underscoring state power to assist parents in determining the publications to which their children would be exposed, as well as the absence in the challenged law of any attempt to regulate what erotica parents shared with their children, a majority ruled that a state could classify as obscene for minors material considered nonobscene for adults.

Later cases drew similar distinctions. In *New York v. Ferber* (1982), for example, the Supreme Court under Chief Justice Warren Burger reinstated the conviction of a Manhattan adult bookstore proprietor who sold an undercover police officer two films devoted almost entirely to scenes of young boys masturbating. The New York court of appeals had overturned as an overly broad infringement on First Amendment rights the statute Ferber was convicted of violating—a law making it a crime to knowingly promote a sexual performance by a child under sixteen through the distribution of materials depicting such activities. But the Supreme Court, speaking through Justice Byron R. White, deferred to the state's important interest in safeguarding the physical and psychological well-being of minors, while tying distribution of child pornography to child sexual abuse. Not only did such materials provide a scarring permanent record of the child's participation, declared White, but production of child pornography could be effectively controlled only if its distribution networks were closed.

On similar grounds, the Rehnquist court held in *Osborne v. Ohio* (1990) that a state could make private possession of child pornography a crime. In *Stanley v. Georgia* (1969), the Warren court had invoked privacy and First Amendment principles in upholding the right of people to possess obscenity in the privacy of their homes. But the *Osborne* majority confined *Stanley* to obscenity involving adults, holding that the state interests underlying the control and prevention of child pornography far surpassed those at issue in *Stanley*. In dissent, on the other hand, Justices William J. Brennan, Thurgood Marshall, and John Paul Stevens argued that the many laws forbidding production, sale, and distribution were surely adequate means for dealing with the admittedly serious problem of child pornography.

Beginning with *Young v. American Mini Theatres* (1976), the Court has also upheld the imposition of special zoning regulations on adult-oriented businesses. *Young* sustained, for example, Detroit ordinances prohibiting operation of any adult movie theater, bookstore, or similar establishment within a thousand feet of another such business, or within five hundred feet of a residential area. And in *City of Renton v. Playtime Theatres, Inc.* (1986), a 7-2 majority upheld an ordinance prohibiting any adult movie theater from locating within a thousand feet of any residence, residential area, church, park, or school. Suggesting that sexually oriented expression is not entitled to the same degree of constitutional protection as other types of speech, and emphasizing that the ordinances at issue did not bar such businesses completely, the Court declared such controls reasonable time, place, and manner regulations.

Finally, the Court has long assigned broadcasting considerably less First Amendment protection than its print, motion picture, and related counterparts enjoy. Most such rulings have involved governmental authority to control access to the airwaves and assure full and fair treatment of public issues. In *FCC v. Pacifica Foundation* (1978), however, a divided Court upheld federal power to cleanse the airwaves of "indecent" speech, at least during daytime hours. After a radio station broadcast comedian George Carlin's twelve-minute "Filthy Words" monologue one midafternoon weekday, a father complained to the Federal Communications Commission (FCC) that his young son had heard the broadcast on the car radio. The FCC proceeded to inform the station that it would consider possible sanctions if it received further complaints from listeners. A divided federal appeals court overturned the agency's action, but the Supreme Court reversed. Speaking in part for a majority and in part for a plurality composed of Chief Justice Warren E. Burger, Justice William H. Rehnquist, and himself, Justice Stevens asserted that the repetitive use of four-letter words devoid of a political or satirical context enjoyed minimal First Amendment protection, that broadcasts confronted citizens in the privacy of their homes as well as in public, and that broadcasts were "uniquely accessible" to children. But Justice Brennan, joined by Justice Marshall, scored the Court's "patent" misapplication of First Amendment principles and contended that whatever minimal discomfort an offensive broadcast might cause listeners could be eliminated by a simple flick of the "off" button. The ruling, added Brennan, would also have the anomalous effect of eliminating from the airwaves material that, under the Court's prior rulings, could not be kept from children.

Other decisions, however, had generally made clear that the government's interest in protecting juveniles and unconsenting adults from exposure to erotic material could not be accomplished through regulations that were so vague or sweeping in reach they unduly interfered with the free expression rights of consenting adults. In *Butler v. Michigan* (1957), the Court overturned a statute that forbade the sale of reading matter considered inappropriate for children, the justices declaring that the effect of such a statute was "to burn the house to roast the pig." *Erznoznik v. City of Jacksonville* (1975) struck down an ordinance prohibiting drive-in theaters from exhibiting films containing nudity from screens visible from the public streets or other public places. Such a regulation, the Court held, would even forbid the display of a baby's bottom. Those offended by nudity could easily avert their eyes and thus could hardly be deemed a captive audience subject to the government's protection. In *Sable Communications v. FCC* (1989), moreover, the Court struck down a 1988 congressional statute that banned "indecent" telephone "dial-a-porn" services. The justices in that case held that individuals, even minors, could not be prosecuted for communicating offensive speech over the telephone.

It was against the backdrop of such decisions that the Supreme Court under Chief Justice William Rehnquist confronted, in *Reno v. American Civil Liberties Union* (1997), First Amendment and related constitutional issues raised by provisions of the Communications Decency Act (CDA) of 1996, Congress's first attempt to regulate erotic expression, or "cyberporn," on the Internet. The CDA was adopted as Title V of the Telecommunications Act of 1996, an omnibus statute concerned primarily with reducing regulation and encouraging the rapid deployment of new telecommunications tech-

nologies. But the decency provisions were not an original part of the larger bill. Instead, they were added in committee or as amendments offered during floor debate on the legislation. Section 223 (a) of the CDA, known as the "indecent transmission" provision, prohibited the "knowing transmission" over the elaborate web of computer interconnections known as the Internet "of obscene or indecent messages to any recipient under eighteen years of age." Section 223(d) forbade the "knowing sending" or display of "patently offensive" messages in a manner available to persons under age eighteen. As affirmative defenses against prosecution under the CDA, people were obliged to take "good faith, reasonable, effective, and appropriate actions" to restrict minors' access to the prohibited communications, or to restrict access by requiring certain designated forms of age proof, such as a verified credit card or an adult identification number or code.

Immediately after President Bill Clinton signed the telecommunications statute into law, the American Civil Liberties Union and nineteen other plaintiffs filed a suit against Attorney General Janet Reno and the Department of Justice, challenging the constitutionality of the "indecent transmissions" and "patently offensive" sending and display provisions of the law and seeking an injunction against their enforcement. A week later, a federal district judge issued a temporary restraining order based on his conclusion that the term "indecent" was simply too vague to provide a basis for criminal prosecution under the CDA. At that point, twenty-seven plaintiffs, including the American Library Association and various Internet providers, filed a separate suit, which was then consolidated with the first case for trial before a special three-judge district court panel. Following an evidentiary hearing, that court issued a preliminary injunction forbidding enforcement of the challenged provisions.

Although the district court's decision was unanimous, each member of the panel wrote a separate opinion. One judge agreed that the government might have a compelling interest justifying regulation of some of the material covered by the CDA, but concluded that its broad language imposed a "chilling effect" on the expression of adults and that the terms "patently offensive" and "indecent" were "inherently vague." A second member of the panel found those terms so vague that their use in a criminal prosecution would violate both the First Amendment and the notice requirements implicit in the Fifth Amendment's due process clause. And the third judge concluded that the CDA would impose severe economic and related burdens on protected speech, especially by noncommercial speakers, while "perversely" leaving largely unaffected commercial pornographers who would obviously want a credit card identification from their potential customers and thus would have no difficulty establishing the affirmative defense the CDA allowed. The district court expressly preserved the government's authority, however, to investigate obscenity or child pornography under the statute.

Under the CDA's special expedited review provisions, the government filed an appeal of the district court's decision in the U.S. Supreme Court. The case was quickly scheduled for oral argument on March 19, 1997. At oral argument, the justices appeared knowledgeable about the Internet, raising numerous questions of counsel for both sides regarding ways to restrict the access of minors, limits on the effectiveness of devices to assure adult verification for Internet users, and the heavy financial burdens the CDA's affirmative defenses might pose for noncommercial Internet providers. Deputy Solicitor General Seth P. Waxman's defense of the challenged law was subjected to particularly close scrutiny. Justices Sandra Day O'Connor and Ruth Bader Ginsburg seemed skeptical, for example, of Waxman's assertion that libraries could generally afford to install age-screening technologies and that such identification schemes would be effective. At one point, moreover, Justice John Paul Stevens asked Waxman whether a library could lawfully permit access to adults who told librarians they planned to show proscribed material to a minor. When the deputy solicitor general suggested that a library might violate the CDA by transmitting the material in such circumstances, Justice Antonin Scalia interrupted: "So any adult has a 'heckler's veto,' just by saying that their [sic] child is watching?"

On June 26, 1997, the Court, speaking through Justice Stevens, invalidated the transmission, sending, and display provisions of the CDA as unconstitutionally sweeping on their face to the extent they applied to "indecent" expression, but held that the portion of the law forbidding the transmission of obscene (as opposed to indecent) material to minors was not "overbroad." Thus, although particular prosecutions of allegedly obscene transmissions under the CDA might fail on the ground that the erotica at issue was not in fact obscene, the Court declined to invalidate that portion of the law on its face, an action that would have prohibited all enforcement of its provisions. The justices refused to save, however, Section 223(d)'s prohibition of the knowing sending or displaying to minors of "patently offensive" material, even though the prevailing definition of obscenity, first announced in *Miller v. California* (1973), had included "patently offensive" erotica within its scope. To be declared obscene under the *Miller* standard, declared Justice Stevens, material also had to appeal to a "prurient interest" in sex and have no "serious literary, artistic, political, or scientific value." Section 223(d) lacked those requirements. To limit the scope of the patent-offensiveness standard, moreover, the *Miller* decision had insisted that such descriptions or depictions of sexual conduct be "specifically defined by the applicable state law"—a safeguard also absent from the CDA's sending and display provisions.

The government's attempts to draw on other earlier precedents were equally unavailing. In fact, asserted Justice Stevens, a close look at the *Ginsberg, Pacifica Foundation,* and *Renton* cases "raise[d]—rather than relieve[d]—doubts concerning" the CDA's constitutionality. The ban on the sale of erotica to minors at issue in *Ginsberg,* for example, did not bar parents from purchasing such material for their children. Moreover, *Ginsberg* applied only to commercial transactions; its ruling limited the reach of materials sold to those that were obscene in the context of their distribution to minors; and it imposed a less restrictive age requirement than the CDA's provisions. The FCC order at issue in *Pacifica* dealt with a medium—broadcasting—long subject to regulation, was more concerned with the timing than substance of the comedic monologue at issue there, did not involve a criminal sanction, and concerned a medium that historically had enjoyed extremely limited First Amendment protection largely because of its highly invasive character. In contrast, the access to the Internet to view any proscribed material involved a series of affirmative steps. In fact, in the *Sable* case the Court had distinguished *Pacifica Foundation* in striking down government regulation of "indecent" telephone "dial-a-porn" conversations and upholding only the law's prohibition on obscene messages.

Contrary to the government's assertions, Stevens further asserted, the CDA could not be viewed as imposing the sort of zoning regulations upheld in *Renton* and other cases. The ordinances at issue there, after all, were primarily concerned with the secondary effects of sexually oriented businesses (such as declining property values and crime) and did not completely forbid the activities subjected to special zoning requirements.

Justice O'Connor, joined by Chief Justice William H. Rehnquist, filed an opinion concurring in only portions of the Court's judgment. O'Connor viewed the CDA as little more than a congressional attempt to create "adult zones" on the Internet, thought creation of such zones could be kept within the Constitution's bounds, but agreed that certain of the provisions the majority had invalidated, though not others, exceeded those limits. To the extent the CDA made it a crime for a person knowingly to send a patently offensive message or image to a specific person under age eighteen, the law, in O'Connor's judgment, passed constitutional muster. In such situations, she explained, "the party initiating the communication knows that all the recipients are minors." In that context, the challenged provisions were no different from the law forbidding the sale of erotica to minors upheld in *Ginsberg*. Nor would the justice agree that the law was a "facially overbroad" infringement on the First Amendment rights of minors—a claim the majority had neither accepted nor rejected. In *Broadrick v. Oklahoma* (1973), the Court determined that a statute could be declared unconstitutionally broad on its face only if its overbreadth was "substan-

tial," and not merely because the sweep of its language was susceptible to unconstitutional application in certain cases. To O'Connor, by contrast, "the universe of speech constitutionally protected as to minors but banned by the CDA—*i.e.*, the universe that is 'patently offensive,' but which nonetheless has some redeeming value for minors or does not appeal to their prurient interest—is a very small one."

The CDA was only Congress's first attempt to regulate cyberporn. Even so, the decision and rationale of the *Reno* case clearly suggest that the protection of minors from Internet erotica, other than that considered obscene for adults, must largely be confined to blocking devices installed by parents and other Internet users rather than be extended to government restrictions on Internet "indecency." Just as curious and resourceful minors may overcome even the most sophisticated blocking technologies, the risk remains that certain parents and surrogates will not exercise what many would consider responsible judgment in such matters. Absent fundamental changes in the nature of family law, however, that is precisely where responsibility for the welfare of children primarily rests.

In a footnote to *Reno v. ACLU*, Congress in April 2000 passed the Children's Online Privacy Protection Act. This law requires that commercial Internet sites that seek information from children known to be younger than thirteen must first obtain written parental consent. The statute is intended to allow parents to monitor what family information their children provide to companies wishing to solicit business. Although this law's principal rationale is to allow parents to restrict, if they choose, what information is released to businesses, a desirable secondary consequence may be to make parents more sensitive to what their sons and daughters are viewing as they "surf the net."

Selected Bibliography

Jacques, Stephen C. "*Reno v. ACLU*: Insulating the Internet, the First Amendment, and the Marketplace of Ideas." *American University Law Review* 46 (1997): 1945–1992.

Other Civil Liberties Issues

The Court and the Committee

———◄○►———

Jerold L. Simmons

Department of History
University of Nebraska at Omaha

Watkins v. United States, 354 U.S. 178 (1957) [U.S. Supreme Court]

◄○► THE CASE IN BRIEF ◄○►

Date
  1957

Location
  Chicago; District of Columbia

Court
  U.S. Court of Appeals
  U.S. Supreme Court

Principal Participants
  John T. Watkins; House Un-American
  Activities Committee; Chief Justice Earl
  Warren

Significance of the Case
  The Court reversed the conviction of a
  man cited for contempt of Congress
  when he refused to testify against alleged
  communists. This marked the first time
  the Court attempted to deal with the
  constitutionality of Congress's
  investigations into communism.

On April 29, 1954, John T. Watkins, an organizer for the United Auto Workers, appeared before a subcommittee of the House Un-American Activities Committee (HUAC) investigating Communist activities in the Chicago area. It was one of the committee's many "road shows," designed to demonstrate to the locals the widespread influence of Communists in the union movement and, at the same time, garner headlines for committee members. Watkins proved a cooperative witness. While denying membership in the party, he spoke candidly of his past work for Communist causes and participation in Communist meetings.

When committee counsel began to read a list of names, however, Watkins balked. He turned to a statement prepared by his lawyer, Joseph Rauh Jr., and, with the committee's indulgence, read it into the record: "I am not going to plead the fifth amendment, but I refuse to answer certain questions that I believe are outside the proper scope of your committee's activities. I will answer any questions which this committee puts to me about myself. I will also answer questions about those persons whom I knew to be members of the Communist Party and whom I believe still are. I will not, however, answer any questions with respect to others with whom I associated in the past. . . . I do not believe that such questions are relevant to the work of this committee nor do I believe that this committee has the right to undertake the public exposure of persons because of their past activities."

It was a principled statement carefully drafted by Rauh to convince both the committee and the public that Watkins was sincerely concerned about Communist infiltration of the labor movement but could not bring himself to subject "innocents" to the committee's brand of exposure. It was not a new tactic. Lillian Hellman, also a Rauh client, had taken a similar position before the committee in 1952. Hellman, though, covered herself with frequent references to the Fifth Amendment, as had several witnesses in the famous Hollywood hearings of 1951. The committee had been inconsistent in citing those who took this stand, and Rauh hoped his client might escape the hearings without a citation for contempt of Congress and with his reputation and conscience unsullied.

It was a position that appealed to Rauh's sense of what was right. A cofounder of Americans for Democratic Action, Rauh supported vigorous measures to fight communism, but, like most liberals, he resented the unprincipled tactics used by congressional inquisitors. He especially resented the "degradation ceremonies" in which ex-Communists and other leftists were forced to inform on associates, many of whom had long since left the party. To him, naming names was a dirty business, often forcing honorable men and women to inform on other honorable individuals who had made innocent mistakes in the past. And it seemed to serve no real purpose. Invariably, the individuals named were known to the committee, so the procedure seemed little more than a pointless ritual, a rite designed to show whether a witness had fully rejected his or her political heresy.

Yet those "degradation ceremonies" had become the committee's raison d'etre in the 1950s; they served to justify the committee's ever-growing appropriations and staff, to keep the files of black-listing agencies filled, and to satisfy the public's desire for retribution. It was the committee's business to collect names, to use its power to expose as a form of punishment. Witnesses could "take the Fifth" and thereby avoid answering the committee's questions, but taking the Fifth implied an admission of guilt and carried serious consequences. Many employers, including the United Auto Workers, automatically discharged "Fifth Amendment Communists," and the label invited private harassment. To avoid the harsh alternatives of taking the Fifth or naming names, a number of mid-1950s witnesses began to search for other options. Several, like college instructor Lloyd Barenblatt, challenged HUAC's authority to inquire into their private political beliefs and associations under the First Amendment. Others, like John Watkins and Arthur Miller (another Rauh client), simply refused to name the "innocents."

HUAC's chairman, Harold Velde, rejected Watkins's statement and the House of Representatives cited him for contempt of Congress. A federal district court found Watkins guilty, and the sentence, a $500 fine and one year in prison, was suspended. The case was appealed to the Court of Appeals for the District of Columbia, where a three-judge panel reversed the ruling, but on rehearing the full bench upheld the conviction. In 1956 the U.S. Supreme Court granted certiorari.

Traditionally, the Supreme Court had shown a marked reluctance to tamper with the authority of congressional inquiries. Prior to *Watkins*, the only substantive limit on Congress's power to investigate was contained in *Kilbourn v. Thompson* (1880), which required that investigations be directed at a "valid legislative purpose." During the late 1940s, the Vinson Court had denied certiorari to a series of petitions challenging HUAC's power to subpoena documents and compel testimony. By granting Watkins certiorari in 1956, the Warren court seemed to indicate its determination to abandon this tradition of tolerance.

Rauh's Supreme Court brief concentrated on challenging the committee's power to punish through exposure. He argued that, because Congress may investigate only as an aid to legislation and because the exposure of the beliefs and associations of witnesses could not serve that purpose, the questions put to Watkins had exceeded the committee's authority. The brief also raised two subsidiary points: that questions probing political beliefs intruded on areas protected by the First Amendment, and that the House resolution under which HUAC operated was unconstitutionally vague. On each of these secondary points, Rauh solicited assistance in the form of amicus curiae briefs.

The American Civil Liberties Union submitted a brief arguing that the committee's questions exceeded the bounds of legislative power under the First Amendment and that its conduct in general had a chilling effect on free expression. Telford Taylor, lawyer for Robert M. Metcalf, who had been convicted for taking a stand similar to that of Watkins, submitted an amicus brief arguing that the questions put to Watkins were beyond the scope of the committee's authority. The House resolution creating HUAC authorized investigations into "the extent, character, and objects of un-American propaganda activities in the United States," but, Taylor argued, the questions put to Watkins had nothing to do with propaganda. Since the statute governing contempt provided that witnesses need only answer questions pertinent to the inquiry, Watkins should not have been required to answer. Ironically, none of the briefs questioned the power of Congress to authorize an investigation into the "propaganda activities" of private citizens.

On June 17, 1957, the Court reversed Watkins's conviction and, for the first time, attempted to deal with the difficult constitutional issues raised by congressional investigations of communism. Chief Justice Earl Warren's discursive majority opinion incorporated most of the arguments contained in the three briefs. He agreed that HUAC's mandate from the House of Representatives was dangerously vague, that the First Amendment did constitute a substantive limitation on the investigative power, and that the naming of names could have a chilling effect on free expression. The chief justice was obviously appalled at HUAC's use of its public hearings to punish political dissidents, especially for past sins, and denied the existence of any "congressional power to expose for the sake of exposure."

Yet having said this, Warren backed away from the implications of his obiter dicta (other words: language not essential to the holding of the case). Instead of reversing Watkins's conviction on these grounds, he merely asked Congress to exercise closer supervision of its probes and to establish a more judicious system of procedures for its committees. "A measure of added care on the part of the House and the Senate" was all that was necessary to resolve the problem.

The reversal of Watkins's conviction rested on a narrow procedural point raised only indirectly in the briefs. Both Rauh and Taylor claimed that the questions asked Watkins were not pertinent to any purpose within the committee's authority. The Court did not specifically agree with this assertion, but it did rule that a witness must be able to determine with certainty whether or not the questions were pertinent. Since HUAC's mandate from the House was too vague to afford guidance and the comments of the subcommittee chair during the hearings failed to establish that pertinence, Watkins was not given sufficient information to make that determination. Consequently, he was deprived of due process of law under the Fifth Amendment.

It was a curiously confusing ruling. Warren had rambled on about the dangers of the investigative power for twenty-five pages then resolved the case on a narrow procedural point having little to do with the substantive issues raised. Warren may have intended his expansive dicta as a warning to Congress, a threat of stronger, more restrictive rulings in the future if Congress failed to curb the excesses of its committees. The narrowness of the holding, however, suggests that the chief justice lacked the votes to issue a more definitive ruling. Warren may have wanted to go further and probably had the support of Hugo Black, William Douglas, and William Brennan. But to hold the votes of Felix Frankfurter and John Marshall Harlan, the ruling had to be narrow. The Court's two most consistent advocates of judicial restraint apparently agreed with the holding but must have had reservations about Warren's dicta. (Harold Burton and Charles Whittaker did not participate.) In any event, Warren's opinion bred confusion. Justice Frankfurter found it necessary to write a concurrence in order "to state what I understand to be the Court's holding." He omitted all references to the larger questions raised in Warren's dicta and summarized the ruling in three paragraphs. Justice Clark wrote a stinging dissent, denouncing Warren's opinion as "a trespass upon the fundamental American principle of separation of powers," and criticized the majority for having placed itself in the position of "grand inquisitor and supervisor of congressional investigations."

Predictably, public reaction was governed far more by the dicta than by the holding. In this instance, the response was intensified because the ruling was delivered on the same day that the Court reversed the convictions of identified Communists in two other controversial cases, *Yates v. U.S.* and *Sweezy v. New Hampshire.* These "Red Monday" decisions outraged conservatives like David Lawrence, who entitled a three-page editorial in *U.S. News and World Report* "Treason's Biggest Victory." Representative Harold Jackson, a member of HUAC, charged that the Court had rendered both his committee and its counterpart in the Senate "innocuous as two kittens in a cageful of rabid dogs." Liberals also read *Watkins* as "a landmark" ruling. The *Washington Post* praised the Court for "action long overdue," and the *New York Times* called *Watkins* "an admirable opinion." John M. Coe told members of the National Lawyers Guild that while *Watkins* might not have "completely castrated" the House committee, "it has at least seriously impaired its virility."

Five weeks after the ruling, Senator William E. Jenner of Indiana introduced a bill designed to remove five types of cases from the appellate jurisdiction of the Supreme Court, including all cases involving contempt of Congress. The measure was soon tabled, and the movement to curb the Court was eventually blocked by the congressional leadership. Ironically, though, the whole affair had little impact on the conduct of HUAC. Its chairman recognized that the Court had demanded very little of his committee. It merely required that HUAC include a statement of legislative purpose at the beginning of each hearing and explain the pertinence of individual questions when challenged by a witness. This the committee did. Beyond this, its procedures were not altered.

The promise of Warren's dicta never materialized. Two years later the Court once again confronted the HUAC question, but this time with the chief justice and his liberal supporters in the minority. In *Barenblatt v. U.S.* (1959), the Court stepped back from the implications of *Watkins* and confirmed the committee's powers almost without exception. So *Watkins* remained little more than a lecture, a promise unfulfilled, and HUAC continued its harassment of the Left without interruption.

Selected Bibliography

Alfange, Dean, Jr. "Congressional Investigations and the Fickle Court." *University of Cincinnati Law Review* 30 (Spring 1961): 113–171.

Beck, Carl. *Contempt of Congress: A Study of the Prosecutions Initiated by the Committee on Un-American Activities.* New Orleans: Hauser Press, 1959.

Goodman, Walter. *The Committee: The Extraordinary Career of the House Committee on Un-American Activities.* New York: Farrar, Straus and Giroux, 1968.

Millikan, Kent B. "Congressional Investigations: Imbroglio in the Court." *William and Mary Law Review* 8 (Spring 1967): 400–420.

Murphy, Walter F. *Congress and the Courts: A Case Study in the American Political Process.* Chicago: University of Chicago Press, 1962.

Pritchett, Charles Herman. *Congress Versus the Supreme Court, 1957–1960.* Minneapolis: University of Minnesota Press, 1961.

Sabin, Arthur J. *In Calmer Times: The Supreme Court and Red Monday.* Philadelphia: University of Pennsylvania Press, 1999.

The Court and the Committee: Part Two

—◄◦►—

Jerold L. Simmons

Department of History
University of Nebraska at Omaha

Barenblatt v. United States, 360 U.S. 109 (1959) [U.S. Supreme Court]

◄◦► THE CASE IN BRIEF ◄◦►

Date
1959

Location
District of Columbia

Court
U.S. Supreme Court

Principal Participants
Lloyd Barenblatt
American Civil Liberties Union
House Un-American Activities
  Committee
Justice John Marshall Harlan

Significance of the Case
A case of a teacher brought before the House Un-American Activities Committee saw the Court soften its earlier stance against the committee. The Court limited itself to a ruling on procedure and not on the legality of the committee.

In *Watkins v. U.S.* (1957), U.S. Supreme Court Chief Justice Earl Warren delivered a stern lecture to Congress on the constitutional dangers implicit in legislative investigations of communism. He affirmed the First Amendment as a substantive limit on congressional inquiries and denied the existence of any congressional power "to expose for the sake of exposure." While the exact holding in *Watkins* turned on a narrow legal point (the fact that the House Un-American Activities Committee [HUAC] had failed to inform the witness of the pertinence of the questions he was required to answer), Warren's expansive dicta led to speculation that the Court would soon deal the committee a lethal blow. Security-conscious conservatives blasted the ruling and introduced a succession of Court-curbing bills in Congress. HUAC's opponents hailed the decision as a turning point, a signal that the Court had finally decided to place limits on the excesses of McCarthyism. Yet two years later, in *Barenblatt v. U.S.*, the *Watkins* majority splintered and the Warren court stepped back from its confrontation with the House Un-American Activities Committee.

Lloyd Barenblatt, a thirty-one-year-old psychology instructor recently dismissed from Vassar, appeared before the committee in June 1954 during its hearings on Communist infiltration of education. While specifically rejecting the protections afforded by the Fifth Amendment, he refused to answer any questions concerning his past or present membership in the Communist Party. Instead, he denied the committee's authority to conduct investigations into higher education or to inquire into his political affiliations. Unlike Watkins, Barenblatt failed to challenge the pertinence of the committee's questions, so his case rested largely on claims of academic freedom and the First Amendment. His conviction for contempt of Congress was upheld by the Court of Appeals for the District of Columbia in January 1957, and a petition for review was remanded to that court for rehearing in light of *Watkins* the following June. When the Court of Appeals again upheld the conviction, the Supreme Court granted certiorari.

Barenblatt's case appeared quite strong. The 1954 hearings were clearly designed to punish radical teachers, and the House committee made no effort to hide that fact. HUAC's stated purpose in the hearings was to identify Communist educators, and its annual report for 1954 noted with obvious approval that "most of the teachers called have been suspended or permanently removed from their positions." Given Warren's pronouncements against this kind of punishment by exposure in *Watkins*, critics of HUAC hoped that the Court would use *Barenblatt* to place substantive limits on the committee's conduct.

The Court's ruling, handed down on June 8, 1959, dashed all such hopes. Justice John Marshall Harlan's opinion, joined by Justices Felix Frankfurter, Tom Clark, Charles Whittaker, and Potter Stewart, specifically rejected Barenblatt's claims and in the process dramatically reversed the thrust of the *Watkins* ruling. The plaintiff's brief, prepared by the American Civil Liberties Union, concentrated on three points: that HUAC had called Barenblatt to testify strictly to punish him; that the forced disclosure of private political beliefs violated Barenblatt's First Amendment rights; and that the committee had no authority to harass teachers or invade the sanctity of educational institutions.

Harlan dispatched each of these contentions. He rejected any notion that the Court could or should attempt to judge the committee's motives in calling Barenblatt. In other words, exposure might have been a consequence of the committee's actions, but the Court would not inquire into the workings of congressmen's minds. While admitting that HUAC's activities might intrude on protected freedoms, Harlan also insisted that Barenblatt's right to silence under the First Amendment had to be balanced against the nation's right of self-preservation. Because the Communist Party was part of a recognized international conspiracy, Barenblatt's rights had to give way to Congress's need to know the details of that conspiracy. Barenblatt's academic freedom argument was also summarily dismissed. Harlan conceded that freedom of the laboratory and lecture hall was a value important to American society, but an educational institution was "not a constitutional sanctuary."

Harlan's opinion prompted a stinging dissent written by Justice Hugo Black and joined by Earl Warren, William Douglas, and, in part, William Brennan. Black criticized the majority for failing "to see what is here for all to see—that exposure and punishment is the aim of this committee and the reason for its existence." He added: "I cannot believe that the nature of our judicial office requires us to be so blind." Black also rejected the entire notion of balancing First Amendment rights, arguing that the Court virtually always used the balancing test to reject claims of individual freedoms.

The *Barenblatt* ruling pleased conservatives and puzzled Court observers. Most attributed the Court's retreat from *Watkins* as a case of judicial timidity, a tactical withdrawal in the face of mounting public and congressional pressures. The Court-curbing proposals in Congress had given the justices a scare, the story went, and to protect the institution, they stepped back from the confrontation. Obviously, this explanation cannot account for the actions of the four dissenters. In *Barenblatt*, Black, Warren, Douglas, and Brennan adopted an impressively radical position. Yet it may explain the nature of Harlan's ruling. All Harlan had to do in *Baren-*

blatt was to distinguish the two cases on the basis of fact. Watkins had challenged the pertinence of the questions, Barenblatt had not. But the ruling went much further, in effect confirming the validity of HUAC's mandate to inquire into "propaganda activities" and its power to compel testimony to that end. For the first time, the committee's activities received clear constitutional sanction. Harlan may have felt it necessary to draft his opinion in such a way as to reject the implications of Warren's ruling in *Watkins* and at the same time pacify the Court's congressional critics.

Whatever the reason, *Barenblatt* ended speculation about the legality of HUAC, and thereafter the Court limited its consideration to matters of committee procedure. The confrontation between the Court and the committee continued through the 1960s, and in the more liberal atmosphere of that decade, the justices reversed a succession of contempt citations. But in every case, the ruling turned on a narrow procedural point. The Court never again seriously weighed the constitutionality of congressional investigations of communism.

Selected Bibliography

Kalven, Harry, Jr. "Mr. Alexander Meiklejohn and the *Barenblatt* Opinion." *University of Chicago Law Review* 27 (Winter 1960): 321–325.

Millikan, Kent B. "Congressional Investigations: Imbroglio in the Courts." *William and Mary Law Review* 8 (Spring 1967): 400–420.

Murphy, Walter F. *Congress and the Courts: A Case Study in the American Political Process.* Chicago: University of Chicago Press, 1962.

Pritchett, Charles Herman. *Congress Versus the Supreme Court. 1957–1960.* Minneapolis: University of Minnesota Press, 1961.

Sabin, Arthur J. *In Calmer Times: The Supreme Court and Red Monday.* Philadelphia: University of Pennsylvania Press, 1999.

Slotnick, Michael C. "The Congressional Investigating Power: Ramifications of the *Watkins-Barenblatt* Enigma." *University of Miami Law Review* 14 (Spring 1960): 381–411.

The Right to Travel

—◦—

Jerold L. Simmons

Department of History
University of Nebraska at Omaha

Aptheker v. Secretary of State, 378 U.S. 500 (1964) [U.S. Supreme Court]

◦ THE CASE IN BRIEF ◦

Date
  1964

Location
  District of Columbia

Court
  U.S. Supreme Court

Principal Participants
  Elizabeth Gurley Flynn
  Herbert Aptheker
  Secretary of State

Significance of the Case
  When Communists were refused the right to travel abroad because of their party membership, the Supreme Court struck down part of a law limiting these rights under the Fifth Amendment.

For over five decades, Elizabeth Gurley Flynn defied established authority. As a teenager she harangued street corner crowds with socialist dogma and recruited mill workers for the Industrial Workers of the World ("Wobblies"). In her twenties, she helped orchestrate the violent textile strikes in Lawrence, Massachusetts, and Paterson, New Jersey, and led antiwar protests against the Wilson administration. Devoting her life to labor activism and political radicalism meant frequent disappointment and official harassment. Often jailed for her work with the Wobblies and later with the American Civil Liberties Union, she learned to confront authority with an engaging smile and firm defiance. After Sacco and Vanzetti, the Passaic strike, and other lost causes of the 1920s, she dropped out of radical activities for a decade. Returning in 1937, Flynn joined the Communist Party, an action that prompted her ouster from the ACLU three years later. She rose rapidly in the party's hierarchy and, by the early 1950s, was its most prominent female advocate. In 1961 she succeeded Eugene Dennis as chair of the party's Central Committee; months later her passport was revoked.

For better than a decade, the State Department had attempted to restrict the foreign travel of American Communists. In February 1951, under pressure from Joseph McCarthy and the "China Lobby," the department began denying passports to party members and anyone else considered to be under Communist influence. In *Kent v. Dulles* (1958), the Supreme Court instructed the department to abandon the policy. Justice William O. Douglas declared the right to travel to be one of the liberties protected by the due process clause of the Fifth Amendment, but he chose to base the ruling on much narrower grounds—on the fact that Congress had not authorized the secretary of state to deny passports on political grounds.

Four years later the policy was revived, this time with congressional sanction. The Internal Security Act of 1950, popularly known as the McCarran Act, made it a crime for any member of an organization under order to register with the Subversive Activities Control Board (SACB) to use or seek to obtain a passport. When the Supreme Court upheld a SACB order against the American Communist Party in June 1961, the State Department again canceled the passports of party leaders.

Flynn and Herbert Aptheker, noted historian and editor of one of the party's journals, brought suit for the return of their passports. A three-judge district court upheld the ban as a reasonable action against "the threat posed by the world Communist movement," and, in December 1963, the U.S. Supreme Court agreed to review the case. In the oral argument, John J. Abt, counsel for Flynn and Aptheker, drew heavily on Justice Douglas's comments in *Kent v. Dulles*. He maintained that the passport restriction denied his clients due process and that Section VI of the Internal Security Act was unconstitutionally broad. Calling the provision "preventive detention," he argued that Congress lacked the authority "to confine people to this country unless they had done something illegal."

His arguments found instant support among the members of the Court. Justice Hugo Black voiced his opinion, expressed on numerous occasions, that the entire McCarran Act was unconstitutional. Other justices concentrated on Section VI and pressed the State Department's counsel, Abram Chaves, to explain why the act banned the travel of all Communists in all situations. Chaves defended the law as a rational expression of the government's right of self-preservation. All Communists were potential agents of a foreign power, he argued, and federal officials were in no position to determine which party members were the most dangerous. Therefore, the only rational plan consistent with national security was to ban the travel of all.

By a vote of 6-3, the Court sided with Flynn and Aptheker. Justice Arthur Goldberg, writing for Chief Justice Earl Warren, and Justices William Douglas, Hugo Black, William Brennan, and Potter Stewart, struck down Section VI of the Internal Security Act on the ground that it "too broadly and indiscriminately restricts the right to travel and thereby abridges the liberty guaranteed by the Fifth Amendment." To Goldberg, the statute made irrelevant the degree of a member's involvement in the party and therefore condemned the innocent along with the guilty. Under the law's provisions, it was a crime for any Communist "to apply for a passport to travel abroad to visit a sick relative, to receive medical treatment, or for any other wholly innocent purpose." Goldberg then applied the principle that a governmental purpose may not be achieved by means that "invade the area of protected freedoms" if a less objectionable means exists to achieve the same purpose. Since Congress might have distinguished between active and passive members of the party and between those traveling for innocent purposes and those whose activities might harm the country, the statute was arbitrary, overly broad, and void on its face.

The dissenters, led by Justice Tom Clark, objected that the majority had ruled on the potential dangers of the law rather than its application in this case. "We have no 'innocent members' before us," he claimed. Flynn and Aptheker were active party members, and their stated purpose for going abroad was to lecture and attend meetings. Clark maintained that such activities could harm U.S. interests and that the government was justified in prohibiting their travel.

The decision prompted little comment in the press. On the same day it decided *Aptheker* (June 22, 1964), the Court handed down two more controversial rulings: *Jacobellis v. Ohio,* which limited state powers to censor movies, and *Escobedo v. Illinois,* which extended the right to counsel to pretrial questioning. These two cases drove *Aptheker v. Secretary of State* to the back pages of the nation's newspapers. Nevertheless, Elizabeth Gurley Flynn and her colleagues considered it a major victory for the party and for the right to travel freely. The passport ban was lifted, and six weeks later Flynn journeyed to the Soviet Union, where she received a hero's welcome. The following month she died in a Moscow hospital at the age of seventy-four.

Selected Bibliography

Baxandall, Rosalyn Fraad. *Words on Fire: The Life and Writing of Elizabeth Gurley Flynn.* New Brunswick, NJ: Rutgers University Press, 1987.

"The Future of American Passports as Restrictions on Travel." *Northwestern University Law Review* 60 (1965): 511–530.

"Limitations of the Right to Travel Abroad and the Implications on First Amendment Rights of the Individual." *Oklahoma City University Law Review* 8 (1983): 469–504.

Family Welfare Rights and the Right to Travel

—◄○►—

Thomas E. Baker

School of Law
Drake University

Dandridge v. Williams, 397 U.S. 471 (1970) and *Saenz v. Roe*, 526 U.S. 489 (1999) [U.S. Supreme Court]

◄○► THE CASE IN BRIEF ◄○►

Date
1970, 1999

Location
Maryland
California

Court
U.S. Supreme Court

Principal Participants
Edmund P. Dandridge Jr.; Linda Williams;
Rita L. Saenz, Director of the California
Dept. of Social Services; Brenda Roe;
Anna Doe

Significance of the Case
The Supreme Court deferred the power to
limit welfare benefit payments to states
and revived the privileges and immunities
clause after 130 years, thus guaranteeing
all United States citizens the right to
travel between states.

These two cases highlight the intersection between statutory rights to governmental subsistence payments and the constitutional right to travel from state to state. The Supreme Court has been careful not to constitutionalize the social welfare system elaborated in detail in statutes and regulations. Consequently, this area of public policy is committed to the Congress and the state legislatures, as well as to the relevant federal and state administrative agencies. The text of the Fourteenth Amendment, however, affords every individual—rich and poor alike—the privilege and immunity to travel freely from state to state. Welfare policies, like any other legislative policy, may not interfere with the full exercise of civil rights and civil liberties.

That this area of public policy is primarily committed to the legislative prerogative is illustrated by the facts and holding in *Dandridge v. Williams*. Maryland, like all the other states, participated in the federal Aid to Families with Dependent Children program, which originated with the Social Security Act of 1935 and was jointly funded by the federal government and the states. As originally conceived, each state established the standard of need for eligible families, within federal guidelines. Some states provided that every family would receive payments to meet the full standard of need. Maryland provided for payments to every family in proportion to the standard of need, but imposed an upper limit on the total amount any one family could receive, no matter how many children were in the family. Thus, a family with four children and a family with eight children would receive the same maximum amount, which was about $250 in the late 1960s, when *Dandridge* arose. Plaintiffs with larger families complained that their actual needs far exceeded the upper limitation and, consequently, that they were being discriminated against.

The Court majority in *Dandridge* upheld the Maryland program. The Court held that the state was furthering a legitimate purpose by encouraging employment and seeking to minimize economic discrimination between welfare families and families of the working poor. In the area of economics or social welfare policies, the Court held that it would defer to legislative judgments of sound, reasonable policies. The fact that larger families were being discriminated against, in effect being paid less per child than smaller families, was not enough of a reason to invalidate the Maryland law. The majority concluded: "[T]he intractable economic, social, and even philosophical problems presented by public welfare assistance programs are not the business of this Court."

Nevertheless, the Supreme Court will go out of its way to protect fundamental rights of individuals. Over the years, different justices have relied upon different sources of constitutional authority to protect the fundamental right to travel: the privileges and immunities clause of Article IV, the commerce clause of Article I, the due process and equal protection clauses of the Fourteenth Amendment, and, by implication, the historical conditions at the time of the formation of the union and even the historical experience before the drafting of the Constitution. Given this confusion, therefore, it is noteworthy that in *Saenz v. Roe* every member of the Supreme Court appeared to admit that the best textual authority for the right was to be found in the privileges or immunities clause of the Fourteenth Amendment.

The majority opinion identified three components of the right to travel: the right to enter and leave a state; the right to be treated as a welcomed visitor while temporarily visiting another state; and the right to move to another state to become a permanent resident and be treated like other citizens of that state. The third component figured in the *Saenz* decision. As a consequence, an important part of the 1996 federal reforms of the welfare system was struck down.

With the legislative approval of Congress, California adopted a statute providing that families moving into the state from another state with lower welfare benefits would continue to receive the same amount of benefits during the first year after moving to California. For example, a family moving to California from Mississippi would receive the Mississippi maximum of $144 instead of the California maximum of $673. The *Saenz* case resulted from a class action lawsuit challenging the federal constitutionality of California's durational residency requirement.

The Court read the Fourteenth Amendment to equate citizenship with residency and to forbid hierarchies or subclasses based either on the duration of a citizen's residency in the new state or the identity of the state of prior residence. A person who permanently moves to another state immediately becomes a citizen of the new state for all purposes, and is entitled to the same treatment and benefits afforded other citizens.

While this may seem only commonsensical, the decision is important because it appears to revive the privileges and immunities clause. That clause was virtually read out of the Constitution in the *Slaughterhouse Cases* (1873), decided just five years after the Fourteenth Amendment was ratified. Since then, the clause had been used to invalidate state legislation only once, in 1935, and even that decision was overruled a few years later. Therefore, the Supreme Court's 1999 decision in *Saenz v. Roe* to rely on the privileges and immunities clause signals something of a revival of federal privileges and immunities including, but perhaps not limited to, the right to travel.

Whatever one thinks of judicial activism that reads rights into the Constitution, judicial activism that reads rights out of the Constitution is far more serious in terms of freedom and liberty. Perhaps what is more remarkable than the invalidation of the California law under the privileges and immunities clause is that for 130 years the Supreme Court managed to ignore one of the three great clauses in the Fourteenth Amendment. It must be left to future decisions to see if the justices will make up for lost time and "discover" other privileges and immunities besides the right to travel.

Selected Bibliography

Ely, John Hart. *Democracy and Distrust.* Cambridge: Harvard University Press, 1980.

Nelson, William E. *The Fourteenth Amendment.* Cambridge: Harvard University Press, 1988.

Tribe, Laurence H. "*Saenz* sans Prophecy: Does the Privileges or Immunities Revival Portend the Future—or Reveal the Structure of the Present?" *Harvard Law Review* 113 (1999) 110–198.

Privacy

———◄o►———

Meaningful Shadows? The Right of Privacy Achieves Constitutional Status

——◄○►——

John W. Johnson
Department of History
University of Northern Iowa

Griswold et al. v. Connecticut, 381 U.S. 479 (1965) [U.S. Supreme Court]

◄○► THE CASE IN BRIEF ◄○►

Date
  1965

Location
  Connecticut

Court
  U.S. Supreme Court

Principal Participants
  Dr. C. Lee Buxton; Estelle T. Griswold;
  Planned Parenthood League of
  Connecticut; State of Connecticut;
  Justice William O. Douglas

Significance of the Case
  Two Connecticut birth-control laws from
  1879 remained on the statute books until
  after World War II when a doctor and
  women's rights advocate challenged them
  in court. The Supreme Court established a
  "right to privacy" by drawing on selective
  portions of the Bill of Rights.

This mid-1960s Supreme Court decision occupies an important place in the history of the protean but still not clearly delineated "right of privacy." It also provides a context for examining starkly contrasting approaches to constitutional construction by members of the nation's highest court. Some legal commentators hailed the precedent that emerged from *Griswold v. Connecticut* as creative constitutionalism; others found it to be a prime example of judicial overreaching.

The *Griswold* case involved the U.S. Supreme Court's review of two Connecticut statutes, originally passed in 1879. The first made it illegal for a person to employ artificial means of contraception; the other made it a crime to "assist, abet or counsel" someone else to use birth control technology. These laws grew out of the prudishness of the Victorian era, particularly the moralism of Anthony Comstock, an active and influential private citizen from New York. Comstock abhorred birth control and felt that it was not a fit subject for polite discussion by ladies and gentlemen. His crusade resulted in the passage of federal legislation against obscenity and contraception.

These "Comstock Laws" had their analogues at the state level, such as the Connecticut legislation at issue in *Griswold*.

For the first third of the twentieth century, reformers and women's rights advocates such as Margaret Sanger and Emma Goldman fought tirelessly for the repeal of anti-contraception laws and in favor of the increased dissemination of birth control information. It was, however, the World War II public health movement, aimed at eradicating venereal disease, which spelled the end to most of the state anti-contraception laws. In the early 1960s, with birth control being widely practiced throughout the United States, Connecticut remained one of the last states in the nation with a law banning contraception still on its books.

Many times in the twentieth century bills had been introduced in Connecticut's General Assembly to overturn the anti-birth control statutes. All these attempts failed. Yet, with contraceptive devices for sale in drugstores in most cities throughout the state, the lingering impact of the nineteenth-century legislation was more symbolic than real. The laws, nevertheless, did serve to deter physicians from counseling on birth control to people in their childbearing years. This particularly impacted poor and uneducated couples. The only documented attempt to enforce the laws occurred as the result of a prosecution orchestrated to test the "assist, abet, or counsel" language of the statute. In the late 1930s, two physicians and a nurse were charged with providing birth control advice to married couples. Their conviction was upheld by the Connecticut Supreme Court in *State v. Nelson* (1940) because a majority of the judges found the ban on birth control to be "a legitimate exercise of the state's police power to preserve and protect public morals."

Prior to *Griswold*, two other judicial efforts were mounted by Connecticut defenders of birth control who were striving to blunt the consequences of the nineteenth-century legislation. In the first, a physician sought a declaratory judgment that he be permitted to prescribe contraceptive devices to married women in situations where pregnancy would be a serious danger to life and health. This effort resulted in a per curiam opinion by the U.S. Supreme Court in *Tile-*

ston v. Ullman (1943), holding that the doctor did not have standing to sue because his own life was not in danger. In an attempt to circumvent the procedural roadblock identified in *Tileston*, a more broadly gauged attempt was made two decades later. In separate suits, a physician and three of his patients sought a declaratory judgment pertaining to the constitutionality of the statutes forbidding the prescription and use of contraceptive devices. The factual record in the case showed that all three of the doctor's patients faced serious health risks should they become pregnant. Once again, on appeal, the U.S. Supreme Court avoided taking a position on the merits of the issue. In *Poe v. Ullman* (1961) the Court held that the suits did not present "cases or controversies" under the U.S. Constitution because neither the doctor nor his patients had actually been charged with violations of the statutes. Speaking for the Court majority, Justice Felix Frankfurter noted that the long-standing failure of Connecticut to seek enforcement of the nineteenth-century anti-contraception legislation made it unlikely that the three women or the doctor would be charged, and thus deprived the situation of any immediacy. "This Court," Frankfurter wrote, "cannot be umpire to debates concerning harmless, empty shadows."

Later in 1961, the physician involved in *Poe*, Dr. C. Lee Buxton, together with the executive director of the Planned Parenthood League of Connecticut, Estelle T. Griswold, opened an office in New Haven and began dispensing "information, instruction, and medical advice to married persons as to the means of preventing conception." After operating their office for ten days, Dr. Buxton and Mrs. Griswold were arrested and charged with violating the aiding and abetting portion of the anti-contraception law. They were convicted, fined $100 each, and closed their office. Their conviction was upheld by Connecticut appeals courts and the case was accepted for a hearing before the U.S. Supreme Court. The position of Buxton and Griswold in the Supreme Court was aggressively supported by amicus curiae briefs prepared by the Planned Parenthood Federation of America, the American Civil Liberties Union, and the Catholic Council on Civil Liberties. Finally, after a quarter-century of unsuccessful legal challenges, it appeared that a definitive judicial resolution beckoned for Connecticut's anti-contraception statute.

In one form or another, each of the justices who eventually wrote an opinion in *Griswold* expressed distaste for the Connecticut proscription on birth control. The six justices in the majority, in a series of opinions arising from quite different rationales, found the statutes to be in violation of the U.S. Constitution. The two dissenters also saw the anti-contraception legislation as bad public policy, but they felt that the statutes' ultimate fate should lie in the hands of elected state legislators rather than members of the judiciary. Justice Tom Clark did not participate.

The "opinion of the Court" was written by William O. Douglas. As the Court's most liberal member, Douglas took the opportunity in *Griswold* to expand upon sentiments that he had expressed a few years earlier in his dissent in *Poe.* He ruled that the two Connecticut anti-contraception statutes violated a "right of privacy" that, he submitted, is protected by the U.S. Constitution. Although the word "privacy" is not mentioned in the Constitution, the concept had been discussed by the justices on numerous prior occasions. In *Griswold,* Douglas held that a constitutional right of privacy can be drawn from the emanations or "penumbra" of certain provisions of the Bill of Rights. The term "penumbra" has its origin in the field of astronomy: it refers to a murky region between complete light and perfect darkness of an eclipse; or it can describe the shaded area surrounding the dark central portion of a sunspot. Employed as a metaphor, "penumbra" usually denotes an area of emanation or shadows. Douglas was not the first member of the Supreme Court to employ this unusual word in an opinion. In fact, the term found its way into Supreme Court opinions at least twenty times prior to 1965. Besides Douglas himself, the justice most disposed to speak of penumbra was Oliver Wendell Holmes, who served on the Court from 1902 to 1932.

According to Douglas, selected provisions of the Bill of Rights cast shadows that educe a "right of privacy." Another way of expressing Douglas's point is to say that the substantive

spirit, as opposed to the literal letter, of a few provisions of the Bill of Rights to the U.S. Constitution strongly augur for a right of privacy. The First Amendment's freedom of expression, for example, logically shades into a freedom to associate and a freedom to keep those associations out of the public eye. The Third Amendment's interdiction against requiring private citizens to quarter soldiers in their homes calls to mind another aspect of privacy. The Fourth Amendment's prohibition of "unreasonable searches and seizures" and the Fifth Amendment's protection of a person's right not to be compelled to incriminate himself in a judicial proceeding also create zones of privacy. To illustrate the long recognition of a right of privacy by the American legal community, Douglas mentioned an 1890 law review article by Louis Brandeis and Samuel Warren, titled "The Right to Privacy." Finally, Douglas found that the Ninth Amendment's wording, that "The enumeration in the Constitution, of certain rights, shall not be construed to deny or disparage others retained by the people," permitted certain residual rights, privacy among them.

Having established, at least for the purpose of the Court majority, a right of privacy, Douglas had no difficulty finding that the fact situation in *Griswold* fell within the limits of the right of privacy that he had identified. To uphold the Connecticut legislation would, in effect, sanction the police to search "the sacred precincts of the marital bedrooms." For Douglas, such a prospect, albeit unlikely, given the experience of Connecticut under the 1879 law, was "repulsive to the notions of privacy surrounding the marriage relationship."

For a major constitutional departure, as Douglas's opinion for the Court in *Griswold* surely was, his rationale was maddeningly brief and lacked extensive judicial citation. The ensuing legal commentary on the opinion took Douglas to task for sloppily creating a significant new constitutional right from the shadows of bits and pieces of the Bill of Rights. Robert Bork, former solicitor general and later appeals court judge, was perhaps the staunchest critic of Douglas's loose decision-making in *Griswold.* But Douglas had many supporters as well. For those individuals, his demarcation of a constitutional right of privacy was creative and long overdue.

The second opinion in *Griswold* was a concurrence written by Justice Arthur Goldberg and joined by Chief Justice Earl Warren and Associate Justice William Brennan. Goldberg agreed with Douglas that there existed a constitutional right of privacy that had been violated by the Connecticut legislation, but he identified a different source of that right. He and his cosigners argued that it was more properly extracted from the Ninth Amendment's reservation of "certain rights" as "retained by the people" rather than by Douglas's penumbral pastiche of Bill of Rights guarantees. Goldberg quoted extensively from James Madison and Alexander Hamilton, eminent drafters of the Constitution, and John Marshall and Joseph Story, distinguished early Supreme Court justices, to support his position. Near the end of his concurrence Goldberg emphasized that the Ninth Amendment "shows a belief of the Constitution's authors that fundamental rights exist that are not expressly enumerated in the first eight amendments." This language placed him in a different camp from those justices and several constitutional scholars who have maintained that the Fourteenth Amendment's due process language "incorporated" just the provisions of the first eight amendments as protections for individual freedoms over and against state as well as federal infringement.

Neither of the other justices filing concurring opinions—John Marshall Harlan and Byron White—had much good to say about the incorporation doctrine. Both were willing to accept the existence of protected liberties outside the scope of the Bill of Rights. Harlan found the right of privacy grounded in the due process clause of the Fourteenth Amendment. His test for determining which protections should be covered was drawn from the "implicit in the concept of ordered liberty" language proposed by Justice Benjamin Cardozo in the 1930s. White agreed with Harlan that protected individual rights should not be limited to those expressly enumerated in the Bill of Rights. For him, a statute that touched a value as cherished as marital privacy could be found constitutional only if it survived a "strict scrutiny" de-

gree of analysis. Most of the decisions that White cited to illustrate the application of his position concerned state laws with racial classifications; not surprisingly, all these laws fell prey to this high standard of review.

In separate dissenting opinions, Justices Hugo Black and Potter Stewart took the majority to task for trying to create protected individual rights out of thin air. The longer of the two opinions, Justice Black's, was particularly biting. As a literalist, Black did not perceive any constitutional basis for a right of privacy—whether stemming from the emanations of selected provisions of the Bill of Rights, from the Ninth Amendment's general verbiage, or from a vague concept of fundamental rights. As the Court's staunchest defender of the incorporation doctrine, Black felt that the only protections for citizens' individual liberty vis-à-vis their own state governments stemmed from state constitutions and the enumerated protections of the first eight amendments to the federal constitution as made applicable to the states through the due process clause of the Fourteenth Amendment. For the *Griswold* majority to create rights not grounded in the state or federal constitution was, Black contended, akin to what the Court so unwisely attempted in the early twentieth century in its "substantive due process" pro-business holdings, such as *Lochner v. New York* (1905). Why, Black asked rhetorically, is it not equally as inappropriate for justices to impose personal preferences for public policy in the sphere of personal rights as in the sphere of economic regulation? As bad as the Connecticut anti-contraception legislation might be, Black felt that it should be up to legislators, not a court, to modify or abolish it. Taking their cue from Black's dissent, legal critics of the majority opinions in *Griswold* began referring to the holding in the case as a "new substantive due process" or a "*Lochner*izing" of the Bill of Rights.

Justice Stewart's dissent generally tracked Black's analysis. Terming the Connecticut statute "an uncommonly silly law," Stewart was, nevertheless, unwilling to join the Court's majority because the state's General Assembly had had many opportunities to amend or abolish the restrictive legislation and had, for whatever reasons, chosen not to do so. He concluded his short dissent thus: "If, as I should surely hope, the law before us does not reflect the standards of the people of Connecticut, the people of Connecticut can freely exercise their true Ninth and Ten Amendment rights to persuade their elected representatives to repeal it. That is the constitutional way to take this law off the books."

Few Court watchers mourned the demise of the Connecticut anti-contraception law. But many were uncomfortable with the shaky grounding of the right of privacy. Whether emerging from the penumbra of several provisions of the Bill of Rights, from the general "retained by the people" language of the Ninth Amendment, or the unspecified fundamental rights, the constitutional establishment of a right of privacy was one of the major stories of the 1964–1965 October term of the Supreme Court.

Once out of the bottle, the right of privacy has been hard to contain. The zone of marital privacy articulated in *Griswold* was expanded to permit privacy in birth control choices for unmarried couples in the 1972 Court ruling of *Eisenstadt v. Baird*. More notably, writing for a bitterly divided Court in the landmark 1973 decision of *Roe v. Wade,* Justice Harry Blackmun gave constitutional support for a woman's right to choose an abortion early in her pregnancy. Hedging shrewdly, he based his ruling on the right of privacy "whether it be founded in the Fourteenth Amendment's concept of personal liberty and restrictions upon state action . . . [or] in the Ninth Amendment's reservation of rights to the people." After *Roe,* legal commentators began to talk about a "zone of bodily privacy." Yet recent Supreme Court decisions have severely cut back the sweep of *Roe v. Wade.*

How far does the zone of bodily privacy extend? Does it include the right of individuals of the same sex to engage in sexual activity? In 1986 the Supreme Court said "no" in *Bowers v. Hardwick* when it refused to strike down a Georgia sodomy statute. However, in the 1992 case of *Romer v. Evans,* the Court did void an amendment to the Colorado constitution which prohibited state and local governments from passing laws protecting homosexuals from discrimination, thus suggesting that the Court was moving towards expanding the zone of privacy to protect the rights of gays. Does bodily privacy include a "right to die"? Courts continue to struggle with this issue.

Recently the language and analysis in *Griswold* have served as the basis for discussions of the right of privacy in spheres well beyond intimate bodily matters. Such issues include the confidentiality of credit information and Social Security numbers, privacy in the workplace, confidentiality in the criminal justice system, and, of course, privacy in the new world of the Internet and cyberspace. As the nation enters the twenty-first century, the shadows of *Griswold* lengthen and continue to diffuse.

Selected Bibliography

Bork, Robert H. *The Tempting of America.* New York: Free Press, 1989.

Brandeis, Louis, and Samuel Warren. "The Right to Privacy." *Harvard Law Review* 4 (1890): 193–220.

Buchanan, G. Sidney. "The Right of Privacy: Past, Present, and Future." *Ohio Northern University Law Review* 16 (1989): 403–510.

Dudziak, Mary L. "Just Say No: Birth Control in the Connecticut Supreme Court Before *Griswold v. Connecticut.*" *Iowa Law Review* 75 (May 1990): 915–939.

Emerson, Thomas I. "Nine Justices in Search of a Doctrine." *Michigan Law Review* 64 (December 1965): 219–234.

Garrow, David J. *Liberty and Sexuality: The Right to Privacy and the Making of Roe v. Wade.* Berkeley: University of California Press, 1998.

Strum, Philippa. *Privacy: The Debate in the United States Since 1945.* Fort Worth, TX: Harcourt Brace, 1998.

The Right of Guardians to Terminate Life-Extending Medical Treatment

—◄○►—

Howard Ball

Department of Political Science
University of Vermont

In re Quinlan, 70 NJ 10 (1976) [New Jersey Supreme Court];
Cruzan v. Director, Missouri Department of Health, 497 US 261 (1990) [U.S. Supreme Court]

—◄○► THE CASE IN BRIEF ◄○►—

Date
1976, 1990

Location
New Jersey
Missouri

Court
U.S. Supreme Court

Principal Participants
Karen Ann and Joseph Quinlan
Parents of Nancy Beth Cruzan
State of New Jersey
State of Missouri
Chief Justice William Rehnquist

Significance of the Case
Conflicting decisions in two "right to die" cases focused the debate concerning whether to allow the termination of medical treatment for patients determined to be in a permanent vegetative state.

Persons who have lost cognitive functions but continue to breathe, exist in what doctors, lawyers, ethicists, and judges term a "permanent vegetative state" (PVS). In 1990, there were more than ten thousand PVS patients in American hospitals. Unlike other hospitalized individuals recovering from trauma or serious illness, PVS patients are, as one Supreme Court justice wrote, "devoid of thought, emotion, and sensation." Traditional legal and medical theory considered such patients alive because the heart and lungs were still functioning.

In the last part of the twentieth century, a new definition of death emerged: the "brain death test." It is reflected in the National Conference of Commissioners on Uniform State Laws' Uniform Determination of Death Act (1980). It states, in part, that "An individual who has sustained either (1) irreversible cessation of circulatory and respiratory functions, or (2) irreversible cessation of all functions of the entire brain, including the brain stem, is dead."

Annually, many thousands of families confront the PVS tragedy. Riding accidents, shootings, drownings, car crashes, and other traumatic accidents where the victim's breathing and circulation have been revived after the brain's cognitive functions cease create intense dilemmas for the victim's family. Legally, although still breathing, the victim is brain-dead. Not conscious, the victim is classified as a "grossly incompetent" person in a PVS. Any action taken on behalf of the victim is taken by the legal guardian or by a surrogate designated prior to the accident by the victim.

Does the guardian or the surrogate of an incompetent victim, knowing that the injured person will never again be conscious and will never again use cognitive functions, have a common-law or constitutional right to withdraw the patient from life-extending medical treatment or to refuse life-extending treatment for the victim? Under what circumstances can an incompetent person have surrogates act to terminate life-extending treatment or to refuse medical treatment on his or her behalf? Is the right to die a fundamental right of privacy, because of a person's constitutionally protected "liberty" interest found in both the Fifth and Fourteenth Amendments of the U.S. Constitution? Or must the right to die be balanced against the state's (Tenth Amendment) general interest in protecting and preserving the sanctity of life for all persons within its jurisdiction?

Such questions were first addressed by American courts in 1976, when the New Jersey Supreme Court heard the watershed case of *In re Quinlan*. Karen Ann Quinlan was brought unconscious to Saint Claire's Hospital in Denville, New Jersey, following a drug overdose. For years, as the court's opinion noted, Karen lay in a "debilitated and allegedly moribund state, . . . comatose and in a chronic and persistent 'vegetative' state, having no awareness of anything or anyone around her and existing at a primitive reflex level. . . . No form of treatment which can cure or improve that condition is known or available. . . . She can never be restored to cognitive or sapient life." Her life was sustained by a respirator, antibiotics, a catheter, and tubal feeding. These heroic efforts required around-the-clock care by a team of four nurses.

Karen's father and guardian, Joseph Quinlan, after agonizing discussions with family and his parish priest, requested that physicians disconnect his daughter's life-support systems. They refused, because such action "conflict[ed] with their professional judgment." Mr. Quinlan went to court to seek authorization "to abandon specialized technological procedures . . . [that have] no potential for resumption or continuance of other than a 'vegetative' existence. [These] serve only maintenance functions." He argued that "Karen's interests" must be evaluated by the court as dominant, even in the face of contrary opinions of the attending physicians.

The New Jersey Supreme Court concluded: "We think that the State's interest . . . weakens and the individual's right to privacy grows as the degree of bodily invasion increases and the prognosis dims. Ultimately there comes a point at which the individual's rights overcome the State interest in preserving life. . . . We have no hesitancy in deciding that no external compelling interest of the State could compel Karen to endure the unendurable, . . . with no realistic possibility of returning to any semblance of cognitive or sapient life."

The right of privacy, as the U.S. Supreme Court found in 1965 in *Griswold v. Connecticut*, is a right "broad enough to encompass a patient's decision to decline medical treatment under certain circumstances, in much the same way as it is broad enough to encompass a woman's decision to terminate a pregnancy under certain conditions." The court determined that Karen's right of privacy, given her "grossly incompetent" state, "may be asserted on her behalf by her guardian under the peculiar circumstances here present." The court also submitted that "there would be no criminal liability in the circumstances of this case [because] the ensuing death would not be homicide but rather expiration from existing natural causes. Secondly, even if it were to be regarded as homicide, it would not be unlawful." There is a very real difference, the Court concluded, between "the unlawful taking of the life of another and the ending of artificial life-support systems as a matter of self-determination." The power of the state to punish persons for the taking of human life "does not encompass individuals terminating medical treatment pursuant to their right of privacy." Ironically, after Karen Quinlan's life support was removed pursuant to the order of the New Jersey Supreme Court, she survived for several years.

In 1990, the justices of the U.S. Supreme Court entered the colloquy on the right to die in the case of *Cruzan v. Director, Missouri Department of Health*. Chief Justice William Rehnquist, writing the opinion for the Court, took judicial notice of the fact that until the 1970s, "the number of right to refuse treatment decisions were relatively few.... More recently, however, with the advance of medical technology capable of sustaining life well past the point where natural forces would have brought certain death in earlier times, cases involving the right to refuse life-sustaining treatment have burgeoned."

On a cold winter night in January 1983, Nancy Cruzan, a twenty-five-year-old woman, lost control of her automobile while traveling in Jasper County, Missouri. Thrown from the car, she landed facedown in a water-filled drainage ditch. When found, she was without any detectable respiratory or cardiac function. Paramedics restored her breathing and heartbeat at the scene of the accident and brought her, unconscious, to a nearby hospital. She had been in an anoxic state (lack of oxygen) for about fourteen minutes. She was unconsciousness and kept alive by feeding and hydration tubes. Rehabilitation efforts failed and, in 1990, she was still in a PVS in the same Missouri hospital she had been brought to seven years earlier.

After the PVS status was known, Cruzan's parents asked the hospital to withdraw life support. The hospital refused to do so without court approval. The parents went into state court to plead for authorization to withdraw life support. The trial court authorized the termination, stating that both state and federal constitutions provided a fundamental right to Nancy Cruzan to direct the withdrawal of "death prolonging procedures." That court took notice that Nancy, when she was twenty-four years old, "expressed thoughts" to a friend that she didn't want to continue her life in a PVS.

The state appealed to the Missouri Supreme Court. That court reversed the lower court decision by a divided vote. Although the state recognized a right to refuse treatment found in the common-law concept of "informed consent," it did not believe that Karen's comments to her roommate prior to the accident were "clear and convincing, inherently reliable evidence" about her views of life and death. Because of this lack of clear and convincing evidence, the court declined to support her co-guardians' claim to exercise "substituted judgment" on Nancy's behalf.

The Missouri Supreme Court concluded that the Missouri Living Will Act "embodied a state policy strongly favoring the preservation of life." Without abundantly clear and convincing proof that the victim did not want life-sustaining medical procedures, the right of the state to preserve human life took precedence. It also rejected the argument that the U.S. Constitution contained a broad right of privacy that gave Nancy and her parents the right to refuse medical treatment. Nancy's parents appealed to the U.S. Supreme Court, which granted certiorari to consider the question of whether the U.S. Constitution prohibits Missouri from electing to follow the "rule of reason" (proof by clear and convincing evidence) as a method "to ensure the State's commitment to the protection and preservation of life." The Court decided that the U.S. Constitution does not forbid the establishment of this procedural requirement.

To support this position, the majority used a balancing test: "Whether [Cruzon's] constitutional rights have been violated must be determined by balancing [her] liberty interests against the relevant state interests." The justices concluded that Missouri's demand that "clear and convincing evidence" be produced had to be met before the guardians of an incompetent PVS patient could legally terminate life-sustaining medical treatment. In the absence of patient competency, the Court held that surrogates must adhere to Missouri's procedural safeguard to assure the closest possible conformance to "the wishes expressed by the patient while competent."

Chief Justice Rehnquist's opinion noted that in America "most courts have based a right to refuse treatment either solely on the common law right to informed consent or both on the common law right and a constitutional privacy right. . . . For purposes of this case, we assume that the U.S. Constitution would grant a competent person a constitutionally protected right to refuse lifesaving hydration and nutrition." Justices Sandra Day O'Connor and Antonin Scalia joined the Rehnquist opinion but also wrote concurring opinions.

There were four dissenters: William J. Brennan, Thurgood Marshall, John Paul Stevens, and Harry Blackmun. For Brennan, the *Cruzan* fact situation was a dire consequence of modern medical technology's great advances. He wrote that "medical technology has effectively created a twilight zone of suspended animation where death commences while life, in some form, continues. Some patients, however, want no part of a life sustained only by medical technology. Instead, they prefer a plan of medical treatment that allows nature to take its course and permits them to die with dignity."

Brennan's opinion emphasized that there was a fundamental right—a "liberty" interest—a person must terminate in order to refuse medical treatment. Furthermore, incompetency does not deprive a patient of that fundamental right. Nancy Cruzan was in that twilight zone for seven years, being "kept metabolically alive." Brennan stated further: "Because I believe that Nancy Cruzan has a fundamental right to be free of unwanted artificial nutrition and hydration, which right is not outweighed by any interests of the State, I find that the improperly based procedural obstacles imposed by the Missouri Supreme Court impermissibly burden that right. . . . Nancy Cruzan is entitled to choose to die with dignity."

Surrogates can act on behalf of the person in a PVS. Unlike state officials, they are intimately associated with the patient and may have known of her desire to end all life-sustaining medical treatment if she should ever lapse into a PVS. Furthermore, when a right is fundamental, there can be no balancing of fundamental rights with the generalized, abstract right of the state to preserve and protect life. The state had presented only an abstract, undifferentiated interest in the preservation of life, and yet, wrote Brennan, the U.S. Supreme Court majority allowed that reason to "overwhelm the best interests of Nancy Cruzan."

Stevens's dissent maintained that the Court majority was wrong to "permit the State's abstract, undifferentiated interest in the preservation of life to overwhelm the best interests of Nancy Beth Cruzan, interests which would, according to an undisputed finding, be served by allowing her guardians to exercise her constitutional right to discontinue medical treatment." Using Missouri's standard, Stevens's dissent maintained that there was clear and convincing evidence in the record to indicate the "impossibility" of medical recovery from her PVS. Stevens further agreed with the state trial judge's conclusion that "there is a fundamental natural right, expressed in our Constitution as the 'right to liberty,' which permits an individual to refuse or direct the withholding or withdrawal of artificial death prolonging procedures when the person has no more cognitive brain function . . . and all the physicians agree that there is no hope of further recovery while the deterioration of the brain continues with further overall worsening physical contractures." In such evidentiary circumstances, a statute prohibiting withdrawal or termination of medical procedures violates Cruzan's "constitutional rights by depriving her of liberty without due process." There was not even a "rational relationship" between the Missouri court's ban and a legitimate state end.

Selected Bibliography

Humphrey, Derek, and Mary Clement. *Freedom to Die: People, Politics, and the Right-to-Die Movement.* New York: St. Martin's Press, 1998.

Kamm, R. M. *Morality, Mortality. Vol. 1, Death and Whom to Save from It.* New York: Oxford University Press, 1993.

Physician-Assisted Suicide: Death with Dignity?

——◄○►——

Howard Ball
Department of Political Science
University of Vermont

Vacco v. Quill, 521 U.S. 793 (1997); *Washington v. Glucksberg*, 521 U.S. 702 (1997) [U.S. Supreme Court]

◄○► THE CASE IN BRIEF ◄○►

Date
1997

Location
New York
Washington

Court
U.S. Supreme Court

Principal Participants
Dr. Timothy E. Quill; Dennis Vacco, Attorney General of New York; Harold Glucksberg; State of Washington

Significance of the Case
The Supreme Court ruled against physician-assisted suicide in these two cases, but a majority of the justices indicated that "death with dignity" may receive some constitutional protection in future cases.

Does a terminally ill but competent person have the right to seek a physician's assistance to commit suicide? In America, only one state, Oregon, allows physician-assisted suicide under legislatively mandated guidelines.

Oregon's Death with Dignity Act was adopted by a state initiative in November 1994 by a vote of 51 percent to 49 percent. Before the Oregon law was implemented, a U.S. district court judge permanently enjoined its enforcement, finding that it violated the Fourteenth Amendment's equal protection clause. The injunction was appealed to the Ninth Circuit Court of Appeals. In *Lee v. State of Oregon* (1997), the appellate court ordered the injunction lifted because the plaintiffs lacked standing. The plaintiffs' petition for certiorari to the U.S. Supreme Court was denied on October 14, 1997. Subsequently, the 1997 Oregon legislature enacted HB 2954, which referred the repeal of the Death with Dignity Act to Oregon voters. The repeal effort was defeated by 60 percent to 40 percent on November 4, 1997.

The statute took effect immediately. It allows a competent, suffering, terminally ill patient (defined as a person who will die in six months or less) to seek medication from a physician to end life quickly. The law stipulates that before receiving any medication "to end his or her life in a humane and dignified manner, a qualified patient shall have made an oral request and a written request, and reiterate the oral request to [the] attending physician no less than 15 days after making the initial oral request." At least two physicians (the attending physician and a consulting physician) must make separate determinations that the patient is terminally ill, is competent, is acting voluntarily, has been informed of the "probable result" of taking the prescription, and has been told of "feasible alternatives, including, but not limited to, comfort care, hospice care, and pain control." Additionally, they must request that the patient discuss the choice with next of kin and, if appropriate, refer the patient for psychological counseling. Before writing a medical prescription, the attending physician must affirm that the patient made an "informed decision." At all times until death, the patient can rescind the request for physician assistance to commit suicide. In 1998, the first full year of the act, sixteen patients received physician assistance in committing suicide. In 1999, the number of physician-assisted suicides under the Death with Dignity Act increased to twenty-seven. The majority of these (sixteen) were terminally ill cancer patients; the rest were dying of chronic lung disease, AIDS, or Lou Gehrig's disease. The average age of the Oregon suicides was seventy-one.

The physician-assisted suicide issue came to the U.S. Supreme Court in 1997 when the justices granted certiorari in cases from New York and the state of Washington. Petitioners, medical doctors in both cases, asked the Court to determine whether a competent person had a constitutional right to commit suicide. In *Vacco*, the source of the right to physician-assisted suicide was claimed to be the Fourteenth Amendment's equal protection clause. In *Washington*, the grounds asserted were the "fundamental liberty interest" in the Fourteenth Amendment's due process clause and the hybrid constitutional right of privacy.

In New York, as in most states, it is criminal for one person to aid another competent person

Compassion in Dying leader Barbara Coombs Lee, second from right, meets with reporters after the state's assisted suicide law was upheld by Oregon voters on Tuesday, November 4, 1997. *AP Photo/ Don Ryan.*

in committing or attempting to commit suicide, even though the competent person has the right to refuse or to terminate medical treatment. In *Vacco*, the three respondent physicians maintained that although it would be within their profession's code of behavior to prescribe lethal medication for mentally competent, terminally ill patients suffering great pain who ask a doctor's help in taking their own lives, the physicians were deterred from doing so by the state's ban against assisted suicide.

The doctors and the three terminally ill patients (all of whom had died by the time the case was heard in the U.S. Supreme Court) sued the state's attorney general. They claimed that the ban against aiding a terminally ill patient in committing suicide violated the Fourteenth Amendment's equal protection clause because state law did allow terminally ill patients to refuse or to terminate lifesaving medical treatment. They maintained that refusal or termination of medication is "essentially the same thing" as physician-assisted suicide. Therefore, the New York law banning assisted suicide violated the Fourteenth Amendment's equal protection clause.

The federal district court disagreed with the doctors' constitutional argument, concluding that it is "hardly unreasonable or irrational for the State to recognize a difference between allowing nature to take its course, even in the most severe situations, and intentionally using an artificial death producing device." The state had "obvious legitimate interests in preserving life, and in protecting vulnerable persons."

On appeal, the U.S. circuit court reversed, holding that the New York law violated the U.S. Constitution's equal protection clause. The appeals court concluded that the law does not treat equally all competent persons who are in the final stages of fatal illness and wish to hasten their deaths. Those who are on life-support systems are allowed to hasten their deaths by directing the removal of such systems; but those who are similarly situated, except for no previous attachment of life-sustaining equipment, are not allowed to hasten death by administering lethal drugs. The appeals court held that ending of life (by terminating or refusing life-support systems) is nothing more or less than assisted suicide. Further, the appeals court concluded that the unequal treatment was not "rationally related" to any legitimate state interests. Therefore, the ban against physician-assisted suicide was in violation of the Fourteenth Amendment's "general rule that States must treat like cases alike but may treat unlike cases accordingly."

New York appealed the decision to the U.S. Supreme Court, and on June 26, 1997, the Court announced its decision in an opinion by Chief Justice William Rehnquist. Although the vote was 9-0 to overturn the federal appeals court, only four justices (Sandra Day O'Connor, Antonin Scalia, Anthony Kennedy, and Clarence Thomas) joined Rehnquist's opinion. A quartet of justices—Stephen Breyer, Ruth Bader Ginsburg, David Souter, and John Paul Stevens—wrote separate concurrences.

For Rehnquist, in *Vacco* as in its companion case, *Washington v. Glucksberg,* there was a threshold question that had to be answered: Did the New York statute bar a fundamental right or did it target a suspect class? In *Vacco,* the particular question, as it was in *Washington,* was whether the right to physician assistance in committing suicide was a fundamental right of a terminally ill, competent patient. If the "legislative classification or distinction neither burdens a fundamental right nor targets a suspect class, we will uphold it so long as it bears a rational relation to some legitimate end," wrote Rehnquist. The conclusion that the chief justice reached was that the statutes did not infringe fundamental rights or involve suspect classifications. Thus, they are entitled to a "strong presumption of validity." Every competent person, Rehnquist submitted, regardless of physical condition, is entitled to refuse unwanted lifesaving medical treatment; but no one is permitted to assist a suicide. Laws that apply evenhandedly to all such persons "unquestionably comply" with the equal protection clause.

Further, the U.S. Supreme Court disagreed with the appeals court's drawing of an unconstitutional distinction between the New York laws: "We think the distinction between assisting suicide and withdrawing life sustaining treatment, a distinction widely recognized and endorsed in the medical profession and in our legal traditions, is both important and logical; it is certainly rational [and] comports with fundamental legal principles of causation and intent." Withdrawal leads to death "from an underlying fatal disease or pathology while taking a fatal prescription leads to death "by that medication." States can move legislatively "to protect and promote patients' dignity at the end of life [while] they remain opposed to physician assisted suicide."

The Court concluded that states may "reaffirm the line between 'killing' and 'letting go.' " The respondents' claim that the distinction between letting go and killing was "arbitrary" and "irrational" was flatly rejected by Rehnquist: "New York's reasons for recognizing and acting on this distinction—including prohibiting intentional killing and preserving life; preventing suicide; maintaining physicians' role as their patients' healers; protecting vulnerable people from indifference, prejudice, and psychological and financial pressure to end their lives; and avoiding a possible slide towards euthanasia—[are] valid and important public interests [that] easily satisfy the constitutional requirement that a legislative classification bear a rational relation to some legitimate end."

Justice Sandra Day O'Connor wrote a short, poignant concurring opinion for both cases.

"Death will be different for each of us," she wrote. "For many, the last days will be spent in physical pain and perhaps the despair that accompanies physical deterioration and a loss of control of basic body and mental functions." In both cases, all parties agreed that a competent, terminally ill patient "who is experiencing great pain has no legal barriers to obtaining medication, from qualified physicians, to alleviate that suffering, even to the point of causing unconsciousness and hastening death." Therefore, she concluded, "there is no need to address the question whether suffering patients have a constitutionally cognizable interest in obtaining relief from the suffering that they may experience in the last days of their lives." She found that there is no dispute that dying patients in Washington and New York can obtain palliative care, even if doing so would hasten their deaths. For her, the difficulty in defining terminal illness and the risk that a dying patient's request for assistance in his or her life might not be truly voluntary justify the prohibitions on assisted suicide.

Justice Breyer shared O'Connor's views, but he issued a separate concurrence to show how he differed from the Rehnquist opinion. For Breyer, Rehnquist's formulation of the rejected "liberty" interest was incorrect. Breyer suggested that there should always be a right to die with dignity, that is, "personal control over the manner of death, professional medical assistance, and the avoidance of unnecessary and severe physical suffering." He believed that the respondents in both cases could have established the basis for a right to die with dignity. "I do not believe, however," concluded Breyer, "that this Court need or now should decide whether or not such a right is 'fundamental.' "

Justice Souter also concurred in the two cases. In *Vacco*, he wrote a short opinion taking notice that the "claims of medical doctors and patients [must] be accorded a high degree of importance requiring a commensurate justification." His major essay on the question of physician-assisted suicide was his concurrence in *Washington*.

Finally, Justice Stevens wrote a concurring opinion for both cases. He wrote separately "to make it clear that there is also room for further debate" about the constitutional limits of the states to punish physician-assisted suicide. In both cases, he noted, the Court's analysis was not limited to a particular set of plaintiffs before it. He maintained, drawing analogy to the Court's decisions in capital punishment and abortion cases, that the Court's conclusion that laws banning physician-assisted suicide did not violate the Constitution "does not mean that every possible application of the statute[s] would be valid." Some state intrusions on the right to decide how death will be encountered, Stevens stressed, are simply intolerable. For example, avoiding intolerable pain and the indignity of living one's final days incapacitated and in agony is certainly crucial to "the liberty . . . to define one's own concept of existence, of meaning, of the universe, and of the mystery of human life."

For Stevens, each assisted suicide is different, and the Court must examine the particulars in order to determine whether, based on the medical and human dynamics in that case, a state statute banning physician-assisted suicide is "intolerable" and in violation of either the equal protection clause or the due process clause in the Fourteenth Amendment. "In my judgment," Stevens argued, "it is clear that the so called 'unqualified interest in the preservation of human life' is not itself sufficient to outweigh the interest in liberty that may justify the only possible means of preserving a dying patient's dignity and alleviating her intolerable suffering."

The Washington case, *Washington et al. v. Harold Glucksberg et al.*, involved a challenge by physicians to a law passed in 1975 that provided for criminal prosecution if a person knowingly caused or aided another person to attempt suicide. In 1994, suit was brought in the Federal District Court of Western Washington by a number of terminally ill plaintiffs and four physicians who occasionally treated the terminally ill. They argued that there would have been assisted suicide of the patients by the doctors if not for the 1975 statutory ban on such actions.

The plaintiffs, doctors and patients, sought a declaratory motion from the Court that the 1975 Washington statute was unconstitutional on its face. They asserted that there was a "liberty" interest protected by the Fourteenth Amendment's due process clause that extended to a choice by a terminally ill but competent patient to commit suicide with the passive assistance of physicians by prescribing a lethal dose of medication. Active physician assistance, by contrast, occurs when a medical doctor actually administers a lethal dose to a terminally ill patient, such as the well-publicized Michigan cases involving Dr. Jack Kevorkian.

The district court judge in *Glucksberg* granted the motions for summary judgment, ruling that the statute was unconstitutional because it placed an undue burden on the exercise of the person's asserted and constitutionally protected liberty interest. On appeal, a three-judge circuit court panel reversed, ruling that "in two hundred and five years of our existence no constitutional right to aid in killing oneself has ever been asserted and upheld by a court of final jurisdiction." However, the Ninth Circuit reheard the case en banc and concluded that the summary judgment for the plaintiffs was correct. Their judgment rested on the "general tradition of self sovereignty" arguments, made in the abortion decision of *Planned Parenthood v. Casey* (1992) and in *Cruzan v. Director, Missouri Department of Health* (1990), that the U.S. Constitution "encompasses a due process liberty interest in controlling the time and manner of one's death"—that there is, in short, a constitutionally recognized "right to die." Therefore, the Washington statute was unconstitutional as applied to terminally ill, competent adults who wished to hasten their deaths with medication prescribed by their physicians.

On certiorari to the U.S. Supreme Court, the justices reversed the appeals court decision. The opinion was announced on June 26, 1997, along with *Vacco v. Quill*. The vote in *Glucksberg*, as in *Vacco*, was 9-0, and there were also six opinions written in the case. In the opinion for the Court, Chief Justice Rehnquist concluded that the 1975 Washington statute did not violate the Fourteenth Amendment's due process clause. As he saw it, the threshold question was whether the right to commit suicide with the assistance of a physician was a "fundamental liberty interest" protected by the due process clause. If the right

to commit suicide with physician assistance was a fundamental right, then the Court had to determine, using the "strict scrutiny" standard, whether the state met the heavy burden of showing an overriding, compelling interest in restricting the passage of "narrowly tailored" legislation. However, if the right to commit suicide with physician assistance was not a fundamental liberty interest, then all the state of Washington needed to do to validate its legislation was to show a "rational relationship" between the 1975 statute and the general purposes of the state government.

Rehnquist began his analysis by noting that suicide is not "deeply rooted" in the nation's traditions. "Anglo American law," he wrote, "has punished or otherwise disproved of assisting suicide for over 700 years," and rendering such assistance is still a crime in almost every state. He stated further that prohibitions against assisted suicide have never contained exceptions for those who were near death. In light of that history, the Court, speaking through Rehnquist, concluded that respondents' asserted "right" to assistance in committing suicide is not a fundamental liberty interest protected by the Due Process Clause.

Having reached this conclusion, it was not difficult for Rehnquist to find a "rational relationship" between the 1975 ban on physician assisted suicide and the general functions of state government to legislate for the public's welfare, well-being, and safety. "The state," he argued, "must be able to protect depressed or mentally ill persons, or those who are suffering from untreated pain, from suicidal impulses. The state also has an interest in protecting the integrity and ethics of the medical profession. Physician assisted suicide is fundamentally incompatible with the physician's role as healer." As a result, most medical associations had argued against its legalization. Also, the chief justice submitted, the state has an interest in "protecting vulnerable groups—including the poor, the elderly, and disabled persons—from abuse, neglect, and mistakes." Finally, Rehnquist expressed the view that the state could ban such actions for "fear that permitting assisted suicide will start it down the path to voluntary and perhaps even involuntary euthanasia." Therefore, the Washington ban "does not violate the Fourteenth Amendment, either on its face or as applied to competent, terminally ill adults who wish to hasten their deaths by obtaining medication prescribed by their doctors."

The views of Justices O'Connor, Breyer, Stevens and Ginsburg were the same in their *Glucksberg* concurrences as they expressed in their *Vacco* opinions. Although Justice David Souter wrote separate concurring opinions in both cases, *Glucksberg* contained Souter's substantive views. Souter maintained that the underlying question, not yet ready to be answered by the Court in these two cases, was whether the statutes set up "arbitrary impositions" or "purposeless restraints" at odds with the due process clause of the Fourteenth Amendment. He concluded that the law's application to the doctors in these cases has not been shown to be unconstitutional, but he still felt called upon to write separately to offer his reasons for rejecting this particular due process claim.

According to Souter, the argument made by the *Glucksberg* doctors—that "the state has no substantively adequate justification for barring the assistance sought by the patient and sought to be offered by the physician"—is based on "substantive due process" and the existence of "unenumerated rights." The meaning of due process, Souter asserted strongly "was impossible to construe without recognizing substantive, and not merely procedural, limitations." Substantive due process, for Souter, was "a continuum of rights to be free from arbitrary impositions and purposeless restraints." Souter found the Rehnquist standard of due process to be too arbitrary. Souter felt that his understanding of the concept would allow courts to assess relative weights or dignities of the contending interests. After such a weighing of the competing interests of liberty and authority, the courts could then determine whether a statute in question "falls inside or outside the zone of what is reasonable in the way it resolves the conflict between the interests of state and individual." There is no doubt, wrote Souter, that there is "an [important] liberty interest in bodily integrity" that must be balanced against the interest of the state. To document this point, Souter cited

Supreme Court cases dating back to 1914 and culminating with the abortion decisions of the 1990s. Souter noted in conclusion that hard data from legislative experimentation, such as Oregon's Death with Dignity Act, will throw more light on the substantive questions—political, moral, religious, and medical—associated with physician-assisted suicide. Accordingly, courts should stay their hand to allow reasonable legislative consideration.

Clearly, the Court has not uttered the final words on the constitutionality of physician-assisted suicide. At least five of the justices in *Vacco* and *Glucksberg*—O'Connor, Ginsberg, Breyer, Souter, and Stevens—have allowed the door to remain open to the possibility that "death with dignity" may have some form of constitutional protection in a future case. Even Chief Justice Rehnquist predicted that the Supreme Court's holdings in *Vacco* and *Glucksberg* would not foreclose the debates on this issue: "Throughout the nation," he wrote in the latter case, "Americans are engaged in earnest and profound debate about the morality, legality, and practicality of physician assisted suicide. Our holding permits this debate to continue, as it should in a democratic society." The societal debate mentioned by Rehnquist led in 2000 to proposed congressional legislation banning physician-assisted suicide. Should such a federal law be passed, it will likely face a constitutional challenge in the courts.

Selected Bibliography

Emanuel, Linda L., ed. *Regulating How We Die: The Ethical, Medical, and Legal Issues Surrounding Physician-Assisted Suicide.* Cambridge: Harvard University Press, 1998.

Grisez, Germain, and Joseph M. Boyle, Jr. *Life and Death with Liberty and Justice: A Contribution to the Euthanasia Debate.* Notre Dame, IN: University of Notre Dame Press, 1979.

Hill, T. Patrick, and David Shirley. *A Good Death: Taking More Control at the End of Your Life.* Reading, MA: Addison-Wesley, 1992.

Hoeffler, James M. *Managing Death.* Boulder, CO: Westview Press, 1997.

Nuland, Sherwin B. *How We Die: Reflections on Life's Final Chapter.* New York: Vintage, 1995.

Urofsky, Melvin I. *Lethal Judgments: Assisted Suicide and American Law*. Lawrence: University Press of Kansas, 2000.

Youngner, Stuart J., Robert M. Arnold, and Renie Schapiro. *The Definition of Death: Contemporary Controversies*. Baltimore: Johns Hopkins University Press, 1999.

Abortion: Who Shall Decide?

————◄○►————

Mary K. Bonsteel Tachau

Deceased Professor of History
University of Louisville

Jane Roe et al. v. Henry Wade, 410 U.S. 113 (1973)
and *William L. Webster v. Reproductive Health Services*, 492 U.S. 490 (1989) [U.S. Supreme Court]

◄○► THE CASE IN BRIEF ◄○►

Date
1973, 1989

Location
Texas; Missouri

Court
U.S. Supreme Court

Principal Participants
Norma McCorvey, alias Jane Roe; Dallas District Attorney Henry Wade; Missouri Attorney General Webster; Justice Harry Blackmun

Significance of the Case
In an extremely controversial decision, the Supreme Court ruled that a woman's right to terminate her pregnancy was guaranteed by the Fourteenth Amendment. The issue of abortion is, perhaps, the most divisive and hotly contested topic in the United States, and this case brought the conflict to a boil.

The experiences of Justice Harry Blackmun give pause to anyone who harbors an ambition to become a member of the U.S. Supreme Court. It was Justice Blackmun's fate to write the majority opinion in *Roe v. Wade* (1973). Although six other justices joined in that decision, it was Justice Blackmun, not they, who became the object of angry demonstrations over the following decades.

Roe v. Wade may be the most controversial decision of the Court since the 1857 *Dred Scott* decision. By sweeping away state laws that stringently limited or absolutely prohibited abortion, it evoked a vigorous and widespread protest movement. Calling themselves "pro-life," rather than "antiabortion," some of its members publicized their convictions by bombing abortion clinics and threatening the life of Justice Blackmun. Until the 1989 decision in *Webster v. Reproductive Health Services*, those who supported *Roe v. Wade* had been, by comparison, relatively quiet and politically inactive.

Yet opposition to *Roe v. Wade* in American society goes beyond the tactics of single-issue, antiabortion activists. It includes many (but not all) religious conservatives, from fundamentalists to the Roman Catholic hierarchy. Among opponents are prominent national leaders, usually those identified with the conservative wings of the major political parties, especially the Republican Party. During the Reagan administration, candidates for appointment by the executive branch often found that their position on *Roe v. Wade* was a major determinant of their success: an antiabortion stance was necessary to pass the administration's "litmus test." Interestingly, most members of the bar and bench who disagree with the *decision* of the Court nevertheless focus their criticism on the *opinion* written by Justice Blackmun, both for its breadth and for its specificity.

The case involved an unmarried pregnant woman who wanted to terminate her pregnancy by an abortion to be preformed by a competent, licensed physician under safe, clinical conditions. In all of the proceedings, the woman was identified as "Jane Roe" to protect her anonymity, thus conforming to the traditional Anglo-American legal convention of using pseudonyms such as "John Doe" or "Richard Roe." However, the plaintiff was subsequently identified in newspapers and on television as Norma McCorvey. It was rare for a pregnant woman who wanted an abortion to be a plaintiff because, during the time that commonly elapses between initiating a suit and having it come to trial, the woman is likely to have given birth—thus presenting the court an opportunity to say that the case is "moot" and avoid the issue entirely.

Roe asserted that she was unable to get a legal abortion in Texas because her life did not appear to be threatened by the continuation of her pregnancy, a necessary condition under the Texas statutes, which prohibited procuring or attempting to procure an abortion except on medical advice for the purpose of saving the mother's life. The Texas statute had not been substantively changed since its passage in 1854. Roe stated that she could not afford to travel to another state in order to secure a safe, legal abortion. She further claimed that the Texas criminal abortion statutes were unconstitutionally vague and that they abridged her right of personal privacy, which was protected by the First, Fourth, Fifth, Ninth, and Fourteenth Amendments.

The action was brought in 1970 against Henry Wade, district attorney for Dallas County, in the U.S. District Court for the Northern District of Texas. Roe asked for a declaratory judgment that the Texas abortion statutes were unconstitutional and for an injunction restraining Wade from enforcing them. In an amendment to her original complaint, Roe sued on behalf of herself and all other women similarly situated. Thus the litigation was a "class action suit," a case in which a plaintiff sues on behalf of other people, as well as herself/himself, who can be identified as members of the same group because they are affected by the same laws.

Two other parties joined in the suit. One was a physician who had been arrested for violating the Texas abortion laws and had two prosecutions pending against him. The district court allowed him to intervene, but the Supreme Court did not, on the grounds that a defendant in a pending state criminal case cannot challenge the statutes under which the state is prosecuting him in a federal court.

The other party was a married, childless couple, who stated that if the wife became pregnant, they would want to terminate her pregnancy by abortion because of a permanent condition that rendered her health precarious. The district court denied their request on the grounds that they did not have standing (the right to come before a court because of a personal stake in the outcome of the controversy). The Supreme Court agreed, saying that the allegation of a possible injury that had not yet occurred did not present an actual case or controversy, as is necessary for adjudication.

Roe v. Wade was only one of dozens of challenges to state abortion laws that had been raised since 1965. In that year, the Supreme Court's decision in *Griswold v. Connecticut* declared unconstitutional state laws which prohibited the sale or use of contraceptives, or advising or counseling their use. The *Griswold* majority held that such laws abridged the right to privacy. Justice William O. Douglas's opinion for the Court in *Griswold* stated that the right to privacy could be inferred from the First, Third, Fourth, Fifth, and Ninth Amendments, although it was not specifically mentioned anywhere in them or elsewhere in the

Constitution. In Justice Douglas's controversial analysis, the right to privacy exists because of "emanations" from the "penumbras" of various Bill of Rights guarantees. Supporters of Douglas's holding in *Griswold* cited his creative jurisprudence; critics attacked the opinion as an example of the worst of modern judicial activism.

The *Griswold* opinion would prove to be central to the efforts of those who wished to change restrictive state abortion laws. For fifteen years, they had focused on state legislatures, with uneven results. As several writers pointed out in influential law review articles, the Court's assertion of a right to privacy suggested a litigation strategy that might be more successful in challenging abortion statutes than the legislative strategy pursued thus far.

The modern doctrine of privacy—the "right to be let alone"—was first enunciated by Louis D. Brandeis and Samuel D. Warren in an 1890 article in *Harvard Law Review*. Justice Brandeis developed the doctrine further in a dissenting opinion in *Olmstead v. United States* (1928). He based his disapproval of governmental invasion of privacy on the Fourth Amendment's guarantees against unreasonable searches and seizures and the Fifth Amendment's protection against self-incrimination. In 1961, the Supreme Court had held in *Mapp v. Ohio* that those guarantees were applicable to state governments, as well as the federal government, because of the Fourteenth Amendment's requirement that states could not deprive any person of liberty without due process of law. Justice Douglas's *Griswold* opinion provided additional grounds for assertions of a constitutional right of privacy by citing the Third and Ninth Amendments as well. Perhaps the most significant expansion was that suggested by the Ninth Amendment, which alludes to rights retained by the people that are not enumerated anywhere in the Constitution.

By 1970, when *Roe v. Wade* was heard in the federal district court in Dallas, legal actions against state abortion laws were pending in thirteen states. The difficulties inherent in so controversial an issue as abortion were compounded by the nature of the litigative process. Since *Eric v. Tompkins* (1938), lower federal courts have been obliged to follow the decisional law of the states in which they are located; state courts, which make the decisions that constitute decisional law, are generally expected to uphold state statutes (although that is an unproven assumption). Women who had abortions were seldom prosecuted; challenges to state abortion laws were typically brought by physicians who were in a relatively weak position from which to protest.

Given those circumstances and the generally conservative cast of Texas, the decision of its federal district court was unexpected. A three-judge panel held that the right to choose whether to have children was protected by the Ninth Amendment, made applicable to the states through the due process clause of the Fourteenth Amendment. It also said that the Texas criminal abortion statutes were void because they were unconstitutionally vague and constituted an "overboard" infringement of the plaintiffs' Ninth Amendment rights. The court did deny Roe's request for an injunction that would have prohibited the district attorney from bringing other prosecutions under the law. That minor setback proved to be an advantage as the case proceeded.

The case was appealed to the U.S. Court of Appeals for the Fifth Circuit, which ordinarily would have been the proper body to hear the case next. In *Roe v. Wade*, however, a direct appeal to the Supreme Court was allowed because of the district court's denial of the injunction.

The Supreme Court had seemed reluctant to hear abortion cases, although the post-*Griswold* litigation had led to mixed decisions in both state and lower federal courts. Some courts declared abortion laws unconstitutional, other upheld them; some granted injunctions against continued enforcement, others did not. It was clear that a decision by the nation's highest court was needed to bring uniformity and predictability in this area of law. Yet the Court had dismissed or upheld lower court dismissals of six cases by the end of its 1970 term, when it was presented with six more requests for review. It accepted two: the Texas case of *Roe v. Wade* and *Doe v. Bolton*, a challenge to the Georgia abortion law.

The Court first heard *Roe v. Wade* in December 1971. According to some reports, the initial vote was 5-2 to strike down the abortion laws. Justices John Marshall Harlan and Hugo Black had died the previous summer, and Justices Lewis Powell and William Rehnquist had not yet joined the Court. Usually the senior justice in the majority chooses whether to write the opinion or to assign it to someone else. In this case, however, Chief Justice Warren Burger is generally said to have voted with the minority, but nevertheless assigned the writing of the majority opinion to Justice Blackmun. Because the internal proceedings of the Court are confidential, it is impossible to verify what went on in the judges' deliberations, and it should be noted that the Chief Justice voted with the majority when the decision was announced. In any event, the selection of Justice Blackmun was consistent with the practice of assigning opinions to members of the Court with expertise in the subject. Blackmun, prior to his appellate judicial service, had been counsel to the Mayo Clinic and was quite conversant with medical matters.

For whatever reasons, no decision was announced during the term. Instead, the case was set for reargument in October 1972, when the two new members of the Court were present. Afterward, the vote to declare the Texas statutes unconstitutional became 7-2. Only Justices Byron White and William Rehnquist were in the minority.

The Court at last announced its decision on January 22, 1973. Justice Blackmun's majority opinion addressed not only the legal issues involved but also the history of abortion laws. He later told Roe's attorney that he had spent the entire previous summer doing research. His analysis of history, combined with his knowledge of modern medical practice, led to a formula for appropriate governmental intervention in abortions. Blackmun began by quoting Justice Oliver Wendell Holmes, Jr.'s statement in *Lochner v. New York* (1905): "[The Constitution] is made for people of fundamentally differing views, and the accident of our finding certain opinions natural and familiar or novel and even shocking ought not to conclude our judgment upon the question whether the statutes embodying them conflict with the Constitution of the United States."

Justice Blackmun answered Wade's claim that the case must now be moot because neither Roe nor any other members of her class were still subject to a 1970 pregnancy by stating that "pregnancy provides a classic justification for a conclusion of nonmootness" because it is a condition capable of repetition. Roe had an actual case and controversy when she filed it, and, as a pregnant woman thwarted by Texas abortion statutes, she had standing to challenge those laws.

He continued by pointing out that laws restricting abortion are of very recent origin in human history. The proscription against abortion in the Hippocratic Oath reflected a minority view: abortions were generally accepted in the ancient world, and were not prohibited by religious precepts. Later, English common law did not prohibit abortion before "quickening" (sometime after the sixteenth week). Most authorities agree that abortion, even after quickening, was not established as a crime in common law. The first English criminal abortion statute (1803) made abortion of a quick fetus a capital offense, but provided lesser penalties for the felony of abortion before quickening.

The American colonies, and later states, followed the English model with an important exception: abortion necessary to save the life of the mother was not a crime. Although statutes varied from state to state, over the next fifty years they became more restrictive as the quickening distinction disappeared and penalties increased. In some jurisdictions, the emphasis changed from preserving the life of the mother to preserving that of the fetus. These trends continued until the 1950s, when about a third of the states adopted less stringent laws based upon the American Law Institute's Model Penal Code of 1959, which allowed abortion under some circumstances. The opinion noted that modern medical techniques, especially when performed early in pregnancy, made abortion far safer than it had once been.

Justice Blackmun then discussed the line of court decisions regarding privacy. He concluded that the right to privacy was not absolute but did encompass the abortion decision, which he found met the Court's standard of a fundamental right "implicit in the concept

Norma McCorvey revisits the U.S. Supreme Court in April, 1989, twenty-six years after her landmark decision in *Roe v. Wade,* to hear an abortion case seeking to limit the decision of her case. *AP Photo.*

of ordered liberty." Whether the right to privacy was grounded in the Fourteenth Amendment's concept of personal liberty and its restrictions on state action, as he believed it to be, or on the Ninth Amendment, as the district court had ruled, it was broad enough to encompass a woman's decision whether or not to terminate her pregnancy.

Justice Blackmun thought it inadvisable for the judiciary to try to resolve the question of when life begins, and he found no constitutional basis for applying the Fourteenth Amendment's protection of persons to the unborn. But even a woman's fundamental right to abortion could be limited, he submitted, by "a compelling state interest" to protect her health. Medical evidence placed the "compelling point" to be at the end of the first trimester. Before that time, the mortality rate for abortion performed under clinical conditions is lower than in normal childbirth, and the state had no interest in the termination of a pregnancy. During the second trimester, Blackmun ruled, the state might regulate abortion in ways that are reasonably related to maternal

health. Because of its interest in promoting the potentiality of life, the state might regulate or even proscribe abortion during the third trimester, except where it is necessary to preserve the life or health of the mother. Until the point where a compelling state interest justifies governmental intervention, Blackmun concluded, the abortion decision is inherently and primarily a medical one. The Texas law, by failing to distinguish between early and late abortions and providing only one ground for legal abortion, swept too broadly and thus interfered with basic constitutional rights. Yet, in a cryptic footnote, Blackmun stated that the Court would not, in this decision, determine the constitutionality of state laws requiring written permission of spouses or of the parents of minors.

Justices Lewis Powell, William Brennan, and Thurgood Marshall supported the majority opinion without qualification; Justices William Douglas and Potter Stewart and Chief Justice Warren Burger supported it with concurring opinions. Justices William Rehnquist and Byron White dissented.

The chief justice emphasized that the decision did not license abortion on demand. Justice Stewart's concurring opinion was an exegesis upon personal liberty. Justice Douglas expanded upon the doctrine of privacy and continued with a philosophically organized grouping of the liberties already recognized as coming under constitutional protection in order to demonstrate that the right to choose abortion fit reasonably within their number.

Justice Rehnquist and Justice White joined in a dissent objecting to the "raw judicial power" in the majority's decision, which they believed gave greater protection to the life of the mother than to the life of the fetus. Justice Rehnquist added his own dissent, protesting what he saw as "judicial legislation" in the trimester test to be applied to a determination of compelling state interests. To him, a century's experience with restrictions on abortion countered the assertion of the court's majority that such limitations were not traditional. He further objected to placing the right to abortion within the scope of the Fourteenth Amendment because he considered that contrary to the intent of its drafters. Finally, he thought that it was unnecessary to strike down the entire Texas statute when it might be applicable to later stages of pregnancy.

The Court's decision brought immediate reaction from the public and further politicization of the issues. Women's rights groups worked to see that poor women had access to abortions in public hospitals. Those who opposed abortion pressed the "pro-life" aspect of their position, opposed candidates who were "pro-choice," and supported state laws that might come within the scope of the majority's footnote. A flood of state legislation was passed, but until 1989, most of it was found too restrictive and was declared unconstitutional by the courts.

The composition of the Supreme Court had changed dramatically by the late 1980s when it heard *Webster v. Reproductive Health Services*, a case concerning a Missouri law placing significant restrictions on the right to secure an abortion. The statute banned the use of public facilities or public employees in performing abortions and required physicians to determine viability of any fetus thought to be twenty weeks or older.

A majority of five justices led by now Chief Justice Rehnquist upheld the ban on public facilities and public employees, but they declined to address the constitutionality of a "finding" in the preamble of the statute declaring that life begins at conception. The Chief Justice and Justices White and Anthony Kennedy upheld the viability test, even though it would fall within the second trimester, when, under *Roe*, regulations must be related to the health of the mother. Justice Sandra Day O'Connor found it unnecessary to reexamine the trimester framework; and Justice Antonin Scalia preferred to repudiate *Roe* outright.

There was more unanimity among the dissenters. Justice John Paul Stevens emphasized his disapproval of the preamble's "finding," declaring that, as an endorsement of a Christian religious tenet, it violated the First Amendment's establishment clause. Justice Blackmun, writing for Justices Brennan and Marshall, reiterated his support for *Roe* and wrote a brief but eloquent conclusion: "For today, at least the law of abortion stands undisturbed. For today,

the women of this Nation still retain the liberty to control their destinies. But the signs are evident and very ominous, and a chill wind blows."

The six opinions among nine justices in *Webster v. Reproductive Health Services* assured a continuation of the controversy over the right to abortion. This was clearly demonstrated by two more key Supreme Court abortion decisions, *Planned Parenthood of Southeastern Pennsylvania v. Casey* (1992) and *Stenberg v. Carhart* (2000). It may be useful to recall that the desegregation of public education ceased to be an issue only when the Supreme Court reached an unshakable unanimity that endured until well after a supportive national consensus developed. In time, the Court and the public may find a similar degree of tolerance or acquiescence to establish an acceptable public policy regarding abortion. It is not likely to be found, however, in a return to home remedies and back-alley abortions, with their tragically high human cost, or in laws that deny safe medical procedures to women who are poor.

Selected Bibliography

Emerson, Thomas I. "Nine Justices in Search of a Doctrine." *Michigan Law Review* 64 (December 1965): 219–234.

Garrow, David. *Liberty and Sexuality: The Right to Privacy and the Making of Roe v. Wade.* Berkeley: University of California Press, 1994.

Goodman, Janice, et al. "Doe and Roe: Where Do We Go from Here?" *Women's Rights Law Review* 1 (Spring 1973): 2–38.

Gordon, Linda. *Woman's Body, Woman's Right.* New York: Penguin Books, 1977.

Lucas, Roy. "Federal Constitutional Limitations on the Enforcement and Administration of State Abortion Statutes." *North Carolina Law Review* 46 (June 1968): 730–778.

Mohr, James C. *Abortion in America: The Origins and Evolution of National Policy.* New York: Oxford University Press, 1978.

Rubin, Eva R. *Abortion, Politics, and the Courts: Roe v. Wade and Its Aftermath.* Westport, CT: Greenwood Press, 1982.

Preserving the "Essence" of *Roe v. Wade*: The Rehnquist Court and Abortion

Tinsley E. Yarbrough
Department of Political Science
East Carolina University

and

John W. Johnson
Department of History
University of Northern Iowa

Planned Parenthood of Southeastern Pennsylvania v. Casey, 505 U.S. 833 (1992);
Stenberg v. Carhart, 530 U.S. 914 (2000) [U.S. Supreme Court]

-o- THE CASE IN BRIEF -o-

Date
1992, 2000

Location
Pennsylvania; Nebraska

Court
U.S. Supreme Court

Principal Participants
Dr. Leroy Carhart; Don Stenberg, Attorney General of Nebraska; Planned Parenthood of Southeastern Pennsylvania; Robert Casey, Governor of Pennsylvania

Significance of the Case
In the two most important decisions by the Supreme Court on abortion since *Roe v. Wade* the Court set a new standard for assessing the constitutionality of abortions and struck down a state ban on partial abortions.

The *Casey* and *Carhart* decisions mark the U.S. Supreme Court's most important rulings on abortion since *Roe v. Wade* (1973). In *Casey*, the Court announced a new standard for assessing the constitutionality of legislation regulating abortion. In *Carhart*, perhaps the most eagerly awaited civil liberties decision of the new century, the Court's majority followed the *Casey* reasoning and struck down a state ban on "partial birth" abortion procedures. Both decisions were issued by bare 5-4 majorities, thus making the future status of abortion legislation subject to a single shift in Court personnel or the change of heart of one sitting justice.

At issue in *Casey* were five provisions of Pennsylvania's abortion statute, as amended in 1988 and 1989: (1) a requirement that a woman seeking an abortion give her informed consent and be provided with information about the risks involved and available alternatives at least twenty-four hours before the procedure was to be performed; (2) a parental consent provision, with a "judicial bypass option," for minors seeking abortions; (3) a medical emergency exemption from the waiting period and informed-consent requirements; (4) a provision obliging a married woman, except under certain circumstances, to notify her spouse before securing an abortion; and (5) reporting and record-keeping requirements placed upon abortion facilities.

Invoking the *Roe* trimester framework, a federal district judge struck down each of those provisions except the reporting requirements. Emphasizing the complex lineup of justices in such recent Supreme Court cases as *Webster v. Reproductive Health Services* (1989) and *Hodgson v. Minnesota* (1990), a panel of the Court of Appeals for the Third Circuit rejected the trial court's application of the trimester formula, concluding instead that the appropriate current standard for the resolution of abortion claims was the "undue burden" approach that Justice Sandra Day O'Connor had advanced in recent cases. Under that formula, as the appeals court construed it, only abortion controls that imposed an undue burden on a woman's decision to abort a pregnancy were to be subjected to the strict, compelling-interest scrutiny required by *Roe*; other regulations would be upheld if rationally related to a legitimate governmental purpose. Invoking its version of the undue-burden approach, the Court of Appeals sustained the challenged statute's informed consent, waiting period, parental consent, and reporting requirements, but held that the spousal notice provision imposed an undue burden that was not narrowly tailored to a compelling governmental interest.

Kathryn Kolbert, counsel for the plaintiffs in *Casey*, spent most of her time during oral argument before the Supreme Court urging the justices to reaffirm *Roe*'s strict standard of review. When Justice Antonin Scalia, a *Roe* opponent, intimated that the only fundamental rights the Court should recognize were those mentioned in the Constitution's text, Kolbert responded that the "liberty" guaranteed specifically in the Fourteenth Amendment's due process clause "logically and necessarily" included a woman's right to decide whether to carry a pregnancy to term. To Justice Anthony Kennedy's suggestion that the challenged regulations could be upheld without undercutting *Roe*, she replied that abandoning strict scrutiny of abortion controls would be "the same as overruling *Roe*." Pennsylvania's

attorney general, Ernest Preate, Jr., contended that *Roe* should be overruled if it could not be construed to accommodate the challenged provisions. Preate urged the Court's adoption of the undue-burden standard—prompting a skeptical Justice Scalia to wonder aloud what law books he might consult in determining whether a law imposed an "undue" restriction on abortion rights.

The justices ultimately forming the five-member majority in *Casey* either reaffirmed the "essence" of *Roe*, embraced *Roe* entirely, or came close to endorsing *Roe*. In a joint opinion, Justices O'Connor, Kennedy, and David Souter spoke for the Court in certain respects and for themselves on other issues. Speaking for a majority, they reaffirmed *Roe*'s recognition of a woman's general right to obtain an abortion before a fetus becomes viable (that is, capable of surviving outside of the womb). They also reaffirmed *Roe*'s acceptance of state authority to forbid nontherapeutic abortions after viability, as well as legitimate state interests in protecting the woman's health and fetal life from the outset of a pregnancy. Speaking for themselves, however, they rejected *Roe*'s "rigid" trimester framework, concluding that states were merely forbidden to impose an undue burden on a woman's abortion decision prior to viability. In refusing to overrule *Roe*, the plurality also stressed the importance of honoring long-established precedent. They seemed equally bent on convincing abortion opponents that the Court would not cave in to intense public disapproval of its rulings. "A decision to overrule *Roe*'s essential holding under the existing circumstances," they declared, "would address error, if error there was, at the cost of both profound and unnecessary damage to the Court's legitimacy, and to the Nation's commitment to the rule of law."

Roe's author, Justice Harry A. Blackmun, and Justice John Paul Stevens provided the fourth and fifth votes to reaffirm at least *Roe*'s "essence" and strike down the spousal notification requirement. For Stevens, the critical question, presumably at every stage of a pregnancy, was whether asserted state interests underlying abortion regulations outweighed the woman's interest in personal liberty. Applying such an approach convinced Stevens that the twenty-four-hour waiting period and counseling provisions, as well as the spousal notification requirement, were unconstitutional. Those provisions, concluded Stevens, unduly burdened a woman's abortion decision. While continuing to embrace *Roe* and contending that all the Pennsylvania provisions violated its trimester framework, Justice Blackmun praised the joint opinion of O'Connor, Kennedy, and Souter as "an act of personal courage and constitutional principle." But Blackmun also recognized that the distance between the Court's approach and *Roe*'s complete dismantling was "the distance [of] but a single vote," and acknowledged that, at eighty-three, he could not remain on the bench forever.

Chief Justice William H. Rehnquist, a *Roe* dissenter, and Justice Scalia also filed separate opinions. Joined by Justice Byron R. White, another *Roe* dissenter, and the recently appointed Justice Clarence Thomas, Rehnquist and Scalia tracked arguments they and other *Roe* critics had advanced for years—that neither the Constitution's text nor deeply rooted national traditions justified recognition of an abortion right, at least not one of a fundamental character entitled to vigorous judicial protection; and that *Roe* and its progeny unduly encroached upon the domain of elected policy makers, contrary to majoritarian democratic principles. Scalia scorned as "frightening," moreover, the joint opinion's suggestion "that we would decide a case differently than the way we otherwise would have in order to show that we can stand firm against public disapproval."

The retirements of Justice White in 1993 and Justice Blackmun in 1994 removed from the Court one of the two *Roe* dissenters (White) and the only justice entirely committed to *Roe* (Blackmun). They were replaced by Ruth Bader Ginsburg and Stephen Breyer, appointees of President Bill Clinton.

Following *Planned Parenthood v. Casey*, the Court successfully avoided hearing abortion cases for the remainder of the 1990s. In the first year of the new century, however, the Court was confronted with a tough case involving a Nebraska statute that banned certain abortion procedures. The Court's decision in this case, *Stenberg v. Carhart* (2000), may turn out to be the most

memorable in the 1999–2000 October term. In total, eight of the nine justices felt compelled to write separate opinions in *Carhart*. Amicus curiae briefs were filed by the American Civil Liberties Union, the American College of Obstetricians and Gynecologists, the American Nurses Association, numerous state attorneys general, and several members of Congress.

At issue in *Carhart* was a 1997 Nebraska statute that made performing a "partial birth abortion" a Class III felony, carrying a prison term of up to twenty years and a fine of up to $25,000, unless the procedure was deemed "necessary to save the life of the mother whose life is endangered by a physical disorder, physical illness, or physical injury, including a life-endangering physical condition caused by or arising from the pregnancy itself." The statute defined a "partial birth abortion" as any procedure "in which the person performing the abortion partially delivers vaginally a living unborn child before killing the unborn child and completing the delivery." Twenty-nine other states have enacted similar bans on partial birth abortions.

The prohibited abortion technique, referred to as "dilation and extraction" (D&X), is relatively rare. According to the Alan Guttmacher Institute, of the estimated 1.4 million abortions performed in the United States in 1996, only about 650 were accomplished by the D&X technique. D&X is almost always performed in the second trimester of pregnancy, and it is usually employed in cases where the pregnant woman suffers from a life-threatening illness such as diabetes or heart disease. D&X is performed, as opposed to less intrusive procedures, because it is considered by most medical authorities to be significantly less hazardous to a woman's health than other late-term abortion techniques.

The challenge to the Nebraska law was brought by Dr. Leroy Carhart, a former Air Force physician in private practice in Bellevue, Nebraska. Dr. Carhart was the only Nebraska doctor willing to perform partial birth abortions in the late 1990s and, thus, to defy the statute. Moreover, he is reputedly one of only three physicians in the entire state of Nebraska performing any abortions whatsoever. Dr. Carhart testified at the district court trial that he performs only about twenty D&X procedures a year out of his yearly total of approximately 1,200 abortions. A federal district court saw merit in Dr. Carhart's suit and found the Nebraska statute unconstitutional under the due process clause of the Fourteenth Amendment. The Eighth Circuit Court of Appeals upheld the district court ruling, and the case came to the Supreme Court via a writ of certiorari.

The Supreme Court announced the decision in *Carhart* on the final day of the 1999–2000 term. Justice Stephen Breyer wrote for the five members of the majority coalition, affirming the decisions of the two lower courts to strike down the Nebraska law. Breyer held that the language of the Nebraska statute swept too broadly. As well as prohibiting late term abortions by the D&X technique, Breyer found that the statute's language could also be construed so as to prohibit the normally legal "dilation and evacuation" (D&E) type of abortion in which fetal tissue is suctioned out of the uterus rather than being dismembered. This reading of the statute, Justice Breyer concluded, places an "undue burden upon a woman's right to make an abortion decision" and, therefore, violates the due process clause of the Fourteenth Amendment. In applying the undue-burden approach, Breyer cited with favor the analysis of the plurality in *Casey*.

Breyer's opinion referred extensively to the medical literature on abortion procedures. Among other things, he emphasized the apparent consensus of medical opinion that second trimester abortions, when they were deemed medically necessary, could be accomplished much more safely by the D&X procedure than by D&E. In addition, Breyer accepted the argument of Simon Heller, Dr. Carhart's attorney, that the Nebraska ban on the D&X procedure was so broadly written that it might be interpreted in such a way as to prohibit most second trimester abortions. This, Breyer concluded, meant that the Nebraska law unconstitutionally imperiled a woman's right to an abortion.

Joining Justice Breyer in the majority in *Carhart* were Justices John Paul Stevens, Sandra Day O'Connor, David Souter, and Ruth Bader Ginsburg. Stevens, O'Connor and Gins-

burg filed brief concurring opinions. Justice O'Connor, for example, was most concerned that the Nebraska law did not provide an adequate "health exception." She suggested that she would be willing to find constitutional a more carefully drawn law that banned partial birth abortions if there was an exception granted for those situations in which a pregnant woman's life or health was in jeopardy.

The surprising vote in *Carhart* was that of Justice Anthony Kennedy. Kennedy had sided with the majority in *Casey* but joined the dissenting bloc in *Carhart*. He was particularly appalled by the brutality of the D&X abortion procedure, and therefore he argued in his lengthy opinion that it was fully within the power of the state, and still consistent with the *Casey* ruling, to pass a law prohibiting such a "shocking" procedure as D&X. Justice Antonin Scalia, also in dissent, shared Kennedy's disgust with partial birth abortions. He wrote that he hoped someday the Court could correct the error in this case and that *Carhart* would assume its rightful place in American jurisprudence beside the discredited *Korematsu v. United States* (1944) and *Dred Scott v. Sandford* (1857). Chief Justice William Rehnquist and Justice Clarence Thomas also wrote separate dissents.

The response to *Carhart* was intense but predictable. The decision received front page headlines and was featured on new broadcasts and Internet discussions. Abortion rights groups were gratified by the decision. For example, Colleen Connell, director of the ACLU's Illinois Reproductive Rights Project, stated: "The broad language of these laws was intended not to outlaw a single procedure, but to limit the availability of all abortion services for women. This decision represents a triumph of health care over politics and ideology." Nevertheless, those who agreed with the decision were chastened by the position of Justice Kennedy, whose alignment with the dissenters in *Carhart* meant that his vote on abortion cases was now problematic. Perhaps the most significant voice in opposition to the majority ruling in *Carhart* was that of Republican Party presidential candidate George W. Bush, who said through a spokeswoman that "states should have the right to enact reasonable laws and restrictions, particularly concerning the brutal practice of partial birth abortions. . . . I pledge to fight for a ban on partial birth abortions."

By 2000, several sitting Supreme Court justices were in their seventies or eighties. It thus appeared likely that President George W. Bush, who took office in 2001, would be presented with the opportunity to fill one or more Supreme Court vacancies. The "essence of *Roe*," having been preserved by narrow 5-4 votes in *Casey* and *Carhart*, might not survive indefinitely.

Selected Bibliography

Graber, M. A. *Rethinking Abortion: Equal Choice, the Constitution, and Reproductive Politics*. Princeton: Princeton University Press, 1996.

Yarbrough, Tinsley E. *The Rehnquist Court and the Constitution*. New York: Oxford University Press, 2000.

Index of Cases

———◄○►———

Index of Names and Subjects

----◄o►----

Bold numbers indicate pages on which main article appears.